PEARSON CUSTOM
BUSINESS RESOURCES

Compiled by

Business in Action
Courtland L. Bovee & John V. Thill

Custom Edition for Quinnipiac University
SB 101

This special edition published in cooperation with Pearson Learning Solutions.

Printed in the United States of America.

V0UD

Please visit our website at *www.pearsonlearningsolutions.com*.

Attention bookstores: For permission to return any unsold stock, contact us at *pe-uscustomreturns@pearson.com*.

Pearson Learning Solutions, 501 Boylston Street, Suite 900, Boston, MA 02116
A Pearson Education Company
www.pearsoned.com

PEARSON   ISBN 10: 1-256-58522-X
ISBN 13: 978-1-256-58522-0

Table of Contents

Developing a Business Mindset

Developing a Business Mindset

1. Explain the concept of adding value in a business and identify the major types of businesses

2. List three steps you can take to help make the leap from consumer to business professional

3. Discuss the five major environments in which every business operates

4. Explain the purpose of the six major functional areas in a business enterprise

5. Summarize seven of the most important business professions

6. Identify seven components of professionalism

MyBizLab

Where you see MyBizLab in this chapter, go to www.mybizlab.com for additional activities on the topic being discussed.

BEHIND THE SCENES ENTER THE HAGGIS ENTERS THE MUSIC BUSINESS ON ITS OWN TERMS

Courtesy of Enter the Haggis

The five members of Enter the Haggis need to treat their music as a business to ensure a long and healthy career in the music industry.

www.enterthehaggis.com

Chances are Trevor Lewington, Brian Buchanan, Craig Downie, Mark Abraham, and James Campbell don't wake up every morning and head off to work thinking of themselves as businesspeople. They are musicians first and foremost, members of Enter the Haggis (ETH), a Toronto-based Celtic rock band that has been steadily building a fan base across North America since the lads met in college in the early 2000s.

They're musicians, but they can't help being businesspeople as well. Being a musician can be a lifetime calling and a consuming passion, but earning a living as a professional musician requires much more than artistic inspiration and talent. Musicians who want to survive and thrive in today's fragmented media landscape are increasingly taking control and managing their careers as business operations.

Any music fan who has been purchasing music over the past decade or so knows that the music industry has been undergoing some profound changes. Sales of compact discs have dropped in half since their peak in 2000, as online sales through digital downloads and digital streaming services have grown rapidly. Legal sales of digital music are increasing, although the vast majority of downloads are illegal. However, not all musicians are dead-set against unauthorized downloading, and many openly encourage it as a way to build audiences for their music and increase demand for concert ticket sales.

As revolutionary as it has been, the transition to digital song files is not the only seismic shake-up affecting the music industry. Behind the scenes, a battle is raging between a handful of large record labels (companies that produce and promote recorded music) and hundreds of smaller independent companies, usually known as the "indies." Musicians who can't get signed by one of the majors—or who don't care for the terms of a major label contract—can try to find a home at an indie label instead.

If you were a member of ETH, what path would you like the group to take? Would you try to sign with a major label or go with an indie? What stance would you take on unauthorized music downloads? How would you build a business to support your dreams of a successful career in music?[1]

INTRODUCTION

Like all other professional bands, Enter the Haggis (profiled in the chapter-opening Behind the Scenes) is more than just an artistic endeavor. It is also a business—with customers, suppliers, payroll, production costs, taxes, legal issues, and almost everything else that comes with being in business. And like all other businesses, it is affected by external forces, from population trends to new technologies. This chapter gets you ready for the whirlwind tour of the business world you'll get in this course, starting with a quick overview of what businesses do and then some advice on making the leap from consumer to business professional.

Understanding What Businesses Do

The term *business* is used in a number of ways:

- As a label for the overall field of business concepts, as in "I plan to major in business."
- As a collective label for the activities of many companies, as in "This legislation is viewed as harmful to American business."
- As a way to indicate specific activities or efforts, as in "Our furniture business earned record profits last year, but our housewares business has lost money for the third year in a row."
- As a synonym for *company*, as in "Apple is a successful business." Other common synonyms here are *firm* and *enterprise*.

In this last sense, a **business** is any profit-seeking organization that provides goods and services designed to satisfy customers' needs. Enter the Haggis, for example, satisfies an important aspect of consumers' entertainment needs. Although the band is not in it primarily for the money, generating positive financial outcomes is essential to the group's survival in the music industry.

ADDING VALUE: THE BUSINESS OF BUSINESS

A good way to understand what any business does is to view it as a system for satisfying customers by transforming lower-value inputs into higher-value outputs (see Exhibit 1). If you want a loaf of bread, for instance, a silo full of wheat isn't of much value to you. After that wheat has been milled into flour, it gets one step closer but is valuable only if you want to bake your own bread. A bakery can take care of the baking, but that helps only if you're willing to travel to the bakery instead of go to the supermarket where you normally shop. At every stage, a company adds value to create the product in a way that makes it appealing to the next customer in the chain.

1 LEARNING OBJECTIVE

Explain the concept of adding value in a business, and identify the major types of businesses.

business Any profit-seeking organization that provides goods and services designed to satisfy customers' needs

EXHIBIT 1	Adding Value to Satisfy Customers

Every company in this chain adds value for the next customer and for the ultimate consumer.

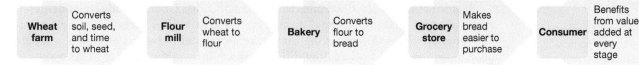

| **Wheat farm** Converts soil, seed, and time to wheat | **Flour mill** Converts wheat to flour | **Bakery** Converts flour to bread | **Grocery store** Makes bread easier to purchase | **Consumer** Benefits from value added at every stage |

revenue Money a company brings in through the sale of goods and services

Each company in this chain has made certain choices about what it will do to generate **revenue**, money the company brings in through the sale of goods and services. The result of these decisions is a company's **business model**, a clear, simple outline of how the business intends to generate revenue. Of course, generating revenue isn't enough; the business model must also indicate how the company is going to realize **profit**, the amount of money left over after *expenses*—all the costs involved in doing business—have been deducted from revenue.

business model A concise description of how a business intends to generate revenue

profit Money left over after all the costs involved in doing business have been deducted from revenue

Competing to Attract and Satisfy Customers

As businesses create their value-added products and offer them for sale to customers, they obviously don't do so in a vacuum. Other companies are also trying to sell their products to those same customers, and the result is competition. Competition gives customers a wider range of options, and it tends to increase quality, improve customer service, and lower prices.

One of the beauties of a free-market economy is that companies generally have considerable freedom in deciding which customers they want to focus on and how they want to compete. For instance, one bakery might decide to compete on price and structure its business model in such a way as to mass-produce bread at the lowest possible cost. Another might decide to compete on quality or uniqueness and structure its business model around handcrafted "artisan" bread that costs two or three times as much as the mass-produced bread. Each company seeks a **competitive advantage** that makes its products or the company as a whole more appealing to its chosen customers. Consumers benefit from better products and more choices, and companies get to focus on what they do best.

REAL-TIME UPDATES
Learn More by Reading This Article

Ten technology trends that are turning business models upside down

See whether these developments have the potential to enable entirely new business models or knock over old models. Go to http://real-timeupdates.com/bia6 and click on Learn More. If you are using MyBizLab, you can access Real-Time Updates within the chapter or under Student Study Tools.

competitive advantage Some aspect of a product or company that makes it more appealing to target customers

Accepting Risks in the Pursuit of Rewards

Take another look at Exhibit 1. Notice how every company from the farmer to the grocery store must accept some level of risk in order to conduct its business. Bad weather or disease could destroy the wheat crop. A shift in consumer behavior, such as cash-strapped families in a recession switching to bakery-outlet stores instead of regular grocery stores, could leave some bakers, distributors, and retailers with bread nobody wants to buy. Businesses take these risks in anticipation of future rewards.

This linking of risk and reward is critical for two reasons. The first and more obvious reason is that without the promise of rewards, businesses would have no incentive to take on the risks. And without entrepreneurs and companies willing to accept risk, very little would get done in the economy. The second reason that the risk associated with business decisions needs to "stay attached" to those decisions is to encourage smart and responsible decision making. If individuals and companies believe they can pursue rewards without facing the risks that should be attached to those pursuits, they are more likely to engage in irresponsible and even unethical behavior—a situation known as *moral hazard* (see Exhibit 2).

not-for-profit organizations Organizations that provide goods and services without having a profit motive; also called *nonprofit organizations*

IDENTIFYING MAJOR TYPES OF BUSINESSES

The driving forces behind most businesses are the prospects of earning profits and building *assets*, which are anything of meaningful value, from patents and brand names to real estate and company stock. In contrast, **not-for-profit organizations** (also known as *nonprofit organizations*) such as museums, most universities, and charities do not have a profit motive. However, they must operate efficiently and effectively to achieve their goals, and successful nonprofits apply many of the business-management principles you'll learn in this course.

goods-producing businesses Companies that create value by making "things," most of which are tangible (digital products such as software are a notable exception)

Businesses can be classified into two broad categories. **Goods-producing businesses** create value by making "things," from Pop-Tarts to school furniture to spacecraft. Most goods are *tangible*, meaning they have a physical presence, although software, music downloads, and other digital products are intangible. **Service businesses** create value by performing activities that deliver some benefit to the customer, such

service businesses Companies that create value by performing activities that deliver some benefit to customers

EXHIBIT 2   Risk, Reward, and the Problem of Moral Hazard

The relationship between risk and reward is fundamental to every modern economy. A company needs to see some promise of reward before it will decide to accept the risks involved in creating and selling products. However, to ensure responsible behavior, these risks need to stay attached to those decisions, meaning if a decision turns out bad, that company should suffer the consequences. If the risk gets disconnected from the decision—meaning someone else will suffer if the decision turns out bad—a situation known as *moral hazard* is created. A significant recent example of this problem involved home-mortgage companies lending money to homeowners who were practically guaranteed to default on their loans but then selling those loans as investments and thereby transferring the risk of nonpayment to someone else.

Proper connection between risk and reward

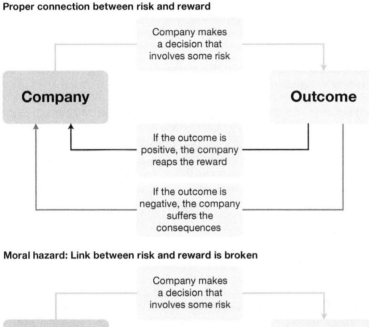

Moral hazard: Link between risk and reward is broken

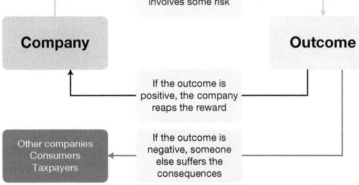

as finance, insurance, transportation, construction, utilities, wholesale and retail trade, banking, entertainment, health care, maintenance and repair, and information. Twitter, Jiffy Lube, HBO, and Verizon Wireless are examples of service businesses. Many companies are both goods-producing and service businesses.

Over the past few decades, the U.S. economy has undergone a profound transformation from being dominated by manufacturing to being dominated by services. The service sector now accounts for roughly three-quarters of the nation's economic output.[2] Although the United States remains one of the world's manufacturing powerhouses, more than half of the 100 largest U.S. companies are now primarily service providers.[3]

Because they require large amounts of money, equipment, land, and other resources to get started and to operate,

Capital-intensive businesses often have high barriers to entry, given the amount of money needed to start operations.

JIM BRYANT/UPI/Landov

barrier to entry Any resource or capability a company must have before it can start competing in a given market

goods-producing businesses are often *capital-intensive businesses*. The capital needed to compete in these industries is a **barrier to entry**, a resource or capability a company must have before it can start competing in a given market. Other barriers to entry include government testing and approval, tightly controlled markets, strict licensing procedures, limited supplies of raw materials, and the need for highly skilled employees. Service businesses tend to be *labor-intensive businesses*, in that they rely more on human resources than on buildings, machinery, and equipment to prosper. However, the Internet and other technologies have reduced the labor required to operate many types of service businesses.

✓ Checkpoint

LEARNING OBJECTIVE 1: Explain the concept of adding value in a business, and identify the major types of businesses.

SUMMARY: Businesses add value by transforming lower-value inputs to higher-value outputs. In other words, they make goods and services more attractive from the buyer's perspective, whether it's creating products that are more useful or simply making them more convenient to purchase. Companies fall into two general categories: goods-producing businesses, which create tangible things (except in the case of digital goods), and service businesses, which perform various activities of value to customers. Many companies are both goods-producing and service businesses. Businesses can also be categorized as capital intensive or labor intensive.

CRITICAL THINKING: (1) What inputs does a musical group use to create its outputs? (2) Can not-for-profit organizations benefit from practices used by for-profit companies? Why or why not?

IT'S YOUR BUSINESS: (1) Think back to the last product you purchased; how did the companies involved in its manufacture and sale add value in a way that benefited you personally? (2) Can you see yourself working for a not-for-profit organization after you graduate? Why or why not?

KEY TERMS TO KNOW: business, revenue, business model, profit, competitive advantage, not-for-profit organizations, goods-producing businesses, service businesses, barrier to entry

2 | LEARNING OBJECTIVE

List three steps you can take to help make the leap from consumer to business professional.

Making the Leap from Buyer to Seller

Even if this course is your first formal exposure to the business world, you already know a lot about business, thanks to your experiences as a consumer. You understand the impact of poor customer service, for example. You have a sense for product value and why some products meet your needs and others don't. In fact, you're an expert in the entire experience of searching for, purchasing, and owning products.

SEEING BUSINESS FROM THE INSIDE OUT

business mindset A view of business that considers the myriad decisions that must be made and the many problems that must be overcome before companies can deliver the products that satisfy customer needs

As you progress through this course, you'll begin to look at things through the eyes of a business professional rather than those of a consumer. Instead of thinking about the cost of buying a particular product, you'll start to think about the cost of making it, promoting it, and distributing it. You'll think about what it takes to make a product stand out from the crowd and recognize the importance of finding opportunities in the marketplace. You'll begin to see business as an integrated system of inputs, processes, and outputs. You'll start to develop a **business mindset** as you gain an appreciation for the many decisions that must

EXHIBIT 3 **The Business Mindset**

Your experiences as a consumer have taught you a great deal about business already. Now the challenge is to turn those experiences around and view the world from a manager's perspective. Here are a few examples of how a business professional approaches some of the questions you've asked as a consumer.

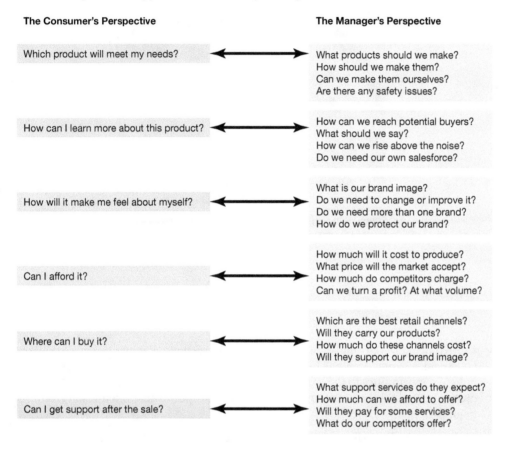

The Consumer's Perspective	The Manager's Perspective
Which product will meet my needs?	What products should we make? How should we make them? Can we make them ourselves? Are there any safety issues?
How can I learn more about this product?	How can we reach potential buyers? What should we say? How can we rise above the noise? Do we need our own salesforce?
How will it make me feel about myself?	What is our brand image? Do we need to change or improve it? Do we need more than one brand? How do we protect our brand?
Can I afford it?	How much will it cost to produce? What price will the market accept? How much do competitors charge? Can we turn a profit? At what volume?
Where can I buy it?	Which are the best retail channels? Will they carry our products? How much do these channels cost? Will they support our brand image?
Can I get support after the sale?	What support services do they expect? How much can we afford to offer? Will they pay for some services? What do our competitors offer?

be made and the many challenges that must be overcome before companies can deliver the products that satisfy customer needs (see Exhibit 3).

APPRECIATING THE ROLE OF BUSINESS IN SOCIETY

Your experiences as a consumer, an employee, and a taxpayer have also given you some insights into the complex relationship between business and society. For now, just consider some of the major elements of this relationship. Business has the potential to contribute to society in many useful ways, including the following (see Exhibit 4 on the next page):

- **Offering valuable goods and services.** If you look around in your daily life, you'll probably realize that most of the goods and services you consider essential to your quality of life were made possible by someone with a profit motive.
- **Providing employment.** U.S. businesses pay out more than $2 trillion in salaries and wages every year, giving millions of employees the means to provide for themselves and their families.[4] In addition, many companies help their employees meet the costs of health care, child care, insurance, retirement, and other living expenses.
- **Paying taxes.** U.S. businesses pay roughly $500 billion dollars in taxes every year,[5] money that helps build highways, fund education, further scientific research, enhance public safety and national defense, and support other vital functions of government.

EXHIBIT 4	Positive and Negative Effects of Business

The relationship between business and society is complex and far reaching. Individuals, communities, and entire nations benefit in multiple ways from the efforts of businesses, but even responsibly managed companies can at times have negative impacts on society in return.

Potential contributions

- Offering valuable goods and services
- Providing employment
- Paying taxes
- Contributing to growth, stability, and security

Potential negative effects

- Generating pollution and creating waste
- Creating health and safety risks
- Disrupting communities
- Causing financial instability

- **Contributing to national growth, stability, and security.** Beyond the mere dollars of taxes paid, a strong economy helps ensure a strong country. As one example, by providing job opportunities to the vast majority of people who want to work, businesses help the country avoid the social unrest and family disruptions that often result from high unemployment.

Unfortunately, businesses don't always operate in ways that benefit society. As you progress into positions of increasing responsibility in your career, be aware of the potentially negative effects that business can have on society:

- **Generating pollution and creating waste.** Just like all individuals, all companies consume resources and produce waste and therefore have an impact on the natural environment and the soil, air, and water upon which all living creatures depend.
- **Creating health and safety risks.** Many business operations involve an element of risk to the health and safety of employees and surrounding communities. For instance, some of the products you use every day, from your digital music player to your laptop computer, contain many toxic materials. If these materials are not created, handled, and disposed of properly, they can cause serious illness or death.
- **Disrupting communities.** From occupying land to displacing existing businesses to overloading schools and roads with employees and their children, growing businesses can disrupt communities even as they provide employment and other benefits. And when businesses fall into decline, they can leave behind everything from abandoned buildings to laid-off workers.
- **Causing financial instability.** Irresponsible or poorly managed companies can become a liability to society if they are unable to meet their financial obligations and need assistance from the government, for example.

The potential negative effects of business are serious matters, but the good news is that you have a say in how business operates. Even as an employee early in your career, you can conduct yourself in ways that balance the profit motive with society's shared interests. And as you climb the corporate ladder or perhaps launch your own business, you'll be in a position to make decisions that help your company prosper in an ethical and sustainable manner.

USING THIS COURSE TO JUMP-START YOUR CAREER

No matter where your career plans take you, the dynamics of business will affect your work and life in innumerable ways. If you aspire to be a manager or an entrepreneur, knowing how to run a business is vital, of course. If you plan a career in a professional specialty such as law, engineering, or finance, knowing how businesses operate will help you interact with clients and colleagues more effectively. Even if you plan to work in government, education, or some other noncommercial setting, business awareness can help you; many of these organizations look to business for new ideas and leadership techniques. *Social entrepreneurs*, people who apply entrepreneurial strategies to enable large-scale social change, use business concepts as well.

As you progress through this course, you'll develop a fundamental business vocabulary that will help you keep up with the latest news and make better-informed decisions. By participating in classroom discussions and completing the chapter exercises, you'll gain some valuable critical-thinking, problem-solving, team-building, and communication skills that you can use on the job and throughout your life.

This course will also introduce you to a variety of jobs in business fields such as accounting, economics, human resources, management, finance, and marketing. You'll see how people who work in these fields contribute to the success of a company as a whole. You'll gain insight into the types of skills and knowledge these jobs require—and you'll discover that a career in business today is fascinating, challenging, and often quite rewarding.

In addition, a study of business management will help you appreciate the larger context in which businesses operate and the many legal and ethical questions managers must consider as they make business decisions. Government regulators and society as a whole have numerous expectations regarding the ways businesses treat employees, shareholders, the environment, other businesses, and the communities in which they operate.

✔ Checkpoint

LEARNING OBJECTIVE 2: List three steps you can take to help make the leap from consumer to business professional.

SUMMARY: To accelerate your transition from consumer to professional, develop a business mindset that views business from the inside out rather than the outside in, recognize the positive and negative effects that business can have on society, and use this course to develop a business vocabulary and explore the wide variety of jobs in the field of business.

CRITICAL THINKING: (1) How can consumer experiences help a business professional excel on the job? (2) If organized businesses didn't exist and the economy were composed of individual craftspeople, would the result be more or less pollution? Explain your answer.

IT'S YOUR BUSINESS: (1) Have you thought about how you might contribute to society as a business professional? (2) What is your view of business at this point in your life? Negative? Positive? A mixture of both?

KEY TERM TO KNOW: business mindset

Recognizing the Multiple Environments of Business

3 LEARNING OBJECTIVE

Discuss the five major environments in which every business operates.

The potential effects of business, both positive and negative, highlight the fact that no business operates in a vacuum. Every company operates within a number of interrelated environments that affect and are affected by business (see Exhibit 5 on the next page).

| EXHIBIT 5 | The Multiple Environments of Business |

Every business operates in an overlapping mix of dynamic environments that continuously create both opportunities and constraints.

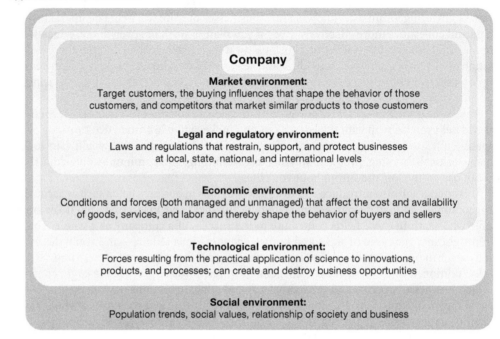

Company

Market environment:
Target customers, the buying influences that shape the behavior of those customers, and competitors that market similar products to those customers

Legal and regulatory environment:
Laws and regulations that restrain, support, and protect businesses at local, state, national, and international levels

Economic environment:
Conditions and forces (both managed and unmanaged) that affect the cost and availability of goods, services, and labor and thereby shape the behavior of buyers and sellers

Technological environment:
Forces resulting from the practical application of science to innovations, products, and processes; can create and destroy business opportunities

Social environment:
Population trends, social values, relationship of society and business

THE SOCIAL ENVIRONMENT

social environment Trends and forces in society at large

Every business operates within the broad **social environment**, the trends and forces in society at large. For instance, all companies are affected by population trends that change the composition of consumer markets and the workforce. One great example of this is the so-called Baby Boom generation, a generational "bulge" in the population made up of people born between 1946 and 1964. This large group of people has affected business in numerous ways as it has moved through childhood, then into adulthood as consumers and workers, and finally back out of the workforce now that the first wave of boomers has reached retirement age. This population bulge has occupied a large number of middle- and upper-management positions, frustrating younger professionals who would like to climb the company ladder and causing many to leave and start their own companies.[6]

stakeholders Internal and external groups affected by a company's decisions and activities

In addition to aggregate numbers of consumers and employees, various segments of society also have expectations about the appropriate relationship of business and society. The responsibility of a company to its **stakeholders**, all those groups affected by its activities, from employees to local communities to advocacy groups, is a subject of ongoing controversy.

THE TECHNOLOGICAL ENVIRONMENT

technological environment Forces resulting from the practical application of science to innovations, products, and processes

The story of ETH highlights the influence of the **technological environment**, forces resulting from the practical application of science to innovations, products, and processes. Technological changes have the potential to change every facet of business, from altering internal processes to creating or destroying market opportunities. *Disruptive technologies*, those that fundamentally change the nature of an industry, can be powerful enough to create or destroy entire companies.

The fact that music can even be recorded and played back in a different time and place is a profound advance made possible by technology. (Imagine how different your life would sound if the only way to hear music were for it to be played live.) In the 130 years or so that recorded music has been around, it has been available on numerous technological platforms, from wax cylinders and wire recorders to vinyl discs, a variety of tape formats, compact discs, and finally digital formats such as MP3. And each new technology has created opportunities for some businesses and destroyed opportunities for others. For example, if music weren't available as individual digital files, Apple might still be just a computer company and not the biggest music retailer in the United States (through its iTunes store).[7]

Speaking of media, social media might turn out to be some of the most disruptive technologies that ever hit the business world. In addition to redefining the relationships between businesses and their stakeholders, social media are redefining companies themselves by redistributing power from vertical hierarchies to horizontal networks.[8]

THE ECONOMIC ENVIRONMENT

Directly or indirectly, virtually every decision a company makes is influenced by the **economic environment**, the conditions and forces that (1) affect the cost and availability of goods, services, and labor and (2) thereby shape the behavior of buyers and sellers. For example, a growing economy can help companies by increasing demand and supporting higher prices for their products, but it can also raise the costs of labor and the materials the companies need to do business. A strong economy can also prompt managers to make decisions that turn out to be unwise in the long term, such as adding costly facilities or employee benefits that the company can't afford when the economy slows down again. A shrinking economy, on the other hand, can damage even well-run, financially healthy companies by limiting demand for their products or the availability of loans or investments needed to expand operations.

economic environment The conditions and forces that affect the cost and availability of goods, services, and labor and thereby shape the behavior of buyers and sellers

THE LEGAL AND REGULATORY ENVIRONMENT

Every business is affected by the **legal and regulatory environment**, the sum of laws and regulations at local, state, national, and even international levels. Some businesses, such as electricity and other basic utilities, are heavily regulated, even to the point of government agencies determining how much such companies can charge for their services. The degree to which various industries should be regulated remains a point of contention, year in and year out.

The policies and practices of government bodies also establish an overall level of support for businesses operating within their jurisdictions. Taxation, fees, efforts to coordinate multiple regulatory agencies, the speed of granting permits and licenses, labor rules, environmental restrictions, protection for assets such as patents and brand names, roads and other infrastructure, and the transparency and consistency of decision making all affect this level of support. Not surprisingly, businesses prefer to locate and do business in jurisdictions that offer lower costs, lower complexity, and greater stability and predictability.

legal and regulatory environment Laws and regulations at local, state, national, and even international levels

THE MARKET ENVIRONMENT

Within the various other environments just discussed, every company operates within a specific **market environment** composed of three important groups: (1) its *target customers*, (2) *buying influences* that shape the behavior of those customers, and (3) *competitors*—other companies that market similar products to those customers. The nature and behavior of these groups and their effect on business strategy vary widely from industry to industry.

In commercial air travel, for instance, airlines have two choices for purchasing large passenger planes: the U.S. company Boeing and the European consortium Airbus. The barriers to entry in commercial aviation are extremely high, and the customer decision-making process is lengthy and driven almost entirely by financial considerations. So while Boeing and Airbus have to make major investment decisions years in advance of launching new products, they can do so with the reasonable assumption that a new competitor isn't going to pop up overnight and that their target customers will behave in fairly predictable ways.

In sharp contrast, clothing fashions and fads can change in a matter of weeks or days, and the behavior of celebrities and other buying influences can have a major impact on consumer choices. Moreover, because it is much easier to launch a new line of clothing than a new airplane, competitors can appear almost literally overnight.

market environment A company's target customers, the buying influences that shape the behavior of those customers, and competitors that market similar products to those customers

✔ Checkpoint

LEARNING OBJECTIVE 3: Discuss the five major environments in which every business operates.

SUMMARY: Business influences and is influenced by (1) the social environment, trends and forces in society at large; (2) the technological environment and its ability to create and destroy markets and alter business processes; (3) the economic environment, the conditions and forces that affect the cost and availability of goods, services, and labor and thereby shape the behavior of buyers and sellers; (4) the legal and regulatory environment, comprising all the rules and regulations relating to business activities; and (5) the market environment, composed of target customers, buying influences, and competitors.

CRITICAL THINKING: (1) Is it wise for cities and states to compete with each other to be more business friendly, specifically with regard to lower tax rates on businesses? Why or why not? (2) Even though it never sells directly to consumers, does a company such as Boeing need to pay attention to population trends? Why or why not?

IT'S YOUR BUSINESS: (1) How has technology made your educational experience in college different from your experience in high school? (2) Have current economic conditions affected your career-planning decisions in any way?

KEY TERMS TO KNOW: social environment, stakeholders, technological environment, economic environment, legal and regulatory environment, market environment

---

4 LEARNING OBJECTIVE

Explain the purpose of the six major functional areas in a business enterprise.

Identifying the Major Functional Areas in a Business Enterprise

Throughout this course, you'll have the opportunity to learn more about the major functional areas within a business enterprise. In the meantime, the following sections offer a brief overview to help you see how all the pieces work together (see Exhibit 6).

RESEARCH AND DEVELOPMENT

research and development (R&D)
Functional area responsible for conceiving and designing new products

Products are conceived and designed through **research and development (R&D)**, sometimes known as *product design* or *engineering*. Of course, not all companies have an R&D function; many companies simply resell products that other firms make, for example. However, for companies that do develop products, R&D is essential to their survival because it provides the ideas and designs that allow these firms to meet customer needs in competitive markets.

information technology (IT)
Systems that promote communication and information usage through the company or that allow companies to offer new services to their customers

Companies can also engage in *process* R&D to design new and better ways to run their operations. Much of this effort goes into **information technology (IT)** systems that promote communication and information usage through the company or allow companies to offer new services to their customers.

MANUFACTURING, PRODUCTION, AND OPERATIONS

Variously called *manufacturing*, *production*, or *operations*, this area is where the company makes whatever it makes (for goods-producing businesses) or does whatever it does (for service businesses). In addition to supervising the actual production activity, operations managers are responsible for a wide range of other strategies and decisions, including *purchasing* (arranging to buy the necessary materials for manufacturing), *logistics* (coordinating the incoming flow of materials and the outgoing flow of finished products), and *facilities management* (everything from planning new buildings to maintaining them).

EXHIBIT 6   **Major Functional Areas in a Business Enterprise**

The functional areas in a business coordinate their efforts to understand and satisfy customer needs. Note that this is a vastly simplified model, and various companies organize their activities in different ways.

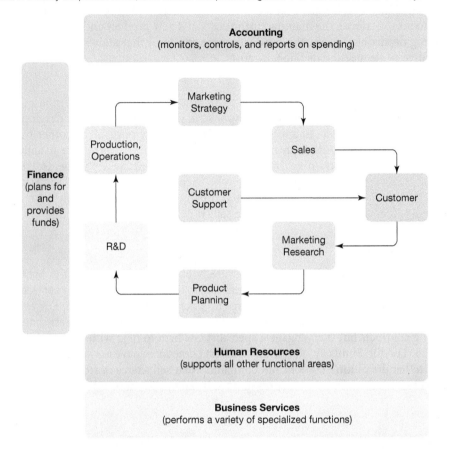

MARKETING, SALES, DISTRIBUTION, AND CUSTOMER SUPPORT

Your experience as a consumer probably gives you more insight into marketing, sales, distribution, and customer support than any other functional area in business. Although the lines separating these three activities are often blurry, generally speaking, *marketing* is charged with identifying opportunities in the marketplace, working with R&D to develop the products to address those opportunities, creating branding and advertising strategies to communicate with potential customers, and setting prices. The *sales* function develops relationships with potential customers and persuades customers, transaction by transaction, to buy the company's goods and services. Depending on the type of product, a *distribution* function can be involved both before the sale (helping to promote products to retailers, for example) and after (to physically deliver products). After products are in buyers' hands, *customer support* then goes to work after the sale, making sure customers have the support and information they need.

Perhaps no aspect of business has been changed as dramatically by recent technological advances as these marketing, sales, distribution, and customer support activities. The advent of *social media* has enabled customers to participate in a multidirectional conversation with companies and with each other rather than being passive recipients of broadcast advertising messages. The result is a profound power shift that puts buyers on much more equal footing with sellers.

FINANCE AND ACCOUNTING

The finance and accounting functions are responsible for virtually every aspect of a firm's finances, including ensuring that the company has the funds it needs to operate, monitoring and controlling how those funds are spent, and drafting reports for company management and outside audiences such as investors and government regulators. Roughly speaking, *financial managers* are responsible for planning, while *accounting managers* are responsible for monitoring and reporting.

Accounting specialists work closely with other functional areas to ensure profitable decision making. For instance, accountants coordinate with the R&D and production departments to estimate the manufacturing costs of a new product and then work with the marketing department to set the product's price at a level that allows the company to be competitive while meeting its financial goals.

HUMAN RESOURCES

The human resources (HR) function is responsible for recruiting, hiring, developing, and supporting employees. Like finance and accounting, HR supports all the other functional areas in the enterprise. Although managers in other functional areas are usually closely involved with hiring and training the employees in their respective departments, HR usually oversees these processes and supports the other departments as needed. The HR department is also charged with making sure the company is in compliance with the many laws concerning employee rights and workplace safety.

BUSINESS SERVICES

In addition to these core functions, a wide variety of *business services* exist to help companies with specific needs in law, banking, real estate, and other areas. These services can be performed by in-house staff, external firms, or a combination of the two. For example, a company might have a small permanent legal staff to handle routine business matters such as writing contracts but then engage a specialist law firm to help with a patent application or a major lawsuit. Similarly, all but the smallest companies have accounting professionals on staff to handle routine matters, but companies that sell shares of stock to the public are required to have their financial records *audited* by an outside accounting firm.

✔ Checkpoint

LEARNING OBJECTIVE 4: Explain the purpose of the six major functional areas in a business enterprise.

SUMMARY: (1) Research and development (R&D) creates the goods and services that a company can manufacture or perform for its customers. (2) Manufacturing, production, or operations is the part of the company where the firm makes whatever it makes or performs whatever services it performs. (3) The related group of functions in marketing, sales, distribution, and customer support are responsible for identifying market opportunities, crafting promotional strategies, and making sure customers are supplied and satisfied with their purchases. (4) Finance and accounting plan for the company's financial needs, control spending, and report on financial matters. (5) Human resources recruits, hires, develops, and supports employees. (6) A variety of business services provide expertise in law, real estate, and other areas.

CRITICAL THINKING: (1) Do service companies ever need to engage in research and development, since they're not creating tangible products? Why or why not? (2) Why is good customer support essential to the success of marketing and sales activities?

IT'S YOUR BUSINESS: (1) Think of a strongly positive or strongly negative experience you've had with a product or company. What feedback would you like to give the company, and to which functional area would you direct your feedback? (2) Have you already chosen the functional area where you want to work after graduation? If so, what led you to that choice?

KEY TERMS TO KNOW: research and development (R&D), information technology (IT)

Exploring Careers in Business

5 **LEARNING OBJECTIVE**

Summarize seven of the most important business professions.

Whether you're getting ready to start your career or you've been in the workforce for a while, use this course as an opportunity to explore the many career track options in the world of business. To help stimulate your thinking, this section offers a quick overview of six major business fields.[9] However, don't limit yourself to these six by any means. For just about any professional interest you might have, you can probably find a business-related career to pursue, from entertainment and sports to health care and sciences and everything in between. Also, pay attention to employment trends; as the business environment evolves, employment opportunities in various fields grow and shrink at different rates (see Exhibit 7).

EXHIBIT 7 | **Business Occupations: Where the Opportunities Are**

As conditions in the various business environments change, employment outlook rises and falls in specific professions. This chart shows projected gains and losses among selected business occupations.

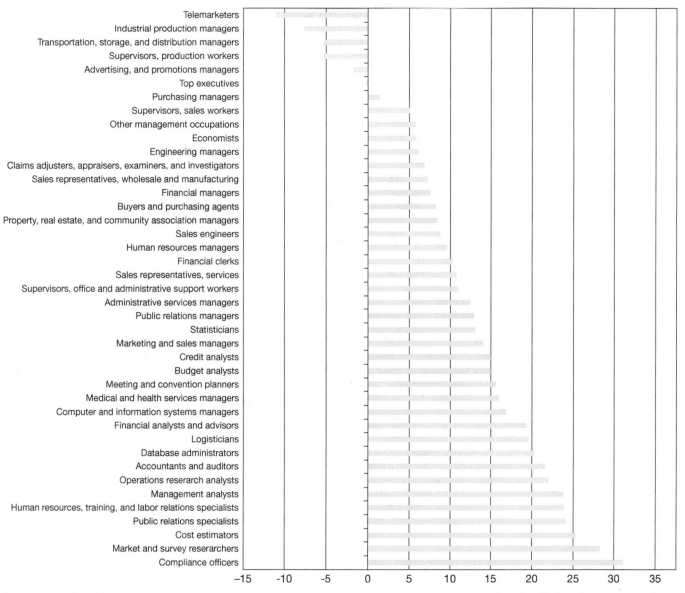

Career Opportunities
% Change in U.S. Employment, 2008–2018

Source: Adapted from T. Alan Lacey and Benjamin Wright, "Occupational Employment Projections to 2018," *Monthly Labor Review*, November 2009 (revised 22 December 2010), 3–10.

OPERATIONS MANAGER

Operations management encompasses all the people and processes used to create the goods and perform the services that a company sells. The work can involve a wide range of tasks and disciplines, including production engineering, assembly, testing, scheduling, quality assurance, information technology, forecasting, finance, logistics, and customer support. Some degree of technical acumen is always required, and many managers begin their careers in technical positions such as industrial engineering.

The work can be stressful as the organization deals with fluctuating demand levels and process and supply problems. On the other hand, if you want to balance your business interests with being involved in creating a company's products, one of these management positions might be perfect for you.

HUMAN RESOURCES SPECIALIST

HR specialists and managers plan and direct human resources activities that include recruiting, training and development, compensation and benefits, employee and labor relations, and health and safety. In addition, HR managers develop and implement human resources systems and practices to accommodate a firm's strategy and to motivate and manage diverse workforces. In the past, top executives and professionals in other functional areas sometimes viewed HR as a tactical function concerned mostly with processing employee records and other non-strategic duties. However, in many companies, the HR function is becoming more strategic and focused on the global competition to find, attract, and keep the best talent on the market.[10]

INFORMATION TECHNOLOGY MANAGER

Like HR, information technology (IT) is evolving from a tactical support function to a critical strategic component. Reflecting IT's strategic importance, many midsize and large companies now have a *chief information officer* (CIO) position at the executive level to plot IT strategy. IT specialists design, implement, and maintain systems that help deliver the right information at the right time to the right people in the organization. Jobs in IT typically require a degree in a technical field, but an understanding of business processes, finance, and management is also important—particularly as you progress up through the ranks of IT management. Many IT managers and executives also have a business degree, although not all companies require one.[11]

MARKETING SPECIALIST

A wide range of career opportunities exist in the interrelated tasks of identifying and understanding market opportunities and shaping the product, pricing, and communication strategies needed to pursue those opportunities. Whether your interests lie in branding strategy, electronic commerce, advertising, public relations, creative communication, interpersonal relations, or social media, chances are you can find a good fit somewhere in the world of marketing.

Many small companies and virtually all midsize and large companies have a variety of marketing positions, but many of these jobs are also found in advertising agencies, public relations (PR) firms, and other companies that offer specialized services to clients. Some marketing jobs are highly specialized (advertising copywriter and e-commerce architect, for instance), whereas others encompass many different aspects of marketing (brand managers, for example, deal with multiple aspects of the marketing and sales functions).

SALES PROFESSIONAL

If you thrive on competition, enjoy solving problems, and get energized by working with a wide range of people, you should definitely consider a career in sales, becoming one of the professionals responsible for building relationships with customers and helping them make purchase decisions. As a consumer, your exposure to sales might be limited to the retail sector of professional selling, but the field is much more diverse. Salespeople sell everything from design services to pharmaceuticals to airliners.

Many salespeople enjoy a degree of day-to-day freedom and flexibility not usually found in office-bound jobs. On the other hand, the pressure is usually intense; few jobs have the immediate indicators of success or failure that sales has, and most salespeople have specific targets, or *quotas*, they are expected to meet.

The qualifications for professional selling depend on the industry and the types of goods and services being sold. Personal characteristics are of the utmost importance in a sales professional as well, including the ability to listen carefully to customers' needs and communicate information about solutions clearly and persuasively.

REAL-TIME UPDATES
Learn More by Visiting This Website

Explore the wide range of career choices

Don't limit yourself to familiar career choices. Explore the full range at this comprehensive website. On MyBizLab (www.mybizlab.com), you can access Real-Time Updates within the chapter or under Student Study Tools. Otherwise, go to http://real-timeupdates .com/bia6 and click on Learn More.

ACCOUNTANT

If working at the intersection of mathematics and business sounds appealing, a career in accounting or finance could be just right for you. Accounting tasks vary by job and industry, but in general, *management accountants* are responsible for collecting, analyzing, and reporting on financial matters—such as analyzing budgets, assessing the manufacturing costs of new products, and preparing state and federal tax returns. *Internal auditors* verify the work of the company's accounting effort and look for opportunities to improve efficiency and cost-effectiveness. *Public accountants* offer accounting, tax preparation, and investment advice to individuals, companies, and other organizations. *External auditors* verify the financial reports of public companies as required by law, and *forensic accountants* investigate financial crimes.

Accounting professionals need to have an affinity for numbers, analytical minds, and attention to detail. Their work can have wide-ranging effects on investors, employees, and executives, so accuracy and timeliness are critical. Communication skills are important in virtually every accounting function. Computer skills are also increasingly important, particularly for accountants closely involved with the design or operation of accounting systems.

FINANCIAL MANAGER

Financial managers perform a variety of leadership and strategic functions. *Controllers* oversee the preparation of income statements, balance sheets, and other financial reports; they frequently manage accounting departments as well. *Treasurers* and *finance officers* have a more strategic role, establishing long-term financial goals and budgets, investing the firm's funds, and raising capital as needed. Other financial management positions include *credit managers*, who supervise credit accounts established for customers, and *cash managers*, who monitor and control cash flow.

Unlike accounting tasks, for which there is a long tradition of outsourcing, the work of financial managers is generally kept in-house, particularly in midsize and large companies. The work of a financial manager touches every part of the company, so a broad understanding of the various functional areas in business is a key attribute for this position. The ability to communicate with people who aren't financial experts is also vital. Moreover, awareness of information technology developments is important for chief financial officers (CFOs) and other top financial managers, so that they can direct their companies' investments in new or improved accounting systems as needed.

✓ Checkpoint

LEARNING OBJECTIVE 5: Summarize seven of the most important business professions.

SUMMARY: (1) Operations managers oversee all the people and processes involved in creating the goods and services that a company sells. (2) HR specialists and managers plan and direct human resources activities such as recruiting, training and development, compensation and benefits, employee and labor relations, and health and safety. (3) IT managers oversee the design, implementation, and maintenance of systems that help deliver the right information at the right time to the right people in the organization. (4) Marketing specialists perform one or more tasks involved in identifying and understanding market opportunities and shaping the product, pricing, and promotional strategies needed to pursue those opportunities. (5) Sales professionals build relationships with customers and help them make purchase decisions. (6) Accountants collect, analyze, and report on financial matters; they also perform audits to verify financial reports or find ways to lower costs. (7) Financial managers plan for the company's financial needs, invest funds, and raise capital.

CRITICAL THINKING: (1) Why are communication skills essential in all seven of the functional areas discussed in this section? (2) Why would financial managers be in a good position to rise up the company ladder?

IT'S YOUR BUSINESS: (1) Which of these seven general career areas appeals to you the most? Why? (2) What is your view of the sales profession? If it is not entirely positive, what would you do as a sales professional to change that public image?

KEY TERM TO KNOW: operations management

6 **LEARNING OBJECTIVE**

Identify seven components of professionalism.

professionalism The quality of performing at a high level and conducting oneself with purpose and pride

Achieving Professionalism

As you map out your career, think about what kind of businessperson you want to be. Will you be someone who just puts in the hours and collects a paycheck? Or will you be someone who performs on a higher plane, someone who wants to make a meaningful contribution and be viewed as a true professional? **Professionalism** is the quality of performing at a high level and conducting oneself with purpose and pride. True professionals exhibit seven distinct traits: striving to excel, being dependable and accountable, being a team player, communicating effectively, demonstrating a sense of etiquette, making ethical decisions, and maintaining a positive outlook (see Exhibit 8).

STRIVING TO EXCEL

Pros are good at what they do, and they never stop improving. No matter what your job might be at any given time—even if it is far from where you aspire to be—strive to perform at the highest possible level. Not only do you have an ethical obligation to give your employer and your customers your best effort, but excelling at each level in your career is the best way to keep climbing up to new positions of responsibility. Plus, being good at what you do delivers a sense of satisfaction that is hard to beat.

In many jobs and in many industries, performing at a high level requires a commitment to continuous learning and improvement. The nature of the work often changes as markets and technologies evolve, and expectations of quality tend to increase over time as well. View this constant change as a positive thing, as a way to avoid stagnation and boredom.

BEING DEPENDABLE AND ACCOUNTABLE

Develop a reputation as somebody people can count on. This means meeting your commitments, including staying on schedule and staying within budgets. These are skills that take some time to develop as you gain experience with how much time and money are required to accomplish various tasks and projects. With experience, you'll learn to be conservative with your commitments. You don't want to be known as someone who overpromises and underdelivers.

EXHIBIT 8	Elements of Professionalism

To develop a reputation as a true professional, develop these seven attributes—and keep improving all the way through your career.

Be the best	• Pros strive to excel, to be the best they can be at everything they do. • Excelling at every level is how you build a great career.
Be dependable	• Pros keep their promises and meet their commitments. • Pros learn from their mistakes and take responsiblity for their errors.
Be a team player	• Pros know how to contribute to a larger cause. • Team players make others around them better.
Be clear	• Communication is the single most important skill you can develop. • Learn to listen as well as you speak and write.
Be respectful	• Good business etiquette is a sign of respect for those around you. • Respecting others is not only good, it's good for your career.
Be ethical	• Responsible professionals work to avoid ethical lapses. • Pros weigh their options carefully when facing ethical dilemmas.
Be positive	• Successful people believe in what they're doing and in themselves. • Pros don't complain about problems; they find them and fix them.

Being accountable also means owning up to your mistakes and learning from failure so that you can continue to improve. Pros don't make excuses or blame others. When they make mistakes—and everybody does—they face the situation head on, make amends, and move on.

BEING A TEAM PLAYER

Professionals know that they are contributors to a larger cause, that it's not all about them. Just as in athletics and other team efforts, being a team player in business is something of a balancing act. On the one hand, you need to pay enough attention to your own efforts and skills to make sure you're pulling your own weight. On the other hand, you need to pay attention to the overall team effort to make sure the team succeeds. Remember that if the team fails, you fail, too.

Great team players know how to make those around them more effective, whether it's lending a hand during crunch time, sharing resources, removing obstacles, making introductions, or offering expertise. In fact, the ability to help others improve their performance is one of the key attributes executives look for when they want to promote people into management.

Being a team player also means showing loyalty to your organization and protecting your employer's reputation—one of the most important assets any company has. Pros don't trash their employers in front of customers or in their personal blogs. When they have a problem, they solve it; they don't share it.

COMMUNICATING EFFECTIVELY

If you're looking for a surefire way to stand out from your competition and establish yourself as a competent professional, improving your communication skills may be the most important step you can take. Follow these guidelines to improve your effectiveness as a communicator:

- **Listen actively.** Active listening means making a conscious effort to turn off your own filters and biases to truly hear and understand what someone else is saying.
- **Provide practical information.** Give people useful information that is adapted to their specific needs.
- **Give facts rather than vague impressions.** Use concrete language, specific detail, and supporting information that is clear, convincing, accurate, and ethical.
- **Don't present opinions as facts.** If you are offering an opinion, make sure the audience understands that.
- **Present information in a concise, efficient manner.** Audiences appreciate—and respond more positively to—high-efficiency messages.
- **Clarify expectations and responsibilities.** Clearly state what you expect from your readers or listeners and what you can do for them.
- **Offer compelling, persuasive arguments and recommendations.** Make it clear to people how they will benefit from responding to your messages the way you want them to.

DEMONSTRATING ETIQUETTE

etiquette The expected norms of behavior in any particular situation

A vital element of professionalism is **etiquette**, the expected norms of behavior in any particular situation. The way you conduct yourself, interact with others, and handle conflict can have a profound influence on your company's success and on your career. Etiquette blunders can have serious financial costs through lower productivity and lost business opportunities.[12] When executives hire and promote you, they expect your behavior to protect the company's reputation. The more you understand such expectations, the better chance you have of avoiding career-damaging mistakes. Moreover, etiquette is an important way to show respect for others and contribute to a smooth-running workplace.

Long lists of etiquette "rules" can be overwhelming, and you'll never be able to memorize all of them. Fortunately, you can count on three principles to get you through any situation: respect, courtesy, and common sense. Moreover, following these principles will encourage forgiveness if you do happen to make a mistake. As you prepare to encounter new situations, take some time to learn the expectations of the other people involved. Travel guidebooks are a great source of information about norms and customs in other countries. Check to see if your library has online access to the Culture-Grams database or review the country etiquette guides available through the Real-Time Updates Learn More item on this page. Don't be afraid to ask questions, either. People will respect your concern and curiosity. You will gradually accumulate considerable knowledge, which will help you feel comfortable and be effective in a wide range of business situations.

MAKING ETHICAL DECISIONS

True professionals conduct themselves with a clear sense of right and wrong. They avoid committing *ethical lapses*, and they carefully weigh all the options when confronted with *ethical dilemmas*.

REAL-TIME UPDATES
Learn More by Reading This Article

Doing business globally with local sensitivity

Get insider tips on how to get along in business cultures around the world. Go to http://real-timeupdates.com/bia6 and click on Learn More. If you are using MyBizLab, you can access Real-Time Updates within the chapter or under Student Study Tools.

MAINTAINING A CONFIDENT, POSITIVE OUTLOOK

Spend a few minutes around successful people in any field, and chances are you'll notice how optimistic they are. They believe in what they're doing, and they believe in themselves and their ability to solve problems and overcome obstacles.

Being positive doesn't mean displaying mindless optimism or spewing happy talk all the time. It means acknowledging that things may be difficult but then buckling down and getting the job done anyway. It means no whining and no slacking off, even when the going gets tough. We live in an imperfect world, no question—jobs can be boring or difficult, customers can be unpleasant, and bosses can be unreasonable. But when you're a pro, you find a way to power through.

Your energy, positive or negative, is also contagious. Both in-person and online, you'll spend as much time with your colleagues as you spend with family and friends. Personal demeanor is therefore a vital element of workplace harmony. No one expects (or wants) you to be artificially upbeat and bubbly every second of the day, but one negative personality can make an entire office miserable and unproductive. Every person in a company has a responsibility to contribute to a positive, energetic work environment.

For the latest information on developing a business mindset and becoming a successful professional, visit http://real-timeupdates.com/bia6.

✔ Checkpoint

LEARNING OBJECTIVE 6: Identify seven components of professionalism.

SUMMARY: Professionalism is the quality of performing at a high level and conducting yourself with purpose and pride. Seven key traits of professionalism are striving to excel, being dependable and accountable, being a team player, communicating effectively, demonstrating a sense of etiquette, making ethical decisions, and maintaining a positive outlook.

CRITICAL THINKING: (1) How much loyalty do employees owe to their employers? Explain your answer. (2) Would it be unethical to maintain a positive public persona if you have private doubts about the path your company is pursuing? Why or why not?

IT'S YOUR BUSINESS: (1) In what ways do you exhibit professionalism as a student? (2) You can see plenty of examples of unprofessional business behavior in the news media and in your own consumer and employee experiences. Why should you bother being professional yourself?

KEY TERMS TO KNOW: professionalism, etiquette

BEHIND THE SCENES

BUILD A BAND, THEN BUILD A BUSINESS

MyBizLab

The beginnings of the Celtic rock band Enter the Haggis (ETH) coincided with the beginning of the revolution in the music industry. Millions of music listeners were fed up with the business model that had been in place for decades, in which record labels forced customers to purchase entire albums for $15 to $20, even when they might want only one or two songs on an album—and usually without the opportunity to listen to the rest of the album first.

Within the music business, thousands of musicians were fed up with the mainstream business model as well. The industry was dominated by a small number of large record companies, also known as *record labels*. These labels made major

investments in the careers of a small number of musicians, from paying for recording sessions to promoting the music to radio stations, which to a large degree dictated the music the public got to hear.

This business model worked out nicely for those musicians lucky enough to get signed by one of the major labels, lucky enough to get significant radio airplay, lucky enough to get significant album and concert sales as a result of that radio exposure, and lucky or smart enough to sign a contract that actually passed some of the resulting profits back to the musicians.

However, the dominant business model was far less satisfying for thousands of other musical acts. With a business model built around big investments made in the hope of big paybacks, the big labels focused on acts with the best chance of appealing to a wide audience. Musicians and groups without a mainstream sound usually needed to look elsewhere. And when the major labels did sign an act, they often exerted a lot of creative and financial control, influencing the sound, the public image, and the career track of the artists in which they invested. Moreover, they recouped their costs before the artist saw any money from album sales, meaning an artist usually had to sell a huge pile of albums to start seeing any money at all from a recording contract. In other words, for many artists, the chances of getting a major label contract were slim, and the chances of being satisfied with such a contract were even slimmer.

Against this backdrop of widespread dissatisfaction on the part of both consumers and creators, a number of forces in the technological environment were turning the industry upside down. The compact disc (CD) gradually replaced most sales of vinyl albums, but it triggered something much more disruptive than simply replacing one album format with another. CDs, of course, store music in digital format, which means the music can be transferred to and played on computers and other digital devices—and distributed over computer networks. The introduction of widely accepted standard file formats, most notably MP3, made it easy to copy and share song files from one device to another. The rapid spread of high-speed Internet connections, low-cost digital music players such as the iPod, and social media such as MySpace and Last.fm added the final pieces of the puzzle. The music industry would never be the same again.

ETH stepped right into this upheaval and embraced a new way of thinking. The group signed with United for Opportunity (UFO), which describes itself as "an organization of experienced, independent-thinking music industry activists that have come together to create a new model for a record label/music distribution company." Not only does UFO support the band's philosophy of giving musicians and their fans more control, but signing with an indie makes more financial sense, too. According to ETH's Brian Buchanan, "The average independent musician sees more real cash from 10,000 independent sales than many major artists see from a million sales."

Will ETH ever become filthy rich playing Celtic-influenced music? Probably not. However, as Buchanan puts it, "Success is making any kind of a living doing the thing you love." By meshing their business model with the changing business environment and working tirelessly to connect with their customers, ETH stands a good chance of making enough money to keep doing what they love for as long as they love doing it.

Critical Thinking Questions

1. Assume that ETH really were in it for the money and not the music. Would it still make sense to stick with an indie label, or should the band pursue a major label contract and all the potential marketing exposure that comes with it? Explain your answer.
2. Search online for "Enter the Haggis" and identify how many ways you can listen to the band's music for free. Why is it in the group's long-term interest to make its music available for free like this?
3. If the band had begun its professional existence 10 years earlier, how might its business strategy be different from the path it took?

LEARN MORE ONLINE

Explore the band's website, at www.enterthehaggis.com, and its presence on Facebook, YouTube, MySpace, Twitter, and iLike. How does the band use its online presence to build a relationship with fans?

MyBizLab

Log on to www.mybizlab.com to access study and assessment aids associated with this chapter.

KEY TERMS

barrier to entry
business
business mindset
business model
competitive advantage
economic environment
etiquette
goods-producing businesses
information technology (IT)
legal and regulatory environment
market environment

not-for-profit organizations
operations management
professionalism
profit
research and development (R&D)
revenue
service businesses
social environment
stakeholders
technological environment

TEST YOUR KNOWLEDGE

Questions for Review

1. What is a business model?
2. What are four ways that business can benefit society?
3. Do all companies have an R&D function? Explain your answer.
4. How does the role of a financial manager differ from the role of an accountant?
5. What is professionalism?

Questions for Analysis

6. Why is it often easier to start a service business than a goods-producing business?
7. Does a downturn in the economy hurt all companies equally? Provide several examples to support your answer.
8. Do laws and regulations always restrict or impede the efforts of business professionals, or can they actually help businesses? Explain you answer.

9. Why is it important for IT specialists and managers to understand business in addition to information technology?
10. **Ethical Considerations.** Is managing a business in ways that reflect society's core values always ethical? Explain your answer.

Questions for Application

11. How will you be able to apply your experience as a consumer of educational services to the challenges you'll face in your career after graduation?
12. What are some of the ways a company in the health-care industry could improve its long-term planning by studying population trends?
13. Identify at least five ways in which your life would be different without digital technology. Would it be more or less enjoyable? More or less productive?
14. Identify three ways in which the principles of professionalism described in this chapter can make you a more successful student.

EXPAND YOUR KNOWLEDGE

Discovering Career Opportunities

Your college's career center offers numerous resources to help you launch your career. Imagine that you write a blog for students at your college, and you want to introduce them to the center's services. Write a blog post of 300 to 400 words, summarizing what the center can do for students.

Improving Your Tech Insights: Digital Products

The category of digital products encompasses an extremely broad range of product types, from e-books to music and movie files to software and instruction sets for automated machinery. Digital products are commonplace these days, but the ability to remotely deliver product value is quite a staggering concept when you think about it. (As just one example, consider that a single iPod or other digital music players can carry the equivalent of several thousand tapes or CDs.)

Supplying music over the Internet is amazing enough, but today even *tangible* products can be delivered electronically: The technology that deposits layers of ink in inkjet printers is being adapted to deposit layers of other liquefied materials, including plastics and metals. Called *3D printing, inkjet fabrication*, or *additive fabrication*, this technology is already being used to "print" product prototypes, architectural models, and a variety of electronic and mechanical components. As the price of the technology continues to drop, don't be surprised if one day you'll be able to download product description files from the Internet and fabricate physical items right on your own home "printer." For more about this technology, visit Dimension 3D Printing (www.dimensionprinting.com), Stratasys (www.stratasys.com), or Z Corporation (www.zcorp.com).

Choose a category of products that has been changed dramatically by the ability to deliver value digitally. In a brief email message to your instructor, explain how digital technology revolutionized this market segment.[13]

PRACTICE YOUR SKILLS

Sharpening Your Communication Skills

Select a local service business where you have been a customer. How does that business try to gain a competitive advantage in the marketplace? Write a brief summary describing whether the company competes on speed, quality, price, innovation, service, or a combination of those attributes. Be prepared to present your analysis to your classmates.

Building Your Team Skills

In teams assigned by your instructor, each member should first identify one career path (such as marketing or accounting) that he or she might like to pursue after graduation and share that choice with the rest of the team. Each team member should then research the others' career options to find at least one significant factor, positive or negative, that could affect someone entering that career. For example, if there are four people on your team, you will research the three careers identified by your three teammates. After the research is complete, convene an in-person or online meeting to give each member of the team an informal career counseling session based on the research findings.

Developing Your Research Skills

Gaining a competitive advantage in today's marketplace is critical to a company's success. Research any company that sounds interesting to you and identify the steps it has taken to create competitive advantages for individual products or the company as a whole.

1. What goods or services does the company manufacture or sell?
2. How does the company set its goods or services apart from those of its competitors? Does the company compete on price, quality, service, innovation, or some other attribute?
3. How do the company's customer communication efforts convey those competitive advantages?

REFERENCES

1. Adapted from Enter the Haggis website, accessed 28 July 2011, www.enterthehaggis.com; United for Opportunity website, accessed 28 July 2011, www.ufomusic.com; Bill Palladino, "Music Business Economics 101," Claudia Schmidt website, accessed 10 May 2009, www.claudiaschmidt.com; Brian Buchanan, "21st Century Rockstardom," blog post, 7 April 2008, www.enterthe-haggis.com; Christopher Knab, "Oh, How the Music Business Keeps Changing," Music Biz Academy.com, January 2009, www.musicbizacademy.com; Ethan Smith, "Can He Save Rock 'n' Roll?" *Wall Street Journal*, 21 February 2009, http://online.wsj.com.
2. "Gross-Domestic-Product-by-Industry Accounts," U.S. Bureau of Economic Analysis website, Release Date: 26 April 2011, www.bea.gov.
3. "The 2011 Fortune 500," *Fortune*, accessed 27 July 2011, http://money.cnn.com.
4. "SOI Tax Stats–Integrated Business Data," IRS website, accessed 27 July 2011, www.irs.gov.
5. "SOI Tax Stats–Integrated Business Data."
6. Cheryl Winokur Munk, "4 Generations," *Community Banker*, January 2009, 30–33.
7. Ed Christman, "Digital Divide," *Billboard*, 22 May 2010, www.billboard.biz.
8. David Kirkpatrick, "Social Power and the Coming Corporate Revolutions," *Forbes*, 7 September 2011, www.forbes.com.
9. Career profiles in this section adapted from U.S. Bureau of Labor Statistics, *Occupational Outlook Handbook, 2008–2009 Edition*, www.bls.gov/oco.
10. Kris Dunn, "The Five Sweetest Jobs in HR and Talent Management," *Workforce*, July 2008, www.workforce.com.
11. Meredith Levinson, "Should You Get an MBA?" *CIO*, 5 July 2007, www.cio.com.
12. Susan G. Hauser, "The Degeneration of Decorum," *Workforce Management*, January 2011, 16–18, 20–21.
13. Adapted from Dimension 3D Printing website, accessed 28 July 2011, www.dimensionprinting.com; Stratasys website, accessed 28 July 2011, www.stratasys.com; Z Corporation, accessed 28 July 2011, www.zcorp.com.

GLOSSARY

barrier to entry Any resource or capability a company must have before it can start competing in a given market

business Any profit-seeking organization that provides goods and services designed to satisfy customers' needs

business mindset A view of business that considers the myriad decisions that must be made and the many problems that must be overcome before companies can deliver the products that satisfy customer needs

business model A concise description of how a business intends to generate revenue

competitive advantage Some aspect of a product or company that makes it more appealing to target customers

economic environment The conditions and forces that affect the cost and availability of goods, services, and labor and thereby shape the behavior of buyers and sellers

etiquette The expected norms of behavior in any particular situation

goods-producing businesses Companies that create value by making "things," most of which are tangible (digital products such as software are a notable exception)

information technology (IT) Systems that promote communication and information usage through the company or that allow companies to offer new services to their customers

legal and regulatory environment Laws and regulations at local, state, national, and even international levels

market environment A company's target customers, the buying influences that shape the behavior of those customers, and competitors that market similar products to those customers

not-for-profit organizations Organizations that provide goods and services without having a profit motive; also called nonprofit organizations

operations management Management of the people and processes involved in creating goods and services

professionalism The quality of performing at a high level and conducting oneself with purpose and pride

profit Money left over after all the costs involved in doing business have been deducted from revenue

research and development (R&D) Functional area responsible for conceiving and designing new products

revenue Money a company brings in through the sale of goods and services

service businesses Companies that create value by performing activities that deliver some benefit to customers

social environment Trends and forces in society at large

stakeholders Internal and external groups affected by a company's decisions and activities

technological environment Forces resulting from the practical application of science to innovations, products, and processes

Organization and Teamwork

LEARNING OBJECTIVES   After studying this chapter, you will be able to

1 Explain the major decisions needed to design an organization structure

2 Define four major types of organization structure

3 Explain how a team differs from a group and describe the six most common forms of teams

4 Highlight the advantages and disadvantages of working in teams and list the characteristics of effective teams

5 Review the five stages of team development and explain why conflict can arise in team settings

6 Explain the concept of an unstructured organization and identify the major benefits and challenges of taking this approach

MyBizLab

Where you see MyBizLab in this chapter, go to www.mybizlab.com for additional activities on the topic being discussed.

BEHIND THE SCENES REINVENTING THE RETAIL EXPERIENCE AT THE CONTAINER STORE

© Wiskerke/Alamy

Effective team communication behind the scenes is key to creating positive customer experiences at The Container Score.

www.containerstore.com

Let's face it: Frontline jobs in retail don't have the greatest reputation. From an employee's perspective, these sales positions often combine low pay with high stress, leading to rapid burnout and frequent turnover. From a customer's perspective, frontline retail employees in some stores seem to fall into two categories: poorly trained, poorly motivated rookies or aggressive staffers who seem more intent on getting commissions than helping customers.

What if you wanted to put a new face on retailing? What if you wanted shopping to be a pleasant, welcome experience for both employees and customers? Too much to ask, perhaps?

This is the challenge Garrett Boone and Kip Tindell set for themselves when they opened the first The Container Store in Dallas, Texas. The chain, which has now expanded to several dozen locations across the country, carries a staggering array of products that help customers organize their lives. The Container Store has storage solutions for every room in the house, from the kitchen to the garage to the home office. Employees are expected to help customers solve every storage problem imaginable, from sweaters to DVDs to rubber stamps to tax records, with a variety of boxes, baskets, hangers, hooks, closet organizers, and more.

If you were in Boone's and Tindell's shoes, what steps would you take to break out of the retail rut and create a business that is satisfying for both customers and employees? How would you attract the best and the brightest employees and pull off a minor miracle in retailing—hanging on to them year after year? How would you organize the staffs in your stores? How much information would you share with them, and how would you communicate it?[1]

INTRODUCTION

Organization might not seem like the most exciting topic in the business world, but as Garrett Boone and Kip Tindell (profiled in the chapter-opening Behind the Scenes) would no doubt tell you, it is one of the most important. This chapter discusses the most important issues to consider in designing an organization structure, introduces you to the most common ways companies structure themselves, and explores the important matter of teamwork. It concludes with a look at the *unstructured organization*, which may be the structure of the future for many businesses. And if organization structures do strike you as a less-than-exhilarating topic, you might be surprised by some of the intriguing innovations going on with new technology-enabled work patterns.

Designing an Effective Organization Structure

A company's **organization structure** has a dramatic influence on the way employees and managers make decisions, communicate, and accomplish important tasks. This structure helps the company achieve its goals by providing a framework for managers to divide responsibilities, effectively distribute the authority to make decisions, coordinate and control the organization's work, and hold employees accountable for their work. In contrast, a poorly designed structure can create enormous waste, confusion, and frustration for employees, suppliers, and customers.

When managers design an organization's structure, they use an **organization chart** to provide a visual representation of how employees and tasks are grouped and how the lines of communication and authority flow (see Exhibit 1). An organization chart depicts the official design for accomplishing tasks that lead to achieving the organization's goals, a framework known as the *formal organization*. Every company also has an *informal organization*—the network of interactions that develop on a personal level among workers. Sometimes the interactions among people in the informal organization parallel their relationships in the formal organization, but often interactions transcend formal boundaries, such as when employees from various parts of the company participate in sports, social, or charitable activities together or use social media to reach across organizational barriers.

In the past, organizations were usually designed around management's desire to control workers, with everything set up in a hierarchy. Today, however, the goal of many companies is an **agile organization** that allows employees to respond quickly to customer needs and changes in the business environment and to bring the best mix of talents and resources to every challenge.

To identify the best structure for their organization, managers need to identify the organization's core competencies, clarify job responsibilities, define the chain of command, and organize the workforce in a way that maximizes effectiveness and efficiency.

IDENTIFYING CORE COMPETENCIES

Before they can decide how to organize, companies need to identify which business functions they should focus on themselves and which they should *outsource* to other companies. For instance, many companies outsource the payroll function because it doesn't make sense for them to invest the time needed to stay on top of frequent changes in income tax laws and related financial matters.[2] Many others outsource parts or all of the manufacturing process and concentrate on product design and marketing.

Core competencies are those activities in which a company excels and has the potential to create competitive advantages. For example, it's a virtual certainty that you've seen or used a product designed by Frog (www.frogdesign.com), a global design consultancy with talents in consumer research, design, and the commercialization phase of bringing new products to market. Frog has worked behind the scenes for many of the world's best-known companies, from Apple to Disney to Sony, but it stays focused on its core competencies in the research and development phase rather than becoming a manufacturer or consumers goods company itself.[3]

IDENTIFYING JOB RESPONSIBILITIES

Once a company knows what it wants to focus on, it can design each job needed to deliver those competencies. A key decision here is finding the optimal level of **work specialization**,

1 **LEARNING OBJECTIVE**

Explain the major decisions needed to design an organization structure.

organization structure A framework that enables managers to divide responsibilities, ensure employee accountability, and distribute decision-making authority

organization chart A diagram that shows how employees and tasks are grouped and where the lines of communication and authority flow

agile organization A company whose structure, policies, and capabilities allow employees to respond quickly to customer needs and changes in the business environment

core competencies Activities that a company considers central and vital to its business

work specialization Specialization in or responsibility for some portion of an organization's overall work tasks; also called division of labor

EXHIBIT 1   **Simplified Organization Chart**

An organization chart portrays the division of activities and responsibilities across a company.

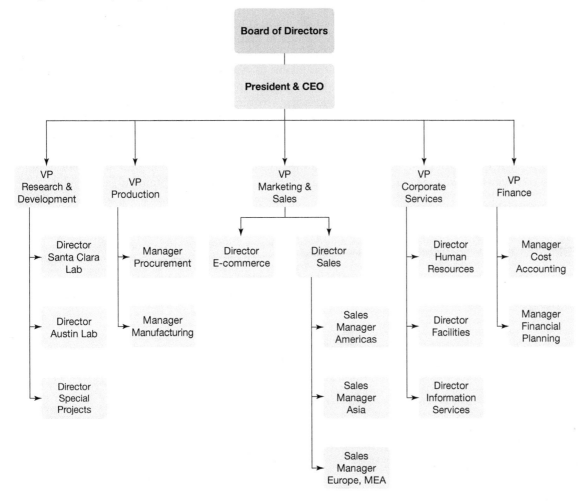

sometimes referred to as the *division of labor*—the degree to which organizational tasks are broken down into separate jobs.[4] Work specialization can improve organizational efficiency by enabling each worker to perform tasks that are well defined and that require specific skills. When employees concentrate on the same specialized tasks, they can perfect their skills and perform their tasks more quickly. In addition to aligning skills with job tasks, specialization prevents overlapping responsibilities and communication breakdowns.

However, organizations can overdo specialization. If a task is defined too narrowly, employees may become bored with performing the same limited, repetitive job over and over. They may also feel unchallenged and alienated. As you'll see later in the chapter, many companies are adopting a team-based approach to give employees a wider range of work experiences and responsibilities.

DEFINING THE CHAIN OF COMMAND

With the various jobs and their individual responsibilities identified, the next step is defining the **chain of command**, the lines of authority that connect the various groups and levels within the organization. The chain of command helps the organization function smoothly by making two things clear: who is responsible for each task and who has the authority to make decisions.

All employees have a certain amount of *responsibility*—the obligation to perform the duties and achieve the goals and objectives associated with their jobs. As they work toward the organization's goals, employees must also maintain their *accountability*, their obligation to report the results of their work to supervisors or team members and to justify any

chain of command A pathway for the flow of authority from one management level to the next

27

outcomes that fall below expectations. Managers ensure that tasks are accomplished by exercising *authority*, the power to make decisions, issue orders, carry out actions, and allocate resources. Authority is vested in the positions that managers hold, and it flows down through the management pyramid. *Delegation* is the assignment of work and the transfer of authority, responsibility, and accountability to complete that work.[5]

The simplest and most common chain-of-command system is known as **line organization** because it establishes a clear line of authority flowing from the top down, as Exhibit 1 depicts. Everyone knows who is accountable to whom, as well as which tasks and decisions each is responsible for. However, line organization sometimes falls short because the technical complexity of a firm's activities may require specialized knowledge that individual managers don't have and can't easily acquire. A more elaborate system, called **line-and-staff organization**, was developed to address the need to combine specialization with management control. In such an organization, managers in the chain of command are supplemented by functional groupings of people known as *staff*, who provide advice and specialized services but who are not in the line organization's overall chain of command (see Exhibit 2).

line organization A chain-of-command system that establishes a clear line of authority flowing from the top down

line-and-staff organization An organization system that has a clear chain of command but that also includes functional groups of people who provide advice and specialized services

---

EXHIBIT 2   **Simplified Line-and-Staff Structure**

A line-and-staff organization divides employees into those who are in the direct line of command and those who provide staff (support) services to line managers at various levels. In this simplified example, the government affairs and legal departments report to the CEO but would provide support to any department in the company, as needed.

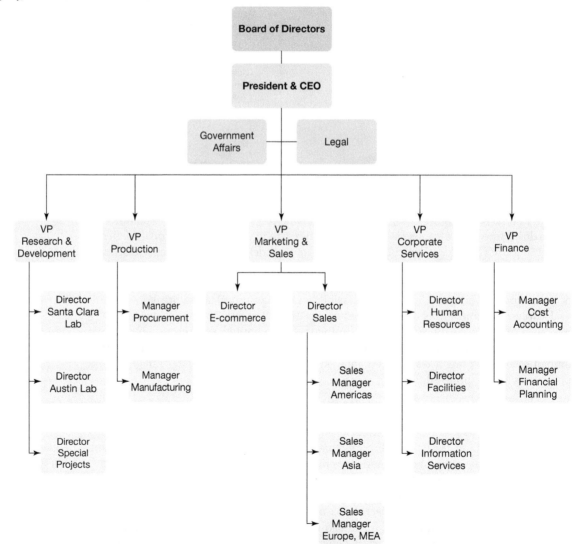

Span of Management

The number of people a manager directly supervises is called the **span of management**, or *span of control*. When a large number of people report directly to one person, that person has a wide span of management. This situation is common in *flat organizations* with relatively few levels in the management hierarchy. In contrast, *tall organizations* have many hierarchical levels, typically with fewer people reporting to each manager than is the case in a flat organization. In these organizations, the span of management is narrow.

To reduce the time it takes to make decisions, many companies are now flattening their organization structures by removing layers of management and pushing responsibilities and authority to lower levels (see Exhibit 3). Such moves have the additional benefit of putting senior executives in closer contact with customers and the daily action of the business.[6]

However, a flatter structure is not necessarily better in all respects. For example, it increases the demand on individual managers and gives them less time to spend with each employee. The Container Store, for instance, recently *added* a layer of management specifically to reduce the span of management in order to give each manager more time "to nurture and develop and train and counsel" his or her employees. "I think it's the best thing we ever did," Kip Tindell said, noting that even with the added costs, financial performance improved even more.[7]

Moreover, the deep experience base that midlevel managers have accrued, regarding both external market dynamics and internal working knowledge of the company itself, can be lost when these positions are eliminated. These managers can be particularly crucial in knowledge-driven industries, where insight and creative thinking are crucial to strategic decision making.[8]

span of management The number of people under one manager's control; also known as span of control

Centralization Versus Decentralization

Organizations that focus decision-making authority near the top of the chain of command are said to be centralized. **Centralization** can benefit a company by utilizing top

centralization Concentration of decision-making authority at the top of an organization

EXHIBIT 3	Flattening an Organization

In this simplified example, a layer of management (the business units) was removed to flatten the organization. In theory, this move reduces costs and speeds communication and decision making. Two obvious downsides are the increased span of management for the two group managers and the loss of knowledge and relationships that the business unit managers brought to the organization.

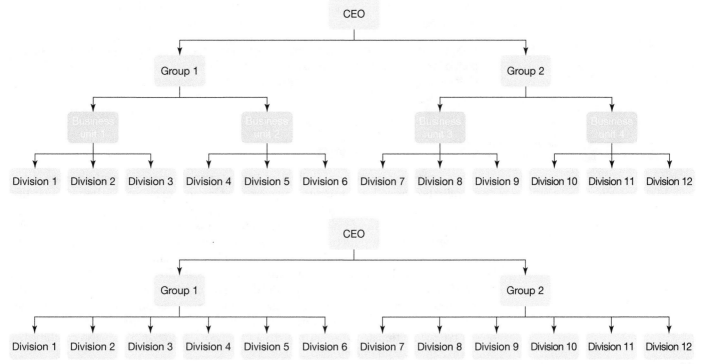

management's experience and broad view of organizational goals. In addition, it can help companies coordinate large undertakings more efficiently, accelerate decisions that might otherwise get bogged down in discussions and disagreements, and reduce the number of overlapping capabilities.

In contrast, **decentralization** pushes decision-making authority down to lower organizational levels—such as department heads—while control over essential companywide matters remains with top management. Implemented properly, decentralization can stimulate responsiveness because decisions don't have to be referred up the hierarchy.[9] However, decentralization does not work in every situation or in every company. At times, strong authority from the top of the chain of command may be needed to keep the organization focused on immediate goals. In other cases, a company may need strong central decision making to coordinate efforts on complex projects or to present a unified image to customers. Decentralization can also lead to inefficiencies, if multiple parts of a firm are doing the same basic task or replicating resources such as information systems. Managers should select the level of decision making that will most effectively serve the organization's needs, given the particular circumstances.[10]

decentralization Delegation of decision-making authority to employees in lower-level positions

---

✔ Checkpoint

LEARNING OBJECTIVE 1: Explain the major decisions needed to design an organization structure.

SUMMARY: The first major decision in designing an organization structure is identifying core competencies, those functions where the company excels and wants to focus. From there, managers can identify job responsibilities (who does what and how much work specialization is optimum), the chain of command, the span of management for each manager, and the degree of centralization or decentralization of decision-making authority.

CRITICAL THINKING: (1) What are the risks of a poorly designed organization structure? (2) How does a flat structure change the responsibilities of individual managers?

IT'S YOUR BUSINESS: (1) What would you say are your two or three core competencies at this point in your career? (2) Would you function better in a highly centralized or in a highly decentralized organization? Why?

KEY TERMS TO KNOW: organization structure, organization chart, agile organization, core competencies, work specialization, chain of command, line organization, line-and-staff organization, span of management, centralization, decentralization

---

2 LEARNING OBJECTIVE

Define four major types of organization structure.

departmentalization Grouping people within an organization according to function, division, matrix, or network

Organizing the Workforce

The decisions regarding job responsibilities, span of management, and centralization versus decentralization provide the insights managers need in order to choose the best organization structure. The arrangement of activities into logical groups that are then clustered into larger departments and units to form the total organization is known as **departmentalization**.[11] The choice must involve both the *vertical structure*—how many layers the chain of command is divided into from the top of the company to the bottom—and the *horizontal structure*—how the various business functions and work specialties are divided across the company.

Variations in the vertical and horizontal designs of organizations can produce an almost endless array of structures—some flat, some wide; some simple and clear; others convoluted and complex. Within this endless variety of structure possibilities, most designs fall into one of four types: functional, divisional, matrix, and network. Companies can also combine two or more of these types in *hybrid structures*.

FUNCTIONAL STRUCTURES

The **functional structure** groups employees according to their skills, resource use, and job requirements. Common functional subgroups include research and development (R&D), production or manufacturing, marketing and sales, and human resources.

Splitting the organization into separate functional departments offers several advantages: (1) Grouping employees by specialization allows for the efficient use of resources and encourages the development of in-depth skills, (2) centralized decision making enables unified direction by top management, and (3) centralized operations enhance communication and the coordination of activities within departments. Despite these advantages, functional departmentalization can create problems with communication, coordination, and control, particularly as companies grow and become more complicated and geographically dispersed.[12] Moreover, employees may become too narrowly focused on departmental goals and may lose sight of larger company goals. Firms that use functional structures often try to counter these weaknesses by using *cross-functional teams* to coordinate efforts across functional boundaries, as you'll see later in the chapter.

functional structure Grouping workers according to their similar skills, resource use, and expertise

DIVISIONAL STRUCTURES

The **divisional structure** establishes self-contained suborganizations that encompass all the major functional resources required to achieve their goals—such as research and design, manufacturing, finance, and marketing.[13] In some companies, these divisions operate with great autonomy; such divisions are often called *business units*.

Many organizations use a structure based on *product divisions*—grouping around each of the company's products or family of products. In contrast, *process divisions* are based on the major steps of a production process. For example, Chevron has divisions (including separate companies in some cases) for such process steps as exploration, refining, pipeline distribution, shipping, and marketing.[14] The third approach, *customer divisions*, concentrates activities on satisfying specific groups of customers (see Exhibit 4). Finally, *geographic divisions* help companies respond more easily to local customs, styles, and product preferences.

Divisional structures offer both advantages and disadvantages. First, because divisions are self-contained, they can react quickly to change, making the organization more flexible. In addition, because each division focuses on a limited number of products, processes, customers, or locations, divisions can often provide better service to customers.

However, divisional departmentalization can also increase costs through duplication (if every product division has its own human resources department, for example). Furthermore, poor coordination between divisions may cause them to focus too narrowly on divisional goals and to neglect the organization's overall goals. Finally, divisions may compete with one another for resources and customers, causing rivalries that hurt the organization as a whole.[15]

divisional structure Grouping departments according to similarities in product, process, customer, or geography

EXHIBIT 4	Customer Division Structure

Focusing each division on a single type of customer can help a company market its products more efficiently and serve customers more responsively.

EXHIBIT 5	Matrix Structure

In a matrix structure, each employee is assigned to both a functional group (with a defined set of basic functions, such as production management) and a project team (which consists of members of various functional groups working together on a project, such as bringing out a new consumer product). Even in this simplified model, you can sense how complex matrix management can be, when employees have multiple managers, and managers share employees with other projects and departments.

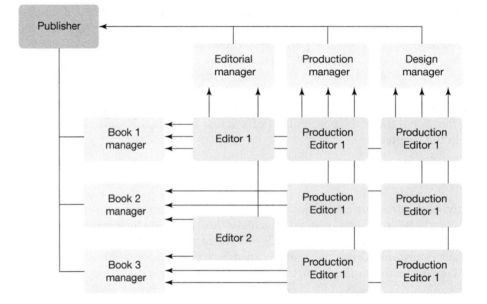

MATRIX STRUCTURES

matrix structure A structure in which employees are assigned to both a functional group and a project team (thus using functional and divisional patterns simultaneously)

A **matrix structure** is an organizational design in which employees from functional departments form teams to combine their specialized skills (see Exhibit 5). This structure allows the company to pool and share resources across divisions and functional groups. The matrix may be a permanent feature of the organization's design, or it may be established to complete a specific project.

The matrix structure can help big companies function like smaller ones by allowing teams to devote their attention to specific projects or customers without permanently reorganizing the company's structure. A matrix can also make it easier to deploy limited resources where they're needed the most and to bring a mix of skills to bear on important tasks. The pharmaceutical giant Bristol-Myers Squibb, for example, makes extensive uses of matrix structures to share expertise and to take advantage of resources spread throughout its global organization. According to executive Jane Luciano, "the matrix helps us to gain control of issues as they travel around the globe and to leverage economies of scale."[16]

On the downside, people in a matrix structure have to get used to reporting to two bosses, more communication and coordination is usually required, and struggles over resources can foster unhealthy competition between the two sides of the matrix.[17] Strong support from upper management, a culture that values collaboration, and hands-on attention from managers to make sure employees don't get lost in the matrix are essential to using this structural form successfully.[18]

REAL-TIME UPDATES
Learn More by Watching This Video

Surviving and thriving in the matrix

This brief overview identifies the portfolio of skills needed to make matrix management work for employees and manager alike. Go to http://real-timeupdates.com/bia6 and click on Learn More. If you are using MyBizLab, you can access Real-Time Updates within the chapter or under Student Study Tools.

NETWORK STRUCTURES

network structure A structure in which individual companies are connected electronically to perform selected tasks for a small headquarters organization

A **network structure** stretches beyond the boundaries of a company to connect a variety of partners and suppliers that perform selected tasks for a headquarters organization. Also called a *virtual organization*, a network organization can outsource engineering, marketing, research, accounting, production, distribution, or other functions. The design of a network structure stems from decisions about core competencies, with executives deciding which functions to focus on internally and which to outsource.

The network structure presents an intriguing blend of benefits and risks. A virtual structure can lower costs and increase flexibility, allowing a company to react more quickly to market demands. It can also boost competitiveness by taking advantage of specific skills and technologies available in other companies. On the other hand, relying too heavily on outsiders can render the company vulnerable to events beyond its control, such as key suppliers going out of business, offering the same goods and services to its competitors, or going into direct competition with the company. Moreover, outsourcing too many fundamental tasks, such as product design, can leave a company without any real competitive distinctions to speak of.[19] For more on contemporary uses of network structures, see "Managing an Unstructured Organization" later in this chapter.

✔ Checkpoint

LEARNING OBJECTIVE 2: Define four major types of organization structure.

SUMMARY: Companies can organize in four primary ways: by function, which groups employees according to their skills, resource use, and expertise; by division, which establishes self-contained departments formed according to similarities in product, process, customer, or geography; by matrix, which assigns employees from functional departments to interdisciplinary project teams and requires them to report to both a department head and a team leader; and by network, which connects separate companies that perform selected tasks for a headquarters organization.

CRITICAL THINKING: (1) Should The Container Store use the same organization structure in each of its stores around the country? Why or why not? (2) Why does a matrix structure create potential problems in the chain of command?

IT'S YOUR BUSINESS: (1) Do you think you would function well in a matrix structure, where you would need to report to two bosses simultaneously? Why or why not? (2) What about as a manger—could you share control with another manager?

KEY TERMS TO KNOW: departmentalization, functional structure, divisional structure, matrix structure, network structure

Organizing in Teams

3 **LEARNING OBJECTIVE**

Explain how a team differs from a group, and describe the six most common forms of teams.

While the vertical chain of command is a tried-and-true method of organizing for business, it is limited by the fact that decision-making authority is often located high up the management hierarchy, while real-world feedback from customers is usually located at or near the bottom of the hierarchy. Companies that organize vertically may become slow to react to change, and high-level managers may overlook many great ideas for improvement that originate in the lower levels of the organization. In addition, many business tasks and challenges demand the expertise of people who work in many parts of the company, isolated by the formal chain of command. To combat these issues, organizations such as The Container Store work to involve employees from all levels and functions of the organization in the decision-making process, using a variety of team formats in day-to-day operations.

This section looks at the most common types of teams, and the following two sections address the challenges of improving team productivity and fostering teamwork.

WHAT IS A TEAM?

A **team** is a unit of two or more people who work together to achieve a shared goal. Teams differ from work groups in that work groups interact primarily to share information and to make decisions to help one another perform within each member's area of responsibility.

team A unit of two or more people who share a mission and collective responsibility as they work together to achieve a goal

In other words, the performance of a work group is merely the summation of all group members' individual contributions.[20] In contrast, the members of a team have a shared mission and are collectively responsible for their work. By coordinating their individual efforts, the members of a successful team accomplish more together than they could individually, a result known as *synergy*.[21]

Although a team's goals may be set by either the team itself or someone in the formal chain of command, it is the job of the team leader to make sure the team stays on track to achieve those goals. Team leaders are often appointed by senior managers, but sometimes they emerge naturally as the team develops. Some teams complete their work and disband in a matter of weeks or months, while those working on complex projects can stay together for years.

TYPES OF TEAMS

The type, structure, and composition of individual teams within an organization depend on the organization's strategic goals and the objective for forming the team. Six common forms of teams are problem-solving teams, self-managed teams, functional teams, cross-functional teams, virtual teams, and social networks and virtual communities. Such classifications are not exclusive, of course. A problem-solving team may also be self-managed and cross-functional.

Problem-Solving Teams

problem-solving team A team that meets to find ways of improving quality, efficiency, and the work environment

A **problem-solving team** is assembled to find ways of improving quality, efficiency, or other performance measures. In some cases, a team attacks a single, specific problem and disbands after presenting or implementing the solution. In other cases, the team continues to meet over time, evaluating trends and fixing new problems as they crop up. At the Massachusetts Eye & Ear Infirmary, for example, a team charged with addressing insurance claim denials meets regularly to solve individual cases and to investigate systematic issues that might be causing problems with multiple patient cases.[22]

Self-Managed Teams

self-managed team A team in which members are responsible for an entire process or operation

As the name implies, a **self-managed team** manages its own activities and requires minimal supervision. Typically, these teams control the pace of work and determination of work assignments. Fully self-managed teams select their own members. Self-managed teams represent a significant change for organizations and managers accustomed to rigid command-and-control structures. However, the potential advantages include lower costs, faster decision making, greater flexibility and innovation, and improved quality (stemming from the increased pride of ownership that an independent team feels in its work).[23]

Functional Teams

functional team A team whose members come from a single functional department and that is based on the organization's vertical structure

A **functional team**, or *command team*, is organized along the lines of the organization's vertical structure and thus may be referred to as a *vertical team*. Such teams are composed of managers and employees within a single functional department, and the structure of a vertical team typically follows the formal chain of command. In some cases, the team may include several levels of the organizational hierarchy within the same functional department.[24]

Cross-Functional Teams

cross-functional team A team that draws together employees from different functional areas

In contrast to functional teams, a **cross-functional team**, or *horizontal team*, draws together employees from various functional areas and expertise. Cross-functional teams can facilitate information exchange, help coordinate multiple organizational units, encourage new solutions for organizational problems, and aid the development of new organizational policies and procedures.[25] However, collaborating across organizational boundaries can be challenging, particularly if participation on a cross-functional team conflicts with an individual's regular departmental workload or performance incentives.[26] Cross-functional teams often involve some form of matrix structure, even if temporarily, which brings with it the advantages and challenges of that form.

A cross-functional team can take on a number of formats. A **task force** is formed to work on a specific activity with a completion point. Several departments are usually involved so that all parties who have a stake in the outcome of the task are able to provide input. In contrast, a **committee** usually has a long life span and may become a permanent part of the organization structure. Committees typically deal with regularly recurring tasks, such as addressing employee grievances.

Virtual Teams

A **virtual team** is composed of members at two or more geographic locations. Research indicates that virtual teams can be as effective as face-to-face teams, as long as they take steps to overcome the disadvantages of not being able to communicate face to face.[27] For instance, some virtual teams meet in person at least once to allow the members to get to know one another before diving into their work.

To be successful, virtual teams should follow three basic rules. First, a virtual team should take full advantage of the diverse viewpoints, experiences, and skills of the various team members. One of the major benefits of virtual teams, in fact, is the opportunity to assemble teams of experts wherever they may be rather than rely on the people who happen to work in a given geographic location. Second, a virtual team should use technology to replicate resources that in-person teams rely on. *Shared online workspaces* are one of the most popular tools for virtual teams because they give everyone access to information and documents the team uses. Email and instant messaging (IM) can be effective for occasional communication, but many teams discover that either some people are left out of important message exchanges or everybody is deluged with every message. Blogs and wikis can cut down on the message overload and keep everyone in the loop. Third, a virtual team should take extra care to keep the team functioning effectively. The lack of the *nonverbal cues*, such as facial expressions and body language, which people rely on heavily when communicating in person, makes virtual communication especially challenging. Teleconferencing and videoconferencing can help in this regard.[28]

Social Networks and Virtual Communities

Social networking technologies are redefining teamwork and team communication by helping erase the constraints of geographic and organization boundaries. In addition to enabling and enhancing teamwork, social networks have numerous other business applications and benefits (see Exhibit 6 on the next page). While they are not always teams in the traditional sense, social networks and virtual communities often function as teams, helping people coordinate their efforts in pursuit of a shared goal. In addition, social networking has become an essential tool for many teams, matrix organizations, temporary organizations, and other structures.

Some companies use social networking technologies to form *virtual communities* or *communities of practice* that link employees with similar professional interests throughout the company and sometimes with customers and suppliers as well. The huge advantage that social networking brings is in identifying the best people to collaborate on each problem or project, no matter where they are around the world or what their official roles are in the organization. Such communities are similar to teams in many respects, but one major difference is in the responsibility for accumulating organizational knowledge over the long term. For example, the pharmaceutical company Pfizer has a number of permanent product safety communities that provide specialized advice on drug safety issues to researchers across the company.[29]

MyBizLab

Gain hands-on experience through an interactive, real-world scenario. This chapter's simulation entitled Team Management is located at **www.mybizlab.com.**

task force A team of people from several departments who are temporarily brought together to address a specific issue

committee A team that may become a permanent part of the organization and is designed to deal with regularly recurring tasks

virtual team A team that uses communication technology to bring together geographically distant employees to achieve goals

EXHIBIT 6	Business Uses of Social Networking Technology

Social networking has emerged as a powerful technology for enabling teamwork and enhancing collaboration in a variety of ways.

Business Challenge	Example of Social Networking in Action
Assembling teams	Identifying the best people, both inside the company and in other companies, to collaborate on projects
Fostering the growth of communities	Helping people with similar—or complementary—interests and skills find each other in order to provide mutual assistance and development
Accelerating the evolution of teams	Accelerating the sometimes slow process of getting to know one another and identifying individual areas of expertise
Maintaining business relationships	Giving people an easy way to stay in contact after meetings and conferences
Supporting customers	Allowing customers to develop close relationships with product experts within the company
Integrating new employees	Helping new employees navigate their way through the organization, finding experts, mentors, and other important contacts
Easing the transition after reorganizations and mergers	Helping employees connect and bond after internal staff reorganizations or mergers with other organizations
Overcoming structural barriers in communication channels	Bypassing the formal communication system in order to deliver information where it is needed in a timely fashion
Solving problems	Finding "pockets of knowledge" within the organization—the expertise and experience of individual employees
Preparing for major meetings and events	Giving participants a way to meet before an event takes place, helping to ensure that the meeting or event becomes more productive more quickly
Sharing and distributing information	Making it easy for employees to share information with people who may need it—and for people who need information to find employees who might have it
Finding potential customers, business partners, and employees	Identifying strong candidates by matching user profiles with current business needs and linking from existing member profiles

Sources: Adapted from Courtland L. Bovée and John V. Thill, *Business Communication Today*, 11th ed., (Upper Saddle River, N.J.: Pearson Prentice Hall, 2012), 181, 184; Christopher Carfi and Leif Chastaine, "Social Networking for Businesses & Organizations," white paper, Cerado website, accessed 13 August 2008, www.cerado.com; Anusorn Kansap, "Social Networking," PowerPoint presentation, Silpakorn University, accessed 14 August 2008, http://real-timeupdates.com; "Social Network Websites: Best Practices from Leading Services," white paper, 28 November 2007, FaberNovel Consulting www.fabernovel.com.

Social networking can also help a company maintain a sense of community even as it grows beyond the size that normally permits a lot of daily interaction. At the online retailer Zappos, fostering a supportive work environment is the company's top priority. To encourage the sense of community among its expanding workforce, Zappos uses social networking tools to track employee connections and encourage workers to reach out and build relationships.[30]

✓ Checkpoint

LEARNING OBJECTIVE 3: Explain how a team differs from a group, and describe the six most common forms of teams.

SUMMARY: The primary difference between a team and a work group is that the members of a team work toward a shared goal, whereas members of a work group work toward individual goals. The six most common forms of teams are (1) problem-solving teams, which seek ways to improve a situation and then submit their recommendations; (2) self-managed teams, which manage their own activities and seldom require supervision; (3) functional teams, which are composed of employees within a single functional department; (4) cross-functional teams, which draw together employees from various departments and expertise in a number of formats such as task forces and committees; (5) virtual teams, which bring together employees from distant locations; and (6) social networks and virtual communities, which are typically less structured than teams but nonetheless share many aspects of teamwork and promote shared goals.

CRITICAL THINKING: (1) How might the work of a task force or committee disrupt the normal chain of command in an organization? (2) Should new hires with no business experience be assigned to virtual teams? Why or why not?

IT'S YOUR BUSINESS: (1) Would you function well in a virtual team setting that offered little or no chance for face-to-face contact with your colleagues? Why or why not? (2) If you had two similar job offers, one with a company that stresses teamwork and another with a company that stresses independent accomplishment, which would you choose? Why?

KEY TERMS TO KNOW: team, problem-solving team, self-managed team, functional team, cross-functional team, task force, committee, virtual team

Ensuring Team Productivity

4 **LEARNING OBJECTIVE**

Highlight the advantages and disadvantages of working in teams, and list the characteristics of effective teams.

Even though teams can play a vital role in helping an organization reach its goals, they are not appropriate for every situation, nor do they automatically ensure higher performance. Understanding the advantages and disadvantages of working in teams and recognizing the characteristics of effective teams are essential steps in ensuring productive teamwork.

ADVANTAGES AND DISADVANTAGES OF WORKING IN TEAMS

Managers must weigh the pros and cons of teams when deciding whether and how to use them. A well-run team can provide a number of advantages:[31]

- **Higher-quality decisions.** Many business challenges require the input of people with diverse experiences and insights, and using teams can be an effective way to bring these multiple perspectives together. Working in teams can unleash new levels of creativity and energy in workers who share a sense of purpose and mutual accountability. Effective teams can be better than top-performing individuals at solving complex problems.[32]
- **Increased diversity of views.** Team members can bring a variety of perspectives to the decision-making process, which can result in more successful actions and decisions, as long as these diverse viewpoints are guided by a shared goal.[33]
- **Increased commitment to solutions and changes.** Employees who feel they've had an active role in making a decision are more likely to support the decision and encourage others to accept it.
- **Lower levels of stress and destructive internal competition.** When people work together toward a common goal rather than competing for individual recognition, their efforts and energies tend to focus on the common good. The sense of belonging to a group and being involved in a collective effort can also be a source of job satisfaction for most people.
- **Improved flexibility and responsiveness.** Because they don't have the same degree of permanence as formal departments and other structural elements, teams are easier to reformulate to respond to changing business needs.

REAL-TIME UPDATES
Learn More by Listening to This Podcast

Taking teams to the top

Listen to these hands-on techniques for developing, launching, leading, and evaluating world-class teams. Go to http://real-timeupdates.com/bia6 and click on Learn More. If you are using MyBizLab, you can access Real-Time Updates within the chapter or under Student Study Tools.

Furthermore, teams fill an individual worker's need to belong to a group, reduce employee boredom, increase feelings of dignity and self-worth, and reduce stress and tension among workers. While the advantages of teamwork help explain the wide spread popularity of teams in today's business environment, teams also present a number of potential disadvantages, particularly if they are poorly structured or poorly managed:[34]

- **Inefficiency.** Even successful teams need to be on constant watch for inefficiency—spending more time than necessary on their decisions and activities or simply losing sight of the team's ultimate goal. Potential sources of inefficiency include internal politics, too much emphasis on consensus, and excessive socializing among team members.
- **Groupthink.** Like all social structures, business teams can generate tremendous pressures to conform with accepted norms of behavior. **Groupthink** occurs when these peer pressures cause individual team members to withhold contrary or unpopular opinions. The result can be decisions that are worse than the team members might have made individually. Overcoming fear of conflict is essential to avoiding groupthink, which may require some coaching from experienced managers and continued attention to rules of engagement when conflict does arise.
- **Diminished individual motivation.** Balancing the need for group harmony with individual motivation is a constant issue with teams. Without the promise of individual recognition and reward, high-performance individuals may feel less incentive to keep working at high levels.
- **Structural disruption.** Teams can become so influential within an organization that they compete with the formal chain of command, in effect superimposing a matrix on the existing structure.
- **Excessive workloads.** The time and energy required to work on teams isn't free, and when team responsibilities are layered on top of individuals' regular job responsibilities, the result can be overload.

groupthink Uniformity of thought that occurs when peer pressures cause individual team members to withhold contrary or unpopular opinions

CHARACTERISTICS OF EFFECTIVE TEAMS

To be successful, teams need to be designed as carefully as any other part of an organization structure. Establishing the size of the team is one of the most important decisions; the optimal size for teams is generally thought to be between 5 and 12 members. Teams with fewer members may lack the necessary range of skills, while members of larger teams may have difficulty bonding properly and communicating efficiently. However, managers sometimes have no choice; complex challenges such as integrating two companies or designing complicated products can require teams of up to 100 people or more.[35]

The types of individuals on a team is also vital. People who assume the *task-specialist role* focus on helping the team reach its goals. In contrast, members who take on the *socioemotional role* focus on supporting the team's emotional needs and strengthening the team's social unity. Some team members are able to assume dual roles, contributing to the task and still meeting members' emotional needs. These members often make effective team leaders. At the other end of the spectrum are members who are *nonparticpators*, contributing little to reaching the team's goals or to meeting members' socioemotional needs. Obviously, a team staffed with too many inactive members isn't going to accomplish much of anything. Exhibit 7 outlines the behavior patterns associated with each of these roles.

Beyond the right number of the right sort of people, effective teams share a number of other characteristics:[36]

- **Clear sense of purpose.** Team members clearly understand the task at hand, what is expected of them, and their respective roles on the team.
- **Open and honest communication.** The team culture encourages discussion and debate. Team members speak openly and honestly, without the threat of anger, resentment, or retribution. They listen to and value feedback from others. As a result, all members participate. Conversely, members who either don't share valuable information because they don't understand that it's valuable or, worse, withhold information as a way to maintain personal power can undermine the team's efforts.[37]
- **Creative thinking.** Effective teams encourage original thinking, considering options beyond the usual.

EXHIBIT 7	Team Member Roles

Team members assume one of these four roles. Members who assume a dual role—emphasizing both task progress and people needs—often make the most effective team leaders.

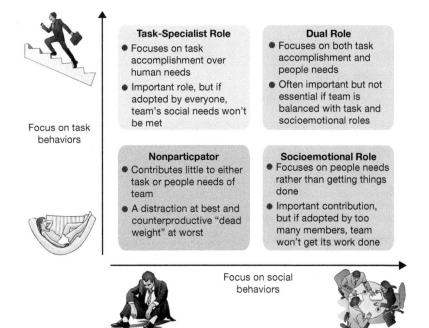

Focus on task behaviors

Task-Specialist Role
- Focuses on task accomplishment over human needs
- Important role, but if adopted by everyone, team's social needs won't be met

Dual Role
- Focuses on both task accomplishment and people needs
- Often important but not essential if team is balanced with task and socioemotional roles

Nonparticpator
- Contributes little to either task or people needs of team
- A distraction at best and counterproductive "dead weight" at worst

Socioemotional Role
- Focuses on people needs rather than getting things done
- Important contribution, but if adopted by too many members, team won't get its work done

Focus on social behaviors

- **Accountability.** Team members commit to being accountable to each other.
- **Focus.** Team members get to the core issues of the problem and stay focused on key issues.
- **Decision by consensus.** On effective teams, all decisions are arrived at by consensus. But this point comes with a warning: Teams that worry too much about consensus can take a long time to make decisions. In many cases, members need to commit to the group's decision even though they may not support it 100 percent.

For a brief review of characteristics of effective teams, see Exhibit 8 on the next page.

✔Checkpoint

LEARNING OBJECTIVE 4: Highlight the advantages and disadvantages of working in teams, and list the characteristics of effective teams.

SUMMARY: Teamwork has the potential to produce higher-quality decisions, increase commitment to solutions and changes, lower stress and destructive internal competition, and improve flexibility and responsiveness. The potential disadvantages include inefficiency, groupthink, diminished individual motivation, structural disruption, and excessive workloads. Effective teams have a clear sense of purpose, communicate openly and honestly, build a sense of fairness in decision making, think creatively, maintain accountability, stay focused on key issues, and emphasize consensus (while balancing the need for quick decision making).

CRITICAL THINKING: (1) Is groupthink similar to peer pressure? Why or why not? (2) Is supporting a group decision you don't completely agree with always a case of groupthink? Explain your answer.

IT'S YOUR BUSINESS: (1) How would you characterize the experience you've had working in teams throughout your high school and college years? (2) How can you apply experience gained on athletic teams and other collaborative activities to the business world?

KEY TERM TO KNOW: groupthink

EXHIBIT 8	Characteristics of Effective Teams

Effective teams practice these good habits.

Make Effective Teamwork a Top Management Priority

- Recognize and reward group performance where appropriate
- Provide ample training opportunities for employees to develop team skills

Select Team Members Wisely

- Involve key stakeholders and decision makers
- Limit team size to the minimum number of people needed to achieve team goals
- Select members with a diversity of views
- Select creative thinkers

Build a Sense of Fairness in Decision Making

- Encourage debate and disagreement without fear of reprisal
- Allow members to communicate openly and honestly
- Consider all proposals
- Build consensus by allowing team members to examine, compare, and reconcile differences—but don't let a desire for 100 percent consensus bog the team down
- Avoid quick votes
- Keep everyone informed
- Present all the facts

Manage Conflict Constructively

- Share leadership
- Encourage equal participation
- Discuss disagreements openly and calmly
- Focus on the issues, not the people
- Don't let minor disagreements boil over into major conflicts

Stay on Track

- Make sure everyone understands the team's purpose
- Communicate what is expected of team members
- Stay focused on the core assignment
- Develop and adhere to a schedule
- Develop rules and follow norms

---

5 **LEARNING OBJECTIVE**

Review the five stages of team development, and explain why conflict can arise in team settings.

Fostering Teamwork

Because teams are composed of unique individuals with different perspectives, the interpersonal relationships among team members require careful consideration. Two particularly important issues are team development and team conflict.

TEAM DEVELOPMENT

Teams often require some time and developmental change to reach full productive speed, and team leaders need to understand this process to help groups reach their potential as quickly as possible. Several models of team development have been proposed over the years. One well-known model defined by researcher Bruce Tuckman identifies five stages of development, nicknamed *forming, storming, norming, performing,* and *adjourning*:[38]

- **Forming.** The forming stage is a period of orientation and ice-breaking. Members get to know each other, determine what types of behaviors are appropriate within the group, identify what is expected of them, and become acquainted with each other's task orientation.
- **Storming.** In the storming stage, members show more of their personalities and become more assertive in establishing their roles. Conflict and disagreement often arise during the storming stage, as members jockey for position or form coalitions to promote their own perceptions of the team's mission. While it is necessary for this storming to occur, team members need to make sure the team doesn't lapse into counterproductive behaviors before it has a chance to resolve these emerging conflicts.
- **Norming.** During the norming stage, conflicts are resolved, and team harmony develops. Members come to understand and accept one another, reach consensus on who the leader is (if that hasn't already been established formally), and reach agreement on member roles.
- **Performing.** In the performing stage, members are really committed to the team's goals. Problems are solved, and disagreements are handled in the interest of task accomplishment.
- **Adjourning.** Finally, if the team has a specific task to perform, it goes through the adjourning stage after the task has been completed. In this stage, issues are wrapped up, and the team is dissolved.

As a team moves through these stages of development, two important developments occur. First, it develops a certain level of **cohesiveness**, a measure of how committed the members are to the team's goals. Cohesiveness is reflected in meeting attendance, team interaction, work quality, and goal achievement. Cohesiveness is influenced by many factors, particularly competition and evaluation. If a team is in competition with other teams, cohesiveness increases as the team strives to excel. In addition, if a team's efforts and accomplishments are recognized by the organization, members tend to be more committed to the team's goals. Strong team cohesiveness generally results in high morale. Moreover, when cohesiveness is coupled with strong management support for team objectives, teams tend to be more productive.

cohesiveness A measure of how committed team members are to their team's goals

The second development is the emergence of **norms**, informal but often powerful standards of conduct that members share and use to guide their behavior. Norms define acceptable behavior by setting limits, identifying values, and clarifying expectations. By encouraging consistent behavior, norms boost efficiency and help ensure the group's survival. Individuals who deviate from these norms can find themselves ridiculed, isolated, or even removed from the group entirely. (This fear is the leading cause of groupthink, by the way.) Norms can be established in various ways: from early behaviors that set precedents for future actions, from significant events in the team's history, from behaviors that come to the team through outside influences, and from a leader's or member's explicit statements that have an impact on other members.[39]

norms Informal standards of conduct that guide team behavior

TEAM CONFLICT

As teams mature and go about their work, conflicts can arise. Although the term *conflict* sounds negative, conflict isn't necessarily bad. It can be *constructive* if it brings important issues into the open, increases the involvement of team members, and generates creative ideas for solving a problem. Teamwork isn't necessarily about happiness and harmony; even teams that have some interpersonal friction can excel if they have effective leadership and team players committed to strong results. As teamwork experts Andy Boynton and Bill Fischer put it, "Virtuoso teams are not about getting polite results."[40]

REAL-TIME UPDATES

Learn More by Listening to This Podcast

Collaboration done right

Hear UC Berkeley's Morten Hansen explain the difference between good collaboration and bad collaboration. Go to http://real-timeupdates.com/bia6 and click on Learn More. If you are using MyBizLab, you can access Real-Time Updates within the chapter or under Student Study Tools.

In contrast, conflict is *destructive* if it diverts energy from more important issues, destroys the morale of teams or individual team members, or polarizes or divides the team.[41] Destructive conflict can lead to *win-lose* or *lose-lose* outcomes, in which one or both sides lose, to the detriment of the entire team. If you approach conflict with the idea that both sides can satisfy their goals to at least some extent (a *win-win strategy*), you can minimize losses for everyone. For a win-win strategy to work, everybody must believe that (1) it's possible to find a solution that both parties can accept, (2) cooperation is better for the organization than competition, (3) the other party can be trusted, and (4) greater power or status doesn't entitle one party to impose a solution.

Causes of Team Conflict

Team conflict can arise for a number of reasons. First, individuals may feel they are in competition for scarce or declining resources, such as money, information, and supplies. Second, team members may disagree over responsibilities. Third, poor communication can lead to misunderstandings and misperceptions. In addition, withholding information can undermine trust among members. Fourth, basic differences in values, attitudes, and personalities may lead to clashes. Fifth, power struggles may result when one party questions the authority of another or when people or teams with limited authority attempt to increase their power or exert more influence. Sixth, conflicts can arise because individual team members are pursuing different goals.[42]

Solutions to Team Conflict

As with any other human relationship, the way a team approaches conflict depends to a large degree on how well the team was functioning in the first place. A strong, healthy team is more likely to view a conflict as simply another challenge to overcome—and it can emerge from the conflict even stronger than before. In contrast, a generally dysfunctional team can disintegrate even further when faced with a new source of conflict.

The following seven measures can help team members successfully resolve conflict:

- **Proactive attention.** Deal with minor conflict before it becomes major conflict.
- **Communication.** Get those directly involved in a conflict to participate in resolving it.
- **Openness.** Get feelings out in the open before dealing with the main issues.
- **Research.** Seek factual reasons for a problem before seeking solutions.
- **Flexibility.** Don't let anyone lock into a position before considering other solutions.
- **Fair play.** Insist on fair outcomes and don't let anyone avoid a fair solution by hiding behind the rules.
- **Alliance.** Get opponents to fight together against an "outside force" instead of against each other.

Team members and team leaders can also take several steps to prevent conflicts. First, by establishing clear goals that require the efforts of every member, the team reduces the chance that members will battle over their objectives or roles. Second, by developing well-defined tasks for each member, the team leader ensures that all parties are aware of their responsibilities and the limits of their authority. Finally, by facilitating open communication, the team leader can ensure that all members understand their own tasks and objectives as well as those of their teammates. Communication builds respect and tolerance, and it provides a forum for bringing misunderstandings into the open before they turn into full-blown conflicts.

✓ Checkpoint

LEARNING OBJECTIVE 5: Review the five stages of team development, and explain why conflict can arise in team settings.

SUMMARY: Several models have been proposed to describe the stages of team development; the well-known model defined by researcher Bruce Tuckman identifies the stages as *forming*, *storming*, *norming*, *performing*, and *adjourning*. In the forming stage, team members become acquainted with each other and with the group's purpose. In the storming stage, conflict often arises as coalitions and power struggles develop. In the norming stage, conflicts are resolved and harmony develops. In the performing stage, members focus on achieving the team's goals. In the adjourning stage, the team dissolves upon completion of its task. Conflict can arise from competition for scarce resources; confusion over task responsibility; poor communication and misinformation; differences in values, attitudes, and personalities; power struggles; and incompatible goals.

CRITICAL THINKING: (1) How can a team leader know when to step in when conflict arises and when to step back and let the issue work itself out? (2) What are the risks of not giving new teams the time and opportunity to "storm" and "norm" before tackling the work they've been assigned?

IT'S YOUR BUSINESS: (1) Have you ever had to be teammates (in any activity) with someone you simply didn't like on a personal level? If so, how did this situation affect your performance as a team member? (2) Have you ever had to adapt your personality in order to succeed on a particular team? Was this a positive or negative experience?

KEY TERMS TO KNOW: cohesiveness, norms

Managing an Unstructured Organization

6 | **LEARNING OBJECTIVE**

Explain the concept of an unstructured organization, and identify the major benefits and challenges of taking this approach.

Much of the thinking in past decades about organization strategies in business centered on the best way to structure a company to compete effectively and operate efficiently. However, a number of companies are concluding that the best way to organize might be with little or no structure at all, at least in terms of the traditional forms. Such **unstructured organizations** are using digital technologies—and global socioeconomic changes enabled by these technologies—to rapidly form and re-form work patterns that bear almost no resemblance to the classic structures.

unstructured organization An organization that doesn't have a conventional structure but instead assembles talent as needed from the open market; the virtual and networked organizational concepts taken to the extreme

These innovators are experimenting with various combinations of virtual organizations, networked organizations, crowdsourcing, outsourcing, and *hyperspecialization*, the division of work into narrowly focused tasks that can be assigned to specialists who become highly skilled at those discrete tasks.[43] The new "formless forms" are enabled by cloud computing, mobile communication, online collaboration platforms, and all manner of social networking tools. All of these elements have been in use for some time, but the mashup of new thinking and new technology promises to unleash them in revolutionary ways. In a sense, by binding together a temporary organization, these technologies take the place of the lines and boxes that define a traditional organization chart.

Just about any category and skill level of work seems a possible candidate for these new approaches—and particularly those that can be expressed digitally. Professions and functions already being affected include software development, product design, visual design, scientific research, legal research, business writing, clerical work, and customer support.[44]

For example, a solo entrepreneur can now quickly assemble a product development team to conceptualize and design a product, then immediately disassemble that team and build a manufacturing team to make the product, and then assemble a sales and customer support team to get the product on the market—all without hiring a single employee. Moreover, this entrepreneur could tap into some of the best technical talent in the world, with top scientists, engineers, and software developers competing to see who can do the best job on the new product. And rather than taking months to establish a company by recruiting employees, leasing office space, hiring supervisors, buying computers, setting up a payroll system, training staffers, and doing all the many other tasks involved in running a conventional company, this entrepreneur could sit at home in his or her pajamas and in a matter of days create an essentially formless company that successfully competes in the global marketplace.

The software development company TopCoder (www.topcoder.com) offers a great illustration of the potential of this new way of working. Billing itself as "The world's largest competitive community for software development and digital creation," TopCoder boasts a membership of more than 300,000 computer scientists and software engineers (including many who are still in college), representing virtually every country in the world. Clients such as our pajama-clad entrepreneur present TopCoder with one or more design challenges, and the members then compete to come up with the best solutions.[45] Instead of auditioning several regular vendors and hoping to make the right choice or hiring a small staff of generalists and hoping they'll be able to handle the many specialized tasks involved in developing the software for a new product, our entrepreneur could get the best of the best working on each part of the design. And when the design work is completed, the various TopCoder members move on to compete on other client projects, and the entrepreneur moves on to assembling teams of manufacturing and marketing specialists.

Just where these changes are taking the business enterprise is difficult to guess because the revolution is still underway. Some firms may adopt these structureless approaches extensively, while others may use them for specific projects. Even if you spend your career in a conventionally structured company, these changes are likely to affect you because they are accelerating the pace of business, influencing the worldwide talent market, and even changing the nature of work itself in some cases (such as introducing project-by-project talent competition).

The following sections take a look at some of the potential benefits and points of concern that are emerging in relation to these new approaches to organization (see Exhibit 9 for a summary).

POTENTIAL BENEFITS OF UNSTRUCTURED ORGANIZATIONS

Unstructured organization promises a number of benefits for firms of all sizes, from entrepreneurs who apply the concept to their entire operations to larger firms that use it for specific parts of the company or individual projects:[46]

- **Increased agility.** In many instances, virtual organizations can be assembled, reconfigured as needed, and disassembled much faster than a conventional employee-based organization can be created, changed, or dismantled. This agility makes it easier to jump on emerging market trends and then change course when the market changes again.
- **Lower fixed costs and more flexible capacity management.** Hiring employees to build organizational capacity increases a company's *fixed costs*, those costs that are incurred regardless of production or sales volumes. With the unstructured approach, companies have much more flexibility in adjusting their expense levels to match revenue levels.
- **Access to otherwise unreachable talent.** "Talent markets" such as TopCoder give many more companies access to these highly developed and often hyperspecialized talents. Companies that might never be able to attract or afford top experts in a field can essentially rent them project by project instead.
- **Benefits of competition.** While most employees are motivated to do good work most of the time, independent individuals working through TopCoder, Guru (www.guru.com), LiveOps (www.liveops.com), and other aggregators must do their best on every single project—and compete with other independents in what is essential a global marketplace—or risk not getting more assignments. Companies that engage contract talent clearly benefit from this competition. In addition, talent markets such as TopCoder and InnoCentive actually structure projects as competitions, in which potential solution providers compete to offer the best ideas and work products.

For workers, the unstructured model also offers several potential benefits:[47]

- **Performance-based evaluation.** Workers tend to be evaluated almost entirely on measurable performance, project by project—on what they can do for a client, not on who they know in the executive suite, where they went to college, or what they did last year.

EXHIBIT 9	Benefits and Challenges of Unstructured Organizations

The unstructured organization is an extreme version of the virtual and networked models, in which a company assembles freelance talent as needed from the open market rather than hiring and organizing employees in a conventional organizational structure.

Potential Benefits		Potential Challenges	
For Companies	**For Workers**	**For Companies**	**For Workers**
• **Increased agility:** Companies can respond to or create opportunities faster and then reorganize and move on when needed. • **Lower fixed costs:** Fewer employees means fewer bills to pay every month. • **More flexible capacity management:** Firms can ramp capacity up and down more quickly and with less trauma. • **Access to star talent:** Managers can "rent" top talent that is too expensive to hire full time or unwilling to work full time. • **Benefitting from competition:** Firms can stage competitions in talent markets to see who can devise the best solutions to problems.	• **Performance-based evaluation:** The only thing that matters is getting the job done. • **Freedom and flexibility:** Workers have more leeway in choosing which projects they want and how much they want to work. • **Access to more interesting and more fulfilling work:** Workers can get access to opportunities that might be unreachable otherwise.	• **Complexity and control issues:** Workers often have competing demands on their time and attention, and managers lack many of the organizational control and incentive "levers" that a regular company has. • **Uncertainty:** Without staff at the ready, companies won't always know if they'll be able to get the talent they need. • **Diminished loyalty:** Managers have to deal with a workforce that doesn't have the same sense of loyalty to the organization that many full-time employees do. • **Management succession:** Companies with fewer employees will find it harder to groom replacement managers and executives. • **Accountability and liability:** Unstructured organizations lack the built-in accountability of conventional structures, and the distribution of work among multiple independent parties could create liability concerns.	• **Uncertainty:** Workers can't be sure they'll have work from one project to the next. • **Loss of meaning and connection:** Independent workers don't get the same sense of working together for a larger, shared purpose that employees get. • **Diminished loyalty:** Workers don't have the same sense employees often do that an organization is looking out for them and will reward sacrifices and effort above and beyond contractual obligations. • **Career development:** Without full-time employers to guide, support, and train them, workers are left to fend for themselves and to keep their skills current at their own expense.

Sources: Adapted in part from Darren Dahl, "Want a Job? Let the Bidding Begin," *Inc.*, March 2011, 93–96; Thomas W. Malone, Robert J. Laubacher, and Tammy Johns, "The Age of Hyperspecialization," *Harvard Business Review*, July-August 2011, 56–65; Jennifer Wang, "The Solution to the Innovator's Dilemma," *Entrepreneur*, August 2011, 24–32; Marjorie Derven, "Managing the Matrix in the New Normal," *T+D*, July 2010, 42–47.

- **Freedom and flexibility.** The flip side of agility for companies is extreme flexibility for workers, particularly after they establish themselves in a field. Within the limits of financial need and project availability, of course, independent contractors can often pick and choose the clients and projects that interest them most and decide how much or how little they want to work.
- **Access to jobs that might be otherwise unattainable.** For people geographically removed from major employment centers, finding decent employment can be a serious challenge. The distributed, virtual approach gives people in rural areas and small towns greater access to job opportunities.

POTENTIAL CHALLENGES OF UNSTRUCTURED ORGANIZATIONS

For all its benefits, the unstructured approach presents some potential drawbacks, some of them considerable. These challenges will discourage many companies and workers from taking this route, and they'll make it more difficult for those who do:[48]

- **Complexity and control issues.** Unstructured organizations can be even more complex than matrix organizations because workers not only have multiple bosses but report to multiple bosses in multiple companies. In addition, even though companies can in effect hire and fire independent contractors more easily, they have less control over this talent than they have over permanent employees.

- **Uncertainty.** Without full-time staff at the ready, companies won't always know if they can get the talent they need for upcoming projects. Conversely, workers won't always know if they'll have a job from one project to the next.

- **Loss of meaning and connection.** Being a full-time employee of an organization means more than just employment to many people. Companies also provide a social structure that is as close as family for some employees. Moreover, the opportunity to help an organization succeed over the long haul, to work with others for a greater purpose, is an important motivator and provides a sense of pride for many employees. Independent contractors who move from project to project don't have the chance to form such bonds.

- **Diminished loyalty.** The bond that develops between employers and employees over time creates a sense of loyalty that can carry both parties through hard times. Employers often make accommodations for employees going through tough personal circumstances, for instance. And many employees are willing to make or at least accept short-term sacrifices that benefit their companies in the long term (such as helping colleagues in addition to doing their own work or accepting pay reductions during periods of slow sales). However, this sense of "all for one and one for all" is not likely to factor heavily in most unstructured scenarios, where workers are more like competing vendors than members of a family.

- **Career development.** Conventional organizations do much more than just put resources in place to tackle one project after another. They invest in employees over months or years, giving them time and opportunities to develop deep knowledge and skills, with the idea that the investment will pay off in the long term. However, independent contractors are responsible for developing themselves, while they're busy making a living, so keeping up with developments in their professions presents a greater burden than it does for typical employees.

- **Management succession.** As companies develop their employees, they also groom future managers and executives who understand both the company internally and its multiple external environments. Without these development channels in place, companies could be hard pressed to replace upper managers when the time comes.

- **Accountability and liability.** Conventional structures tend to have clear lines of accountability up and down the chain of command (meaning who is responsible if things go awry) and clear assignments of legal or financial liability in the event of major foul-ups. However, the situation might not be quite so clear in an unstructured organization that relies on a temporary assemblage of independent companies and contractors.

While these challenges should not be taken lightly by companies or workers, they are likely to be manageable in enough different scenarios that the unstructured approach will catch on in more and more industries. Exactly where unstructured organizations will take the world of business will be interesting to see.

✓ Checkpoint

LEARNING OBJECTIVE 6: Explain the concept of an unstructured organization, and identify the major benefits and challenges of taking this approach.

SUMMARY: An unstructured organization doesn't rely on conventional organizational structures to assemble the resources needed to pursue business goals. Instead, it assembles independent contractors or companies, as needed, for specific tasks or functions, relying on electronic communications to replace much of the structural linkages in a conventional company. The potential benefits for companies are increased agility, lower fixed costs and more flexible capacity management, access to otherwise unreachable talent, and the benefits of competition among workers or service providers. For workers, the benefits include performance-based evaluation of their efforts, more freedom and flexibility to choose which projects to work on and how much to work, and access to jobs that might be otherwise unattainable. The potential disadvantages of the unstructured approach include complexity and control issues for managers, greater uncertainty for companies and workers, the loss of meaning and connection to a greater purpose for employees, diminished loyalty for both employers and employees, uncertainties in career development and management succession, and concerns over accountability and liability.

CRITICAL THINKING: (1) "Unstructured organization" is something of a contradiction in terms; are such companies still "organized" if they have no permanent structure? Why or why not? (2) How can workers develop marketable skills if they work as independent contractors?

IT'S YOUR BUSINESS: (1) Where do you think you would be most comfortable, as a regular employee in a conventionally structured firm or as an independent contractor, moving from project to project? Why? (2) Assume that you went to work for a conventional employer and then left to work as an independent contractor as soon as you developed enough of a skill set to make it on your own. (Assume as well that you were not violating any sort of employment contract and were free to leave.) Would you have any ethical concerns about leaving an employer who had invested in your professional development? Why or why not?

KEY TERM TO KNOW: unstructured organization

BEHIND THE SCENES

TEAMING UP FOR SUCCESS AT THE CONTAINER STORE

MyBizLab

The Container Store was not started with a modest goal. Founders Garrett Boone and Kip Tindell set out to become the "best retail store in the United States." Judging by feedback from customers and employees, they just might have succeeded.

As millions of frustrated consumers know all too well, though, delivering great customer service in retail environments isn't easy. The Container Store does it with strong company values, respect for employees, and a structure that promotes teamwork over individual competition. The company's values flow from the idea that people are its greatest asset because they are the key to exceptional service. The notion that "people are our greatest asset" is repeated often in the business world and often without substance to back it up, but The Container Store goes to extraordinary lengths to practice what it preaches. The company isn't bashful about saying employees are its number-one priority, either, saying that while business involves "an interdependent set of stakeholders—employees, customers, vendors, the community and shareholders. At The Container Store, we firmly believe our employee is the #1 stakeholder. In doing so, employees take better care of customers and ultimately the shareholders experience greater benefit from this approach to business."

To put employees first, however, the company makes sure it has the best employees it can find. Far from viewing employees as interchangeable parts, Tindell even says, "I choose employees and friends the same way." The Container Store uses a comprehensive interviewing and selection process to find the perfect person for each position, driven by the belief that "one great person equals three good people in terms of business productivity." Most employees are college educated, almost half come from employee referrals, and most have been customers of the store. They are also self-motivated, team oriented, and passionate about customer service.

Those traits are enhanced by extensive employee development: New full-time employees receive over 200 hours of training in their first year and nearly that much every year thereafter. In comparison, most retailers give new workers less than 10 hours of training per year. As a result, employees feel extremely confident in their ability to help customers, and positive feedback from customers continues to build that confidence.

The Container Store also pays three to four times the minimum wage, offering wages as much as 50 to 100 percent above those of other retailers. The financial security builds loyalty and helps keep annual turnover at a fraction of the typical turnover rates in the industry. What's more, salespeople are not paid commissions, unlike retail staffs in many other companies. Without the constant pressure to "make the numbers," it's easier for employees to take their time with customers, using their creative instincts and extensive training to design complete solutions to customers' storage problems. By not paying commissions, The Container Store also helps employees sense that they're all part of a team rather than being in competition with one another.

That emphasis on teamwork is reinforced twice a day, before opening and after closing, through a meeting called "the huddle." Similar to a huddle in football, it helps give everyone a common purpose: set goals, share information, boost morale, and bond as a team. Morning sessions feature spirited discussions of sales goals and product applications and may include a chorus of "Happy Birthday" for celebrating team members. Evening huddles include more team building and friendly competitions such as guessing the daily sales figures. Tindell believes that full, open communication with employees takes courage but says, "The only way that people feel really, really a part of something is if they know everything."

The Container Store differs dramatically from many other retail establishments in the way it embraces part-time employees. These workers are essential at the busiest times, such as evenings and holiday seasons, but they are treated as second-class citizens in some companies. Not at The Container Store. To begin with, the company refers to them as "prime-time" employees, not part-time, since these staffers are most valuable in those prime-time rush periods. And these people also receive extensive training and are treated as equal members of the team at each store. As one prime-timer in Houston puts it, "Everyone is treated as an important human being. I don't feel like a part-time employee at all—I feel like a professional. They make belonging easy and a source of pride."

By aligning its corporate values with its management practices and its organization structure, The Container Store paves the way for its employees to deliver great customer service. And by frequently astonishing its employees with enlightened leadership, the company sets a strong example for the people in blue aprons who are expected to astonish customers every day.

People outside the company notice, too. The Container Store has become a consistent winner in such nationwide forums as the annual Performance Through People Award, presented by Northwestern University, and *Fortune* magazine's annual list of "The 100 Best Companies to Work For."[49] And it all starts with teamwork. As Tindell says, "I think we do team as well as anybody I've ever seen."

Critical Thinking Questions

1. Based on what you've learned about the way employees at The Container Store interact with customers, do you think that the company emphasizes centralized or decentralized decision making? Explain your answer.
2. How might the company's emphasis on teamwork affect accountability and authority?
3. What effect might a change to commission-based compensation have on the team structure at The Container Store?

LEARN MORE ONLINE

Visit The Container Store's website, at www.containerstore.com, and read about the company's history, its culture, and the benefits it offers employees. What do you think of the company's belief that one great person equals three good people? What kinds of jobs are available in stores, the home office, and the distribution center?

MyBizLab

Log on to www.mybizlab.com to access study and assessment aids associated with this chapter.

KEY TERMS

agile organization	line-and-staff organization
centralization	matrix structure
chain of command	network structure
cohesiveness	norms
committee	organization chart
core competencies	organization structure
cross-functional team	problem-solving team
decentralization	self-managed team
departmentalization	span of management
divisional structure	task force
functional structure	team
functional team	unstructured organization
groupthink	virtual team
line organization	work specialization

TEST YOUR KNOWLEDGE

Questions for Review

1. What is an agile organization?
2. What are the characteristics of tall organizations and flat organizations?
3. What are the advantages and disadvantages of work specialization?
4. What are the advantages and disadvantages of functional departmentalization?
5. What are the potential benefits and potential disadvantages of the unstructured organizational model?

Questions for Analysis

6. Why is it important for companies to decide on their core competencies before choosing an organization structure?
7. How can a virtual organization reduce costs?
8. What can managers do to help teams work more effectively?
9. How can companies benefit from using virtual teams?
10. **Ethical Considerations.** You were honored to be selected to serve on the salary committee of the employee negotiations task force. As a member of that committee, you reviewed confidential company documents listing the salaries of all department managers. You discovered that other managers at your level are earning $25,000 more than you, even though you've been at the company the same amount of time. You feel that a raise is justified on the basis of this confidential information. How will you handle this situation?

Questions for Application

11. You are the leader of a cross-functional work team whose goal is to find ways of lowering production costs. Your team of eight employees has become mired in the storming stage. The team members disagree on how to approach the task, and they are starting to splinter into factions, each pursuing its own goal. What can you do to help the team move forward?
12. You've recently accepted a job as the U.S. sales manager for a German manufacturing company. One of your first assignments is serving on a virtual problem-solving team with colleagues from Germany, France, Japan, and South Korea. Budgets are tight, so you won't have the opportunity to meet with your teammates in person to get to know one another. What steps can you take to help the team develop into a cohesive and efficient unit?
13. **Concept Integration.** One of your competitors has approached you with an intriguing proposition. The company would like to merge with your company. The economies of scale are terrific. So are the growth possibilities. There's just one issue to be resolved. Your competitor is organized under a flat structure and uses lots of cross-functional teams. Your company is organized under a traditional tall structure that is departmentalized by function. Using your knowledge about culture clash, what are the likely issues you will encounter if these two organizations are merged?
14. This question was intentionally excluded from this edition.

EXPAND YOUR KNOWLEDGE

Discovering Career Opportunities

Whether you're a top manager, first-line manager (supervisor), or middle manager, your efforts will impact the success of your organization. To get a closer look at what the responsibilities of a manager are, log on to the Prentice Hall Student Success Super-Site, at www.prenhall.com/success. Click on Majors Exploration and select Business and then Management in the drop-down boxes. Then scroll down and read about careers in management.

1. What can you do with a degree in management?
2. What is the future outlook for careers in management?
3. Scroll down to "Advice from a Management Professor." After reading this information, does management appeal to you as a major? Why or why not?

Improving Your Tech Insights: Wireless Connectivity

Wireless connectivity—both local area Wi-Fi and wide area mobile phone networks—gives businesses three major benefits.

The first is making information available where and when it can be most useful. The second is untethering workers from physical locations, allowing them to be productive wherever they want or need to be. The third major benefit is simplifying the connection between people and computers. This technology can help in a variety of ways, from making it easier to add networking to an older building that doesn't have wires running through the walls to enabling business teams to move around large corporate campuses (to attend team meetings, for example) without losing their connections to the company network. Research the ways businesses are using wireless connectivity to overcome organizational boundaries, enhance teamwork, improve customer service, or improve meetings. Identify three examples in a brief email to your instructor.

PRACTICE YOUR SKILLS

Sharpening Your Communication Skills

In group meetings, some of your colleagues have a habit of interrupting and arguing with the speaker, taking credit for ideas that aren't theirs, and shooting down ideas they don't agree with. You're the newest person in the group and not sure if this is accepted behavior in this company, but it concerns you both personally and professionally. Should you go with the flow and adopt their behavior or stick with your own communication style, even though you might get lost in the noise? In two paragraphs, explain the pros and cons of both approaches.

Building Your Team Skills

What's the most effective organization structure for your college or university? With your team, obtain a copy of your school's organization chart. If this chart is not readily available, gather information by talking with people in administration and then draw your own chart of the organization structure.

Analyze the chart in terms of span of management. Is your school a flat or a tall organization? Is this organization structure appropriate for your school? Does decision making tend to be centralized or decentralized in your school? Do you agree with this approach to decision making?

Finally, investigate the use of formal and informal teams in your school. Are there any problem-solving teams, task forces, or committees at work in your school? Are any teams self-directed or virtual? How much authority do these teams have to make decisions? What is the purpose of teamwork in your school? What kinds of goals do these teams have?

Share your team's findings during a brief classroom presentation and then compare the findings of all teams. Is there agreement on the appropriate organization structure for your school?

Developing Your Research Skills

Although teamwork can benefit many organizations, introducing and managing team structures can be a real challenge. Search past issues of business journals or newspapers (print or online editions) to locate articles about how an organization has overcome problems with teams.

1. Why did the organization originally introduce teams? What types of teams are being used?
2. What problems did each organization encounter in trying to implement teams? How did the organization deal with these problems?
3. Have the teams been successful from management's perspective? From the employees' perspective? What effect has teamwork had on the company, its customers, and its products?

REFERENCES

1. "Container Store's Hiring Secret," *Fortune* video, accessed 23 August 2011, http://money.cnn.com; The Container Store website, accessed 23 August 2011, www.containerstore.com; "100 Best Companies to Work For," *Fortune*, accessed 14 April 2009, www.fortune.com; Bob Nelson, "Can't Contain Excitement at The Container Store," BizJournals.com, accessed 11 March 2005, www.bizjournals.com; Mike Duff, "Top-Shelf Employees Keep Container Store on Track," *DSN Retailing Today*, 8 March 2004, 7, 49; Bob Nelson, "The Buzz at The Container Store," *Corporate Meetings & Incentives*, June 2003, 32; Jennifer Saba, "Balancing Act," *Potentials*, 1 October 2003, www.highbeam.com; Peter S. Cohan, "Corporate Heroes," *Financial Executive*, 1 March 2003, www.highbeam.com; Margaret Steen, "Container Store's Focus on Training a Strong Appeal to Employees," *Mercury News* (San Jose, Calif.), 6 November 2003, www.highbeam.com; Holly Hayes, "Container Store Brings Clutter Control to San Jose, Calif.," 17 October 2003, *Mercury News* (San Jose, Calif.), 1F; "Performance Through People Award," press release, 10 September 2003; David Lipke, "Container Store's CEO: People Are Most Valued Asset," *HFN*, 13 January 2003, www.highbeam.com; Lorrie Grant, "Container Store's Workers Huddle Up to Help You Out," 30 April 2002, *USA Today*, B1.
2. "Benefits of Outsourcing Payroll," *Practical Accountant*, November 2008, SR9.
3. "Capabilities" and "History," Frog Design website, accessed 16 August 2011, www.frogdesign.com.
4. Stephen P. Robbins and David A. DeCenzo, *Management*, 4th ed. (Upper Saddle River, N.J.: Pearson Prentice Hall, 2004), 142–143.
5. Charles R. Greer and W. Richard Plunkett, *Supervision: Diversity and Teams in the Workplace*, 10th ed. (Upper Saddle River, N.J.: Prentice Hall, 2003), 77.
6. Caroline Ellis, "The Flattening Corporation," *MIT Sloan Management Review*, Summer 2003, 5.

7. "Container Store's Hiring Secret."
8. "Why Middle Managers May Be the Most Important People in Your Company," Knowledge@Wharton, 25 May 2011, http://knowledge.wharton.upenn.edu.
9. Gareth R. Jones, *Organizational Theory, Design, and Change*, 4th ed. (Upper Saddle River, N.J.: Pearson Prentice Hall, 2004), 109.
10. Jones, *Organizational Theory, Design, and Change*, 109–111.
11. Richard L. Daft, *Management*, 6th ed. (Mason, Ohio: South-Western, 2003), 320.
12. Jones, *Organizational Theory, Design, and Change*, 163.
13. Jones, *Organizational Theory, Design, and Change*, 167.
14. "Our Businesses," Chevron website, accessed 16 August 2011, www.chevron.com.
15. Daft, *Management*, 324–327.
16. Marjorie Derven, "Managing the Matrix in the New Normal," *T+D*, July 2010, 42–47.
17. Jerald Greenberg and Robert A. Baron, *Behavior in Organizations*, 8th ed. (Upper Saddle River, N.J.: Prentice Hall, 2003), 558–560; Daft, *Management*, 329.
18. Derven, "Managing the Matrix in the New Normal."
19. Pete Engardio and Bruce Einhorn, "Outsourcing Innovation," *BusinessWeek*, 21 March 2005, 84–94.
20. Stephen P. Robbins, *Essentials of Organizational Behavior*, 6th ed. (Upper Saddle River, N.J.: Prentice Hall, 2000), 105.
21. Greer and Plunkett, *Supervision*, 293.
22. "Attacking Claim Denials," *Receivables Report for America's Health Care Financial Managers*, October 2007, 1–6.
23. Steven A. Frankforter and Sandra L. Christensen, "Finding Competitive Advantage in Self-Managed Work Teams," *Business Forum*, 2005, Vol. 27, Issue 1, 20–24.
24. Daft, *Management*, 594; Robbins and DeCenzo, *Fundamentals of Management*, 336.

25. Daft, *Management*, 618; Robbins and DeCenzo, *Fundamentals of Management*, 262.
26. Morten T. Hansen, "When Internal Collaboration Is Bad for Your Company," *Harvard Business Review*, April 2009, 82–88.
27. Jerry Fjermestad, "Virtual Leadership for a Virtual Workforce," *Chief Learning Officer*, March 2009, 36–39.
28. Jenny Goodbody, "Critical Success Factors for Global Virtual Teams," *Strategic Communication Management*, February/March 2005, 18–21; Ann Majchrzak, Arvind Malhotra, Jeffrey Stamps, and Jessica Lipnack, "Can Absence Make a Team Grow Stronger?" *Harvard Business Review*, May 2004, 131–137.
29. Richard McDermott and Douglas Archibald, "Harnessing Your Staff's Informal Networks," *Harvard Business Review*, March 2010, 82–89.
30. Tony Hsieh, "Why I Sold Zappos," *Inc.*, 1 June 2010, www.inc.com.
31. Robbins and DeCenzo, *Fundamentals of Management*, 257–258; Daft, *Management*, 634–636.
32. "Groups Best at Complex Problems," *Industrial Engineer*, June 2006, 14.
33. Max Landsberg and Madeline Pfau, "Developing Diversity: Lessons from Top Teams," *Strategy + Business*, Winter 2005, 10–12.
34. Derven, "Managing the Matrix in the New Normal"; Robert Kreitner, *Management*, 9th ed. (Boston: Houghton Mifflin, 2004), 475–481; Daft, *Management*, 635–636.
35. Lynda Gratton and Tamara J. Erickson, "8 Ways to Build Collaborative Teams," *Harvard Business Review*, November 2007, 100–109.
36. Jon R. Katzenbach and Douglas K. Smith, "The Discipline of Teams," *Harvard Business Review*, July/August 2005, 162–171; Laird Mealiea and Ramon Baltazar, "A Strategic Guide for Building Effective Teams," *Public Personnel Management*, Summer 2005, 141–160; Larry Cole and Michael Cole, "Why Is the Teamwork Buzz Word Not Working?" *Communication World*, February/March 1999, 29; Patricia Buhler, "Managing in the 90s: Creating Flexibility in Today's Workplace," *Supervision*, January 1997, 24+; Allison W. Amason, Allen C. Hochwarter, Wayne A. Thompson, and Kenneth R. Harrison, "Conflict: An Important Dimension in Successful Management Teams," *Organizational Dynamics*, Autumn 1995, 20+.
37. Jared Sandberg, "Some Ideas Are So Bad That Only a Team Effort Can Account for Them," *Wall Street Journal*, 29 September 2004, B1.
38. Mark K. Smith, "Bruce W. Tuckman—Forming, Storming, Norming, and Performing in Groups," Infed.org, accessed 5 July 2005, www.infed.org; Robbins and DeCenzo, *Fundamentals of Management*, 258–259; Daft, *Management*, 625–627.
39. Jones, *Organizational Theory, Design, and Change*, 112–113; Greenberg and Baron, *Behavior in Organizations*, 280–281; Daft, *Management*, 629–631.
40. Andy Boynton and Bill Fischer, *Virtuoso Teams: Lessons from Teams That Changed Their Worlds* (Harrow, UK: FT Prentice Hall, 2005), 10.
41. Thomas K. Capozzoli, "Conflict Resolution—A Key Ingredient in Successful Teams," *Supervision*, November 1999, 14–16.
42. Daft, *Management*, 631–632.
43. Darren Dahl, "Want a Job? Let the Bidding Begin," *Inc.*, March 2011, 93–96; Thomas W. Malone, Robert J. Laubacher, and Tammy Johns, "The Age of Hyperspecialization," *Harvard Business Review*, July–August 2011, 56–65.
44. Malone, et al., "The Age of Hyperspecialization."
45. "How Does It Work?" TopCoder website, accessed 18 August 2011, www.topcoder.com.
46. Adapted from Dahl, "Want a Job? Let the Bidding Begin," Malone, et al., "The Age of Hyperspecialization"; Jennifer Wang, "The Solution to the Innovator's Dilemma," *Entrepreneur*, August 2011, 24–32; Derven, "Managing the Matrix in the New Normal."
47. "LiveOps and Vision Perry Create New Work Opportunities for Rural Tennessee," LiveOps press release, 18 July 2011, www.liveops.com; Malone, et al., "The Age of Hyperspecialization."
48. Adapted from Dahl, "Want a Job? Let the Bidding Begin," Malone, et al., "The Age of Hyperspecialization"; Wang, "The Solution to the Innovator's Dilemma"; "Managing the Matrix in the New Normal."
49. See note 1.

GLOSSARY

agile organization A company whose structure, policies, and capabilities allow employees to respond quickly to customer needs and changes in the business environment

centralization Concentration of decision-making authority at the top of an organization

chain of command A pathway for the flow of authority from one management level to the next

cohesiveness A measure of how committed team members are to their team's goals

committee A team that may become a permanent part of the organization and is designed to deal with regularly recurring tasks

core competencies Activities that a company considers central and vital to its business

cross-functional team A team that draws together employees from different functional areas

decentralization Delegation of decision-making authority to employees in lower-level positions

departmentalization Grouping people within an organization according to function, division, matrix, or network

divisional structure Grouping departments according to similarities in product, process, customer, or geography

functional structure Grouping workers according to their similar skills, resource use, and expertise

functional team A team whose members come from a single functional department and that is based on the organization's vertical structure

groupthink Uniformity of thought that occurs when peer pressures cause individual team members to withhold contrary or unpopular opinions

line organization A chain-of-command system that establishes a clear line of authority flowing from the top down

line-and-staff organization An organization system that has a clear chain of command but that also includes functional groups of people who provide advice and specialized services8

matrix structure A structure in which employees are assigned to both a functional group and a project team (thus using functional and divisional patterns simultaneously)

network structure A structure in which individual companies are connected electronically to perform selected tasks for a small headquarters organization

norms Informal standards of conduct that guide team behavior

organization chart A diagram that shows how employees and tasks are grouped and where the lines of communication and authority flow

organization structure A framework that enables managers to divide responsibilities, ensure employee accountability, and distribute decision-making authority

problem-solving team A team that meets to find ways of improving quality, efficiency, and the work environment

self-managed team A team in which members are responsible for an entire process or operation

span of management The number of people under one manager's control; also known as span of control

task force A team of people from several departments who are temporarily brought together to address a specific issue

team A unit of two or more people who share a mission and collective responsibility as they work together to achieve a goal

unstructured organization An organization that doesn't have a conventional structure but instead assembles talent as needed from the open market; the virtual and networked organizational concepts taken to the extreme

virtual team A team that uses communication technology to bring together geographically distant employees to achieve goals

work specialization Specialization in or responsibility for some portion of an organization's overall work tasks; also called division of labor

Forms of Ownership

From Chapter 5 of *Business in Action*, Sixth Edition. Courtland L. Bovée, John V. Thill. Copyright © 2013 by Pearson Education, Inc. Published by Pearson Business. All rights reserved.

Forms of Ownership

LEARNING OBJECTIVES   After studying this chapter, you will be able to

1 Define *sole proprietorship* and explain the six advantages and six disadvantages of this ownership model

2 Define *partnership* and explain the six advantages and three disadvantages of this ownership model

3 Define *corporation* and explain the four advantages and six disadvantages of this ownership model

4 Explain the concept of *corporate governance* and identify the three groups responsible for ensuring good governance

5 Identify the potential advantages of pursuing mergers and acquisitions as a growth strategy, along with the potential difficulties and risks

6 Define *strategic alliance* and *joint venture* and explain why a company would choose these options over a merger or an acquisition

MyBizLab

Where you see MyBizLab in this chapter, go to www.mybizlab.com for additional activities on the topic being discussed.

BEHIND THE SCENES   SCANNING THE SKIES FOR HELP AT SIRIUS SATELLITE RADIO

Faced with mounting competition and a tough financial environment, Sirius CEO Mel Karmazin began exploring ways to join forces with rival satellite radio service XM Radio.

www.siriusxm.com

From the beginning, business had been up in the air—literally and figuratively—for Sirius and XM. Both companies used satellites to broadcast multiple radio channels, and both companies struggled financially. Satellites are about the most expensive pieces of business equipment imaginable, costing more than $300 million each to build and launch. At one point, Sirius had three in the sky, XM had four, and both companies kept a spare on the ground, so satellite costs alone pushed $3 billion. And the technology to transmit signals was only part of the cost. The companies spent millions more to snag high-profile personalities and popular sporting events.

With costs like these, a company obviously needs a mammoth revenue stream to have any hope of turning a profit. However, that side of the equation wasn't any easier. Accessing satellite radio requires a special receiver and a monthly subscription fee, which puts the service at a disadvantage when consumers compare it to free *terrestrial* radio (the regular old kind of radio). Sirius and XM countered that satellite is commercial free and uncensored, and it offers content not available anywhere else. However, with the U.S. economy in the worst shape it had been in for decades, millions of consumers were cutting back on discretionary purchases such as entertainment.

If you were Mel Karmazin, CEO of Sirius, how would you address this challenge? Keeping costs under control as much as possible and aggressive marketing are obvious options, but is it time to rethink things from the ground up? Can the relatively small satellite radio market even support two independent providers, both of whom struggle with high costs? Would it make more sense to join forces with XM? If so, what would be the best approach—merge the two firms? Attempt to buy XM outright? Cooperate as two independent companies?[1]

INTRODUCTION

One of the most fundamental decisions you must make when starting a business is selecting a form of business ownership. This decision can be complex and can have far-reaching consequences for owners, employees, and customers. Picking the right ownership structure involves knowing your long-term goals and how you plan to achieve them. Your choice also depends on your desire for control and your tolerance for risk. Then as your business grows, you may need to modify the original structure, as Mel Karmazin of Sirius contemplated in the chapter-opening Behind the Scenes. And even if you have no plans to start a business, knowing the legal structure of the companies where you might work is vital information to have.

The three most common forms of business ownership are sole proprietorship, partnership, and corporation. Each form has its own characteristic internal structure, legal status, size, and fields to which it is best suited. Each has key advantages and disadvantages for the owners (see Exhibit 1).

1 LEARNING OBJECTIVE

Define *sole proprietorship,* and explain the six advantages and six disadvantages of this ownership model.

Sole Proprietorships

A **sole proprietorship** is a business owned by one person (although it may have many employees). Many farms, retail establishments, and small service businesses are sole proprietorships, as are many home-based businesses, such as those operated by caterers,

sole proprietorship A business owned by a single person

EXHIBIT 1	Forms of Business Ownership

Each of the major forms of business ownership has distinct advantages and disadvantages.

Structure	Control	Profits and Taxation	Liability Exposure	Ease of Establishment
Sole proprietorship	One owner has complete control	Profits and losses flow directly to the owners and are taxed at individual rates	Owner has unlimited personal liability for the business's financial obligations	Easy to set up; typically requires just a business license and a form to register the company name
General partnership	Two or more owners; each partner is entitled to equal control unless agreement specifies otherwise	Profits and losses flow directly to the partners and are taxed at individual rates; partners share income and losses equally unless the partnership agreement specifies otherwise	All partners have unlimited liability, meaning their personal assets are at risk for mistakes made by others partners	Easy to set up; partnership agreement not required but strongly recommended
Limited partnership	Two or more owners; one or more general partners manage the business; limited partners don't participate in the management	Same as for general partnership	Limited partners have limited liability (making them liable only for the amount of their investment); general partners have unlimited liability	Same as for general partnership
Corporation	Unlimited number of shareholders; no limits on stock classes or voting arrangements; ownership and management of the business are separate (shareholders in public corporations are not involved in management decisions; in private or closely held corporations, owners are more likely to participate in managing the business)	Profits are taxed at corporate rates; profits are taxed again at individual rates when (or if) they are distributed to investors as dividends	Investor's liability is limited to the amount of his or her investment	More complicated and expensive to establish than a sole proprietorship; requirements vary from state to state

consultants, and freelance writers. Many of the local businesses you frequent around your college campus are likely to be sole proprietorships. You may be a sole proprietor yourself: If you are paid for performing any kind of service, from babysitting to website design, without being on a company's payroll, you are legally classified as a sole proprietor.[2]

ADVANTAGES OF SOLE PROPRIETORSHIPS

Operating as a sole proprietorship offers six key advantages:

- **Simplicity.** A sole proprietorship is easy to establish and requires far less paperwork than other structures. About the only legal requirement for establishing a sole proprietorship is obtaining the necessary business licenses and permits required by the city, county, and state. Otherwise, just by starting business operations without creating a partnership or a corporation, you legally establish yourself as a sole proprietor.[3]
- **Single layer of taxation.** Income tax is a straightforward matter for sole proprietorships. The federal government doesn't recognize the company as a taxable entity; all profit "flows through" to the owner, where it is treated as personal income and taxed accordingly.
- **Privacy.** Beyond filing tax returns and certain other government reports that may apply to specific businesses, sole proprietors generally aren't required to report anything to anyone. Your business is your business. Of course, if you apply for a loan or solicit investors, you will need to provide detailed financial information to these parties.
- **Flexibility and control.** As a sole proprietor, you aren't required to get approval from a business partner, your boss, or a board of directors to change any aspect of your business strategy or tactics. You can make your own decisions, from setting your own hours to deciding how much of the work you'll do yourself and how much you'll assign to employees. It's all up to you (within the limits of whatever contractual obligations you might have, of course, such as a franchising agreement). Also, as the sole owner, whatever financial value exists in the business is yours. You can keep the business, sell it, give it away, or bequeath it to your children.
- **Fewer limitations on personal income.** As a partner in a partnership or an employee in a corporation, your income is established by various agreements and compensation policies. As a sole proprietor, you keep all the after-tax profits the business generates; if the business does extremely well, you do extremely well. Of course, if the business doesn't generate any income, you don't get a paycheck.
- **Personal satisfaction.** For many sole proprietors, the main advantage is the satisfaction of working for themselves—of taking the risks and enjoying the rewards. If you work hard, make smart decisions, and have a little bit of luck, you get to see and enjoy the fruits of your labor.

DISADVANTAGES OF SOLE PROPRIETORSHIPS

For all its advantages, sole proprietorship also has six significant disadvantages:

unlimited liability A legal condition under which any damages or debts incurred by a business are the owner's personal responsibility

- **Financial liability.** In a sole proprietorship, the owner and the business are legally inseparable, which gives the proprietor **unlimited liability**: Any legal damages or debts incurred by the business are the owner's personal responsibility. If you aren't covered by appropriate insurance and run into serious financial or legal difficulty, such as getting sued for an accident that happened on your premises, you could lose not only the business but everything else you own, including your house, your car, and your personal investments.
- **Demands on the owner.** There's quite a bit of truth to the old joke that working for yourself means you get to set your own hours—you can work whichever 80 hours a week you want. In addition to the potential for long hours (certainly, not all sole proprietors work crazy hours), you often have the stress of making all the major decisions, solving all the major problems, and being tied so closely to the company that taking time off is sometimes impossible. Plus, business owners can feel isolated and unable to discuss problems with anyone.[4] Fortunately, social media sites have been a huge

blessing for sole proprietors in this and many other respects. Business owners can reach out for advice, fresh ideas, useful contacts, or simply the socialization that is missing for many small-business owners. General-purpose business networks such as LinkedIn (www.linkedin.com) and specialized networks such Biznik (http://biznik.com), which focuses on small-business challenges, can be tremendous resources for sole proprietors.

- **Limited managerial perspective.** Running even a simple business can be a complicated effort that requires expertise in accounting, marketing, information technology, business law, and many other fields. Few individual owners possess enough skills and experience to make consistently good decisions. To get broader input for important decisions, small-business owners can turn to a variety of sources for input, including networks and support groups designed specifically for proprietors to counsel each other on key decisions.[5]

- **Resource limitations.** Because they depend on a single owner, sole proprietorships usually have fewer financial resources and fewer ways to get additional funds from lenders or investors. This lack of capital can hamper a small business in many ways, limiting its ability to expand, to hire the best employees, and to survive rough economic periods.

- **No employee benefits for the owner.** Moving from a corporate job to sole proprietorship can be a shock for employees accustomed to paid vacation time, sick leave, health insurance, and other benefits that many employers offer. Sole proprietors get none of these perks without paying for them out of their own pockets.

- **Finite life span.** Although some sole proprietors pass their businesses on to their heirs, the owner's death may mean the demise of the business. And even if the business does transfer to an heir, the founder's unique skills may have been crucial to its successful operation.

✓ Checkpoint

LEARNING OBJECTIVE 1: Define *sole proprietorship*, **and explain the six advantages and six disadvantages of this ownership model.**

SUMMARY: A sole proprietorship is a business owned by a single individual and legally inseparable from that person. The six advantages of this structure are simplicity, a single layer of taxation, privacy, flexibility and control, fewer limitations on personal income, and personal satisfaction. The six disadvantages are unlimited financial liability, demands on the owner, limited managerial perspective, resource limitations, no employee benefits for the owner, and a finite life span.

CRITICAL THINKING: (1) How many sole proprietors do you know? Do they seem satisfied with the choice of working for themselves? Why or why not? (2) Would you ever consider going into business as a sole proprietor? Why or why not?

IT'S YOUR BUSINESS: (1) In your everyday consumer interactions, would you rather do business with a sole proprietorship or a corporation? Why? (2) What would be the potential advantages and disadvantages from a consumer's point of view?

KEY TERMS TO KNOW: sole proprietorship, unlimited liability

Partnerships

A **partnership** is a company that is owned by two or more people but is not a corporation. The partnership structure is appropriate for firms that need more resources and leadership talent than a sole proprietorship but don't need the fundraising capabilities or other advantages of a corporation. Many partnerships are small, with just a handful of owners, although a few are very large; the accounting and consulting firm PwC (www.pwc.com), for example, has more than 8,000 partners.[6] (Note that some companies refer to their employees as "partners," but that isn't the same thing as legal business partners.)

2 LEARNING OBJECTIVE

Define *partnership,* and explain the six advantages and three disadvantages of this ownership model.

partnership An unincorporated company owned by two or more people

general partnership A partnership in which all partners have joint authority to make decisions for the firm and joint liability for the firm's financial obligations

limited partnership A partnership in which one or more persons act as *general partners* who run the business and have the same unlimited liability as sole proprietors

limited liability A legal condition in which the maximum amount each owner is liable for is equal to whatever amount each invested in the business

master limited partnership (MLP) A partnership that is allowed to raise money by selling units of ownership to the general public

limited liability partnership (LLP) A partnership in which each partner has unlimited liability only for his or her own actions and at least some degree of limited liability for the partnership as a whole

Partnerships come in two basic flavors. In a **general partnership**, all partners have *joint authority* to make decisions for the firm and *joint liability* for the firm's financial obligations.[7] If the partnership gets sued or goes bankrupt, all the partners have to dig into their own pockets to pay the bills, just as sole proprietors must.

To minimize personal liability exposure, some organizations opt instead for a **limited partnership**. Under this type of partnership, one or more persons act as *general partners* who run the business and have the same unlimited liability as sole proprietors. The remaining owners are *limited partners* who do not participate in running the business and who have **limited liability**—the maximum amount they are liable for is whatever amount each invested in the business.

Two additional types of partnerships have been created in recent years to accommodate the needs of particular industries or professions. A **master limited partnership (MLP)** is allowed to raise money by selling *units* of ownership to the general public, in the same way corporations sell shares of stock to the public. This gives MLPs the fundraising capabilities of corporations without the double-taxation disadvantage (see "Disadvantages of Corporations"). Strict rules limit the types of companies that qualify for MLP status; most are in the energy industry.[8]

The **limited liability partnership (LLP)** form of business was created to help protect individual partners in certain professions from major mistakes (such as errors that trigger malpractice lawsuits) by other partners in the firm. In an LLP, each partner has unlimited liability only for his or her own actions and at least some degree of limited liability for the partnership as a whole. Restrictions on who can form an LLP—and how much liability protection is offered under this structure—vary from state to state. In California, for example, only architects, consulting engineers, land surveyors, lawyers, and public accountants are allowed to form LLPs.[9]

ADVANTAGES OF PARTNERSHIPS

Partnerships offer two of the same advantages as sole proprietorship plus four more that overcome some important disadvantages of being a sole owner:

- **Simplicity.** Strictly speaking, establishing a partnership is almost as simple as establishing a sole proprietorship: You and your partners just say you're in business together, apply for the necessary business licenses, and get to work. However, while this approach is legal, it is not safe or sensible. Partners need to protect themselves and the company with a partnership agreement (see "Keeping It Together: The Partnership Agreement").
- **Single layer of taxation.** Income tax is straightforward for partnerships. Profit is split between or among the owners based on whatever percentages they have agreed to. Each owner then treats his or her share as personal income.
- **More resources.** One of the key reasons to partner up with one or more co-owners is to increase the amount of money you have to launch, operate, and grow the business. In addition to the money that owners invest themselves, a partnership can potentially raise more money because partners' personal assets support a larger borrowing capacity.
- **Cost sharing.** An important financial advantage in many partnerships is the opportunity to share costs. For example, a group of lawyers or doctors can share the cost of facilities and support staff while continuing to work more or less independently.
- **Broader skill and experience base.** Pooling the skills and experience of two or more professionals can overcome one of the major shortcomings of the sole proprietorship.

    If your goal is to build a business that can grow significantly over time, a partnership can be much more effective than trying to build it up as a sole owner.[10]

Partnerships can bring together business professionals with diverse skill sets and perspectives.

- **Longevity.** By forming a partnership, you increase the chances that the organization will endure because new partners can be drawn into the business to replace those who die or retire. For example, even though the original partners in the several accounting firms that eventually became PricewaterhouseCoopers (the roots of which stretch back to 1849) died many years ago, the company continues.[11]

DISADVANTAGES OF PARTNERSHIPS

Anyone considering the partnership structure needs to be aware of three potentially significant disadvantages:

- **Unlimited liability.** All owners in a general partnership and the general partners in a limited partnership face the same unlimited liability as sole proprietors. However, the risk of financial wipeout can be even greater because a partnership has more people making decisions that could end in catastrophe (unless the company is formed as an LLP).
- **Potential for conflict.** More bosses equals more chances for disagreement and conflict. Partners can disagree over business strategy, the division of profits (or the liability for losses), hiring and firing of employees, and other significant matters. Even simple interpersonal conflict between partners can hinder a company's ability to succeed. Given the potential for conflict, some experts recommend against equal ownership splits where everyone has an equal vote in how things are run.[12]
- **Expansion, succession, and termination issues.** Partnerships need to consider how they will handle such issues as expanding by bringing in an additional partner, replacing a partner who wants to sell out or retire, and terminating a partner who is unable or unwilling to meet the expectations of his or her role in the organization. Such issues can destroy partnerships if the owners don't have clear plans and expectations for addressing them.

KEEPING IT TOGETHER: THE PARTNERSHIP AGREEMENT

A carefully written *partnership agreement* can maximize the advantages of the partnership structure and minimize the potential disadvantages. Although state laws (everywhere except Louisiana) specify some basic agreements about business partnerships, these laws are generic and therefore not ideal for many partnerships.[13] At a minimum, a partnership agreement should address investment percentages, profit-sharing percentages, management responsibilities and other expectations of each owner, decision-making strategies, succession and exit strategies (if an owner wants to leave the partnership), criteria for admitting new partners, and dispute-resolution procedures (including dealing with owners who aren't meeting their responsibilities).[14]

A clear and complete agreement is important for every partnership, but it can be particularly important when you are going into business with a friend, a spouse, or anyone else with whom you have a personal relationship. While you might have a great personal partnership, the dynamics of that relationship could get in the way of a successful business partnership. For instance, a couple who are accustomed to sharing decisions and responsibilities equally in their personal relationship could struggle in a business relationship in which one of them is the clear leader of the company. In addition, stresses and strains in the business relationship can filter into the personal relationship. To protect both the personal and professional partnerships, make sure you start with a clear understanding of what the business relationship will be.

✔ **Checkpoint**

LEARNING OBJECTIVE 2: Define *partnership*, **and explain the six advantages and three disadvantages of this ownership model.**

SUMMARY: Partnership is a business structure in which two or more individuals share ownership of the firm. The two basic forms of partnership are *general partnership*, in which all owners play an active role and have unlimited liability, and the *limited partnership*, in which only the general partner or partners have active management roles and unlimited liability. Six key advantages of partnership are simplicity, a single layer of taxation, more resources, cost sharing, broader skill and experience base, and longevity. Three potential disadvantages are unlimited liability for general partners; potential for conflict; and expansion, succession, and termination issues.

CRITICAL THINKING: (1) Would you prefer going into a business with a seasoned professional you don't know well or someone you know, like, and trust but who doesn't have a lot of business experience? Why? (2) What are the three most important qualifications you would look for in a potential business partner?

IT'S YOUR BUSINESS: (1) Would you consider entering into a business partnership with your best friend? Why or why not? (2) Now turn the question around: Would your best friend consider having *you* as a business partner?

KEY TERMS TO KNOW: partnership, general partnership, limited partnership, limited liability, master limited partnership (MLP), limited liability partnership (LLP)

---

3 | LEARNING OBJECTIVE

Define *corporation,* and explain the four advantages and six disadvantages of this ownership model.

corporation A legal entity, distinct from any individual persons, that has the power to own property and conduct business

shareholders Investors who purchase shares of stock in a corporation

private corporation A corporation in which all the stock is owned by only a few individuals or companies and is not made available for purchase by the public

public corporation A corporation in which stock is sold to anyone who has the means to buy it

liquidity A measure of how easily and quickly an asset such as corporate stock can be converted into cash by selling it

Corporations

A **corporation** is a legal entity, distinct from any individual persons, that has the power to own property and conduct business. It is owned by **shareholders**, investors who purchase shares of stock. The stock of a **private corporation**, also known as a *closely held corporation*, is owned by only a few individuals or companies and is not made available for purchase by the public. In contrast, the stock of a **public corporation** is sold to anyone who has the means to buy it—individuals, investment companies such as mutual funds, not-for-profit organizations, and other companies. These companies are said to be *publicly held* or *publicly traded*.

With their unique ability to pool money from outside investors, corporations can grow to enormous size. The annual revenues of the world's largest corporations, such as Walmart, ExxonMobil, Royal Dutch Shell, and Sinopec Group, are bigger than the entire economies of many countries.[15] However, many small firms and even individuals also take advantage of the unique benefits of corporate organization.

ADVANTAGES OF CORPORATIONS

Corporations have become a major economic force because this structure offers four major advantages over sole proprietorships and partnerships:

- **Ability to raise capital.** The ability to pool money by selling shares of stock to outside investors is the reason corporations first came into existence and remains one of the key advantages of this structure. A number of firms have raised a billion dollars or more by selling stock to the public for the first time.[16] The potential for raising vast amounts gives corporations an unmatched ability to invest in research, marketing, facilities, acquisitions, and other growth strategies.

- **Liquidity.** The stock of publicly traded companies has a high degree of **liquidity**, which means that investors can easily and quickly convert their stock into cash by selling it on the open market. In contrast, *liquidating* (selling) the assets of a sole proprietorship or a partnership can be slow and difficult. Liquidity helps make corporate stocks an attractive investment, which increases the number of people and institutions willing to invest in such companies. In addition, because shares have value established in the open market, a corporation can use shares of its own stock to acquire other companies.

- **Longevity.** Liquidity also helps give corporations a long life span; when shareholders sell or bequeath their shares, ownership simply passes to a new generation, so to speak. Finding willing buyers for a corporation's stock is generally much easier than finding willing buyers for a sole proprietorship or stakes in a partnership.
- **Limited liability.** A corporation itself has unlimited liability, but the various shareholders who own the corporation face only limited liability—their maximum potential loss is only as great as the amount they've invested in the company. Like liquidity, limited liability offers protection that helps make corporate stocks an attractive investment.

DISADVANTAGES OF CORPORATIONS

The advantages of the corporate structure are compelling, but six significant disadvantages must be considered carefully:

- **Cost and complexity.** Starting a corporation is more expensive and more complicated than starting a sole proprietorship or a partnership, and "taking a company public" (selling shares to the public) can be extremely expensive for a firm and time-consuming for upper managers. For a large firm, the process can cost many hundreds of thousands of dollars and consume months of executive time.
- **Reporting requirements.** To help investors make informed decisions about stocks, government agencies require publicly traded companies to publish extensive and detailed financial reports. These reports can eat up a lot of staff and management time, and they can expose strategic information that might benefit competitors or discourage investors unwilling to wait for long-term results.
- **Managerial demands.** Top executives must devote considerable time and energy to meeting with shareholders, financial analysts, and the news media. By one estimate, CEOs of large publicly held corporations can spend as much as 40 percent of their time on these externally focused activities.[17]
- **Possible loss of control.** Outside investors who acquire enough of a company's stock can gain seats on the board of directors and therefore begin exerting their influence on company management. In extreme cases, outsiders can take complete control and even replace the company founders if they believe a change in leadership is needed.
- **Double taxation.** A corporation must pay federal and state corporate income tax on its profits, and individual shareholders must pay income taxes on their share of the company's profits received as *dividends* (periodic payments that some corporations opt to make to shareholders).
- **Short-term orientation of the stock market.** Publicly held corporations release their financial results once every quarter, and this seemingly simple requirement can have a damaging impact on the way companies are managed. The problem is that executives feel the pressure to constantly show earnings growth from quarter to quarter so that the stock price keeps increasing—even if smart, strategic reasons exist for sacrificing earnings in the short term, such as investing in new product development or retaining talented employees instead of laying them off during slow periods. Managers sometimes wind up zigzagging from one short-term fix to the next, trying to prop up the stock price for investors who don't have the patience for strategic, long-term plans to bear fruit. When executive compensation is closely tied to stock prices, managers may have even more incentive to compromise the long-term health of the company in order to meet quarterly expectations.[18] To escape this pressure, corporate leaders sometimes choose to take their companies private, meaning they buy all the shares held by the public and convert to privately held status.

SPECIAL TYPES OF CORPORATIONS

As with the partnership structure, special types of corporations have been created to aid companies in particular situations. An **S corporation**, or *subchapter S corporation*, combines the capital-raising options and limited liability of a corporation with the federal

S corporation A type of corporation that combines the capital-raising options and limited liability of a corporation with the federal taxation advantages of a partnership

taxation advantages of a partnership (although a few states tax S corporations like regular corporations).[19] Corporations seeking "S" status must meet certain criteria, including a maximum of 100 investors, all of whom must be U.S. residents.[20]

limited liability company (LLC) A structure that combines limited liability with the pass-through taxation benefits of a partnership; the number of shareholders is not restricted, nor is members' participation in management

As its name suggests, the **limited liability company (LLC)** structure offers the advantages of limited liability, along with the pass-through taxation benefits of a partnership. Furthermore, LLCs are not restricted in the number of shareholders they can have, and members' participation in management is not restricted as it is in limited partnerships. Given these advantages, the LLC structure is recommended for most small companies that aren't sole proprietorships.[21] Although LLCs are favored by many small companies, they are by no means limited to small firms. Some large and well-known firms have gone the LLC route, including BMW of North America, the Albertsons grocery store chain, and GMAC, a $2 billion finance company.[22]

Finally, an intriguing new type of corporate structure supports the goals of businesspeople who want their companies to pursue social and environmental goals while still pursuing profits as any other corporation does. A **benefit corporation** has most of the attributes of a regular corporation but adds the legal requirement that the company must also pursue a stated nonfinancial goal, such as hiring workers whose life histories make employment difficult to attain or reducing the environmental impact of particular products. The corporation's performance toward meeting that goal must be independently verified as well. These requirements offer key advantages to founders and other stakeholders. Entrepreneurs who launch a corporation with social or environmental objectives in mind are assured that, even if they give up or lose voting control of the corporation, the company is still legally required to pursue its social or environmental goal. In addition, the transparency offered by third-party verification assures customers who want to buy from companies that support causes they value. Maryland was the first state to recognize benefit corporations, and several other states have since followed suit.[23]

benefit corporation A profit-seeking corporation whose charter specifies a social or environmental goal that the company must pursue in addition to profit

The labels applied to various types of corporations can be a bit confusing. The most important points to remember are the difference between privately and publically held corporations and the basic features of S corporations and LLCs. Exhibit 2 summarizes these features, along with some other terms you may run across in the business media.

| EXHIBIT 2 | Corporate Structures |

Different types of corporate structures serve different purposes for their owners. The first five terms are the most important to remember.

Structure	Characteristics
Public corporation (also known *as publicly held* or *publicly traded*)	Corporation whose stock is sold to the general public
Private corporation (also known as *closely held*)	Corporation whose stock is held by a small number of owners and is not available for sale to the public
S corporation (also known as *subchapter S corporation*)	Corporation allowed to sell stock to a limited number of investors while enjoying the pass-through taxation of a partnership
Limited liability company (LLC)	Corporate structure with benefits similar to those of an S corporation, without the limitation on the number of investors
Benefit corporation	Profit-seeking corporation whose charter also requires it to pursue a stated social or environmental goal
Subsidiary	Corporation primarily or wholly owned by another company
Parent company	Corporation that owns one or more subsidiaries
Holding company	Special type of parent company that owns other companies for investment reasons and usually exercises little operating control over those subsidiaries
Alien corporation	Corporation that operates in the United States but is incorporated in another country
Foreign corporation (sometimes called an *out-of-state corporation*)	Company that is incorporated in one state (frequently the state of Delaware, where incorporation laws are more lenient) but that does business in several other states where it is registered
Domestic corporation	Corporation that does business only in the state where it is chartered (incorporated)

Checkpoint

LEARNING OBJECTIVE 3: Define *corporation*, **and explain the four advantages and six disadvantages of this ownership model.**

SUMMARY: A corporation is a legal entity with the power to own property and conduct business. The four primary advantages of this structure are the ability to raise capital by selling shares of ownership, liquidity (meaning it is easy to convert shares of ownership to cash), longevity, and limited liability for owners. Six disadvantages are startup costs and complexity, ongoing reporting requirements, extra demands on top managers, potential loss of control, double taxation, and the short-term orientation of the stock market.

CRITICAL THINKING: (1) Why is the LLC structure recommended for most small companies that aren't sole proprietorships? (2) How can the demands of the stock market affect managerial decision making?

IT'S YOUR BUSINESS: Assume you own stock in a large, publicly traded corporation that is hiring a new CEO. All other things being equal, who would be a better choice: a brilliant strategic thinker who is a weak communicator with poor "people skills" or a gifted public speaker and motivator who is competent but perhaps not brilliant when it comes to strategy? Explain your answer.

KEY TERMS TO KNOW: corporation, shareholders, private corporation, public corporation, liquidity, S corporation, limited liability company (LLC), benefit corporation

Corporate Governance

Although a corporation's shareholders own the business, few of them are typically involved in managing it, particularly if the corporation is publicly traded. Instead, shareholders who own *common stock* elect a **board of directors** to represent them, and the directors, in turn, select the corporation's top officers, who actually run the company (see Exhibit 3). The term **corporate governance** can be used in a broad sense to describe all the policies, procedures, relationships, and systems in place to oversee the successful and legal operation of the enterprise. However, media coverage and public discussion tend to define governance in a more narrow sense, as the responsibilities and performance of the board of directors specifically. Because serious corporate blunders can wreak havoc on employees, investors, and the economy as a whole, effective corporate governance has become a vital concern for society as a whole, not just for the individual companies themselves.

EXHIBIT 3	**Corporate Governance**

Shareholders of a corporation own the business, but their elected representatives on the board of directors hire the corporate officers who run the company and hire other employees to perform the day-to-day work. (Note that corporate officers are also employees.)

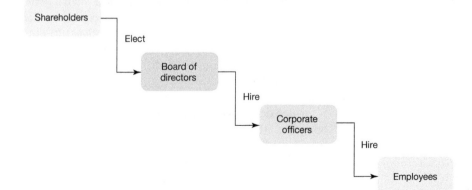

4 **LEARNING OBJECTIVE**

Explain the concept of *corporate governance,* and identify the three groups responsible for ensuring good governance.

board of directors A group of professionals elected by shareholders as their representatives, with responsibility for the overall direction of the company and the selection of top executives

corporate governance In a broad sense, describes all the policies, procedures, relationships, and systems in place to oversee the successful and legal operation of the enterprise; in a narrow sense, refers to the responsibilities and performance of the board of directors specifically

SHAREHOLDERS

Even though most don't have any direct involvement in company management, shareholders play a key role in corporate governance. All shareholders who own common stock are invited to an annual meeting where top executives present the previous year's results and plans for the coming year and shareholders vote on various resolutions that may be before the board. Those who cannot attend the annual meeting in person can vote by **proxy**, authorizing management to vote on their behalf.

proxy A document that authorizes another person to vote on behalf of a shareholder in a corporation

Because shareholders elect the directors, in theory they are the ultimate governing body of the corporation. However, a major corporation may have thousands or even millions of shareholders, so unless they own a large number of shares, individual shareholders usually have little influence. Notable exceptions are *institutional investors*, such as pension funds, insurance companies, mutual funds, religious organizations, and college endowment funds. Those with large holdings of stock can have considerable influence over management. For example, the 300 institutions that make up the Interfaith Center on Corporate Responsibility (ICCR) collectively control $100 billion in corporate stock, giving them a powerful voice.[24]

shareholder activism Activities taken by shareholders (individually or in groups) to influence executive decision making in areas ranging from strategic planning to social responsibility

Shareholder activism, in which shareholders pressure management on matters ranging from executive pay to corporate social responsibility to overall company performance, has become an increasingly visible factor in corporate governance. Activist shareholders are becoming better organized and more sophisticated in proposals they present, forcing boards to pay more attention to the concerns they raise.[25] At the same time, more boards seem to recognize the benefits to be gained by engaging activists and listening to their concerns.[26] However, not everyone is happy with this development. Those who lean toward the minimalist view of corporate social responsibility worry that such activism is beginning to undermine the ability of corporate boards to do their work effectively.[27]

BOARD OF DIRECTORS

As the representatives of the shareholders, the board of directors is responsible for selecting corporate officers, guiding corporate affairs, reviewing long-term plans, making major strategic decisions, and overseeing financial performance. Boards are typically composed of major shareholders (both individuals and representatives of institutional investors), philanthropists, and executives from other corporations. Directors are often paid a combination of an annual fee and *stock options*, the right to buy company shares at an advantageous price.

Much of the attention focused on corporate reform in recent years has zeroed in on boards, with various boards being accused of not paying close enough attention to what their companies were doing, approving management proposals without analyzing them carefully, being allied too closely with management to serve as the independent representatives of shareholders, or simply failing to add enough value to strategy planning. In response to both outside pressure and management's recognition of how important an effective board is, corporations are wrestling with a variety of board-related issues:

- **Composition.** Identifying the type of people who should be on the board can be a major challenge. The ideal board is a balanced group of seasoned executives, each of whom can "bring something to the table" that helps the corporation, such as extensive contacts in the industry, manufacturing experience, insight into global issues, and so on. The ratio of insiders (company executives) to outsiders (independent directors) is another hot topic. Federal law now requires that the majority of directors be independent, but to be effective, these outsiders must have enough knowledge about the inner workings of the organization to make informed decisions. Diversity is also important, to ensure that adequate attention is paid to issues that affect stakeholders who have been historically underrepresented on corporate boards. Women hold only 12 percent of all the seats on U.S. corporate boards, and members of ethnic minorities hold only 10 percent.[28]

REAL-TIME UPDATES
Learn More by Listening to This Podcast

Corporate governance and the management of financial risk

Listen in as industry experts discuss vital issues in corporate governance. Go to http://real-timeupdates.com/bia6 and click on Learn More. If you are using MyBizLab, you can access Real-Time Updates within the chapter or under Student Study Tools.

- **Education.** Overseeing a modern corporation is an almost unimaginably complex task. Board members are expected to understand everything from government regulations to financial management to executive compensation strategies—in addition to the inner workings of the corporation itself. Various companies offer special training programs or orientation sessions for directors in such areas as financial reporting (to make sure directors who aren't well versed in finance can understand their company's own financial statements), compliance challenges, product research, manufacturing, and human resources issues.[29]
- **Liability.** One of the more controversial reform issues has been the potential for directors to be held legally and financially liable for misdeeds of the companies they oversee and even for simply failing to investigate "red flags" in company financial reports.[30]
- **Independent board chairs.** The *board chair* (or *chairman*, as many companies refer to the position) oversees the other members of the board of directors—who are supposed to oversee the corporate officers who make up the top management team, while the CEO oversees the top management team. However, in many corporations, one person acts as both board chair and CEO (meaning that in a sense, the CEO is his or her own boss), leading critics to ask how effectively such boards can oversee top management. The majority of large European companies now divide these responsibilities between two people, but that trend has not yet caught on widely in the United States. An emerging alternative is a *lead director*, an independent board member who guides the operation of the board and helps maintain its role as an independent voice in governance.[31]
- **Recruiting challenges.** Being an effective director in today's business environment is a tough job—so tough that good candidates may start to think twice about accepting directorships. Well-chosen board members are more vital than ever, though, so corporate and government leaders have no choice but to solve these challenges.

CORPORATE OFFICERS

The third and final group that plays a key role in governance are the **corporate officers**, the top executives who run the company. Because they implement major board decisions, make numerous other business decisions, ensure compliance with a dizzying range of government regulations, and perform other essential tasks, the executive team is the major influence on a company's performance and financial health. The highest-ranking officer is the **chief executive officer (CEO)**, and that person is aided by a team of other "C-level" executives, such as the chief financial officer (CFO), chief information officer (CIO), chief technology officer (CTO), and chief operating officer (COO)—titles vary from one corporation to the next.

Corporate officers are hired by the board and generally have legal authority to conduct the company's business, in everything from hiring the rest of the employees to launching new products. The actions of these executives can make or break the company, so it is obviously in the board's interest to hire the best talent available, help them succeed in every way possible—and pay attention to what these managers are doing.

corporate officers The top executives who run a corporation

chief executive officer (CEO) The highest-ranking officer of a corporation

✓ Checkpoint

LEARNING OBJECTIVE 4: Explain the concept of *corporate governance*, and identify the three groups responsible for ensuring good governance.

SUMMARY: Corporate governance involves all the policies, procedures, relationships, and systems in place to oversee the successful and legal operation of the enterprise. More narrowly, it refers specifically to the responsibilities and performance of the board of directors. The three groups responsible for good governance are (1) the shareholders, who elect (2) the board of directors, who approve overall strategy and hire (3) the corporate officers who run the company.

CRITICAL THINKING: (1) Why are some shareholder activists pressuring corporations to increase the number of board seats held by women and minorities? (2) Why do so many European corporations now divide board chair and CEO responsibilities between two people?

IT'S YOUR BUSINESS: Should the qualifications of the board of directors play a role in your decision whether to buy the stock of a particular corporation? Why or why not?

KEY TERMS TO KNOW: board of directors, corporate governance, proxy, shareholder activism, corporate officers, chief executive officer (CEO)

Mergers and Acquisitions

5 LEARNING OBJECTIVE

Identify the potential advantages of pursuing mergers and acquisitions as a growth strategy, along with the potential difficulties and risks.

merger An action taken by two companies to combine as a single entity

acquisition An action taken by one company to buy a controlling interest in the voting stock of another company

hostile takeover Acquisition of another company against the wishes of management

leveraged buyout (LBO) Acquisition of a company's publicly traded stock, using funds that are primarily borrowed, usually with the intent of using some of the acquired assets to pay back the loans used to acquire the company

If a company determines that it doesn't have the right mix of resources and capabilities to achieve its goals and doesn't have the time or inclination to develop them internally, it can purchase or partner with a firm that has what it needs. Businesses can combine permanently through either *mergers* or *acquisitions*. The two terms are often discussed together, usually with the shorthand phrase "M&A," or used interchangeably (although they are technically different, and the legal and tax ramifications can be quite different, depending on the details of the transaction).

In a **merger**, two companies join to form a single entity. Companies can merge either by pooling their resources or by one company purchasing the assets of the other.[32] Although not strictly a merger, a *consolidation*, in which two companies create a new, third entity that then purchases the two original companies, is often lumped together with the other two merger approaches.[33] (Adding to the confusion, businesspeople and the media often use the term *consolidation* in two general senses: to describe any combination of two companies, merger or acquisition, and to describe situations in which a wave of mergers and acquisitions sweeps across an entire industry, reducing the number of competitors.)

In an **acquisition**, one company buys a controlling interest in the voting stock of another company. In most acquisitions, the selling parties agree to be purchased; management is in favor of the deal and encourages shareholders to vote in favor of it as well. Because buyers frequently offer shareholders more than their shares are currently worth, sellers are often motivated to sell. However, in some situations, a buyer attempts to acquire a company against the wishes of management. In such a **hostile takeover**, the buyer tries to convince enough shareholders to go against management and vote to sell.

To finance an acquisition, buyers can offer sellers cash, stock in the acquiring company, or a combination of the two. Another option involves debt. A **leveraged buyout (LBO)** occurs when someone purchases a company's publicly traded stock primarily by using borrowed funds, sometimes using the target company's assets as collateral for these loans. The debt is expected to be repaid with funds generated by the company's operations and, often, by the sale of some of its assets. An LBO is an aggressive move and can be quite risky if the buyer takes on so much debt that repayment demands deplete the cash the company has for operations and growth.

ADVANTAGES OF MERGERS AND ACQUISITIONS

Companies pursue mergers and acquisitions for a variety of reasons: They might hope to increase their buying power as a result of their larger size, increase revenue by cross-selling products to each other's customers, increase market share by combining product lines to provide more comprehensive offerings, or gain access to new expertise, systems, and teams of employees who already know how to work together. Bringing a company under new ownership can also be an opportunity to replace or improve inept management and thereby help a company improve its performance.[34] In many cases, the primary

EXHIBIT 4   **Types of Mergers**

A *vertical merger* occurs when a company purchases a complementary company at a different stage or level in an industry, such as a furniture maker buying a lumber supplier. A *horizontal merger* involves two similar companies at the same level; companies can merge to expand their product offerings or their geographic market coverage. In a *conglomerate merger,* a parent company buys companies in unrelated industries, often to diversify its assets to protect against downturns in specific industries.

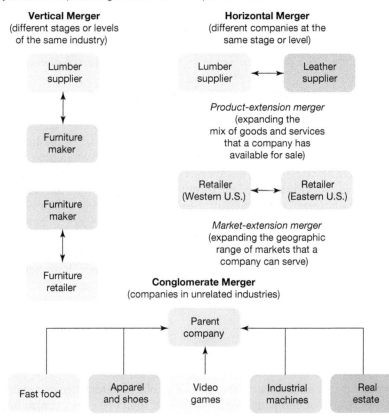

goal is to reduce overlapping investments and capacities in order to lower ongoing costs, which is the main reason Sirius's Mel Karmazin pursued a merger with rival XM Satellite Radio (see Behind the Scenes at the beginning of the chapter). Exhibit 4 identifies the most common types of mergers.

For many firms, a merger or an acquisition is a rare event, but some other companies use acquisitions as a strategic tool to expand year after year. Microsoft, for example, has acquired nearly 140 companies since 1987, including such mammoth deals as the $8.5 billion purchase of Skype in 2011.[35]

DISADVANTAGES OF MERGERS AND ACQUISITIONS

While the advantages can be compelling, joining two companies is a complex process because it involves virtually every aspect of both organizations. Here are just some of the daunting challenges that must be overcome:

- Executives have to agree on how the merger will be financed—and then come up with the money to make it happen.
- Managers need to decide who will be in charge after they join forces.
- Marketing departments need to figure out how to blend product lines, branding strategies, and advertising and sales efforts.
- Incompatible information systems (including everything from email to websites to accounting software) may need to be rebuilt or replaced in order to operate together seamlessly.

- Companies must often deal with layoffs, transfers, and changes in job titles and work assignments.
- The *organizational cultures* of the two firms must be harmonized somehow, which can result in clashes between different values, management styles, communication practices, workplace atmosphere, and approaches to managing the changes required to implement the merger.[36]

Moreover, while managers and employees are wrestling with all these challenges, they need to continue manufacturing products, satisfying customers, and tending to all the other daily details of business. Mergers can drive customers away if they feel neglected while the two companies are busy with all the internal chores of stitching themselves together.

Because of these risks and difficulties, somewhere between two-thirds and three-quarters of all mergers fail to meet their stated business goals.[37] The worst deals can waste millions or billions of dollars and destroy massive amounts of *market valuation* (the total value of a company's stock). For example, Sprint acquired Nextel in the hope that combining these two wireless phone networks would create a more competitive alternative to AT&T and Verizon Wireless. However, problems such as incompatible technologies and conflicting cultures probably doomed the combination from the start, and only three years later Sprint *wrote off* (essentially declaring as lost) most of the $35 billion it had spent on the deal.[38]

Even with the risks and long odds, managers continue to pursue mergers and acquisitions, and some companies have become quite proficient at the process. Companies that beat the odds, such as tech stalwarts IBM and Cisco, for instance, have developed comprehensive processes for evaluating and implementing acquisitions. In fact, "acquisition skill" can be considered a competitive advantage for the companies that do it frequently and do it well.[39]

MERGER AND ACQUISITION DEFENSES

Every corporation that sells stock to the general public is potentially vulnerable to takeover by any individual or company that buys enough shares to gain a controlling interest. However, as mentioned earlier, most takeovers are friendly acquisitions welcomed by the acquired company. A hostile takeover can be launched in one of two ways: by tender offer or by proxy fight. In a *tender offer*, the buyer, or *raider*, as this party is sometimes called, offers to buy a certain number of shares of stock in the corporation at a specific price. The price offered is generally more, sometimes considerably more, than the current stock price, so that shareholders are motivated to sell. The raider hopes to get enough shares to take control of the corporation and to replace the existing board of directors and management. In a *proxy fight*, the raider launches a public relations battle for shareholder votes, hoping to enlist enough votes to oust the board and management.

Corporate boards and executives have devised a number of schemes to defend themselves against unwanted takeovers. With a *poison pill* defense, a targeted company invokes some move that makes it less valuable to the potential raider, with the hope of discouraging the takeover. A common technique is to sell newly issued stock to current stockholders at prices below the market value of the company's existing stock, thereby instantly increasing the number of shares the raider has to buy.[40] With the *white knight* tactic, a third company is invited to acquire a company that is in danger of being swallowed up in a hostile takeover.

Some critics believe that poison pills and other defenses are bad for shareholders because they can entrench weak management and discourage takeover attempts that would improve company value. For example, Yahoo!, which has been struggling in recent years and has become vulnerable to takeover, tried to enact a provision that would give employees such generous severance packages in the event of a takeover that buying the company would become prohibitively expensive. After shareholders sued, a judge forced Yahoo! to change the policy.[41]

✓ Checkpoint

LEARNING OBJECTIVE 5: Identify the potential advantages of pursuing mergers and acquisitions as a growth strategy, along with the potential difficulties and risks.

SUMMARY: Mergers and acquisitions can help companies reduce costs by eliminating redundancies and increasing buying power, increase revenue by cross-selling goods and services to each other's customers or expanding into new markets, and compete more effectively by adding new technologies or talented employees. However, the difficulties and risks are considerable: coming up with the money, deciding which managers will be in charge, merging marketing and sales efforts, reconciling information systems, dealing with redundant employees, and meshing different corporate cultures.

CRITICAL THINKING: (1) If you were on the board of directors at a company and the CEO proposed a merger with a top competitor, what types of questions would you want answered before you gave your approval? (2) If a CEO has an opportunity to merge with or acquire another company and is reasonably certain that the transaction will benefit shareholders, is the CEO obligated to pursue the deal? Why or why not?

IT'S YOUR BUSINESS: (1) Have you (or someone you know) ever experienced a merger or an acquisition as an employee? Was your job affected? (2) Have you ever experienced a merger or an acquisition as a customer? Did customer service suffer during the transition of ownership?

KEY TERMS TO KNOW: merger, acquisition, hostile takeover, leverage buyout (LBO)

Strategic Alliances and Joint Ventures

A **strategic alliance** is a long-term partnership between companies to jointly develop, produce, or sell products and a **joint venture** is a separate legal entity established by the strategic partners. Both of these options can be more attractive than a merger or acquisition in certain situations.

STRATEGIC ALLIANCES

Strategic alliances can accomplish many of the same goals as a merger or an acquisition but with less risk and work than permanently integrating two companies.[42] They can help a company gain credibility in a new field, expand its market presence, gain access to technology, diversify offerings, and share best practices without forcing the partners to become permanently entangled.

For example, Cisco's core business is networking technologies that allow people to share information of all types over the Internet. Because a complete information system usually requires more than just networking, Cisco has formed a number of strategic alliances with companies that specialize in computers, mobile phones, software, business consulting, and other products and services. These relationships let Cisco focus on its core strengths while offering customers complete solutions.[43]

Strategic alliances aren't restricted to just two partners. To help electric companies and other utilities deliver energy more efficiently, Cisco teamed up with five other large companies to form the Smart Energy Alliance.[44] A merger on this scale would've been unimaginably complex, but this strategic partnership allows the companies to collaborate in this area without formally combining.

---

6 | LEARNING OBJECTIVE

Define *strategic alliance* and *joint venture,* and explain why a company would choose these options over a merger or an acquisition.

strategic alliance A long-term partnership between companies to jointly develop, produce, or sell products

joint venture A separate legal entity established by two or more companies to pursue shared business objectives

JOINT VENTURES

While strategic alliances avoid much of the work and risk of formal mergers, they don't create a unified entity that functions with a single management structure, information system, and other organizational elements. In contrast, a joint venture lets companies create an operation that is more tightly integrated than a strategic alliance but without disrupting the original companies to the extent that a merger or acquisition does. In fact, after the spotty record of mergers and acquisitions in recent years, more companies are now considering joint ventures as a more attractive way to collaborate.[45] A good example is clearXchange, a system that enables person-to-person payments via email or text messaging. It was launched by three large banks that compete with one another as a matter of course but that cooperated on the new venture as a way to compete against PayPal.[46]

Exhibit 5 offers a quick graphical summary of the major ways businesses can join forces. For the latest information on company structure, corporate governance, and related issues, visit http://real-timeupdates.com/bia6.

EXHIBIT 5	Options for Joining Forces

Companies can choose from a variety of ways to combine resources and capabilities.

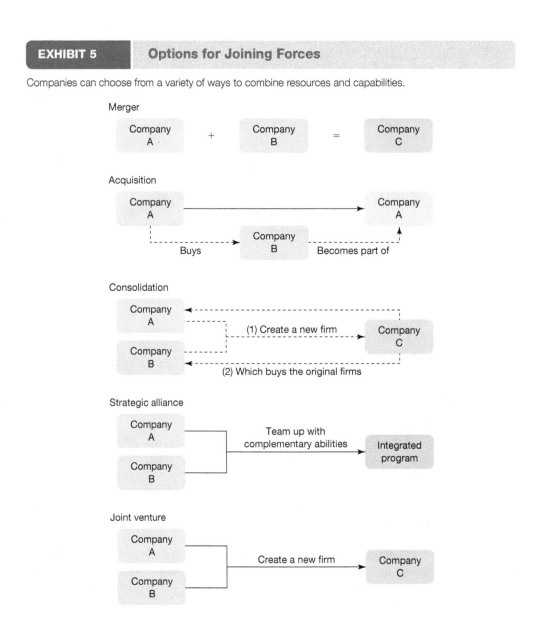

✔ Checkpoint

LEARNING OBJECTIVE 6: Define *strategic alliance* **and** *joint venture,* **and explain why companies would choose these options over a merger or an acquisition.**

SUMMARY: Strategic alliances can accomplish many of the same goals as a merger or an acquisition but with less risk and work than permanently integrating two companies. A joint venture lets companies create an operation that is more tightly integrated than a strategic alliance but without disrupting the original companies to the extent that a merger or acquisition does.

CRITICAL THINKING: Why are an increasing number of companies considering joint ventures rather than mergers and acquisitions?

IT'S YOUR BUSINESS: Assume that you've worked for years to build up a strong and independent company; would you be comfortable sharing power with another company in a strategic alliance or joint venture? Why or why not?

KEY TERMS TO KNOW: strategic alliance, joint venture

BEHIND THE SCENES

TEAMING UP FOR SURVIVAL AT SIRIUS XM

MyBizLab

Mergers and acquisitions can be exciting opportunities to expand by adding new product capabilities or greater market coverage. Unfortunately, such was not the case when Sirius CEO Mel Karmazin and his counterpart at XM, Hugh Panero, pondered the difficulties they were facing in the satellite radio business. Neither company had ever turned a profit, both were deeply in debt, costs were going nowhere but up, and the U.S. economy was slowing down.

Karmazin and Panero needed to join forces just to survive, and in early 2007, the companies announced plans to merge. (Although the deal was announced as a "merger of equals," it certainly looked more like an acquisition of XM by Sirius. Karmazin became the CEO of the combined Sirius XM, XM Satellite Radio became a subsidiary of Sirius XM, and Panero left the company later that year. Acquisitions are often presented to the public as mergers to allow the company being acquired to save a little face.)

By combining their competing efforts in both technical development and marketing, Karmazin and Panero expected to save $400 million in the first year. Outside analysts figured the two companies could eventually save anywhere from $3 billion to $7 billion overall. From a cost perspective, a merger clearly seemed to make sense.

A merger might have been the best choice, but it certainly wasn't an easy one. For starters, when the Federal Communications Commission (FCC) granted Sirius and XM licenses to begin service in 1997, the licenses came with the stipulation that the two firms never merge. In addition, numerous members of Congress, consumer advocates, and other media companies spoke out against the merger on the grounds that allowing the country's only two satellite radio companies to merge would create a monopoly in that market.

Karmazin and his colleagues had to convince both the FCC and the antitrust regulators at the Department of Justice (DOJ) that the public now had so many entertainment choices that merging would not hurt consumers or restrain competition. The good news/bad news situation for Sirius and XM was that the competitive landscape was indeed so crowded—with terrestrial radio, inexpensive or free Internet radio, digital music players, and music-enabled smartphones—that the two companies were able to convince government officials to approve the deal.

The DOJ didn't put any conditions on the approval, but the FCC did. First, the company had to agree not to raise prices for three years, a significant matter, given the ongoing struggle for profitability. Second, it had to give consumers more flexibility in tailoring subscriptions with the specific channels they want. Third, it had to allow any manufacturer to produce and sell radios capable of receiving Sirius XM signals, a move designed to broaden consumer options and lower equipment prices. Fourth, the company had to increase educational programming and make 24 of its satellite channels available for lease by minority- and women-owned media providers.

The newly christened Sirius XM made it over all the regulatory hurdles, but life didn't get any easier. In fact, it got a lot worse almost immediately. The company relied on new car sales for a significant portion of its new subscribers—many new cars come with satellite radios as a standard or optional feature, and buyers often get free satellite service for a few months, after which the company hopes they've enjoyed it enough to become paying subscribers. Unfortunately, when the economy collapsed

71

in late 2008, new car sales collapsed with it, squeezing the major source of new customers. To its great credit, the company did manage to keep adding new subscribers in the tough market, but not nearly enough to become profitable.

As if that weren't enough, the collapse of the global credit market in 2008 also threw a serious wrench into the company's financial management model. To finance those expensive satellites and on-air personalities, the company had been relying on a rolling series of short-term loans. However, those credit faucets dried up practically overnight.

By early 2009 Sirius XM was perilously close to bankruptcy, its stock value had plunged to mere pennies per share, and it was vulnerable to a hostile takeover by Dish Network, one of the two major satellite television services. With disaster looming, Karmazin found help in the form of a massive infusion of cash from Liberty Media, which—not coincidentally—controls DirecTV, Dish Network's major competitor in satellite television. Liberty's money (partly a loan and partly an investment that gave Liberty a 40 percent share of ownership) gave Sirius XM a second chance, but the company's long-range future looked anything but secure. The loan from Liberty came with an eye-popping 15 percent interest rate, and it was only a short-term solution.

To prevent anyone else from gaining control while they worked on implementing the merger and pushing the company toward profitability, Karmazin and the Sirius XM board adopted a poison pill shortly after the Liberty deal that would be triggered if any uninvited buyer acquired more than 4.9 percent of the outstanding stock.

Sirius XM was on life support—but it lived. The potential synergies of the merger began to kick in as Karmazin and Panero had predicted, lowering capital and operating costs as the company could now serve a combined subscriber base through a single satellite network and administrative infrastructure. Satellites need to be replaced on a regular schedule, and Sirius XM completed a satellite replacement cycle at the end of 2011, so it won't need to make this massive capital investment again until 2016 or 2017. Operating and marketing efficiencies improved, lowering the cost of *subscriber acquisition* (the average amount of money spent to add a new customer). The company renegotiated its contract with General Motors on more favorable terms, and it was said to be pursuing amendments with the other automakers as well. The fees paid for on-air talent are another area of potentially significant cost savings. Although terms of these contracts usually aren't disclosed, on-air personalities who want to be on satellite can no longer play Sirius and XM against each other for bargaining leverage.

The revenue side of the balance sheet began looking up as well. In 2010, the economy began to recover, ever so slightly and perhaps not permanently, and car sales started edging up with it. More than 60 percent of new U.S. car models now have Sirius XM radios built in, and nearly half of those new owners opt for a paid Sirius XM subscription after their initial free trial period. Plus, the first wave of satellite-equipped cars have now cycled through to the used-car market, creating a whole new population of potential customers. In 2010, Sirius XM passed the 20 million subscriber mark, and its average revenue per subscriber increased as well.

In fact, thanks to the combination of cost reductions and revenue growth, Sirius began turning things around even while the recession was in full force. Except for some extraordinary one-time expenses involving debt retirement, the company had put together a string of profitable quarters, and its stock price was rebounding in 2011 as well.

Liberty, meanwhile, still has its share of the company, and its $530 million investment was worth in the neighborhood of $5 billion by 2011, giving it a "once-in-a-lifetime home run," in the words of one market observer.

Sirius XM continues to expand its product offering and availability, with its music, sports, talk, weather, and traffic channels now available on more than 800 devices, from in-dash radios to iPads to smartphones. The company's newest product and technology initiative, which includes such features as the ability to buy songs heard over the satellite radio service and to pause, record, and replay audio (much as TiVo and other DVRs do with television service), is dubbed Sirius 2.0. For a company that was pushed to the edge of collapse but found a way to reinvent itself, the "2.0" label is apt in more ways than one.[47]

Critical Thinking Questions

1. Other than for purely financial reasons (interest on the loan and potential gains from its investment), why might Liberty Media have wanted to help Sirius XM?

2. The poison pill defense that Sirius XM put in place after the merger expired in 2011, made it at least theoretically possible for another company to buy enough shares to complete a takeover. With its finances on much stronger footing and its stock price rebounding, the company has started to look like an attractive investment. If another party (including Liberty Media) eventually acquires Sirius XM because of its attractive stock price and growth prospects, does that mean the merger of Sirius and XM was a failure? Why or why not?

3. In 2011, Sirius XM's stock was added to the NASDAQ 100 stock market index (NASDAQ's index of its 100 largest nonfinancial companies). One intriguing outcome is that it forces mutual fund companies that offer *index funds* that mimic this particular market index to buy Sirius XM stock. What effect might this change have on the potential for an outsider—welcome or not—to take control of the company?

LEARN MORE ONLINE

How has Sirius XM fared since its merger and the assistance from Liberty Media? Get the latest financial information from the company's website, at **www.siriusxm.com** (look under "Investor Relations"). How is the company faring today? Does it continue to be profitable? Has it managed to preserve the benefits of the merger by keeping costs in line with revenue growth?

MyBizLab

Log on to www.mybizlab.com to access study and assessment aids associated with this chapter.

KEY TERMS

acquisition
benefit corporation
board of directors
chief executive officer (CEO)
corporate governance
corporate officers
corporation
general partnership
hostile takeover
joint venture
leveraged buyout (LBO)
limited liability
limited liability company (LLC)
limited liability partnership (LLP)

limited partnership
liquidity
master limited partnership (MLP)
merger
partnership
private corporation
proxy
public corporation
S corporation
shareholder activism
shareholders
sole proprietorship
strategic alliance
unlimited liability

TEST YOUR KNOWLEDGE

Questions for Review

1. What are the three basic forms of business ownership?
2. How does unlimited liability put a business owner at risk?
3. What is the difference between a general partnership and a limited partnership?
4. What is a closely held corporation, and why do some companies choose this form of ownership?
5. What is the role of a company's board of directors?

Questions for Analysis

6. Why is it advisable for partners to enter into a formal partnership agreement?
7. To what extent do shareholders control the activities of a corporation?
8. How might a company benefit from having a diverse board of directors that includes representatives of several industries, countries, and cultures?
9. Why might two companies choose to form a strategic alliance rather than pursue a merger or an acquisition?
10. Ethical Considerations. Are poison pill defenses ethical? If a potential acquirer buys company stock legally, thereby becoming a part owner of the company, should management be allowed to entrench itself against the wishes of this owner? Explain your answer.

Questions for Application

11. Suppose you and some friends want to start a business to take tourists on wilderness backpacking expeditions. None of you has much extra money, so you plan to start small. However, if you are successful, you would like to expand into other types of outdoor tours and perhaps even open branches in other locations. What form of ownership should your new enterprise take, and why?
12. Do you own or have you ever considered owning stock? If so, what steps have you taken to ensure that company management has shareholders' interests in mind?
13. Visit Liberty Media's website, www.libertymedia.com, and find the company's corporate governance guidelines. Assume that you're going to start a company that you plan to incorporate. Identify at least five principles of good governance from Liberty's website that you will use to guide the board of your new corporation.
14. Concept Integration. You've developed considerable expertise in setting up new manufacturing plants, and now you'd like to strike out on your own as a consultant who advises other companies. However, you recognize that manufacturing activity tends to expand and contract at various times during the business cycle. Do you think a single-consultant sole proprietorship or a small corporation with a half dozen or more consultants would be better able to ride out tough times at the bottom of a business cycle?

EXPAND YOUR KNOWLEDGE

Discovering Career Opportunities

Are you best suited to working as a sole proprietor, as a partner in a business, or as an employee or a manager in a corporation? For this exercise, select three businesses with which you are familiar: one run by a single person, such as a dentist's practice or a local landscaping firm; one run by two or three partners, such as a small accounting firm; and one that operates as a corporation, such as Target or Walmart.

1. Write down what you think you would like about being the sole proprietor, one of the partners, the corporate manager, or an employee in the businesses you have selected. For example, would you like having full responsibility for the sole proprietorship? Would you like being able to consult with other partners in the partnership before making decisions? Would you settle for less autonomy to get the benefits of being a corporate employee?

2. Now write down what you might dislike about each form of business. For example, would you dislike the risk of bearing all legal responsibility in a sole proprietorship? Would you dislike having to talk with your partners before spending the partnership's money? Would you dislike having to write reports for top managers and shareholders of the corporation?

3. Weigh the pluses and minuses you have identified in this exercise. In comparison, which form of business most appeals to you?

Improving Your Tech Insights: Groupware

Groupware, software that lets people communicate, share files, present materials, and work on documents simultaneously, is changing the way employees interact—and even the way businesses work together. For example, *shared workspaces* are "virtual offices" that give everyone on a team access to the same set of resources and information: databases, calendars, project plans, archived instant messages and emails, reference materials, and team documents. These workspaces (which are typically accessed through a web browser) make it easy for geographically dispersed team members to access shared files anytime, anywhere. Employees no longer need to be in the same office or even in the same time zone. They don't even need to be employees. Groupware makes it easy for companies to pull together partners and temporary contractors on a project-by-project basis. Groupware is often integrated with *web-based meeting systems* that combine instant messaging, shared workspaces, video-conferencing, and other tools.

Pick a company you might like to work for someday, and with that company in mind, conduct research to identify a currently available groupware system. (Groupware systems aren't always identified as such, so you might want to search for "project collaboration systems" or similar terms.) In a brief email message to your instructor, explain how this particular groupware system could help the employees and managers in the company you've chosen be more productive.[48]

PRACTICE YOUR SKILLS

Sharpening Your Communication Skills

You have just been informed that your employer is going to merge with a firm in Germany. Using online or library resources, find information on German business culture and customs and prepare a short report that would help your U.S. colleagues work effectively with your new German colleagues.

Building Your Team Skills

Imagine that the president of your college or university has just announced plans to retire. Your team, playing the role of the school's board of directors, must decide how to choose a new president to fill this vacancy next semester.

First, generate a list of the qualities and qualifications you think the school should seek in a new president. What background and experience would prepare someone for this key position? What personal characteristics should the new president have? What questions would you ask to find out how each candidate measures up against the list of credentials you have prepared?

Now list all the stakeholders that your team, as directors, must consider before deciding on a replacement for the retiring president. Of these stakeholders, whose opinions do you think are most important? Whose are least important? Who will be directly and indirectly affected by the choice of a new president? Of these stakeholders, which should be represented as participants in the decision-making process?

Select a spokesperson to deliver a brief presentation to the class, summarizing your team's ideas and the reasoning behind your suggestions. After all the teams have completed their presentations, discuss the differences and similarities among credentials proposed by all the teams for evaluating candidates for the presidency. Then compare the teams' conclusions about stakeholders. Do all teams agree on which stakeholders should participate in the decision-making process? Lead a classroom discussion on a board's responsibility to its stakeholders.

Developing Your Research Skills

Review recent issues of business newspapers or periodicals (print or online editions) to find an article or series of articles illustrating one of the following business developments: merger, acquisition, hostile takeover, or leveraged buyout.

1. Explain in your own words what steps or events led to this development.
2. What results do you expect this development to have on (a) the company, (b) consumers, and (c) the industry the company is part of? Write down your answers, along with today's date.
3. Follow your story in the business news over the next month (or longer, as your instructor requests). What problems, opportunities, or other results are reported? Were these developments anticipated at the time of the initial story, or did they seem to catch industry analysts by surprise? How well did your answers to question 2 predict the results?

REFERENCES

1. Adapted from "Corporate Overview," Sirius XM website, accessed 6 August 2011, www.siriusxm.com; *2010 Sirius Proxy Statement and Annual Report*, www.siriusxm.com; John Kell, "Sirius Profit Jumps with Added Subscribers," *Wall Street Journal*, 3 May 2011, www.ebsco.com; Russell Adams, "Liberty Media Bids for Barnes," *Wall Street Journal*, 20 May 2011, B1; Relmor Demitrius, "Sirius XM's NASDAQ 100 Inclusion Good Timing," King of All Trades blog, 8 July 2011, www.kingofalltrades .com; Robert Holmes, "Sirius XM Sets Poison-Pill Plan," The Street, 30 April 2009, www.thestreet.com; Relmor Demitrius, "Can Liberty Media Lose Control of Sirius XM?" King of All Trades blog, 7 March 2011, www.kingofalltrades.com; Steve Garcia, "Synergy: Sirius, Liberty Media and Dish Network, Part 1," Seeking Alpha blog, 3 May 2011, http://seekingalpha .com; Steve Garcia, "Sirius XM's Major Synergies Are Finally Being Realized," Seeking Alpha blog, 27 July 2011, http://seekingalpha .com; "Sirius XM Radio Inc.," Google Finance, accessed 6 August

2011, www.google.com/finance; Olga Kharif, "Serious Threats to Sirius Radio," *BusinessWeek*, 30 March 2009, www.businessweek.com, Greg Avery, "Malone's Liberty Media Invests $530M in Sirius XM Radio," *Denver Business Journal*, 17 February 2009, www.bizjournals.com; Ronald Grover, "John Malone: King of Satellite?" *BusinessWeek*, 18 February 2009, www.businessweek.com; David Goldman, "XM–Sirius Merger Approved by DOJ," CNN.com, 24 March 2008, http://money.cnn.com; Olga Kharif, "More Static for Sirius–XM Deal, *BusinessWeek*, 8 May 2008, www.businessweek.com; Jeffrey H. Birnbaum, "Radio Merger Under Fire from Black Lawmakers," *Washington Post*, 17 June 2008, www.washingtonpost.com; Kim Hart, "Satellite Radio Merger Approved," *Washington Post*, 26 July 2008, www.washingtonpost.com; "Sirius Completes Acquisition of XM Satellite," Reuters, 29 July 2008, www.reuters.com; Olga Kharif, "Sirius XM Is in a Serious Bind," *BusinessWeek*, 17 September 2008, www.businessweek.com; Olga Kharif, "Sirius-XM: A Long, Challenging Road Ahead," *BusinessWeek*, 11 November 2008, www.businessweek.com; Andrew Ross Sorkin and Zachery Kouwe, "Sirius XM Prepares for Possible Bankruptcy," *New York Times*, 11 February 2009, www.nytimes.com; "Sirius Satellite Radio: Corporate Overview.

2. "Sole Proprietorship Basics," Nolo, accessed 10 March 2009, www.nolo.com.

3. "Sole Proprietorship FAQ," Nolo, accessed 10 March 2009, www.nolo.com.

4. William Atkinson, "Emotional Exhaustion: When You Have No Energy Left to Give," *LP/Gas*, June 2005, 17–20.

5. "Join the Club," *Entrepreneur*, December 2008, 89.

6. "Facts and Figures," PwC website, accessed 5 August 2011, www.pwc.com.

7. "Partnership Basics," Nolo, accessed 10 March 2009, www.nolo.com.

8. Michael Cumming, "What Is a Master Limited Partnership?" Morningstar, 9 August 2007, www.morningstar.com.

9. California Secretary of State website, accessed 5 August 2011, www.sos.ca.gov.

10. Kelly K. Spors, "So, You Want to Be an Entrepreneur," *Wall Street Journal*, 23 February 2009, http://online.wsj.com.

11. "Facts and Figures," PwC.

12. Stephanie Clifford, "10 Questions to Ask Your Partner (Before You Sign an Agreement)," *Inc.*, November 2006, www.inc.com.

13. "Creating a Partnership Agreement," Nolo, accessed 11 March 2009, www.nolo.com.

14. "Creating a Partnership Agreement."

15. "2011 Fortune Global 500," *Fortune*, accessed 5 August 2011, http://money.cnn.com; "The World Factbook," Central Intelligence Agency, accessed 5 August 2011, www.cia.gov.

16. "Largest US IPOs," Renaissance Capital IPO Home, accessed 12 March 2009, www.ipohome.com.

17. Geoffrey Colvin and Ram Charan, "Private Lives," *Fortune*, 27 November 2006, 190–198.

18. Sanford M. Jacoby and Sally Kohn, "Japan's Management Approaches Offer Lessons for U.S. Corporations," *Seattle Times*, 27 March 2009, www.seattletimes.com.

19. "S Corporation Facts," Nolo, accessed 13 March 2009, www.nolo.com

20. "Business Subchapter S Corporation," Lawfirms.com, accessed 13 March 2009, www.lawfirms.com.

21. "How to Choose the Right Legal Structure," *Inc.*, January–February 2009, www.inc.com.

22. Hoovers, accessed 13 March 2009, www.hoovers.com.

23. Alex Goldmark, "The Benefit Corporation: Can Business Be About More Than Profit?" *Good*, 1 July 2011, www.good.is; "Maryland First State in Union to Pass Benefit Corporation Legislation," B Corporation press release, 14 April 2010, www.crswire.com; B Corporation website, accessed 5 August 2011, www.bcorporation.net.

24. Interfaith Center on Corporate Responsibility website, accessed 5 August 2011, www.iccr.org; William J. Holstein, "Unlikely Allies," *Directorship*, 3 October 2006, www.forbes.com.

25. Jena McGregor, "Activist Investors Get More Respect," *BusinessWeek*, 11 June 2007, 34–35.

26. "Posner and Sherman on the Transformation of the Activist Investor," The Deal.com, 11 November 2008, www.thedeal.com.

27. Martin Lipton, "Shareholder Activism and the 'Eclipse of the Public Corporation,'" *The Corporate Board*, May/June 2007, 1–5.

28. Carol Bowie, "Independent Board Chairs: A Trend Picks Up Speed," *The Corporate Governance Advisor*, March–April 2009, 14–16; Cora Daniels, "Finally in the Director's Chair," *Fortune*, 4 October 2004, 42–44; David A. Nadler, "Building Better Boards," *Harvard Business Review*, May 2004, 102–111; Judy B. Rosener, "Women on Corporate Boards Make Good Business Sense," *Directorship*, May 2003, www.womensmedia.com.

29. "The Case for Customized Board Education," Susan Ellen Wolf, Robert J. Bertolini, Thomas J. Colligan, Fred Hassan, and Thomas J. Sabatino, Jr. *The Corporate Governance Advisor*, January/February 2011, 1–6; Joann S. Lublin, "Back to School," *Wall Street Journal*, 21 June 2004, R3.

30. Bill Baker, Larry West, Brian Cartwright, and Brian Nysenbaum, "Liability of Outside Directors in SEC Enforcement Actions," *The Corporate Governance Advisor*, May/June 2011, 16–21.

31. Jeffrey M. Stein and Parth S. Munshi, "The Changing Role of the Lead Director," *The Corporate Governance Advisor*, November–December 2008, 11–18.

32. "Mergers & Acquisitions Explained," Thomson Investors Network, accessed 8 April 2004, www.thomsoninvest.net.

33. *The PSI Opportunity* (online newsletter), PSI website, accessed 8 April 2004, www.psiusa.com.

34. "Spring Merger Fever," *Wall Street Journal*, 22 May 2007, A14.

35. Kevin Maney, "Skype: The Inside Story of the Boffo $8.5 Billion Deal," Fortune, 25 July 2011, 125–128; "Microsoft Corporation M&A Summary," Alacra, accessed 5 August 2011, www.alacrastore.com.

36. Greta Roberts, "The Soft Things That Make Mergers Hard," *Harvard Business Review* Blog Network, 12 July 2011. http://blogs.hbr.org.

37. Tim Merrifield, "Six Tips for Succeeding with the Art of Acquisition," Cisco website, accessed 5 August 2011, www.cisco.com; "The Contra Team," *Business 2.0*, April 2006, 83.

38. "Sprint-Nextel Joins the 'Worst Mergers in History' Club," Portfolio.com, 28 February 2008, www.portfolio.com.

39. Merrifield, "Six Tips for Succeeding with the Art of Acquisition."

40. Investopedia, accessed 5 August 2011, www.investopedia.com.

41. Nancy Gohring, "Judge OKs Settlement in Yahoo 'Poison Pill' Shareholder Suit," *Computerworld*, 9 March 2009, www.computerworld.com

42. Michael Hickins, "Searching for Allies," *Management Review*, January 2000, 54–58.

43. "Strategic Alliances," Cisco Systems, accessed 14 March 2009, www.cisco.com.

44. Smart Energy Alliance website, accessed 5 August 2011, www.smart-energy-alliance.com.

45. "Joint Ventures Overtake M&A," PricewaterhouseCoopers 12th Annual Global CEO Survey, accessed 14 March 2009, www.pwc.com.

46. Aaron Smith and Blake Ellis, "New Cash Transfer Service Rivals PayPal," CNNMoney, 25 May 2011, http://money.cnn.com.

47. See note 1.

48. Adapted from 37Signals website, accessed 2 July 2007, www.37signals.com; Tony Kontzer, "Learning to Share," *InformationWeek*, 5 May 2003, 28; Jon Udell, "Uniting Under Groove," *InfoWorld*, 17 February 2003, www.elibrary.com; Alison Overholt, "Virtually There?" *Fast Company*, 14 February 2002, 108. 6

GLOSSARY

acquisition An action taken by one company to buy a controlling interest in the voting stock of another company

benefit corporation A profit-seeking corporation whose charter specifies a social or environmental goal that the company must pursue in addition to profit

board of directors A group of professionals elected by shareholders as their representatives, with responsibility for the overall direction of the company and the selection of top executives

chief executive officer (CEO) The highest-ranking officer of a corporation

corporate governance In a broad sense, describes all the policies, procedures, relationships, and systems in place to oversee the successful and legal operation of the enterprise; in a narrow sense, refers to the responsibilities and performance of the board of directors specifically

corporate officers The top executives who run a corporation

corporation A legal entity, distinct from any individual persons, that has the power to own property and conduct business

general partnership A partnership in which all partners have joint authority to make decisions for the firm and joint liability for the firm's financial obligations

hostile takeover Acquisition of another company against the wishes of management

joint venture A separate legal entity established by two or more companies to pursue shared business objectives

leveraged buyout (LBO) Acquisition of a company's publicly traded stock, using funds that are primarily borrowed, usually with the intent of using some of the acquired assets to pay back the loans used to acquire the company

limited liability company (LLC) A structure that combines limited liability with the pass-through taxation benefits of a partnership; the number of shareholders is not restricted, nor is members' participation in management

limited liability partnership (LLP) A partnership in which each partner has unlimited liability only for his or her own actions and at least some degree of limited liability for the partnership as a whole

limited liability A legal condition in which the maximum amount each owner is liable for is equal to whatever amount each invested in the business

limited partnership A partnership in which one or more persons act as general partners who run the business and have the same unlimited liability as sole proprietors

liquidity A measure of how easily and quickly an asset such as corporate stock can be converted into cash by selling it

master limited partnership (MLP) A partnership that is allowed to raise money by selling units of ownership to the general public

merger An action taken by two companies to combine as a single entity

private corporation A corporation in which all the stock is owned by only a few individuals or companies and is not made available for purchase by the public

proxy A document that authorizes another person to vote on behalf of a shareholder in a corporation

public corporation A corporation in which stock is sold to anyone who has the means to buy it

S corporation A type of corporation that combines the capital-raising options and limited liability of a corporation with the federal taxation advantages of a partnership

shareholder activism Activities taken by shareholders (individually or in groups) to influence executive decision making in areas ranging from strategic planning to social responsibility

shareholders Investors who purchase shares of stock in a corporation

sole proprietorship A business owned by a single person

strategic alliance A long-term partnership between companies to jointly develop, produce, or sell products

partnership An unincorporated company owned by two or more people

unlimited liability A legal condition under which any damages or debts incurred by a business are the owner's personal responsibility

Entrepreneurship and Small-Business Ownership

Entrepreneurship and Small-Business Ownership

LEARNING OBJECTIVES   After studying this chapter, you will be able to

 Highlight the contributions small businesses make to the U.S. economy

 List the most common reasons people start their own companies and identify the common traits of successful entrepreneurs

3 Explain the importance of planning a new business and outline the key elements in a business plan

4 Identify the major causes of business failures and identify sources of advice and support for struggling business owners

5 Discuss the principal sources of small-business private financing

6 Explain the advantages and disadvantages of franchising

MyBizLab

Where you see MyBizLab in this chapter, go to www.mybizlab.com for additional activities on the topic being discussed.

BEHIND THE SCENES  BRINGING TRADITIONAL HEALING WISDOM TO MODERN CONSUMERS AT SISTER SKY

Monica Simeon and Marina TurningRobe, the sisters behind Sister Sky bath and body products, have turned their business dreams into reality but still face some important challenges as they continue to grow.

www.sistersky.com

For entrepreneurial inspiration, Monica Simeon didn't have to look very far. She learned how to run a business by helping her father operate one of the first Native American casinos. She got the inspiration for her business while preparing batches of skin lotions based on traditional herbal remedies after commercial products didn't help with her son's severe eczema. And the opportunity to form a business partnership was as close as her sister, Marina TurningRobe.

Thus was born Sister Sky, which makes natural bath and body products based on recipes and natural plant knowledge handed down from generation to generation. The company is based on the Spokane Indian Reservation in northeast Washington state, where the sisters grew up—and grew into their entrepreneurial lifestyle.

Like many other entrepreneurs, the sisters' vision is much broader than simply earning a living. They emphasize purity and authenticity in their products, whether that means using more-expensive distilled water to avoid risks of contamination, shunning the cheaper petroleum-based ingredients used in many mass-produced bath and body products, or staying true to the wisdom they have inherited from their ancestors. In addition, the sisters believe they have a duty to "promote cultural sharing in a positive way by educating consumers about the indigenous essence and spirit of the plant botanicals contained in our products." Finally,

Simeon says, "One of our main goals is to improve the tribal economy by expanding opportunities for jobs beyond the casino."

If you were Simeon or TurningRobe, what steps would you take to make sure your young business made it through the launch stage and onto a path of sustainable growth and profitability? Where might you turn for advice and support if you needed it? How would you stay true to your vision of authentic and purposeful products while pursuing the goal of providing job opportunities—and still meet the unrelenting demands of managing a business in a highly competitive industry?[1]

INTRODUCTION

Since you're studying business, chances are you've already had an idea or two for a new business. Are you ready to commit yourself fully to a business idea, as Monica Simeon and Marina TurningRobe (profiled in the chapter-opening Behind the Scenes) have done? Are you ready to make sacrifices and do whatever it takes to get your company off the ground? Should you start something from scratch or buy an existing business? Being an entrepreneur is one of the most exciting and important roles in business, but it requires high energy and some tough decision making, as you'll discover in this chapter.

The Big World of Small Business

Many businesses start out the way Sister Sky did: with an entrepreneur (or two, in this case), a compelling idea, and the drive to succeed. Small-business ownership gives people like Monica Simeon and Marina TurningRobe the opportunity to pursue their dreams while making lasting and important contributions to their communities. Entrepreneurship also provides the platform for launching companies that grow to be quite large. With the exception of operations spun off from existing companies, even the biggest corporations begin life as small businesses. The importance of small businesses in the U.S. economy is reflected in their sheer number: While there are roughly 17,000 large companies in the United States, there are more than 27 million small companies.[2]

Defining just what constitutes a small business is surprisingly tricky, but it is vitally important because billions of dollars are at stake when it comes to such things as employment regulations—from which the smallest companies are often exempt—and government contracts reserved for small businesses.[3] Roughly speaking, a **small business** is an independently owned and operated company that employs fewer than 500 people and "is not dominant in its field of operation," in the words of the U.S. Small Business Administration (SBA). Beyond that general starting point, the SBA defines the maximum size of "small" through either annual revenue or number of employees, and the limits vary by industry.[4]

ECONOMIC ROLES OF SMALL BUSINESSES

From employing millions of people to creating essential products, small businesses play a vital role in the U.S. economy. Here are some of the major contributions small firms make (see Exhibit 1 for some key facts and figures):

- **They provide jobs.** Although most small businesses have no employees, those that do employ about half of the private-sector workforce in this country and create roughly two-thirds of all new jobs.[5]
- **They introduce new products.** The freedom to innovate that is characteristic of many small firms continues to yield countless advances: Among all firms that apply for U.S. patents on new inventions, small businesses receive 13 times more patents per employee than larger firms.[6]
- **They meet the needs of larger organizations.** Many small businesses act as distributors, servicing agents, and suppliers to larger corporations and to numerous government agencies (which often reserve a certain percentage of their purchasing contracts for small businesses).
- **They inject a considerable amount of money into the economy.** Small businesses pay nearly half the private-sector payroll in the United States and produce half the country's gross domestic product.[7]

MyBizLab

Gain hands-on experience through an interactive, real-world scenario. This chapter's simulation entitled Getting Your Business off the Ground is located at **www.mybizlab.com**.

1 | **LEARNING OBJECTIVE**

Highlight the contributions small businesses make to the U.S. economy.

small business A company that is independently owned and operated, is not dominant in its field, and employs fewer than 500 people (although this number varies by industry)

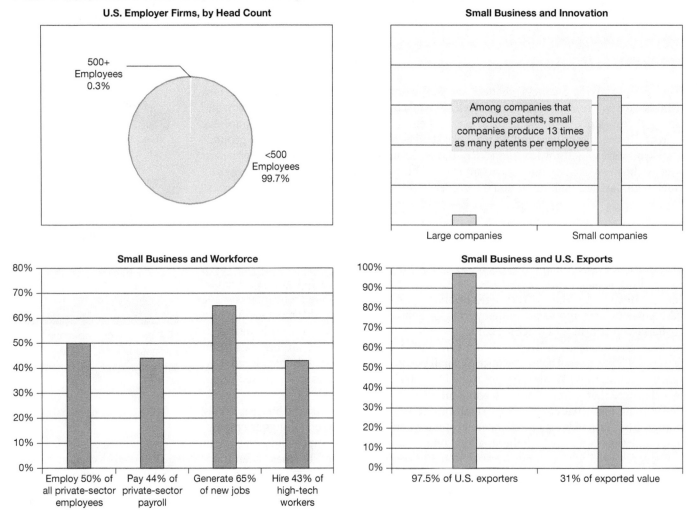

EXHIBIT 1 **The Big Economic Impact of Small Business**

In terms of employment, innovation, and exports, there is nothing small about small business in the United States.

Source: Adapted from "FAQs: Advocacy Small Business Statistics and Research," U.S. Small Business Administration, accessed 9 August 2011, www.sba.gov.

- **They take risks that larger companies sometimes avoid.** Entrepreneurs play a significant role in the economy as risk takers—people willing to try new and unproven ideas.
- **They provide specialized goods and services.** Small businesses frequently spring up to fill niches that aren't being served by existing companies.

CHARACTERISTICS OF SMALL BUSINESSES

The majority of small businesses are modest operations with little growth potential, although some have attractive income potential for the solo businessperson. Small businesses such as a self-employed consultant, a corner florist, or a small e-commerce venture are sometimes called *lifestyle businesses* because they are built around the personal and financial needs of an individual or a family. In contrast, other firms are small simply because they are young, but they have ambitious plans to grow. These *high-growth ventures* are usually run by a team rather than by one individual, and they expand rapidly by obtaining a sizable supply of investment capital and by introducing new products or services to a large market.

Regardless of their primary objectives, small companies tend to differ from large ones in a variety of important ways. First, most small firms have a narrow focus, offering fewer goods and services to fewer market segments. Second, unless they are launched with generous financial backing, which is rare, small businesses have to get by with limited resources. Third, smaller businesses often have more freedom to innovate and move quickly. As they grow larger, companies tend to get slower and more bureaucratic. In contrast, entrepreneurial firms usually find it easier to operate "on the fly," making decisions quickly and reacting to changes in the marketplace.

FACTORS CONTRIBUTING TO THE INCREASE IN THE NUMBER OF SMALL BUSINESSES

Three factors are contributing to the increase in the number of small businesses today: e-commerce, social media, and other technological advances; the growing diversity in entrepreneurship; and corporate downsizing and outsourcing.

E-Commerce, Social Media, and Other Technologies

Technology has always played a major role in business formation, but the rapid growth of e-commerce and social media in recent years has revolutionized the way many companies operate. Companies such as Pandora and Facebook couldn't exist without web technologies, of course, because their connection to customers happens entirely online. In other instances, technology enables innovation in one or more functional areas. For example, thousands of companies use the web to replace physical retail stores while continuing to use conventional production and distribution systems in the physical world. Online technology also allows an operation such as handcrafts marketplace Etsy (www.etsy.com) to give "very-very small businesses" a unified presence online, as well as making it easier for shoppers to find products of interest.[8] In fact, avoiding the high cost of establishing a physical presence while being able to market to the entire world is one of the most significant and lasting changes that technology has brought to small business.

Similarly, social media have dramatically changed the marketing and selling functions for many companies. While Facebook, YouTube, and other online media tools are used by companies of every size, they are particularly vital to small companies whose minuscule marketing budgets prohibit them from doing much advertising or other traditional promotional activities.

Growing Diversity in Entrepreneurship

Small-business growth is being fueled by women, minorities, immigrants, military veterans who want to apply their leadership skills, older workers who can't find employment to fit their interests or skills, and young people who want alternatives to traditional employment. For instance, women now own more than 10 million U.S. businesses.[9] Minority business ownership is also on the rise across the United States, with members of ethnic minority groups now owning 15 percent of all U.S. businesses.[10]

Young people are one of the strongest forces in entrepreneurship and launch the majority of new businesses.[11] It's never too early to start. Facebook, Google, and Dell are just a few of the significant companies started by college students. In the words of Joseph Keeley, who formed College Nannies and Tutors (www.collegenannies.com) when he was a freshman at the University of St. Thomas, "As a young entrepreneur, the risk is relatively low. If you have a well-thought-out plan, don't be afraid to execute it. The risk only gets higher as you get older." Keeley's initiative has paid off: His company recently celebrated its tenth year in business and has franchise operations and corporate child-care programs across the country.[12] If you'd like to network with other aspiring entrepreneurs, look into such groups as the Collegiate Entrepreneurs Organization (www.c-e-o.org).

Downsizing and Outsourcing

Business start-ups often soar when the economy sours. During hard times, many companies downsize or lay off

REAL-TIME UPDATES
Learn More by Listening to This Podcast

What does it take to make it as a young entrepreneur?

Listen in as six recent Stanford graduates discuss their experiences as entrepreneurs. Go to http://real-timeupdates.com/bia6 and click on Learn More. If you are using MyBizLab, you can access Real-Time Updates within the chapter or under Student Study Tools.

REAL-TIME UPDATES
Learn More by Visiting This Website

See how Sister Sky uses social media to connect with customers

Visit the Facebook page of Sister Sky, the company featured in this chapter's Behind the Scenes. Go to http://real-timeupdates.com/bia6 and click on Learn More. If you are using MyBizLab, you can access Real-Time Updates within the chapter or under Student Study Tools.

Wayne Erbsen turned his passion for preserving and performing traditional music into a business that reaches customers all over the world from his home in Asheville, North Carolina. Native Ground Books & Music (www.nativeground.com) offers books and recordings of songs and folklore from the Civil War, the Old West, Appalachia, railroading, gospel, and many other elements of America's heritage.

Photo by Tim Barnwell

talented employees, who then have little to lose by pursuing self-employment. Tech titans William Hewlett and David Packard joined forces in Silicon Valley in 1938 during the Great Depression, and Microsoft launched during the 1975 recession.[13] During the recent global recession, another wave of entrepreneurs took their turn. As companies were trimming staff, Mark Cannice, who runs the entrepreneurship program at the University of San Francisco, said, "If there is a silver lining, the large-scale downsizing from major companies will release a lot of new entrepreneurial talent and ideas—scientists, engineers, business folks now looking to do other things."[14]

Outsourcing, the practice of engaging outside firms to handle either individual projects or entire business functions also creates numerous opportunities for small businesses and entrepreneurs. Some companies subcontract special projects and secondary business functions to experts outside the organization, while others turn to outsourcing as a way to permanently eliminate entire departments, and some laid-off employees even become entrepreneurs and sell services to their former employers.

✓ Checkpoint

LEARNING OBJECTIVE 1: Highlight the contributions small businesses make to the U.S. economy.

SUMMARY: Small businesses provide jobs, employing about half the private-sector workforce. They introduce new and innovative products, they supply many of the needs of larger organizations, they inject considerable amounts of money into the economy, they often take risks that larger organizations avoid, and they provide many specialized goods and services.

CRITICAL THINKING: (1) Why do you think many companies grow more risk averse as they grow larger? (2) If they wanted to, could large businesses take the place of small businesses in the U.S. economy? For instance, could someone build a nationwide landscaping company? Why or why not?

IT'S YOUR BUSINESS: If you can't land the right job soon after graduation, would you consider starting a business? Why or why not?

KEY TERMS TO KNOW: small business

---

2 | LEARNING OBJECTIVE

List the most common reasons people start their own companies, and identify the common traits of successful entrepreneurs.

entrepreneurial spirit The positive, forward-thinking desire to create profitable, sustainable business enterprises

The Entrepreneurial Spirit

To some people, working for themselves or starting a company seems a perfectly natural way to earn a living. To others, the thought of working outside the structure of a regular company might seem too scary to even contemplate. However, every professional should understand the **entrepreneurial spirit**—the positive, forward-thinking desire to create profitable, sustainable business enterprises—and the role it can play in *every* company, not just small or new firms. The entrepreneurial spirit is vital to the health of the economy and to everyone's standard of living, and it can help even the largest and oldest companies become profitable and competitive.

WHY PEOPLE START THEIR OWN COMPANIES

Starting a company is nearly always a difficult, risky, exhausting endeavor that requires significant sacrifice. Why do people do it? Some want more control over their future; others are simply tired of working for someone else. Some, such as Monica Simeon and Marina

TurningRobe of Sister Sky, have new product ideas that they believe in with such passion that they're willing to risk everything on a start-up enterprise. Some start companies to pursue business goals that are important to them on a personal level. Jennie Baird, cofounder of Generation Grownup (www.generationgrownup .com), which publishes parenting-related websites, had two important reasons—reasons shared by Simeon, TurningRobe, and many others: "I wanted to take the opportunity to be the one in control of innovation and work on something that I believe in."[15]

Another reason, one that becomes more common during tough job markets, is the inability to find attractive employment anywhere else. Alex Andon searched for months after being laid off from his job in the biotech industry. Out of frustration as much as anything else ("I hate looking for work," he explained), he became an entrepreneur, putting his biology background to work launching Jellyfish Art (www.jellyfishart.com) to create and sell jellyfish aquariums.[16]

Frustrated in a tough job market, Alex Andon used his expertise in biology and aquarium design to launch Jellyfish Art (www.jellyfishart.com). The company specializes in the unique and demanding field of aquariums for jellyfish.

QUALITIES OF SUCCESSFUL ENTREPRENEURS

While it's impossible to lump millions of people into a single category, successful entrepreneurs tend to share a number of characteristics (see Exhibit 2). If you have many of these traits, successful entrepreneurship could be in your future, too—if you're not already a hard-working entrepreneur.

INNOVATING WITHOUT LEAVING: INTRAPRENEURSHIP

The entrepreneur's innovative spirit is so compelling that many large companies and individuals within companies now try to express it through *intrapreneurship*, a term coined by business consultant Gifford Pinchot (www.intrapreneur.com) to designate entrepreneurial efforts within a larger organization.[17]

EXHIBIT 2	Qualities Shared by Successful Entrepreneurs

While there is no single personality profile that fits all successful entrepreneurs, here are the qualities that entrepreneurs tend to have.

- Like to control their destiny—and believe they can
- Curious and eager to learn to reach their goals
- Learn from mistakes and view failure as a chance to grow
- Highly adaptable and in tune with their markets
- Willing to take sensible risks but are not "gamblers"

- Love what they do and are driven by a passion to succeed
- Often don't measure success in strictly financial terms
- Have a high degree of confidence and optimism
- Relate well with diverse personalities
- Have a talent for inspiring others

- Willing to work hard for sustained periods of time
- Extremely disciplined; no one has to motivate them
- Willing to make sacrifices in other areas of their lives

However, innovating within a larger organization is often much easier said than done because companies tend to become more analytical, more deliberate, more structured, and more careful as they mature. Mechanisms put in place to prevent mistakes can also hamper innovative thinking by restricting people to tried-and-true methods. Organizations can develop habits based on behaviors and decisions that made sense in the past but that no longer make sense as the business environment changes. Injecting the entrepreneurial spirit sometimes means going against the accepted wisdom.[18] In other words, it can be risky behavior that may or may not be rewarded. Companies sometimes need to take special steps to encourage, protect, and reward the entrepreneurial spirit.

✔ Checkpoint

LEARNING OBJECTIVE 2: List the most common reasons people start their own companies, and identify the common traits of successful entrepreneurs.

SUMMARY: People start businesses for a variety of reasons, including gaining more control over their futures, wanting to avoid working for someone else, having new product ideas that they are deeply passionate about, pursuing business goals that are important to them on a personal level, or seeking income alternatives during tough employment markets. The entrepreneurial spirit, the positive, forward-thinking desire to create profitable, sustainable business enterprises, is a good way to summarize the entrepreneurial personality. Specifically, successful entrepreneurs tend to love what they do and are driven by a passion to succeed at it, they are disciplined and willing to work hard, they are confident and optimistic, and they like to control their own destiny. Moreover, they relate well to others and have the ability to inspire others, they are curious, they learn from their mistakes without letting failure drag them down, they are adaptable and tuned into their environments, and they are moderate but careful risk takers.

CRITICAL THINKING: (1) Would someone who excels at independent entrepreneurship automatically excel at an intrapreneurial effort? Why or why not? (2) Does the inability or unwillingness to work within the constraints of a typical corporation mean someone is naturally suited to entrepreneurship? Why or why not?

IT'S YOUR BUSINESS: If you had to start a business right now and generate profit as quickly as possible, what kind of business would you start? Explain your answer.

KEY TERMS TO KNOW: entrepreneurial spirit

3 LEARNING OBJECTIVE

Explain the importance of planning a new business, and outline the key elements in a business plan.

The Start-Up Phase: Planning and Launching a New Business

The start-up phase is an exciting time because entrepreneurs and small-business owners love to roll up their sleeves and get to work, but it's also an exhausting time because a lot of work must be done. Focusing that start-up energy and making sure essential tasks get completed calls for careful decision making and planning, starting with choosing the best ownership option and creating an effective business plan.

SMALL-BUSINESS OWNERSHIP OPTIONS

People who have an entrepreneurial urge sometimes jump to the conclusion that starting a new company is the best choice, but it's definitely not the only choice—and not always the right choice. Before you decide, consider all three options: creating a new business, buying an existing business, or buying a franchise. Creating a new business has many advantages, but it can also be the most difficult option (see Exhibit 3 on the next page).

EXHIBIT 3 | **Business Start-Up Options**

Creating an all-new, independent business can be an exciting prospect, but this brief comparison highlights how much work it requires and how many risks are involved. (You can read more about franchising later in this chapter.)

Start-Up Strategy	Financial Outlay at Start-Up	Possibilities for Borrowing Start-Up Capital or Getting Investors	Owner's Freedom and Flexibility	Business Processes and Systems	Support Networks	Workforce	Customer Base, Brand Recognition, and Sales
Create a new, independent business	Some businesses can be started with very little cash; others, particularly in manufacturing, may require a lot of capital	Usually very limited; most lenders and many investors want evidence that the business can generate revenue before they'll offer funds; venture capitalists invest in new firms, but only in a few industries	Very high, particularly during early phases, although low capital can severely restrict the owner's ability to maneuver	Must be designed and created from scratch, which can be time-consuming and expensive	Suppliers, bankers, and other elements of the network must be selected; the good news is that the owner can select and recruit ones that he or she specifically wants	Must be hired and trained at the owner's expense	None; must be built from the ground up, which can put serious strain on company finances until sales volume builds
Buy an existing independent business	Can be considerable; some companies sell for multiples of their annual revenue, for example	Banks are more willing to lend to "going concerns," and investors are more likely to invest in them	Less than when creating a new business because facilities, workforce, and other assets are already in place—more than when buying a franchise	Already in place, which can be a plus or minus, depending on how well they work	Already in place; may need to be upgraded	Already in place, which could be a positive or a negative, but at least there are staff to operate the business	Assuming that the business is at least somewhat successful, it has a customer base with ongoing sales and some brand reputation (which could be positive or negative)
Buy into a franchise system	Varies widely, from a few thousand to several hundred thousand dollars	Varies, but many franchisors do not allow franchisees to buy a franchise with borrowed funds, so they must have their own capital	Low to very low; most franchisors require rigid adherence to company policies and processes	One of the key advantages of buying a franchise is that it comes with an established business system	Varies; some franchise companies specify which suppliers a franchisee can use	Must be hired and trained, but a franchisor usually provides training or training support	Customer base and repeat sales must be built up, but one of the major advantages of a franchise is established brand recognition

Compared to starting a new business, buying an existing business can involve less work and less risk—provided, of course, that you check out the company carefully. When you buy a healthy business, you generally purchase an established customer base, functioning business systems, proven products or services, and a known location. In addition, financing an existing business is often much easier because lenders are reassured by the company's history and existing assets and customer base.

Still, buying an existing business is not without disadvantages and risks. You may need a considerable amount of financing to buy a fully functioning company, for example, and you will inherit any problems the company has, from unhappy employees to obsolete equipment to customers with overdue accounts. Thorough research is a must.[19]

The third option, buying a franchise, combines many of the benefits of independent business ownership with the support that comes with being part of a larger organization.

BLUEPRINT FOR AN EFFECTIVE BUSINESS PLAN

Although many successful entrepreneurs claim to have done little formal planning, they all have at least *some* intuitive idea of what they're trying to accomplish and how they hope to do it. In other words, even if they haven't produced a formal printed document, chances are they've thought through the big questions, which is just as important. As FedEx founder Fred Smith put it, "Being entrepreneurial doesn't mean [you] jump off a ledge and figure out how to make a parachute on the way down."[20]

business plan A document that summarizes a proposed business venture, goals, and plans for achieving those goals

A **business plan** summarizes a proposed business venture, communicates the company's goals, highlights how management intends to achieve those goals, and shows how customers will benefit from the company's goods or services. Preparing a business plan serves three important functions. First, it guides the company operations and outlines a strategy for turning an idea into reality. Second, it helps persuade lenders and investors to finance your business if outside money is required. Third, it can provide a reality check in case an idea just isn't feasible.

Business plans can be written before the company is launched, when the founders are defining their vision of what the company will be, when the company is seeking funding, and after the company is up and running, when the plan serves as a monitor-and-control mechanism to make sure operations are staying on track. At any stage, a comprehensive business plan forces you to think about personnel, marketing, facilities, suppliers, distribution, and a host of other issues vital to a company's success. (For an alternative view on the value of business plans and how much time you should spend writing one, watch the video in the Real-Time Updates Learn More on this page.) The specific elements to include in a business plan can vary based on the situation; here are the sections typically included in a plan written to attract outside investors:[21]

- **Summary.** In one or two paragraphs, summarize your business concept, particularly the *business model*, which defines how the company will generate revenue and produce a profit. The summary must be compelling, catching the investor's attention and giving him or her reasons to keep reading. Describe your product or service and its market potential. Highlight some things about your company and its leaders that will distinguish your firm from the competition. Summarize your financial projections and indicate how much money you will need from investors or lenders and where it will be spent.
- **Mission and objectives.** Explain the purpose of your business and what you hope to accomplish.
- **Company overview.** Give full background information on the origins and structure of your venture.
- **Products or services.** Concisely describe your products or services, focusing on their unique attributes and their appeal to customers.
- **Management and key personnel.** Summarize the background and qualifications of the people most responsible for the company's success.
- **Target market.** Provide data that will persuade an investor that you understand your target market. Be sure to identify the strengths and weaknesses of your competitors.
- **Marketing strategy.** Provide projections of sales volume and market share; outline a strategy for identifying and reaching potential customers, setting prices, providing customer support, and physically delivering your products or services. Whenever possible, include evidence of customer acceptance, such as advance product orders.
- **Design and development plans.** If your products require design or development, describe the nature and extent of what needs to be done, including costs and possible problems.
- **Operations plan.** Provide information on facilities, equipment, and personnel requirements.
- **Start-up schedule.** Forecast development of the company in terms of completion dates for major aspects of the business plan.

REAL-TIME UPDATES
Learn More by Watching This Video

Is it necessary—or even smart—to spend months writing a business plan?

Some entrepreneurs don't agree that writing a comprehensive business plan is always a good idea. See what Kevin Ryan has to say in this interview. Go to http://real-timeupdates.com/bia6 and click on Learn More. If you are using MyBizLab, you can access Real-Time Updates within the chapter or under Student Study Tools.

- **Major risk factors.** Identify all potentially negative factors and discuss them honestly.
- **Financial projections and requirements.** Include a detailed budget of start-up and operating costs, as well as projections for income, expenses, and cash flow for the first three years of business. Identify the company's financing needs and potential sources.
- **Exit strategy.** Explain how investors will be able to cash out or sell their investment, such as through a public stock offering, sale of the company, or a buyback of the investors' interest.

REAL-TIME UPDATES
Learn More by Reading This PDF

Want to pitch to investors? Learn from the pros first

Guy Kawasaki and his partners at Garage Technology Ventures offer invaluable advice on presenting a business idea to potential investors. Go to http://real-timeupdates.com/bia6 and click on Learn More. If you are using MyBizLab, you can access Real-Time Updates within the chapter or under Student Study Tools.

Veteran Silicon Valley entrepreneur and investor Guy Kawasaki advises entrepreneurs to create a concise *executive summary* of their business plan to use when presenting their ideas to investors for the first time. Entrepreneurs often have as little as 20 minutes (and sometimes even less) to make these pitches, so a compelling presentation backed up by an executive summary no longer than 20 pages is ideal. The most important part of the entire package is "the grab," a compelling one- or two-sentence statement that gets an investor's attention. If an investor is intrigued, he or she can then read the executive summary to get a better sense of the opportunity and then review the full business plan before making a decision to provide funds.[22]

✓ Checkpoint

LEARNING OBJECTIVE 3: Explain the importance of planning a new business, and outline the key elements in a business plan.

SUMMARY: Planning is essential because it forces you to consider the best ownership strategy for your needs and circumstances (creating a new company, buying an existing company, or buying a franchise), and it forces you to think through the factors that will lead to success. An effective business plan should include your mission and objectives, company overview, management, target market, marketing strategy, design and development plans, operations plan, start-up schedule, major risk factors, and financial projections and requirements.

CRITICAL THINKING: (1) Why is it important to identify critical risks and problems in a business plan? (2) Many experts suggest that you write the business plan yourself, rather than hiring a consultant to write it for you. Why is this a good idea?

IT'S YOUR BUSINESS: (1) Think of several of the most innovative or unusual products you currently own or have recently used (don't forget about services as well). Were these products created by small companies or large ones? (2) Optimism and perseverance are two of the most important qualities for entrepreneurs. On a scale of 1 (lowest) to 10 (highest), how would you rate yourself on these two qualities? How would your best friend rate you?

KEY TERM TO KNOW: business plan

The Growth Phase: Nurturing and Sustaining a Young Business

4 LEARNING OBJECTIVE

Identify the major causes of business failures, and identify sources of advice and support for struggling business owners.

So far, so good. You've done your planning and launched your new enterprise. Now the challenge is to keep going and keep growing toward your goals. To ensure a long and healthy life for your business, start by understanding the reasons new businesses can fail.

THE NEW BUSINESS FAILURE RATE

You may have heard some frightening "statistics" about the failure rate of new businesses, with various sources saying that 70, 80, or even 90 percent of new business ventures fail. Unfortunately, calculating a precise figure that represents all types of businesses across all industries is probably impossible. First, the definition of "failure" can be hard to pin down and varies from one business owner to the next. For example, business owners may retire, return to the corporate workforce to get away from the grind of running a business alone, or simply decide to pursue a different path in life. All of these closures would count as failures in a typical survey, but they wouldn't count as failures to the business owners themselves. Second, establishing a time frame is essential for a failure rate to have any meaning. For example, ill-conceived or undercapitalized businesses often don't survive the first year, so the early failure rate is quite high. However, after the bad ideas collide with reality and disappear, the rate of failure slows down, and the companies that fail do so for a wide variety of reasons, some internal and some external. Third, structural changes in the economy or in a particular industry can deal a fatal blow to nearly every company in a particular category, both upstarts and established players. For example, the rapid growth of online travel shopping is hammering traditional in-person travel agencies. The fact that some newer agencies are closing is probably more the result of this structural change in the industry than of some "new business failure" phenomenon.

In other words, view every failure statistic with skepticism unless you can find out how it was calculated. For instance, in the notoriously difficult restaurant industry, "90 percent of new restaurants fail" is repeated so often that many people assume that it must be true. However, one in-depth study showed the rate to be only 60 percent after four years—still a serious number, but considerably less than the near-certain failure rate of 90 percent.[23]

Another study—this one a comprehensive analysis using data from the U.S. Census Bureau—found that 50 percent of all new employer firms (those that hire employees) were still in business after four years, and another 17 percent were no longer in operation but had closed "successfully," meaning that the owner retired, sold the company, or otherwise ended the enterprise on a positive note. In other words, averaged across all industries, only 33 percent actually "failed" during this time frame.[24]

Although the statistics may not be quite as gloomy as many people think, even a 33 percent failure rate should demand the careful entrepreneur's attention. To help make sure you don't become a statistic, start by understanding why businesses tend to fail (see Exhibit 4 on the next page) and figure out how to avoid making the same mistakes.

Perhaps one of the most important reasons companies fail is something that doesn't always show up in surveys. It's a simple matter of "motivational collapse," when the would-be entrepreneur encounters one too many setbacks and simply doesn't have the drive to keep going.[25] A truly committed entrepreneur, in contrast, keeps pushing onward, experimenting, making adjustments, and keeping his or her enthusiasm level high until things start to click. One would be hard-pressed to improve on the insight and advice offered by Marina TurningRobe of Sister Sky: "In business, you must have the courage and honesty to admit when you fall short. This helps you refine, reformulate, redesign and come back stronger and better. If you can't admit your shortcomings you will become stagnant, irrelevant, or just plain arrogant. In a competitive business environment, being any of these will be your demise."[26]

ADVICE AND SUPPORT FOR BUSINESS OWNERS

Keeping a business going is no simple task, to be sure. Fortunately, entrepreneurs can get advice and support from a wide variety of sources.

Government Agencies and Not-for-Profit Organizations

A number of city, state, and federal government agencies offer business owners advice, assistance, and even financing in some cases. For instance, many cities and states have an office of economic development chartered with helping companies prosper so that they might contribute to the local or regional economy. At the federal level, small businesses can apply for SBA-backed loans, get management and financing advice, and learn about selling to the federal government at www.sba.gov. The Minority Business Development Agency

EXHIBIT 4	Why New Businesses Fail

These twelve blunders are among the most common reasons for the failure of new businesses.

Leadership Issues	Marketing and Sales Issues	Financial Issues	Systems and Facilities Issues
Managerial incompetence: Owner doesn't know how to plan, lead, control, or organize **Lack of strategic planning:** Owner didn't think through all the variables needed to craft a viable business strategy **Lack of relevant experience:** Owner may be experienced in business but not in the particular markets or technologies that are vital to the new firm's success **Inability to make the transition from corporate employee to entrepreneur:** Owner can't juggle the multiple and diverse responsibilities or survive the lack of support that comes with going solo	**Ineffective marketing:** Small companies—especially *new* small companies—face a tremendous challenge getting recognition in crowded markets **Uncontrolled growth:** Company may add customers faster than it can handle them, leading to chaos, or may even "grow its way into bankruptcy" if it spends wildly to capture and support customers **Overreliance on a single customer:** One huge customer can disappear overnight, leaving the company in dire straits	**Inadequate financing:** Being undercapitalized can prevent a company from building the scale required to be successful or sustaining operations until sales revenues increase enough for the firm to be self-funding **Poor cash management:** A company may spend too much on nonessentials, fail to balance expenditures with incoming revenues, fail to use loan or investment funds wisely, or fail to budget enough to pay its bills **Too much overhead:** Putting in place too many fixed expenses that are directly related to creating or selling products leaves the firm vulnerable to any slowdown in the economy	**Poor location:** Being in the wrong place will doom a retail operation and can raise costs for other types of business as well **Poor inventory control:** Company may build too much or buy too much, raising costs too high—or it may do the opposite and be unable to satisfy demand

(www.mbda.gov) offers advice and programs to minority-owned businesses. Many state agencies also have offices to help small firms compete.

Some of the best advice available to small businesses is delivered by thousands of volunteers from the Service Corps of Retired Executives (SCORE), a resource partner of the SBA. These experienced business professionals offer free advice and one-to-one counseling to entrepreneurs. You can learn more at www.score.org.

Many colleges and universities also offer entrepreneurship and small-business programs. Check with your college's business school to see whether resources are available to help you launch or expand a company. The U.S. Chamber of Commerce (www.chamberofcommerce.com) and its many local chambers offer advice and special programs for small business as well.

Business Partners

Banks, credit card companies, software companies, and other firms you do business with can also be a source of advice and support. For example, the Open Forum (www.openforum.com), hosted by American Express, offers a variety of videos, articles, and online network tools to help small business owners, as well as online tutorials and forums where business owners can post questions.[27] As you might expect, the free resources from these companies are part of their marketing strategies and so include a certain amount of self-promotion, but don't let that stop you from taking advantage of all the free advice you can get.

Mentors and Advisory Boards

Many entrepreneurs and business owners take advantage of individual mentors and advisory boards. Mentoring can

REAL-TIME UPDATES
Learn More by Listening to This Podcast

Increase your chances of success by learning from other entrepreneurs

SCORE advisor Lou Davenport shares the wisdom he has gained from helping struggling entrepreneurs. Go to http://real-timeupdates.com/bia6 and click on Learn More. If you are using MyBizLab, you can access Real-Time Updates within the chapter or under Student Study Tools.

happen through both formal programs such as SCORE and informal relationships developed in person or online (see Exhibit 5 for a list of top social networks for entrepreneurs). In either case, the advice of a mentor who has been down the road before can be priceless.

An **advisory board** is a form of "group mentoring" in which you assemble a team of people with subject-area expertise or vital contacts to help review plans and decisions. Unlike a corporate board of directors, an advisory board does not have legal responsibilities, and you don't have to incorporate to establish an advisory board. In some cases, advisors will agree to help for no financial compensation. In other cases, particularly for growth companies that want high-profile experts, advisors agree to serve in exchange for either a fee or a small portion of the company's stock (up to 3 percent is standard).[28]

Print and Online Media

Your local library and the Internet offer information to help any small-business owner face just about every challenge imaginable. For instance, blogs written by business owners, investors, and functional specialists such as marketing consultants can offer valuable insights. Websites such as www.entrepreneurship.org provide free advice on every aspect of managing an entrepreneurial organization. Also, the websites affiliated with these well-known business magazines should be on every small-business owner's regular reading list:

- *Inc.* (www.inc.com)
- *Business 2.0* (http://money.cnn.com/magazines/business2)
- *Bloomberg Businessweek* (www.businessweek.com/small-business)
- *Fortune* and *Money* (http://money.cnn.com/smallbusiness)

EXHIBIT 5	Social Networking for Entrepreneurs

Here are just a few of the many online networks that provide advice and vital connections for entrepreneurs.

Network	Special Features	URL
Entrepreneur Connect	Social network created by *Entrepreneur* magazine	http://econnect.entrepreneur.com
PartnerUp	Helps entrepreneurs looking for people and resources	www.partnerup.com
StartupNation	Provides articles, forums, blogs, seminars, and podcasts	www.startupnation.com
LinkedIn	Not specifically for entrepreneurs, but so many business professionals are members of this popular network that most entrepreneurs should have a presence as well	www.linkedin.com
Biznik	Social network focused on collaboration, with entrepreneurs and small-business owners helping one another	http://biznik.com
Perfect Business	Resource-rich site that can help with all phases of starting a business	www.perfectbusiness.com
Go BIG Network	Bills itself as the world's biggest community of start-up companies	www.gobignetwork.com
Cofoundr	Private members-only network (you can't view other profiles without joining) for programmers, designers, investors, and others in the entrepreneurial community	http://cofoundr.com
The Funded	Lets entrepreneurs share information on venture capitalists and angel investors, including the amounts and terms they've been offered	http://thefunded.com
Young Entrepreneur	Popular site for active entrepreneurs and those considering entrepreneurship	www.youngentrepreneur.com

Networks and Support Groups

No matter what industry you're in or what stage your business is in, you can probably find a local or an online network of people with similar interests. Many cities across the country have local networks; search online for "entrepreneur network." Some entrepreneurs meet regularly in small groups to analyze each other's progress month by month. Being forced to articulate your plans and decisions to peers—and to be held accountable for results—can be an invaluable reality check. Some groups focus on helping entrepreneurs hone their presentations to potential investors. In addition to local in-person groups, social networking technology gives entrepreneurs an endless array of opportunities to connect online (see Exhibit 5).

Business Incubators

Business incubators are centers that provide "newborn" businesses with various combinations of advice, financial support, access to industry insiders and connections, facilities, and other services a company needs to get started. Some incubators are not-for-profit organizations affiliated with the economic development agencies of local or state governments or universities, some are for-profit enterprises, some companies have internal incubators to encourage new ventures, and some are run by venture capitalists.

One of the best-known incubators, Y Combinator (http://ycombinator.com), has helped to fund and nurture more than 300 companies in digital media and related industries. In exchange for a small share of ownership, it makes small investments in companies; more important, it helps founders refine their ideas, develop products, polish their pitches to investors, connect with industry experts, handle incorporation issues to avoid legal trouble later on, hire the right kind of employees, and even mediate disputes between company founders. If all this help sounds priceless, Y Combinator would certainly agree with you: "The kind of advice we give literally can't be bought, because anyone qualified to give it is already rich. You can only get it from investors."[29]

To learn more about incubators or to find one in your area, visit the National Business Incubation Association website, at www.nbia.org.

business incubators Facilities that house small businesses and provide support services during the company's early growth phases

---

✔ Checkpoint

LEARNING OBJECTIVE 4: Identify the major causes of business failures, and identify sources of advice and support for struggling business owners.

SUMMARY: Ten common reasons for failure are managerial incompetence, inexperience, inadequate financing, poor cash management, lack of strategy planning, ineffective marketing, uncontrolled growth, poor location, poor inventory control, and the inability to make the transition from corporate employee to independent entrepreneur. Another factor that can contribute to any of these explicit reasons is motivational collapse, when the entrepreneur simply gives up. For help and advice, business owners can turn to a variety of government agencies, not-for-profit organizations, business partners, mentors and advisory boards, print and online media, networks and support groups, and business incubators.

CRITICAL THINKING: (1) Why would a state or local government invest taxpayer dollars in a business incubator? (2) Can you think of any risks of getting advice from other entrepreneurs?

IT'S YOUR BUSINESS: (1) Have you ever shopped at a store or eaten in a restaurant and said to yourself, "This place isn't going to make it"? What factors caused you to reach that conclusion? (2) Does your college have an entrepreneur program or participate in a business incubator? If you wanted to start a business, how might such services help you?

KEY TERMS TO KNOW: advisory board, business incubators

5 **LEARNING OBJECTIVE**

Discuss the principal sources of small-business private financing.

Financing Options for Small Businesses

Figuring out *how much* you'll need in order to start a business requires good insights into the particular industry you plan to enter. Figuring out *where* to get the money is a creative challenge no matter which industry you're in. Financing a business enterprise is a complex undertaking, and chances are you'll need to piece together funds from multiple sources, possibly using a combination of *equity* (in which you give investors a share of the business in exchange for their money) and *debt* (in which you borrow money that must be repaid). Exhibit 6 identifies, in broad terms, the major types of financing available to businesses at various stages in their life cycle.

SEEKING PRIVATE FINANCING

seed money The first infusion of capital used to get a business started

Private financing covers every source of funding except selling stocks and bonds. Nearly all companies start with private financing, even those that eventually "go public." The range of private financing options is diverse, from personal savings to investment funds set up by large corporations looking for entrepreneurial innovations. Many firms get **seed money**, their very first infusion of capital, through family loans. If you go this route, be sure to make the process as formal as a bank loan would be, complete with a specified repayment plan. Otherwise, problems with the loan can cause problems in the family.[30]

An intriguing combination of private and public financing is *crowdfunding*, in which an entrepreneur invites people to fund a share of a new business venture or a new product. For instance, Alex Andon, the founder of Jellyfish Art featured earlier in the chapter, used the funding platform Kickstarter (www.kickstarter.com) to solicit money to begin production of a new desktop aquarium. Depending on the amount given, donors received recognition on the company's website, Jellyfish Art clothing, or the new product itself. Andon set a one-month goal to raise the money—but in one day the site brought in more than double what he asked for.[31] Crowdfunding on Kickstarter and other sites is popular with not-for-profit organizations as well.

EXHIBIT 6	**Financing Possibilities Over the Life of a Small Business**

The potential funding sources available to a business owner vary widely, depending on where the business is in its life cycle. Note that this is a general map only and covers only the most common funding sources. Individual lending opportunities depend on the specific business owner(s), the state of the economy, and the type of business and its potential for growth. For example, venture capital is available only to firms with the potential to grow rapidly and only in a few industries.

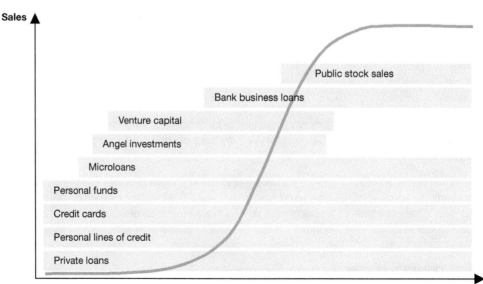

Four common categories of private financing are banks and microlenders, venture capitalists, angel investors, and personal credit cards and lines of credit.

Banks and Microlenders

Bank loans are one of the most important sources of financing for small business—but there's an important catch: In most cases, banks won't lend money to a start-up that hasn't established a successful track record.[32] As your company grows, a bank will usually be a good long-term partner, helping you finance expansions and other major expenses. However, just about your only chance of getting a bank loan is by putting up marketable collateral, such as buildings or equipment, to back the loan.[33]

In response to the needs of entrepreneurs who don't qualify for standard bank loans or who don't need the amount of a regular loan, hundreds of organizations now serve as **microlenders**, offering loans up to $35,000 or so. You can learn more at the Association for Enterprise Opportunity website, at www.microenterpriseworks.org.[34]

> **microlenders** Organizations, often not-for-profit, that lend smaller amounts of money to business owners who might not qualify for conventional bank loans

Venture Capitalists

At the other end of the funding scale are **venture capitalists (VCs)**, investment specialists who raise pools of capital from large private and institutional sources (such as pension funds) to finance ventures that have high growth potential and need large amounts of capital. VC funding provides a crucial stimulus to the economy by making risky, early-stage investments in firms that are likely to become major employers if their products succeed in the marketplace. Because one-third of VC-funded start-ups don't succeed, those that do succeed need to really pay off to compensate. VCs are therefore extremely focused and selective; they invest in only a few thousand companies in the United States every year.[35]

Given the amounts of money involved and the expectations of sizable returns, VCs usually invest in high-potential areas such as information technology, energy, biotechnology, and digital media. Unlike banks or most other financing sources, VCs do more than simply provide money. They also provide management expertise in return for a sizable ownership interest in the business. Once the business becomes profitable, VCs reap the reward by selling their interest to long-term investors, usually after the company goes public.

> **venture capitalists (VCs)** Investors who provide money to finance new businesses or turnarounds in exchange for a portion of ownership, with the objective of reselling the business at a profit

Angel Investors

Start-up companies that can't attract VC investment (perhaps because they are too early in their product development) often look for **angel investors**, private individuals who put their own money into start-ups, with the goal of eventually selling their interest for a profit. These individuals are willing to invest smaller amounts than VCs and often stay involved with the company for a longer period of time. Many of these investors join *angel networks* or *angel groups* that invest together in chosen companies. Angel investing tends to have a more local focus than venture capitalism, so you can search for angels through local business contacts and organizations. You can also find angel groups at the Angel Capital Association website, at www.angelcapitalassociation.org.[36]

> **angel investors** Private individuals who invest money in start-ups, usually earlier in a business's life and in smaller amounts than VCs are willing to invest or banks are willing to lend

Credit Cards and Personal Lines of Credit

Although they tend to be one of the most expensive forms of financing, credit cards are also widely available and sometimes the only source of funding an entrepreneur has. Consequently, roughly half of all entrepreneurs and small business owners use their cards to get cash for start-up or ongoing expenses.[37]

Funding a business with credit cards or a personal line of credit might be the only option many people have, but it is extremely risky. Unfortunately, there is no simple answer about whether to use credit cards; some entrepreneurs have used them to launch successful, multimillion-dollar businesses, while others have destroyed their credit ratings and racked up debts that take years to pay off.

REAL-TIME UPDATES
Learn More by Watching This Video

Learn how to talk to an angel

Successful entrepreneur and angel investor David Rose offers advice on making your pitch to angle capitalists. Go to http://real-timeupdates.com/bia6 and click on Learn More. If you are using MyBizLab, you can access Real-Time Updates within the chapter or under Student Study Tools.

Small Business Administration Assistance

The SBA offers a number of financing options for small businesses. To get an SBA-backed loan, you apply to a regular bank or credit union, which actually provides the money. The SBA guarantees to repay most of the loan amount (the percentage varies by program) if you fail to do so. In addition to operating its primary loan guarantee program, the SBA also manages a microloan program in conjunction with nonprofit, community-based lenders.[38]

Another option for raising money is the Small Business Investment Companies (SBICs) created by the SBA. These investment firms offer loans, venture capital, and management assistance, although they tend to make smaller investments and are willing to consider businesses that VCs or angel investors may not want to finance. The SBIC program has helped fund some of the best-known companies in the United States, including Apple, FedEx, Jenny Craig, and Outback Steakhouse.[39]

GOING PUBLIC

initial public offering (IPO)
A corporation's first offering of shares to the public

Companies with solid growth potential may also seek funding from the public at large, although only a small fraction of the companies in the United States are publicly traded. Whenever a corporation offers its shares of ownership to the public for the first time, the company is said to be *going public*. The shares offered for sale at this point are the company's **initial public offering (IPO)**. Going public is an effective method of raising needed capital, but it can be an expensive and time-consuming process with no guarantee of raising the amount of money needed. Public companies must meet a variety of regulatory requirements.

✓ Checkpoint

LEARNING OBJECTIVE 5: Discuss the principal sources of small-business private financing.

SUMMARY: Sources of *private financing* for small businesses include banks and microlenders, venture capitalists, angel investors, credit cards and personal lines of credit, and loan programs from the Small Business Administration. Companies that reach sufficient size with continued growth potential have the additional option of seeking *public financing* by selling shares.

CRITICAL THINKING: (1) Would a profitable small business with only moderate growth potential be a good candidate for venture capitalist funding? Why or why not? (2) Why would angel investors help finance companies privately, rather than buying shares of publicly traded companies?

IT'S YOUR BUSINESS: Would you be willing to take on credit card debt in order to start a company? Why or why not?

KEY TERMS TO KNOW: seed money, microlenders, venture capitalists (VCs), angel investors, initial public offering (IPO)

---

6 LEARNING OBJECTIVE

Explain the advantages and disadvantages of franchising.

franchise A business arrangement in which one company (the franchisee) obtains the rights to sell the products and use various elements of a business system of another company (the franchisor)

The Franchise Alternative

An alternative to creating or buying an independent company is to buy a **franchise**, which enables the buyer to use a larger company's trade name and sell its goods or services in a specific territory. In exchange for this right, the **franchisee** (the small-business owner who contracts to sell the goods or services) pays the **franchisor** (the supplier) an initial start-up fee, then monthly royalties based on sales volume. Franchises are a large and growing presence in the U.S. economy, with roughly 3,000 franchisor systems and a million individual franchised establishments.[40]

TYPES OF FRANCHISES

Franchises are of three basic types. A *product franchise* gives you the right to sell trademarked goods, which are purchased from the franchisor and resold. Car dealers and gasoline stations fall into this category. A *manufacturing franchise*, such as a soft-drink bottling plant, gives you the right to produce and distribute the manufacturer's products, using supplies purchased from the franchisor. A *business-format franchise* gives you the right to open a business using a franchisor's name and format for doing business. This format includes many well-known chains, including Taco Bell, Pizza Hut, The UPS Store, and Curves fitness centers.

ADVANTAGES OF FRANCHISING

Franchising is a popular option for many people because it combines at least some of the freedom of working for yourself with many of the advantages of being part of a larger, established organization. You can be your own boss, hire your own employees, and benefit directly from your hard work. If you invest in a successful franchise, you know you are getting a viable business model, one that has worked many times before. If the franchise system is well managed, you get the added benefit of instant name recognition, national advertising programs, standardized quality of goods and services, and a proven formula for success. Buying a franchise also gives you access to a support network and in many cases a ready-made blueprint for building a business. Depending on the system, your initial investment provides you with such services as site-location studies, market research, training, and technical assistance, as well as assistance with building or leasing your structure, decorating the building, purchasing supplies, and operating the business during your initial ownership phase.

DISADVANTAGES OF FRANCHISING

Although franchising offers many advantages, it is not the ideal vehicle for everyone. Perhaps the biggest disadvantage is the relative lack of control, at several levels. First, when you buy into a franchise system, you typically agree to follow the business format, and franchisors can prescribe virtually every aspect of the business, from the color of the walls to the products you can carry. In fact, if your primary purpose in owning a business is the freedom to be your own boss, franchising probably isn't the best choice because you don't have a great deal of freedom in many systems. Second, as a franchisee, you usually have little control over decisions the franchisor makes that affect the entire system. Disagreements and even lawsuits have erupted in recent years over actions taken by franchisors regarding product supplies, advertising, and pricing.[41] Third, if the fundamental business model of the franchise system no longer works—or never worked in the first place—or if customer demand for the goods and services you sell declines, you don't have the option of independently changing your business in response.

In addition, buying a franchise involves both initial costs associated with buying into a franchise system and regular payments after that, based on a percentage of sales revenue. These costs vary widely, based on the complexity and popularity of the franchise. The start-up costs for a simple home-based franchise can be less than $10,000, but a popular fast-food franchise can run from $250,000 to $2 million, and luxury hotels can top $5 million. Most franchises, however, have initial costs in the $50,000 to $200,000 range.[42]

HOW TO EVALUATE A FRANCHISING OPPORTUNITY

With so much at stake, researching a franchising opportunity carefully is vital (see Exhibit 7). The Federal Trade Commission (FTC) requires franchisors to disclose extensive information about their operations to prospective franchisees, including background information on the company and its executives, the company's financial status, the history of any litigation involving other franchisees, initial and ongoing costs, all restrictions put on franchisees, the availability and cost of training, procedures for ending the franchise agreement, earnings projections, and the names of current and former franchise owners. Study all this information and talk to as many current and former franchise owners as you can before taking the plunge.[43]

franchisee A business owner who pays for the rights to sell the products and use the business system of a franchisor

franchisor A company that licenses elements of its business system to other companies (franchisees)

REAL-TIME UPDATES
Learn More by Reading This PDF

Don't sign that franchise agreement before you read this

Before you commit to a franchise, consult "Buying a Franchise: A Consumer Guide," a free publication from the FTC. Go to http://real-timeupdates.com/bia6 and click on Learn More. If you are using MyBizLab, you can access Real-Time Updates within the chapter or under Student Study Tools.

EXHIBIT 7	Twelve Questions to Ask Before Signing a Franchise Agreement

A franchise agreement is a legally binding contract that defines the relationship between a franchisee and a franchisor. Before signing a franchise agreement, be sure to read the disclosure document and consult an attorney.

1. What are the total start-up costs? What does the initial franchise fee cover? Does it include a starting inventory of supplies and products?

2. Who pays for employee training?

3. How are the periodic royalties calculated, and when are they paid?

4. Are all trademarks and names legally protected?

5. Who provides and pays for advertising and promotional items?

6. Who selects the location of the business?

7. Is the franchise assigned an exclusive territory?

8. If the territory is not exclusive, does the franchisee have the right of first refusal on additional franchises established in nearby locations?

9. Is the franchisee required to purchase equipment and supplies from the franchisor or other suppliers?

10. Under what conditions can the franchisor and/or the franchisee terminate the franchise agreement?

11. What restrictions are placed on the franchisee (such as selecting goods and services for sale, selling online, or moving into new territories)?

12. Can the franchise be assigned to heirs?

✓ Checkpoint

LEARNING OBJECTIVE 6: Explain the advantages and disadvantages of franchising.

SUMMARY: Franchising appeals to many because it combines some of the advantages of independent business ownership with the resources and support of a larger organization. It can also be less risky than starting or buying an independent business because you have some evidence that the business model works. The primary disadvantages are the lack of control and the costs, both the initial start-up costs and the monthly payments based on a percentage of sales.

CRITICAL THINKING: (1) Why might a business owner with a successful concept decide to sell franchises rather than expand the company under his or her own control? (2) Why might someone with strong entrepreneurial spirit be dissatisfied with franchise ownership?

IT'S YOUR BUSINESS: (1) Are you a good candidate for owning and operating a franchise? Why or not? (2) Think about a small-business idea you've had or one of the small businesses you patronize frequently. Could this business be expanded into a national or international chain? Why or why not?

KEY TERMS TO KNOW: franchise, franchisee, franchisor

BEHIND THE SCENES

BUILDING AN AUTHENTIC AND PURPOSEFUL BUSINESS AT SISTER SKY

MyBizLab

Sisters Monica Simeon and Marina TurningRobe have committed themselves to making products that are both authentic and purposeful and in doing so have created a company that shares those same attributes. Of course, like just about every other small business, Sister Sky has required intense dedication and many, many long days.

After Simeon and TurningRobe decided to turn their first homemade lotions into a real business, they started in a leased manufacturing space in Spokane, Washington. Both of their families would pitch in for 12-hour days, seven days a week—mixing, bottling, and boxing. When sales began to take off, they built their own manufacturing facility on the Spokane Indian Reservation, as part of their commitment to help reservation economies diversify beyond gaming. Putting their houses up for collateral, they installed a $100,000 automated manufacturing system to replace much of the manual labor and expand their production volume. Beyond employing and mentoring fellow tribal members, including offering job-readiness training for tribal youth, the sisters also made a point of buying goods and services from other Native American–owned companies and serving as entrepreneurial role models in Native American communities.

In addition to scaling up manufacturing, Simeon and TurningRobe had to adjust their original marketing strategy. They initially focused on the general gift market but found that they were a tiny player in a vast market. Realizing that the cultural heritage of their product line gave them a unique advantage, they refocused on Native American hotels and resorts, particularly those with luxury spa services. They also now offer spa consulting services, helping property owners create culturally authentic environments and experiences for their guests.

As is often the case, the challenges don't stop as a business grows, and Simeon and TurningRobe faced several classic small-business dilemmas, including time management. Simeon's husband joined the company as production manager, which freed up the sisters' time for selling, but as Simeon said recently, "We're so busy selling, we have no time to step back and strategize." A consultant who worked with them during a "business makeover" sponsored by *Fortune Small Business* magazine stressed that they really have no choice on this: They simply have to make time for strategizing, forcing themselves to step away from marketing and sales activities every quarter to review and adjust their business plan.

One of the key strategic decisions Simeon and TurningRobe must make is where to expand next. They've already moved beyond spa sales to high-end boutiques and gift shops, where their unique product concept appeals to consumers looking for something out of the ordinary. Being active in social media is helping them make connections with customers and potential business partners, too. Also, having received Minority Business Enterprise (MBE) certification from the National Minority Supplier Development Council, the company has made its first inroads into having its products used by Wyndham and other major hotel and resort chains. Sister Sky's MBE status helps these large customers meet supplier diversity goals.

More than 10 years into their entrepreneurial adventure, the sisters and their company are going strong with expanding sales but also with rewards that go beyond their own business objectives. By employing fellow tribe members and offering both inspiration and practical training, TurningRobe and Simeon are fulfilling their larger purpose, too. "Wealth building in our tribal communities through entrepreneurship is critical if we are going to improve our conditions and solve our own problems," Simeon explains. TurningRobe also speaks for many passionate entrepreneurs when she says, "If you love what you do and strive to create meaning to what you sell or create, and do it on a professional level, then I think you have found your purpose."[44]

Critical Thinking Questions

1. Which of the qualities of successful entrepreneurs have Simeon and TurningRobe demonstrated?
2. Should Simeon and TurningRobe consider lowering their ingredient costs by switching to petroleum-based ingredients or stopping their use of pure distilled water? Why or why not?
3. Would opening their own retail stores be a risky decision for Sister Sky? How would this change the company's business model?

LEARN MORE ONLINE

Go to http://real-timeupdates.com/bia6, click on Learn More, and then select. "Sister Sky video." Would this video appeal to potential customers of Sister Sky products? Would it appeal to potential investors? Why or why not?

MyBizLab

Log on to www.mybizlab.com to access study and assessment aids associated with this chapter.

KEY TERMS

advisory board
angel investors
business incubators
business plan
entrepreneurial spirit
franchise
franchisee

franchisor
initial public offering (IPO)
microlenders
seed money
small business
venture capitalists (VCs)

TEST YOUR KNOWLEDGE

Questions for Review

1. What are three essential functions of a business plan?
2. What are the advantages of buying a business rather than starting one from scratch?
3. What are the advantages and disadvantages of owning a franchise?
4. What are the key reasons for most small-business failures?
5. What is a business incubator?

Questions for Analysis

6. Why is the entrepreneurial spirit vital to the health of the nation's economy?
7. Do you expect that the number of entrepreneurs in the United States will grow in the next 10 years? Why or why not?
8. What factors should you consider when evaluating a franchise agreement?
9. What factors should you consider before selecting financing alternatives for a new business?
10. **Ethical Considerations.** You're thinking about starting your own chain of upscale, drive-through espresso stands. You have several ideal sites in mind, and you've analyzed the industry and all the important statistics. You have financial backing, and you really understand the coffee market. In fact, you've become a regular at a competitor's operation for

over a month. The owner thinks you're his best customer. But you're not there because you love the espresso. No, you're actually spying. You're learning everything you can about the competition so you can outsmart them. Is this behavior ethical? Explain your answer.

Questions for Application

11. Briefly describe an incident in your life in which you failed to achieve a goal you set for yourself. What did you learn from this experience? How could you apply this lesson to a future experience as an entrepreneur?
12. Based on your total life experience up to this point—as a student, consumer, employee, parent, and any other role you've played—what sort of business would you be best at running? Why?
13. **Concept Integration.** This question was intentionally excluded from this edition.
14. **Concept Integration.** Pick a local small business or franchise that you visit frequently and discuss whether that business competes on price, speed, innovation, convenience, quality, or any combination of those factors. Be sure to provide some examples.

EXPAND YOUR KNOWLEDGE

Discovering Career Opportunities

Would you like to own and operate your own business? Whether you plan to start a new business from scratch or buy an existing business or a franchise, you need certain qualities to be successful. Start your journey to entrepreneurship by reviewing this chapter's section on entrepreneurs.

1. Which of the entrepreneurial characteristics mentioned in the chapter describe you? Which of those characteristics can you develop more fully in advance of running your own business?
2. Visit www.sba.gov, click on "Starting & Managing a Business" and then "Use Our Starting Up Assessment Tool" (look under "Thinking About Starting"). Answer this brief survey and then think about what it says about your entrepreneurial readiness. Do you agree with what the survey says about you? Whether it says you are or are not ready, or

somewhere in between, does this align with your long-term vision for your career?
3. On the SBA website, read the article "Steps to Finding a Mentor" in the "Finding a Mentor or Counselor" section. With these insights in hand, think about your personal, professional, and academic networks. Assume that you want to start a business right now, before you graduate. Is there anybody you already know who could offer you sound advice? What sort of guidance would this person be able to offer? If you don't know anyone, what steps could you take to meet a mentor or counselor?

Improving Your Tech Insights: Social Networking Technology

If you've used Facebook or Google+, you're already familiar with social networking. Business versions of this technology are changing the way many professionals communicate. Social networking applications, which can be either stand-alone software products or websites, help identify potential business connections by indexing online address books, calendars, and message archives.

One of the biggest challenges small-business owners face is finding the right people and making those connections, whether they're looking for a new employee, an investor, a potential customer, or anyone else who might be important to the future of your business. Using social networking, businesspeople can reach more people than they could ever hope to reach via traditional, in-person networking. Visit several of the websites listed in Exhibit 5 and read about the benefits of joining these networks. In a brief email message to your instructor, describe how you could use these networks to locate potential candidates to serve on the advisory board of your small business. (Make up any details you need about your company.)

PRACTICE YOUR SKILLS

Sharpening Your Communication Skills

Effective communication begins with identifying your primary audience and adapting your message to your audience's needs. This is particularly true for business plans. One of the primary reasons for writing a business plan is to obtain financing. With that in mind, what do you think are the most important things investors will want to know? How can you convince them that the information you are providing is accurate? What should you assume investors know about your specific business or industry?

Building Your Team Skills

The questions shown in Exhibit 7 cover major legal issues you should explore before investing money in a franchise. In addition, however, there are many more questions you should ask in the process of deciding whether to buy a particular franchise.

With your team, think about how to investigate the possibility of buying a Papa John's franchise. Go to www.papajohns .com and find the information the company provides about franchising opportunities. First, brainstorm with your team a plan to learn more about the potential positives and negatives of buying a Papa John's franchise. Be sure to consider both regular and nontraditional franchises, as the company calls them. Next, generate a list of at least 10 questions an interested buyer should ask about this potential business opportunity.

Choose a spokesperson to present your team's ideas to the class. After all the teams have reported, hold a class discussion to analyze the lists of questions generated by all the teams. Which questions were on most teams' lists? Why do you think those questions are so important? Can your class think of any additional questions that were not on any team's list but seem important?

Developing Your Research Skills

Scan issues of print or online editions of business journals or newspapers for articles describing problems or opportunities faced by small businesses in the United States. Clip or copy three or more articles that interest you and then answer the following questions.

1. What problem or opportunity does each article present? Is it an issue faced by many businesses, or is it specific to one industry or region?
2. What could a potential small-business owner learn about the risks and rewards of business ownership from reading these articles?
3. How might these articles affect someone who is thinking about starting a small business?

REFERENCES

1. Adapted from "MBDA Helps Sister Sky Tap into a Legacy of Entrepreneurism," *MBDA.gov Newsletter*, March 2011, U.S. Department of Commerce Minority Business Development Agency, accessed 8 August 2011, www.mbda.gov; Sister Sky website, accessed 8 August 2011, www.sistersky.com; Sister Sky Facebook page, accessed 8 August 2011, www.facebook.com/pages/Sister-Sky/230340194280; Patricia Gray, "Conditioning a Firm for Growth," *Fortune Small Business*, 3 December 2007; "Necessity Inspires This Mother's Invention: New Body Lotion Is Nature-Based Eczema Treatment," press release, 2 July 2007, www.theproductrocket.com; A.J. Naff, "Sister Sky: A Perfect Blend of Entrepreneurship and Native Wisdom," *Indian Gaming*, June 2008, 32–33.
2. "Advocacy Small Business Statistics and Research," U.S. Small Business Administration, accessed 9 August 2011, www.sba .gov.
3. Bernard Stamler, "Redefinition of Small Leads to a Huge Brawl," *New York Times*, 21 September 2004, G8.
4. "Small Business Size Regulations," U.S. Small Business Administration, accessed 10 August 2011, www.sba.gov; "Table of Small Business Size Standards Matched to North American Industry Classification System Codes," U.S. Small Business Administration, accessed 30 March 2009, www.sba.gov.
5. "How Important Are Small Businesses to the U.S. Economy?" U.S. Small Business Administration, accessed 30 March 2009, www.sba.gov; Malik Singleton, "Same Markets, New Marketplaces," *Black Enterprise*, September 2004, 34; Edmund L. Andrews, "Where Do the Jobs Come From?" *New York Times*, 21 September 2004, E1, E11.
6. "How Important Are Small Businesses to the U.S. Economy?"
7. "How Important Are Small Businesses to the U.S. Economy?"
8. "About Etsy," Etsy, accessed 11 August 2011, www.etsy.com.
9. National Association of Women Business Owners, accessed 9 August 2011, www.nawbo.com.
10. "Advocacy Small Business Statistics and Research," U.S. Small Business Administration, accessed 30 March 2009, www.sba.gov.
11. Norman Scarborough and Thomas Zimmerer, *Effective Small Business Management* (Upper Saddle River, N.J.: Pearson Prentice Hall, 2002), 16.
12. College Nannies & Tutors, accessed 9 August 2011, www .collegenannies.com; Stacy Perman, "The Startup Bug Strikes Earlier," *BusinessWeek*, 31 October 2005, www.businessweek.com.

13. Jim Hopkins, "Bad Times Spawn Great Start-Ups," *USA Today*, 18 December 2001, 1B; Alan Cohen, "Your Next Business," *FSB*, February 2002, 33–40.

14. Matt Richtel and Jenna Wortham, "Weary of Looking for Work, Some Create Their Own," *New York Times*, 13 March 2009, www.nytimes.com.

15. Heather Green, "Self-Help for Startups," *BusinessWeek*, 5 February 2009, www.businessweek.com.

16. Richtel and Wortham, "Weary of Looking for Work, Some Create Their Own."

17. Intrapreneur, accessed 31 March 2009, www.intrapreneur.com.

18. Jeffrey Bussgang, "Think Like a VC, Act Like an Entrepreneur," *BusinessWeek*, 14 August 2008, www.businessweek.com.

19. "Buy a Business," U.S. Small Business Administration, accessed 3 July 2007, www.sba.gov.

20. Joshua Hyatt, "The Real Secrets of Entrepreneurs," *Fortune*, 15 November 2004, 185–202.

21. Brown, "How to Write a Winning Business Plan"; Michael Gerber, "The Business Plan That Always Works," *Her Business*, May/June 2004, 23–25; J. Tol Broome, Jr., "How to Write a Business Plan," *Nation's Business*, February 1993, 29–30; Albert Richards, "The Ernst & Young Business Plan Guide," *R & D Management*, April 1995, 253; David Lanchner, "How Chitchat Became a Valuable Business Plan," *Global Finance*, February 1995, 54–56; Marguerita Ashby-Berger, "My Business Plan—And What Really Happened," *Small Business Forum*, Winter 1994–1995, 24–35; Stanley R. Rich and David E. Gumpert, *Business Plans That Win $$$* (New York: Harper & Row, 1985).

22. "Writing a Compelling Executive Summary," Garage Technology Ventures, accessed 9 March 2011, www.garage.com; "Crafting Your Wow! Statement," Garage Technology Ventures, accessed 9 March 2011, www.garage.com; Guy Kawasaki website, accessed 9 March 2011, www.guykawasaki.com.

23. Kerry Miller, "The Restaurant-Failure Myth," *BusinessWeek*, 16 April 2007, 19.

24. Brian Headd, "Redefining Business Success: Distinguishing Between Closure and Failure," *Small Business Economics* 21, 51–61, 2003.

25. Joel Spolsky, "Start-Up Static," *Inc.*, March 2009, 33–34.

26. "MBDA Helps Sister Sky Tap into a Legacy of Entrepreneurism."

27. Bank of America website, accessed 1 April 2009, http://smallbusinessonlinecommunity.bankofamerica.com

28. Christine Comaford-Lynch, "Don't Go It Alone: Create an Advisory Board," *BusinessWeek*, 1 February 2007, www.businessweek.com.

29. "What We Do," Y Combinator, accessed 11 August 2011, http://ycombinator.com

30. Paulette Thomas, "It's All Relative," *Wall Street Journal*, 29 November 2004, R4, R8.

31. Alex Andon, "Update #1: We Met Our Goal!" Kickstarter, 11 August 2011, www.kickstarter.com.

32. Reed Albergotti, "Long Shot," *Wall Street Journal*, 29 November 2004, R4; Scarborough and Zimmerer, *Effective Small Business Management*, 439.

33. Bob Zider, "How Venture Capital Works," *Harvard Business Review*, November/December 1998, 131–139.

34. Association for Enterprise Opportunity website, accessed 11 August 2011, www.microenterpriseworks.org.

35. National Venture Capital Association website, accessed 11 August 2011, www.nvca.org.

36. Angel Capital Association, accessed 11 August 2011, www.angelcapitalassociation.org; William Payne, "What to Expect from Angel Networks," *American Venture*, September/October 2004, 38–39; Kaufman Foundation, "Business Angel Investing Groups Growing in North America," October 2002, www.angelcapitalassociation.org.

37. David Port, "APR Hikes Ambush Biz Owners," *Entrepreneur*, 16 March 2009, www.entrepreneur.com; Bobbie Gossage, "Charging Ahead," *Inc.*, January 2004, www.inc.com.

38. U.S. Small Business Administration website, accessed 11 August 2011, www.sba.gov.

39. U.S. Small Business Administration website, accessed 11 August 2011, www.sba.gov.

40. Eddy Goldberg, "The Basics of Franchising," Franchising.com, accessed 11 August 2011, www.franchising.com; Sarah Max, "The Franchising Way to Grow," *BusinessWeek*, 5 December 2008, www.businessweek.com.

41. Douglas MacMillan, "Franchise Owners Go to Court," *BusinessWeek*, 29 January 2007, www.businessweek.com; Jill Lerner, "UPS Store Dispute Escalating," *Atlanta Business Chronicle*, 24 February 2006, www.bizjournals.com.

42. Eddy Goldberg, "The Costs Involved in Opening a Franchise," Franchising.com, accessed 12 August 2011, www.franchising.com; "U.S. Franchising," McDonald's website, accessed 12 August 2011, www.aboutmcdonalds.com.

43. *Buying a Franchise: A Consumer Guide*, U.S. Federal Trade Commission, accessed 12 August 2011, www.ftc.gov

44. See note 1.
ererewrew

GLOSSARY

advisory board A team of people with subject-area expertise or vital contacts who help a business owner review plans and decisions

angel investors Private individuals who invest money in start-ups, usually earlier in a business's life and in smaller amounts than VCs are willing to invest or banks are willing to lend

business incubators Facilities that house small businesses and provide support services during the company's early growth phases

business plan A document that summarizes a proposed business venture, goals, and plans for achieving those goals

entrepreneurial spirit The positive, forward-thinking desire to create profitable, sustainable business enterprises

franchisee A business owner who pays for the rights to sell the products and use the business system of a franchisor

franchise A business arrangement in which one company (the franchisee) obtains the rights to sell the products and use various elements of a business system of another company (the franchisor)

franchisor A company that licenses elements of its business system to other companies (franchisees)

initial public offering (IPO) A corporation's first offering of shares to the public

microlenders Organizations, often not-for-profit, that lend smaller amounts of money to business owners who might not qualify for conventional bank loans

seed money The first infusion of capital used to get a business started

small business A company that is independently owned and operated, is not dominant in its field, and employs fewer than 500 people (although this number varies by industry)

venture capitalists (VCs) Investors who provide money to finance new businesses or turnarounds in exchange for a portion of ownership, with the objective of reselling the business at a profit

Management Roles, Functions, and Skills

Management Roles, Functions, and Skills

LEARNING OBJECTIVES After studying this chapter, you will be able to

1 Explain the importance of management and identify the three vital management roles

2 Describe the planning function and outline the strategic planning process

3 Describe the organizing function and differentiate among top, middle, and first-line management

4 Describe the leading function, leadership style, and organizational culture

5 Describe the controlling function and explain the four steps in the control cycle

6 Identify and explain four important types of managerial skills

MyBizLab

Where you see MyBizLab in this chapter, go to www.mybizlab.com for additional activities on the topic being discussed.

BEHIND THE SCENES WEGMANS SATISFIES CUSTOMERS BY PUTTING EMPLOYEES FIRST

Wegmans Food Markets, Inc.

Wegmans CEO Danny Wegman carries on the family tradition of satisfying customers by paying attention to employees and their needs.

www.wegmans.com

Thousands of companies use slogans such as "The customer is king," proclaiming in various ways that customers are their number-one priority. Not Wegmans, a regional grocery store chain based in Rochester, New York. Wegmans makes a clear statement of its priorities: employees first, customers second.

What do customers think about this, you ask? They love it. Customers routinely drive miles out of their way, past other grocery stores, to shop at Wegmans. The company receives thousands of letters of praise every year from current customers—and several thousand more letters from consumers in cities where it doesn't have stores, begging the chain to open a Wegmans nearby.

Such enthusiasm has helped the company post a solid record of success since its founding in 1915. As a private company, Wegmans isn't required to report its financial results to the public, but the numbers that are available are impressive. Its operating margin (a measure of profitability) is twice as high as that of national chains such as Safeway and Kroger. Sales per square foot, a key measure of selling efficiency, are estimated to be 50 percent higher than the industry average. The *Wall Street Journal* once called Wegmans the "best chain in the country, maybe in the world."

Such results would be impressive in any industry, but they're almost unfathomable in the grocery retailing business, one of the toughest industries on earth. Most grocery retailers struggle with constant price wars that guarantee paper-thin profit margins (making one or two cents on every dollar of revenue is typical), frequent labor troubles, high employee turnover, and a customer base that views most grocery stores as virtually indistinguishable from one another. As if those problems weren't enough, grocers face the steamrolling cost efficiencies of Walmart and other discount mass merchandisers, which have already captured one-third of the grocery business in the United States.

If you were Danny Wegman, the company's third-generation CEO, how would you sustain the Wegmans way of doing business in the face of relentless competitive pressures? How would you hold your own against the giant discounters that have rampaged through the grocery industry? How would you make sure that Wegmans attracts the best employees in the business and keeps them satisfied and productive?[1]

INTRODUCTION

Whether they are front-line supervisors or top executives such as Danny Wegman (profiled in the chapter-opening Behind the Scenes), managers have tremendous influence over the success or failure of the companies they lead. Leading seems to come naturally to Wegman, but he would probably be the first to tell you that **management**, the interrelated tasks of planning, organizing, leading, and controlling in pursuit of organizational goals,[2] is no easy job. In fact, according to one survey, more than one-third of the people who take on new managerial positions fail within the first 18 months.[3] Even those who eventually succeed can struggle with the transition from individual contributor to manager. If you aspire to become a manager, you can improve your chances of success by gaining a thorough understanding of what being a manager really entails. This chapter explores the *roles* that managers play, the *functions* they perform, and the essential *skills* they need.

management The process of planning, organizing, leading, and controlling to meet organizational goals

The Roles of Management

Danny Wegman doesn't buy merchandise from wholesalers, stock shelves, or operate cash registers, but the decisions he makes, the organizational framework he establishes, the expectations he sets, the managers he hires to oversee employees, and the culture he establishes all have enormous impact on the company's success. Likewise, the managers who report to Wegman, including his daughter, company president Colleen Wegman, aren't directly engaged in the tasks of buying and selling groceries. However, within the scope of his or her own responsibilities, each of these managers also has significant influence on the company's fortunes. Although managers don't usually do the hands-on work in an organization, they create the environment and provide the resources that give employees opportunities to excel in their work.

In addition, given the effect that managerial decisions and behaviors have on employees, customers, investors, and other stakeholders, it's no exaggeration to say that management is one of the most vital professions in the contemporary economy. Managers who effectively and ethically guide their companies contribute greatly to our standard of living and our economic security. By the same measure, managers who fail, through poor planning, misguided decisions, or questionable ethics, can create havoc that extends far beyond the walls of their own companies. In other words, management is one of the most important functions in society, not just within the sphere of business.

All the **managerial roles** that leaders must play can be grouped into three main categories: interpersonal, informational, and decisional.

1 LEARNING OBJECTIVE

Explain the importance of management, and identify the three vital management roles.

managerial roles Behavioral patterns and activities involved in carrying out the functions of management; includes interpersonal, informational, and decisional roles

INTERPERSONAL ROLES

Management is largely a question of getting work accomplished through the efforts of other people, so a manager must play a number of interpersonal roles, including providing leadership to employees, building relationships, and acting as a liaison between groups and individuals both inside and outside the company (such as suppliers, government agencies, consumers, labor unions, and community leaders). Effective managers tend to excel at networking, fostering relationships with many people within their own companies and within the industries and communities where their companies do business. In fact, the number of connections a person has becomes an increasingly important asset the higher he or she rises in an organization.

INFORMATIONAL ROLES

Managers spend a fair amount of time gathering information from sources both inside and outside an organization. The higher up they are, the more they rely on subordinates to collect, analyze, and summarize information—and the greater the risk that they will fall out of touch with what is happening on "the front lines," where the essential day-to-day work of the organization is performed. Today's companies have devised powerful and clever ways to collect and process information for managers. A good example is the *executive dashboard*, which, just like the dashboard in a car, provides quick-read summaries of vital performance variables (see Exhibit 1).

The dashboard analogy is also a good way to think about the information challenges that managers face. As you're driving, making split-second decisions while keeping your eyes on the road, you don't need to know how full the water reservoir is or how fast the water pump is turning. Such details would overwhelm your decision making and serve no immediate purpose. However, if your engine is in danger of overheating because the water pump is failing, you need enough advance warning to take corrective action before it's too late, so your dashboard provides a quick summary through a temperature gauge or warning light. Similarly, managers must figure out what they need to know and when they need to know it. Generally speaking, as you progress higher up in an organization, you need to monitor more information sources but see fewer details from each one.

Managers also communicate information to employees, other managers, and other stakeholders. This communication involves virtually every form of information, from technical and administrative information to motivational pep talks to strategic planning sessions. And it involves every form of media, from private conversations to videoconferences that connect managers with employees across the country or around the world.

The increasing use of social media for both internal and external communication is changing the nature of the manager's informational role in many companies. In the past, communication was often concentrated in formal channels that tended to flow in only one direction at a time, such as from a manager down to his or her subordinates or from "the company" to customers. With social media, a more conversational model is emerging, in which more

EXHIBIT 1	Executive Dashboards

To help managers avoid information overload, many companies now use executive dashboards to present carefully filtered highlights of key performance parameters. The latest generation of software makes it easy to customize screens to show each manager the specific summaries he or she needs to see.

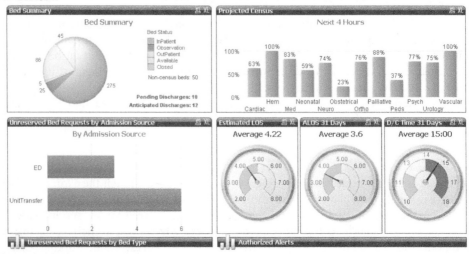

Source: Used with permission of StatCom.

people can participate and communication is more immediate and less formal. For example, on the Southwest Airlines Nuts About Southwest blog (www.blogsouthwest.com), a team of employee and manager bloggers from around the company conduct what amounts to multiple ongoing conversations with thousands of Southwest customers. The smart use of social media is helping managers learn more from employees and customers and communicate back to these and other stakeholder groups more effectively.

DECISIONAL ROLES

Managers up and down the organizational ladder face an endless stream of decisions. Many of these decisions are fairly routine, such as choosing which of several job candidates to hire or setting the prices of new products. Other decisions, however, might occur only once or twice in a manager's career, such as responding to a product-tampering crisis or the threat of a hostile takeover. Some decisions are made after extensive information gathering and analysis; others have to be made on the spot, with little but judgment and intuition to guide the manager's choice. One of the most significant changes occurring in business management in recent years is the effort to push decision making as far down the organizational pyramid as possible, giving whichever employees face a particular situation the authority to make decisions about it. This approach not only accelerates and improves work flow and customer service but also frees up higher-level managers to work on more strategic matters.

Being able to move among these roles comfortably while performing the basic management functions is just one of the many skills that managers must have. The following sections provide a closer look at those four functions—planning, organizing, leading, and controlling.

✔ Checkpoint

LEARNING OBJECTIVE 1: Explain the importance of management, and identify the three vital management roles.

SUMMARY: While managers usually don't do the hands-on work in an organization, they create the environment and provide the resources that give employees the opportunities to excel in their work. Managerial responsibilities include creating the organizational framework, fostering a positive culture, setting expectations, and providing resources. The three vital managerial roles are interpersonal (interacting with others), informational (receiving and sharing information), and decisional (making decisions).

CRITICAL THINKING: (1) How are social media changing the nature of a manager's information role? (2) Would managers get more respect from employees if they "rolled up their sleeves" and pitched in with the daily work more often? Why or why not?

IT'S YOUR BUSINESS: (1) Review the process you went through to choose the college you are currently attending. What lessons from your experience could someone apply to managerial decision making? (2) Do you believe you have the right personality for management? If not, what areas would you work on?

KEY TERMS TO KNOW: management, managerial roles

The Planning Function

Managers engage in **planning** when they develop strategies, establish goals and objectives for the organization, and translate those strategies and goals into action plans. **Strategic plans** outline the firm's long-range (often two to five years) organizational goals and set a course of action the firm will pursue to reach its goals. The *strategic planning process* consists of six interrelated steps: defining the organization's mission, vision, and values; performing a SWOT analysis; developing forecasts; analyzing the competition; establishing goals and objectives; and developing action plans (see Exhibit 2 on the next page).

---

2 | LEARNING OBJECTIVE

Describe the planning function, and outline the strategic planning process.

planning Establishing objectives and goals for an organization and determining the best ways to accomplish them

strategic plans Plans that establish the actions and the resource allocation required to accomplish strategic goals; they're usually defined for periods of two to five years and developed by top managers

| EXHIBIT 2 | The Strategic Planning Process |

Specific firms have their own variations of the strategic planning process, but these six steps offer a good general model. The circular arrangement is no coincidence, by the way. Strategic planning should be a never-ending process, as you establish strategies, measure outcomes, monitor changes in the business environment, and make adjustments as needed.

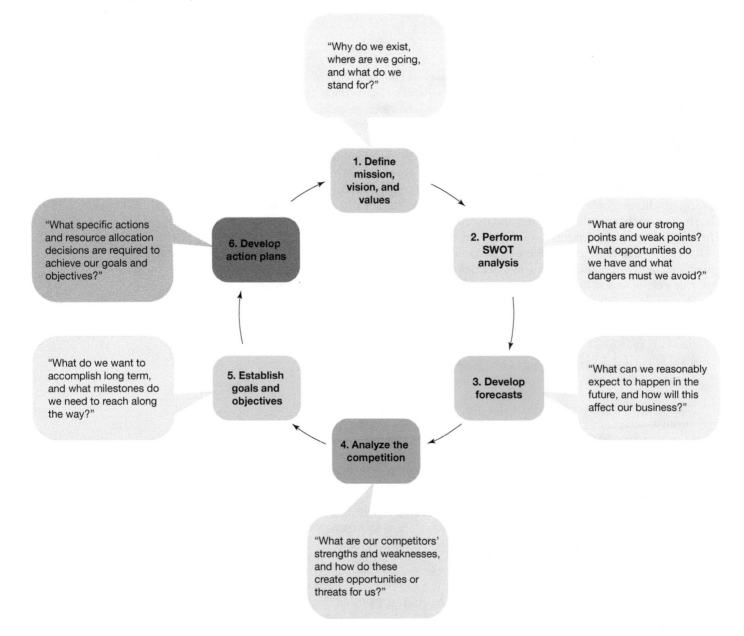

DEFINING THE MISSION, VISION, AND VALUES

To achieve any level of strategic clarity, planners first need to agree on the basic principles that define the organization, and such agreement can be articulated in three interrelated statements. First, a **mission statement** is a brief expression of *why* the company exists.[4] For example, the medical device manufacturer Welch Allyn defines its mission as "helping doctors, nurses, and other healthcare providers across the globe provide the best patient care by developing innovative products, breakthrough technologies, and cutting-edge solutions that help them see more patients, detect more conditions, and improve more lives."[5] This statement clearly defines the scope of the company's activities and its priorities in serving its target customers. Just as important, it eliminates activities the company could pursue, such as consumer products, but chooses not to.

mission statement A brief statement of why an organization exists; in other words, what the organization aims to accomplish for customers, investors, and other stakeholders

Second, a **vision statement** is a brief expression of *what* the company aspires to be. The defense contractor Northrop Grumman puts it this way: "Our vision is to be the most trusted provider of systems and technologies that ensure the security and freedom of our nation and its allies."[6] Notice how this statement differs in both content and tone from the mission statement above. It provides some focus (for example, saying the company wants to be the *most trusted* provider, not necessarily the largest or the most technologically advanced) without getting into the specifics of a mission statement. It also inspires employees with a clear sense of purpose. (Note that these definitions of *mission* and *vision* are not universally agreed upon, and some companies use these terms interchangeably.)

Third, a **values statement** identifies the principles that guide the company's decisions and behaviors and establish expectations for everyone in the organization. For instance, in addition to such attributes as honesty, service, fun, and inclusiveness, Enterprise Rent-a-Car identifies hard work as one of its values: "Learning how to run a successful business from the ground up and delivering our high standard of service is hard work. It's work that demands a deep personal commitment from each employee." In return, the company offers unusual opportunities to learn entrepreneurship and business management early in one's career.[7]

Mission, vision, and values statements are sometimes dismissed as vague "happy talk" that companies spend a lot of time creating but never look at again, and this criticism is sometimes deserved. However, if the statements are (1) crafted with the purpose of truly defining what the company stands for and (2) used in both strategic planning and the ongoing evaluation of the company's performance, they become essential parts of the company's "DNA."

ASSESSING STRENGTHS, WEAKNESSES, OPPORTUNITIES, AND THREATS

Before establishing long-term goals, a company needs to have a clear assessment of its strengths and weaknesses relative to the opportunities and threats it faces. This analysis is commonly referred to as *SWOT* (pronounced "swat"), which stands for strengths, weaknesses, opportunities, and threats (see Exhibit 3).

vision statement A brief and inspirational expression of what a company aspires to be

values statement A brief articulation of the principles that guide a company's decisions and behaviors

EXHIBIT 3	SWOT Analysis

Identifying a firm's strengths, weaknesses, opportunities, and threats is a common strategic planning technique. Here are some examples of the factors a company might identify during a SWOT analysis.

Internal

Strengths
Respected brand
Financial resources
Strong management
Design patents

Weaknesses
Aging facilities
Talent shortage
Narrow customer
base

Positive, helpful ← → **Negative, harmful**

Opportunities
New products
Attractive merger
candidates
New markets in Asia

Threats
Liability lawsuits
Pending regulations
Shrinking demand
for existing products

External
(in some cases, threats
can also come from
internal sources)

Strengths are positive internal factors that contribute to a company's success, which can be anything from a team of expert employees to financial resources to unique technologies. For instance, Southern Cross Healthcare (www.schealthcare.co.uk) is the largest operator of elder-care homes in the United Kingdom. Two of its key strengths are its leading market position and its broad portfolio of services.[8] *Weaknesses* are negative internal factors that inhibit the company's success, such as obsolete facilities, inadequate financial resources to fund growth, or lack of managerial depth and talent. According to analysis by the research firm Datamonitor, one of Southern Cross's weaknesses was a failure to successfully integrate care homes that it acquired, which affected operating costs and service quality.[9] Identifying a firm's internal strengths and weaknesses helps management understand its current abilities so it can set proper goals.

After taking inventory of the company's internal strengths and weaknesses, the next step is to identify the external opportunities and threats that might significantly affect the firm's ability to attain desired goals. *Opportunities* are positive situations that represent the possibility of generating new revenue. As a provider of services to elderly consumers, for example, Southern Cross has significant opportunities to expand its sales based on the demographics of an aging population.[10] Shrewd managers and entrepreneurs recognize opportunities before others do and then promptly act on their ideas.

Threats are negative forces that could inhibit a firm's ability to achieve its objectives, including such external factors as new competitors, new government regulations, economic contraction, changes in interest rates, disruptions in supply, technological advances that render products obsolete, theft of intellectual property, product liability lawsuits, and even the weather. Depending on the company and the industry, it can also be helpful to consider internal threats if they have the potential to disrupt business. Datamonitor identifies increasing labor costs and intense competition as the two primary threats that Southern Cross faces.[11] The combination of rising costs (an internal threat) and increasing competition (an external threat) could put a serious squeeze on the company's profit margins.

DEVELOPING FORECASTS

By its very nature, planning requires managers to make predictions about the future. Forecasting is a notoriously difficult and error-prone part of strategic planning. Managers need to predict not only *what* will (or will not) occur, but *when* it will occur and *how* it will affect their business. Forecasting is crucial to every company's success because it influences the decisions managers make regarding virtually every business activity, and misreading the future can damage or even destroy a company.

Managerial forecasts fall under two broad categories: *quantitative forecasts*, which are typically based on historical data or tests and often involve complex statistical computations, and *qualitative forecasts*, which are based more on intuitive judgments. Neither method is foolproof, but both are valuable tools and are often used together to help managers fill in the unknown variables that inevitably crop up in the planning process. For example, managers can make statistical projections of next year's sales based on data from previous years while factoring in their judgment about the impact of new competitors, changing regulations, or other external forces.

As important as forecasting is, it represents a vexing paradox because, to a significant degree, the future is simply not predictable. Technology, fashion, and other influential forces often move forward in lurches and leaps that are difficult to predict. Extraordinary events—such as wars, economic meltdowns, or natural disasters can play havoc with the best forecasts. Moreover, a single surprising development can trigger a chain reaction of other developments that might have been impossible to envision before. One key element in the art of management, therefore, is crafting plans that are solid enough to move the company forward in a strategically coherent direction while staying alert to changing conditions and being flexible enough to adapt quickly when things do change.

ANALYZING THE COMPETITION

The competitive context in which a company operates needs to be thoroughly understood and factored into the strategic planning process. Performing a SWOT analysis on each of your major competitors is a good first step. Identifying *their* strengths and weaknesses helps pinpoint *your* opportunities and threats. For instance, if you discover that one of your competitors has been suffering customer satisfaction problems, that could be a sign of financial difficulties, product flaws, or other weaknesses that could be opportunities for you to capture additional market share. Similarly, identifying your competitors' opportunities and threats can give you insight into what they might do next, and you can then plan accordingly.

Competitive analysis should always keep the customer's perspective in mind. You may believe you have the best product, the best reputation, and the best customer service, but the only beliefs that matter are the target customer's. Conversely, you might believe that a competitor's less-expensive products are inferior, but those products might well be good enough to meet customers' needs—meaning that the higher cost of your higher-quality products puts you at a disadvantage.

ESTABLISHING GOALS AND OBJECTIVES

Although the terms are often used interchangeably, it helps to think of a **goal** as a broad, long-range accomplishment that the organization wants to attain and to think of an **objective** as a specific, short-range target designed to help reach that goal. For Wegmans, a *goal* might be to capture 15 percent of the grocery market in the mid-Atlantic region over the next five years, and an *objective* in support of that goal might be to open four new stores in Virginia in the next two years.

goal A broad, long-range target or aim

objective A specific, short-range target or aim

Business people are often advised to make their goals and objectives "SMART," as in *specific, measurable, attainable, relevant,* and *time limited.* For example, "substantially increase our sales" is a poorly worded statement because it doesn't define what *substantial* means or when it should be measured. This acronym can be a helpful reminder to set meaningful goals, but as with the paradox of forecasting, it's important to use good judgment and be flexible, too.[12] For example, you may not know whether a goal is really attainable until you try to reach it, or you might reach it easily and realize you set your sights too low.

DEVELOPING ACTION PLANS

With strategic goals and objectives in place, the next step is to develop a plan to reach them. Plans are often organized in a hierarchy, just as a company itself is. For instance, the overall strategic plan might be supported at the next level down by a research and development plan, a manufacturing plan, and a marketing plan, describing how each functional area will help the company reach its strategic goals and objectives.

The names and contents of these *tactical plans* or *operational plans* vary widely by industry, company, and business function. Some address all the actions required in a particular department or functional area over a recurring time frame, such as a quarter or a year, while others address all the tasks involved in a single project or event. For example, a *launch plan* for a new product might cover a period from several months or a year before the product is introduced to the public on through the launch date and several months afterward. Such a plan would identify all the actions needed to coordinate the launch of the product, including the production ramp-up, promotional activities, sales training, physical distribution, and every other task and resource allocation decision needed to get the new product off to a successful start.

By the way, crafting a solid plan and carrying it through to completion are great ways to make a name for yourself early in your career, even for relatively simple projects. Demonstrate that you can figure out what needs to be done, coordinate all the resources, and then bring it in on schedule and on budget. Upper managers will notice and keep you in mind when they need people to take on more challenging and important projects.

✔ Checkpoint

LEARNING OBJECTIVE 2: Describe the planning function, and outline the strategic planning process.

SUMMARY: Planning is the process of developing strategies, establishing goals and objectives for the organization, and translating those strategies and goals into action plans. Plans vary in their time frame and scope, from high-level, long-range strategic plans to lower-level, short-term tactical and operational plans. The strategic planning process consists of six interrelated steps: defining the organization's mission, vision, and values; performing a SWOT analysis; developing forecasts; analyzing the competition; establishing goals and objectives; and developing action plans.

CRITICAL THINKING: (1) Would Boeing and Old Navy develop strategic plans over the same time horizon? Why or why not? (2) How does the vision statement guide the planning process?

IT'S YOUR BUSINESS: (1) What is your personal vision statement for your career and your life? Have you ever thought about your future in this way? (2) Consider a career path that you might pursue upon graduation, and perform a quick SWOT analysis. What are some of your internal strengths and weaknesses and external opportunities and threats?

KEY TERMS TO KNOW: planning, strategic plans, mission statement, vision statement, values statement, goal, objective

---

3 | LEARNING OBJECTIVE

Describe the organizing function, and differentiate among top, middle, and first-line management.

organizing The process of arranging resources to carry out the organization's plans

management pyramid An organizational structure divided into top, middle, and first-line management

The Organizing Function

Organizing, the process of arranging resources to carry out an organization's plans, is the second major function of managers. To organize effectively, managers must think through all the activities that employees perform, as well as all the facilities and equipment employees need in order to complete those activities. Managers also give people the ability to work toward company goals by determining who will have the authority to make decisions, to perform or supervise activities, and to distribute resources. The three levels of management in a typical corporate hierarchy—top, middle, bottom—is commonly known as the **management pyramid** (see Exhibit 4).

EXHIBIT 4 | The Management Pyramid

Here are some of the typical jobs in the three basic levels of management.

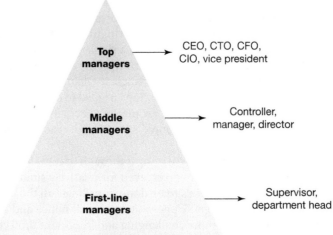

TOP MANAGERS

Top managers are the upper-level managers, such as Danny Wegman, who have the most power and who take overall responsibility for an organization. This tier includes corporate officers and usually the next layer or two of management beneath them, depending on the size and structure of the company. The term *executive* applies to top managers. Typical job titles include the "C" level positions, such as chief marketing officer (CMO) and chief financial officer (CFO) and vice presidents (the largest corporations may have dozens of vice presidents overseeing various divisions or functions).

Top managers establish the structure for the organization as a whole, and they select the people who fill the upper-level positions. Top managers also make long-range plans, establish major policies, and often represent the company to the media, the community, and other stakeholders. Two significant ways in which top management differs from lower management tiers are the long time frames with which executives must work and the magnitude of the decisions they need to make. Given the difficulty and importance of these strategic decisions, the ability to make tough judgment calls is highly valued in top executives.

top managers Those at the highest level of the organization's management hierarchy; they are responsible for setting strategic goals, and they have the most power and responsibility in the organization

MIDDLE MANAGERS

Middle managers have similar responsibilities but on a smaller scale, such as for an individual division or facility. The term *middle management* is somewhat vague, but in general, managers at this level report upward to top executives, while first-line managers report to them. In other words, they usually manage other managers, not workers. A smaller company might have a single layer of middle management (or none at all, in many cases), whereas a large corporation could have a half dozen or more layers of middle managers.

The term "middle management" is sometimes used disparagingly, giving the impression that middle managers are "bureaucrats" who clog up the works without adding much value. Some highly regarded opinion leaders have gone so far as to blame such managers for much that ails the modern corporation.[13] Many companies have also *flattened* their organizational structures by removing one or more layers of middle management.

However, middle managers play the essential role of translating strategic goals and objectives into the actions that allow the company to meet those targets. While they may not do the actual day-to-day work, middle managers are the ones who put the systems and resources in place so that front-line teams can work efficiently and with coordinated purpose. They also provide vital coaching and mentoring for first-line managers who are making the transition into management. As leadership consultant Steve Arneson emphasizes, "It's the leaders in the middle who must communicate and execute strategy, solve problems, create efficiencies, and manage performance."[14] In his analysis of the computer game industry, Wharton management professor Ethan Mollick concluded that middle managers who oversaw new game development had a greater impact on company performance than the top managers who set strategy or the developers who designed and created the games.[15]

middle managers Those in the middle of the management hierarchy; they develop plans to implement the goals of top managers and coordinate the work of first-line managers

FIRST-LINE MANAGERS

At the bottom of the management pyramid are **first-line managers** (or *supervisory managers*). They oversee the work of nonmanagerial employees, and they put into action the plans developed at higher levels. Titles at this level include supervisor, department head, and office manager.[16] The types of employees these managers supervise vary widely, from entry-level workers with limited experience and education to advanced experts in engineering, science, finance, and other professional specialties.

Like managers at the levels above them, first-line managers face challenges unique to their position in the hierarchy. As the direct interface between "management" and the employees, they have the most immediate responsibility for ensuring that necessary work is done according to agreed-upon performance standards. They must also deal with any friction that exists between employees and management. Supervisors are also usually quite involved in recruiting, hiring, and training of employees. In this role, they perform the vital task of making sure employees acquire the skills they need and adapt to the organization's culture.

first-line managers Those at the lowest level of the management hierarchy; they supervise the operating employees and implement the plans set at the higher management levels

✓ Checkpoint

LEARNING OBJECTIVE 3: Describe the organizing function, and differentiate among top, middle, and first-line management.

SUMMARY: The organizing function involves arranging an organization's resources in the best way possible to help reach its goals and objectives. Top managers grapple with long-range, strategic issues and often must make decisions about events and conditions several years into the future. They also have important communication roles, representing the company to external stakeholders. Middle managers usually have responsibility over individual divisions or facilities and are charged with translating strategic plans into the tactical plans that will allow the company to reach its goals and objectives. First-line managers supervise nonmanagement employees; they have the shortest time horizons and greatest tactical perspective.

CRITICAL THINKING: (1) Why might a manager need to deemphasize skills honed in previous positions as he or she rises through the organizational hierarchy? (2) Would top managers or first-line managers typically have more or less of the information they'd like to have for the decisions they need to make? Why?

IT'S YOUR BUSINESS: (1) Have you ever supervised others on the job or in volunteer work? If so, how would you rate your performance as a manager? (2) If you were suddenly promoted to manage the department you've been working in, would you change your "work" personality? Why or why not?

KEY TERMS TO KNOW: organizing, management pyramid, top managers, middle managers, first-line managers

---

4 LEARNING OBJECTIVE

Describe the leading function, leadership style, and organizational culture.

leading The process of guiding and motivating people to work toward organizational goals

The Leading Function

Leading is the process of influencing and motivating people to work willingly and effectively toward common goals. Managers with good leadership skills have greater success in influencing the attitudes and actions of others and motivating employees to put forth their best performance.

All managers have to be effective leaders to be successful, but management and leadership are not the same thing. One way to distinguish between the two is to view management as the rational, intellectual, and practical side of guiding an organization and to view leadership as the inspirational, visionary, and emotional side. Both management and leadership involve the use of power, but management involves *position power* (so called since it stems from the individual's position in the organization), whereas leadership involves *personal power* (which stems from a person's own unique attributes, such as expertise or charisma).[17]

Successful leaders tend to share many of the same traits, but no magical set of personal qualities automatically destines someone for leadership. Nevertheless, in general, good leaders possess a balance of several types of intelligence:

REAL-TIME UPDATES
Learn More by Reading This Article

Do you have what it takes to be a successful leader?

Rate yourself on 10 essential attributes of leadership. Go to http://real-timeupdates.com/bia6 and click on Learn More. If you are using MyBizLab, you can access Real-Time Updates within the chapter or under Student Study Tools.

- *Cognitive intelligence* involves reasoning, problem solving, memorization, and other rational skills. Obviously, leaders need a sufficient degree of cognitive intelligence to understand and process the information required for planning and decision making in their jobs.
- *Emotional intelligence* is a measure of a person's awareness of and ability to manage his or her own emotions. People with high emotional intelligence recognize their own emotional states and the effect those emotions have on others, they are able to regulate their emotional responses

in order to control or reduce disruptive impulses and moods, and they have a high degree of *empathy* (the ability to understand others' feelings).[18]

- *Social intelligence* involves looking outward to understand the dynamics of social situations and the emotions of other people, in addition to your own.[19] Socially adept managers have a knack for finding and building common ground with people of all kinds. Moreover, leaders, in a sense, "infect" their organizations with their own emotions, positive or negative.[20]

All three types of intelligence are essential to building the competencies that lead to success. In fact, various studies suggest that in both leadership and life in general, emotional and social intelligence play a far greater role in success than purely cognitive intelligence.[21]

REAL-TIME UPDATES
Learn More by Listening to This Podcast

Find out why great leaders are made, not born

Explore the factors that produce great leaders and get advice on how to become one yourself. Go to http://real-timeupdates .com/bia6 and click on Learn More. If you are using MyBizLab, you can access Real-Time Updates within the chapter or under Student Study Tools.

DEVELOPING AN EFFECTIVE LEADERSHIP STYLE

Leadership style can be viewed as finding the right balance between *what* the leader focuses on and *how* he or she makes things happen in the organization. Every manager has a definite style, although good leaders usually adapt their approach to match the requirements of the particular situation.[22] Across the range of leadership styles, you can find three basic types (see Exhibit 5). **Autocratic leaders** control the decision-making process in their organizations, often restricting the decision-making freedom of subordinates. Autocratic leadership generally has a bad reputation, and when it's overused or used inappropriately, it can certainly produce bad results or stunt an organization's growth. However, companies

autocratic leaders Leaders who do not involve others in decision making

EXHIBIT 5	Leadership Styles

Leadership styles fall on a continuum from *autocratic* (manager makes the decisions) to *democratic* (manager and subordinates make decisions together) to *laissez-faire* (subordinates make decisions on their own). Each style has strengths and weaknesses, and effective managers often adapt their style to suit specific situations.

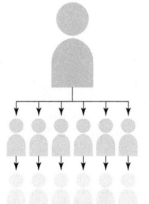

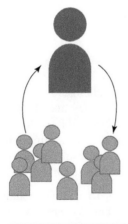

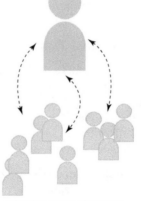

Autocratic leadership:

Manager makes the decisions and issues directives down the chain of command; subordinates have little or no freedom to make decisions, deviate from plans, or provide contrary input.

Democratic leadership:

Manager shares decision-making authority, seeking input and inviting subordinates to participate in a coordinated planning process; group can encourage a change of course if needed.

Laissez-faire leadership:

Manager acts as advisor and supporter, offering input when asked but generally letting subordinates chart and adjust their own course toward meeting agreed-upon goals and objectives.

can find themselves in situations where autocratic leadership is needed to guide the firm through challenging situations or to bring uncooperative units in line.

democratic leaders Leaders who delegate authority and involve employees in decision making

participative management A philosophy of allowing employees to take part in planning and decision making

laissez-faire leaders Leaders who leave most decisions up to employees, particularly those concerning day-to-day matters

employee empowerment Granting decision-making and problem-solving authorities to employees so they can act without getting approval from management

Democratic leaders, in contrast, delegate authority and involve employees in decision making. Also known as *collaborative* leaders, these managers invite and seek out input from anyone in the organization who can add insight to the decision-making process. For example, after Salesforce.com installed an internal social networking application that gave everyone in the company the chance to share information, CEO Mark Benioff began monitoring the flow of insights and realized that some of the most valuable information about customers was coming from employees whom upper management didn't normally communicate with. Inspired by that discovery, he opened the annual strategic planning meeting to the entire company via social networking.[23] This style is often called **participative management**.

The third leadership style takes its name from the French term *laissez-faire*, which can be translated roughly as "hands off." **Laissez-faire leaders** such as Danny Wegman take the role of supporters and consultants, encouraging employees' ideas and offering insights or opinions when asked. After the overall strategic direction and priorities are in place, they emphasize **employee empowerment**—giving employees the power to make decisions that apply to their specific aspects of work. As Wegman puts it, "Once you share a common set of values, you can go and be yourself."[24]

COACHING AND MENTORING

coaching Helping employees reach their highest potential by meeting with them, discussing problems that hinder their ability to work effectively, and offering suggestions and encouragement to overcome these problems

mentoring A process in which experienced managers guide less-experienced colleagues in nuances of office politics, serving as a role model for appropriate business behavior, and helping to negotiate the corporate structure

Leaders have an important responsibility for education and encouragement, which may take the form of coaching and mentoring. **Coaching** involves taking the time to meet with employees, discussing any problems that may hinder their ability to work effectively, and offering suggestions and encouragement to help them find their own solutions to work-related challenges. (Note that the term *executive coaching* usually refers to hiring an outside management expert to help senior managers.)

Mentoring is similar to coaching but is based on long-term relationships between senior and junior members of an organization. The mentor is usually an experienced manager or employee who can help guide other managers and employees through the corporate maze. Mentors have a deep knowledge of the business and can explain office politics, serve as role models for appropriate business behavior, and provide valuable advice about how to succeed within the organization. Mentoring programs are used in a variety of ways, such as helping newly promoted managers make the transition to leadership roles and helping women and minorities prepare for advancement.

MANAGING CHANGE

Change presents a major leadership challenge for one simple reason: Many people don't like it, or at least they don't like being told they need to change. They may fear the unknown, they may be unwilling to give up current habits or benefits, they may not trust the motives of the people advocating change, or they may simply have experienced too many change initiatives that didn't yield the promised results.[25] To improve the chances of success when the organization needs to change, managers can follow these steps:[26]

1. **Identify everything that needs to change.** Changes can involve the structure of the organization, technologies and systems, or people's attitudes, beliefs, skills, or behaviors.[27] One particular challenge for managers advocating change is understanding the ripple effect the change will have throughout the organization.[28]
2. **Identify the forces acting for and against a change.** By understanding these forces, managers can work to amplify the forces that will facilitate the change and remove or diminish the negative forces.
3. **Choose the approach best suited to the situation.** Managers can institute change through a variety of techniques, including communication, education, participation in decision making, negotiation, visible support from top managers or other opinion leaders, or coercive use of authority (usually recommended only for crisis situations). When managers engage people in the change, asking for their input and advice so they

can help design the changes, they'll be much more likely to embrace the new way of doing things.[29]

4. **Reinforce changed behavior and monitor continued progress.** Once a change has been made, managers need to reinforce new behaviors and make sure old behaviors don't creep back in.

BUILDING A POSITIVE ORGANIZATIONAL CULTURE

Strong leadership is a key element in establishing a productive **organizational culture** (sometimes known as *corporate culture*)—the set of underlying values, norms, and practices shared by members of an organization (see Exhibit 6). Culture can be a negative or a

organizational culture A set of shared values and norms that support the management system and that guide management and employee behavior

---

EXHIBIT 6	**Creating the Ideal Culture in Your Company**

You can't create a culture directly, but you can establish the behaviors and values that in turn do create a culture. Use this list of questions to explore the many ways you can foster a positive culture—and avoid the growth of a negative culture.

Company Values

- Have you articulated a compelling vision for the company?
- Have you defined a mission statement, based on that vision, that employees understand and can implement?
- Do employees know how their work relates to this vision?
- Is there a common set of values that binds the organization together?
- Do you and other executives or owners demonstrate these values day in and day out?

People

- How are people treated?
- Do you foster an atmosphere of civility and respect?
- Do you value and encourage teamwork, with all ideas welcomed?
- Do you acknowledge, encourage, and act upon (when appropriate) ideas from employees?
- Do you give employees credit for their ideas?
- Have you shown a positive commitment to a balance between work and life?

Community

- Have you clarified how the company views its relationship with the communities it affects?
- Do your actions support that commitment to community?

Communication

- Do you practice and encourage open communication?
- Do you share operating information throughout the company so that people know how the company is doing?
- Do you regularly survey employees on workplace issues and ask for their input on solutions?
- Is there an open-door policy for access to management?

Employee Performance

- Do you handle personnel issues with fairness and respect?
- Do employees receive feedback regularly?
- Are employee evaluations based on agreed-upon objectives that have been clearly communicated?

Sources: Adapted from Andrew Bird, "Do You Know What Your Corporate Culture Is?" *CPA Insight*, February, March 1999, 25–26; Gail H. Vergara, "Finding a Compatible Corporate Culture," *Healthcare Executive*, January/February 1999, 46–47; Hal Lancaster, "To Avoid a Job Failure, Learn the Culture of a Company First," *Wall Street Journal*, 14 July 1998, B1.

positive force in an organization, and managers set the tone by establishing expectations, defining rules and policies that shape behavior, and acting as role models. When employees at Wegmans see Danny Wegman enthusiastically embrace the challenges of the day and treat customers and colleagues with respect, that positive energy radiates throughout the culture. As employee Elaine Danar puts it, "I have an incredible sense of pride to represent this company."[30]

Positive cultures create an environment that encourages employees to make smart decisions for the good of the company and its customers. At companies with legendary corporate cultures, such as Wegmans, Nordstrom, and Southwest Airlines, employees routinely go the extra mile to make sure customers are treated well. In contrast, negative, dysfunctional cultures can lead employees to make decisions that are bad for customers and bad for the company.

✓ Checkpoint

LEARNING OBJECTIVE 4: Describe the leading function, leadership style, and organizational culture.

SUMMARY: Leading is the art and science of influencing and motivating people to work toward common goals. Leaders can exhibit a range of styles in what they choose to focus on (strategic versus operational matters) and how they make things happen (forcing versus enabling). Three specific leadership styles are autocratic, democratic, and laissez-faire. Organizational culture is the set of underlying values, norms, and practices shared by members of an organization.

CRITICAL THINKING: (1) Are management and leadership the same thing? If not, why not? (2) Can a single individual be an autocratic, a democratic, *and* a laissez-faire leader? Why or why not?

IT'S YOUR BUSINESS: (1) What is your natural inclination in terms of the three basic leadership styles—autocratic, democratic, or laissez-faire? Think about times in school, at work, or in social situations in which you played a leadership role. How did you lead? (2) Does leadership experience in school activities such as student government and athletics help prepare you for business leadership? Why or why not?

KEY TERMS TO KNOW: leading, autocratic leaders, democratic leaders, participative management, laissez-faire leaders, employee empowerment, coaching, mentoring, organizational culture

---

5 | **LEARNING OBJECTIVE**

Describe the controlling function, and explain the four steps in the control cycle.

controlling The process of measuring progress against goals and objectives and correcting deviations if results are not as expected

The Controlling Function

Controlling is the management function of keeping a company's activities on track toward previously established goals. The nature of control varies widely, from directly intervening in a process to modifying policies or systems in a way that enables employees to reach their objectives.

THE CONTROL CYCLE

A good way to understand managerial control is to envision the *control cycle*, a four-step process of (1) establishing performance standards based on the strategic plan, (2) measuring performance, (3) comparing performance to standards, and (4) responding as needed (see Exhibit 7). Of course, the specific steps taken in any situation depend on the industry, the company, the functional area within the company, and the manager's leadership style. In

EXHIBIT 7	The Control Cycle

The control cycle starts with setting strategic goals and then establishing performance standards that will tell managers and employers whether the company is on track to meet those goals. As the company goes about its business, performance is measured along the way and then compared against the standards. If performance meets or exceeds the standards, no corrective action is required. However, if performance is below the standards, management can either take steps to improve performance (if the standards are still considered achievable) or lower the standards and possibly reset the goals (if they are deemed to be unachievable).

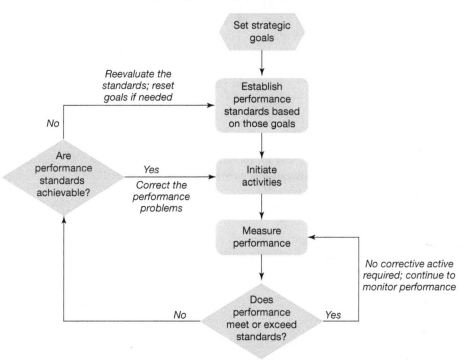

some cases, the control cycle is a formal process with explicit measurements, reports, and other tools. In others, control is subtle.

Establishing Performance Standards

In the first step of the control cycle, managers set **standards**, the criteria against which performance will be measured. Top managers set standards for the organization as a whole, such as revenue and profitability targets. Then for their individual areas of responsibility, middle and first-line managers set standards based on the overall organizational standards of performance.

Knowing which variables to use as standards and the values to set as performance targets can require a lot of experience and experimentation. Choosing variables that are truly meaningful rather than just easy to measure can also be a significant challenge. For example, *web analytics* software can deliver lots of data about online traffic, but it might not answer crucial questions such as why website visitors abandon their online shopping carts without buying anything.

A common approach to setting standards is **benchmarking**, comparing a company's key performance attributes with those of industry leaders.[31] For example, a company might discover that its average revenue per employee (total sales divided by the number of employees) is significantly lower than that of the best company in its industry. With this data point in hand, the company could look for ways to make its selling process more efficient, train sales people to go after bigger deals, or find other ways to improve the cost–revenue ratio.

One of the most important performance variables that fall under managerial control is **quality**—a measure of how closely activities or outcomes conform to predetermined standards and customer expectations. You'll learn more about quality in such areas as product and process quality in manufacturing and operations management and quality of hire in human resources.

standards Criteria against which performance is measured

benchmarking Collecting and comparing process and performance data from other companies

quality A measure of how closely a product conforms to predetermined standards and customer expectations

Measuring Performance and Responding as Needed

In the second step of the control cycle, managers assess performance, using both quantitative (specific, numerical) and qualitative (subjective) performance measures. For example, many companies now use a **balanced scorecard**, which monitors performance from multiple perspectives, including finances, operations, customer relationships, and the growth and development of employees and intellectual property.[32]

In the third step, managers compare performance with the established standards. If the level of performance falls short, the next step is usually to take corrective action to improve performance. However, in some cases, managers might decide that the level of performance originally hoped for is not realistic. For example, a sales department might have set aggressive goals for a new product at the beginning of the year, but then a tough competitor appeared out of nowhere three months later. The department manager may have no choice but to lower the sales target for the rest of the year.

CRISIS MANAGEMENT: MAINTAINING CONTROL IN EXTRAORDINARY CIRCUMSTANCES

No matter how well a company plans for its future, mistakes and catastrophes happen. And although not every specific crisis can be envisioned, managers can plan how the company should respond to each type of possible event. **Crisis management** involves the decisions and actions needed to keep a company functioning smoothly and to tend to stakeholder needs during and after an emergency.

Successful crisis management requires clear thinking and quick action while a crisis is unfolding, but smart companies don't wait until a crisis hits. A *crisis management* plan needs to contain both *contingency plans* to help managers make important decisions in a limited time frame and *communication plans* to reach affected parties quickly and forestall rumors and false information (see Exhibit 8). The plan should clearly specify which people are

balanced scorecard A method of monitoring the performance from four perspectives: finances, operations, customer relationships, and the growth and development of employees and intellectual property

crisis management Procedures and systems for minimizing the harm that might result from some unusually threatening situations

EXHIBIT 8	Communicating in a Crisis

Crisis situations test a manager's ability to make decisions and communicate clearly.

When a Crisis Hits:

Do	Don't
Prepare for trouble ahead of time by identifying potential problems, appointing and training a response team, and preparing and testing a crisis management plan.	Blame anyone for anything.
Get top management involved immediately.	Speculate in public.
	Refuse to answer questions.
Set up a news center for company representatives and the media that is equipped with phones, computers, and other electronic tools for preparing news releases and online updates. At the news center, take the following steps:	Release information that will violate anyone's right to privacy.
	Use the crisis to pitch products or services.
• Issue frequent news updates, and have trained personnel available to respond to questions around the clock.	Play favorites with media representatives.
• Provide complete information packets to the news media as soon as possible.	
• Prevent conflicting statements and provide continuity by appointing a single person trained in advance to speak for the company.	
• Tell receptionists and other employees to direct all phone calls to the designated spokesperson in the news center.	
• Provide updates when new information is available via blog postings, microblog updates, text messaging, Facebook, and other appropriate media.	
Tell the whole story—openly, completely, and honestly. If you are at fault, apologize.	
Demonstrate the company's concern by your statements and your actions.	

authorized to speak for the company, provide contact information for all key executives, and include a list of the news outlets and social media tools that will be used to disseminate information. In today's media-saturated environment, companies need to begin communicating literally within minutes after a crisis hits, to reach those who need information and to avoid the appearance of stonewalling or confusion.

REAL-TIME UPDATES
Learn More by Watching This Video

Crisis management in a social media landscape

Social media are changing every aspect of business communication, including crisis management. Learn how the rules are changing. Go to http://real-timeupdates.com/bia6 and click on Learn More. If you are using MyBizLab, you can access Real-Time Updates within the chapter or under Student Study Tools.

✓ Checkpoint

LEARNING OBJECTIVE 5: Describe the controlling function, and explain the four steps in the control cycle.

SUMMARY: The controlling function consists of the activities and decisions involved in keeping a company's activities on track toward previously established goals. The four steps in the control cycle are establishing performance standards based on the strategic plan, measuring performance, comparing performance to standards, and responding as needed.

CRITICAL THINKING: (1) Why is it important to meet the needs of internal customers? (2) Is lowering performance standards in response to a failure to meet those standards necessarily a sign of "giving up"? Why or why not?

IT'S YOUR BUSINESS: (1) Do you benchmark your performance in any aspect of your personal or academic life? If yes, does it help you improve? If not, can you identify some aspects that could potentially benefit from benchmarking? (2) Think back over any crises you've faced in your life. How well did you respond? What would you do differently in a future crisis?

KEY TERMS TO KNOW: controlling, standards, benchmarking, quality, balanced scorecard, crisis management

Essential Management Skills

6 **LEARNING OBJECTIVE**

Identify and explain four important types of managerial skills.

Managers rely on a number of skills to perform their functions and maintain a high level of quality in their organizations. These skills can be classified as *interpersonal*, *technical*, *conceptual*, and *decision making*. As managers rise through an organization's hierarchy, they may need to deemphasize skills that helped them in lower-level jobs and develop different skills. For instance, staying closely involved with project details is often a plus for first-line supervisors, but it can lead to serious performance issues for higher-level managers who should be spending time on more strategic issues.[33]

INTERPERSONAL SKILLS

The various skills required to communicate with other people, work effectively with them, motivate them, and lead them are **interpersonal skills**. Because managers mainly get things done through people at all levels of the organization, such skills are essential. Encouraging employees to work together toward common goals, interacting with employees and other managers, negotiating with partners and suppliers, developing employee trust and loyalty, and fostering innovation are all activities that require interpersonal skills.

Communication is the most important and pervasive interpersonal skill that managers use. Effective communication not only increases a manager's and an organization's

interpersonal skills Skills required to understand other people and to interact effectively with them

productivity but also shapes the impressions made on colleagues, employees, supervisors, investors, and customers. In your role as a manager, communication allows you to perceive the needs of these stakeholders (your first step toward satisfying them), and it helps you respond to those needs.[34] Moreover, as the workforce becomes more diverse—and as more companies recognize the value of embracing diversity in their workforces—managers need to adjust their interactions with others, communicating in a way that considers the different needs, backgrounds, experiences, and expectations of their workforces.

TECHNICAL SKILLS

technical skills The ability and knowledge to perform the mechanics of a particular job

A person who knows how to operate a machine, prepare a financial statement, or use a web content management system has **technical skills**, the knowledge and ability to perform the tasks required in a particular job. Technical skills are most important at lower organizational levels because managers at those levels work directly with employees who are using the tools and techniques.

However, in today's increasingly technology-driven business environment, managers often need to have a solid understanding of the processes they oversee. One obvious reason is that they need to grasp the technical matters if they are to make smart decisions regarding planning, organizing, leading, and controlling. Another key reason for understanding technical matters is that demonstrating a level of technical aptitude gives managers credibility in the eyes of their employees. Maria Azua, a vice president at IBM, says her experience as a programmer earlier in her career helped her earn respect from the people she now leads. "They don't see me as a stodgy executive who doesn't understand, because I've done the same work they do."[35]

administrative skills Technical skills in information gathering, data analysis, planning, organizing, and other aspects of managerial work

Managers at all levels use **administrative skills**, which are the technical skills necessary to direct an organization, including scheduling, researching, analyzing data, and managing projects. Managers must know how to start a project or work assignment from scratch, map out each step in the process to its successful completion, develop project costs and timelines, and establish checkpoints at key project intervals.

CONCEPTUAL SKILLS

conceptual skills The ability to understand the relationship of parts to the whole

Managers need **conceptual skills** to visualize organizations, systems, markets, and solutions—both as complete entities on their own and as interrelated pieces of a whole. For example, the most visible part of a company's accounting system is probably its accounting software and the reports it produces, but the entire system also includes procedures, policies, and the people who process and use financial information. At the same time, the accounting system is also part of an overall business system and needs to integrate seamlessly with sales, purchasing, production, and other functions.

Conceptual skills are especially important to top managers because they are the strategists who develop the plans that guide the organization toward its goals. Managers use their conceptual skills to acquire and analyze information, identify both problems and opportunities, understand the competitive environment in which their companies operate, and develop strategies and plans. The ability to conceptualize solutions that don't yet exist, to see things as they could be rather than simply as how they are, is a vital skill for executives.

DECISION-MAKING SKILLS

decision-making skills The ability to identify a decision situation, analyze the problem, weigh the alternatives, choose an alternative, implement it, and evaluate the results

Decision-making skills involve the ability to define problems and opportunities and select the best course of action. To ensure thoughtful decision making, managers can follow a formal process such as the six steps highlighted in Exhibit 9:

1. **Recognize and define the problem or opportunity.** Most companies look for problems or opportunities by gathering customer feedback, conducting studies, or monitoring such warning signals as declining sales or profits, excess inventory buildup, or high customer turnover.

EXHIBIT 9 | **Steps in the Decision-Making Process**

Following these six steps will help you make better decisions, particularly if you make a habit of applying what you learn from every decision outcome to the next decision you need to make.

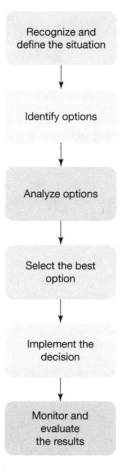

Recognize and define the situation

↓

Identify options

↓

Analyze options

↓

Select the best option

↓

Implement the decision

↓

Monitor and evaluate the results

2. **Identify and develop options.** The goal of this step is to develop a list of alternative courses of action. A problem that is easy to identify, such as a steady decline in sales revenue, might not have any easy answers. This step requires solid conceptual skills. Managers may need to break old thinking habits and throw away long-held assumptions in order to find promising solutions to tough problems.

3. **Analyze the options.** Once the ideas have been generated, they need to be studied and compared using criteria such as cost, feasibility, availability of resources, market acceptance, potential for revenue generation, and compatibility with the company's mission and vision. Some decisions present a simple yes/no choice, but others present multiple options that must be compared.

4. **Select the best option.** For some decisions, quantitative analysis can identify a clear choice from among the available options. For other decisions, however, managers might have to rely on intuition and experience to point the way.

5. **Implement the decision.** After an option has been selected, it's time to implement the decision.

6. **Monitor the results.** Finally, managers monitor the results of decisions over time to see whether the chosen alternative works, whether any new problems or opportunities arise because of the decision, and whether the decision should be modified to meet changing circumstances.

Although this list presents a logical and comprehensive method for decision making, it's important to realize that managers must frequently make decisions with incomplete or imperfect information. In other words, you may not have all the information you need, and you may not have as much time as you'd like to take. In fact, in today's fast-moving markets, the ability to make good decisions with incomplete information has become a highly valued management skill.[36]

For the latest information on managerial skills, visit http://real-timeupdates.com/bia6.

✓ Checkpoint

LEARNING OBJECTIVE 6: Identify and explain four important types of managerial skills.

SUMMARY: Interpersonal skills are the abilities to communicate with, motivate, and lead others. Technical skills involve the "mechanics" of a particular job, including the administrative skills of project management. Conceptual skills are the abilities to visualize organizations, systems, markets, and solutions—even when they may not exist yet. Decision-making skills include defining problems and opportunities and selecting the best course of action to take in each case.

CRITICAL THINKING: (1) Why is trust a vital aspect of a manager's interpersonal skills? (2) What are the risks of defining problems or opportunities poorly prior to making decisions?

IT'S YOUR BUSINESS: (1) Would you succeed as a manager if you started a company right out of college, without having gained any experience as an employee in another company? Why or why not? (2) How would you rate your conceptual skills? Does "seeing the big picture" come easily to you? If not, how might you improve in this area?

KEY TERMS TO KNOW: interpersonal skills, technical skills, administrative skills, conceptual skills, decision-making skills

BEHIND THE SCENES   MyBizLab

CUSTOMERS BELIEVE IN WEGMANS BECAUSE WEGMANS BELIEVES IN ITS EMPLOYEES

The conventional response to all challenges in the retail grocery industry is to just keep squeezing everything—customer service, wages, employee benefits, training, and anything else—to keep prices low and still eke out a profit. However, CEO Danny Wegman and his colleagues are adamant that joining the discounters in a never-ending race to cut, cut, cut is not the Wegmans way. Instead, the company defines its mission as being "the very best at serving the needs of our customers." In pursuit of that mission, the company makes employees its number-one priority and counts on employees to then meet the needs of customers.

To compete successfully against both traditional grocers and Wal-Mart, Wegmans's strategy emphasizes a huge selection of products and employees who know food and love serving customers. The cheese department is a good example. Unlike the typical selection of two or three dozen varieties at other stores,

Wegmans offers four or five *hundred* varieties—and knowledgeable staff who can help customers select and serve the perfect cheese. In fact, chances are the department manager has been sent on a research tour of cheese-producing areas in Europe to gain first hand knowledge of the tastes and traditions of each region.

Such training is expensive, to be sure. Add in higher-than-average wages and employee benefits, and Wegmans's labor costs are higher than those of its competitors. Moreover, Wegmans managers exhibit a degree of personal concern for employees not often found in the hectic retail industry. As an example, when one manager whose job required frequent out-of-town travel learned that her mother had been diagnosed with cancer, Wegmans executives modified her responsibilities so that she could stay in town to care for her mother—before she even asked. Another indicator of the company's care for its employees is the investment it makes in their futures, even if those futures take them outside the company. More than 25,000 employees have received company scholarships, and roughly 4,000 employees attend college every year with financial assistance from Wegmans.

This investment in employees pays off in important ways. For starters, customers buy more when they understand how to use various products and are successful and satisfied with them. These positive experiences with Wegmans employees also help shoppers build emotional bonds with the store, further increasing customer loyalty. And employees who enjoy their work and feel they are treated with respect are more productive and less likely to leave for other jobs. Employee turnover (the percentage of the workforce that leaves and must be replaced every year) is a major expense for retailers, but turnover at Wegmans is a fraction of the industry average. As just one measure of the positive organizational culture at Wegmans, the company has made *Fortune* magazine's list of the 100 Best Companies to Work For every year since the survey began—and it is usually at or near the top of that list.

The mission to be the best at serving consumers extends to the company's decision-making style as well. For day-to-day decisions, laissez-faire management is widespread; executives want front-line employees to make whatever choices are needed to keep customers happy. As a Wegmans executive joked a few years ago, "We're a $3 billion company run by 16-year-old cashiers." The scheme must be working: The company is now approaching $6 billion in sales and shows no signs of slowing down.[37]

Critical Thinking Questions

1. Wegmans has always been managed by members of the Wegman family. Do you think the company could continue its winning ways if the next generation doesn't want to take over, forcing the company to hire someone from outside the family as CEO? Explain your answer.
2. Would the Wegmans approach work for a car dealer? A bookstore? A manufacturer of industrial goods? Explain you answers.
3. How does low employee turnover contribute to the distinct and positive corporate culture at Wegmans?

LEARN MORE ONLINE

Visit the Wegmans website, at www.wegmans.com, and click on "Careers." Read the information and watch the videos to learn more about working at Wegmans. Imagine yourself as someone who wants to join the company. Does the information on this website increase your interest in the company? Could you see yourself launching a career at Wegmans?

MyBizLab

Log on to www.mybizlab.com to access study and assessment aids associated with this chapter.

KEY TERMS

administrative skills
autocratic leaders
balanced scorecard
benchmarking
coaching
conceptual skills
controlling
crisis management
decision-making skills
democratic leaders
employee empowerment
first-line managers
goal
interpersonal skills
laissez-faire leaders
leading
management

management pyramid
managerial roles
mentoring
middle managers
mission statement
objective
organizational culture
organizing
participative management
planning
quality
standards
strategic plans
technical skills
top managers
values statement
vision statement

TEST YOUR KNOWLEDGE

Questions for Review

1. What is management? Why is it so important?
2. What is forecasting, and how is it related to the planning function?
3. What is the goal of crisis management?
4. How does leadership differ from management?
5. Why are interpersonal skills important to managers at all levels?

Questions for Analysis

6. Why is cognitive intelligence alone insufficient for effective leadership?
7. How do the three levels of management differ?
8. How do autocratic, democratic, and laissez-faire leadership styles differ?
9. Why are coaching and mentoring effective leadership techniques?

10. **Ethical Considerations.** When an organization learns about a threat that could place the safety of its workers or its customers at risk, is management obligated to immediately inform these parties of the threat? Explain your answer.

Questions for Application

11. Which would be more difficult to forecast 10 years from now: the number of 60-year-old residents or their average disposable income? Why?
12. What are your long-term goals? Develop a set of long-term career goals for yourself and several short-term objectives that will help you reach those goals. Make sure your goals are SMART.
13. This question was intentionally excluded from this edition.
14. **Concept Integration.** What is the principal difference between a business plan and a strategic plan?

EXPAND YOUR KNOWLEDGE

Discovering Career Opportunities

If you become a manager, how much of your day will be spent performing each of the four basic functions of management? This is your opportunity to find out. Arrange to shadow a manager (such as a department head, a store manager, or a shift supervisor) for a few hours. As you observe, categorize the manager's activities in terms of the four management functions and note how much time each activity takes. If observation is not possible, interview a manager in order to complete this exercise.

1. How much of the manager's time is spent on each of the four management functions? Is this the allocation you expected?
2. Ask whether this is a typical workday for this manager. If it isn't, what does the manager usually do differently? During a typical day, does this manager tend to spend most of the time on one particular function?
3. Of the four management functions, which does the manager believe is most important for good organizational performance? Do you agree?

Improving Your Tech Insights: Business Intelligence Systems

One of the maddening ironies of contemporary business is that many decision makers are awash in data but starved for true information and insights. *Business intelligence* (BI) systems, also called *business analytics*, aim to harness all that data and turn it into the information and insights that managers need.

Explore the business intelligence or business analytics products offered by several of the leading vendors, including Actuate (www.actuate.com), IBM (www.ibm.com), SAP Business Objects (www.sap.com), Information Builders (www.informationbuilders.com), Oracle (www.oracle.com), and SAS (www.sas.com). Research a system offered by one of these vendors, and in a brief email message to your instructor, summarize in your own words the system's benefits for managerial decision makers. (*Business intelligence* is a broad term that describes a variety of approaches, technologies, and specific products, so the field can be a bit confusing. Try several websites, if needed, to find a BI system that you can summarize briefly.)

PRACTICE YOUR SKILLS

Sharpening Your Communication Skills

Potential customers frequently visit your production facility before making purchase decisions. You and the people who report to you in the sales department have received extensive training in etiquette issues because you deal with high-profile clients. However, the rest of the workforce has not received such training, and you worry that someone might inadvertently say or do something that would offend one of these potential customers. In a two-paragraph email, explain to the general manager why you think anyone who might come in contact with customers should receive basic etiquette training.

Building Your Team Skills

With a team of fellow students, perform a SWOT analysis for your college or university, from the perspective of recruiting new students. Identify as many significant strengths and weaknesses as you can think of, being as objective as possible. Next, identify any important opportunities and threats you can find, such as demographic shifts or changes in government funding. Summarize your findings in a chart modeled after Exhibit 3. Finally, evaluate your college's website and other promotional materials, if available, according to how well they present the school's strengths to prospective students.

Developing Your Research Skills

Find two articles in business journals or newspapers (print or online editions) that profile two senior managers who lead a business organization.

1. What experience, skills, and business background do the two leaders have? Do you see any striking similarities or differences in their backgrounds?
2. What kinds of business challenges have these two leaders faced? What actions did they take to deal with those challenges? Did they establish any long-term goals or objectives for their company? Did the articles mention a new change initiative?
3. Describe the leadership strengths of these two people as they are presented in the articles you selected. Is either leader known as a team builder? Long-term strategist? Shrewd negotiator? What are each leader's greatest areas of strength?

REFERENCES

1. Adapted from Wegmans website, accessed 13 August 2011, www .wegmans.com; "100 Best Companies to Work For," *Fortune*, accessed 13 August 2011, http://money.cnn.com/magazines/ fortune; Matthew Boyle, "The Wegmans Way," *Fortune*, 24 January 2005, www.fortune.com; William Conroy, "Rochester, N.Y.–Based Grocer Tops Magazine's Best Employer Rankings," *Asbury Park* (NJ) *Press*, 11 January 2005, www.ebsco.com; Matthew Boyle, "The Wegmans Way," *Fortune*, 24 January 2005, 62–68; "UCCNet Designated as U.S. Data Pool of Choice by Leading Retailers," UCCNet website, accessed 8 March 2005, www.uccnet .org; Joy Davis, "Caring for Employees Is Wegmans' Best Selling Point," (Rochester, NY) *Democrat and Chronicle*, 6 February 2005, www.democratandchronicle.com; Michael A. Prospero, "Employee Innovator: Wegmans," *Fast Company*, October 2004, 88; Matt Glynn, "Employees of Rochester, N.Y.–Based Grocer Celebrate Firm's Top Ranking," *Buffalo* (NY) *News*, 11 January 2005, www.ebsco.com.
2. Richard L. Daft, *Management*, 6th ed. (Mason, Ohio: Thompson South-Western, 2003), 5.
3. Anne Fisher, "Starting a New Job? Don't Blow It," *Fortune*, 24 February 2005, www.fortune.com.
4. Daniel S. Cochran, Fred R. David, and C. Kendrick Gibson, "A Framework for Developing an Effective Mission Statement," *Journal of Business Strategies*, Fall 2008, 27–39.
5. Welch Allyn website, accessed 13 August 2011, www.welchallyn .com.
6. Northrop Grumman website, accessed 13 August 2011, www .northropgrumman.com.
7. Enterprise Rent-A-Car Careers website, accessed 13 August 2011, www.erac.com.
8. Southern Cross Healthcare Group website, accessed 13 August 2011, www.schealthcare.co.uk; Datamonitor, "Southern Cross Healthcare Group SWOT Analysis," accessed 13 August 2011, www.ebsco.com.
9. "Southern Cross Healthcare Systems SWOT Analysis."
10. "Southern Cross Healthcare Systems SWOT Analysis."
11. "Southern Cross Healthcare Systems SWOT Analysis."
12. Alastair Dryburgh, "Don't You Believe It . . . It's Smart to Have SMART Objectives," *Management Today*, June 2011, 14.
13. Dean Foust, "Speaking up for the Organization Man," *BusinessWeek*, 9 March 2009, 78.
14. Steve Arneson, "Lead from the Middle," *Leadership Excellence*, March 2008, 19.
15. Why Middle Managers May Be the Most Important People in Your Company," Knowledge@Wharton, 25 May 2011, http:// knowledge.wharton.upenn.edu.
16. Daft, *Management*, 13.
17. Daft, *Management*, 514–515.
18. "Sometimes, EQ Is More Important Than IQ," CNN.com, 14 January 2005, www.cnn.com; Daniel Goleman, "What Makes a Leader?" *Harvard Business Review*, November–December 1998, 92–102; Shari Caudron, "The Hard Case for Soft Skills," *Workforce*, July 1999, 60–66.
19. James G. Clawson, *Level Three Leadership: Getting Below the Surface*, 2nd ed. (Upper Saddle River, N.J.: Prentice Hall, 2003), 116.
20. Cary Cherniss, "Emotional Intelligence: What It Is and Why It Matters," Consortium for Research on Emotional Intelligence in Organizations website, accessed 4 April 2009, www .eiconsortium.com.
21. Cherniss, "Emotional Intelligence: What It Is and Why It Matters."
22. Daniel Goleman, "Leadership That Gets Results," *Harvard Business Review*, March–April 2000, 78–90.
23. Herminia Ibarra and Morten T. Hansen, "Are You a Collaborative Leader?" *Harvard Business Review*, July/August 2011, 69–74.
24. Wegmans website, accessed 3 April 2009, www.wegmans.com.
25. Jeffrey D. Ford and Laurie W. Ford, "Decoding Resistance to Change," *Harvard Business Review*, April 2009, 99–103; Daft, *Management*, 382; Stephen Robbins and David DeCenzo, *Fundamentals of Management*, 4th ed. (Upper Saddle River, N.J.: Prentice Hall, 2003), 209.
26. Robbins and DeCenzo, *Fundamentals of Management*, 211; Daft, *Management*, 384, 396.
27. Robbins and DeCenzo, *Fundamentals of Management*, 210–211.

28. Ford and Ford, "Decoding Resistance to Change."
29. Paul Hebert, "People Don't Hate Change—They Hate You Trying to Change Them," Fistful of Talent blog, 6 April 2009, www.fistfuloftalent.com.
30. "High Standards," video, Wegmans website, accessed 3 April 2009, www.wegmans.com.
31. "Benchmarking," American Society for Quality, accessed 13 August 2011, http://asq.org.
32. Kevin J. Gregson, "Converting Strategy to Results," *American Venture*, September/October 2004, 16–18.
33. Robert E. Kaplan and Robert B. Kaiser, "Developing Versatile Leadership," *MIT Sloan Management Review*, Summer 2003, 19–26.
34. Courtland L. Bovée and John V. Thill, *Business Communication Today*, 9th ed. (Upper Saddle River, N.J.: Pearson Prentice Hall, 2008), 4.
35. Holly Ocasio Rizzo, "Patently Successful," *Hispanic Business*, April 2007, 34–36.
36. Geoff Gloeckler, "The Case Against Case Studies," *BusinessWeek*, 4 February 2008, 66–67.
37. See note 1.

GLOSSARY

administrative skills Technical skills in information gathering, data analysis, planning, organizing, and other aspects of managerial work

autocratic leaders Leaders who do not involve others in decision making

balanced scorecard A method of monitoring the performance from four perspectives: finances, operations, customer relationships, and the growth and development of employees and intellectual property

benchmarking Collecting and comparing process and performance data from other companies

coaching Helping employees reach their highest potential by meeting with them, discussing problems that hinder their ability to work effectively, and offering suggestions and encouragement to overcome these problems

conceptual skills The ability to understand the relationship of parts to the whole

controlling The process of measuring progress against goals and objectives and correcting deviations if results are not as expected

crisis management Procedures and systems for minimizing the harm that might result from some unusually threatening situations

decision-making skills The ability to identify a decision situation, analyze the problem, weigh the alternatives, choose an alternative, implement it, and evaluate the results

democratic leaders Leaders who delegate authority and involve employees in decision making

employee empowerment Granting decision-making and problem-solving authorities to employees so they can act without getting approval from management

first-line managers Those at the lowest level of the management hierarchy; they supervise the operating employees and implement the plans set at the higher management levels

goal A broad, long-range target or aim

interpersonal skills Skills required to understand other people and to interact effectively with them

laissez-faire leaders Leaders who leave most decisions up to employees, particularly those concerning day-to-day matters

leading The process of guiding and motivating people to work toward organizational goals

management pyramid An organizational structure divided into top, middle, and first-line management

management The process of planning, organizing, leading, and controlling to meet organizational goals

managerial roles Behavioral patterns and activities involved in carrying out the functions of management; includes interpersonal, informational, and decisional roles

mentoring A process in which experienced managers guide less-experienced colleagues in nuances of office politics, serving as a role model for appropriate business behavior, and helping to negotiate the corporate structure

middle managers Those in the middle of the management hierarchy; they develop plans to implement the goals of top managers and coordinate the work of first-line managers

mission statement A brief statement of why an organization exists; in other words, what the organization aims to accomplish for customers, investors, and other stakeholders

objective A specific, short-range target or aim

organizational culture A set of shared values and norms that support the management system and that guide management and employee behavior

organizing The process of arranging resources to carry out the organization's plans

participative management A philosophy of allowing employees to take part in planning and decision making

planning Establishing objectives and goals for an organization and determining the best ways to accomplish them

quality A measure of how closely a product conforms to predetermined standards and customer expectations

standards Criteria against which performance is measured

strategic plans Plans that establish the actions and the resource allocation required to accomplish strategic goals; they're usually defined for periods of two to five years and developed by top managers

technical skills The ability and knowledge to perform the mechanics of a particular job

top managers Those at the highest level of the organization's management hierarchy; they are responsible for setting strategic goals, and they have the most power and responsibility in the organization

values statement A brief articulation of the principles that guide a company's decisions and behaviors

vision statement A brief and inspirational expression of what a company aspires to be

Financial Information and Accounting Concepts

From Chapter 17 of *Business in Action*, Sixth Edition. Courtland L. Bovée, John V. Thill. Copyright © 2013 by Pearson Education, Inc. Published by Pearson Business. All rights reserved.

Financial Information and Accounting Concepts

LEARNING OBJECTIVES   After studying this chapter, you will be able to

1 Define *accounting* and describe the roles of private and public accountants

2 Explain the impact of accounting standards such as GAAP and the Sarbanes-Oxley Act on corporate accounting

3 Describe the *accounting equation* and explain the purpose of *double-entry bookkeeping* and the *matching principle*

4 Identify the major financial statements and explain how to read a balance sheet

5 Explain the purpose of the income statement and the statement of cash flows

6 Explain the purpose of ratio analysis and list the four main categories of financial ratios

MyBizLab

Where you see MyBizLab in this chapter, go to www.mybizlab.com for additional activities on the topic being discussed.

BEHIND THE SCENES REALITY COMES KNOCKING AT THE GOOGLEPLEX

David Eulitt/MCT/Newscom

When expenses began to grow faster than revenues, Google CFO Patrick Pichette began a systematic evaluation of how the company was spending its cash.

www.google.com

You may have received some nice employee benefits somewhere along the line, but did an armored truck ever back up to your company's front door to hand out $1,000 to every employee at Christmas time?

As Google's dominance in the profitable search engine market grew in recent years and its stock price soared, the company looked like it just might end up with all the cash in the world. To create one of the world's best places to work, the Mountain View, California, Internet giant sometimes spent money as if it had unlimited cash, too. Employee perks ranged from a companywide ski trip and an annual cash bonus—which really was delivered by armored truck—to free meals cooked by gourmet chefs and on-site massages, doctors, and car service.

Beyond these mere amenities, Google created one of the most interesting and stimulating workplaces imaginable. Engineers were allowed to spend up to 20 percent of their time exploring whatever fascinated them, even if those adventures weren't directly related to the company's current business efforts. Those explorations often did lead to new products and features, though, as Google's product line expanded far beyond its original search engine.

As it launched new projects and business initiatives right and left, Google kept hiring the best and the brightest; by 2008, the company had 20,000 employees and another 10,000 contractors. It had also acquired more than 50 other companies, paying from a few million dollars to get small niche companies on up to $1.65 billion to buy YouTube and $3.1 billion to buy the online advertising company DoubleClick.

Cash was flowing in, cash was flowing out, and all was good in the Googleplex, as the company's headquarters complex is known. But reality has a way of catching up to even the highest-flying companies, and Google would prove no exception. Internally, after a decade of rampant growth, expenses were eating up an ever-larger share of revenue. Externally, the global economy was cooling off quickly, and one company after another began trimming advertising budgets. Despite its many product innovations and explorations, Google

still depended on search engine advertising for nearly all its revenue. Online advertising wasn't getting chopped quite as severely as ads for television and other traditional media, but the spending reductions were serious enough to slow Google's sales growth. With expenses growing faster than revenue, something had to give.

If you were Patrick Pichette, Google's chief financial officer, how would you bring spending under control without alienating a workforce that has come to expect a certain level of pampering—and without stifling innovation, the engine behind the company's spectacular growth?[1]

INTRODUCTION

With years of experience managing complex business operations, Google's Patrick Pichette (profiled in the chapter-opening Behind the Scenes) could tell you how vital it is to have accurate, up-to-date accounting information. After providing an introduction to what accountants do and the rules they are expected to follow, this chapter explains the fundamental concepts of the accounting equation and double-entry bookkeeping. It then explores the primary "report cards" used in accounting: the balance sheet, income statement, and statement of cash flows. The chapter wraps up with a look at trend analysis and ratio analysis, the tools that managers, lenders, and investors use to predict a company's ongoing health.

MyBizLab

Gain hands-on experience through an interactive, real-world scenario. This chapter's simulation entitled OBM & Financial Statements is located at **www.mybizlab.com.**

Understanding Accounting

1 LEARNING OBJECTIVE

Define *accounting*, and describe the roles of private and public accountants.

Accounting is the system a business uses to identify, measure, and communicate financial information to others, inside and outside the organization. Accurate and timely financial information is important to businesses such as Google for two reasons: First, it helps managers and owners plan and control a company's operations and make informed business decisions. Second, it helps outsiders evaluate a business. Suppliers, banks, and other lenders want to know whether a business is creditworthy; investors and shareholders are concerned with its profit potential; government agencies are interested in its tax accounting.

accounting Measuring, interpreting, and communicating financial information to support internal and external decision making

Because outsiders and insiders use accounting information for different purposes, accounting has two distinct facets. **Financial accounting** is concerned with preparing financial statements and other information for outsiders such as stockholders and *creditors* (people or organizations that have lent a company money or have extended its credit); **management accounting** is concerned with preparing cost analyses, profitability reports, budgets, and other information for insiders such as management and other company decision makers. To be useful, all accounting information must be accurate, objective, consistent over time, and comparable to information supplied by other companies.

financial accounting The area of accounting concerned with preparing financial information for users outside the organization

management accounting The area of accounting concerned with preparing data for use by managers within the organization

WHAT ACCOUNTANTS DO

Some people confuse the work accountants do with **bookkeeping**, which is the clerical function of recording the economic activities of a business. Although some accountants do perform bookkeeping functions, their work generally goes well beyond the scope of this activity. Accountants prepare financial statements, analyze and interpret financial information, prepare financial forecasts and budgets, and prepare tax returns. Some accountants specialize in certain areas of accounting, such as *cost accounting* (computing and analyzing production and operating costs), *tax accounting* (preparing tax returns and interpreting tax law), *financial analysis* (evaluating a company's performance and the financial implications of strategic decisions such as product pricing, employee benefits,

bookkeeping Recordkeeping; the clerical aspect of accounting

and business acquisitions), or *forensic accounting* (combining accounting and investigating skills to assist in legal and criminal matters).

In addition to traditional accounting work, accountants may also help clients improve business processes, plan for the future, evaluate product performance, analyze profitability by customer and product groups, design and install new computer systems, assist companies with decision making, and provide a variety of other management consulting services. Performing these functions requires a strong business background and a variety of business skills beyond accounting.

PRIVATE ACCOUNTANTS

private accountants In-house accountants employed by organizations and businesses other than a public accounting firm; also called *corporate accountants*

controller The highest-ranking accountant in a company, responsible for overseeing all accounting functions

certified public accountants (CPAs) Professionally licensed accountants who meet certain requirements for education and experience and who pass a comprehensive examination

public accountants Professionals who provide accounting services to other businesses and individuals for a fee

Private accountants work for corporations, government agencies, and not-for-profit organizations. Their titles vary by function and include *corporate accountant, managerial accountant,* and *cost accountant.*[2] Private accountants generally work together as a team under the supervision of the organization's **controller**, who reports to the vice president of finance or the chief financial officer (CFO). Exhibit 1 shows the typical finance department of a large company. In smaller organizations, the controller may be in charge of the company's entire finance operation and report directly to the president.

Although certification is not required of private accountants, many are licensed **certified public accountants (CPAs)**. Specific requirements vary by state, but to receive a CPA license, an individual must complete a certain number of hours of college-level coursework, have a minimum number of years of work experience in the accounting field, and pass the Uniform CPA Exam.[3] A growing number of private accountants are becoming *certified management accountants (CMAs)*; to do so, they must pass an intensive exam sponsored by the Institute of Management Accountants.[4]

PUBLIC ACCOUNTANTS

In contrast to private accountants, **public accountants** are independent of the businesses, organizations, and individuals they serve. Most public accountants are employed by public

---

EXHIBIT 1   **Typical Finance Department**

Here is a typical finance department of a large company. In smaller companies, the controller may be the highest-ranking accountant and report directly to the president. The top executive in charge of finance is often called the chief financial officer (CFO).

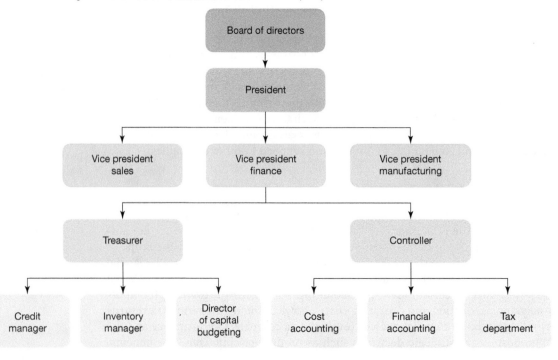

accounting firms that provide a variety of accounting and consulting services to their clients. The largest of these, four international networks known as the "Big Four," are Deloitte Touche Tohmatsu (www.deloitte.com), Ernst & Young (www.ey.com), KPMG (www.kpmg.com), and PricewaterhouseCoopers, or PwC (www.pwc.com). Whether they belong to one of these giant networks (each of which employs over 100,000 people) or to a smaller independent firm, public accountants generally are CPAs and must obtain CPA and state licensing certifications before they are eligible to conduct an **audit**—a formal evaluation of a company's accounting records and processes to ensure the integrity and reliability of a company's financial statements.

By the way, if you've shied away from accounting as a career choice because of popular stereotypes about it being a dull job fit only for "bean counters," it's time to take another look. Partly as a consequence of financial scandals in recent years and the growing complexity of accounting regulations, accounting specialists are now in demand in many industries. Employment is growing faster than average for all accounting occupations, while salaries and benefits are increasing as everybody from the Big Four to the FBI to corporations both large and small actively recruits accountants to help navigate the challenging landscape of contemporary business finance.[5]

audit Formal evaluation of the fairness and reliability of a client's financial statements

✓ Checkpoint

LEARNING OBJECTIVE 1: Define *accounting*, **and describe the roles of private and public accountants.**

SUMMARY: Accounting is the system a business uses to identify, measure, and communicate financial information to others, inside and outside the organization. Accountants perform a wide variety of tasks, including preparing financial statements, analyzing and interpreting financial information, preparing financial forecasts and budgets, preparing tax returns, interpreting tax law, computing and analyzing production costs, evaluating a company's performance, and analyzing the financial implications of business decisions. Private accountants work for corporations, government agencies, and not-for-profit organizations, performing various accounting functions for their employers. Public accountants, in contrast, sell their services to individuals and organizations. One of the most important functions of public accountants is performing audits, a formal evaluation of a company's accounting records and processes.

CRITICAL THINKING: (1) Why would a private accountant bother with becoming a CPA? (2) What effect can unreliable or uncertain accounting have on the economy?

IT'S YOUR BUSINESS: (1) How rigorous are your personal bookkeeping and accounting efforts? Do you keep accurate records, analyze spending, and set budgets? (2) If you don't really account for your personal finances, how might doing so help you, now and in the future?

KEY TERMS TO KNOW: accounting, financial accounting, management accounting, bookkeeping, private accountants, controller, certified public accountants (CPAs), public accountants, audit

The Rules of Accounting

2 **LEARNING OBJECTIVE**

In order to make informed decisions, investors, bankers, suppliers, and other parties need some means to verify the quality of the financial information that companies release to the public. They also need some way to compare information from one company to the next. To accommodate these needs, financial accountants are expected to follow a number of rules, some of which are voluntary and some of which are required by law.

Explain the impact of accounting standards such as GAAP and the Sarbanes-Oxley Act on corporate accounting.

ACCOUNTING STANDARDS: GAAP AND IFRS

Accounting is based on numbers, so it might seem like a fairly straightforward task to tally up a company's revenues and costs to determine its net profits. However, accounting is often anything but simple. For instance, *revenue recognition*, how and when a company records incoming revenue, is a particularly complex topic.[6] As just one example, should a company record revenue (a) when it ships products to customers, (b) when it bills customers, (c) when customers actually pay, or (d) after everyone has paid and any products that are going to be returned for refunds have been returned (since refunds reduce revenue)? If customers are in financial trouble and taking a long time to pay or are not paying at all, or if a poorly designed product is generating a lot of returns, the differences can be substantial.

Standardizing Through GAAP

From booking revenues and expenses to placing a value on assets and liabilities, the decisions just discussed affect just about every aspect of a company's stated financial picture. That picture in turn affects how much tax the company has to pay, how attractive it is as an investment opportunity, how creditworthy it is from a lender's point of view, and other significant outcomes.

To help ensure consistent financial reporting so that all stakeholders understand what they're looking at, over the years regulators, auditors, and company representatives have agreed on a series of accounting standards and procedures. **GAAP (generally accepted accounting principles)**, overseen in the United States by the Financial Accounting Standards Board (FASB), aims to give a fair and true picture of a company's financial position and enable outsiders to make confident analyses and comparisons. GAAP can't prevent every reporting abuse, but it does make distorting financial results in order to fool outsiders more difficult.[7] Companies can still provide "non-GAAP" financial results to investors in addition to their GAAP figures—as Google does, for example—but they must label these figures as non-GAAP data.

Companies whose stock is publicly traded in the United States are required to file audited financial statements with the Securities and Exchange Commission (SEC). During an audit, CPAs who work for an independent accounting firm, also known as **external auditors**, review a client's financial records to determine whether the statements that summarize these records have been prepared in accordance with GAAP. The auditors then summarize their findings in a report attached to the client's published financial statements. Sometimes these reports disclose information that might materially affect the client's financial position, such as the bankruptcy of a major supplier, a large obsolete inventory, costly environmental problems, or questionable accounting practices. When a company receives a clean audit report, this means that to the best of the auditors' knowledge the company's financial statements are accurate.

To assist with the auditing process, many large organizations use *internal auditors*—employees who investigate and evaluate the organization's internal operations and data to determine whether they are accurate and whether they comply with GAAP, federal laws, and industry regulations. Although this self-checking process is vital to an organization's financial health, an internal audit is not a substitute for having an independent auditor look things over and render an unbiased opinion.

The Evolution Toward Global Accounting Standards

GAAP has helped standardize accounting and financial reporting for companies in the United States, but the situation is more complex at the international level because GAAP standards are not used in most other countries. The lack of global standardization creates extra work for U.S. multinationals, essentially forcing them to keep two sets of books.[8] In addition, it complicates cross-border transactions, mergers, and investments because companies don't have a single set of benchmarks to compute assets, liabilities, and other vital quantities.

For the past decade, the FASB has been working with the London-based International Accounting Standards Board to harmonize GAAP with the **international financial reporting standards (IFRS)** now used in most countries. At present, the earliest the SEC plans to require or at least allow U.S. corporations to begin using IFRS-compatible standards is 2015,

GAAP (generally accepted accounting practices) Standards and practices used by publicly held corporations in the United States and a few other countries in the preparation of financial statements; on course to converge with IFRS

external auditors Independent accounting firms that provide auditing services for public companies

international financial reporting standards (IFRS) Accounting standards and practices used in many countries outside the United States

and many details remain to be worked out. However, it is clear that the eventual standards will bring pervasive changes to the accounting profession, financial management, information systems, stock-based compensation and bonuses, and other aspects of managing a public corporation.[9]

Just how complex and expensive it will be for U.S. companies to shift from GAAP to IFRS (or an IFRS-friendly version of GAAP) isn't clear yet. In general, the shift could take several years of work and will require a comprehensive reevaluation of a company's finances. The implications could be significant. For example, corporate income tends to come out higher under IFRS than it does under GAAP, which could conceivably increase companies' tax obligations.[10]

Changing to IFRS should help investors who want to purchase stocks of companies based in other countries, help U.S. stock exchanges by making them more competitive in world capital markets, help foreign companies that want to sell stock in the United States, and help multinational companies by letting them settle on a single set of accounting standards. Another key potential benefit is that companies will find it easier to staff financial positions around the world because everyone will be trained in the same financial language.[11]

REAL-TIME UPDATES
Learn More by Reading This Article

Follow the convergence

If you're considering a career in accounting or finance, use this site to stay on top of the convergence of GAAP and IFRS. Go to http://real-timeupdates.com/bia6 and click on Learn More. If you are using MyBizLab, you can access Real-Time Updates within the chapter or under Student Study Tools.

SARBANES-OXLEY

The need for and complexity of financial reporting standards is highlighted in the controversial story of **Sarbanes-Oxley**, the informal name of the Public Company Accounting Reform and Investor Protection Act. (You'll hear it referred to as "Sox" or "Sarbox" as well.) Passed in 2002 in the wake of several cases of massive accounting fraud, most notably involving the energy company Enron and the telecom company WorldCom, Sarbanes-Oxley changed public company accounting in the United States in a number of important ways. Its major provisions include[12]

Sarbanes-Oxley
The informal name of comprehensive legislation designed to improve integrity and accountability of financial information

- Outlawing most loans by corporations to their own directors and executives
- Creating the Public Company Accounting Oversight Board (PCAOB) to oversee external auditors
- Requiring corporate lawyers to report evidence of financial wrongdoing
- Prohibiting external auditors from providing certain nonaudit services
- Requiring that audit committees on the board of directors have at least one financial expert and that the majority of board members be independent (not employed by the company in an executive position)
- Prohibiting investment bankers from influencing stock analysts
- Requiring CEOs and CFOs to sign statements attesting to the accuracy of their financial statements
- Requiring companies to document and test their internal financial controls and processes

The last item in particular, the result of the brief "Section 404" of the legislation, generated considerable controversy. Representative Michael Oxley, co-sponsor of the legislation, says that "99.9 percent of the complaints you hear are about 404." Oxley adds that it's not the two paragraphs in this section of the legislation that caused so much grief but rather the several hundred pages of regulations the PCAOB generated to enforce it.[13] As one financial writer put it, the requirements were so sweeping that they left financial executives "awash in a vast sea of details, with little ability to set priorities about what to focus on in their compliance efforts."[14]

After a lot of initial criticism about the costs of compliance and a shift in the PCAOB's stance to let companies focus on monitoring the riskiest financial decisions instead of every mundane transaction, complaints about Sarbox have leveled off in recent years.[15]

REAL-TIME UPDATES
Learn More by Visiting This Website

Get the latest in international accounting news

This site from Deloitte bills itself as the number one website for international accounting news. Go to http://real-timeupdates.com/bia6 and click on Learn More. If you are using MyBizLab, you can access Real-Time Updates within the chapter or under Student Study Tools.

✓ Checkpoint

LEARNING OBJECTIVE 2: Explain the impact of accounting standards such as GAAP and the Sarbanes-Oxley Act on corporate accounting.

SUMMARY: Accounting standards such as GAAP help ensure consistent financial reporting, which is essential for regulators and investors to make informed decisions. To ensure consistency on a global scale, GAAP is likely to be merged with the international financial reports standards (IFRS) in the coming years. Sarbanes-Oxley introduced a number of rules covering the way publicly traded companies manage and report their finances, including restricting loans to directors and executives, creating a new board to oversee public auditors, requiring corporate lawyers to report financial wrongdoing, requiring CEOs and CFOs to sign financial statements under oath, and requiring companies to document their financial systems.

CRITICAL THINKING: (1) Should U.S. public companies with no significant overseas business activity be forced to follow international accounting standards? Why or why not? (2) How does requiring CEOs to personally attest to the accuracy of financial statements eliminate errors and misrepresentations?

IT'S YOUR BUSINESS: (1) How might the convergence of GAAP and IFRS in the coming years affect you as an investor? (2) If you were considering buying stock in a company, would you support rigorous and detailed financial accountability such as that called for by Section 404 of Sarbanes-Oxley? Why or why not?

KEY TERMS TO KNOW: GAAP (generally accepted accounting principles), external auditors, international financial reporting standards (IFRS), Sarbanes-Oxley

---

3 LEARNING OBJECTIVE

Describe the *accounting equation*, and explain the purpose of *double-entry bookkeeping* and the *matching principle*.

assets Any things of value owned or leased by a business

liabilities Claims against a firm's assets by creditors

owners' equity The portion of a company's assets that belongs to the owners after obligations to all creditors have been met

accounting equation The basic accounting equation, stating that assets equal liabilities plus owners' equity

Fundamental Accounting Concepts

In their work with financial data, accountants are guided by three basic concepts: the *fundamental accounting equation*, *double-entry bookkeeping*, and the *matching principle*. Here is a closer look at each of these essential ideas.

THE ACCOUNTING EQUATION

For thousands of years, businesses and governments have kept records of their **assets**—valuable items they own or lease, such as equipment, cash, land, buildings, inventory, and investments. Claims against those assets are **liabilities**, or what the business owes to its creditors—such as lenders and suppliers. For example, when a company borrows money to purchase a building, the lender has a claim against the company's assets. What remains after liabilities have been deducted from assets is **owners' equity**:

$$\text{Assets} - \text{Liabilities} = \text{Owners' equity}$$

As a simple example, if your company has $1,000,000 in assets and $800,000 in liabilities, your equity would be $200,000:

$$\$1,000,000 - \$800,000 = \$200,000$$

Using the principles of algebra, this equation can be restated in a variety of formats. The most common is the simple **accounting equation**, which serves as the framework for the entire accounting process:

$$\text{Assets} = \text{Liabilities} + \text{Owners' equity}$$
$$\$1,000,000 = \$800,000 + \$200,000$$

This equation suggests that either creditors or owners provide all the assets in a corporation. Think of it this way: If you were starting a new business, you could contribute cash to the company to buy the assets you needed to run your business or you could borrow money from a bank (the creditor) or you could do both. The company's liabilities are placed before owners' equity in the accounting equation because creditors get paid first. After liabilities have been paid, anything left over belongs to the owners. As a business engages in economic activity, the dollar amounts and composition of its assets, liabilities, and owners' equity change. However, the equation must always be in balance; in other words, one side of the equation must always equal the other side.

REAL-TIME UPDATES
Learn More by Reading This Article

Introduction to the accounting equation

Get a better feel for the accounting equation with these practical examples. Go to http://real-timeupdates.com/bia6 and click on Learn More. If you are using MyBizLab, you can access Real-Time Updates within the chapter or under Student Study Tools.

DOUBLE-ENTRY BOOKKEEPING AND THE MATCHING PRINCIPLE

To keep the accounting equation in balance, most companies use a **double-entry bookkeeping** system that records every transaction affecting assets, liabilities, or owners' equity. Each transaction is entered twice, once as a *debit* and once as a *credit*, and they must offset each other to keep the accounting equation in balance. The double-entry method predates computers by hundreds of years and was originally created to minimize errors caused by entering and adding figures by hand; accounting software typically handles all this behind the scenes now.

The **matching principle** requires that expenses incurred in producing revenues be deducted from the revenue they generated during the same accounting period. This matching of expenses and revenue is necessary for the company's financial statements to present an accurate picture of the profitability of a business. Accountants match revenue to expenses by adopting the **accrual basis** of accounting, which states that revenue is recognized when you make a sale or provide a service, not when you get paid. Similarly, your expenses are recorded when you receive the benefit of a service or when you use an asset to produce revenue—not when you pay for it.

Accrual accounting focuses on the economic substance of an event rather than on the movement of cash. It's a way of recognizing that revenue can be earned either before or after cash is received and that expenses can be incurred when a company receives a benefit (such as a shipment of supplies) either before or after the benefit is paid for.

If a business runs on a **cash basis**, the company records revenue only when money from the sale is actually received. Your checking account is a simple cash-based accounting system: You record checks, debit card charges, and ATM withdrawals at the time of purchase and record deposits at the time of receipt. Cash-based accounting is simple, but it can be misleading. It's easy to inflate income, for example, by delaying the payment of bills. For that reason, public companies are required to keep their books on an accrual basis.

Depreciation, or the allocation of the cost of a tangible long-term asset over a period of time, is another way that companies match expenses with revenue. (For intangible assets, this allocation over time is known as *amortization*.) When Google buys a piece of real estate, for example, instead of deducting the entire cost of the item at the time of purchase, the company *depreciates* it, or spreads the cost over a certain number of years as specified by tax regulations because the asset will likely generate income for many years. If the company were to expense long-term assets at the time of purchase, its apparent financial performance would be distorted negatively in the year of purchase and positively in all future years when these assets generate revenue.

double-entry bookkeeping A method of recording financial transactions that requires a debit entry and credit entry for each transaction to ensure that the accounting equation is always kept in balance

matching principle The fundamental principle requiring that expenses incurred in producing revenue be deducted from the revenues they generate during an accounting period

accrual basis An accounting method in which revenue is recorded when a sale is made and an expense is recorded when it is incurred

cash basis An accounting method in which revenue is recorded when payment is received and an expense is recorded when cash is paid

depreciation An accounting procedure for systematically spreading the cost of a tangible asset over its estimated useful life

✓ Checkpoint

LEARNING OBJECTIVE 3: Describe the *accounting equation*, and explain the purpose of *double-entry bookkeeping* and the *matching principle*.

SUMMARY: The basic accounting equation is Assets = Liabilities + Owners' equity. Double-entry bookkeeping is a system of recording every financial transaction as two counterbalancing entries in order to keep the accounting equation in balance. The matching principle makes sure that expenses incurred in producing revenues are deducted from the revenue they generated during the same accounting period.

CRITICAL THINKING: (1) How does double-entry bookkeeping help eliminate errors? (2) Why is accrual-based accounting considered more fraud-proof than cash-based accounting?

IT'S YOUR BUSINESS: (1) Does looking at the accounting equation make you reconsider your personal spending habits? (Think about taking on liabilities that don't create any long-term assets, for example.) (2) How would accrual basis accounting give you better insights into your personal finances?

KEY TERMS TO KNOW: assets, liabilities, owners' equity, accounting equation, double-entry bookkeeping, matching principle, accrual basis, cash basis, depreciation

---

4 | LEARNING OBJECTIVE

Identify the major financial statements, and explain how to read a balance sheet.

closing the books
Transferring net revenue and expense account balances to retained earnings for the period

Using Financial Statements: The Balance Sheet

As a company conducts business day after day, sales, purchases, and other transactions are recorded and classified into individual accounts. After these individual transactions are recorded and then summarized, accountants must review the resulting transaction summaries and adjust or correct all errors or discrepancies before **closing the books**, or transferring net revenue and expense items to *retained earnings*. Exhibit 2 illustrates the *accounting cycle* that companies go through during a given accounting period, such as a month.

In a way, this is what you do every month when you get your bank statement. You might think you have $50 left in your account but then see your statement and realize with delight that you forgot to record depositing the $100 check your grandmother sent you, and your true balance is $150. Or you might realize with dismay that you forgot to record the $300 ATM withdrawal you made on spring break, and your true balance is –$250. Before you know how much money you'll have to spend next month—your retained earnings—you have to accurately close the books on this month.

UNDERSTANDING FINANCIAL STATEMENTS

Financial statements consist of three separate but interrelated reports: the *balance sheet*, the *income statement*, and the *statement of cash flows*. These statements are required by law for all publicly traded companies, but they are vital management tools for every company, no matter how large or small. Together, these statements provide information about an organization's financial strength and ability to meet current obligations, the effectiveness of its sales and collection efforts, and its effectiveness in managing its assets. Organizations and individuals use financial statements to spot opportunities and problems, to make business decisions, and to evaluate a company's past performance, present condition, and future prospects.

The following sections examine the financial statements of Computer Central Services, a hypothetical company engaged in direct sales and distribution of personal computers and accessories. In the past year, the company shipped more than 2.3 million orders, amounting to more than $1.7 billion in sales—a 35 percent increase in sales over the prior year. The company's daily sales volume has grown considerably over the last decade—from $232,000 to $6.8 million. Because of this tremendous growth and the increasing demand for new computer products, the company recently purchased a 276,000-square-foot building.

BALANCE SHEET

balance sheet
A statement of a firm's financial position on a particular date; also known as a *statement of financial position*

The **balance sheet**, also known as the *statement of financial position*, is a snapshot of a company's financial position on a particular date (see Exhibit 3). In effect, it freezes all business actions and provides a baseline from which a company can measure change from that point forward. This statement is called a balance sheet because it includes

EXHIBIT 2   **The Accounting Cycle**

Here are the general steps in the accounting process, or *accounting cycle*, from recording transactions to making sure the books are in balance to closing the books for a particular accounting period (usually a month). Steps 1 through 3 are done as transactions occur; steps 4 through 8 are usually performed at the end of the accounting period.

1. Perform *transactions*
A transaction is any relevant accounting event, including making a sale, making a purchase, or making a debt payment.

2. Analyze and record transactions in a *journal*
Journalizing means analyzing the *source document* (e.g., a sales receipt or a customer invoice) for each transaction, then separating the transaction, into its debit and credit components and recording these chronologically in a journal.

8. *Close the books* for the accounting period
Transfer the balances from temporary ledger accounts to the permanent balance sheet and income statement. Record *reversing entries* as needed to start fresh temporary accounts at the beginning of the next period.

3. *Post* journal entries to the *ledger*
Entries from the chronological journals are moved to the account-based ledger. Over the course of the month or other accounting period, each account (e.g., sales revenue or expenses) in the ledger fills up with the various transaction records posted from the journals. These accounts are considered temporary because they are closed out at the end of the accounting period (see step 8).

7. Prepare *financial statements*
With the accounts adjusted and in balance for the accounting period, various managerial and government compliance reports can now be generated.

6. Prepare an adjusted trial balance
This is the same procedure as in step 4 but includes the adjusting entries made in step 5. Again, if the debits total and the credits total don't match, the error needs to be investigated and corrected.

4. Prepare a *trial balance*
At the end of the accounting period, the debits and credits in the ledger are totaled, and then the two amounts are compared. If they don't equal, one or more errors have crept in somewhere in the previous three steps and need to be found and corrected.

5. Make *adjusting entries*, as needed
Not all relevant changes are generated by transaction records during the accounting period, so accountants enter items such as asset depreciation or transactions whose revenues or expenses occur before or after the accounting period.

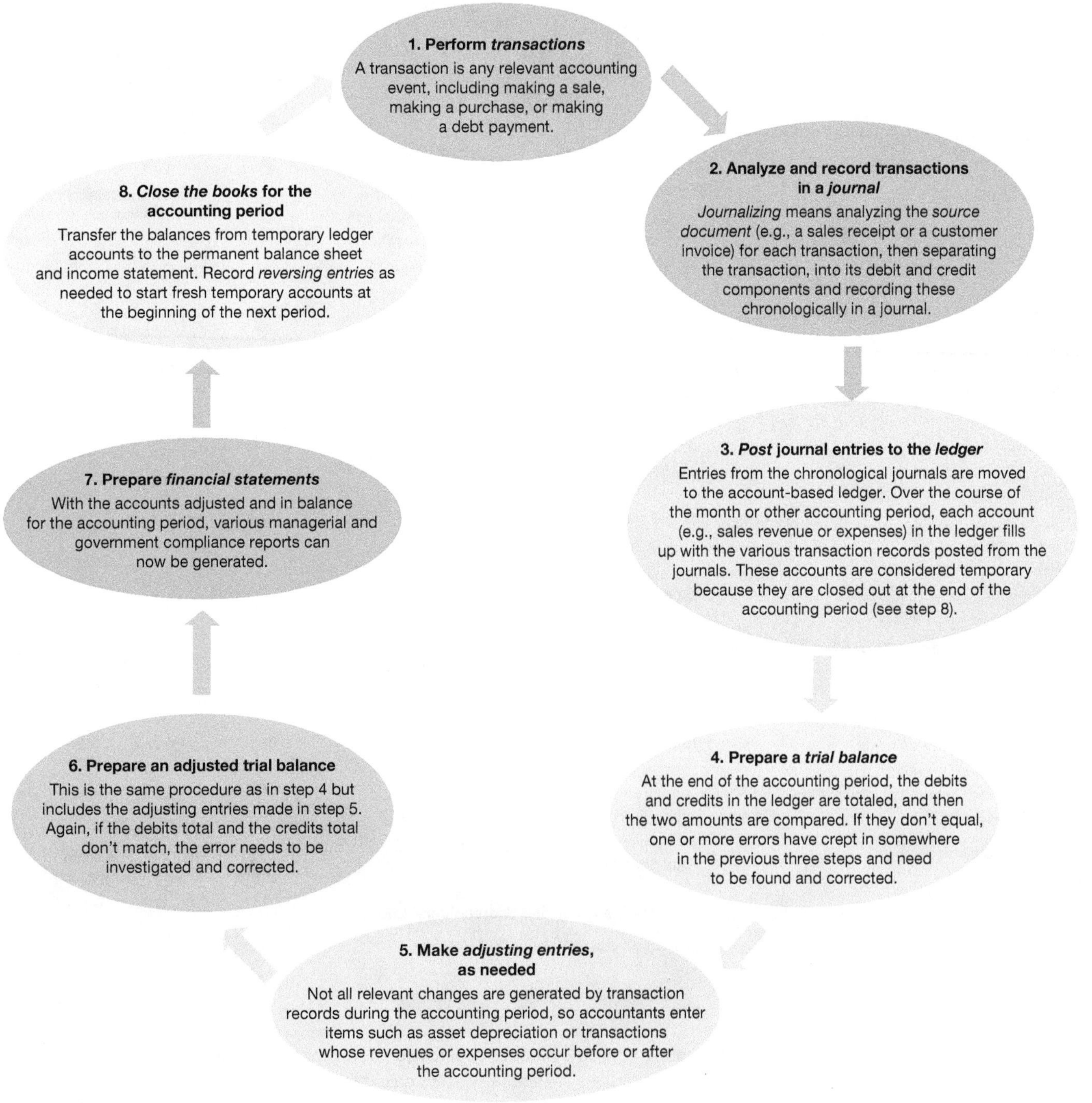

Sources: Adapted from Jeffery Slater, *College Accounting: A Practical Approach*, 11th ed. (Upper Saddle River, N.J.: Pearson Prentice Hall, 2010), 78, 104, 148; "The Accounting Process," NetMBA, www.netmba.com; Bob Schneider, "Accounting Basics: The Accounting Process," Investopedia.com, www.investopedia.com.

all elements in the accounting equation and shows the balance between assets on one side of the equation and liabilities and owners' equity on the other side.

Every company prepares a balance sheet at least once a year, most often at the end of the **calendar year**, covering January 1 to December 31. However, many business and government bodies use a **fiscal year**, which may be any 12 consecutive months. Some companies prepare a balance sheet more often than once a year, such as at the end of each month or quarter. Every balance sheet is dated to show the exact date when the financial snapshot was taken.

calendar year
A 12-month accounting period that begins on January 1 and ends on December 31

fiscal year
Any 12 consecutive months used as an accounting period

EXHIBIT 3 | **Balance Sheet for Computer Central Services**

The categories used on the year-end balance sheet for Computer Central Services are typical.

Computer Central Services

Balance Sheet
As of December 31, 2012
($ thousands)

Amounts for the various subcategories are shown in this column

ASSETS

Cash and other items that will or can be converted to cash within one year, plus expenses paid in advance

Current Assets		
Cash	$ 5,000	
Marketable Securities	40,000	
Accounts Receivable	100,000	
Inventory	50,000	
Miscellaneous Prepaid Items	5,000	
Total Current Assets		**$200,000**

Total for the category is shown in this column (e.g., here, the five items to the left add up to $200,000)

Assets such as buildings, equipment, furniture, and other property expected to be used for longer than one year

Fixed Assets		
Property and Equipment	53,000	
Less: Accumulated Depreciation	−3,000	
Total Fixed Assets		50,000
Total Assets		**$250,000**

Current and fixed assets are totaled here

LIABILITIES AND SHAREHOLDERS' EQUITY

Amounts owed that are due to be repaid within one year

Current Liabilities		
Accounts Payable	$ 50,000	
Accrued Expenses	30,000	
Total Current Liabilities		$ 80,000

Debts that are due a year or more after the date of the balance sheet

Long-Term Liabilities		
Loans Payable	20,000	
Total Long-Term Liabilities		20,000
Total Liabilities		100,000

Current and long-term liabilities are totaled here

Money invested in the company for ownership interest, plus accumulated earnings

Shareholders' Equity		
Common Stock	125,000	
Retained Earnings	25,000	
Total Shareholders' Equity		150,000
Total Liabilities and Shareholders' Equity		**$250,000**

Liabilities plus shareholders' equity equals assets

By reading a company's balance sheet, you should be able to determine the size of the company, the major assets owned, any asset changes that occurred in recent periods, how the company's assets are financed, and any major changes that have occurred in the company's debt and equity in recent periods.

Assets

As discussed earlier in the chapter, an asset is something owned by a company with the intent to generate income. Assets can be *tangible* or *intangible*. Tangible assets include land, buildings, and equipment. Intangible assets include intellectual property (such as patents and business methods), *goodwill* (which includes company reputation), brand awareness and recognition, workforce skills, management talent, and even customer relationships.[16]

As you might expect, assigning value to intangible assets is not an easy task (and is one of the major points of difference between GAAP and IFRS, incidentally), but these assets make up an increasingly important part of the value of many contemporary companies.[17] For instance, much of the real value of a company such as Google is not in its tangible assets but in its search engine algorithms, software designs, brand awareness, and the brainpower of its workforce. For example, a recent balance sheet for the company listed over $8 billion in goodwill and other intangibles.[18]

The asset section of the balance sheet is often divided into *current assets* and *fixed assets*. **Current assets** include cash and other items that will or can become cash within the following year. **Fixed assets** (sometimes referred to as *property, plant, and equipment*) are long-term investments in buildings, equipment, furniture and fixtures, transportation equipment, land, and other tangible property used in running the business. Fixed assets have a useful life of more than one year.

Assets are listed in descending order by *liquidity*, or the ease with which they can be converted into cash. Thus, current assets are listed before fixed assets. The balance sheet gives a subtotal for each type of asset and then a grand total for all assets. The current assets of Computer Central Services consist primarily of cash, investments in short-term marketable securities such as money-market funds, *accounts receivable* (amounts due from customers), and inventory (such as computers, software, and other items the company sells to customers).

current assets Cash and items that can be turned into cash within one year

fixed assets Assets retained for long-term use, such as land, buildings, machinery, and equipment; also referred to as *property, plant, and equipment*

Liabilities

Liabilities may be current or long term, and they are listed in the order in which they will come due. The balance sheet gives subtotals for **current liabilities** (obligations that will have to be met within one year of the date of the balance sheet) and **long-term liabilities** (obligations that are due one year or more after the date of the balance sheet), and then it gives a grand total for all liabilities.

Current liabilities include accounts payable, short-term financing, and accrued expenses. *Accounts payable* includes the money the company owes its suppliers as well as money it owes vendors for miscellaneous services (such as electricity and telephone charges). *Accrued expenses* are expenses that have been incurred but for which bills have not yet been received. For example, because salespeople at Computer Central Services earn commissions, the company has a liability to those employees after the sale is made—regardless of when a check is issued to the employee. If such expenses and their associated liabilities were not recorded, the company's financial statements would be misleading and would violate the matching principle because the commission expenses earned at the time of sale would not be matched to the revenue generated from the sale.

Long-term liabilities include loans, leases, and bonds. A borrower makes principal and interest payments to the lender over the term of the loan, and its obligation is limited to these payments. Rather than borrow money to make purchases, a firm may enter into a *lease*, under which the owner of an item allows another party to use it in exchange for regular payments. Bonds are certificates that obligate the company to repay a certain sum, plus interest, to the bondholder on a specific date. Bonds are traded on organized securities exchanges.

current liabilities Obligations that must be met within a year

long-term liabilities Obligations that fall due more than a year from the date of the balance sheet

Owners' Equity

The owners' investment in a business is listed on the balance sheet under owners' equity (or *shareholders' equity* or *stockholders' equity* for corporations). Sole proprietorships list owner's equity under the owner's name with the amount (assets minus liabilities). Small partnerships list each partner's share of the business separately, and large partnerships list the total of all partners' shares. In a corporation, the shareholders' total investment value is

retained earnings
The portion of shareholders' equity earned by the company but not distributed to its owners in the form of dividends

the sum of two amounts: the total value of the all the shares currently held, plus **retained earnings**—cash that is kept by the company rather than distributed to shareholders in the form of dividends. As Exhibit 3 shows, Computer Central Services has retained earnings of $25 million. The company doesn't pay dividends—many small and growing corporations don't—but rather builds its cash reserves to fund expansion in the future. (Shareholders' equity can be slightly more complicated than this, depending on how the company's shares were first created, but this summary gives you the basic idea of how the assets portion of the balance sheet works.)

✓ Checkpoint

LEARNING OBJECTIVE 4: Identify the major financial statements, and explain how to read a balance sheet.

SUMMARY: The three major financial statements are the balance sheet, the income statement, and the statement of cash flows. The balance sheet provides a snapshot of the business at a particular point in time. It shows the size of the company, the major assets owned, the ways the assets are financed, and the amount of owners' investment in the business. Its three main sections are assets, liabilities, and owners' equity.

CRITICAL THINKING: (1) Why do analysts need to consider different factors when evaluating a company's ability to repay short-term versus long-term debt? (2) Would the current amount of the owners' equity be a reasonable price to pay for a company? Why or why not?

IT'S YOUR BUSINESS: (1) What are your current and long-term financial liabilities? Are these liabilities restricting your flexibility as a student or consumer? (2) As a potential employee, what intangible assets can you offer a company?

KEY TERMS TO KNOW: closing the books, balance sheet, calendar year, fiscal year, current assets, fixed assets, current liabilities, long-term liabilities, retained earnings

---

5 **LEARNING OBJECTIVE**

Explain the purpose of the income statement and the statement of cash flows

Using Financial Statements: Income and Cash Flow Statements

In addition to the balance sheet, the two other fundamentally important financial statements are the income statement and the statement of cash flows.

INCOME STATEMENT

income statement A financial record of a company's revenues, expenses, and profits over a given period of time; also known as a *profit and loss statement*

expenses Costs created in the process of generating revenues

net income Profit earned or loss incurred by a firm, determined by subtracting expenses from revenues; casually referred to as the *bottom line*

If the balance sheet is a snapshot, the income statement is a movie. The **income statement**, or *profit-and-lose statement* or simply "P&L," shows an organization's profit performance over a period of time, typically one year. It summarizes revenue from all sources as well as all **expenses**, the costs that have arisen in generating revenues. Expenses and income taxes are then subtracted from revenues to show the actual profit or loss of a company, a figure known as **net income**—also called profit or, informally, the *bottom line*. By briefly reviewing a company's income statements, you should have a general sense of the company's size, its trend in sales, its major expenses, and the resulting net income or loss. Owners, creditors, and investors can evaluate the company's past performance and future prospects by comparing net income for one year with net income for previous years. Exhibit 4 shows the income statement for Computer Central Services.

Expenses include both the direct costs associated with creating or purchasing products for sale and the indirect costs associated with operating the business. If a company manufactures or purchases inventory, the cost of storing the product for sale (such as heating the warehouse, paying the rent, and buying insurance on the storage facility) is added to the difference between the cost of the beginning inventory and the cost of the ending inventory

EXHIBIT 4	Income Statement for Computer Central Services

An income statement summarizes the company's financial operations over a particular accounting period, usually a year.

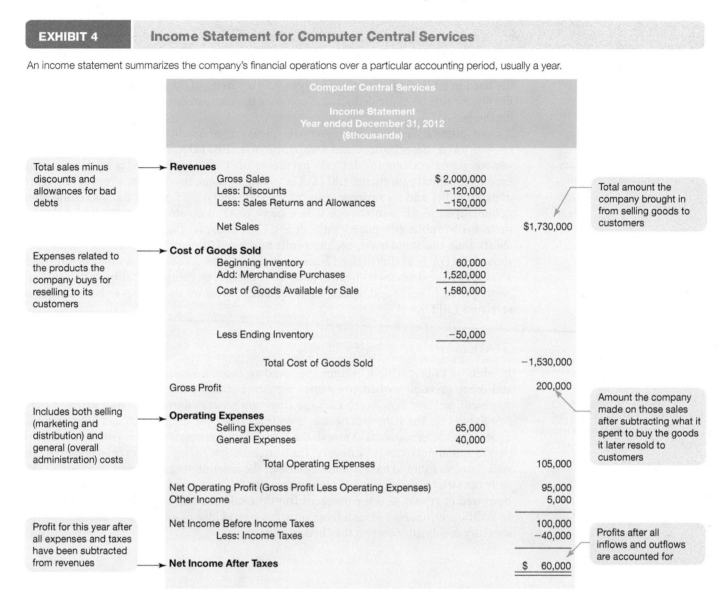

Computer Central Services

Income Statement
Year ended December 31, 2012
($thousands)

Total sales minus discounts and allowances for bad debts

Revenues

Gross Sales	$ 2,000,000	
Less: Discounts	−120,000	
Less: Sales Returns and Allowances	−150,000	
Net Sales		$1,730,000

Total amount the company brought in from selling goods to customers

Expenses related to the products the company buys for reselling to its customers

Cost of Goods Sold

Beginning Inventory	60,000	
Add: Merchandise Purchases	1,520,000	
Cost of Goods Available for Sale	1,580,000	
Less Ending Inventory	−50,000	
Total Cost of Goods Sold		−1,530,000
Gross Profit		200,000

Includes both selling (marketing and distribution) and general (overall administration) costs

Operating Expenses

Selling Expenses	65,000	
General Expenses	40,000	
Total Operating Expenses		105,000
Net Operating Profit (Gross Profit Less Operating Expenses)		95,000
Other Income		5,000

Amount the company made on those sales after subtracting what it spent to buy the goods it later resold to customers

Profit for this year after all expenses and taxes have been subtracted from revenues

Net Income Before Income Taxes		100,000
Less: Income Taxes		−40,000
Net Income After Taxes		$ 60,000

Profits after all inflows and outflows are accounted for

in order to compute the actual cost of items that were sold during a period—or the **cost of goods sold**. The computation can be summarized as follows:

Cost of goods sold = Beginning inventory + Net purchases − Ending inventory

As shown in Exhibit 4, cost of goods sold is deducted from sales to obtain a company's **gross profit**—a key figure used in financial statement analysis. In addition to the costs directly associated with producing goods, companies deduct **operating expenses**, which include both *selling expenses* and *general expenses*, to compute a firm's *net operating income*. Net operating income is often a better indicator of financial health because it gives an idea of how much cash the company is able to generate. For instance, a company with a sizable gross profit level can actually be losing money if its operating expenses are out of control—and if it doesn't have enough cash on hand to cover the shortfall, it could soon find itself bankrupt.[19]

Selling expenses are operating expenses incurred through marketing and distributing the product (such as wages or salaries of salespeople, advertising, supplies, insurance for the sales operation, depreciation for the store and sales equipment, and other sales department expenses such as telephone charges). *General expenses* are operating expenses incurred in the overall administration of a business. They include such items as professional services (such as accounting and legal fees), office salaries, depreciation of office equipment, insurance for office operations, and supplies.

cost of goods sold The cost of producing or acquiring a company's products for sale during a given period

gross profit The amount remaining when the cost of goods sold is deducted from net sales; also known as *gross margin*

operating expenses All costs of operation that are not included under cost of goods sold

A firm's net operating income is then adjusted by the amount of any nonoperating income or expense items such as the gain or loss on the sale of a building. The result is the net income or loss before income taxes (losses are shown in parentheses), a key figure used in budgeting, cash-flow analysis, and a variety of other financial computations. Finally, income taxes are deducted to compute the company's after-tax net income or loss for the period.

An alternative—and controversial—measure of profitability is *earnings before interest, taxes, depreciation, and amortization*, or **EBITDA**. Because it doesn't include various items such as the interest payments on loans or the effects of depreciating expensive capital equipment, EBITDA is viewed by some investors as a "purer" measure of profitability and an easier way to compare financial performance across companies or industries. And even though it is a non-GAAP indicator and must be labeled as such, many public companies publish EBITDA because it can suggest greater profitability than the standard operating profit number. However, for those very same reasons, EBITDA is also criticized because it doesn't reflect some costs that could mask a company's real financial health, such as the large, ongoing capital investments that are required in some industries. Consequently, investors should never base decisions solely on EBITDA.[20]

EBITDA
Earnings before interest, taxes, depreciation, and amortization

STATEMENT OF CASH FLOWS

statement of cash flows
A statement of a firm's cash receipts and cash payments that presents information on its sources and uses of cash

In addition to preparing a balance sheet and an income statement, all public companies and many privately owned companies prepare a **statement of cash flows**, or *cash flow statement*, to show how much cash the company generated over time and where it went (see Exhibit 5). The statement of cash flows tracks the cash coming into and flowing out of a company's bank accounts. It reveals the increase or decrease in the company's cash for the period and summarizes (by category) the sources of that change. From a brief review of this statement, you should have a general sense of the amount of cash created or consumed by daily operations, the amount of cash invested in fixed or other assets, the amount of debt borrowed or repaid, and the proceeds from the sale of stock or payments for dividends. In addition, an analysis of cash flows provides a good idea of a company's ability to pay its short-term obligations when they become due.

✓ Checkpoint

LEARNING OBJECTIVE 5: Explain the purpose of the income statement and the statement of cash flows.

SUMMARY: The income statement, also known as the profit and loss statement, reflects the results of operations over a period of time. It gives a general sense of a company's size and performance. The statement of cash flows shows how a company's cash was received and spent in three areas: operations, investments, and financing. It gives a general sense of the amount of cash created or consumed by daily operations, fixed assets, investments, and debt over a period of time.

CRITICAL THINKING: (1) How could two companies with similar gross profit figures end up with dramatically different net operating income? (2) How might a statement of cash flows help a turnaround expert decide how to rescue a struggling company?

IT'S YOUR BUSINESS: (1) What would your personal income statement look like today? Are you operating "at a profit" or "at a loss"? (2) What steps could you take to reduce your "operating expenses"?

KEY TERMS TO KNOW: income statement, expenses, net income, cost of goods sold, gross profit, operating expenses, EBITDA, statement of cash flows

EXHIBIT 5 | **Statement of Cash Flows for Computer Central Services**

A statement of cash flows shows a firm's cash receipts and cash payments as a result of three main activities—operating, investing, and financing—for an identified period of time (such as the year indicated here).

Computer Central Services

Statement of Cash Flows
Year ended December 31, 2012
($ thousands)

Most companies start with net income and make adjustments for various inflows and outflows throughout the year

Cash Flows from Operating Activities*

Net Income		$ 60,000
Adjustments to Reconcile Net Income to		
Net Cash Provided by Operating Activities	−40,000	
Net Cash Provided by or Used in Operating Activities		$20,000

The company had positive cash flow in two of the three cash flow categories

Cash from buying or selling property and securities

Cash Flows from Investing Activities

Purchase of Property and Equipment	−30,000	
Purchase of Securities	−115,000	
Redemption of Securities	125,000	
Net Cash Provided by or Used in Operating Activities		−20,000

Cash from borrowing or repaying existing debts

Cash Flows from Financing Activities

Loan Proceeds	15,000	
Payment of Long-Term Debt	−10,000	
Net Cash Provided by or Used in Operating Activites		5,000
Net (Decrease) Increase in Cash		5,000
Cash and Cash Equivalents at Beginning of Year		$18,000
Cash and Cash Equivalents at End of Year		$23,000

The company experienced a net increase in cash of $5 million over the course of the year

As a result of the $5 million cash inflow, the company ended the year with $23 million in cash

*Numbers preceded by minus sign indicate cash outflows.

Analyzing Financial Statements

6 **LEARNING OBJECTIVE**

Explain the purpose of ratio analysis, and list the four main categories of financial ratios.

After financial statements have been prepared, managers, investors, and lenders use these statements to evaluate the financial health of the organization, make business decisions, and spot opportunities for improvements by looking at the company's performance in relation to its past performance, the economy as a whole, and the performance of its competitors.

TREND ANALYSIS

The process of comparing financial data from year to year is known as *trend analysis*. You can use trend analysis to uncover shifts in the nature of a business over time. Of course, when you are comparing one period with another, it's important to take into account the effects of extraordinary or unusual items such as the sale of major assets, the purchase of a new line of products from another company, weather, or economic conditions that may have affected the company in one period but not the next. These extraordinary items are usually disclosed in the text portion of a company's annual report or in the notes to the financial statements.

RATIO ANALYSIS

Unlike trend analysis, which tracks *absolute* numbers from one year to the next, ratio analysis creates *relative* numbers by comparing sets of figures from a single year's performance. By using ratios rather than absolute amounts, analysts can more easily assess a company's performance from one year to the next or compare it with other companies. A variety of commonly used ratios help companies understand their current operations and answer some key questions: Is inventory too large? Are credit customers paying too slowly? Can the company pay its bills? Ratios also allow comparison with other companies within an industry, which helps gauge how well a company is doing relative to its competitors. Every industry tends to have its own "normal" ratios, which act as yardsticks for individual companies.

TYPES OF FINANCIAL RATIOS

Financial ratios can be organized into the following groups, as Exhibit 6 shows: profitability, liquidity, activity, and leverage (or debt).

Profitability Ratios

You can analyze how well a company is conducting its ongoing operations by computing *profitability ratios*, which show the state of the company's financial performance or how well it's generating profits. Three of the most common profitability ratios are **return on sales**, or *profit margin* (the net income a business makes per unit of sales); **return on equity** (net income divided by owners' equity); and **earnings per share** (the profit earned for each share of stock outstanding). Exhibit 6 shows how to compute these profitability ratios by using the financial information from Computer Central Services.

Liquidity Ratios

Liquidity ratios measure a firm's ability to pay its short-term obligations. As you might expect, lenders and creditors are keenly interested in liquidity measures. A company's **working capital** (current assets minus current liabilities) is an indicator of liquidity because it represents current assets remaining after the payment of all current liabilities. The dollar amount of working capital can be misleading, however. For example, it may include the value of slow-moving inventory items that cannot be used to help pay a company's short-term debts.

A different picture of the company's liquidity is provided by the **current ratio**—current assets divided by current liabilities. This figure compares the current debt owed with the current assets available to pay that debt. The **quick ratio**, also called the *acid-test ratio*, is computed by subtracting inventory from current assets and then dividing the result by current liabilities. This ratio is often a better indicator of a firm's ability to pay creditors than the current ratio because the quick ratio leaves out inventories—which at times might be difficult to sell. Analysts generally consider a quick ratio of 1.0 to be reasonable, whereas a current ratio of 2.0 is considered a safe risk for short-term credit. Exhibit 6 shows that both the current and quick ratios of Computer Central Services are well above these benchmarks and industry averages.

Activity Ratios

Activity ratios analyze how well a company is managing and making use of its assets. For companies that maintain inventories, the most common activity ratio is the **inventory turnover ratio**, which measures how fast a company's inventory is turned into sales. Inventory is a constant balancing act—hold too little, and you risk being out of stock when orders arrive; hold too much, and you raise your costs. When inventory sits on the shelf, money is tied up without earning interest; furthermore, the company incurs expenses for its storage, handling, insurance, and taxes. In addition, there is often a risk that the inventory will become obsolete or go out of style before it can be converted into finished goods and sold. Car dealers, for example, face the never-ending challenge of selling this year's models before next year's arrive. Newer models usually make the older models a lot less attractive in buyers' eyes, often requiring dealers to resort to steep discounts just to get rid of aging inventory.[21]

A recent study of U.S. manufacturers found wide disparities in inventory turnover, with the best performers moving their inventory four or five times faster than lower performers.[22] As with all ratios, however, it's important to dig below the surface after making an initial

---

return on sales The ratio between net income after taxes and net sales; also known as the *profit margin*

return on equity The ratio between net income after taxes and total owners' equity

earnings per share A measure of a firm's profitability for each share of outstanding stock, calculated by dividing net income after taxes by the average number of shares of common stock outstanding

working capital Current assets minus current liabilities

current ratio A measure of a firm's short-term liquidity, calculated by dividing current assets by current liabilities

quick ratio A measure of a firm's short-term liquidity, calculated by adding cash, marketable securities, and receivables, then dividing that sum by current liabilities; also known as the *acid-test ratio*

inventory turnover ratio A measure of the time a company takes to turn its inventory into sales, calculated by dividing cost of goods sold by the average value of inventory for a period

EXHIBIT 6 — How Well Does This Company Stack Up?

Financial ratios offer a quick and convenient way to evaluate how well a company is performing in relation to prior performance, the economy as a whole, and the company's competitors.

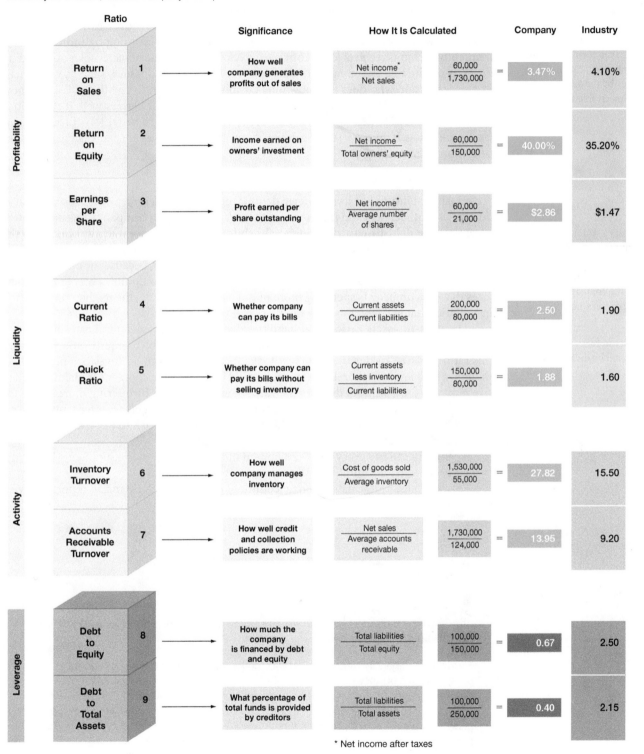

	Ratio		Significance	How It Is Calculated			Company	Industry
Profitability	Return on Sales	1	How well company generates profits out of sales	Net income* / Net sales	60,000 / 1,730,000	=	3.47%	4.10%
	Return on Equity	2	Income earned on owners' investment	Net income* / Total owners' equity	60,000 / 150,000	=	40.00%	35.20%
	Earnings per Share	3	Profit earned per share outstanding	Net income* / Average number of shares	60,000 / 21,000	=	$2.86	$1.47
Liquidity	Current Ratio	4	Whether company can pay its bills	Current assets / Current liabilities	200,000 / 80,000	=	2.50	1.90
	Quick Ratio	5	Whether company can pay its bills without selling inventory	Current assets less inventory / Current liabilities	150,000 / 80,000	=	1.88	1.60
Activity	Inventory Turnover	6	How well company manages inventory	Cost of goods sold / Average inventory	1,530,000 / 55,000	=	27.82	15.50
	Accounts Receivable Turnover	7	How well credit and collection policies are working	Net sales / Average accounts receivable	1,730,000 / 124,000	=	13.95	9.20
Leverage	Debt to Equity	8	How much the company is financed by debt and equity	Total liabilities / Total equity	100,000 / 150,000	=	0.67	2.50
	Debt to Total Assets	9	What percentage of total funds is provided by creditors	Total liabilities / Total assets	100,000 / 250,000	=	0.40	2.15

* Net income after taxes

comparison. For instance, a decline in a manufacturer's inventory turnover ratio could indicate that sales are slowing down, or it could mean sales are steady but the company made some forecasting errors and as a result produced more goods than it needed. Conversely, a company with a high ratio could be discounting heavily and not making as much money as it could by raising prices and lowering its sales volume.

Another useful activity ratio is the **accounts receivable turnover ratio**, which measures how well a company's credit and collection policies are working by indicating how frequently accounts receivable are converted to cash. The volume of receivables outstanding depends on the financial manager's decisions regarding several issues, such as who qualifies for credit and who does not, how long customers are given to pay their bills, and how aggressive the firm is in collecting its late payments. Be careful here as well. If the ratio is going up, you need to determine whether the company is doing a better job of collecting or if sales are rising. If the ratio is going down, it may be because sales are decreasing or because collection efforts are lagging.

Leverage, or Debt, Ratios

A company's ability to pay its long-term debts is reflected in its *leverage ratios*, also known as *debt ratios*. Both lenders and investors use these ratios to judge a company's risk and growth potential. The **debt-to-equity ratio** (total liabilities divided by total equity) indicates the extent to which a business is financed by debt as opposed to invested capital (equity). From a lender's standpoint, the higher this ratio is, the riskier the loan, because the company must devote more of its cash to debt payments. From an investor's standpoint, a higher ratio indicates that the company is spending more of its cash on interest payments than on investing in activities that will help raise the stock price.[23]

The **debt-to-assets ratio** (total liabilities divided by total assets) indicates how much of the company's assets are financed by creditors. As with the debt-to-equity ratio, the higher this ratio gets, the riskier the company looks to a lender. From an investor's perspective, though, a high level of debt relative to assets could indicate that a company is making aggressive moves to grow without diluting the value of existing shares by offering more shares for sale.[24] However, having a high level of debt to assets, or being *highly leveraged*, puts a company at risk. Those assets may not be able to generate enough cash to pay back the debt, or lenders and suppliers might cut off the company's credit.

Again, you can use every ratio as a helpful initial indicator but be sure to dig below the surface to see what the number really means.

For the latest information on accounting practices and financial reporting, visit http://real-timeupdates.com/bia6.

accounts receivable turnover ratio A measure of the time a company takes to turn its accounts receivable into cash, calculated by dividing sales by the average value of accounts receivable for a period

debt-to-equity ratio A measure of the extent to which a business is financed by debt as opposed to invested capital, calculated by dividing the company's total liabilities by owners' equity

debt-to-assets ratio A measure of a firm's ability to carry long-term debt, calculated by dividing total liabilities by total assets

✔ Checkpoint

LEARNING OBJECTIVE 6: Explain the purpose of ratio analysis, and list the four main categories of financial ratios.

SUMMARY: Financial ratios provide information for analyzing the health and future prospects of a business. Ratios facilitate financial comparisons among different-size companies and between a company and industry averages. Most of the important ratios fall into one of four categories: profitability ratios, which show how well the company generates profits; liquidity ratios, which measure the company's ability to pay its short-term obligations; activity ratios, which analyze how well a company is managing its assets; and debt ratios, which measure a company's ability to pay its long-term debt.

CRITICAL THINKING: (1) Why is it so important to be aware of extraordinary items when analyzing a company's finances? (2) Why is the quick ratio frequently a better indicator than the current ratio of a firm's ability to pay its bills?

IT'S YOUR BUSINESS: (1) Assume that you are about to make a significant consumer purchase, and the product is available at two local stores, one with high inventory turnover and one with low. Which store would you choose based on this information? Why? (2) If you were applying for a home mortgage loan today, would a lender view your debt-to-assets ratio favorably? Why or why not?

KEY TERMS TO KNOW: return on sales, return on equity, earnings per share, working capital, current ratio, quick ratio, inventory turnover ratio, accounts receivable turnover ratio, debt-to-equity ratio, debt-to-assets ratio

BEHIND THE SCENES

MyBizLab

GOOGLE THIS: "COST CONTROL"

By just about any measure you can think of, Google is one of the most spectacular success stories in the history of business. However, even a company as wealthy as Google has to control its spending.

Google's case is unusual in the sense of its sheer scale, but the story is not unique. When a young company is growing quickly and money is pouring in from sales or from investors, the natural tendency is to focus on building the business and capturing market opportunities. The less exciting—but ultimately no less important—task of creating a sustainable cost structure with rigorous expense management often doesn't get as much attention in the early years.

In some companies, rapid growth in a hot economy can mask serious underlying problems that threaten the long-term viability of the enterprise. In the dot-com boom of the late 1990s, for instance, more than a few high-flying companies fell to earth when investors who had enjoyed a rocket ride in the stock market realized the companies didn't have workable business models.

During the mid-2000s, Google's revenue had been increasing at a spectacular pace, from $10.6 billion in 2006, to $16.6 billion in 2007, to $21.8 billion in 2008. However, expenses were growing at an even faster rate. As a result, the company's profit margin dropped from 29 percent in 2006 to around 20 percent in 2008 (still 5 percentage points better than the industry average); 2008 ended with the first-ever drop in quarterly profits in the company's history.

The cooling economy and slowing profits didn't expose any fatal flaws in the Google business model, but the drop certainly was a wake-up call that emphasized the need to transition to the next stage of organizational development. It was time for the accounting and financial management functions to play a more prominent role and to transform a wild and wooly entrepreneurial success story into a major corporation with stable finances.

Back in 2001, Google cofounders Larry Page and Sergey Brin brought in Eric Schmidt, a seasoned technology industry executive, to guide the company's growth beyond its initial start-up stage. Under Schmidt's leadership, Google expanded from 200 employees to more than 20,000 and secured its place as one of the world's most influential companies. In 2008, facing the need for a more methodical approach to accounting and financial management, Schmidt brought in another executive with a proven track record in corporate leadership. Patrick Pichette made his name helping Bell Canada reduce operating expenses by $2 billion, and his proven ability to bring expenses in line with revenue was just what Google needed.

Pichette and other executives tackled expenses at three levels: employee perks, staffing, and project investment. It's safe to say the employee perks at Google are still better than you'll find just about anywhere, but they have been trimmed back to save money. The company no longer pays for the annual trip, and the $1,000 annual cash bonus was replaced with a $400 smartphone. The 50 percent discount on Google-branded clothes and other products was reduced to 20 percent, and the subsidy on hybrid vehicles was trimmed as well. On the plus side, employees still get free gourmet meals and subsidized concierge services to take some of the hassle out of handling life's little chores.

At the staffing level, Google is taking a much harder look at hiring practices to better align staffing with project needs. Tellingly, the first layoffs in the company's history, in January 2009, involved 100 recruiters whose services were no longer needed because Google's hiring rate had slowed so dramatically. Thousands of contract workers were let go as well. The vaunted "20 percent time" was reevaluated, too, with the company deciding to focus engineers' time more directly on core projects.

At the project and program levels, Google is scrutinizing its investments more carefully and pulling the plug on less-promising activities. Some of the higher-profile shutdowns in the past few years include Lively, a virtual world that would have competed with SecondLife; dMarc Broadcasting, a radio advertising company; Google Wave, a collaboration platform; and Google Labs, which did a lot of the company's speculative tinkering and experimentation. "More wood behind fewer arrows" is how Google describes its new emphasis on putting its resources into the projects most likely to have sizable long-term success.

Pichette leads by example when it comes to cost control, too—flying economy class in North America and riding to work on a bicycle that is so beat up he says he doesn't even bother to lock it up.

While continuing to manage costs more carefully, the company is also stepping up its efforts to generate more revenue. Key areas of focus include expanding the company's activities in mobile phone advertising and display advertising (graphical ads as opposed to the text-only ads that now appear next to Google searches), expanding Google+ to take on the mighty Facebook in social networking, growing its software and e-book revenue, and continuing to push YouTube toward profitability.

To say the effort has been a success would be a bit of an understatement. Expenses are down, and free cash flow is up dramatically. Even after that rough patch when the economy slowed ad sales, Google still ended 2008 with over $20 billion in current assets—and it raised that to almost $30 billion in 2009, over $40 billion in 2010 and headed for $50 billion and beyond.

Asked why the company was sitting on so much cash, Pichette explains that in the fast-changing world of search and other digital services, Google might need to jump on an acquisition almost overnight, with potentially billions of dollars of cash in hand. It might not have an infinite supply of money, but with a new focus on careful accounting, Google will have plenty of cash to keep its innovation engine churning out new ideas for years to come.[25]

Critical Thinking Questions

1. Given the eventual need for rigorous financial management, should every company have extensive cost controls in place from the first moment of operation? Explain your answer.
2. Google recently had a debt-to-equity ratio of 0.04. Microsoft, one of its key competitors, had a debt-to-equity ratio of 0.15. From a bank's point of view, which of the two companies is a more attractive loan candidate, based on this ratio? Why?
3. At the end of 2008, Google's current ratio was 8.77. Midway through 2009, the current ratio was up to 11.91. Does this make Google more or less of a credit risk in the eyes of potential lenders? Why?

LEARN MORE ONLINE

Visit Google's "Investor Relations" section, at http://investor.google.com. Peruse the latest financial news. How does the company's financial health look at present? What do the trends for revenue, expenses, and income look like? Does the company report both GAAP and non-GAAP financial results? Why does it report non-GAAP figures?

MyBizLab

Log on to www.mybizlab.com to access study and assessment aids associated with this chapter.

KEY TERMS

accounting
accounting equation
accounts receivable turnover ratio
accrual basis
assets
audit
balance sheet
bookkeeping
calendar year
cash basis
certified public accountants (CPAs)
closing the books
controller
cost of goods sold
current assets
current liabilities
current ratio
debt-to-assets ratio
debt-to-equity ratio
depreciation
double-entry bookkeeping
earnings per share
EBITDA
expenses
external auditors

financial accounting
fiscal year
fixed assets
GAAP (generally accepted accounting principles)
gross profit
income statement
international financial reporting standards
　(IFRS)
inventory turnover ratio
liabilities
long-term liabilities
management accounting
matching principle
net income
operating expenses
owners' equity
private accountants
public accountants
quick ratio
retained earnings
return on equity
return on sales
Sarbanes-Oxley
statement of cash flows
working capital

TEST YOUR KNOWLEDGE

Questions for Review

1. What is GAAP?
2. What is an audit, and why are audits performed?
3. What is the matching principle?
4. What are the three main profitability ratios, and how is each calculated?
5. What is the value of an income statement?

Questions for Analysis

6. Why are the GAAP and IFRS standards being converged?
7. Why would a company bother with double-entry bookkeeping?
8. Why are the costs of fixed assets depreciated?
9. Why would a bank lending officer be interested in the cash flow statement of a company that is applying for a loan?
10. Ethical Considerations. In the process of closing the company books, you encounter a problematic transaction. One of the company's customers was invoiced twice for the same project materials, resulting in a $1,000 overcharge. You immediately notify the controller, whose response is, "Let it go, it happens often. It'll probably balance out on some future transaction." What should you do now?

Questions for Application

11. The senior partner of an accounting firm is looking for ways to increase the firm's business. What other services besides traditional accounting can the firm offer to its clients? What new challenges might this additional work create?
12. Visit the websites of Google and Microsoft and retrieve their annual reports. Using these financial reports, compute the working capital, current ratio, and quick ratio for each company. Does one company appear to be more liquid than the other? Why?
13. If you were asked to lend money to your cousin's clothing store to help her through a slow sales period, would you be more interested in looking at the current ratio or the quick ratio as a measure of liquidity? Why?
14. Concept Integration. Your appliance manufacturing company recently implemented a just-in-time inventory system for all parts used in the manufacturing process. How might you expect this move to affect the company's inventory turnover rate, current ratio, and quick ratio?

EXPAND YOUR KNOWLEDGE

Discovering Career Opportunities

People interested in entering the field of accounting can choose among a wide variety of careers with diverse responsibilities and challenges. Visit the Accountants and Auditors page at www .bls.gov/oco/ocos001.htm to read more about career opportunities in accounting.

1. What are the day-to-day duties of this occupation? How would these duties contribute to the financial success of a company?
2. What skills and educational qualifications would you need to enter this occupation? How do these qualifications fit with your current plans, skills, and interests?
3. What kinds of employers hire people for this position? According to your research, does the number of employers seem to be increasing or decreasing? How do you think this trend will affect your employment possibilities if you choose this career?

Improving Your Tech Insights: GRC Software

The Sarbanes-Oxley Act's requirement that publicly traded companies regularly verify their internal accounting controls spurred the development of software tools to help companies flag and fix problems in their financial systems. In the past few years, a number of software vendors have gone beyond Sarbox compliance to integrate the monitoring of a wide range of legal and financial issues that require management attention. This new category of software is generally known as *governance, risk, and compliance (GRC) software*. GRC capabilities can either be built into other software packages (such as accounting and finance software, process management software, or business intelligence software) or offered as standalone compliance programs. Vendors that offer GRC capabilities include Oracle (www.oracle.com), SAP (www.sap.com), and OpenPages (www.openpages.com), among many others.

Explore one GRC software solution. In a brief email message to your instructor, describe the benefits of using this particular software package.[26]

PRACTICE YOUR SKILLS

Sharpening Your Communication Skills

Obtain a copy of the annual report of a business and examine what the report shows about finances and current operations.

- Consider the statements made by the CEO regarding the past year: Did the company do well, or are changes in operations necessary to its future well-being? What are the projections for future growth in sales and profits?
- Examine the financial summaries for information about the fiscal condition of the company: Did the company show a profit?

- If possible, obtain a copy of the company's annual report from the previous year and compare it with the current report to determine whether past projections were accurate.
- Prepare a brief written summary of your conclusions.

Building Your Team Skills

Divide into small groups and compute the following financial ratios for Alpine Manufacturing, using the company's balance sheet and income statement. Compare your answers to those of your classmates:

- Profitability ratios: return on sales; return on equity; earnings per share
- Liquidity ratios: current ratio; quick ratio
- Activity ratios: inventory turnover; accounts receivable turnover
- Leverage ratios: debt to equity; debt to total assets

ALPINE MANUFACTURING INCOME STATEMENT YEAR ENDED DECEMBER 31, 2012	
Sales	$1,800
Less: Cost of Goods Sold	1,000
Gross Profit	$ 800
Less: Total Operating Expenses	450
Net Operating Income Before Income Taxes	350
Less: Income Taxes	50
Net Income after Income Taxes	$ 300

ALPINE MANUFACTURING BALANCE SHEET DECEMBER 31, 2012		
ASSETS		
Cash	$ 100	
Accounts Receivable (beginning balance $350)	300	
Inventory (beginning balance $250)	300	
Current Assets	700	
Fixed Assets	2,300	
Total Assets		$3,000
LIABILITIES AND SHAREHOLDERS' EQUITY		
Current Liabilities (beginning balance $300)	$ 400	
Long-Term Debts	1,600	
Shareholders' Equity (100 common shares outstanding valued at $12 each)	1,000	
Total Liabilities and Shareholders' Equity		$3,000

Developing Your Research Skills

Select an article from a business journal or newspaper (print or online editions) that discusses the quarterly or year-end performance of a company that industry analysts consider notable for either positive or negative reasons.

1. Did the company report a profit or a loss for this accounting period? What other performance indicators were reported? Is the company's performance improving or declining?
2. Did the company's performance match industry analysts' expectations, or was it a surprise? How did analysts or other experts respond to the firm's actual quarterly or year-end results?
3. What reasons were given for the company's improvement or decline in performance?

REFERENCES

1. James Manyika, "Google's CFO on Growth, Capital Structure, and Leadership," McKinsey Quarterly, August 2011, www.mckinseyquarterly.com; Google financial profile on Trefis, accessed 10 September 2011, www.trefis.com; Bill Coughran, "More Wood Behind Fewer Arrows," Google blog, 20 July 2011, http://googleblog.blogspot.com; Julianne Pepitone, "Google Beats Profit Estimates," CNNMoney.com, 16 April 2009, http://money.cnn.com; "Frugal Google," Fortune, 22 January 2009, http://money.cnn.com/magazines/fortune; Miguel Helft, "Google's Profit Surges in Quarter," New York Times, 16 July 2009, www.nytimes.com; Catherine Clifford, "Layoffs Hit Google: 200 Jobs Cut," CNNMoney.com, 26 March 2009, http://money.cnn.com; Adam Lashinsky, "Belt-Tightening at Google," Fortune, 22 January 2009, http://money.cnn.com/magazines/fortune; Adam Lashinsky, "The Axman Comes to Google," Fortune, 23 March 2009, http://money.cnn.com/magazines/fortune; Google website, accessed 23 August 2009, www.google.com; Jessica E. Vascellaro and Scott Morrison, "Google Gears Down for Tougher Times," Wall Street Journal, 3 December 2008, http://online.wsj.com; Abbey Klaassen, "A Maturing Google Buckles Down and Searches for Cost Savings," Advertising Age, 1 December 2008, 3, 29.

2. "Accountants and Auditors," Occupational Outlook Handbook, 2010–11 Edition, U.S. Bureau of Labor Statistics website, www.bls.gov.

3. "Frequently Asked Questions," American Institute of Certified Public Accountants website, accessed 19 August 2009, www.aicpa.org.

4. "CMA: The Essential Credential," Institute of Management Accountants, accessed 10 September 2011, www.imanet.org.
5. "Accountants and Auditors," *Occupational Outlook Handbook, 2010-11 Edition*; Nanette Byrnes, "Green Eyeshades Never Looked So Sexy," *BusinessWeek*, 10 January 2005, 44; "Rules Make Accountants Newly Hot Commodity," *Oregonian*, 13 April 2005, www.ebsco.com.
6. Sarah Johnson, "Goodbye GAAP," *CFO*, 1 April 2008, www.cfo.com.
7. "Detecting Two Tricks of the Trade," Investopedia.com, accessed 19 August 2009, www.investopedia.com.
8. Johnson, "Goodbye GAAP."
9. American Institute of CPAs, "International Financial Reporting Standards (IFRS): An AICPA Backgrounder," 2011; PricewaterhouseCoopers, "IFRS and US GAAP: Similarities and Differences," September 2010; KPMG, "IFRS Compared to US GAAP: An Overview," September 2010.
10. American Institute of CPAs, "International Financial Reporting Standards (IFRS): An AICPA Backgrounder"; Johnson, "Goodbye GAAP."
11. Johnson, "Goodbye GAAP."
12. "Summary of SEC Actions and SEC Related Provisions Pursuant to the Sarbanes-Oxley Act of 2002," SEC website, accessed 9 May 2004, www.sec.gov; "Sarbanes-Oxley Act's Progress," *USA Today*, 26 December 2002, www.highbeam.com.
13. Scott Leibs, "Five Years and Counting," *CFO*, 1 July 2007, www.cfo.com.
14. David M. Katz, "CFOs Seek Sarbox Triage," *CFO*, 9 February 2006, www.cfo.com.
15. Sarah Johnson, "PCAOB Chairman Mark Olson to Retire," *CFO*, 9 June 2009, www.cfo.com.
16. Thayne Forbes, "Valuing Customers," *Journal of Database Marketing & Customer Strategy Management*, October 2007, 4–10.
17. Baruch Lev, "Sharpening the Intangibles Edge," *Harvard Business Review*, June 2004, 109–116.
18. "Google Inc. Financial," Google Finance, accessed 10 September 2011, www.google.com/finance.
19. "How to Spot Trouble in Your Financials," *Inc.*, October 2004, 96.
20. Ben McClure, "A Clear Look at EBITDA," Investopedia.com, 17 April 2010, www.investopedia.com; "Bobbie Gossage," Cranking Up the Earnings," *Inc.*, October 2004, 54; Lisa Smith, "EBITDA: Challenging the Calculation," Investopedia.com, 20 November 2009, www.investopedia.com.
21. Amy Wilson, "Old Vehicles Clog Dealer Lots," *Automotive News*, 11 May 2009, 4.
22. "Inventory Turnover," *Controller's Report*, October 2008, 13–14.
23. Jeffery Slater, *College Accounting: A Practical Approach*, 11th ed. (Upper Saddle River N.J.: Pearson Prentice Hall, 2010), 741.
24. Slater, *College Accounting: A Practical Approach*, 735.
25. See note 1.
26. Adapted from Mary Hayes Weier, "Companies Look to Contain Risk with GRC Software," *InformationWeek*, 5 April 2008, www.informationweek.com; OpenPages website, accessed 24 August 2009, www.openpages.com; Oracle website, accessed 24 August 2009, www.oracle.com; GRC Software Seems to be Rising," *FierceComplianceIT*, 12 March 2007, www.fiercecomplianceit.com; James Kobielus, "Compliance-Enabling Technologies via SOA on the Rise," *ITWorldCanada*, 8 March 2007, www.itworldcanada.com.

GLOSSARY

accounting equation The basic accounting equation, stating that assets equal liabilities plus owners' equity

accounting Measuring, interpreting, and communicating financial information to support internal and external decision making

accounts receivable turnover ratio A measure of the time a company takes to turn its accounts receivable into cash, calculated by dividing sales by the average value of accounts receivable for a period

accrual basis An accounting method in which revenue is recorded when a sale is made and an expense is recorded when it is incurred

assets Any things of value owned or leased by a business

audit Formal evaluation of the fairness and reliability of a client's financial statements

balance sheet A statement of a firm's financial position on a particular date; also known as a *statement of financial position*

bookkeeping Recordkeeping; the clerical aspect of accounting

calendar year A 12-month accounting period that begins on January 1 and ends on December 31

cash basis An accounting method in which revenue is recorded when payment is received and an expense is recorded when cash is paid

certified public accountants (CPAs) Professionally licensed accountants who meet certain requirements for education and experience and who pass a comprehensive examination

closing the books Transferring net revenue and expense account balances to retained earnings for the period

controller The highest-ranking accountant in a company, responsible for overseeing all accounting functions

cost of goods sold The cost of producing or acquiring a company's products for sale during a given period

current assets Cash and items that can be turned into cash within one year

current liabilities Obligations that must be met within a year

current ratio A measure of a firm's short-term liquidity, calculated by dividing current assets by current liabilities

debt-to-assets ratio A measure of a firm's ability to carry long-term debt, calculated by dividing total liabilities by total assets

debt-to-equity ratio A measure of the extent to which a business is financed by debt as opposed to invested capital, calculated by dividing the company's total liabilities by owners' equity

depreciation An accounting procedure for systematically spreading the cost of a tangible asset over its estimated useful life

double-entry bookkeeping A method of recording financial transactions that requires a debit entry and credit entry for each transaction to ensure that the accounting equation is always kept in balance

earnings per share A measure of a firm's profitability for each share of outstanding stock, calculated by dividing net income after taxes by the average number of shares of common stock outstanding

EBITDA Earnings before interest, taxes, depreciation, and amortization

expenses Costs created in the process of generating revenues

external auditors Independent accounting firms that provide auditing services for public companies

financial accounting The area of accounting concerned with preparing financial information for users outside the organization

fiscal year Any 12 consecutive months used as an accounting period

fixed assets Assets retained for long-term use, such as land, buildings, machinery, and equipment; also referred to as *property, plant, and equipment*

GAAP (generally accepted accounting practices) Standards and practices used by publicly held corporations in the United States and a few other countries in the preparation of financial statements; on course to converge with IFRS

gross profit The amount remaining when the cost of goods sold is deducted from net sales; also known as *gross margin*

income statement A financial record of a company's revenues, expenses, and profits over a given period of time; also known as a *profit and loss statement*

international financial reporting standards (IFRS) Accounting standards and practices used in many countries outside the United States

inventory turnover ratio A measure of the time a company takes to turn its inventory into sales, calculated by dividing cost of goods sold by the average value of inventory for a period

liabilities Claims against a firm's assets by creditors

long-term liabilities Obligations that fall due more than a year from the date of the balance sheet

management accounting The area of accounting concerned with preparing data for use by managers within the organization

matching principle The fundamental principle requiring that expenses incurred in producing revenue be deducted from the revenues they generate during an accounting period

net income Profit earned or loss incurred by a firm, determined by subtracting expenses from revenues; casually referred to as the *bottom line*

operating expenses All costs of operation that are not included under cost of goods sold

owners' equity The portion of a company's assets that belongs to the owners after obligations to all creditors have been met

private accountants In-house accountants employed by organizations and businesses other than a public accounting firm; also called *corporate accountants*

public accountants Professionals who provide accounting services to other businesses and individuals for a fee

quick ratio A measure of a firm's short-term liquidity, calculated by adding cash, marketable securities, and receivables, then dividing that sum by current liabilities; also known as the *acid-test ratio*

retained earnings The portion of shareholders' equity earned by the company but not distributed to its owners in the form of dividends

return on equity The ratio between net income after taxes and total owners' equity

return on sales The ratio between net income after taxes and net sales; also known as the *profit margin*

Sarbanes-Oxley The informal name of comprehensive legislation designed to improve integrity and accountability of financial information

statement of cash flows A statement of a firm's cash receipts and cash payments that presents information on its sources and uses of cash

working capital Current assets minus current liabilities

The Art and Science of Marketing

From Chapter 13 of *Business in Action*, Sixth Edition. Courtland L. Bovée, John V. Thill. Copyright © 2013 by Pearson Education, Inc. Published by Pearson Business. All rights reserved.

The Art and Science of Marketing

LEARNING OBJECTIVES   After studying this chapter, you will be able to

1 Define *marketing* and explain its role in society

2 Identify three trends that help define contemporary marketing

3 Differentiate between consumer buying behavior and organizational buying behavior

4 Define *strategic marketing planning* and identify the four basic options for pursuing new marketing opportunities

5 Identify the four steps in crafting a marketing strategy

6 Describe the four main components of the marketing mix

MyBizLab

Where you see MyBizLab in this chapter, go to www.mybizlab.com for additional activities on the topic being discussed.

BEHIND THE SCENES RED ANTS PANTS GIVE WORKING WOMEN A CHOICE THAT FITS

Sarah Calhoun of Red Ants Pants crafted a successful marketing mix to fulfill her mission of providing hardwearing pants for hardworking women.

Photo By Erik Peterson, Courtesy of Sarah Calhoun

www.redantspants.com

Something doesn't add up here:

1. Thousands and thousands of women work in heavy labor jobs, from farming and ranching to welding, construction, and pile driving. In fact, a quarter of the workforce in the building trades, agriculture, fishing, and forestry are women.
2. The kind of work these women perform quickly shreds regular clothing. They need heavy duty duds.
3. Carhartt and other work clothing suppliers sell heavy-duty pants that can stand up to the rigors of tough work, but when Sarah Calhoun surveyed the market, these suppliers focused on work pants made for men.
4. Women aren't shaped like men.

Calhoun wasn't a clothing designer, didn't work in the business, and wasn't chasing some lifelong entrepreneurial dream. But she was fed up—with men's work pants that didn't fit or women's regular pants that didn't hold up under the stress and strain of clearing trails, peeling logs, and doing the other sorts of work she took on in her adopted home state of Montana.

Tired of constantly putting down her tools so she could pull up her misfit britches, Calhoun decided to solve the problem herself. She launched Red Ants Pants with the single-minded goal of outfitting women who need rugged workwear.

Why "Red Ants Pants," by the way? In a conversation with a biologist about the social behaviors of ants, she learned that in red ant colonies, females do most of the work. In keeping with the

154

cheeky style she adopted for all her company's communication, she uses the name as a salute to hardworking women everywhere.

Calhoun was convinced she had spotted a business opportunity, but what was the best way to pursue it? How could a total outsider—based in White Sulphur Springs, Montana, no less—break into the clothing industry? How could she design a product that would meet the needs of her target customers?

How many choices should she offer in terms of colors, styles, and sizes? What could she do to craft a compelling message and get that message in front of the buying public? How should she price the high-quality product she had in mind? What about distribution and the rest of the marketing mix? If you were in Calhoun's position, how would you go about marketing Red Ants Pants?[1]

INTRODUCTION

Sarah Calhoun's experience in introducing the Red Ants Pants brand (profiled in the chapter-opening Behind the Scenes) illustrates the complex challenge of fashioning an appealing blend of products, prices, distribution methods, and customer communication efforts—the essential elements of marketing. This chapter introduces the basic concepts of marketing.

My BizLab

Gain hands-on experience through an interactive, real-world scenario. This chapter's simulation entitled Market Research Matters is located at **www.mybizlab.com.**

Marketing in a Changing World

Marketing requires a wide range of skills, from research and analysis to strategic planning to persuasive communication. On the job and in the media, you will encounter many uses of the term *marketing*, from the broad and strategic to the narrow and tactical. However, noted marketing professors Philip Kotler and Gary Armstrong offer a definition that does a great job of highlighting the contemporary flavor of customer-focused marketing: **Marketing** is "the process by which companies create value for customers and build strong customer relationships in order to capture value from customers in return."[2] The ideas of *value*, the *exchange* of value, and lasting *relationships* are essential elements of successful marketing.

In addition to goods and services, marketing applies to not-for-profit organizations, people, places, and causes. Politicians and celebrities constantly market themselves. So do places that want to attract residents, tourists, and business investments. **Place marketing** describes efforts to market geographic areas ranging from neighborhoods to entire countries. **Cause-related marketing** promotes a cause or a social issue—such as physical fitness, cancer awareness, environmental sustainability—while also promoting a company and its products.

1 LEARNING OBJECTIVE

Define *marketing*, and explain its role in society.

marketing The process of creating value for customers and building relationships with those customers in order to capture value back from them

place marketing Marketing efforts to attract people and organizations to a particular geographical area

cause-related marketing Identification and marketing of a social issue, cause, or idea to selected target markets

THE ROLE OF MARKETING IN SOCIETY

Marketing plays an important role in society by helping people satisfy their needs and wants and by helping organizations determine what to produce.

Needs and Wants

Individuals and organizations have a wide variety of needs, from food and water necessary for survival to transaction processing systems that make sure a retail store gets paid for all the credit card purchases it records. As a consumer, you experience **needs** any time there are differences or gaps between your actual state and your ideal state. You're hungry and you don't want to be hungry: You need to eat. Needs create the motivation to buy products and are, therefore, at the core of any discussion of marketing.

Your **wants** are based on your needs but are more specific. Producers do not create needs, but they do try to shape your wants by exposing you to attractive choices. For instance, when you *need* some food, you may *want* a Snickers bar, an orange, or a seven-course dinner at the swankiest restaurant in town. If you have the means, or *buying power*, to purchase the product you want, you create *demand* for that product.[3]

needs Differences between a person's actual state and his or her ideal state; they provide the basic motivation to make a purchase

wants Specific goods, services, experiences, or other entities that are desirable in light of a person's experiences, culture, and personality

Avon has made breast cancer awareness and research funding a focus of its cause-related marketing.

exchange process The act of obtaining a desired object or service from another party by offering something of value in return

transaction An exchange of value between parties

utility The power of a good or service to satisfy a human need

Exchanges and Transactions

When you participate in the **exchange process**, you trade something of value (usually money) for something else of value. When you make a purchase, you encourage the producer of that item to create or supply more of it. In this way, supply and demand tend toward balance, and society obtains the goods and services that are most satisfying. When the exchange actually occurs, it takes the form of a **transaction**. Party A gives Party B $1.29 and gets a medium Coke in return. A trade of values takes place.

Most transactions in today's society involve money, but money is not necessarily required. Bartering or trading, which predates the use of cash, is making a big comeback thanks to the Internet. Hundreds of online barter exchanges are now in operation in the United States alone. Intermediaries such as BizXchange (www.bizx.com) facilitate cashless trading among multiple members through a system of credits and debits. For instance, an advertising agency might trade services to a dairy farm, which then trades products to a catering company, which then trades services to the advertising agency. By eliminating the need for trading partners to have exactly complimentary needs at exactly the same time, these exchanges make it easy for companies to buy and sell without using cash.[4]

The Four Utilities

To encourage the exchange process, marketers enhance the appeal of their goods and services by adding **utility**, which is any attribute that increases the value that customers place on the product (see Exhibit 1). When organizations change raw materials into finished goods, they are creating *form utility* desired by consumers. When supermarkets provide fresh, ready-to-eat dishes as an alternative to food ingredients, they are creating form utility. In other cases, marketers try to make their products available when and where customers want to buy them, creating *time utility* and *place utility*. Overnight couriers such as FedEx create time utility, whereas coffee carts in office buildings and ATMs in shopping malls create place utility. Services such as Apple's iTunes create both time and place utility: You can purchase music almost instantly, without leaving your computer. The final form of utility is *possession utility*—the satisfaction that buyers get when they actually possess a product, both legally and physically. Mortgage companies, for example, create possession utility by offering loans that allow people to buy homes they could otherwise not afford.

marketing concept An approach to business management that stresses customer needs and wants, seeks long-term profitability, and integrates marketing with other functional units within the organization

THE MARKETING CONCEPT

Business's view of the marketing function has evolved rather dramatically over the decades. In years past, many companies pursued what was known as the *product concept*, which was essentially to focus on the production of goods and count on customers to figure out which products they needed and take the steps to find and purchase them. In other words, the product concept views the primary purpose of a business as making things, not satisfying customers. As markets evolved and competition heated up, the *sales concept* began to take over, which emphasizes building a business by generating as many sales transactions as possible. The customer features more prominently in the sales concept, but only as a target to be sold to, not as a partner in a mutually satisfying relationship.

In contrast, today's most successful companies tend to embrace the **marketing concept**, the idea that companies should respond to customers' needs and wants while seeking long-term profitability and coordinating their own marketing

EXHIBIT 1	Examples of the Four Utilities

The utility of a good or service has four aspects, each of which enhances the product's value to the consumer.

Utility	Example
Form utility	Kettle Valley's Fruit Snack (www.kettlevalley.net) bars provide the nutritional value of real fruit in a form that offers greater convenience and longer storage life.
Time utility	LensCrafters (www.lenscrafters.com) has captured a big chunk of the market for eyeglasses by providing on-the-spot, one-hour service.
Place utility	By offering convenient home delivery of the latest fashion apparel and accessories, dELiA*s (www.delias.com) catalog and website have become favorites of teenage girls.
Possession utility	RealNetworks's Rhapsody music streaming service (www.rhapsody.com) gives customers the option of buying individual songs.

efforts to achieve the company's long-term goals (see Exhibit 2). These *customer-focused* companies build their marketing strategies around the goal of long-term relationships with satisfied customers.[5] The term **relationship marketing** is often applied to these efforts to distinguish them from efforts that emphasize production or sales transactions. One of the most significant goals of relationship marketing is **customer loyalty**, the degree to which customers continue to buy from a particular retailer or buy the products offered by a particular manufacturer. The payoff from becoming customer focused can be considerable, but the process of transforming a product-or sales-driven company into one that embraces the

relationship marketing A focus on developing and maintaining long-term relationships with customers, suppliers, and distribution partners for mutual benefit

customer loyalty The degree to which customers continue to buy from a particular retailer or buy the products of a particular manufacturer or service provider

EXHIBIT 2	The Selling Concept Versus the Marketing Concept

Firms that practice the selling concept sell what they make rather than making what the market wants. In contrast, firms that practice the marketing concept determine the needs and wants of a market and deliver the desired product or service more effectively and efficiently than competitors do.

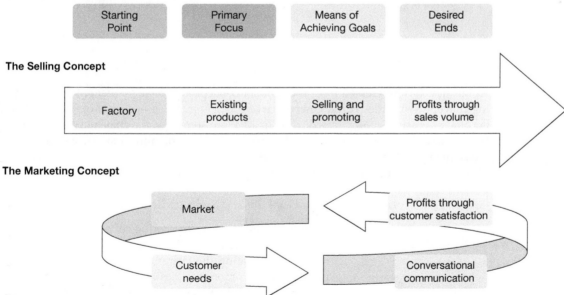

Source: Adapted in part from Philip Kotler and Gary Armstrong, *Principles of Marketing*, 13th ed. (Upper Saddle River, N.J.: Pearson Prentice Hall, 2010), 10.

marketing concept can take years and may involve changes to major systems and processes throughout the company, as well as the basic culture of the company.[6]

Why all the emphasis on customer service and customer satisfaction in the marketing concept? It's not just about being nice and helpful; satisfying customers is simply smart business. For one thing, keeping your existing customers is usually much cheaper and easier than finding new customers. For another, satisfied customers are the best promotion a company can hope for, particularly given the power of social media and social commerce.

✓ Checkpoint

LEARNING OBJECTIVE 1: Define *marketing*, and explain its role in society.

SUMMARY: Marketing can be defined as "the process by which companies create value for customers and build strong customer relationships in order to capture value from customers in return." The marketing function guides a company in selecting which products to offer, how much to charge for them, how to distribute them to customers, and how to promote them to potential buyers. Marketing plays an important role in society by helping people satisfy their needs and wants and by helping organizations determine what to produce.

CRITICAL THINKING: (1) Should every company see long-term relationships with customers to the same degree? Why or why not? (2) Would a company that already dominates its markets ever care about the marketing concept? Why or why not?

IT'S YOUR BUSINESS: (1) What is your reaction when you feel as though you're being "sold to" by a company that is clearly more interested in selling products than in meeting your needs as an individual consumer? (2) Do you want to have a "relationship" with any of the companies that you currently patronize as a customer? Why or why not?

KEY TERMS TO KNOW: marketing, place marketing, cause-related marketing, needs, wants, exchange process, transaction, utility, marketing concept, relationship marketing, customer loyalty

---

2 | **LEARNING OBJECTIVE**

Identify three trends that help define contemporary marketing.

Challenges in Contemporary Marketing

As business has progressed from the product concept to the sales concept to the marketing concept—with the critical emergence of social commerce—the role of marketing has become increasingly complicated. You'll read about some specific challenges in this chapter, but here are three general issues that many marketing organizations are wrestling with today: involving the customer in the marketing process, making data-driven decisions, and conducting marketing activities with greater concern for ethics and etiquette.

INVOLVING THE CUSTOMER IN THE MARKETING PROCESS

REAL-TIME UPDATES
Learn More by Reading This Article

Read the inside story on being customer focused

Tony Hsieh, CEO of Zappos, explains how a culture deeply rooted in customer focus (and employee empowerment) is the foundation of the company's success. Go to http://real-timeupdates.com/bia6 and click on Learn More. If you are using MyBizLab, you can access Real-Time Updates within the chapter or under Student Study Tools.

A central element in the marketing concept is involving the customer as a partner in a mutually beneficial relationship rather than treating the customer as a passive recipient of products and promotional messages. Involving the customer has always been relatively easy for small, local companies and for large companies with their major customers. For instance, a neighborhood bistro or coffee shop can prepare foods and drinks just the way its regular customers want, and satisfied customers are happy to tell friends and relatives about their favorite places to eat and drink. At the other extreme, a maker of jet engines such as Pratt & Whitney or Rolls-Royce works closely with its airplane manufacturing customers to create exactly the products those customers want.

The challenge has been to replicate this level of intimacy on a broader scale, when a company has thousands of customers spread across the country or around the world. Two sets of technologies have helped foster communication and collaboration between companies and their customers. The first is **customer relationship management (CRM)** systems, which capture, organize, and capitalize on all the interactions that a company has with its customers, from marketing surveys and advertising through sales orders and customer support. A CRM system functions like an institutional memory for a company, allowing it to record and act on the information that is pertinent to each customer relationship.

CRM can be a powerful means to foster relationships, but to a certain degree, conventional CRM simply computerizes an existing way of doing business. A more dramatic step is enabling **social commerce**, using blogs, wikis, *user-generated content* such as online videos or customer-created advertising, and other social media technologies. These tools let customers communicate with companies, with each other, and with other influences in the marketplace such as prominent bloggers and journalists. For example, social networks such as Facebook have the potential to redefine advertising because consumers tend to view friends and peers as more reliable sources of product information than advertising.[7] Another valuable use of social media is listening to feedback from customers.[8] Innovative companies are beginning to integrate these two relationship technologies, combining the data capture and retrieval of CRM with the interactivity of social media.[9]

customer relationship management (CRM) A type of information system that captures, organizes, and capitalizes on all the interactions that a company has with its customers

social commerce The creation and sharing of product-related information among customers and potential customers

MAKING DATA-DRIVEN MARKETING DECISIONS

Learning more about customers is one aspect of the larger challenge of collecting, analyzing, and using data to make marketing decisions. Marketers in every industry would like to have better insights for making decisions and better ways of measuring the results of every marketing initiative. Pioneering retailer John Wannamaker said 100 years ago that "half the money I spend on advertising is wasted. The trouble is, I don't know which half."[10] Actually, Wannamaker was probably overly optimistic. In one extensive study, advertising was found to increase revenue for just over half of new products but for only one-third of existing products.[11] In other words, according to this research, the advertising campaigns for two-thirds of established products in the marketplace don't bring in more revenue.

Understandably, top executives are demanding that marketing departments do a better job of justifying their budgets and finding the most effective ways of meeting marketing objectives. However, this accountability challenge is not a simple one, and the problem may never be completely solvable for many companies. With so many sources of information in the marketplace, particularly with the continuing growth of online and mobile marketing channels, identifying which sources influence which aspects of buyer behavior can be difficult.

To get a better idea of how well their marketing budgets are being spent, companies can use a class of tools and techniques called *marketing analytics*. For example, Google Analytics helps online advertisers measure the effectiveness of specific search-term keywords and track the behavior of website visitors from their initial landing on an e-commerce site on through to a purchase.[12] By integrating such tools into an overall measurement system that evaluates both online and offline marketing activities, a company can improve its decision making and focus its time and money in the most productive marketing efforts.

The process of gathering and analyzing *market intelligence* about customers, competitors, and related marketing issues through any combination of methods is known as **marketing research**. As markets grow increasingly dynamic and open to competition from all parts of the globe, today's companies realize that information is the key to successful action. Without it, they're forced to use guesswork, analogies from other markets that may or may not apply, or experience from the past that may not correspond to the future.[13]

At the same time, however, marketing research can't provide the answer to every strategic or tactical question. As

marketing research The collection and analysis of information for making marketing decisions

REAL-TIME UPDATES
Learn More by Reading This Article

Marketing research tutorial

This three-part series offers a great overview of research strategies and techniques. Go to http://real-timeupdates.com/bia6 and click on Learn More. If you are using MyBizLab, you can access Real-Time Updates within the chapter or under Student Study Tools.

a manager or an entrepreneur, you'll find yourself in situations that require creative thinking and careful judgment to make the leap beyond what the data alone can tell you. Research techniques range from the basic to the exotic, from simple surveys to advanced statistical techniques to neurological scanning that tries to discover how and why customers' brains respond to visual and verbal cues about products. You can see a sample of techniques in Exhibit 3.

MARKETING WITH GREATER CONCERN FOR ETHICS AND ETIQUETTE

Under pressure to reach and persuade buyers in a business environment that gets more fragmented and noisy all the time, marketers occasionally step over the line and engage in practices that are rude, manipulative, or even downright deceptive. The result is an increasing degree of skepticism of and hostility toward advertising and other marketing activities.[14]

To avoid intensifying the vicious circle in which marketers keep doing the same old things, only louder and longer—leading customers to get more angry and more

EXHIBIT 3	Marketing Research Techniques

Marketers can use a wide variety of techniques to learn more about customers, competitors, and threats and opportunities in the marketplace.

Technique	Examples
Observation	Any in-person, mechanical, or electronic technique that monitors and records behavior, including website usage tracking and monitoring of blogs and social networking websites.
Surveys	Data collection efforts that measure responses from a representative subset of a larger group of people; can be conducted in person (when people with clipboards stop you in a mall, that's called a *mall intercept*), over the phone, by mail or email, or online. Designing and conducting a meaningful survey requires thorough knowledge of statistical techniques such as *sampling* to ensure valid results that truly represent the larger group. For this reason, many of the simple surveys that you see online these days do not produce statistically valid results.
Interviews and focus groups	One-on-one or group discussions that try to probe deeper into issues than a survey typically does. *Focus groups* involve a small number of people guided by a facilitator while being observed or recorded by researchers. Unlike surveys, interviews and focus groups are not designed to collect statistics that represent a larger group; their real value is in uncovering issues that might require further study.
Process data collection	Any method of collecting data during the course of other business tasks, including warranty registration cards, sales transaction records, gift and loyalty program card usage, and customer service interactions.
Experiments	Controlled scenarios in which researchers adjust one or more variables to measure the effect these changes have on customer behavior. For instance, separate groups of consumers can be exposed to different ads to see which ad is most effective. *Test marketing*, the launch of a product under real-world conditions but on a limited scale (such as in a single city), is a form of experimental research.
Ethnographic research	A branch of anthropology that studies people in their daily lives to learn about their needs, wants, and behaviors in real-life settings.
Neuromarketing studies	Research that measures brain activity while customers are viewing or interacting with product, websites, or other elements.

Sources: Adapted from Ken Anderson, "Ethnographic Research: A Key to Strategy," *Harvard Business Review*, March 2009, 24; Emily R. Murphy, Judy Illes, and Peter B. Reiner, "Neuroethics of Neuromarketing," *Journal of Consumer Behaviour*, July–October 2008, 293–302; Dick Bucci, "Recording Systems Add More Depth When Capturing Answers," *Marketing News*, 1 March 2005, 50; Laurence Bernstein, "Enough Research Bashing!" *Marketing*, 24 January 2005, 10; Naresh K. Malhotra, *Basic Marketing Research* (Upper Saddle River, N.J.: Pearson Prentice Hall, 2002), 110–112, 208–212, 228–229.

defensive—some marketers are looking for a better way. Social commerce shows a lot of promise for redefining marketing communication from one-way promotion to two-way conversation. Another hopeful sign is **permission-based marketing**, in which marketers invite potential or current customers to receive information in areas that genuinely interest them. Many websites now take this approach, letting visitors sign up for specific content streams with the promise that they won't be bombarded with information they don't care about.

The widespread adoption of social media has also increased the attention given to transparency, which in this context refers to a sense of openness, of giving all participants in a conversation access to the information they need to accurately process the messages they are receiving. A key aspect of transparency is knowing who is behind the messages one receives. Consider the promotional event that Netflix staged in Toronto to announce the launch of its streaming video service in Canada. The outdoor news conference seemed to attract dozens of curious people who were excited about the availability of Netflix. However, many of these people who "spontaneously" showed up were actually paid actors with instructions to "look really excited, particularly if asked by media to do any interviews about the prospect of Netflix in Canada." The company apologized when the stunt was exposed.[15]

A major issue in business communication transparency is **stealth marketing**, which involves attempting to promote products and services to customers who don't know they're being marketed to. A common stealth marketing technique is rewarding someone for promoting products to his or her friends without telling them it's a form of advertising. Critics—including the U.S. Federal Trade Commission (FTC) and the Word of Mouth Marketing Association—assert that such techniques are deceptive because they don't give their targets the opportunity to raise their instinctive defenses against the persuasive powers of marketing messages.[16]

Aside from ethical concerns, trying to fool the public is simply bad for business. As LaSalle University professor Michael Smith puts it, "The public backlash can be long, deep, and damaging to a company's reputation."[17]

permission-based marketing
A marketing approach in which firms first ask permission to deliver messages to an audience and then promise to restrict their communication efforts to those subject areas in which audience members have expressed interest

stealth marketing The delivery of marketing messages to people who are not aware that they are being marketed to; these messages can be delivered by either acquaintances or strangers, depending on the technique

✔ Checkpoint

LEARNING OBJECTIVE 2: Identify three trends that help define contemporary marketing.

SUMMARY: Three general issues that many marketing organizations are wrestling with today are involving the customer in the marketing process, making data-driven decisions, and conducting marketing with greater concern for ethics and etiquette. Allowing customers greater involvement is essential to relationship marketing and the marketing concept. Increasingly, this involvement is enabled by *social commerce*—customers using social media to converse with companies and each other. Data-driven decision making is a top priority as many companies struggle to justify and optimize marketing expenditures. Public opinion of business in general and marketing in particular is at a low point these days, prompting many professionals to take a closer look at their business practices and relationships with customers.

CRITICAL THINKING: (1) How can technology help companies replicate the community feel of a small neighborhood business on a global scale? (2) Why do some critics consider stealth marketing to be unethical?

IT'S YOUR BUSINESS: (1) Are you so loyal to any brands or companies that you refuse to accept substitutes—so much so that if you can't have your favorite product, you'll do without? What is it about these products that earns your continued loyalty? (2) Have you ever been a target of stealth marketing? If so, how did you feel about the company after you learned you had been marketed to without your knowledge?

KEY TERMS TO KNOW: customer relationship management (CRM), social commerce, marketing research, permission-based marketing, stealth marketing

Differentiate between consumer
buying behavior and
organizational buying behavior.

consumer market Individuals or
households that buy goods and
services for personal use

organizational market
Companies, government agencies,
and other organizations that buy
goods and services either to resell
or to use in the creation of their
own goods and services

Understanding Today's Customers

To implement the marketing concept, companies must have good information about what
customers want. Today's customers, both individual consumers and organizational buyers,
are a diverse and demanding group, with little patience for marketers who do not understand
them or will not adapt business practices to meet their needs. For instance, consumers faced
with complex purchase decisions such as cars can now find extensive information online about
products, prices, competitors, customer service rankings, safety issues, and other factors.

The first step toward understanding customers is recognizing the purchase and ownership habits of the **consumer market**, made up of individuals and families who buy for
personal or household use, and the **organizational market**, composed of companies and a
variety of noncommercial institutions, from local school districts to the federal government.

Exhibit 4 models two decision-making paths that buyers can take when they perceive
the need to make a purchase, one for routine purchases and one for new, unusual, or highly
significant purchases. Consumers and organizations can follow either path, depending on
a specific purchase. Broadly speaking, however, organizational buyers tend to approach
purchasing in a more rational, data-driven fashion, simply because organizational choices
are nearly always about functional and financial value.

THE CONSUMER DECISION PROCESS

Think about several purchase decisions you've made recently. Classical economics suggests
that your behavior would follow a rational process of first recognizing a need and then gathering information, identifying alternative solutions, and finally making your choice from
those alternatives. But how often do you really make decisions in this way? Researchers now
understand that consumer behavior tends to be far less logical and far more complicated—
and more interesting—than this model suggests. In fact, some research suggests that as
much as 95 percent of the decision-making process is subconscious and that sensory cues
can play a much larger role than objective information.[18] The emerging field of *behavioral
economics* is starting to offer better insights into consumer behavior by incorporating a
broader (and somewhat less-flattering) view of the way people really make decisions.[19]

EXHIBIT 4	Buyer Decision Making

The steps buyers go through on the way to making a purchase vary widely, based on the magnitude of the purchase and the significance of the
outcome. In general, businesses and other organizations use a more formal and more rational process than consumers, and nonroutine decisions
in either sector require more time and energy than routine decisions. Defining *routine* is not a simple matter, however; a company might make huge
resupply purchases automatically while a consumer spends days agonizing over a pair of jeans.

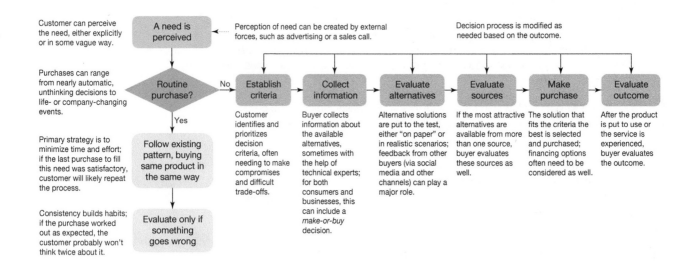

Even in situations in which consumers gather lots of information and appear to be making a well-thought-out, rational decision, they often are acting more on gut feelings and emotional responses. For instance, you might see some jaw-dropping sports car glide past you on the street, and in that split second—before you even start "thinking" about it—you've already decided to buy one just like it. Sure, you'll gather brochures, do research on the Internet, test-drive other models, and so on, but chances are you're not really evaluating alternatives. Instead, your rational, conscious brain is just looking for evidence to support the decision that your emotional, semiconscious brain has already made.

Moreover, consumers make all kinds of decisions that are hard to explain by any rational means. We might spend two weeks gathering data on $200 music players but choose a college with a $20,000 annual tuition simply because a best friend is going there. Sometimes we buy things for no apparent reason other than the fact that we have money in our pockets. As a result, at one time or another, all consumers suffer from **cognitive dissonance**, which occurs when one's beliefs and behaviors don't match. A common form of this situation is *buyer's remorse*, in which one makes a purchase and then regrets doing so—sometimes immediately after the purchase.

You can start to understand why so many decisions seem mysterious from a rational point of view if you consider all the influences that affect purchases:

- **Culture.** The cultures (and subgroups within cultures) that people belong to shape their values, attitudes, and beliefs and influence the way they respond to the world around them.
- **Socioeconomic level.** In addition to being members of a particular culture, people also perceive themselves as members of a certain social class—be it upper, middle, lower, or somewhere in between. In general, members of various classes pursue different activities, buy different goods, shop in different places, and react to different media—or at least like to believe they do.
- **Reference groups.** Individuals are influenced by *reference groups* that provide information about product choices and establish values that they perceive as important. Reference groups can be either *membership* or *aspirational*. As the name suggests, membership groups are those to which consumers actually belong, such as families, networks of friends, clubs, and work groups. In contrast, consumers are not members of aspirational reference groups but use them as role models for style, speech, opinions, and various other behaviors.[20] For instance, millions of consumers buy products that help them identify with popular musicians or professional athletes.
- **Situational factors.** These factors include events or circumstances in people's lives that are more circumstantial but that can influence buying patterns. Such factors can range from having a coupon to celebrating a holiday to being in a bad mood. If you've ever indulged in "retail therapy" to cheer yourself up, you know all about situational factors—and the buyer's remorse that often comes with it.
- **Self-image.** Many consumers tend to believe that "you are what you buy," so they make or avoid choices that support their desired self-images. Marketers capitalize on people's need to express their identity through their purchases by emphasizing the image value of goods and services.

THE ORGANIZATIONAL CUSTOMER DECISION PROCESS

The purchasing behavior of organizations is easier to understand than the purchasing behavior of consumers because it's more clearly driven by economics and influenced less by subconscious and emotional factors. Here are some of the significant ways in which organizational purchasing differs from consumer purchasing:[21]

- **An emphasis on economic payback and other rational factors.** Much more so than with consumer purchases, organizational purchases are carefully evaluated for financial impact, reliability, and other objective factors. Organizations don't always make the

REAL-TIME UPDATES
Learn More by Reading This Article

Take a closer look at consumer buying behavior

This tutorial dives into the "why" and "how" of consumer choices. Go to http://real-timeupdates.com/bia6 and click on Learn More. If you are using MyBizLab, you can access Real-Time Updates within the chapter or under Student Study Tools.

cognitive dissonance Tension that exists when a person's beliefs don't match his or her behaviors; a common example is *buyer's remorse*, when someone regrets a purchase immediately after making it

REAL-TIME UPDATES
Learn More by Reading This Article

Take a closer look at organizational buying behavior

Learn more about how businesses make purchasing decisions. Go to http://real-timeupdates.com/bia6 and click on Learn More. If you are using MyBizLab, you can access Real-Time Updates within the chapter or under Student Study Tools.

best choices, of course, but their choices are usually based on a more rational analysis of needs and alternatives. This isn't to say that emotions play little or no role in the purchase decision, however; organizations don't make decisions, people do. Fear of change, fear of failure, excitement about new technologies, and the pride of being associated with world-class suppliers are just a few of the emotions that can influence organizational purchases.

- **A formal buying process.** From office supplies to new factories, most organizational purchases follow a formal buying process, particularly in mid- to large-size companies.

- **Greater complexity in product usage.** The Apple iPhone is a great example of how consumer and organizational markets differ. It was instantly popular with vast numbers of consumers, but breaking into the corporate market was a much greater challenge for Apple because organizational buyers must address such issues as compatibility with corporate communication systems and legal requirements of data retention and security.[22] In addition, the *network effect*, in which the value of a product increases with the number of customers who use it, can be a key decision driver.[23] A major reason that other software providers have so much trouble putting a dent in Microsoft's dominance of the corporate market is that business users need compatibility, so it is simpler to select the tools that more people already use. Also, organizations sometimes continue to use products long after better substitutes become available if the costs and complexity of updating outweigh the advantages of the newer solutions.

- **The participation and influence of multiple people.** Except in the very smallest businesses, the purchase process usually involves a group of people. This team can include end users, technical experts, the manager with ultimate purchasing authority, and a professional purchasing agent whose job includes researching suppliers, negotiating prices, and evaluating supplier performance. Multiple family members play a part in many consumer purchases, of course, but not with the formality apparent in organizational markets.

- **Close relationships between buyers and sellers.** Close relationships between buyers and sellers are common in organizational purchasing. In some cases, employees of the seller even have offices inside the buyer's facility to promote close interaction.

✓ Checkpoint

LEARNING OBJECTIVE 3: Differentiate between consumer buying behavior and organizational buying behavior.

SUMMARY: Classical economic theory suggests that consumers follow a largely rational process of recognizing a need, searching for information, evaluating alternatives, making a purchase, and evaluating the product after use or consumption. However, recent research into behavioral economics and consumer psychology suggests that many consumer purchases are far less rational. Much of this decision making happens subconsciously and is driven to a large degree by emotion, culture, and situational factors. Organizational buying behavior comes much closer to the rational model of classical economics because purchases are usually judged by their economic value to the organization. The most significant ways in which organizational purchasing differs from consumer purchasing are an emphasis on economic payback, a formal buying process, greater complexity in product usage, purchasing groups, and close relationships between buyers and sellers.

CRITICAL THINKING: (1) Can business-to-business marketers take advantage of new insights into consumer buying behavior? Why or why not? (2) How could families and individual consumers benefit from adopting some elements of organizational buying behavior?

IT'S YOUR BUSINESS: (1) Do you read product reviews online before making important purchases? Why or why not? Have you ever contributed to social commerce by posting your own reviews or product advice? (2) Why did you buy the clothes you are wearing at this very moment?

KEY TERMS TO KNOW: consumer market, organizational market, cognitive dissonance

Identifying Market Opportunities

With insights into your customers' needs and behaviors, you're ready to begin planning your marketing strategies. **Strategic marketing planning** is a process that involves three steps: (1) examining the current marketing situation, (2) assessing opportunities and setting objectives, and (3) crafting a marketing strategy to reach those objectives (see Exhibit 5). Companies often record the results of their planning efforts in a formal *marketing plan*.

EXAMINING THE CURRENT MARKETING SITUATION

Examining your current marketing situation includes reviewing your past performance (how well each product is doing in each market where you sell it), evaluating your competition, examining your internal strengths and weaknesses, and analyzing the external environment.

4 | LEARNING OBJECTIVE

Define *strategic marketing planning*, and identify the four basic options for pursuing new marketing opportunities.

strategic marketing planning
The process of examining an organization's current marketing situation, assessing opportunities and setting objectives, and then developing a marketing strategy to reach those objectives

EXHIBIT 5	The Strategic Marketing Planning Process

Strategic marketing planning can involve a range of major decisions that fall into three general steps: (1) examining the current marketing situation, (2) assessing opportunities and setting objectives, and (3) developing a marketing strategy. The nature of these steps can vary widely depending on the products and markets involved; for example, emerging markets and mature markets have very different sets of customer and competitor dynamics.

1. Examine current marketing situation

- Review past performance
- Evaluate competition
- Examine strengthes and weaknesses
- Analyze the business environment

2. Assess opportunities and set objectives

- Explore product and market opportunities
- Set sales targets that are invigorating while being realistic

3. Develop marketing strategy

- Divide market into strategically productive segments
- Choose best-fit segments
- Decide how to position in minds of target customers
- Develop marketing mix

Reviewing Performance

Unless you're starting a new business, your company has a history of marketing performance. Maybe sales have slowed in the past year, maybe you've had to cut prices so much that you're barely earning a profit, or maybe sales have been strong and you have money to invest in new marketing activities. Reviewing where you are and how you got there is critical because you want to learn from your mistakes and repeat your successes—without getting trapped in mindsets and practices that need to change for the future, even if they were successful in the past.

Evaluating Competition

In addition to reviewing past performance, you must evaluate your competition. If you own a Burger King franchise, for example, you need to watch what McDonald's and Wendy's are doing. You also have to keep an eye on Taco Bell, KFC, Pizza Hut, and other restaurants, as well as pay attention to any number of other ways your customers might satisfy their hunger—including fixing a sandwich at home. Furthermore, you need to watch the horizon for trends that could affect your business, such as consumer interest in organic foods or in locally produced ingredients.

Examining Internal Strengths and Weaknesses

Successful marketers try to identify sources of competitive advantage and areas that need improvement. They look at such factors as financial resources, production capabilities, distribution networks, brand awareness, business partnerships, managerial expertise, and promotional capabilities. On the basis of your internal analysis, you will be able to decide whether your business should (1) limit itself to those opportunities for which it possesses the required strengths or (2) challenge itself to reach higher goals by acquiring and developing new strengths.

Analyzing the External Environment

Marketers must also analyze trends and conditions in the business environment when planning their marketing strategies. For example, customer decisions are greatly affected by interest rates, inflation, unemployment, personal income, and savings rates. During recessions, consumers still aspire to enjoy the good life, but they are forced by circumstances to alter their spending patterns.[24] "Affordable luxuries" become particularly appealing during these times, for example. Recessions also create opportunities for agile and aggressive companies to take business away from companies weakened by poor sales and deteriorating finances.[25]

ASSESSING OPPORTUNITIES AND SETTING OBJECTIVES

After you've examined the current marketing situation, you're ready to assess your marketing opportunities and set your objectives. Successful companies are always on the lookout for new marketing opportunities, which can be classified into four options (see Exhibit 6).[26] **Market penetration** involves selling more of your existing products into the markets you already serve. **Product development** is creating new products for those current markets, while **market development** is selling your existing products to new markets. Finally, **diversification** involves creating new products for new markets.

Generally speaking, these four options are listed in order of increasing risk. Market penetration can be the least risky because your products already exist and the market has already demonstrated some level of demand for your products. At the other extreme, creating new products for new markets is usually the riskiest choice of all because you encounter uncertainties in both dimensions (you may fail to create the product you need, and the market might not be interested in it).

After you've framed the opportunity you want to pursue, you are ready to set your marketing objectives. A common marketing objective is to achieve a certain level of **market share**, which is a firm's portion of the total sales within a market (market share can be defined by either number of units sold or by sales revenue).

market penetration Selling more of a firm's existing products into the markets it already serves

product development Creating new products for a firm's current markets

market development Selling existing products to new markets

diversification Creating new products for new markets

market share A firm's portion of the total sales in a market

EXHIBIT 6	Pursuing Market Opportunities

Every company has four basic options when it comes to pursuing market opportunities. The arrows show the increasing level of risk, from the lowest to the highest.

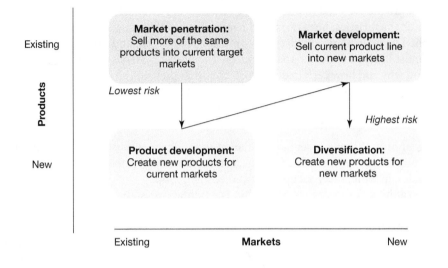

Checkpoint

LEARNING OBJECTIVE 4: Define *strategic marketing planning*, and identify the four basic options for pursuing new marketing opportunities.

SUMMARY: Strategic marketing planning involves three steps: (1) examining the current marketing situation (including past performance, competition, internal strengths and weaknesses, and the external environment); (2) assessing market opportunities and setting marketing objectives; and (3) developing a marketing strategy to reach those objectives. The four basic options for pursuing market opportunities are *market penetration* (selling more existing products into the current markets), *product development* (creating new products for current markets), *market development* (selling existing products to new markets), and *diversification* (creating new products for new markets).

CRITICAL THINKING: (1) Why is it important to analyze past performance before assessing market opportunities and setting objectives? (2) Why is diversification considered riskier than market penetration, product development, and market development strategies?

IT'S YOUR BUSINESS: (1) Do you see yourself as a trendsetter in any aspect of your life? (2) How could the four options for pursuing market opportunities be applied to your career planning at various stages in your career? (Think of your skills as the products you have to offer.)

KEY TERMS TO KNOW: strategic marketing planning, market penetration, product development, market development, diversification, market share

Crafting a Marketing Strategy

Using the current marketing situation and your objectives as your guide, you're ready to develop a **marketing strategy**, which consists of dividing your market into *segments*, choosing your *target markets* and the *position* you'd like to establish in those markets, and then developing a *marketing mix* to help you get there.

5	LEARNING OBJECTIVE

Identify the four steps in crafting a marketing strategy.

marketing strategy An overall plan for marketing a product; includes the identification of target market segments, a positioning strategy, and a marketing mix

DIVIDING MARKETS INTO SEGMENTS

market A group of customers who need or want a particular product and have the money to buy it

market segmentation The division of a diverse market into smaller, relatively homogeneous groups with similar needs, wants, and purchase behaviors

A **market** contains all the customers who might be interested in a product and can pay for it. However, most markets contain subgroups of potential customers with different interests, values, and behaviors. To maximize their effectiveness in reaching these subgroups, many companies subdivide the total market through **market segmentation**, grouping customers with similar characteristics, behaviors, and needs. Each of these market segments can then be approached by offering products that are priced, distributed, and promoted in a unique way that is most likely to appeal to that segment. The overall goal of market segmentation is to understand why and how certain customers buy what they buy so that you use your finite resources to create and market products in the most efficient manner possible.[27]

Four fundamental factors marketers use to identify market segments are demographics, psychographics, geography, and behavior:

demographics The study of statistical characteristics of a population

psychographics Classification of customers on the basis of their psychological makeup, interests, and lifestyles

geographic segmentation Categorization of customers according to their geographical location

behavioral segmentation Categorization of customers according to their relationship with products or response to product characteristics

- **Demographics.** When you segment a market using **demographics**, the statistical analysis of a population, you subdivide your customers according to characteristics such as age, gender, income, race, occupation, and ethnic group.
- **Psychographics.** Whereas demographic segmentation is the study of people from the outside, **psychographics** is the analysis of people from the inside, focusing on their psychological makeup, including attitudes, interests, opinions, and lifestyles. Psychographic analysis focuses on why people behave the way they do by examining such issues as brand preferences, media preferences, values, self-concept, and behavior.
- **Geography.** When differences in buying behavior are influenced by where people live, it makes sense to use **geographic segmentation**. Segmenting the market into geographic units such as regions, cities, counties, or neighborhoods allows companies to customize and sell products that meet the needs of specific markets and to organize their operations as needed.
- **Behavior. Behavioral segmentation** groups customers according to their relationship with products or response to product characteristics. To identify behavioral segments, marketers study such factors as the occasions that prompt people to buy certain products, the particular benefits they seek from a product, their habits and frequency of product usage, and the degree of loyalty they show toward a brand.[28]

Starting with these variables, researchers can also combine different types of data to identify target segments with even greater precision, such as merging geographic, demographic, and behavioral data to define specific types of consumer neighborhoods.

CHOOSING YOUR TARGET MARKETS

target markets Specific customer groups or segments to whom a company wants to sell a particular product

After you have segmented your market, the next step is to find appropriate target segments, or **target markets**, on which to focus your efforts. Marketers use a variety of criteria to narrow their focus to a few suitable market segments, including the magnitude of potential sales within each segment, the cost of reaching those customers, fit with a firm's core competencies, and any risks in the business environment.

Exhibit 7 diagrams four strategies for reaching target markets. Companies that practice *undifferentiated marketing* (also known as *mass marketing*) ignore differences among buyers and offer only one product or product line and present it with the same communication, pricing, and distribution strategies to all potential buyers. Undifferentiated marketing has the advantages of simplicity and economies of scale, but it can be less effective at reaching some portions of the market.

By contrast, companies that manufacture or sell a variety of products to several target customer groups practice *differentiated marketing*. This is Toyota's approach, for example, with the Scion brand aimed at young buyers, the Toyota brand designed for its core audience, and the Lexus brand targeted to those wanting luxury cars. Differentiated marketing is a popular strategy, but it requires substantial resources because the company has to tailor products, prices, promotional efforts, and distribution arrangements for each customer group. The differentiation should be based on meaningful differences that don't alienate any audiences.

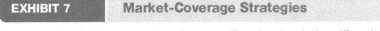

EXHIBIT 7   **Market-Coverage Strategies**

Four alternative market-coverage strategies are undifferentiated marketing, differentiated marketing, concentrated marketing, and micromarketing.

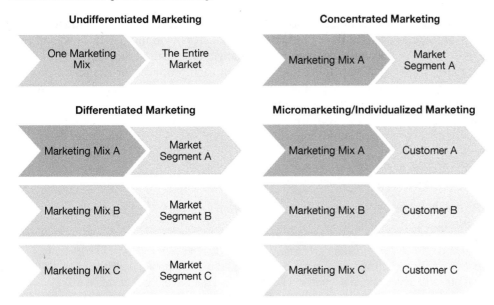

Source: Adapted from Philip Kotler and Gary Armstrong, *Principles of Marketing*, 13th ed. (Upper Saddle River, N.J.: Pearson Prentice Hall, 2010), 201–207.

Concentrated marketing focuses on only a single market segment. With this approach, you acknowledge that various other market segments may exist but you choose to target just one. The biggest advantage of concentrated marketing is that it allows you to focus all your time and resources on a single type of customer (which is why this approach is usually the best option for start-up companies, by the way). The strategy can be risky, however, because you've staked your fortunes on just one segment.

Micromarketing, or *individualized marketing*, is the narrowest strategy of all, in which firms target a single location or even a single customer.[29] This approach can range from customizable products to *major accounts* sales teams that craft entire marketing programs for each of their largest customers.

Achieving success in any market segment can take time and significant investment, so embracing market segments for the long term is essential. For example, Procter & Gamble, the company behind the Pampers brand of disposable diapers, targets women before their babies are born and maintains a relationship with them for years afterward.[30] In fact, many companies now think in terms of *customer lifetime value*: the total potential revenue from each customer over a certain time span minus the cost of attracting and keeping that customer. This approach lets companies focus on their most valuable customers while deciding what to do with their less-profitable customers (such as abandoning those customers or changing marketing strategies to make pursuing them more profitable).[31]

STAKING OUT A POSITION IN YOUR TARGET MARKETS

After you have decided which segments of the market to enter, your next step is to decide what *position* you want to occupy in those segments. **Positioning** is the process of designing a company's offerings, messages, and operating policies so that both the company and its products occupy distinct and desirable competitive positions in your target customers' minds. For instance, for every product category that you care about as a consumer, you have some ranking of desirability in your mind—you believe that certain colleges are more prestigious than others, that certain brands of shoes are more fashionable than others, that one video game system is better than the others, and so on. Successful marketers are careful to choose the position they'd like to occupy in buyers' minds.

positioning Managing a business in a way designed to occupy a particular place in the minds of target customers

In their attempts to secure favorable positions, marketers can emphasize such variables as product attributes, customer service, brand image (such as reliability or sophistication), price (such as low cost or premium), or category leadership (such as the leading online bookseller). For example, BMW and Porsche work to associate their products with performance, Mercedes Benz with luxury, and Volvo with safety.

A vital and often overlooked aspect of positioning is that although marketers take all kinds of steps to position their products, it is *customers* who ultimately decide on the positioning: They're the ones who interpret the many messages they encounter in the marketplace and decide what they think and feel about each product. For example, you can advertise that you have a luxury product, but if consumers aren't convinced, it's not really positioned as a luxury product. The only result that matters is what the customer believes. One auto industry marketing executive put it this way: "Everyone works so hard to control and define what their brand stands for, when they ought to just let the consumer do it."[32]

✔ Checkpoint

LEARNING OBJECTIVE 5: Identify the four steps in crafting a marketing strategy.

SUMMARY: Crafting a marketing strategy involves dividing your market into *segments*, choosing your *target markets* and the *position* you'd like to establish in those markets, and developing a *marketing mix* to help you get there. Segmentation (using demographics, psychographics, geography, and behavior) allows a company to select parts of the market most likely to respond to specific marketing programs. Companies can use one of four approaches to selecting target markets: undifferentiated (mass) marketing, differentiated marketing (with a different marketing mix for each segment), concentrated marketing (focusing on a single market segment), and micromarketing or individualized marketing. A *position* refers to the position a company or brand occupies in the mind of the target market segments. In creating a *marketing mix*, companies define the products they will offer, the prices they will charge, distribution methods, and customer communication efforts.

CRITICAL THINKING: (1) Would two companies interested in the same group of customers automatically use the same target market approach (such as differentiated or concentrated)? Why or why not? (2) Why aren't marketers ultimately in control of the positions their products achieve in the marketplace?

IT'S YOUR BUSINESS: (1) Think of three car brands or specific models. How are these products positioned in your mind? What terms do you use to describe them? (2) Given your transportation needs in the near future (assuming you will need a car), which model is the most desirable? The least desirable?

KEY TERMS TO KNOW: marketing strategy, market, market segmentation, demographics, psychographics, geographic segmentation, behavioral segmentation, target markets, positioning

---

6 **LEARNING OBJECTIVE**

Describe the four main components of the marketing mix.

marketing mix The four key elements of marketing strategy: product, price, distribution, and customer communication

The Marketing Mix

After you've segmented your market, selected your target market, and taken steps to position your product, your next task is to develop a marketing mix. A firm's **marketing mix** consists of product, price, distribution, and customer communication (see Exhibit 8). (You might also hear references to "the four Ps" of the marketing mix, which is short for products, pricing, place or physical distribution, and promotion. However, with the advent of digital goods and services, distribution is no longer exclusively a physical concern. And many companies now view customer communication as a broader and more interactive activity than the functions implied by *promotion*.)

EXHIBIT 8	The Marketing Mix

The marketing mix consists of four key elements: the products a company offers to potential buyers, the price it asks in return, its methods of distributing those products to customers, and the various efforts it makes to communicate with customers before and after the sale.

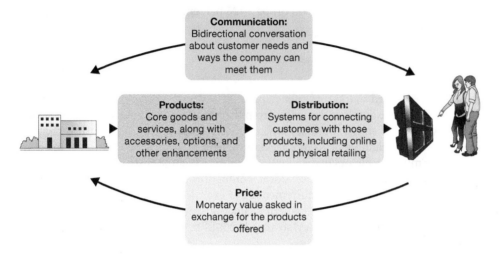

PRODUCTS

In common usage, *product* usually refers to a tangible good, while *service* refers to an intangible performance. However, for the purposes of studying marketing, it is helpful to define **product** as the bundle of value offered for the purpose of satisfying a want or a need in a marketing exchange. In this expanded definition, both tangible goods and intangible services are considered products. The reason for taking this broader view of *product* is that it encourages a more holistic look at the entire offering, which can include the brand name, design, packaging, support services, warranty, the ownership experience, and other attributes.

product A bundle of value that satisfies a customer need or want

For example, if you buy a pair of $200 Dolce & Gabbana sunglasses with the brand's prominent "DG" initials on the side, you are buying much more than a device that holds a couple of protective lenses in front of your eyes. You are buying a shopping and ownership experience that is distinctly different from that for buying a pair of $5 sunglasses from a discount drugstore. You are buying the opportunity to feel a particular way about yourself and to present a particular image to the world around you. You are buying the right to brand yourself with the Dolce & Gabbana brand and everything that brand means to you. All these elements constitute the Dolce & Gabbana product. You'll explore products in more detail in Chapter 14.

PRICING

Price, the amount of money customers pay for the product (including any discounts), is the second major component of a firm's marketing mix. Looking back at Kotler and Armstrong's definition of marketing, price is the *value captured* from customers in exchange for the value offered in the product. Setting and managing a product's price is one of the most critical decisions a company must make because price is the only element in a company's marketing mix that produces revenue; all other elements represent costs. Moreover, setting a product's price not only determines income but also can differentiate a product from the competition. Determining the right price is not an easy task, and marketers constantly worry whether they've turned away profitable customers by charging too much or "left money on the table" by charging too little.

price The amount of money charged for a product or service

A number of factors influence pricing decisions, including marketing objectives, government regulations, production costs, customer perceptions, competition, and customer demand. A company's costs establish the minimum amount it can charge, and the various external forces establish the maximum. Somewhere in between those two extremes lies an optimum price point. Products also exhibit different levels of *price elasticity*, which is a measure of how sensitive customers are to changes in price. If you don't have a smart phone yet and the price of such phones drops by 25 percent, you might well be tempted to buy one. In contrast, if the price of broccoli drops by 25 percent, chances are you won't eat more veggies as a result.

DISTRIBUTION

distribution channels Systems for moving goods and services from producers to customers; also known as marketing channels

Distribution is the third marketing-mix element. It covers the organized network of firms and systems that move goods and services from the producer to the customer. This network is also known as *marketing channels*, *marketing intermediaries*, or **distribution channels**. As you can imagine, channel decisions are interdependent with virtually everything else in the marketing mix. Key factors in distribution planning include customer needs and expectations, market coverage, distribution costs, competition, positioning, customer support requirements, and sales support requirements. For example, when AstraZeneca introduced a cancer drug that required careful patient evaluation and education, it released the drug through a single specialty pharmacy so that it could manage pharmacist training more closely.[33]

Marketing intermediaries perform a variety of essential marketing functions, including providing information to customers, providing feedback to manufacturers, providing sales support, gathering assortments of goods from multiple producers to make shopping easier for customers, and transporting and storing goods. These intermediaries fall into two general categories: *wholesalers* and *retailers*. The basic distinction between them is that wholesalers sell to other companies whereas retailers sell to individual consumers. Across industries, you can find tremendous variety in the types of wholesalers and retailers, from independent representatives who sell products from several manufacturers to huge distribution companies with national or international scope to purely digital retailers such as Apple's iTunes service.

CUSTOMER COMMUNICATION

promotion A wide variety of persuasive techniques used by companies to communicate with their target markets and the general public

In traditional marketing thought, the fourth element of the marketing mix is **promotion**, all the activities a firm undertakes to promote its products to target customers. The goals of promotion include *informing, persuading,* and *reminding.* Among these activities are advertising in a variety of media, personal selling, public relations, and sales promotion. Promotion may take the form of direct, face-to-face communication or indirect communication through such media as television, radio, magazines, newspapers, direct mail, billboards, transit ads, social media, and other channels.

However, as "Involving the Customer in the Marketing Process" points out, forward-thinking companies have moved beyond the unidirectional approach of promotion to interactive customer communication. By talking *with* their customers instead of *at* their customers, marketers get immediate feedback on everything from customer service problems to new product ideas. As you'll read in the Behind the Scenes at the end of the chapter, Sarah Calhoun of Red Ants Pants literally sits in customers' living rooms, listening to their thoughts about work pants.

Promotion is still a vital part of customer communication, but by encouraging two-way conversations, whether it's two people talking across a desk or an online network spread across the globe, marketers can also learn while they are informing, persuading, and reminding. Moreover, by replacing "sales pitches" with conversations and giving customers some control over the dialog, marketers can also help break down some of the walls and filters that audiences have erected after years of conventional marketing promotion.[34] Chapter 16 offers a closer look at customer communication.

For the latest information on marketing principles, visit http://real-timeupdates.com/bia6.

Checkpoint

LEARNING OBJECTIVE 6: Describe the four main components of the marketing mix.

SUMMARY: The four elements of the marketing mix are product, price, distribution, and customer communication. Products are goods, services, persons, places, ideas, organizations, or anything else offered for the purpose of satisfying a want or need in a marketing exchange. Price is the amount of money customers pay for the product. Distribution is the organized network of firms that move the goods and services from the producer to the customer. Customer communication involves the activities used to communicate with and promote products to target markets.

CRITICAL THINKING: (1) Why is price sometimes referred to as *captured value*? (2) Why do companies that embrace relationship marketing focus on "customer communication" rather than "promotion"?

IT'S YOUR BUSINESS: (1) If you could buy a product from a website or a store right down the street and the prices were the same, where would you make your purchase? Why? (2) When buying products, do you tend to seek out products with visible logos (such as the Nike swoosh or the Dolce & Gabbana initials), or do you shun such products? Or do you not care one way or the other? Why?

KEY TERMS TO KNOW: marketing mix, product, price, distribution channels, promotion

BEHIND THE SCENES   MyBizLab

AGGRAVATION LEADS TO INSPIRATION FOR SARAH CALHOUN OF RED ANTS PANTS

Like many other entrepreneurs, frustration was the source of inspiration for Sarah Calhoun. When she couldn't find rugged work pants designed for women, she decided to meet this unmet market need herself. A chance encounter in a coffee shop with an experienced apparel industry insider (who noticed she was reading *Starting a Business for Dummies*) convinced her that a real opportunity was there and waiting for someone to pursue it.

Calhoun based all three key elements of her marketing strategy—segmentation, target markets, and positioning—on her mission of pursuing this opportunity. She founded Red Ants Pants with the singular focus on providing hardwearing pants for hardworking women, meeting the needs of customers whose work makes clothing a matter of practical utility and even on-the-job safety.

Red Ants Pants are made from tough, heavy cloth and in both "straight" and "curvy" styles to provide a better fit for more women. In addition, they come in two or three times as many

waist/inseam combinations as typical pants, greatly increasing the chance that every woman will find exactly the size she needs.

In keeping with the capacity of a small business and the nature of her product offerings, simplicity is the key word in the product mix. Pants are available in exactly one color: chocolate brown. (It was only after buying $45,000 worth of the practical fabric that Calhoun learned "chocolate brown is the new black" in the fashion world.) A few years after introducing the pants, she expanded the product portfolio with a handful of complementary products, including shirts, hats, and belts.

Calhoun is adamant about keeping production in the United States, too, a rarity in the clothing business, which outsources most of its production to low-cost labor centers in other countries. Instead, she chose a mother/daughter-owned factory two states over, in Seattle, and she views supporting quality jobs in this country as "part of my responsibility as a business owner."

Referring to her production partners, she says, "They have 23 employees who are treated well, paid well and enjoy good working conditions."

At $129 a pair, the pants are not bargain-bin items, to be sure. However, like many purveyors of high-quality products, Calhoun emphasizes value, noting that customers would wear out several pairs of cheaper pants in the time they might wear out a single pair of Red Ants. Plus, the price reflects the structure she has chosen for her business: not offshoring in pursuit of the lowest possible production costs. At the rate her sales are growing, customers apparently agree that it's a fair price to pay for pants that keep them safe and comfortable on the job.

Distribution strategy was one of Calhoun's most important marketing and business decisions. Clothes in general and pants in particular are products for which individual fit and function can't be absolutely confirmed until the customer tries them on. Having her products available in hundreds of retail outlets would let more customers try them on—and give her tremendous visibility in the market. However, it would also put her at the mercy of retailers' demands regarding price and inventory. She opted to function as her own distribution channel, selling from her website, over the phone, and from her storefront operation in White Sulphur Springs, Montana. Having so many sizing options helps ensure that pants fit when customers receive them, but as with most online clothing retailers, she invites customers to exchange pants that don't fit.

Like millions of other small companies in recent years, Red Ants Pants has taken advantage of technology to overcome distribution hurdles. Calhoun explains, "The old quote of retail being location, location, location doesn't hold up as much. I have Internet and I have UPS and mail service, and that's all I need."

Customer communication is another aspect of the marketing mix in which Calhoun demonstrates both the greater flexibility that small companies often have compared to their larger, "more corporate" competitors—and the need to exercise creative brain power over brute-force budget power. Her communication style is more fun and more daring that the typical corporation would attempt, for example, and it seems to resonate with buyers. How many clothing companies would use photographs (discreetly staged, to be sure) to suggest that hardworking women would rather wear no pants than wear pants that don't fit?

Without a significant marketing budget, Calhoun looks for low-cost, high-visibility ways to reach customers. Her most

unusual has been the Anthill, an ant-decorated Airstream travel trailer that she and her sales manager take on the road on trips they call the "Tour de Pants." They invite women to stage in-home gatherings, much like old-school Tupperware parties. Visiting customers in their homes and hearing stories about women working in what are often male-dominated professions, Calhoun also gets invaluable marketing research insights. And the Anthill is rolling advertising at its best. Some people even follow her down the highway to learn more about the company and its wares.

Calhoun's most ambitious communication effort so far has been sponsoring the Red Ants Pants Music Festival in 2011, which attracted such major Americana artists as Lyle Lovett and Guy Clark. All profits went to the Red Ants Pants Foundation, which she started to "support family farms and ranches, women in business, and rural initiatives."

The combination of meeting customer needs with quality products and a creative marketing effort is paying off. Red Ants Pants now has customers all across the country and around the world, from Europe to Australia, and even women working the research stations in Antarctica. Are customers satisfied with the product? "Putting on these pants was a religious experience," is how one phrased it.[35]

Critical Thinking Questions

1. How might Calhoun's decision to keep production in the United States help solidify her market position in the minds of her target customers?

2. If Red Ants Pants had investors looking for a quick return, how might that influence Calhoun's decision to continuing functioning as her own retail channel, rather than going through established retailers?

3. How could meeting small groups of women in their homes to talk about pants possibly be an efficient communication strategy?

LEARN MORE ONLINE

Visit the Red Ants Pants website, at **www.redantspants.com**, and its page on Facebook (search for "Red Ants Pants"). How are the various elements of the marketing mix represented? How does the style of communication help Red Ants Pants connect with customers? What sort of practical information is provided to help customers select and order products?

MyBizLab

Log on to www.mybizlab.com to access study and assessment aids associated with this chapter.

KEY TERMS

behavioral segmentation
cause-related marketing
cognitive dissonance
consumer market
customer loyalty

customer relationship management (CRM)
demographics
distribution channels
diversification
exchange process

geographic segmentation
market
market development
market penetration
market segmentation
market share
marketing
marketing concept
marketing mix
marketing research
marketing strategy
needs
organizational market
permission-based marketing
place marketing

positioning
price
product
product development
promotion
psychographics
relationship marketing
social commerce
stealth marketing
strategic marketing planning
target markets
transaction
utility
wants

TEST YOUR KNOWLEDGE

Questions for Review

1. Why are companies pushing for more accountability from the marketing function?
2. How does the organizational market differ from the consumer market?
3. What is strategic marketing planning, and what is its purpose?
4. What external environmental factors affect strategic marketing decisions?
5. What are the four basic components of the marketing mix?

Questions for Analysis

6. Why would consumers knowingly buy counterfeit luxury brands?
7. How can marketing research help companies improve their marketing efforts?
8. Why does a company need to consider its current marketing situation, including competitive trends, when setting objectives for market share?

9. Why do companies segment markets?
10. Ethical Considerations. Is it ethical to observe shoppers for the purposes of marketing research without their knowledge and permission? Why or why not?

Questions for Application

11. How might a retailer use relationship marketing to improve customer loyalty?
12. Think of a product you recently purchased and review your decision process. Why did you need or want that product? How did the product's marketing influence your purchase decision? How did you investigate the product before making your purchase decision? Did you experience cognitive dissonance after your decision?
13. If you were launching a new manufacturing company, would you draft your marketing plan or design your production processes first? Why?
14. Concept Integration. How might the key economic indicators, including consumer price index, inflation, and unemployment, affect a company's marketing decisions?

EXPAND YOUR KNOWLEDGE

Discovering Career Opportunities

Jobs in marketing cover a wide range of activities, including a variety of jobs such as personal selling, advertising, marketing research, product management, and public relations. You can get more information about various marketing positions by consulting the *Occupational Outlook Handbook* (www.bls.gov/oco), job-search websites such as Career Builder (www.careerbuilder.com) and Monster (www.monster.com), and other online resources.

1. Select a specific marketing job that interests you, and use the sites mentioned above to find out more about this career

path. What specific duties and responsibilities do people in this position typically handle?
2. Search through help-wanted ads in newspapers, specialized magazines, or websites to find two openings in the field you are researching. What educational background and work experience are employers seeking in candidates for this position? What kind of work assignments are mentioned in these ads?
3. Now think about your talents, interests, and goals. How do your strengths fit with the requirements, duties, and responsibilities of this job? Do you think you would find this field enjoyable and rewarding? Why?

Improving Your Tech Insights: Search Engines

As most every web user knows, search engines identify individual webpages that contain specific words or phrases you've asked for. Search engines have the advantage of scanning millions of individual webpages, and they use powerful ranking algorithms to present the pages that are probably the most relevant to your search request. Because each engine uses a proprietary and secret algorithm to rank the displayed results, multiple engines can display different result sets for the same query.

To see how search engines can return markedly different results, search on the phrase "Apple computer market share" (use the quotation marks) using Google, Bing, and Yahoo!. In a brief email message to your instructor, describe the differences and similarities among the three search results. Which search engine gave you the best results? How many of the search results were more than a year out of date? How might the differences among the search engines affect the work of a businessperson preparing a report on Apple's share of the personal computer market?

PRACTICE YOUR SKILLS

Sharpening Your Communication Skills

In small groups, as assigned by your instructor, take turns interviewing each person in the group about a product that each person absolutely loves or detests. Try to probe for the real reasons behind the emotions, touching on all the issues you read about in this chapter, from self-image to reference groups. Do you see any trends in the group's collective answers? Do people learn anything about themselves when answering the group's questions? Does anyone get defensive about his or her reasons for loving or hating a product? Be prepared to share with the class at least two marketing insights you learned through this exercise.

Building Your Team Skills

In the course of planning a marketing strategy, marketers need to analyze the external environment to consider how forces outside the firm may create new opportunities and challenges. One important environmental factor for merchandise buyers at Sears is weather conditions. For example, when merchandise buyers for lawn and garden products think about the assortment and number of products to purchase for the chain's stores, they don't place any orders without first poring over long-range weather forecasts for each market. In particular, temperature and precipitation predictions for the coming 12 months are critical to the company's marketing plan, because they offer clues to consumer demand for barbecues, lawn furniture, gardening tools, and other merchandise.

What other products would benefit from examining weather forecasts? With your team, brainstorm to identify at least three types of products (in addition to lawn and garden items) for which Sears should examine the weather as part of its analysis of the external environment. Share your recommendations with the entire class. How many teams identified the same products your team did?

Developing Your Research Skills

From recent issues of business journals and newspapers (print or online editions), select an article that describes in some detail a particular company's attempt to build relationships with its customers (either in general or for a particular product or product line).

1. Describe the company's market. What geographic, demographic, behavioral, or psychographic segments of the market is the company targeting?
2. How does the company communicate with and learn about its customers?
3. According to the article, how successful has the company been in understanding its customers?

REFERENCES

1. Adapted from Red Ants Pants website, accessed 8 September 2011, www.redantspants.com; Becky Warren, "Ants on the Pants," *Country Woman*, February–March 2011, www.countrywomanmagazine.com; Dan Testa, "Red Ants Pants: By Working Women, for Working Women," *Flathead Beacon*, 4 March 2010, www.flatheadbeacon.com; Sammi Johnson, "Outdoor Woman: Red Ants Pants," *406 Woman*, April/May 2010, 52–53; Beth Judy, "Fit for Her," *Montana Magazine*, March–April 2010, 14–16; *Montana Quarterly*, Summer 2010, www.redantspants.com; Devan Grote, "Red Ants Pants," *Gettysburg*, Spring 2009, www.redantspants.com.
2. Philip Kotler and Gary Armstrong, *Principles of Marketing*, 13th ed. (Upper Saddle River, N.J.: Pearson Prentice Hall, 2010), 5.
3. Kotler and Armstrong, *Principles of Marketing*, 6.
4. BizXchange website, accessed 13 July 2009, www.bizx.com.
5. June Lee Risser, "Customers Come First," *Marketing Management,* November/December 2003, 22–26.
6. Ranjay Gulati and James B. Oldroyd, "The Quest for Customer Focus," *Harvard Business Review*, April 2005, 92–101.
7. Jonathan L. Yarmis, "How Facebook Will Upend Advertising," *BusinessWeek*, 28 May 2008, www.businessweek.com
8. Paul Gunning, "Social Media Reality Check," *Adweek*, 8 June 2008, 18.
9. Jeremiah Owyang, "When Social Media Marries CRM Systems," Web Strategy blog, 3 June 2008, www.web-strategist.com.
10. "Sorry, John," *Adweek*, 22 June 2009, 9.
11. Dominique M. Hanssens, Daniel Thorpe, and Carl Finkbeiner, "Marketing When Customer Equity Matters," *Harvard Business Review*, May 2008, 117–123.

12. Google Analytics, accessed 24 October 2011, www.google.com/analytics.
13. Eric Almquist, Martin Kon, and Wolfgang Bock, "The Science of Demand," *Marketing Management*, March/April 2004, 20–26; David C. Swaddling and Charles Miller, "From Understanding to Action," *Marketing Management*, July/August 2004, 31–35.
14. "Marketing Under Fire," *Marketing Management*, July/August 2004, 5.
15. Michael Oliveira, "Netflix Apologizes for Using Actors to Meet Press at Canadian Launch," *Globe and Mail*, 22 September 2010, www.theglobeandmail.com.
16. Word of Mouth Marketing Association, "WOM 101," http://womma.org; Nate Anderson, "FTC Says Stealth Marketing Unethical," *Ars Technica*, 13 December 2006, http://arstechnica.com; "Undercover Marketing Uncovered," CBSnews.com, 25 July 2004, www.cbsnews.com; Stephanie Dunnewind, "Teen Recruits Create Word-of-Mouth 'Buzz' to Hook Peers on Products," *Seattle Times*, 20 November 2004, www.seattletimes.com.
17. Pophal, "Tweet Ethics: Trust and Transparency in a Web 2.0 World."
18. Dan Hill, "Why They Buy," *Across the Board*, November–December 2003, 27–32; Eric Roston, "The Why of Buy," *Time*, April 2004.
19. Dan Ariely, "The End of Rational Economics," *Harvard Business Review*, July/August 2009, 78–84.
20. Michael R. Solomon, *Consumer Behavior*, 6th ed. (Upper Saddle River, N.J.: Pearson Prentice Hall, 2004), 366–372.
21. Based in part on James C. Anderson and James A. Narus, *Business Market Management: Understanding, Creating, and Delivering Value*, 2nd ed. (Upper Saddle River, N.J.: Pearson Prentice Hall, 2004), 114–116.
22. Daniel Lyons, "Tough Customers," *Forbes Asia*, 7 April 2008, 69.
23. Gerard J. Tellis, Eden Yin, and Rakesh Niraj, "Does Quality Win? Network Effects Versus Quality in High-Tech Markets," *Journal of Marketing Research*, May 2009, 135–149.
24. Eric Beinhocker, Ian Davis, and Lenny Mendonca, "The 10 Trends You Have to Watch," *Harvard Business Review*, July/August 2009, 55–60.
25. Beinhocker, et al., "The 10 Trends You Have to Watch."
26. Kotler and Armstrong, *Principles of Marketing*, 43–46.
27. Gordon A. Wyner, "Pulling the Right Levers," *Marketing Management*, July/August 2004, 8–9.
28. Kotler and Armstrong, *Principles of Marketing*, 196–197.
29. Kotler and Armstrong, *Principles of Marketing*, 205–207.
30. Jeneanne Rae, "New Thinking About Consumer Marketing," *BusinessWeek*, 30 June 2009, 16.
31. Detlef Schoder, "The Flaw in Customer Lifetime Value," *Harvard Business Review*, December 2007, 26.
32. Mark Rechtin, "Scion's Dilemma," *AutoWeek*, 23 May 2006, www.autoweek.com.
33. Ben Comer, "AstraZeneca Signs Exclusive Distribution Deal for Vandetanib," PharmExec.com, 27 April 2011, http://blog.pharmexec.com.
34. Paul Gillin, *The New Influencers: A Marketer's Guide to the New Social Media* (Sanger, Calif.: Quill Driver Books, 2007), xi.
35. See note 1.

GLOSSARY

behavioral segmentation Categorization of customers according to their relationship with products or response to product characteristics

cause-related marketing Identification and marketing of a social issue, cause, or idea to selected target markets

cognitive dissonance Tension that exists when a person's beliefs don't match his or her behaviors; a common example is *buyer's remorse*, when someone regrets a purchase immediately after making it

consumer market Individuals or households that buy goods and services for personal use

customer loyalty The degree to which customers continue to buy from a particular retailer or buy the products of a particular manufacturer or service provider

customer relationship management (CRM) A type of information system that captures, organizes, and capitalizes on all the interactions that a company has with its customers

demographics The study of statistical characteristics of a population

distribution channels Systems for moving goods and services from producers to customers; also known as marketing channels

diversification Creating new products for new markets

exchange process The act of obtaining a desired object or service from another party by offering something of value in return

geographic segmentation Categorization of customers according to their geographical location

market A group of customers who need or want a particular product and have the money to buy it

market development Selling existing products to new markets

market penetration Selling more of a firm's existing products into the markets it already serves

market segmentation The division of a diverse market into smaller, relatively homogeneous groups with similar needs, wants, and purchase behaviors

market share A firm's portion of the total sales in a market

marketing concept An approach to business management that stresses customer needs and wants, seeks long-term profitability, and integrates marketing with other functional units within the organization

marketing mix The four key elements of marketing strategy: product, price, distribution, and customer communication

marketing research The collection and analysis of information for making marketing decisions

marketing strategy An overall plan for marketing a product; includes the identification of target market segments, a positioning strategy, and a marketing mix

marketing The process of creating value for customers and building relationships with those customers in order to capture value back from them

needs Differences between a person's actual state and his or her ideal state; they provide the basic motivation to make a purchase

organizational market Companies, government agencies, and other organizations that buy goods and services either to resell or to use in the creation of their own goods and services

permission-based marketing A marketing approach in which firms first ask permission to deliver messages to an audience and then promise to restrict their communication efforts to those subject areas in which audience members have expressed interest

place marketing Marketing efforts to attract people and organizations to a particular geographical area

positioning Managing a business in a way designed to occupy a particular place in the minds of target customers

price The amount of money charged for a product or service

product A bundle of value that satisfies a customer need or want

product development Creating new products for a firm's current markets

promotion A wide variety of persuasive techniques used by companies to communicate with their target markets and the general public

psychographics Classification of customers on the basis of their psychological makeup, interests, and lifestyles

relationship marketing A focus on developing and maintaining long-term relationships with customers, suppliers, and distribution partners for mutual benefit

social commerce The creation and sharing of product-related information among customers and potential customers

stealth marketing The delivery of marketing messages to people who are not aware that they are being marketed to; these messages can be delivered by either acquaintances or strangers, depending on the technique

strategic marketing planning The process of examining an organization's current marketing situation, assessing opportunities and setting objectives, and then developing a marketing strategy to reach those objectives

target markets Specific customer groups or segments to whom a company wants to sell a particular product

transaction An exchange of value between parties

utility The power of a good or service to satisfy a human need

wants Specific goods, services, experiences, or other entities that are desirable in light of a person's experiences, culture, and personality

Product and Pricing Strategies

From Chapter 14 of *Business in Action*, Sixth Edition. Courtland L. Bovée, John V. Thill. Copyright © 2013 by Pearson Education, Inc. Published by Pearson Business. All rights reserved.

LEARNING OBJECTIVES After studying this chapter, you will be able to

1 Identify the main types of consumer and organizational products and describe the four stages in the life cycle of a product

2 Describe six stages in the product development process

3 Define *brand* and explain the concepts of brand equity and brand loyalty

4 Identify four ways of expanding a product line and discuss two risks that product-line extensions pose

5 List the factors that influence pricing decisions and explain break-even analysis

6 Identify nine common pricing methods

MyBizLab

Where you see MyBizLab in this chapter, go to www.mybizlab.com for additional activities on the topic being discussed.

BEHIND THE SCENES TRANSFORMING A WORLD-CLASS ATHLETE INTO A WORLD-CLASS BRAND

Photo by Marc Serota/Getty Images

Professional golfer Annika Sorenstam is building a brand image to power her postgolf business career.

www.annikasorenstam.com

Start reading a list of Annika Sorenstam's accomplishments on the golf course, and you might have to stop halfway through and take a nap. Here's the short version: 89 tournament wins worldwide, including 10 major championships, and more than $20 million in prize winnings, with many millions more in product endorsements. Before she stepped away from competitive golf in late 2008, she dominated the woman's professional circuit as no one in recent memory had done before. And she rose high enough to achieve that ultimate badge of celebrity: one-name status. Millions of golf fans don't need to hear a last name; for them, she is simply Annika.

Her career on the course has clearly been a resounding success. But having achieved more before age 40 than most people could hope to achieve in several lifetimes, Sorenstam isn't ready to stop. In fact, she's starting all over again, this time in a multifaceted business career.

Sorenstam likes to measure herself against the best of the best. In fact, after dominating women's golf, she was the first woman to play in a professional men's tournament in more than 50 years. She did so not to make any kind of grand statement but simply to see how her skills compared to those of her male counterparts.

In her new career, Sorenstam is once again measuring herself against top performers, including such figures as basketball star Michael Jordan and golfers Arnold Palmer and Jack Nicklaus. Palmer and Nicklaus are particularly apt role models, both having built golf-centric business empires and having remained vibrant public figures years after hitting their last competitive shots.

Sorenstam believes it's high time a woman joined their ranks. "Ask a person on the street to name five male athletes who have made a name for themselves outside their sport—no problem," she says. "Ask the same question about women athletes? They can't name one." She plans to be the first. What advice would you give her to make the transition from golf star to business star, from Annika the athlete to Annika the brand?[1]

INTRODUCTION

This chapter explores two of the four elements in the marketing mix, product and price. Annika Sorenstam's challenge in defining the Annika brand (profiled in the chapter-opening Behind the Scenes) is an essential part of product strategy. She also faces another challenge that you'll read more about in this chapter: assembling the right mix of goods and services as part of a firm's overall product mix. Finally, as in every business, Sorenstam has to engage in careful financial analysis and make shrewd pricing decisions to stay both competitive and profitable.

MyBizLab

Gain hands-on experience through an interactive, real-world scenario. This chapter's simulation entitled Pricing Strategies and Objectives is located at **www.mybizlab.com**.

Characteristics of Products

As the central element in every company's exchanges with its customers, products naturally command a lot of attention from managers planning new offerings and coordinating the marketing mixes for existing offerings. To understand the nature of these decisions, it's important to recognize the various types of products and the stages that products go through during their "lifetime" in the marketplace.

1 | LEARNING OBJECTIVE

Identify the main types of consumer and organizational products, and describe the four stages in the life cycle of a product.

TYPES OF PRODUCTS

Think about Doritos tortilla chips, Intel semiconductors, and your favorite musical artist. You wouldn't market all these products in the same way, because buyer behavior, product characteristics, market expectations, competition, and other elements of the equation are entirely different.

Classifying products on the basis of tangibility and application can provide useful insights into the best ways to market them. Some products are predominantly tangible; others are mostly intangible. Most products, however, fall somewhere between those two extremes. The *product continuum* indicates the relative amounts of tangible and intangible components in a product (see Exhibit 1).

EXHIBIT 1 | **The Product Continuum**

Products contain both tangible and intangible components; predominantly tangible products are categorized as goods, whereas predominantly intangible products are categorized as services.

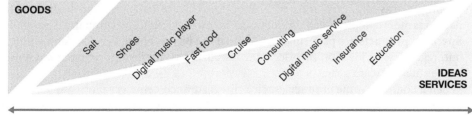

Tangible dominant

Intangible dominant

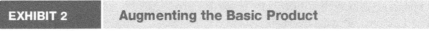

EXHIBIT 2   **Augmenting the Basic Product**

Product decisions also involve how much or how little to augment the core product with additional goods and services.

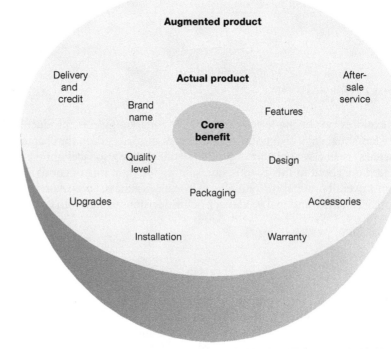

Source: Adapted from Philip Kotler and Gary Armstrong, *Principles of Marketing*, 10th ed. (Upper Saddle River, N.J.: Pearson Prentice Hall, 2004), 279.

To provide a more complete solution to customer needs, many companies find success by *augmenting* a core product with accessories, services, and other elements (see Exhibit 2). For example, when GlaxoSmithKline introduced its Alli weight-loss pill, the company augmented Alli with a weight-loss program that included counseling, online networking, and other tools to help people use the product successfully.[2] In some cases, these enhancements are included in the price of the product, but product augmentation can also be a way to increase revenue, by offering new services and accessories or by charging for enhancements that were previously included at no charge.[3]

Consumer Products

Organizations and consumers use many of the same products, but they can use them for different reasons and in different ways. Products that are primarily sold to individuals for personal consumption are known as *consumer products*. Consumer products can be classified into four subgroups, depending on how people shop for them:

- Everyday goods and services that people buy frequently, usually without much conscious planning, are known as **convenience products**.
- **Shopping products** are fairly important goods and services that people buy less frequently, such as computers and college educations. Because the stakes are higher and the decisions more complex, such products require more thought and comparison shopping.
- **Specialty products** are particular brands that the buyer especially wants and will seek out, regardless of location or price, such as Suzuki violin lessons or Bang & Olufsen home entertainment gear.
- When it comes to some products, such as life insurance, cemetery plots, and items that are new to the marketplace, consumers aren't looking for them. The marketing challenges for these *unsought products* include making consumers aware of their existence and convincing people to consider them.

convenience products Everyday goods and services that people buy frequently, usually without much conscious planning

shopping products Fairly important goods and services that people buy less frequently with more planning and comparison

specialty products Particular brands that the buyer especially wants and will seek out, regardless of location or price

Industrial and Commercial Products

Organizational products, or *industrial and commercial products*, are generally purchased by organizations in large quantities and are used to create other products or to operate the organization. **Expense items** are relatively inexpensive goods that are generally used within a year of purchase, such as printer cartridges and paper. **Capital items** are more expensive products with a longer useful life. Examples include computers, vehicles, production machinery, and even entire factories. Businesses and other organizations also buy a wide variety of services, from facilities maintenance to temporary executives.

Aside from dividing products into expense and capital items, industrial buyers and sellers often classify products according to their intended use:

- *Raw materials* such as iron ore, crude petroleum, lumber, and chemicals are used in the production of final products.
- *Components* such as semiconductors and fasteners also become part of the manufacturers' final products.
- *Supplies* such as pencils, nails, and lightbulbs that are used in a firm's daily operations are considered expense items.
- *Installations* such as factories, power plants, and airports are major capital projects.
- *Equipment* includes items such as desks, computers, and factory robots.
- *Business services* range from landscaping and cleaning to complex services such as management consulting and auditing.

expense items Inexpensive products that organizations generally use within a year of purchase

capital items More expensive organizational products with a longer useful life, ranging from office and plant equipment to entire factories

THE PRODUCT LIFE CYCLE

Most products undergo a **product life cycle**, passing through four distinct stages in sales and profits: introduction, growth, maturity, and decline (see Exhibit 3). The marketing challenge changes from stage to stage, sometimes dramatically.

The product life cycle can describe a product class (gasoline-powered automobiles), a product form (sport utility vehicles), or a brand or model (Ford Explorer). Product classes and forms tend to have the longest life cycles, specific brands somewhat shorter life cycles,

product life cycle Four stages through which a product progresses: introduction, growth, maturity, and decline

---

EXHIBIT 3	The Product Life Cycle

Most products and product categories move through a life cycle similar to the one represented by the curve in this diagram, with new innovations pushing existing products along the time axis. However, the duration of each stage varies widely from product to product. Automobiles have been in the maturity stage for decades, but faxing services barely made it into the introduction stage before being knocked out of the market by low-cost fax machines that every business and home office could afford—which were themselves pushed along the curve by digital document formats.

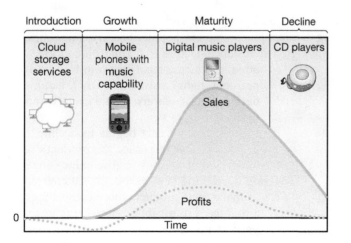

Source: Adapted from Philip Kotler and Gary Armstrong, *Principles of Marketing*, 10th ed. (Upper Saddle River, N.J.: Pearson Prentice Hall, 2004), 330.

and individual products even shorter cycles. The amount of time that a product remains in any one stage depends on customer needs and preferences, economic conditions, the nature of the product, and the marketer's strategy. The proliferation of new products, changing technology, globalization, and the ability to quickly imitate competitors is hurtling many product forms and brands through their life cycles much faster today than in the past. In categories such as smartphones, individual models can go through the entire life cycle in as little as nine months.[4]

Introduction

The first stage in the product life cycle is the *introductory stage*, which extends from the research-and-development (R&D) phase through the product's first commercial availability. The introductory stage is a crucial phase that requires careful planning and often considerable investment. Marketing staffs often work long hours for weeks or months before a product launch, preparing promotional materials, training sales staff, completing packaging, finalizing the price, and wrapping up countless other tasks. Some markets offer the luxury of building demand over time if the introduction isn't a blockbuster, but in others, a weak introduction can doom a product. The opening weekend for a movie, for instance, often determines its success or failure—a tremendously stressful scenario for people who have invested months or years and many millions of dollars making the film.

Growth

After the introductory stage comes the *growth stage*, marked by a rapid jump in sales—if the product is successful—and, usually, an increase in the number of competitors and distribution outlets. As competition increases, so does the struggle for market share. This situation creates pressure to maintain large promotional budgets and competitive prices. With enough growth, however, a firm may be able to reach economies of scale that allow it to create and deliver its products less expensively than in the introduction phase. The growth stage can reap handsome profits for those who survive.

Maturity

During the *maturity stage*, usually the longest in the product life cycle, sales begin to level off. Markets tend to get saturated with all the supply that buyers demand, so the only way a firm can expand its sales in this phase is to win sales away from other suppliers. Because the costs of introduction and growth have diminished in this stage, most companies try to keep mature products alive so they can use the resulting profits to fund the development of new products (often referred to as "milking a cash cow").

Decline

Although maturity can be extended for many years, most products eventually enter the *decline stage*, when sales and profits slip and then fade away. Declines occur for several reasons: changing demographics, shifts in popular taste, overwhelming competition, and advances in technology. For instance, feature-rich smartphones are pushing a bunch of other product categories toward or into decline, including personal digital assistants (PDAs), handheld GPS navigation devices, music players, digital cameras, and portable gaming devices.[5]

When a product begins to decline, the company must decide whether to reduce the product's costs to compensate for declining sales or to discontinue it altogether and focus on developing newer products. Of course, companies can try to make their products more compelling and competitive at any stage. From subtle refinements to complete makeovers, product improvements can sometimes be a way to maintain competitiveness and maximize the returns on the money and effort invested in a product.

✓ Checkpoint

LEARNING OBJECTIVE 1: Identify the main types of consumer and organizational products, and describe the four stages in the life cycle of a product.

SUMMARY: Consumer products can be identified as *convenience*, *shopping*, *specialty*, or *unsought*, distinguished primarily by the amount of thought and effort that goes into buying them. Organizational products are divided into *expense items*, less-expensive goods used in production or operations; *capital items*, more expensive goods and facilities with useful lives longer than a year; and *business services*. The product life cycle consists of (1) the introductory stage, during which marketers focus on stimulating demand for the new product; (2) the growth stage, when marketers focus on increasing the product's market share; (3) the maturity stage, during which marketers try to extend the life of the product by highlighting improvements or by repackaging the product in different sizes; and (4) the decline stage, when firms must decide whether to reduce the product's costs to compensate for declining sales or to discontinue it.

CRITICAL THINKING: (1) Do manufacturers have a responsibility to create safe products even if customers don't care and don't want to pay for safety features? Why or why not? (2) Do automobiles ever enter the decline stage of the product life cycle? Explain your answer.

IT'S YOUR BUSINESS: (1) Have you ever had the urge to be "the first one on the block" to buy a new product, try a new fashion, or discover a new musical artist? If so, were you pleased or displeased when "the masses" began to imitate your choice? What does your reaction say about you as a consumer? (2) Have you ever replaced a product (such as a computer or smartphone) that was still functional, just because a newer version had hit the market? What influenced your decision?

KEY TERMS TO KNOW: convenience products, shopping products, specialty products, expense items, capital items, product life cycle

The New-Product Development Process

2 LEARNING OBJECTIVE

Describe six stages in the product development process.

product development process
A formal process of generating, selecting, developing, and commercializing product ideas

Mad scientists and basement inventors still create new products, but many of today's products appear on the market as a result of a rigorous, formal **product development process**—a method of generating, selecting, developing, and commercializing product ideas (see Exhibit 4 on the next page).

IDEA GENERATION

The first step in the new-product development process is to come up with some ideas that will satisfy unmet needs. Customers, competitors, and employees are often the best source of new-product ideas. Companies can also hire *trend watchers*, can monitor social media to spot shifts in consumer tastes, or can use *crowdsourcing* to invite the public to submit ideas or product designs. Some ideas are more or less sheer luck: The popular photo-sharing website Flickr (www.flickr.com) started as a feature in a massively multiplayer online game; developers soon realized the photo-sharing tool was a better business opportunity than the game they were creating.[6] Of course, many "new" product ideas are simply improvements to or variations on existing products, but even those slight alterations can generate big revenues.

IDEA SCREENING

From all the ideas under consideration, the company selects those that appear to be worthy of further development, applying broad criteria such as whether the product can use existing production facilities and how much technical and marketing risk is involved. Research suggests that sharply narrowing the possibilities at this stage is better than keeping a large

EXHIBIT 4   The Product Development Process

The product development process aims to identify the product ideas most likely to succeed in the marketplace. The process varies widely by company, of course; entrepreneurs and start-ups sometimes begin with a single product idea and take it all the way through to commercialization.

| Idea generation | Idea screening | Business analysis | Prototyping | Test marketing | Commercialization |

| Brainstorm product concepts that could satisfy unmet market needs or enhance the company's product portfolio | Subject those ideas to *feasibility* or *concept testing* to identify those with the best chance of turning into successful products | Subject those ideas to a *business-case analysis* based on estimates of production costs, sales volumes, and selling price | Develop functioning "pre-release" versions that can be used by target customers to check for design flaws, market appeal, and so on | Release a finished or nearly finished *(beta)* version to selected customers or market segments and measure customer reaction | Fine-tune the product design and the rest of the marketing mix and then officially launch the product and push sales in all target markets |

number of ideas alive, since each idea competes for attention or resources until it is abandoned or implemented as a real product.[7] This is often referred to as a *feasibility study*, in which the product's features are defined and its workability is tested. In the case of consumer products, marketing consultants and advertising agencies are often called in to help evaluate new ideas. In some cases, potential customers are asked what they think of a new product idea—a process known as *concept testing*. Some companies involve customers early in the design process to make sure new products truly meet customer needs instead of the design team's perception of customer needs. Xerox's Chief Technology Officer Sophie Vandebroek refers to her company's approach as "customer-led innovation" and says that "dreaming with the customer" is essential to creating the right products.[8]

BUSINESS ANALYSIS

A product idea that survives the screening stage is subjected to a business analysis. During this stage, the company reviews the sales, costs, and profit projections to determine whether they meet the company's objectives. In addition, it estimates the costs associated with various levels of production. Given these projections, analysts calculate the potential profit that will be achieved if the product is introduced. If the product meets the company's objectives, it can then move to the prototype development stage.

PROTOTYPE DEVELOPMENT

prototypes Preproduction samples of products used for testing and evaluation

At this stage, the firm may actually develop a product concept into a functioning "prerelease" product. For physical goods, the firm creates and tests a few samples, or **prototypes**, of the product, including its packaging. These units are rigorously analyzed for usability, durability, manufacturability, customer appeal, and other vital criteria, depending on the type of product. In addition, the company begins to plan for large-scale manufacturing (for tangible goods) or *scalability* (for digital services, for example), then identifies the resources required to bring the product to market.

TEST MARKETING

test marketing A product development stage in which a product is sold on a limited basis to gauge its market appeal

During **test marketing**, the firm introduces the product in selected markets and monitors consumer reactions. Test marketing gives the marketer experience with marketing the product before going to the expense of a full introduction. For instance, producers of television programs can test shows in local or regional markets to gauge viewer appeal before going nationwide. Companies can also release products early to get feedback from potential customers before finalizing features and functions. Software developers often do so through *beta* versions. Test marketing can be expensive and time-consuming, however, so not all companies choose to take this step with every new product.

COMMERCIALIZATION

It's go time. The final stage of development is **commercialization**, the large-scale production and distribution of products that have survived the testing process. This phase (also referred to as a *product launch*) requires the coordination of many activities—manufacturing, packaging, distribution, pricing, media relations, and customer communication.

commercialization Large-scale production and distribution of a product

✔ Checkpoint

LEARNING OBJECTIVE 2: Describe six stages in the product development process.

SUMMARY: The first two stages of product development involve generating and screening ideas to isolate those with the most potential. In the third stage, promising ideas are analyzed to determine their likely profitability. Those that appear worthwhile enter the fourth stage, the prototype development stage, in which a limited number of the products are created. In the fifth stage, the product is test marketed to determine buyer response. Products that survive the testing process are then commercialized, the final stage.

CRITICAL THINKING: (1) Apple claims to never do any marketing research for new product ideas but instead creates products that Apple employees themselves would be excited to have. What are the risks of this approach? Would it work for all consumer and organizational markets? (2) Consumers and government regulators sometimes complain about identical products being sold at different prices to different customers as part of test marketing efforts. Are such tests ethical? Why or why not?

IT'S YOUR BUSINESS: (1) What currently unavailable service can you think of that could be offered on mobile phones? (2) In addition to the mobile phone itself, what other product elements (such as a website or phone accessories) would be required to launch such a service?

KEY TERMS TO KNOW: product development process, prototypes, test marketing, commercialization

Product Identities

Creating an identity for products is one of the most important decisions marketers make. That identity is encompassed in the **brand**, which can have meaning at three levels: (1) a unique name, symbol, or design that sets the product apart from those offered by competitors; (2) the legal protections afforded by a trademark and any relevant intellectual property; and (3) the overall company or organizational brand.[9] For instance, the Nike "swoosh" symbol is a unique identifier on every Nike product, a legally protected piece of intellectual property, and a symbol that represents the entire company.

Branding helps a product in many ways. It gives customers a way of recognizing and specifying a particular product so that they can choose it again or recommend it to others. It provides consumers with information about the product. It facilitates the marketing of the product. And it creates value for the product. This notion of the value of a brand is also called **brand equity**. In fact, a brand name can be an organization's most valuable asset, and major brands are worth billions of dollars—and that's just the intangible value of the brand name.[10] Strong brands simplify marketing efforts because the target audience tends to associate

3 LEARNING OBJECTIVE

Define *brand*, and explain the concepts of brand equity and brand loyalty.

brand A name, term, sign, symbol, design, or combination of those used to identify the products of a firm and to differentiate them from competing products

brand equity The value that a company has built up in a brand

Brands help consumers make confident choices from the thousands of products available in today's supermarkets.

positive qualities with any product that carries a respected brand name—and vice versa.

Customers who buy the same brand again and again are evidence of the strength of **brand loyalty**, or commitment to a particular brand. Brand loyalty can be measured in degrees. The first level is *brand awareness*, which means that people are more likely to buy a product because they are familiar with it. The next level is *brand preference*, which means people will purchase the product if it is available, although they may still be willing to experiment with alternatives if they cannot find the preferred brand. The third and ultimate level of brand loyalty is *brand insistence*, the stage at which buyers will accept no substitute. Some brands, such as Harley-Davidson motorcycles and American Girl dolls, can acquire such a deep level of meaning to loyal consumers that the brands become intertwined with the narratives of the consumers' life stories.[11]

brand loyalty The degree to which customers continue to purchase a specific brand

brand names The portion of brands that can be expressed orally, including letters, words, or numbers

brand marks The portion of brands that cannot be expressed verbally

logo A graphical and/or textual representation of a brand

BRAND NAME SELECTION

Jeep, Levi's 501, and iPod are **brand names**, the portion of a brand that can be spoken, including letters, words, or numbers. Annika Sorenstam uses her first name in all capital letters as her brand name. In contrast, the McDonald's golden arches and the Nike "swoosh" symbol are **brand marks**, the portion of a brand that cannot be expressed verbally. The term **logo** (from *logotype*) once referred to typesetting treatment of a brand name but is now used more variably to refer to the nonverbal brand mark, the visual treatment of the brand name, or the combination of the two (see Exhibit 5).

The choice of a brand name and any associated brand marks can be a critical success factor. Imagine if Nike has chosen a cute fuzzy duckling or a static shape of some kind, rather than the dynamic and "athletic" swoosh shape—not to mention naming the brand after the Greek goddess of victory.

trademarks Brands that have been given legal protection so that their owners have exclusive rights to their use

Brand names and brand symbols may be registered with the Patent and Trademark Office as **trademarks**, brands that have been given legal protection so that their owners have exclusive rights to their use. The Lanham Trademark Act prohibits the unauthorized use of a trademark on goods or services when the use would likely confuse consumers as to the origin of those goods and services.[12] Companies zealously protect their brand names because if a name becomes too widely used in a general sense, it no longer qualifies for protection under trademark laws. Cellophane, kerosene, linoleum, escalator, zipper, and shredded wheat are just a few of the many brand names that have since lost trademark protection and can now be used by anyone.[13]

BRAND OWNERSHIP

national brands Brands owned by manufacturers and distributed nationally

private brands Brands that carry the label of a retailer or a wholesaler rather than a manufacturer

Brand names may be associated with a manufacturer, a retailer, a wholesaler, or a combination of business types. Brands offered and promoted by a national manufacturer, such as Procter & Gamble's Tide detergent and Pampers disposable diapers, are called **national brands**. **Private brands** are not linked to a manufacturer but instead carry a wholesaler's or a retailer's brand. DieHard batteries and Kenmore appliances are private brands sold by Sears. As an alternative to branded products, some retailers also offer *generic products*, which are packaged in plain containers that bear only the name of the product. Note that

| EXHIBIT 5 | Product Identities |

Toyota's Facebook page shows its brand mark, brand name, and a *tagline*, often referred to as a *slogan*.

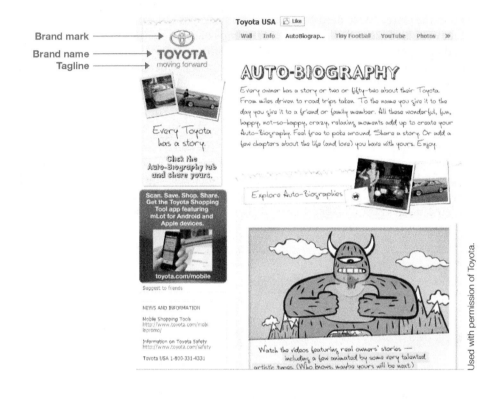

Used with permission of Toyota.

"generics" is also a term used in the pharmaceutical industry to describe products that are copies of an original drug (other companies are allowed to make these copies after the patent on the original drug expires).

Co-branding occurs when two or more companies team up to closely link their names in a single product, usually to leverage the brand associations and awareness of one product onto the other. Companies can also **license**, or offer to sell, the rights to well-known brand names and symbols. Mainstream movies, for example, often hit the market with an array of licensing deals with fast-food chains and other consumer products companies.

co-branding A partnership between two or more companies to closely link their brand names together for a single product

license An agreement to produce and market another company's product in exchange for a royalty or fee

PACKAGING

Most tangible products need some form of packaging to protect them from damage or tampering, but packaging can also play an important role in a product's marketing strategy. Packaging makes products easier to display, facilitates the sale of smaller products, serves as a means of product differentiation, and enhances the product's overall appeal and convenience. Packaging can significantly influence buyer perceptions, too, sometimes in surprising ways. For instance, packages with simple geometric lines (such as cylinders or rectangles) are perceived as being larger than geometrically complex packages of the same volume. Package designers can use these perceptual effects to create particular images for their products.[14]

Packaging can also involve decisions about which items to include as the product offering and in what quantities. For example,

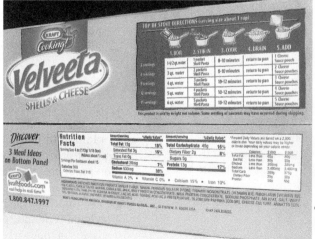

© Sarah-Maria Vischer / The Image Works

Product packaging usually has a number of functions, from promoting and protecting the product to displaying legally required health and safety information to providing instructions for use.

189

Costco and other warehouse-style retailers offer many of the same products available through regular grocery stores but in packages of larger quantities.

In the retailing environment, packaging plays a key role in reducing shoplifting; retailers have put a lot of pressure on manufacturers to adopt packages that are difficult to conceal or to open in the store. Those hard-to-open plastic packages known as "clamshells" that consumers love to hate—and that account for hundreds of injuries every year as people attempt to slice them open—are one such response to shoplifting.[15] Packaging is also a major environmental concern, in both the resources used and waste generated, so expect innovations and new regulations in this area in the coming years.

LABELING

Labeling is an integral part of packaging. Whether the label is a separate element attached to the package or a printed part of the container, it serves to identify a brand and communicate multiple types of information, from promotional messages to legally required safety or nutritional data. The labeling of foods, drugs, cosmetics, and many health products is regulated under various federal laws, which often require disclosures about potential dangers, benefits, and other issues consumers need to consider when making a buying decision.

✔ Checkpoint

LEARNING OBJECTIVE 3: Define *brand*, **and explain the concepts of brand equity and brand loyalty.**

SUMMARY: *Brand* encompasses the various elements of product identity and meaning. *Brand equity* reflects the value of a brand name based on its strength and appeal in the marketplace and its power as a communication vehicle. *Brand loyalty* can be defined at three levels: brand awareness, in which the buyer is familiar with the product; brand preference, in which the buyer will select the product if it is available; and brand insistence, in which the buyer will accept no substitute.

CRITICAL THINKING: (1) Can a brand with a bad reputation be rescued? Would a company be wiser to just drop a "bad brand" and start fresh with something new? (2) Is staying with the same product only a case of brand "loyalty"? Could other factors be in play that lead consumers or organizations not to switch brands? Explain your answer.

IT'S YOUR BUSINESS: (1) How many visible brand marks are you currently wearing? Are these common brands? (2) What do you think these brands say about you?

KEY TERMS TO KNOW: brand, brand equity, brand loyalty, brand names, brand marks, logo, trademarks, national brands, private brands, co-branding, license

---

4 LEARNING OBJECTIVE

Identify four ways of expanding a product line, and discuss two risks that product-line extensions pose.

brand managers Managers who develop and implement the marketing strategies and programs for specific products or brands

Product-Line and Product-Mix Strategies

In addition to developing product identities, a company must continually evaluate what kinds of products it will offer. To stay competitive, most companies continually add and drop products to ensure that declining items will be replaced by growth products. Companies that offer more than one product also need to pay close attention to how those products are positioned in the marketplace relative to one another. The responsibility for managing individual products, product lines, and product mixes is usually assigned to one or more managers in the marketing department. In a smaller company, the *marketing manager* tackles this effort; in larger companies with more products to manage, individual products or groups of products are usually assigned to **brand managers**, known in some companies as *product managers* or *product line managers*.

PRODUCT LINES

A **product line** is a group of products from a single manufacturer that are similar in terms of use or characteristics. The General Mills (www.generalmills.com) snack-food product line, for example, includes Bugles, Cascadian Farm organic snacks, and Nature Valley Granola Bars. Within each product line, a company confronts decisions about the number of goods and services to offer. On the one hand, offering additional products can help a manufacturer boost revenues and increase its visibility in retail stores. On the other hand, creating too many products and product variations can be expensive for everyone in the supply chain and can be confusing to buyers.

product line A series of related products offered by a firm

PRODUCT MIX

An organization with several product lines has a **product mix**—a collection of diverse goods or services offered for sale. The General Mills product mix includes cereals, baking products, desserts, snack foods, and entrees (see Exhibit 6). Three important dimensions of

product mix The complete portfolio of products that a company offers for sale

---

EXHIBIT 6	The Product Mix at General Mills (selected products)

These selected products from General Mills illustrate the various dimensions of its product mix. The mix is *wide* because it contains multiple product lines (cereals, fruit snacks, pasta, soup, yogurt, and more). The cereal product line is *long* because it contains many individual brands (only four of which are shown here). And these four cereal brands show different depths. The Trix brand is a shallow line, whereas the Cheerios brand is *deep*.

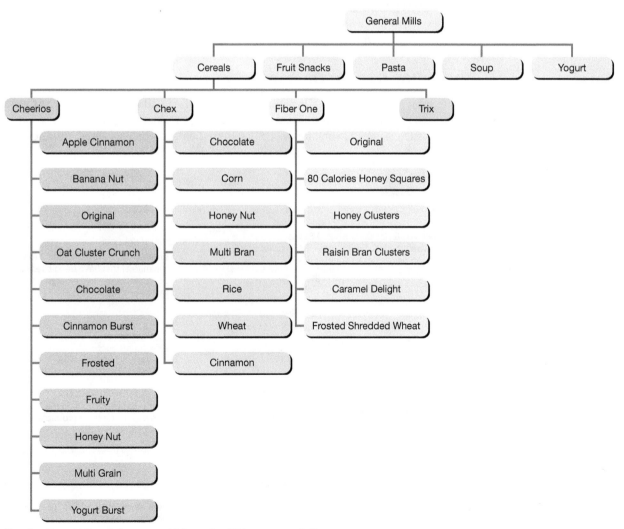

Source: Based on General Mills website, accessed 6 September 2011, www.generalmills.com.

a product mix are *width*, *length*, and *depth*, and each dimension presents its own set of challenges and opportunities. A product mix is *wide* if it has several product lines. A product mix is *long* if it carries several items in its product lines. For instance, General Mills produces multiple cereal brands within the ready-to-eat cereal line. A product mix is *deep* if it has a number of versions of *each* product in a product line. The Cheerios brand, for example, currently has about a dozen different varieties.[16]

When deciding on the dimensions of a product mix, a company must weigh the risks and rewards associated with various approaches. Some companies limit the number of product offerings and focus on selling a few items in higher quantities. Doing so can keep production and marketing costs lower through economies of scale. However, counting too heavily on a narrow set of products leaves a company vulnerable to competitive threats and market shifts. Other companies diversify their product offerings as a protection against shifts in consumer tastes, economic conditions, and technology, or as a way to build marketing synergy by offering complementary products.[17]

Retailers often have considerable influence in manufacturers' product line decisions, particularly in the store-based retail channel. In general, the more revenue a manufacturer represents, the better chance it has of getting all-important shelf space. Consequently, retail store aisles tend to be dominated by a few large brands, and manufacturers look for ways to build portfolios of best sellers that can command attention at the retail level.

Online retailing presents much better opportunities for large numbers of specialized and low-volume products. Without the physical limitations of a "bricks and mortar" facility, online retailers can offer a much greater variety of products. For example, the average physical bookstore might offer 40,000 volumes, whereas the major online book retailers offer several million.[18] While these products may individually sell at lower volumes, collectively they represent a substantial business opportunity that has been termed the *long tail* (referring to a sales volume graph in which a vast number of low-volume products stretches out toward infinity).[19]

PRODUCT EXPANSION STRATEGIES

As Exhibit 7 shows, you can expand your product line and mix in a number of ways. One approach is to introduce additional items in a given product category under the same brand name—such as new flavors, forms, colors, ingredients, or package sizes. Another approach

EXHIBIT 7	Expanding a Product Line

Companies use one or more of these product-line expansion methods to pursue new opportunities.

Example: Taylor Guitars's 200 Series, priced between the 100 Series entry-level models and the company's professional series

Line filling: Developing items to fill gaps in the market that have been overlooked by competitors or have emerged as consumer tastes and needs shift

Example: Crest Pro-Health Enamel Shield Toothpaste

Line extension: Creating variations of an existing product

Example: Iams pet insurance (Iams is a brand of pet food)

Brand extension: Using the brand of existing products on products in a new category

Example: Volkswagen Passat CC (priced above the regular Passat models)

Line stretching: Adding items with price points above or below the current product line

is to expand a product line to add new and similar products with the same product name—a strategy known as **family branding**.

Conversely, in a **brand extension**, a company applies a successful brand name to a new product category in the hopes that the recognition and reputation of the brand will give it a head start in the new category. Building on the name recognition of an existing brand cuts the costs and risks of introducing new products. However, product-line extensions present two important risks that marketers need to consider carefully. First, stretching a brand to cover too many categories or types of products can dilute the brand's meaning in the minds of target customers. For instance, if the sports broadcaster ESPN were to branch out into business and financial news, its original sports audience might wonder whether the company is still committed to being a leader in sports journalism, and the business news audience might wonder what value a sports media company could bring to financial news. Second, additional products do not automatically guarantee increased sales revenue. Marketers need to make sure that new products don't simply *cannibalize*, or take sales away from, their existing products.

family branding Using a brand name on a variety of related products

brand extension Applying a successful brand name to a new product category

PRODUCT STRATEGIES FOR INTERNATIONAL MARKETS

Product adaptation is one of the key changes that companies need to consider when moving into other countries. First, managers must decide on which products and services to introduce in which countries. When selecting a country, they must take into consideration the type of government, market-entry requirements, tariffs and other trade barriers, cultural and language differences, consumer preferences, foreign-exchange rates, and differing business customs. Then, they must decide whether to standardize the product, selling it everywhere, or to customize the product to accommodate the lifestyles and habits of local target markets. A company may change only the product's name or packaging, or it can modify the product's components, size, and functions.

For example, the social network site hi5 (www.hi5.com) has become one of the world's most popular gaming and entertainment websites through extensive adaption, including localization in more than 50 languages around the world.[20] Similarly, French consumers have been eating at McDonald's (www.mcdonalds.fr) since the company first arrived in 1972, but the burger giant has a unique look in that country. To accommodate a culture known for its cuisine and dining experience, many McDonald's outlets in France have upgraded their decor to a level that would make them almost unrecognizable in the United States. And while the basic burger offerings remain roughly the same, menus include local cheeses, brioche (a soft bread), and *croques monsieurs* (a traditional grilled ham-and-cheese sandwich).[21]

For the latest information on product and branding strategies, visit http://real-timeupdates .com/bia6.

✓ Checkpoint

LEARNING OBJECTIVE 4: Identify four ways of expanding a product line, and discuss two risks that product-line extensions pose.

SUMMARY: A product line can be expanded by filling gaps in the market, extending the line to include new varieties of existing products, extending the brand to new product categories, and stretching the line to include lower- or higher-priced items. Two of the biggest risks with product-line extensions are losing brand identity and coherence (weakening of the brand's meaning) and cannibalizing of sales of other products in the product line.

CRITICAL THINKING: (1) If McDonald's had been relatively unknown to French diners when the company entered that market in 1972, would it have made more sense to use a different and more "French-sounding" brand name? Why or why not? (2) Would a consumer-products manufacturer ever want to create more product extensions and variations than it could explain in terms of pure market appeal? Why or why not?

| 5 | LEARNING OBJECTIVE |

List the factors that influence pricing decisions, and explain break-even analysis.

Pricing Strategies

The second key element in the marketing mix is pricing. Pricing involves *capturing value* back from the customer in exchange for the value provided in the product. Setting and managing prices is a combination of strategic considerations and careful financial analysis.

STRATEGIC CONSIDERATIONS IN PRICING

Managers must consider a variety of internal and external factors when establishing prices:

- **Marketing objectives**. The first step in setting a price is to match it to the objectives set in the strategic marketing plan. Is the goal to increase market share, increase sales, improve profits, project a particular image, or combat competition? Price is a flexible tool that can help a firm achieve a wide variety of marketing objectives.
- **Government regulations**. To protect consumers and encourage fair competition, governments around the world have enacted various price-related laws over the years. These regulations are particularly important in three areas of prohibited behavior: (1) *price discrimination*, unfairly offering attractive discounts to some customers but not to others; (2) *deceptive pricing*, pricing schemes that are considered misleading; and (3) *price fixing*, an agreement among two or more companies supplying the same type of products as to the prices they will charge. For example, the U.S. government recently fined 21 airlines more than $1.7 billion—and sent several airline executives to jail—for an extensive price-fixing scheme on flights to and from the United States. The scheme operated for more than five years, until two of the airlines, Lufthansa and Virgin Atlantic, took advantage of an amnesty program and turned themselves in.[22]
- **Customer perceptions**. Another consideration in setting price is the perception of quality and value that a price elicits from customers. An unexpectedly low price can trigger fears of low quality, but a high price can connote quality and even exclusivity. Specific numbers can have perceptual effect as well, such as the well-known "9 effect." You've probably noticed that many prices end in a 9, such as $9.99 or $5,999. Your conscious mind says, "Gimme a break; we all know that's really $10 or $6,000." However, research suggests that our minds equate that 9 with a bargain—even when it isn't. In one experiment, for example, a dress sold more when priced at $39 than when it was priced at $34.[23]
- **Market demand**. The discussion of supply and demand in Chapter 2 points out that market demand usually fluctuates as prices fluctuate. However, some goods and services are relatively *insensitive* to changes in price; others are highly *sensitive*. Buyers can also exhibit individual levels of price sensitivity. For instance, brand-loyal customers tend to be less sensitive to price, meaning they will stick with a brand even as the price increases, whereas other buyers will begin switching to cheaper alternatives.[24] Marketers refer to this sensitivity as **price elasticity**—how responsive demand will be to a change in price.
- **Competition**. Competitive prices are obviously a major consideration whenever a firm is establishing or changing its prices. Technology has profoundly shifted the balance of power in this respect from sellers to buyers in recent years, as social commerce websites

price elasticity A measure of the sensitivity of demand to changes in price

Prices that end in 9 (such as $9.99 or $5,499) try to convey a "bargain" message. However, marketers of higher-quality products often use even-numbered prices that end in 0 to emphasize a sense of luxury over low cost.

and mobile Internet access make it easy to find the lowest prices for a wide variety of goods and services. The easier it is for buyers to compare prices, for instance, the more important competitive prices become—particularly when buyers don't perceive much difference among the available products.

COST STRUCTURE AND BREAK-EVEN ANALYSIS

Every company has a particular *cost structure* that determines how much it must spend to create and market its products. Some costs remain the same regardless of production and sales volume. Such **fixed costs** include rent or mortgage payments, insurance premiums, real estate taxes, and salaries. These are costs incurred just to "keep the doors open," without creating or selling anything. In contrast, **variable costs**, including raw materials, supplies consumed during production, shipping, and sales commissions, vary with changes in production and sales volume. Obviously, the more a company can lower its cost structure, the more flexibility it has in setting prices and ensuring desirable levels of profit.

The cost to create and sell each product is a combination of fixed and variable costs. A critical calculation in setting prices is **break-even analysis**, determining the number of units a firm must sell at a given price to recoup both fixed and variable costs—to "break even," in other words. The **break-even point** is the minimum sales volume the company must achieve to avoid losing money. Sales volume beyond the break-even point will generate profits; sales volume below the break-even amount will result in losses.

You can determine the break-even point in number of units with this simple calculation:

$$\text{Break-even point} = \frac{\text{Fixed costs}}{\text{Selling price} - \text{Variable costs per unit}}$$

For example, if you wanted to price haircuts at $20 and you had fixed costs of $60,000 and variable costs per haircut of $5, you would need to sell 4,000 haircuts to break even:

$$\text{Break-even point} = \frac{\$60,000}{\$20 - \$5} = 4,000 \text{ units}$$

fixed costs Business costs that remain constant regardless of the number of units produced

variable costs Business costs that increase with the number of units produced

break-even analysis A method of calculating the minimum volume of sales needed at a given price to cover all costs

break-even point Sales volume at a given price that will cover all of a company's costs

Naturally, $20 isn't your only pricing option. Why not charge $30 instead? At that price, you need to sell only 2,400 haircuts to break even (see Exhibit 8). Of course, you would have to convince 2,400 people to pay the higher price, and depending on market dynamics and your cost structure, you might make more money selling at the lower price.

Note that break-even analysis doesn't dictate what price you *should* charge; rather, it provides some insight into the price you *can* charge and begin to generate profit. With the break-even point in hand, you can then factor in the various strategic considerations to determine price using one of the methods discussed in the next section.

EXHIBIT 8	**Break-Even Analysis**

The break-even point is the point at which revenues just cover costs. After fixed costs and variable costs have been met, any additional income represents profit. The graphs show that at $20 per haircut, the break-even point is 4,000 haircuts; charging $30 yields a break-even point at only 2,400 haircuts.

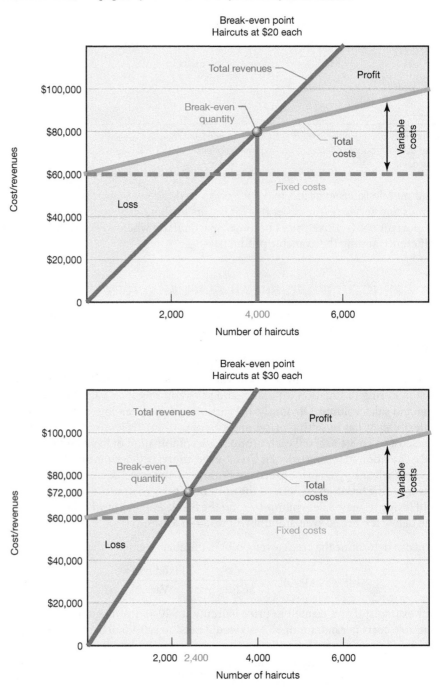

✓ Checkpoint

LEARNING OBJECTIVE 5: List the factors that influence pricing decisions, and explain break-even analysis.

SUMMARY: Strategic considerations in pricing include marketing objectives, government regulations, customer perceptions, market demand, and competition. *Break-even analysis* is a way to determine how many units (the *break-even point*) a firm needs to produce in order to begin turning a profit by covering its fixed and variable costs. The break-even point is calculated by dividing fixed costs by the difference between the selling price and the variable costs per unit.

CRITICAL THINKING: (1) Why wouldn't a firm just drop any product that isn't selling in high enough volume to reach its break-even point? (2) Is "9" style pricing ethical? Why or why not?

IT'S YOUR BUSINESS: (1) Do you factor in the value of your time when you price-comparison shop? Why or why not? (2) As a consumer taking charge of your own financial future, what lessons could you take from the business concepts of fixed and variable costs?

KEY TERMS TO KNOW: price elasticity, fixed costs, variable costs, break-even analysis, break-even point

Pricing Methods

6 LEARNING OBJECTIVE

Identify nine common pricing methods.

Break-even analysis and the various strategic considerations help managers establish an overall framework of pricing possibilities. You can think of costs as establishing the pricing "floor," whereas demand, competition, and other factors establish the "ceiling." Somewhere between those two limits lies the ideal price for each product. Managers can apply a variety of methods to pinpoint specific prices. Note that some of these methods aren't mutually exclusive; companies can use two or more methods, either in succession or at the same time.

COST-BASED PRICING

Some companies simplify the pricing task by using **cost-based pricing**, also known as *cost-plus pricing*, in which they start with the cost of producing a good or a service and then add a *markup* to arrive at the selling price. Cost-based pricing is simple, but it suffers from a major weakness: It doesn't consider any external factors such as customer demand or competitive prices. The price could be too high for market conditions, leaving the company uncompetitive, or it could be too low, generating less profit than it could otherwise.

cost-based pricing A method of setting prices based on production and marketing costs, rather than conditions in the marketplace

VALUE-BASED PRICING

In contrast to cost-based pricing, **value-based pricing** establishes a price on a product's potential or perceived value in the marketplace. In other words, rather than starting with cost and then figuring out a price, this method starts with a target price and works backward to identify a cost structure that will yield acceptable profit margins. The disadvantage of this method is that it requires more information and more analysis, because managers need to measure or at least estimate perceptions of customer value in order to establish the price. If a company lacks the information to establish a realistic price point based on value, one option is to introduce the product using cost-based pricing and then gradually shift to a value-based model as more is learned about how customers perceive the product.[25]

An additional challenge with value-based pricing is that perceptions of value change over time. For example, in a recession or depression, consumers take a much harder look at

value-based pricing A method of setting prices based on customer perceptions of value

the value they are receiving for the money they spend. Many want more product value while paying the same price or the same product value at a lower price, while others are willing to give up some product value in exchange for lower prices. In all these cases, the perception of value changes, and companies that understand and can deliver on the new perceptions of value stand the best chance of surviving or even thriving during tough times.[26]

OPTIMAL PRICING

optimal pricing A computer-based pricing method that creates a demand curve for every product to help managers select a price that meets specific marketing objectives

Optimal pricing attempts to minimize the errors and guesswork of other methods by using computer software to generate the ideal price for every item, at each individual store, at any given time. A price-optimization program feeds reams of data from checkout scanners, seasonal sales figures, competitors, and other sources into probability algorithms to come up with an individual demand curve for each product in each store. From that, retailers can identify which products are the most price sensitive. Then they can adjust prices up or down according to each store's priorities—profit, revenue, or market share. Some systems also let store managers conduct "what if" analyses based on past sales data, helping them see the potential effect of proposed price changes.[27]

SKIM PRICING

skim pricing Charging a high price for a new product during the introductory stage and lowering the price later

During the introductory phase of the product life cycle, a company may opt to take advantage of strong demand before competitors can enter the market and exert downward pressure on prices. To achieve this goal, the company can charge a high initial price—a practice known as **skim pricing**—with the intention of dropping the price later. *Early adopters* are often willing to pay a premium to get their hands on new products as soon as possible. In consumer markets, some people simply want to have the latest and greatest before anyone else; in organizational markets, new types of equipment can give companies a short-term competitive advantage.

PENETRATION PRICING

penetration pricing Introducing a new product at a low price in hopes of building sales volume quickly

Skim prices are set high with the understanding that many customers won't be willing to pay them. In contrast, companies use **penetration pricing** to build sales volume by charging a low initial price. This approach has the added advantage of discouraging competition, because the low price—which competitors would be pressured to match—limits the profit potential for everyone. (If the intent of penetration is to drive competitors out of business, though, companies open themselves up to charges of illegal *predatory pricing*.)

However, penetration pricing doesn't work if the company can't sustain the low price levels profitably, if prices for a particular product are inelastic, or if customers weigh other factors more heavily than price. Moreover, as mentioned earlier, prices that are far below the market's expectations can raise concerns about quality, reliability, and safety. Everyone would like to pay less for medical care, but many people would be unwilling to go to cut-rate clinics if they thought their health might be jeopardized.

LOSS-LEADER PRICING

loss-leader pricing Selling one product at a loss as a way to entice customers to consider other products

As part of a larger marketing plan, some companies occasionally resort to **loss-leader pricing**, setting a price on one product so low that they lose money on every sale but recoup that loss by enticing customers to try a new product or buy other products. For instance, grocery stores can use milk and other staples as loss leaders to encourage shoppers to visit. (And there's a reason these products are often all the way at the back of the store—you have to walk past hundreds of higher-margin products that you might suddenly decide you can't live without.)

AUCTION PRICING

In an *auction*, the seller doesn't set a firm price but allows buyers to competitively bid on the products being sold. Auctions used to be confined to a few market sectors such as fine art, agricultural products, and government bonds, but that all changed when eBay turned selling and buying via auctions into a new national pastime. Many companies now use eBay and other auction sites to sell everything from modular buildings to tractors to industrial equipment. In *procurement auctions* or *reverse auctions*, potential buyers identify the goods or services they need and the prices they're willing to pay, then suppliers respond with offers at the prices they're willing to charge. The travel website Priceline.com, for example, lets buyers enter a price they're willing to pay and then see whether airlines, hotels, and other providers are willing to sell at that price (see Exhibit 9).[28]

EXHIBIT 9	Reverse Auction Pricing

Priceline was a pioneer in the concept of reverse auction pricing.

PARTICIPATIVE PRICING

participative pricing Allowing customers to pay the amount they think a product is worth

One of the most unusual pricing strategies is **participative pricing**, sometimes known as "pay what you want," in which customers literally get to pay as much as they think a product is worth. While it might sound like a strategy for financial disaster, with participative pricing, buyers sometimes pay *more* than the company would normally charge.[29] When the band Radiohead let buyers name their own price for one of its downloadable albums, the band made more money from that album than from downloads on all their other studio albums combined.[30]

FREE AND FREEMIUM PRICING

freemium pricing A hybrid pricing strategy of offering some products for free while charging for others, or offering a product for free to some customers while charging others for it

Even more radical than participative pricing is no price at all. However, giving away goods and services can make a lot of sense in the right situation, such as when a new company is trying to make a name for itself in the marketplace.[31] Another use of free pricing is when some customers are charged enough to provide free goods and services for other customers, a tactic known as **freemium pricing** (*free + premium*).[32] For example, a number of smartphone and tablet apps offer a free version with fewer capabilities and a paid version of the full product. Giving away some products while maintaining full prices for others (the common "buy one, get one free" approach) is also a way to effectively offer discounted pricing without the risk of creating expectations of lower prices.[33]

PRICE ADJUSTMENT TACTICS

discounts Temporary price reductions to stimulate sales or lower prices to encourage certain behaviors such as paying with cash

After they've established initial price points, companies need to stay on the lookout for potential advantages that can be gained by adjusting prices up or down over time. They can offer a variety of **discounts**, such as temporary price reductions to stimulate sales, price reductions for paying early or paying in cash, or *volume discounts* for buying in bulk.

Although offering discounts is a popular way to boost sales of a product, the downside is that discounts can set off *price wars* between competitors. Price wars can occur when (1) one supplier believes that underpricing the competition is the best way—or perhaps the only way—for it to increase sales volume and (2) customers believe that price is the only meaningful differentiator among the various suppliers. This situation occurs frequently in the air travel industry, which is why it has been wracked with price wars ever since it was deregulated years ago. Price wars present two significant dangers: that customers will begin to believe that price is the only factor to care about in the market and that desperate competitors will cut prices so far that they'll damage their finances—perhaps beyond repair.

bundling Offering several products for a single price that is presumably lower than the total of the products' individual prices

Sometimes sellers combine several of their products and sell them at one reduced price. This practice, called **bundling**, can also promote sales of products consumers might not otherwise buy—especially when the combined price is low enough to entice them to purchase the bundle. Examples of bundled products are season tickets, vacation packages, computer software with hardware, and wrapped packages of shampoo and conditioner.

dynamic pricing Continually adjusting prices to reflect changes in supply and demand

Finally, companies can constantly reprice their products in response to supply and demand fluctuations, a tactic known as **dynamic pricing**. Dynamic pricing not only enables companies to move slow-selling merchandise instantly but also allows companies to experiment with different pricing levels. Because price changes are immediately distributed via computer networks, customers always have the most current price information. Airlines and hotels have used this type of continually adjusted pricing for years, a technique often known as *yield management*. However, companies need to be careful not to alienate customers by creating so much pricing uncertainty that purchasing becomes a frustrating cat-and-mouse game. In fact, noted brand strategist Al Ries calls dynamic pricing the "ultimate brand destruction machine" because it rewards buyers for price shopping rather than being loyal to a single brand.[34]

For the latest information on pricing strategies and tactics, visit http://real-timeupdates.com/bia6.

REAL-TIME UPDATES
Learn More by Reading This Article

Can the business world survive Groupon?

Coupons have been a pricing dilemma for years, but Groupon and other social coupon schemes are turning couponing into a blessing for some companies and a nightmare for others. Go to http://real-timeupdates.com/bia6 and click on Learn More. If you are using MyBizLab, you can access Real-Time Updates within the chapter or under Student Study Tools.

✔ Checkpoint

LEARNING OBJECTIVE 6: Identify nine common pricing methods.

SUMMARY: (1) *Cost-based* or *cost-plus pricing* takes the cost of producing and marketing a product and adds a markup to arrive at the selling price. (2) *Value-based pricing* seeks to establish the perceived value of the product in the eyes of target customers and sets a price based on that. (3) *Optimal pricing* is a computer-based method that uses sales data to create a demand curve for every product, allowing managers to select prices based on specific marketing objectives. (4) *Skim pricing* involves setting an initial price that is relatively high in order to capitalize on pent-up demand or the lack of direct competition for a new product. (5) *Penetration pricing* is setting a price low enough to achieve targeted sales volumes. (6) *Loss-leader pricing* is setting the price artificially low on one product in order to attract buyers for other products. (7) *Auction pricing* lets buyers determine the selling price by bidding against one another; in a reverse auction, buyers state a price they are willing to pay and sellers choose whether to match it. (8) *Participative pricing* lets buyers pay whatever they think a product is worth. (9) *Freemium pricing* involves giving away products to some customers (as a means of attracting paying customers, for example) or giving away some products but charging for others.

CRITICAL THINKING: (1) What steps could a company take to determine the perceived value of its products in its target markets? (2) How can patterns of temporary price discounts "train" consumers to stop buying at full price?

IT'S YOUR BUSINESS: (1) Have you ever bid on anything on eBay, another online auction site, or an in-person auction? If so, how did you decide how much to bid? Did you set a maximum price you'd allow yourself to spend? Did you get caught up in the competitive emotions of bidding against someone else? (2) Have you ever purchased a hot new product as soon as it hit the market, only to see the price drop a few months later? If so, did you resolve never to buy so quickly again?

KEY TERMS TO KNOW: cost-based pricing, value-based pricing, optimal pricing, skim pricing, penetration pricing, loss-leader pricing, participative pricing, freemium pricing, discounts, bundling, dynamic pricing

---

BEHIND THE SCENES
BUILDING THE ANNIKA BRAND

MyBizLab

Annika Sorenstam is approaching her second career the same way she approached her first. In golf, she reached the top of her sport by learning from the best, surrounding herself with a supportive team, setting ambitious goals, and working as hard as it takes to reach those goals.

A central element in her business plan is the role she herself plays as the core of the "Annika" brand. As a young player in her native Sweden, she was so reluctant to step into the limelight that she would falter toward the end of tournaments to avoid winning and facing the media attention that came with it. She clearly fixed that problem, transforming herself into a quietly confident but ferocious competitor who often left other players in the dust as she went on to win nearly 90 times worldwide.

However, as she was nearing retirement from golf and ramping up her business activities, she realized that the persona she had become known for on the course didn't lend itself to her ambitions for the Annika brand. Research by branding consultant Duane Knapp showed that people respected Sorenstam's competitive drive but really had no sense of who she was as a person. Even her own husband says she was viewed by the public as "the stoic Swede who will step on your throat" on the way to victory and not the "humble, pretty, and hilarious" woman he knew off the course.

Transforming Annika the feared competitor into Annika the warm and welcoming brand icon was a top priority. Good examples of this effort are her blog www.annikablog.com and her Twitter account http://twitter.com/#!/ANNIKA59, which give visitors the chance to know her as she lives off the course, including her love of gourmet cooking, her passion for skiing, and her role as a mother.

Along with crafting an inviting brand image that more accurately reflects her true personality, Sorenstam is busy expanding the Annika product line. She continues to endorse many of the same goods and services she promoted as an active player, including Callaway Golf, Lexus, and Rolex. Other business partnerships include an Annika-branded clothing line with Cutter & Buck, Annika wine, and Annika perfume.

A central element in her product portfolio is the Annika Academy, a golf instruction facility in Reunion, Florida, that offers lessons, corporate outings, golf vacations, and the opportunity to train with the same advisors and coaches who work with Sorenstam. For the ultimate golf experience, a few lucky visitors every year can buy the three-day, $12,000 "Soren-Slam" package, which includes nine holes of golf with Sorenstam herself.

Following another path blazed by her golf-business mentors, Sorenstam also launched a golf course design business, with courses stretching from Turkey to China to the United States. Having had the opportunity to play some of the finest and most historic golf courses in the world, she combines that experience with her insights as a professional to create challenging but playable courses. Her designs also aim to right an aesthetic wrong shared by too many golf courses: The best views of both the playing area and the surrounding landscape are found on the men's tee boxes. (Golf courses have different sets of tee boxes to reflect the different hitting lengths of average male and female players.) On her courses, women enjoy the same quality of experience as the men.

Sorenstam has had an interest in finance since any early age, and that passion is reflected in yet another part of the product mix, the Annika Financial Group. This small advisory firm helps other professional athletes manage their money and achieve financial security in their postathletic lives.

With a recrafted brand image and a growing product portfolio, Sorenstam is off to a hot start in her quest to be the first woman to join the exclusive club of former athletes who have truly made it big in business. Michael Jordan is "Air Jordan," Arnold Palmer is the "The King," Jack Nicklaus is "The Golden Bear," and Greg Norman, another golf empire builder, is "The Shark." Who knows—perhaps Annika is "The Avenger"?[35]

Critical Thinking Questions

1. Golfers who take lessons and purchase other services from the Annika Academy presumably share at least some of Sorenstam's passion for winning. Would toning down the competitive aspect of Sorenstam's public persona negatively affect the Annika brand in the eyes of Academy customers? Explain your answer.
2. Sorenstam's charitable efforts include the Annika Foundation, which you can read about on her website. How does her work with the Make-A-Wish Foundation and other activities contribute to her brand equity?
3. Explain how the brand extension efforts in wine, perfume, and financial advice can reasonably fit under the umbrella of the Annika brand.

LEARN MORE ONLINE

Visit Sorenstam's main website at www.annikasorenstam.com, her blog at www.annikablog.com, her Twitter account at http://twitter.com/#!/ANNIKA59, and the Annika Academy website at www.annikaacademy.com. What is your overall impression of Sorenstam as a businessperson and of the Annika brand as a product identifier? Do these communication efforts help in the effort to shift her public image away from that of the fierce competitor?

MyBizLab

Log on to www.mybizlab.com to access study and assessment aids associated with this chapter.

KEY TERMS

brand
brand equity
brand extension
brand loyalty
brand managers
brand mark
brand names
break-even analysis
break-even point
bundling
capital items
co-branding
commercialization
convenience products
cost-based pricing

discounts
dynamic pricing
expense items
family branding
fixed costs
freemium pricing
license
logo
loss-leader pricing
national brands
optimal pricing
participative pricing
penetration pricing
price elasticity
private brands

product development process	skim pricing
product life cycle	specialty products
product line	test marketing
product mix	trademarks
prototypes	value-based pricing
shopping products	variable costs

TEST YOUR KNOWLEDGE

Questions for Review

1. What are the four stages of the product life cycle?
2. What is test marketing?
3. What are the functions of packaging?
4. How many books will a publisher have to sell to break even if fixed costs are $100,000, the selling price per book is $60, and the variable costs per book are $40?
5. How does cost-based pricing differ from value-based pricing?

Questions for Analysis

6. How does branding help consumers?
7. Why are some well-established brands worth millions or even billions of dollars?
8. Why is cost-based pricing risky?
9. Why is it important to review the objectives of a strategic marketing plan before setting a product's price?
10. **Ethical Considerations.** If your college neighborhood is typical, many companies in the area adorn themselves in your school colors and otherwise seek to identify their names with your school name and thereby encourage business from students. Some of these firms probably have brand licensing agreements with your college or are involved in sponsoring various groups on campus. However, chances are some of them are using school colors and other branding elements without having any formal arrangement with the college. In other words, they may be getting commercial benefit from the association without paying for it.[36] Is this ethical? Why or why not?

Questions for Application

11. In what ways might Mattel modify its pricing strategies during the life cycle of a toy product?
12. Do you consider yourself an *early adopter* when it comes to trying out new products or new fashions, or do you tend to take a wait-and-see attitude? How does your attitude toward new products and new ideas influence your decision-making as a consumer?
13. This question was intentionally excluded from this edition.
14. This question was intentionally excluded from this edition.

EXPAND YOUR KNOWLEDGE

Discovering Career Opportunities

Being a marketing manager is a big responsibility, but it can be a lot of fun at the same time. Read what the U.S. Department of Labor has to say about the nature of the work, working conditions, qualifications, and job outlook for marketing managers by accessing the Bureau of Labor Statistics's *Occupational Outlook Handbook*, at www.bls.gov/oco.

1. What does a marketing manager do?

2. What are some key questions you might want to ask when interviewing for a job in marketing?

3. What training and qualifications should a marketing manager have?

Improving Your Tech Insights: Location and Tracking Technologies

Location and tracking technologies cover a wide range of capabilities. Radio frequency identification (RFID) technology uses small scannable tags attached to products or even people and pets. RFID is being implemented extensively in retail and wholesale distribution systems to enhance inventory management. Parents and caregivers can also use RFID to check on elderly relatives, pets, or children. The Great America amusement park in Santa Clara, California, offers RFID bracelets for $5 so parents and children can reconnect if they get separated in the crowds. The Food and Drug Administration (FDA) has approved an implantable device that stores medical information that emergency personnel could retrieve with a quick scan, even if the patient is unconscious.

The Global Positioning System (GPS) can pinpoint any location on Earth using a network of satellites and small transceivers. Trucking fleets use GPS to keep track of all their vehicles to optimize scheduling and make sure drivers stay on assigned routes. Some rental car companies use GPS to see whether drivers break the speed limit or venture outside of permitted rental territories. *Enhanced 911*, or *E911*, uses either GPS or cell phone towers to let emergency personnel pinpoint the location of people calling on cell phones. GPS-enabled smartphones are creating a dizzying array of new location-based services, from location-based social networking such as Loopt and Foursquare to shopping and dining guides to wireless payment systems.

Using online research tools, identify at least one emerging business opportunity that could take advantage of location and tracking technologies. In an email message to your instructor, describe the opportunity and briefly explain how the technology would be used.[37]

PRACTICE YOUR SKILLS

Sharpening Your Communication Skills

Now's your chance to play the role of a marketing specialist trying to convince a group of customers that your product concept is better than the competition's. You're going to wade into the industry battle over digital photo printing. Choose a side: either the photo printer manufacturers, who want consumers to buy printers to print their own digital photos (visit HP, at www.hp.com, for an overview of photo-quality printers), or the service providers, who claim their way is better (visit one of the many retailers that offer a service-based approach, such as www.cvs.com or www.walmart.com). Prepare a short presentation on why the approach you've chosen is better for consumers. Feel free to segment the consumer market and choose a particular target segment if that bolsters your argument.

Building Your Team Skills

Select a high-profile product with which you and your teammates are familiar. Do some online research to learn more about that brand. Then answer these questions and prepare a short group presentation to your classmates summarizing your findings:

- Is the product a consumer product, an organizational product, or both?
- At what stage in its life cycle is this product?
- Is the product a national brand or a private brand?
- How do the product's packaging and labeling help boost consumer appeal?

- How is this product promoted?
- Is the product mix to which this product belongs wide? Long? Deep?
- Is the product sold in international markets? If so, does the company use a standardized or a customized strategy?
- How is the product priced in relation to competing products?

Developing Your Research Skills

Scan recent business journals and newspapers (print or online editions) for an article related to one of the following:
- New product development
- The product life cycle
- Brand extensions
- Pricing strategies
- Packaging

1. Does this article report on a development in a particular company, several companies, or an entire industry? Which companies or industries are specifically mentioned?
2. If you were a marketing manager in this industry, what concerns would you have as a result of reading the article? What questions do you think companies in this industry (or related ones) should be asking? What would you want to know?
3. In what ways do you think this industry, other industries, or the public might be affected by this trend or development in the next five years? Why?

REFERENCES

1. Annika Sorenstam website, accessed 7 September 2011, www.annikasorenstam.com; Annika Academy website, accessed 7 September 2011, www.theannikaacademy.com; Jeff Chu, "A New Course for Sörenstam," *Time South Pacific* (Australia/New Zealand edition), 12 January 2009, 46–47; Brian McCallen, "Annika on Course," *Forbes*, 8 October 2007, 68–69; Eben Harrell, "Calling Time," *Time South Pacific* (Australia/New Zealand edition), 26 May 2008, 5; Edward Schmidt, Jr., "Fierce Competition," *Meeting News*, 8 October 2007, 60; Barry Janoff, "Sorenstam Scores with Sponsors; Foul Called on NBA's Offseason," *Brandweek*, 1 October 2007, 12; Jessica Shambora, "Stroke of Genius," *Fortune*, 10 November 2008, 62–64.

2. Jeneanne Rae, "New Thinking About Consumer Marketing," *BusinessWeek*, 30 June 2009, 16.
3. Werner Reinartz and Wolfgang Ulaga, "How to Sell Services More Profitably," *Harvard Business Review*, May 2008, 90–96.
4. Jung-Ah Lee and Evan Ramstad, "Samsung Pulls Galaxy Tab from Berlin Trade Show," *Wall Street Journal*, 6 September 2011, http://online.wsj.com.
5. Jenna Wortham, "Sending GPS Devices the Way of the Tape Deck?" *New York Times*, 7 July 2009, www.nytimes.com.
6. Michael V. Copeland and Om Malik, "How to Build a Bulletproof Startup," *Business 2.0*, June 2006, www.business2.com.

7. Nicolas Block, Kara Gruver, and David Cooper, "Slimming Innovation Pipelines to Fatten Their Returns," *Harvard Management Update*, August 2007, 3–5.

8. Nanette Byrnes, "Xerox' New Design Team: Customers," *BusinessWeek*, 7 May 2007, 72.

9. David Haigh and Jonathan Knowles, "How to Define Your Brand and Determine Its Value," *Marketing Management*, May/June 2004, 22–28.

10. David Kiley, "Best Global Brands," *BusinessWeek*, 6 August 2007, 56–64.

11. Nina Diamond, John F. Sherry, Albert M. Muñiz, Mary Ann McGrath, Robert V. Kozinets, and Stefania Borghini, "American Girl and the Brand Gestalt: Closing the Loop on Sociocultural Branding Research," *Journal of Marketing*, May 2009, 118–134.

12. Janell M. Kurtz and Cynthia Mehoves, "Whose Name Is It Anyway," *Marketing Management*, January/February 2002, 31–33.

13. Dictionary.com, accessed 24 October 2011, www.dictionary.com.

14. Lawrence L. Garber Jr., Eva M. Hyatt, and Ünal Ö. Boya, "The Effect of Package Shape on Apparent Volume: An Exploratory Study with Implications for Package Design," *Journal of Marketing Theory & Practice*, Summer 2009, 215–234.

15. Margaret Webb Pressler, "Do Not Pry Open Until Christmas: The Hard Truth About Hated 'Clamshell' Packaging," *Washington Post*, 30 November 2006, A1+; Jennifer Saranow, "The Puncture Wound I Got for Christmas," *Wall Street Journal*, 30 December 2004, D1+.

16. General Mills website, accessed 7 September 2011, www.generalmills.com.

17. Betsy Morris and Joan L. Levinstein, "What Makes Apple Golden," *Fortune*, 17 March 2008, 68–74; Bharat N. Anand, "The Value of a Broader Product Portfolio," *Harvard Business Review*, January 2008, 20–22.

18. Erik Brynjolfsson, Yu (Jeffrey) Hu, and Duncan Simester, "Goodbye Pareto Principle, Hello Long Tail: The Effects of Search Costs on the Concentration of Sales," research paper, February 2007, http://papers.ssrn.com.

19. Chris Anderson, "The Long Tail," *Wired*, October 2004, www.wired.com.

20. "About Us," hi5 Networks, accessed 7 September 2011, www.hi5networks.com; Jessi Hempel, "hi5 Guns for Facebook," *Fortune*, 27 October 2008, 14.

21. Andrew Shanahan, "Why Did France Fall in Love with McDonald's?" *The Guardian*, 24 July 2008, www.guardian.co.uk; Carol Matlack, "What's This? The French Love McDonald's?" *BusinessWeek*, 13 January 2003, 50; Shirley Leung, "Armchairs, TVs and Espresso–Is It McDonald's?" *Wall Street Journal*, 30 August 2002, A1, A6.

22. Alicia A. Caldwell, "21 Airlines Fined for Fixing Passenger, Cargo Fees," *Seattle Times*, 5 March 2011, www.seattletimes.com.

23. Eric Anderson and Duncan Simester, "Mind Your Pricing Cues," *Harvard Business Review*, September 96–103.

24. Edward Ramirez and Ronald E. Goldsmith, "Some Antecedents of Price Sensitivity," *Journal of Marketing Theory & Practice*, Summer 2009, 199–213.

25. Elisabeth A. Sullivan, "Value Pricing: Smart Marketers Know Cost-Plus Can Be Costly," *Marketing News*, 15 January 2008, 8.

26. Peter J. Williamson and Ming Zeng, "Value-for-Money Strategies for Recessionary Times," *Harvard Business Review*, March 2009, 66–74.

27. Revionics website, accessed 27 July 2009, www.revionics.com; Amy Cortese, "The Power of Optimal Pricing," *Business 2.0*, September 2002, 68–70.

28. Priceline website, accessed 7 September 2011, www.priceline.com.

29. Ju-Young Kim, Martin Natter, and Martin Spann, "Pay What You Want: A New Participative Pricing Mechanism," *Journal of Marketing*, January 2009, 44–58.

30. John Varcoe, "Lunatics in Charge," *NZ Marketing Magazine*, June 2009, 10.

31. Don Moyer, "That's Going to Cost You," *Harvard Business Review*, May 2009, 132.

32. Sunil Gupta and Carl F. Mela, "What Is a Free Customer Worth?" *Harvard Business Review*, November 2008, 102–109.

33. "How About Free? The Price Point That Is Turning Industries on Their Heads," Knowledge@Wharton, 4 March 2009, http://knowledge.wharton.upenn.edu.

34. Al Ries, "Variable Pricing Is Ultimate Brand-Destruction Machine," *Advertising Age*, 8 June 2009, 11.

35. See note 1.

36. Aubrey Kent and Richard M. Campbell, Jr., "An Introduction to Freeloading: Campus-Area Ambush Marketing," *Sport Marketing Quarterly* 16, no. 2 (2007), 118–122.

37. Adapted from Valerie Bennett and Andrew Capella, "Location-Based Services," IBM website, accessed 27 July 2009, www.ibm.com; David LaGress, "They Know Where You Are," *U.S. News & World Report*, 8 September 2003, 32–38; Christopher Elliott, "Some Rental Cars Are Keeping Tabs on Drivers," *New York Times*, 13 January 2004, C6; Kristi Heim, "Microchips in People, Packaging and Pets Raise Privacy Questions," *Seattle Times*, 18 October 2004, www.seattletimes.com; Andrew Heining and Christa Case, "Are Book Tags a Threat?" *Christian Science Monitor*, 5 October 2004, www.csmonitor.com; Corie Lok, "Wrist Radio Tags," *Technology Review*, November 2004, 25; Brian Albright, "RFID Dominates Frontline's Supply Chain Week," *Frontline Solutions*, November 2003, 10–13.

GLOSSARY

brand A name, term, sign, symbol, design, or combination of those used to identify the products of a firm and to differentiate them from competing products

brand equity The value that a company has built up in a brand

brand extension Applying a successful brand name to a new product category

brand loyalty The degree to which customers continue to purchase a specific brand

brand managers Managers who develop and implement the marketing strategies and programs for specific products or brands

brand marks The portion of brands that cannot be expressed verbally

brand names The portion of brands that can be expressed orally, including letters, words, or numbers

break-even analysis A method of calculating the minimum volume of sales needed at a given price to cover all costs

break-even point Sales volume at a given price that will cover all of a company's costs

bundling Offering several products for a single price that is presumably lower than the total of the products' individual prices

capital items More expensive organizational products with a longer useful life, ranging from office and plant equipment to entire factories

co-branding A partnership between two or more companies to closely link their brand names together for a single product

commercialization Large-scale production and distribution of a product

convenience products Everyday goods and services that people buy frequently, usually without much conscious planning

cost-based pricing A method of setting prices based on production and marketing costs, rather than conditions in the marketplace

discounts Temporary price reductions to stimulate sales or lower prices to encourage certain behaviors such as paying with cash

dynamic pricing Continually adjusting prices to reflect changes in supply and demand

expense items Inexpensive products that organizations generally use within a year of purchase

family branding Using a brand name on a variety of related products

fixed costs Business costs that remain constant regardless of the number of units produced

freemium pricing A hybrid pricing strategy of offering some products for free while charging for others, or offering a product for free to some customers while charging others for it

license An agreement to produce and market another company's product in exchange for a royalty or fee

logo A graphical and/or textual representation of a brand

loss-leader pricing Selling one product at a loss as a way to entice customers to consider other products

national brands Brands owned by manufacturers and distributed nationally

optimal pricing A computer-based pricing method that creates a demand curve for every product to help managers select a price that meets specific marketing objectives

participative pricing Allowing customers to pay the amount they think a product is worth

penetration pricing Introducing a new product at a low price in hopes of building sales volume quickly

price elasticity A measure of the sensitivity of demand to changes in price

private brands Brands that carry the label of a retailer or a wholesaler rather than a manufacturer

product development process A formal process of generating, selecting, developing, and commercializing product ideas

product life cycle Four stages through which a product progresses: introduction, growth, maturity, and decline

product line A series of related products offered by a firm

product mix The complete portfolio of products that a company offers for sale

prototypes Preproduction samples of products used for testing and evaluation

shopping products Fairly important goods and services that people buy less frequently with more planning and comparison

skim pricing Charging a high price for a new product during the introductory stage and lowering the price later

specialty products Particular brands that the buyer especially wants and will seek out, regardless of location or price

test marketing A product development stage in which a product is sold on a limited basis to gauge its market appeal

trademarks Brands that have been given legal protection so that their owners have exclusive rights to their use

value-based pricing A method of setting prices based on customer perceptions of value

variable costs Business costs that increase with the number of units produced

Customer Communication

LEARNING OBJECTIVES After studying this chapter, you will be able to

1 Describe the three major tasks in crafting a communication strategy and identify four important legal aspects of marketing communication

2 Identify the major types of advertising, the most common advertising appeals, and the most important advertising media

3 Explain how direct marketing differs from advertising and identify the major forms of direct media

4 Describe consultative selling and explain the personal-selling process

5 Define *sales promotion* and identify the major categories of consumer and trade promotions

6 Explain the uses of social media in customer communication and the role of public relations

MyBizLab

Where you see MyBizLab in this chapter, go to www.mybizlab.com for additional activities on the topic being discussed.

BEHIND THE SCENES PULLING IN THE CROWDS AT SEAWORLD SAN ANTONIO

To quickly build interest in the new Journey to Atlantis water ride, SeaWorld San Antonio turned to a new generation of customer communication tools.

http://seaworldparks.com/seaworld-sanantonio

Theme parks offer plenty of ways for visitors to find a few hours of fun in the sun, enjoy some entertainment, and maybe give themselves a good scare on the roller coaster. From a marketing point of view, however, there is a never-ending challenge of creating new reasons to visit. Consumers who've "been there, done that" at a particular theme park are understandably tempted to take their entertainment dollars somewhere else unless the park can offer fresh attractions to lure them back.

One of three SeaWorld parks run by Busch Entertainment Corporation (the other two are in San Diego and Orlando), the 250-acre SeaWorld San Antonio is the world's largest marine life theme park. In addition to having numerous marine life exhibits, shows, and other attractions, the park offers several hair-raising rides, including the eight-story-high Great White roller coaster and the 65-mile-per-hour Steel Eel "hypercoaster." Both are exciting rides, but coaster enthusiasts who've already ridden them might not feel any immediate urge to revisit SeaWorld.

But visitors certainly would be interested in a new ride, and SeaWorld was ready to offer one with Journey to Atlantis, a combination roller coaster/water ride. Although not a thrill ride in the sense of pushing the limits of speed and performing gravity-defying stunts, Journey to Atlantis does offer great views of San

---

From Chapter 16 of *Business in Action*, Sixth Edition. Courtland L. Bovée, John V. Thill. Copyright © 2013 by Pearson Education, Inc. Published by Pearson Business. All rights reserved.

Antonio at the top and a grand splashdown into a lake at the bottom—a perfect way to cool off on a hot Texas afternoon.

With Journey to Atlantis nearing completion ahead of schedule, the customer communication team needed to get the word out quickly about this new attraction. If you were public relations specialist Kami Huyse, how would you identify the right audience and reach out to them with information about the new ride? How would you develop relationships with coaster enthusiasts—people who don't hesitate to travel just about anywhere to try a new ride—and encourage them to add Journey to Atlantis to their must-try lists? And how would you build excitement and energy around a product that really needs to be experienced to be fully appreciated?[1]

My BizLab

Gain hands-on experience through an interactive, real-world scenario. This chapter's simulation entitled Promoting a Product is located at **www .mybizlab.com**.

1 LEARNING OBJECTIVE

Describe the three major tasks in crafting a communication strategy, and identify four important legal aspects of marketing communication.

social communication model An approach to communication based on interactive social media and conversational communication styles

INTRODUCTION

When SeaWorld San Antonio (profiled in the chapter-opening Behind the Scenes) needed to generate awareness for its new Journey to Atlantis ride, the company and its communication team had a dizzying array of options for reaching out to potential park visitors. This chapter, our final discussion of the marketing function, explains how marketers set communication goals, define messages, and choose from the ever-growing array of media options to reach target audiences.

Customer Communication: Challenges, Strategies, and Issues

Not long ago, marketing communication was largely about companies broadcasting carefully scripted messages to a mass audience that often had few, if any, ways to respond. Moreover, customers and other interested parties had few ways to connect with one another to ask questions about products, influence company decisions, or offer each other support.

However, a variety of technologies have enabled and inspired a new approach to customer communication. In contrast to the "we talk, you listen" mindset of the past, this new **social communication model** is *interactive* and *conversational*. Today's audiences are no longer passive recipients of messages; instead, they demand to be active participants in a meaningful conversation. On the surface, this approach might look like it has just added a few new electronic media tools to the traditional arsenal of television, radio, newspapers, and magazines. However, as Exhibit 1 shows, the changes are much deeper and more profound. "Social Media in the Marketing Process" on page 381 discusses this new model in more detail.

In this new world of interactive communication, it's more vital than ever to have a strategy that (1) establishes *clear communication goals*, (2) defines *compelling messages* to help achieve those goals, and (3) outlines a *cost-effective media mix* to engage target audiences.

ESTABLISHING COMMUNICATION GOALS

Communication activities can meet a wide range of marketing goals, but only if these activities are crafted with clear goals based on where the target audience is in the purchasing cycle.[2] Marketers take the following steps to move potential customers toward purchases:

- **Generating awareness.** People obviously can't buy things they don't know about, so creating awareness is essential for new companies and new products.
- **Providing information and creating positive emotional connections.** The next step is to build logical and emotional acceptance for the company and its products. Social media can work for or against companies in a significant way at this stage. If customers are pleased with a product, they'll help spread the message through the virtual word-of-mouth communication of social media. But they'll also spread the word if a product does not meet their expectations.

EXHIBIT 1	The Social Model of Customer Communication

The new social model of customer communication differs from the conventional promotion model in a number of significant ways.

Conventional Promotion Model Tendencies	Social Model Tendencies
Publication	Conversation
Lecture	Discussion
Intrusion	Permission
Unidirectional	Bidirectional, multidirectional
One to many	One to one, many to many
Control	Influence
Low message frequency	High message frequency
Few channels	Many channels
Information hoarding	Information sharing
Static	Dynamic
Hierarchical	Egalitarian
Structured	Amorphous
Isolation	Collaboration
Planned	Reactive
Rigid	Responsive

- **Building preference.** If buyers accept a product as a potential solution to their needs, the next step is to encourage them to prefer it over all other products they may be considering.
- **Stimulating action.** Now comes the most critical step: convincing a consumer or an organization to act on that product preference to make a purchase, using a compelling *call to action*.
- **Reminding past customers.** Past customers are often the best prospects for future sales, so *reminder advertising* tells these buyers that a product is still available or a company is ready to serve their needs.

DEFINING CUSTOMER MESSAGES

After establishing communication goals, the marketer's next step is to define the **core message**. This is the single most important idea the company hopes to convey to the target audience about a product. Ideally, the message can be expressed in a single sentence, such as "The Caterpillar 385C Ultra High Demolition Excavator can increase productivity at every stage of the most demanding demolition projects."[3] Notice how this statement highlights a key customer benefit (productivity) and identifies the target audience (companies that demolish buildings).

Of course, no one is going to shell out a million dollars for a 100-ton piece of equipment based on a single sentence. Think of the core message as the foundation on which the marketing team can build successive layers of detail and explanation, with each communication effort expanding on the core message. For instance, advertisements try to communicate a few key points quickly, without going into great detail. A sales presentation could go into more detail, and a technical brochure or a website can provide extensive information.

As Exhibit 1 notes, one of the most significant changes that the social communication model has brought to marketing is that companies now have far less control of their messages. After a message is released into the wild, so to speak, bloggers, reporters, industry analysts, and other parties will begin to repeat it, enhance it, change it, and even refute it. Starting with a clear and compelling core message increases the chances that the message will reach its target audience intact. If the core message is not clear or not credible, it will surely be altered or refuted as it passes from one outside commentator to the next.

core message The single most important idea an advertiser hopes to convey to the target audience about its products or the company

ASSEMBLING THE COMMUNICATION MIX

communication mix A blend of communication vehicles—advertising, direct marketing, personal selling, sales promotion, social media, and public relations—that a company uses to reach current and potential customers

With clear goals and a compelling message, the next step is to share that message using a **communication mix**, also known as a *media mix* or *promotional mix*, through some combination of advertising, direct marketing, personal selling, sales promotion, social media, and public relations. Crafting the optimal mix is one of the toughest decisions marketing managers face and requires constant monitoring as markets and media choices evolve.

To assemble the best mix, companies have to consider a range of product, market, and distribution channel factors. Product factors include the type of product, its price range, and its stage in the product life cycle. For example, an innovative technical product may require intensive educational efforts in the introduction and growth stages to help customers understand and appreciate its value. Market factors include the type of intended customers (consumers versus organizations), the nature of the competition, and the size and geographic spread of the target market.

push strategy A promotional strategy that focuses on intermediaries, motivating them to promote, or *push*, products toward end users

Channel factors include the need for intermediaries, the type of intermediaries available, and the ability of those companies to help with communication. A key decision is whether to focus communication efforts on the intermediaries or on final customers. With a **push strategy**, a producer focuses on intermediaries, trying to persuade wholesalers or retailers to carry its products and promote those products to *their* customers. Conversely, with a **pull strategy**, the producer appeals directly to end customers. Customers learn of the product through these communication efforts and request it from retailers (in the case of consumers) or wholesalers (in the case of business customers). For example, if a television commercial encourages you to "ask your pharmacist" about a specific product, the company is using a pull strategy. Many companies use both push and pull strategies to increase the impact of their promotional efforts.

pull strategy A promotional strategy that stimulates consumer demand via advertising and other communication efforts, thereby creating a *pull* effect through the channel

integrated marketing communications (IMC) A strategy of coordinating and integrating communication and promotion efforts with customers to ensure greater efficiency and effectiveness

With the number of communication vehicles continuing to expand, the need for companies to "speak with one voice" becomes even greater. **Integrated marketing communications (IMC)** is a strategy of coordinating and integrating all communication and promotional efforts to ensure clarity, consistency, and maximum communications impact.[4] However, companies obviously can't control all the messages their target audiences receive, particularly now that customers are empowered through social media. While the company is working to integrate its outgoing communication efforts, the customer is also integrating all the incoming messages he or she is receiving (see Exhibit 2).

| **EXHIBIT 2** | **Message Integration in Customer Communication** |

To maximize efficiency and consistency, companies need to integrate their customer communication efforts. However, customers also integrate messages on the receiving end—including messages that might contradict messages from the company.

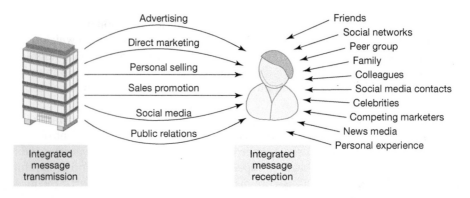

COMMUNICATION LAWS AND ETHICS

As marketing and selling grow increasingly complex, so do the legal ramifications of marketing communication. In the United States, the Federal Trade Commission (FTC) has the authority to impose penalties against advertisers that violate federal standards for truthful advertising. Other federal agencies have authority over advertising in specific industries, such as transportation and financial services. Individual states have additional laws that apply. The legal aspects of promotional communication can be quite complex, and they vary from state to state and from country to country. However, if you are involved in customer communication in any form, at a minimum you need to be aware of these legal issues:[5]

- **Marketing and sales messages must be truthful and nondeceptive.** The FTC considers messages to be deceptive if they include statements that are likely to mislead reasonable customers and the statements are an important part of the purchasing decision. Failing to include important information is also considered deceptive. The FTC also looks at *implied claims*—claims you don't explicitly make but that can be inferred from what you do or don't say.
- **You must back up your claims with evidence.** According to the FTC, offering a money-back guarantee or providing letters from satisfied customers is not enough; you must still be able to support claims for your product with objective evidence such as a survey or scientific study (see Exhibit 3). If you claim that your food product lowers cholesterol, you must have scientific evidence to support that claim.
- **"Bait and switch" advertising is illegal.** Trying to attract buyers by advertising a product that you don't intend to sell—and then trying to sell them another (and usually more expensive) product—is illegal.

EXHIBIT 3	Supporting Marketing Claims with Verifiable Evidence

Merck, the company that makes the hair-loss treatment Propecia, takes care to back up its product claims with solid evidence, out of respect for its audience and to ensure compliance with regulations regarding marketing and sales messages. The series of photos available through the "Evidence of Regrowth" link provides additional visual confirmation of the product's benefits.

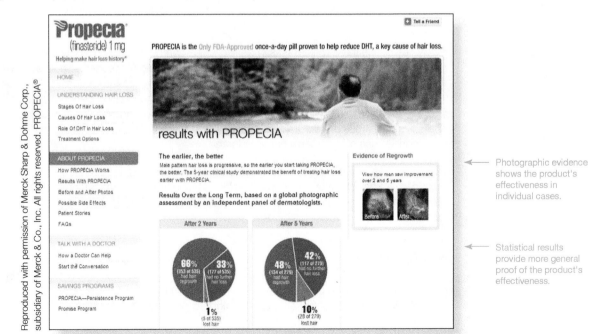

- **Marketing messages and websites aimed at children are subject to special rules.** For example, online marketers must obtain consent from parents before collecting personal information about children under age 13.
- **Marketing and sales messages are considered binding contracts in many states.** If you imply or make an offer and then can't fulfill your end of the bargain, you can be sued for breach of contract.
- **In most cases, you can't use a person's name, photograph, or other identity without permission.** Doing so is considered an invasion of privacy. You can use images of people considered to be public figures as long as you don't unfairly imply that they endorse your message.

Moreover, communicators must stay on top of changing regulations, such as the latest laws governing unsolicited bulk email ("spam"), customer privacy, data security, and disclosure requirements for bloggers who review products. Two of the latest ethical concerns that could produce new legislation are *behavioral targeting*, which tracks the online behavior of website visitors and serves up ads based on what they appear to be interested in, and *remarketing*, in which behaviorally targeted ads follow users even as they move on to other websites.[6]

Regarding privacy and other aspects of communication, responsible companies recognize the vital importance of ethical standards. Professional associations such as the American Association of Advertising Agencies (www.aaaa.org), the Direct Marketing Association (www.the-dma.org), and the American Marketing Association (www.marketingpower.com) devote considerable time and energy to ethical issues in marketing, including ongoing education for practitioners and self-regulation efforts aimed at avoiding or correcting ethical lapses. For instance, the National Advertising Review Council (www.narcpartners.org), whose members include advertisers, agencies, and the general public, works with the Better Business Bureau to investigate and resolve complaints of deceptive advertising in order to foster public trust.[7]

✔ Checkpoint

LEARNING OBJECTIVE 1: Describe the three major tasks in crafting a communication strategy, and identify four important legal aspects of marketing communication.

SUMMARY: The three major tasks in developing a communication strategy are establishing clear communication goals, defining compelling messages to help achieve those goals, and outlining a cost-effective media mix to engage target audiences. Four important issues in communications law are making sure advertising claims are truthful and nondeceptive, supporting claims with real evidence, recognizing that marketing and sales messages are contractual obligations in many cases, and avoiding the unauthorized use of a person's name or image.

CRITICAL THINKING: (1) Why do credit card companies target students even though most of them have little or no income? (2) Would it be wise for a manufacturer that is new to a particular industry (and unknown within it) to invest most of its promotional resources in a pull strategy? Why or why not?

IT'S YOUR BUSINESS: (1) What is your "core message" as a future business professional? How would you summarize, in one sentence, what you can offer a company? (2) Does knowing that advertisers are trying to track your online behavior in order to target you with personalized ads make you want to limit or change your web surfing? Do you think advertisers have the right to do this? Why or why not?

KEY TERMS TO KNOW: social communication model, core message, communication mix, push strategy, pull strategy, integrated marketing communications (IMC)

Advertising

2 LEARNING OBJECTIVE

Identify the major types of advertising, the most common advertising appeals, and the most important advertising media.

Advertising can be defined as the "placement of announcements and persuasive messages in time or space purchased in any of the mass media."[8] In other words, advertisers buy time on radio or television and space in print and online media. Two key points here are that advertising is paid for, and it is carried by someone else's medium. (Companies sometimes own the media in which they advertise, but this is not the usual case.) This section offers a quick overview of the various types of advertising, the appeals most commonly used in advertising, and the advantages and disadvantages of major advertising media.

advertising The delivery of announcements and promotional messages via time or space purchased in various media

TYPES OF ADVERTISING

Companies can use advertising for a variety of purposes. The most common type, *product advertising*, promotes the features and benefits of specific products. The term *comparative advertising* is applied to ads that specifically highlight how one product is better than its competitors. Strong comparative messages can boost sales, but the approach is risky. Competitors are likely to sue if they believe their products have been portrayed unfairly, and sometimes *attack ads* can decrease sales for an entire product category (including the products of the advertiser) by emphasizing the negative aspects of the products in question.[9]

In some countries, comparative ads are tightly regulated and sometimes banned, but that is clearly not the case in the United States. Indeed, the FTC encourages advertisers to use direct product comparisons, with the intent of better informing customers. Comparative advertising is frequently used by competitors vying with the market leader, but it is useful whenever a company believes it has some specific product strengths that are important to customers. However, given the damage that unfair comparative advertising can cause, both federal regulations and industry guidelines established by the American Association of Advertising Agencies address the issues of fairness and accuracy in comparative advertising.[10]

Institutional advertising is designed to create goodwill and build a desired image for a company rather than to promote specific products. For example, a firm might promote its commitment to sustainable business practices or workforce diversity. Institutional ads that address public issues are called **advocacy advertising**. With recent efforts to overhaul health insurance in the United States, for instance, many companies with a financial stake in the outcome have been using advertising to present their points of view.[11]

institutional advertising Advertising that seeks to create goodwill and to build a desired image for a company, rather than to promote specific products

Advertising can also be classified according to the sponsor. *National advertising* is sponsored by companies that sell products on a nationwide basis. The biggest national advertisers spend a *lot* on advertising, with companies such as Verizon and AT&T spending over $1 billion a year.[12] In contrast, *local advertising* is sponsored by a local merchant; grocery store ads are a good example. *Cooperative advertising* involves a financial arrangement in which companies with products sold nationally share the costs of local advertising with local marketing intermediaries.

advocacy advertising Advertising that presents a company's opinions on public issues such as education or health care

ADVERTISING APPEALS

A key decision in planning a promotional campaign is choosing the **advertising appeal**, a creative tactic designed to capture the audience's attention and promote preference for the product or company being advertised. Marketers can choose from seven basic appeals (note that these appeals are not limited to advertising; they are used in other types of persuasive communication as well):[13]

advertising appeal A creative tactic designed to capture the audience's attention and promote preference for the product or company being advertised

- **Logic.** The basic approach with a logical appeal is to make a claim based on a rational argument supported by solid evidence. Not surprisingly, business-to-business advertising relies heavily on logical appeals because businesses have logical concerns— profitability, process improvements, quality, and other financial and technical concerns. However, marketers should not ignore the emotional aspects of business purchasing. Managers put their reputations and sometimes their careers on the line when they make major purchase decisions, so advertisers need to consider these emotional elements. Logical appeals are also used in consumer advertising whenever the purchase decision has a rational component and logic might help persuade buyers to consider or prefer a particular product.

- **Emotion.** An emotional appeal calls on audience feelings and sympathies rather than facts, figures, and rational arguments (see Exhibit 4). Emotional appeals range from sentimental to terrifying. On the lighter side, flowers, greeting cards, and gifts are among the products usually sold with a positive emotional appeal. At the other end of the spectrum are appeals to a broad range of fears: personal and family safety, financial security, social acceptance, and business success or failure. To be effective, appeals to fear must be managed carefully. Laying it on too thick can anger the audience or even cause them to block out the message entirely.
- **Humor.** In a world cluttered with advertising, humor is frequently used to capture people's attention. However, humor can be tricky; sometimes it can offend audiences, tainting the brand, or the humor can be so memorable that audiences remember the joke but not the product being advertised.[14]
- **Celebrity.** The thinking behind celebrity involvement in advertising is that people will be more inclined to use products endorsed by a celebrity because they will identify with and want to be like this person (no matter how far-fetched such aspirations might be at a purely logical level). Celebrities can also bring new excitement, humor, energy, and even perceived value to a product. In addition to being expensive, however, celebrity endorsements can be risky because the brand's image becomes linked to the celebrity's image, including whatever image problems the celebrity experiences in his or her personal life.[15]
- **Sex.** Sex-oriented appeals are the most controversial type of advertising, in terms of both social reaction and promotional effectiveness. Although the phrase "sex sells" is often repeated, it isn't always true. Sexual appeals can definitely be effective, but the degree of effectiveness varies by product, audience, and the role of the sexual imagery or narrative in the advertising. For example, sexual appeals have been shown to be more effective with audiences that have a low level of emotional or intellectual engagement with the purchase than with audiences that are more involved.[16]
- **Music.** With its ability to create emotional bonds and "embed" itself in listeners' memories, music can be a powerful aspect of advertising. Marketers can take several approaches to integrating music into radio, television, or online advertising, including composing *jingles* specifically for commercials, licensing popular songs for use in commercials (although these fees can run into the millions of dollars for hit songs), or working with emerging artists to write songs specifically with advertising use in mind.[17]
- **Scarcity.** If a product is in limited supply or available only for a limited time, advertisers can use this scarcity to encourage consumer responses.

Note that these appeals are not mutually exclusive. For example, ads can use humor to catch an audience's attention and then use an emotional appeal to strengthen the bond with the brand or logic to show the superiority of a product.

ADVERTISING MEDIA

advertising media
Communications channels, such as newspapers, radio, television, and the World Wide Web

media mix A combination of print, broadcast, online, and other media used for an advertising campaign

Choosing **advertising media**, or channels of communication, can be as important as selecting the type of advertising and the advertising appeal. Major advertising media include newspapers, television, radio, magazines, product placement, fixed web (from computers), and mobile web (from mobile phones and other handheld devices). A *media plan* outlines the advertising budget, the schedule of when ads will appear, and a discussion of the **media mix**—the combination of print, broadcast, online, and other media to be used in the campaign. To create the media mix, advertising experts factor in the characteristics of the target audience, the types of media that will reach the largest audience in the most cost-effective way, and the strengths and weaknesses of the various media as they relate to the product and its marketing message (see Exhibit 5).

EXHIBIT 4	**Emotional and Logical Appeals**

All marketing messages strike a balance between logical and emotional appeals. Bigelow Tea uses textual and visual elements to convey the literal and figurative warmth offered by a cup of tea. In contrast, the stock brokerage TD Ameritrade provides a comprehensive, layered message that emphasizes logical supporting points. Investing one's hard-earned money obviously has a strong emotional angle, however, so TD Ameritrade also emphasizes points of safety and security.

Without using any images of people, the solitary teacup (left), the multiple glasses of iced tea (center), and the brunch setting suggested by the tea and food (right) convey both the pleasures of a quiet time alone as well as the pleasures of sharing tea with friends and family.

The red-orange color of the tea, enhanced with the glow of backlighting through the translucent liquid, speaks of warmth and comfort.

Complementary colors suggest freshness and elegance, adding to the emotional appeal.

The text uses the storytelling technique to explain the creation of Bigelow's signature Constant Comment tea flavor and does so in a way that highlights the emotional appeal of drinking tea.

Used with permission of R.C. Bigelow, Inc.

The main idea of "choose TD Ameritrade" is echoed from the webpage tab, through the introductory text, and down to the specific details.

The headline and introductory paragraph address universal concerns among investors.

These six supporting points—each of which reflects a key audience need—back up the top-level message of "A better way to invest."

An endorsement from a well-known source boosts the credibility of the company's promotional message.

Each of the six supporting points is presented at three levels of detail: (1) the short message of the button labels at the far left, (2) a short paragraph with a headline that echoes audience needs, and (3) additional pages (accessed via the link) with full details.

Image Courtesy of TD Ameritrade IP Company, Inc.

215

EXHIBIT 5	Advantages and Disadvantages of Major Advertising Media

Each medium has strengths and weaknesses; companies often combine two or more media in an advertising campaign to maximize their promotional effectiveness.

Medium	Advantages	Disadvantages
Newspapers	Extensive market coverage; low cost; short lead time for placing ads; good local market coverage; geographic selectivity; credibility	Poor graphic quality; short life span; cluttered pages; visual competition from other ads; printed papers have rapidly declining readership in many cities
Television	Great impact; broad reach; appealing to senses of sight, sound, and motion; creative opportunities for demonstration; high attention; entertainment carryover	High cost for production and air time; less audience selectivity; long preparation time; commercial clutter; short life for message; vulnerability to being skipped or muted; losing ground to new media options
Radio	Low cost; high frequency; immediacy; portability; high geographic and demographic selectivity	No visual possibilities; short life for message; commercial clutter; lower attention than television; declining audience share; low level of engagement
Magazines	Good production quality; long life; local and regional market selectivity; authority and credibility; multiple readers extend reach of each issue; close bond with readers	Limited demonstration possibilities; long lead time between placing and publishing ads; lots of ad clutter; high cost; declining readership for many titles
Product placement	Offers a way to get around viewers' advertising filters; chance for high visibility in the right program, movie, or game	Limited choice of vehicles; unpredictable; effectiveness is linked to the popularity of the programming; risk of overuse could reduce effectiveness over time
Fixed web (from stationary computers)	Rich media options and interactivity can make ads more compelling and more effective; changes and additions can be made quickly and easily in most cases; webpages can provide an almost unlimited amount of information; can be measured and personalized through tracking and targeting capabilities; instant links to online retailing and influence on store-based retail sales; growing audiences for Internet radio and video; social media connections can spread marketing messages through word of mouth	Extreme degree of audience fragmentation (millions of websites); increasing clutter (such as pop-up ads); technical glitches can interrupt ad display; not as portable as magazines, newspapers, or mobile web; ad-blocking software can prevent ads from being displayed
Mobile web (from mobile phones and other handheld devices)	In addition to almost every advantage of the fixed web other than display size: portability; constant, "always-on" presence (most people have their phones with them much of the time); opportunity for location-based advertising; possibilities for narrow targeting	Many users won't tolerate advertising intrusions via mobile phone; small screen size limits display possibilities

Sources: Adapted from Jeffrey M. O'Brien, "The Wizards of Apps," *Fortune,* 5 May 2009, 29–30; Christopher Meyer, "The Year of Marketing Dangerously," *Harvard Business Review,* October 2008, 26–27; Magid Abraham, "The Off-line Impact of Online Ads," *Harvard Business Review,* April 2008, 28; Michael A. Wiles and Anna Danielova, "The Worth of Product Placement in Successful Films: An Event Study Analysis," *Journal of Marketing,* July 2009, 44–63; Sarah Chung and Tina Hedges, "Is Your Digital Marketing a Turn-on?" *Global Cosmetic Industry,* July 2009, 22–24; Douglas MacMillan, "What Works in Online Video Advertising?" *BusinessWeek,* 28 January 2009, 26; Guy Yaniv, "Sold on Mobile Marketing: Effective Wireless Carrier Mobile Advertising and How to Make It Even More So," *International Journal of Mobile Marketing,* December 2008, 86–91; Kenneth E. Clow and Donald Baack, *Integrated Advertising, Promotion, and Marketing Communications,* 4th ed. (Upper Saddle River, N.J.: Pearson Prentice Hall, 2010), 219–229.

Three trends are likely to shape advertising media in the coming years. First, the media landscape will continue to fragment as new online and mobile formats emerge and conventional print and broadcast media fight to hang on to their share of advertisers' budgets. The days when advertisers could reach most consumers through a few television networks and major periodicals are long gone. Figuring out how to reach consumers who spread their attention across a variety of media and delivery platforms is one of the biggest challenges facing marketers today. With Facebook emerging as a multibillion-dollar advertising platform, for example, companies have yet another choice to consider when it comes to dividing up their advertising budgets.[18]

Second, the lines between advertising, entertainment, and *value-added content* (such as informative articles and how-to videos) will continue to blur. For example, more advertisers are borrowing storytelling techniques and other methods from the entertainment industry to make their TV commercials, online videos, and other ads more entertaining and thus more likely to be watched.[19] **Product placement**, in which companies pay to have their products displayed or used in television shows, movies, and video games, is already a multibillion-dollar business and is sure to grow as advertisers respond to the increasing number of ways consumers are able to ignore, skip, or block ads—and as content producers look for new cash flow opportunities. Product placement ranges from subtle brand displays in the background of a scene to active engagement with a product.[20]

Third, technical innovations will continue to create new advertising tools and techniques, including the behavioral targeting methods described on page 368 and more sophisticated tracking and pricing models that tie advertising costs to measurable results.[21] To counter the low response rates of conventional banner ads on websites, for instance, marketers are trying new ways of integrating advertising with site content.[22] The number of *hybrid media* will grow; one example is "webified" interactive purchasing systems that merge the television and Internet platforms so that consumers can use their TV remotes to buy products shown in a program.[23] As online video expands, so too will connections with advertising and retailing, including software that turns images of people and products in a video into clickable hyperlinks—so that a viewer can instantly order the same clothes an actor or a host is wearing, for example.[24]

REAL-TIME UPDATES

Learn More by Watching This Video

Inventing new ways to engage the audience

See how prominent television advertisers are responding to the changing world of media. Go to http://real-timeupdates.com/bia6 and click on Learn More. If you are using MyBizLab, you can access Real-Time Updates within each chapter or under Student Study Tools.

product placement The paid display or use of products in television shows, movies, and video games

✔ Checkpoint

LEARNING OBJECTIVE 2: Identify the major types of advertising, the most common advertising appeals, and the most important advertising media.

SUMMARY: The major types of advertising based on the type of message are *product* advertising (which promotes the benefits of a product), *comparative* advertising (which compares a product to competitors' products), *institutional* advertising (which promotes a company or other organization), and *advocacy* advertising (which conveys information and opinions about public issues). Advertising can also be categorized by sponsor, including *national*, *local*, and *cooperative* advertising. The most common advertising appeals are logic, emotion, humor, celebrity, sex, music, and scarcity. Major advertising media include newspapers, television, radio, magazines, product placement, fixed web (from computers), and mobile web (from mobile phones and other handheld devices).

CRITICAL THINKING: (1) Do fragmented media make it easier or harder for marketers to engage in segmented or concentrated marketing? Explain your answer. (2) Why would a company such as McDonald's, which is already well known to virtually all consumers in the United States, continue to spend heavily on advertising?

IT'S YOUR BUSINESS: (1) Have you ever believed that you could create better advertising for a product than the company behind the product created? If so, explain the type of appeal you would've used and why. (2) Do you find that you tend to watch and listen to most television commercials, or do you mute or channel surf during commercials? If you pay attention to commercials, what captures your interest?

KEY TERMS TO KNOW: advertising, institutional advertising, advocacy advertising, advertising appeal, advertising media, media mix, product placement

Explain how direct marketing differs from advertising, and identify the major forms of direct media.

direct marketing Direct communication other than personal sales contacts designed to stimulate a measurable response

Direct Marketing

Although it is similar to advertising in many respects, **direct marketing**, defined as direct communication other than personal sales contacts, can differ from advertising in three important ways. (The lines continue to blur between types of media, so not all these distinctions hold true for every medium.) First, direct marketing often uses *personally addressable* media such as letters and email messages to deliver targeted messages to individual consumers or organizational purchasers. Second, except for infomercials, direct marketing doesn't involve the purchase of time or space in other media. The advertiser usually has control over the delivery mechanism and can decide when, where, and how the message is delivered. Third, direct marketing has a *direct response* aspect that often isn't present in advertising. While effective direct marketing works to build lasting relationships with customers, its primary emphasis is generating sales *now*.

According to the Direct Marketing Association (www.the-dma.org), a trade group of advertisers and marketing agencies, direct marketing efforts, on average, yield twice the return on investment of other marketing efforts.[25] Bear in mind, however, that direct marketing efforts often take place within a broader context of advertising and other activities. While they may get the credit for making the sale, they often don't work in isolation.

DIRECT MARKETING TECHNIQUES

Direct marketing has evolved dramatically from its early days, when pioneering promotional efforts such as the Sears catalog in the late 1800s helped establish *mail order* on a massive scale.[26] Direct marketing is now a computer-intensive multimedia effort that includes mail, telephone, and online media. The heart of any direct marketing effort is a customer database that contains contact histories, purchase records, and profiles of each buyer or potential buyer. (Direct marketing is sometimes referred to as *database marketing*.) The data can range from basic demographic information to records of all customer contacts to detailed purchasing records and other behavioral data. Such databases also play a vital role in relationship marketing because they enable a company to personalize its interaction with every customer.

The *measurability* of direct marketing is one of its greatest appeals. If you mail a promotional flyer to 1,000 people and 36 of them call to place an order, you know the campaign had a 3.6 percent response rate. Because direct responses are directly measurable (unlike many advertising efforts), direct marketing lends itself to constant experimentation and improvement. This is particularly true with online direct marketing efforts, where changes can be made cheaply and quickly.

Just as many retailers now reach out to customers in multiple ways through multichannel retailing (see page 348), many companies now integrate direct marketing with other communication efforts in *multichannel marketing campaigns*. For instance, customer databases are now expanding to include everything from widget usage on social networks to mobile web and phone usage.[27]

DIRECT MARKETING MEDIA

The catalogs that helped launch direct marketing over a hundred years ago are still a force today, as a peek inside any mailbox in the country will confirm. Here is a brief look at the major media used in direct marketing:

direct mail Printed materials addressed to individual consumers, households, or business contacts

- **Mail. Direct mail**, printed material addressed to an individual or a household, has the key advantage of being able to put promotional materials, ranging from simple letters and glossy catalogs to DVDs and product samples, directly into the hands of a target audience.
- **Email.** The ability to send millions of messages in a matter of minutes at almost no cost made email a hit with direct marketers—and practically destroyed email as a viable communication medium in the minds of some users tired of being deluged with unwanted "spam." The spam problem notwithstanding, email marketing remains the fastest-growing direct marketing medium.[28] To minimize the level of annoyance and to help potential customers get the information they really do want, many companies now emphasize *permission-based* email marketing, usually by asking customers or website visitors to *opt-in* to mailing lists.

- **Search engine marketing.** With millions of web users relying on search engines such as Google and Bing every day, **search engine marketing**, or *search advertising*, has become an important marketing medium (see Exhibit 6). Although it doesn't quite fit the traditional categories of either advertising or direct marketing, search engine marketing comes closer to being a direct medium because it is individualized to each web user. Search advertising works in two basic ways. First, advertisers can pay to have small ads presented whenever the keywords they select are used in a search. These are the "sponsored results" that can appear above and to the right of the actual search results. Second, these ads can also appear on the many websites that are in the search engine's *advertising exchange* or *advertising network*, a collection of websites that sell space on their pages for such ads.[29] These ads are triggered by content on a webpage and can appear anywhere on the page, even inserted between sections of an online article.

- **Direct response online.** The interactive, adaptable nature of websites allows them to go far beyond static advertising media to become direct, personalized communication channels. As Amazon.com founder Jeff Bezos explains, referring to the fact that every returning customer is greeted with a customized storefront based on his or her shopping patterns, "If we have 72 million customers, we should have 72 million stores."[30] *Targeted display advertising* involves ads with graphical (as opposed to just textual) content served up on web pages based on some knowledge of an individual's interests or behaviors. While Google is the most common conduit for search engine advertising, Facebook, with its massive user base, is the leader in the rapidly growing sector of online display advertising.[31]

- **Telephone.** The telephone is a major promotional tool in consumer and organizational markets and for both *inbound* (when buyers call in to place orders) and *outbound* (when sellers contact potential buyers with sales offers) marketing. After rising complaints from consumers about telemarketers interrupting them at home, Congress created the National Do Not Call Registry, which gives individuals the opportunity to have their numbers removed from telemarketers' lists. However, marketers can still call businesses as well as consumers who have purchased from them in the past.

- **Direct response television.** More commonly known as *infomercials*, **direct response television** programs have the major advantage of time, allowing companies to demonstrate products and engage viewers in a way that isn't possible with 30- or 60-second commercials.

search engine marketing Automated presentation of ads that are related to either the results of an online search or the content being displayed on other webpages

direct response television The use of television commercials and longer-format infomercials that are designed to stimulate an immediate purchase response from viewers

---

EXHIBIT 6   **Search Engine Marketing**

Sponsored search results display ads based on the terms entered into a search engine.

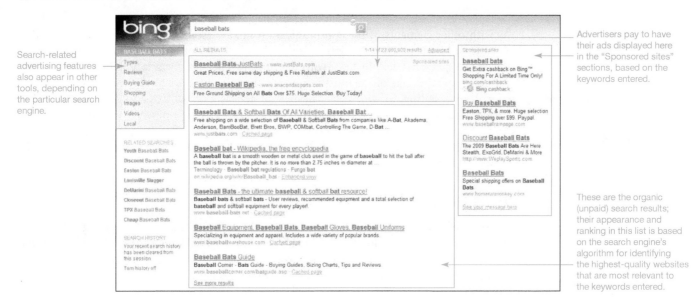

✓ Checkpoint

LEARNING OBJECTIVE 3: Explain how direct marketing differs from advertising, and identify the major forms of direct media.

SUMMARY: Direct marketing differs from advertising in three important ways: (1) It uses *personally addressable* media such as letters and email messages to deliver targeted messages to individual consumers or organizational purchasers, (2) it doesn't involve the purchase of time or space in other media, and (3) it has a *direct response* aspect that often isn't present in advertising. The major categories of direct marketing media are mail (including catalogs), email, search engine marketing, telephone, and direct response television.

CRITICAL THINKING: (1) Would an iPhone app that streams QVC or another shopping channel to mobile phones be an effective direct marketing medium? Why or why not? (2) If direct marketing has a better return on investment than other forms of promotion, why do companies bother with anything but direct marketing?

IT'S YOUR BUSINESS: (1) As a rough guess, what percentage of the direct marketing messages you receive in a given week are effectively targeted to your needs as a consumer? Identify a recent example that was well targeted and one that was not. (2) Have you ever responded to the offer in a "spam" email message? If so, what enticed you to do so?

KEY TERMS TO KNOW: direct marketing, direct mail, search engine marketing, direct response television

---

4 | **LEARNING OBJECTIVE**

Describe consultative selling, and explain the personal-selling process.

personal selling One-on-one interaction between a salesperson and a prospective buyer

Personal Selling

Even with the rapid advance of e-commerce and other marketing technologies, **personal selling**, the one-on-one interaction between a salesperson and a prospective buyer, remains a fundamentally important part of the promotional mix in many consumer and organizational markets. Although a salesforce can't reach millions of customers at once like a website or a direct marketing program can, today's highly trained sales professionals are able to build relationships and solve problems in ways that impersonal media can't match.

CONTEMPORARY PERSONAL SELLING

As with other elements of the communication mix, personal selling has evolved over the years to support the contemporary idea of the customer-oriented marketing concept. In this sense, personal selling has evolved from *peddling products* to *creating partnerships* with customers.[32] One of the most important shifts in the sales profession is the advent of **consultative selling**, in which the salesperson acts as a consultant and advisor who helps current and potential customers find the best solutions to their personal or business needs. And even if a shopper isn't ready to buy something immediately, a good consultative salesperson will view the interaction as a chance to build a long-term relationship that could lead to sales in the future.[33]

consultative selling An approach in which a salesperson acts as a consultant and advisor to help customers find the best solutions to their personal or business needs

THE PERSONAL-SELLING PROCESS

Personal selling varies widely from industry to industry, with some sales being completed in a matter of minutes and others taking weeks or months. Time is often the salesperson's most valuable asset, so it must be spent wisely—focusing on the most valuable prospects who are most likely to purchase. The following steps can be adapted to almost any sales situation (see Exhibit 7):

EXHIBIT 7	The Personal-Selling Process

The personal-selling process can involve up to seven steps, starting with prospecting for sales leads and ending with following up after the sale has been closed. This diagram gives you a general idea of how salespeople approach major sales opportunities.

1. Prospecting	2. Preparing	3. Approaching	4. Aligning with Customer Needs	5. Handling Objections	6. Closing	7. Following Up
Finding and qualifying potential customers; usually involves generating sales, identifying prospects, and qualifying prospects	Getting ready for the sales call; researching the customer in more depth, establishing objectives, and preparing a presentation	Taking steps to make a good first impression; crafting the right appearance, maintaining professional behavior, and preparing an engaging introduction	Listening to the prospect describe what is needed and proposing a solution to meet those needs	Addressing any concerns the prospect might raise; exploring the deeper reasons that might be behind the expressed objections	Asking the prospect to choose the solution being offered	Checking in with the customer after the sale to make sure the solution is working out as expected and to keep building a longterm relationship

- **Step 1: Prospecting.** The process of finding and qualifying potential customers is known as **prospecting**. This step usually involves three activities: (1) *generating sales leads*—names of individuals and organizations that might be likely prospects for the company's product; (2) *identifying prospects*—potential customers who indicate a need or a desire for the seller's product; and (3) *qualifying prospects*—the process of figuring out which prospects have both the authority and the available money to buy.

- **Step 2: Preparing.** With a list of strong prospects in hand, the next step is to prepare for the *sales call* (in person, over the phone, or online via videoconferencing or another method). In this research phase, the sales staff tries to learn more about the people and organizations they will be contacting regarding their buying needs, their motives for buying, and the names of current suppliers. The salesperson then establishes specific objectives to achieve during the sales call, which vary depending on where the buyer is in the decision cycle. Finally, the salesperson often prepares a presentation, which can be as basic as a list of points to discuss or as elaborate as a product demonstration or multimedia presentation.

- **Step 3: Approaching the prospect.** First impressions can make or break a sale, so knowledgeable salespeople take care to (1) craft the appropriate appearance for themselves and for everything that represents them; (2) maintain behaviors and attitudes that are professional, courteous, and confident without being arrogant; and (3) prepare opening lines that include a brief greeting and introduction, followed by a few carefully chosen words that establish a good rapport with the potential customer.

- **Step 4: Uncovering needs and presenting solutions.** After the conversation has been initiated, the next step is understanding the customer's specific needs. The biggest mistake a salesperson can make at this stage is talking instead of listening. The most extreme form of this error is the *canned sales pitch*, in which the salesperson recites or even reads a stock message, with no regard for the customer's unique circumstances. In contrast, today's enlightened sales professionals focus on questioning and listening before offering a solution that meets each prospect's unique needs.

- **Step 5: Handling objections.** Potential customers can express a variety of objections to the products they are considering, and salespeople need to be ready with answers and alternatives.

prospecting The process of finding and qualifying potential customers

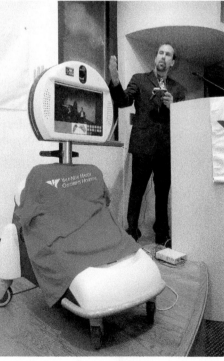

Personal selling is an important promotional element for many business-to-business marketers.

© Peter Hvizdak /The Image Works

- **Step 6: Closing.** Bringing the sales process to a successful conclusion by asking for and receiving an affirmative purchase decision is known as **closing.** Experienced professionals know to look for signs that the prospect is ready to make a decision, and they use a variety of techniques such as offering to write up an order to encourage a definitive answer.[34]

- **Step 7: Following up.** Most companies depend on repeat sales and referrals from satisfied customers, so it's important that salespeople follow up after the sale to make sure customers are satisfied with their purchases. Staying in touch gives a company the opportunity to answer questions, address areas of confusion or dissatisfaction with a purchase, and show customers it is a reliable partner for the long haul.

closing The point at which a sale is completed

✓ Checkpoint

LEARNING OBJECTIVE 4: Describe consultative selling, and explain the personal-selling process.

SUMMARY: Consultative selling is a combination of persuasion and advice, in which the salesperson acts as a consultant and advisor who helps current and potential customers find the best solutions to their personal or business needs. The seven general steps in personal selling are (1) *prospecting*, finding prospects and qualifying them; (2) *preparing*, creating a prospect profile, setting objectives for the call, and preparing a presentation; (3) *approaching* the prospect, with the goal of making a positive first impression; (4) *uncovering* the customer's needs and *presenting* appropriate solutions; (5) *handling objections*, using audience comments as an opportunity to strengthen the presentation; (6) *closing*, focusing on completing the sale; and (7) *following up* after the sale to make sure the buyer is satisfied.

CRITICAL THINKING: (1) Why is the canned approach inadequate for many selling situations? (2) Why should a salesperson take the time to qualify sales leads?

IT'S YOUR BUSINESS: (1) Would you be comfortable in a personal-selling role? Why or why not? (2) What can you learn from professional selling methods to help you in a job interview?

KEY TERMS TO KNOW: personal selling, consultative selling, prospecting, closing

---

5 LEARNING OBJECTIVE

Define *sales promotion*, and identify the major categories of consumer and trade promotions.

Sales Promotion

Sales promotion consists of short-term incentives to build the reputation of a brand, encourage the purchase of a product, or simply enhance relationships with current and potential customers. Sales promotion consists of two basic categories: consumer promotion and trade promotion.

CONSUMER PROMOTIONS

sales promotion A wide range of events and activities designed to promote a brand or stimulate interest in a product

Companies use a variety of consumer promotional tools and incentives to stimulate repeat purchases and to entice new users:

- **Contests and other audience involvement tactics.** Giving consumers the opportunity to participate in contests, games, sweepstakes, surveys, and other activities, particularly if there is a chance for consumers to demonstrate cleverness or creativity, is a great way to build energy around a brand.

- **Coupons.** The biggest category of consumer promotion is **coupons**, printed or electronic certificates that spur sales by giving buyers a discount when they purchase specified products (see Exhibit 8). Paper couponing is an inefficient technique, however; consumers redeem only 1 percent of the 300 billion printed coupons distributed

coupons Printed or electronic certificates that offer discounts on particular items and are redeemed at the time of purchase

EXHIBIT 8 | **Consumer Promotions Using Social Media**

Blimpie is one of many companies that use Facebook as a channel for consumer promotions. "Liking" a company page such as this puts the company's Wall postings into your Facebook feed, making it a convenient way for the firm to reach out to customers.

Courtesy of Kahala Corp.

every year in the United States.[35] The rapid growth of mobile couponing via smartphones and new social systems such as Groupon (www.groupon.com) are revolutionizing couponing. While they are creating opportunities for businesses, the spread of these coupons is changing buyer behavior as more and more consumers now expect stores and restaurants to offer coupons.[36]

- **Rebates.** With **rebates**, companies offer partial reimbursement of the price as a purchase incentive. Rebates can be an effective tool for boosting sales, but they obviously cut into per-unit profits—and the effect can be more or less permanent when frequent rebates in an industry encourage buyers to delay purchases until a rebate program is available.

rebates Partial reimbursement of price, offered as a purchase incentive

- **Point-of-purchase.** A **point-of-purchase (POP) display** is an in-store presentation designed to stimulate immediate sales. POP displays are a vital element in the marketing effort for many products sold at retail stores. Not only do they represent the manufacturer's last chance to communicate with the consumer, but they help capture *impulse purchases*—unplanned purchases that can make up as much as 50 percent of sales in mass merchandise stores and supermarkets.[37]
- **Samples and trial-use versions.** Distributing samples is an effective way to introduce a new product, encourage nonusers to try an existing product, encourage current buyers to use the product in a new way, or expand distribution into new areas. Many software products are also offered as trial versions to let customers try before buying.
- **Special-event sponsorship.** Sponsoring special events has become one of the most popular sales promotion tactics, with thousands of companies spending billions of dollars to sponsor events ranging from golf to opera.
- **Other promotions.** Other popular consumer sales promotion techniques include in-store demonstrations, loyalty and frequency programs such as frequent-flyer programs, and **premiums**, which are free or bargain-priced items offered to encourage the consumer to buy a product. **Specialty advertising** (on pens, calendars, T-shirts, mouse pads, and other items) helps keep a company's name in front of customers for a long period of time.

point-of-purchase (POP) display Advertising or other display materials set up at retail locations to promote products to potential customers as they are making their purchase decisions

premiums Free or bargain-priced items offered to encourage consumers to buy a product

specialty advertising Advertising that appears on various items such as coffee mugs, pens, and calendars, designed to help keep a company's name in front of customers

TRADE PROMOTIONS

trade promotions Sales-promotion efforts aimed at inducing distributors or retailers to push a producer's products

trade allowances Discounts or other financial considerations offered by producers to wholesalers and retailers

Although shoppers are more aware of consumer promotions, **trade promotions** aimed at inducing wholesalers or retailers to sell a company's products actually account for the larger share of promotional spending and can be the single largest item in a manufacturer's marketing budget.[38] The most popular trade promotions are **trade allowances**, which involve discounts on product prices, free merchandise, or other payments, such as the retail slotting allowances. The intermediary can either pocket the savings to increase profits or pass the savings on to the consumer to generate additional sales. Trade allowances are commonly used when adopting a push marketing strategy because they encourage the intermediaries to carry new products or to sell higher volumes of current products.

The chief downside of trade allowances is that they can create the controversial practice of *forward buying*, in which customers load up on merchandise while the price is low. For example, if a producer offers retailers a 20 percent discount for a period of 6 weeks, a retailer might choose to buy enough inventory to last 8 or 10 weeks. Purchasing this excessive amount at the lower price increases the retailer's profit, but at the expense of the producer's profit.

Besides trade allowances, other popular trade promotions are dealer contests and bonus programs designed to motivate distributors or retailers to push particular merchandise. Product samples are also common in many business marketing efforts. For instance, semiconductor manufacturers often provide samples of electronic components to engineers who are designing new products, knowing that if the prototype is successful, it could lead to full-scale production—and orders for thousands or millions of components.

✓ Checkpoint

LEARNING OBJECTIVE 5: Define *sales promotion*, and identify the major categories of consumer and trade promotions.

SUMMARY: The two main types of sales promotion are consumer promotion and trade promotion. Consumer promotions are intended to motivate the final consumer to try new products or to experiment with the company's brands. Examples include contests, coupons, rebates, point-of-purchase displays, samples, special-event sponsorship, premiums, and specialty advertising. Trade promotions are designed to induce wholesalers and retailers to promote a producer's products. Common trade promotions include trade allowances, dealer contests, bonus programs, and samples.

CRITICAL THINKING: (1) If 99 percent of coupons are never used, why do companies keep printing so many? (2) If wholesalers and retailers can make money selling a manufacturer's product, why would the manufacturer need to offer incentives such as sales contests?

IT'S YOUR BUSINESS: (1) How can sales promotions reduce the reluctance that buyers might feel about trying an unfamiliar product? (2) Have you ever participated in a sales promotion without realizing you were doing so? For example, have you ever "liked" a company on Facebook to enter a sweepstakes without realizing that in doing so you were also signing up for all its Wall postings in your Facebook feed?

KEY TERMS TO KNOW: sales promotion, coupons, rebates, point-of-purchase (POP) display, premiums, specialty advertising, trade promotions, trade allowances

Social Media and Public Relations

6 **LEARNING OBJECTIVE**

Explain the uses of social media in customer communication and the role of public relations.

All the communication methods discussed so far in this chapter involve activities by companies themselves to transmit carefully crafted and controlled messages to target audiences. The final two methods, social media and public relations, differ from the traditional methods in two key respects: They rely on others to forward or create promotional messages, and they don't provide anywhere near the level of control over those messages that conventional marketing methods offer.

SOCIAL MEDIA IN THE MARKETING PROCESS

Social media are any electronic media that transform passive audiences into active participants in the communication process by allowing them to share, revise, or respond to existing content, or to contribute new content. These media include social networks, blogs, microblogs such as Twitter, wikis, *user-generated content (UGC)* sites such as Flickr and YouTube, *community Q&A sites* such as LinkedIn Answers and Get Satisfaction's customer support sites, and *community participation websites* such as Yelp. To varying degrees, all of these media play a role in contemporary marketing.

Social media activities combine the newest communication technologies with the oldest form of marketing communication in the world, **word of mouth**—customers and other parties transmitting information about companies and products through personal conversations. Word-of mouth marketing is often called *viral marketing*, in reference to the transmission of messages in much the same way that biological viruses are transmitted from person to person. However, viral marketing is not really an accurate metaphor. As author Brian Solis puts it, "There is no such thing as viral marketing."[39] Real viruses spread from host to host on their own, whereas word-of-mouth marketing spreads *voluntarily* from person to person. The distinction is critical because marketers need to give people a good reason—good content, in other words—to pass along their messages.

The social communication model is by no means limited to the consumer sector. Technical professionals were using the Internet for communication years before the World Wide Web was invented, and now businesspeople in just about every industry use social media to share ideas, conduct research, and evaluate products. In fact, many businesspeople are far more active in social media than the average consumer.[40]

Communication Strategies for Social Media

Audiences in the social media environment are not willing to be passive recipients in a structured, one-way information delivery process—or to rely solely on promotional

social media Any electronic media that transform passive audiences into active participants in the communication process by allowing them to share content, revise content, respond to content, or contribute new content

word of mouth Communication among customers and other parties, transmitting information about companies and products through online or offline personal conversations

REAL-TIME UPDATES
Learn More by Watching This Video

Spending less on media and more on the good stuff

New York City's 4food burger restaurant relies on low-cost social media efforts to spread the word specifically so that it can spend its money on high-quality ingredients. Go to http://real-timeupdates .com/bia6 and click on Learn More. If you are using MyBizLab, you can access Real-Time Updates within each chapter or under Student Study Tools.

messages from marketers. This notion of interactive participation is the driving force behind **conversation marketing**, in which companies *initiate* and *facilitate* conversations in a networked community of customers, journalists, bloggers, Twitter users, and other interested parties. Social media can be a powerful communication channel, but companies should follow these guidelines in order to meet audience expectations:[41]

- **Remember that it's a conversation, not a lecture or a sales pitch.** One of the great appeals of social media is the feeling of conversation, of people talking *with* one another instead of one person talking *at* everyone else.
- **Facilitate community building.** Make sure customers and other audiences can connect with the company and with each other.
- **Initiate and respond to conversations within the community.** Marketers can start or join conversations by providing useful information to current and potential customers. As you can see in the Behind the Scenes wrap-up at the end of the chapter, this effort was key to SeaWorld's success in launching its new water coaster ride.
- **Identify and support champions.** In marketing, *champions* are enthusiastic fans of a company and its products—so enthusiastic that they help spread the company's message, defend it against detractors, and help other customers use its products.
- **Restrict conventional promotional efforts to the right time and right place.** Persuasive communication efforts are still valid for specific communication tasks, such as regular advertising and the product information pages on a website, but efforts to inject "salespeak" into social media conversations will be rejected by the audience.

Brand Communities

Another major impact of social media has been the rapid spread of **brand communities**, people united by their interest in and ownership of particular products (see Exhibit 9). These communities can be formal membership organizations, such as the longstanding Harley Owners Group (HOG), or informal networks of people with similar interests. They can be fairly independent from the company behind the brand or can have the active support and involvement of company management, as is the case of Harley-Davidson's support of the motorcycle enthusiasts who are members of HOG (*hog* is an affectionate nickname for a Harley).[42]

Social media are natural communication vehicles for brand communities because these tools let people bond and share information on their own terms. And because a strong majority of consumers now trust their peers more than any other source of product information—including conventional advertising techniques—formal and informal brand communities are becoming an essential information source in consumer buying behavior.[43]

PUBLIC RELATIONS

Public relations encompasses a wide variety of nonsales communications that businesses have with their many stakeholders, including communities, investors, industry analysts, government agencies, and activists. Companies rely on public relations to build a favorable corporate image and foster positive relations with all these groups.

Public relations efforts often involve the news media, with companies offering information to print, broadcast, and online journalists in the hope that these intermediaries will pass the message along to their audiences. If the information is likely to interest their audiences, journalists will help "spread the word," in the best cases generating high levels of public awareness at a much lower cost than a company could achieve on its own through paid advertising.[44]

Two standard tools for communicating with the media are the press release and the press conference. A traditional **press release** is a short message sent to the media covering topics that are of potential news interest; a *video news release* is a brief video clip sent to television stations. Companies use news releases in the hopes of getting favorable news coverage about themselves and their products. When a business has significant news to announce, it will often arrange a **press conference**, at which reporters can listen to company representatives and ask questions.

---

conversation marketing An approach to customer communication in which companies initiate and facilitate conversations in a networked community of potential buyers and other interested parties

brand communities Formal or informal groups of people united by their interest in and ownership of particular products

public relations Nonsales communication that businesses have with their various audiences (including both communication with the general public and press relations)

press release A brief statement or video program released to the press announcing new products, management changes, sales performance, and other potential news items; also called a *news release*

press conference An in-person or online gathering of media representatives at which companies announce new information; also called a *news conference*

| EXHIBIT 9 | Using Social Media to Promote Brand Communities |

The Segway Social online network connects owners of these unique personal vehicles, including helping teams organize Segway polo matches and other events.

Until recently, press releases were intended only for members of the news media and were crafted in a way to provide information to reporters who would then write their own articles. However, the nature of the press release is changing. Many companies now view it as a general-purpose tool for communicating directly with customers and other audiences, writing *direct-to-consumer press releases*. As news media expert David Meerman Scott puts it, "Millions of people read press releases directly, unfiltered by the media. You need to be speaking directly to them."[45]

The newest twist on news releases is the *social media release*, which has several advantages over the traditional release. First, the social media release emphasizes bullet-point content over narrative paragraphs so that bloggers, editors, and others can assemble their own stories rather than being forced to rewrite the material in a traditional release. Second, as an electronic-only document (a specialized webpage, essentially), the social media release offers the ability to include videos and other multimedia elements. Third, social bookmarking buttons make it easy for people to help publicize the content.[46] Similarly, the traditional press conference is being replaced or augmented in many cases with *webcasts*, online presentations that can reach thousands of viewers at once and be archived for later retrieval.

For the latest information on customer communication strategies, techniques, and tools, visit http://real-timeupdates.com/bia6.

✔ Checkpoint

LEARNING OBJECTIVE 6: Explain the uses of social media in customer communication and the role of public relations.

SUMMARY: Social media have several potential uses in customer communication, including customer service, rumor control, research, and relationship building. They can also be used for promotion, but that should be done in an indirect, customer-focused manner. Because consumers and investors support companies with good reputations, smart companies use public relations to build and protect their images. They communicate with consumers, investors, industry analysts, and government officials through the media. They pursue and maintain press relations with representatives of newspapers, television, and other broadcast media so that they can provide effective news releases (also known as press releases) and hold effective news conferences.

CRITICAL THINKING: (1) If marketers are advised against blatantly promoting their products in social media, why should they bother using these media at all? (2) Why are press relations critical to the launch of many new products?

IT'S YOUR BUSINESS: (1) Have you ever used social media to ask questions about a product or to criticize or compliment a company? Did anyone from the company respond? (2) Do you consider yourself a member of any brand communities (formal or informal)? If so, what effect do these groups have on your purchasing behavior?

KEY TERMS TO KNOW: social media, word of mouth, conversation marketing, brand communities, public relations, press release, press conference

---

BEHIND THE SCENES   MyBizLab

SEAWORLD SAN ANTONIO GETS SOCIAL TO BUILD INTEREST IN NEW RIDE

When SeaWorld San Antonio needed to get the word out quickly about its new Journey to Atlantis water coaster ride, public relations specialist Kami Huyse of My PR Pro (http://myprpro.com) worked with SeaWorld's Director of Communications Fran Stephenson to survey the options. The team had three objectives: (1) build relationships with the community of coaster enthusiasts, (2) create awareness of the new ride, and (3) increase visitor traffic. You can see that these goals stretch across three time frames: long-term relationship building, midterm awareness, and short-term sales. It's a lot to ask of any communication campaign—and particularly a campaign with the time and budget limits that Huyse and Stephenson faced.

Hard-core roller coaster enthusiasts are *really* enthusiastic about their coasters. They like to learn about new rides, compare their impressions of rides they've been on, organize trips to visit

rides around the country, and even work to preserve some of the classic old roller coasters that dot the American landscape. Dozens of websites, forums, blogs, and coaster groups share information, including the 7,000-member American Coaster Enthusiasts (www.aceonline.org). With Huyse's expertise in social media, she recognized an opportunity when she saw one: They would connect with the "thrill ride" community online.

Their research identified 22 blogs and forums that were particularly active and influential in the enthusiast community. "The primary strategy was to treat coaster bloggers as a VIP audience and to create content to suit their needs," Huyse explains. These bloggers were also invited to attend a special prelaunch media day to test-drive Journey to Atlantis.

As part of this effort to provide opinion influencers and the general public with enticing content about the new ride,

SeaWorld's in-house communication staff created 11 videos and a 45-image photo collection that were made available for public use through YouTube, Flickr, and Veoh. The staff also created a content-rich website with social media functionality to add to SeaWorld's existing web presence to serve as the "hub" of the launch campaign.

The results? One of the knocks against social media as a business communication platform is that its effects can be difficult or impossible to measure. While that is true in many cases, Huyse and her colleagues were able to make three specific measurements that highlight the success of SeaWorld's social media effort. First, of the 22 targeted VIP enthusiast groups, more than half covered the opening in their blogs or forums, including the influential Theme Park Insider website (www.themeparkinsider.com). Second, more than 50 other websites created links to the Journey to Atlantis campaign website, and 30 of those were from coaster enthusiast websites. These numbers might sound small, but remember that social media is a game of multiplication: Small numbers of people spreading a message can quickly turn into large numbers.

The third and ultimately most important measurement is the impact on SeaWorld's business. Fortunately for Huyse's team, a measuring device was already in place: the exit surveys that SeaWorld routinely conducts, asking park visitors about their experiences and decisions to visit. Using data from this survey, the team could identify which media efforts drove visitors to the park most effectively and then calculate the cost-effectiveness of each method to see how the social media campaign compared to SeaWorld's other, ongoing promotional efforts. While television was almost as effective as online efforts at driving traffic through the front gate, the net cost to get one visitor through the front gate was nearly five times higher for television. And in terms of actual sales, based on SeaWorld's average per capita revenue figure, the social media campaign generated more than $2.6 million in revenue—for only $44,000 in total costs. From a marketing point of view, that's even more thrilling than a ride on the latest roller coaster.[47]

Critical Thinking Questions

1. With social media proving to be a cost-effective way to attract park visitors, should SeaWorld abandon its other promotional efforts and focus everything on social media? Why or why not?
2. What steps can SeaWorld take to maintain a relationship with coaster enthusiasts, now that the excitement surrounding the new ride has faded?
3. Do coaster fans such as members of American Coaster Enthusiasts constitute a brand community as described in the chapter? Why or why not?

LEARN MORE ONLINE

Search online for commentary and media materials relating to the Journey to Atlantis ride at SeaWorld San Antonio. (Be aware that different rides with the same name exist at the other SeaWorld parks.) Imagine that you're a coaster enthusiast. Based on what you see online, would you consider visiting San Antonio to ride Journey to Atlantis? Why or why not?

MyBizLab

Log on to www.mybizlab.com to access study and assessment aids associated with this chapter.

KEY TERMS

advertising
advertising appeal
advertising media
advocacy advertising
brand communities
closing
communication mix
consultative selling
conversation marketing
core message
coupons
direct mail
direct marketing
direct response television
institutional advertising
integrated marketing communications (IMC)
media mix
personal selling

point-of-purchase (POP) display
premiums
press conference
press release
product placement
prospecting
public relations
pull strategy
push strategy
rebates
sales promotion
search engine marketing
social communication model
social media
specialty advertising
trade allowances
trade promotions
word of mouth

TEST YOUR KNOWLEDGE

Questions for Review

1. What are two key ways in which the social communication model differs from conventional promotional communication?
2. What is the difference between using a push strategy and using a pull strategy to promote products?
3. What are the advantages of personal selling over other forms of customer communication?
4. What is an advertising appeal?
5. What are some common types of consumer promotion?

Questions for Analysis

6. Why is it important for sales professionals to qualify prospects?
7. What are the potential disadvantages of using celebrity appeals in advertising?
8. Why do some companies avoid email marketing, particularly to noncustomers?
9. Do marketers have any control over social media? Why or why not?
10. **Ethical Considerations.** Is your privacy being violated when a website you visit displays ads that are personalized in any way, even if it's just geographically targeted to the local area (based on your computer's Internet address)? Why or why not?

Questions for Application

11. If you were a real estate agent, how would you determine whether it's worth investing a significant amount of time in a particular prospect?
12. Think about an advertisement (in any medium) that had either a strongly positive or strongly negative effect on your attitude toward the product being advertised or the advertiser itself. Why did the ad have this effect? If you responded positively to the ad, do you think you were being manipulated in any way? If you responded negatively—and you are a potential buyer of the product that was advertised—what changes would you make to the ad to make it more successful?
13. Would it be a good idea to "repurpose" conventional press releases as posts on your company blog? Why or why not?
14. **Concept Integration.** Should companies involve their marketing channels in the design of their customer communication programs? What are the advantages and disadvantages of doing so?

EXPAND YOUR KNOWLEDGE

Discovering Career Opportunities

Jobs in customer communication—advertising, direct marketing, personal selling, sales promotion, social media, and public relations—are among the most exciting and challenging in all of marketing. Choose a particular job in one of these areas. Using personal contacts, local directories of businesses or business professionals, or online resources such as company websites or search engines (including Twitter and blog search tools), arrange a brief phone, email, or personal interview with a professional working in your chosen marketing field.

1. What are the daily activities of this professional? What tools and resources does this person use most often on the job? What does this professional like most and least about the job?
2. What talents and educational background does this professional bring to the job? How are the person's skills and knowledge applied to handle the job's daily activities?
3. What advice does the person you are interviewing have for newcomers entering this field? What can you do now to get yourself started on a career path toward this position?

Improving Your Tech Insights: Individualized Advertising

Don't be surprised if you look out the window one morning to see clouds in the sky arranged in letters that spell out your name and invite you to try a refreshing bottle of Coke or remind you to get your oil changed at Jiffy Lube.

Maybe it won't get quite that far, but advertisers are perfecting a variety of technologies that allow them to pinpoint individual audience members with customized messages. One interesting effect of this is that some advertising media or retailing formats are starting to look more like direct marketing media. As the chapter notes, Amazon.com already personalizes a store front for every one of its customers. Here are a few other examples: personalized magazine covers (including one that showed an aerial photograph of each subscriber's neighborhood with his or her home or office circled in red); commercials on digital cable systems that can be targeted to viewers in an individual neighborhood or even an individual household (with messages shaped by the demographics of the residents of the house); narrowly focused audio messages that can be aimed at a single shopper in a retail store; Google's Gmail email service, which serves up ads based on specific words in your email messages; and Google's behavioral targeting technology (its "interest-based advertising"), which displays ads based on your web-surfing patterns.

Identify one form of individualized advertising now in use (you can search for "individualized advertising," "personalized advertising," "behavioral targeting," or "interest-based advertising"). In a brief email message to your instructor, describe the technology, explain how it helps businesses reach customers more effectively, and identify any privacy concerns involved with the medium.[48]

PRACTICE YOUR SKILLS

Sharpening Your Communication Skills

The good news: The current events blog you started as a hobby has become quite popular. The bad news: The blog now takes up so much of your time that you've had to quit a part-time job you were using to supplement your regular income. After some discussions with other bloggers, you decide to join Google's AdSense program (www.google.com/adsense) to help pay for the costs of operating your blog. With this program, small ads triggered by keywords in the content you publish will appear on your site. However, you're worried that your audience will think you've "sold out" because you're now generating revenue from your blog. Write a short message that could be posted on your blog, explaining why you consider it necessary to run ads and assuring your readers of your continued objectivity, even if that means criticizing organizations whose ads might appear on your blog.

Building Your Team Skills

In small groups, discuss three or four recent ads or consumer promotions (in any media) that you think were particularly effective. Using the knowledge you've gained from this chapter, try to come to agreement on which attributes contributed to the success of each ad or promotion. For instance: Was it persuasive? Informative? Competitive? Creative? Did it have logical or emotional appeal? Did it stimulate you to buy the product? Why? Compare your results with those of other teams. Did you mention the same ads? Did you list the same attributes?

Developing Your Research Skills

Choose an article from recent issues of business journals or newspapers (print or online editions) that describes the advertising or promotion efforts of a particular company or trade association.

1. Who is the company or trade association targeting?
2. What specific marketing objectives is the organization trying to accomplish?
3. What role does advertising play in the promotion strategy? What other promotion techniques does the article mention? Are any of them unusual or noteworthy? Why?

REFERENCES

1. SeaWorld San Antonio website, accessed 10 September 2011, http://seaworldparks.com/seaworld-sanantonio; Kami Huyse, "Case Study: ROI of Social Media Campaign for SeaWorld San Antonio—A Year Later," Communication Overtones blog, 18 April 2008, http://overtonecomm.blogspot.com; Shel Israel, "GNTV: Making a Splash with Social Media Measurement," Global Neighbourhoods blog, 28 March 2008, http://redcouch.typepad.com/weblog; American Coaster Enthusiasts website, accessed 18 August 2009, www.aceonline.org.

2. Philip Kotler and Gary Armstrong, *Principles of Marketing*, 13th ed. (Upper Saddle River, N.J.: Pearson Prentice Hall, 2010), 409–140.

3. Adapted from Caterpillar website, accessed 2 August 2009, www.cat.com.

4. Kotler and Armstrong, *Principles of Marketing*, 405.

5. "How to Comply with the Children's Online Privacy Protection Rule," U.S. Federal Trade Commission website, accessed 17 July 2010, www.ftc.gov; "Frequently Asked Advertising Questions: A Guide for Small Business," U.S. Federal Trade Commission website, accessed 17 July 2010, www.ftc.gov.

6. Miguel Helft and Tanzina Vega, "Retargeting Ads Follow Surfers to Other Sites," *New York Times*, 29 August 2010, www.nytimes.com.

7. National Advertising Review Council website, accessed 3 August 2009, www.narcpartners.org.

8. American Marketing Association website, accessed 3 August 2009, www.marketingpower.com.

9. Emily Bryson York, "The Gloves Are Off: More Marketers Opt for Attack Ads," *Advertising Age*, 25 May 2009, 4.

10. William Wells, John Burnett, and Sandra Moriarty, *Advertising: Principles & Practice*, 6th ed. (Upper Saddle River, N.J.: Pearson Prentice Hall, 2003), 47–48.

11. Peter Overby, "Millions Spent on Ad War over Health Care Overhaul," National Public Radio website, 21 July 2009, www.npr.org.

12. Maureen Morrison, "Verizon Tops AT&T as Most-Advertised Brand," *Advertising Age*, 22 June 2009, http://adage.com.

13. Adapted from Kenneth E. Clow and Donald Baack, *Integrated Advertising, Promotion, and Marketing Communications*, 4th ed. (Upper Saddle River, N.J.: Pearson Prentice Hall, 2010), 153–167.

14. Clow and Baack, *Integrated Advertising, Promotion, and Marketing Communications*, 155–156.

15. Steve McKee, "The Trouble with Celebrity Endorsements," *BusinessWeek*, 17 November 2008, 10.

16. Sanjay Putrevu, "Consumer Responses Toward Sexual and Nonsexual Appeals," *Journal of Advertising*, Summer 2008, 57–69.

17. Clow and Baack, *Integrated Advertising, Promotion, and Marketing Communications*, 162–164.

18. Todd Wasserman, "Facebook to Take Number 1 Spot in Display Ad Market This Year," Mashable, 20 June 2011, http://mashable.com.

19. Kotler and Armstrong, *Principles of Marketing*, 436–437.

20. Janet Stilson, "The Clutter Busters," *Adweek*, 2 March 2009, 7.

21. Ben Kunz, "A Pricing Revolution Looms in Online Advertising," *BusinessWeek*, 7 April 2009, 20.

22. Brian Morrissey, "Thinking Beyond the Banner," *Adweek*, 8 June 2009, 9.

23. "The $56 billion Ad Question," *Fortune*, 3 January 2011, http://tech.fortune.cnn.com; Meyer, "The Year of Marketing Dangerously."

24. Douglas MacMillan, "What Works in Online Video Advertising?" *BusinessWeek*, 28 January 2009, 26.

25. "What Is the Direct Marketing Association?" Direct Marketing Association website, accessed 15 August 2009, www.the-dma.org.

26. "History of the Sears Catalog," Sears Archives, accessed 15 August 2009, www.searsarchives.com.

27. "Direct Marketing Association 2008 Annual Report," Direct Marketing Association website, www.the-dma.org.

28. Carol Krol, "E-Mail, Fastest Growing Direct Marketing Segment, Expands Double Digits," *DMNews*, 4 August 2009, www.dmnews.com.

29. "Google Adwords," Google website, accessed 18 August 2007, www.google.com; Danny Sullivan, "Major Search Engines and Directories," *Search Engine Watch*, 28 March 2007, http://searchenginewatch.com; Thomas Claburn, "Google, Yahoo Gain Search

Market Share; Microsoft, Time Warner Lose," *InformationWeek*, 21 November 2006, www.informationweek.com.

30. Kotler and Armstrong, *Principles of Marketing*, 489.

31. Wasserman, "Facebook to Take Number 1 Spot in Display Ad Market This Year."

32. Gerald L. Manning and Barry L. Reece, *Selling Today*, 9th ed. (Upper Saddle River, N.J.: Pearson Prentice Hall, 2004), 7–8.

33. Howard Feiertag, "Build Your Group Sales by Consultative Selling," *Hotel & Motel Management*, 15 June 2009, 10.

34. Kotler and Armstrong, *Principles of Marketing*, 474–475.

35. Dan Balaban, "Will Tough Times Spell Greater Opportunity for Mobile Coupons?" *Cards & Payments*, March 2009, 14–17.

36. Jay Goltz, "Is Groupon Ruining Retailing?" *New York Times*, 16 March 2011, www.nytimes.com.

37. Clow and Baack, *Integrated Advertising, Promotion, and Marketing Communications*, 284.

38. Clow and Baack, *Integrated Advertising, Promotion, and Marketing Communications*, 340.

39. Brian Solis, *Engage!* (Hoboken, N.J.: Wiley, 2010), 86.

40. Josh Bernoff, "Why B-to-B Ought to Love Social Media," *Marketing News*, 15 April 2009, 20.

41. Josh Bernoff, "Social Strategy for Exciting (and Not So Exciting) Brands," *Marketing News*, 15 May 2009, 18; Larry Weber, *Marketing to the Social Web* (Hoboken, N.J.: Wiley, 2007), 12–14; David Meerman Scott, *The New Rules of Marketing and PR* (Hoboken, N.J.: Wiley, 2007), 62; Paul Gillin, *The New Influencers* (Sanger, Calif.: Quill Driver Books, 2007), 34–35; Jeremy Wright, *Blog Marketing: The Revolutionary Way to Increase Sales, Build*

Your Brand, and Get Exceptional Results (New York: McGraw-Hill, 2006), 263–365.

42. Susan Fournier and Lara Lee, "Getting Brand Communities Right," *Harvard Business Review*, April 2009, 105–111.

43. Patrick Hanlon and Josh Hawkins, "Expand Your Brand Community Online," *Advertising Age*, 7 January 2008, 14–15.

44. Steve McKee, "Why PR Is the Prescription," *BusinessWeek*, 13 April 2009, 8.

45. David Meerman Scott, *The New Rules of Marketing and PR* (Hoboken, N.J.: Wiley, 2007), 62.

46. Shel Holz, "Next-Generation Press Releases," CW Bulletin, September 2009, www.iabc.com; Steph Gray, "Baby Steps in Social Media News Releases," Helpful Technology blog, 15 May 2009, http://blog.helpfultechnology.com.

47. See note 1.

48. Adapted from Miguel Helft, "Google to Offer Ads Based on Interests," *New York Times*, 11 March 2009, www.nytimes.com; "Nick Gillespie Discusses the Personalized Cover of *Reason* Magazine and the Possibilities of Database Technology" (interview), Talk of the Nation, National Public Radio, 4 May 2003, www.highbeam.com; Kevin J. Delaney, "Will Users Care if Gmail Invades Privacy?" *Wall Street Journal*, 6 April 2004, B1, B3; Allison Fass, "Spot On," *Forbes*, 23 June 2003, 140; "Hey You! How About Lunch?" *Wall Street Journal*, 1 April 2004, B1, B5.

GLOSSARY

advertising appeal A creative tactic designed to capture the audience's attention and promote preference for the product or company being advertised

advertising media Communications channels, such as newspapers, radio, television, and the World Wide Web

advertising The delivery of announcements and promotional messages via time or space purchased in various media

advocacy advertising Advertising that presents a company's opinions on public issues such as education or health care

brand communities Formal or informal groups of people united by their interest in and ownership of particular products

closing The point at which a sale is completed

communication mix A blend of communication vehicles—advertising, direct marketing, personal selling, sales promotion, social media, and public relations—that a company uses to reach current and potential customers

consultative selling An approach in which a salesperson acts as a consultant and advisor to help customers find the best solutions to their personal or business needs

conversation marketing An approach to customer communication in which companies initiate and facilitate conversations in a networked community of potential buyers and other interested parties

core message The single most important idea an advertiser hopes to convey to the target audience about its products or the company

coupons Printed or electronic certificates that offer discounts on particular items and are redeemed at the time of purchase

direct mail Printed materials addressed to individual consumers, households, or business contacts

direct marketing Direct communication other than personal sales contacts designed to stimulate a measurable response

direct response television The use of television commercials and longer-format infomercials that are designed to stimulate an immediate purchase response from viewers

institutional advertising Advertising that seeks to create goodwill and to build a desired image for a company, rather than to promote specific products

integrated marketing communications (IMC) A strategy of coordinating and integrating communication and promotion efforts with customers to ensure greater efficiency and effectiveness

media mix A combination of print, broadcast, online, and other media used for an advertising campaign

personal selling One-on-one interaction between a salesperson and a prospective buyer

point-of-purchase (POP) display Advertising or other display materials set up at retail locations to promote products to potential customers as they are making their purchase decisions

premiums Free or bargain-priced items offered to encourage consumers to buy a product

press conference An in-person or online gathering of media representatives at which companies announce new information; also called a *news conference*

press release A brief statement or video program released to the press announcing new products, management changes, sales performance, and other potential news items; also called a *news release*

product placement The paid display or use of products in television shows, movies, and video games

prospecting The process of finding and qualifying potential customers

public relations Nonsales communication that businesses have with their various audiences (including both communication with the general public and press relations)

pull strategy A promotional strategy that stimulates consumer demand via advertising and other communication efforts, thereby creating a *pull* effect through the channel

push strategy A promotional strategy that focuses on intermediaries, motivating them to promote, or *push*, products toward end users

rebates Partial reimbursement of price, offered as a purchase incentive

sales promotion A wide range of events and activities designed to promote a brand or stimulate interest in a product

search engine marketing Automated presentation of ads that are related to either the results of an online search or the content being displayed on other webpages

social communication model An approach to communication based on interactive social media and conversational communication styles

social media Any electronic media that transform passive audiences into active participants in the communication process by allowing them to share content, revise content, respond to content, or contribute new content

specialty advertising Advertising that appears on various items such as coffee mugs, pens, and calendars, designed to help keep a company's name in front of customers

trade allowances Discounts or other financial considerations offered by producers to wholesalers and retailers

trade promotions Sales-promotion efforts aimed at inducing distributors or retailers to push a producer's products

word of mouth Communication among customers and other parties, transmitting information about companies and products through online or offline personal conversations

Production Systems

From Chapter 9 of *Business in Action*, Sixth Edition. Courtland L. Bovée, John V. Thill. Copyright © 2013 by Pearson Education, Inc. Published by Pearson Business. All rights reserved.

Production Systems

LEARNING OBJECTIVES After studying this chapter, you will be able to

1 Explain the systems perspective and identify seven principles of systems thinking that can improve your skills as a manager

2 Describe the *value chain* and *value web* concepts and discuss the controversy over offshoring

3 Define *supply chain management* and explain its strategic importance

4 Identify the major planning decisions in production and operations management

5 Explain the unique challenges of service delivery

6 Define *quality*, explain the challenge of quality and product complexity, and identify four major tools and strategies for ensuring product quality

MyBizLab

Where you see MyBizLab in this chapter, go to www.mybizlab.com for additional activities on the topic being discussed.

BEHIND THE SCENES CUSTOMIZING DREAMS AT CARVIN GUITARS

Carvin offers personalized guitars at affordable prices through a combination of sophisticated production systems and old-world handicraft.

www.carvinguitars.com

After beginning guitarists have mastered the nuances of "Mary Had a Little Lamb" and set their sights on making serious music, they often encounter a serious equipment dilemma. Low-cost, beginner guitars lack the materials and workmanship needed to produce top-quality sounds. Some are difficult to keep in tune, and some cannot produce true notes all the way up and down the neck. Plus, they just aren't very cool. Nobody wants to jump on stage in front of 50,000 adoring fans with a guitar purchased at the local discount store.

And so the shopping begins, as the aspiring guitarist looks to find a better "axe." As with just about every product category these days, the array of choices is dizzying. For a few hundred dollars, budding musicians can choose from several imports that offer improved quality. Jumping up toward $1,000 to $2,000, they can enter the world of such classic American brands as Fender, Gibson, and Martin—a world that goes up to $10,000 and beyond for limited-edition models. Musicians with that much to spend and several months to wait can also hire skilled instrument builders known as *luthiers* to create custom guitars that reflect their individual personalities and playing styles. Luthiers can custom-craft just about any attribute a guitarist might want, from the types of wood for the body to the radius of the fingerboard.

But what if our superstar-in-training wants it all: world-class quality, the personalized touch of a custom guitar, and a midrange price tag, without the long delays associated with handcrafted instruments?

That "sweet spot" in the guitar market is the territory staked out by Carvin, a San Diego company that has been in the instrument business for over 60 years. How can Carvin profitably do business in this seemingly impossible market segment? How could the company quickly customize guitars and sell them in the $750 to $1,500 range without compromising quality?[1]

INTRODUCTION

Carvin (profiled in the chapter-opening Behind the Scenes) faced a classic systems challenge: how to design and operate business processes that would enable the company to deliver its unique value to customers. This chapter starts with an overview of systems concepts that every manager can use in any functional area; it then explores systems-related issues in the production function, including value chains and value webs, supply chain management, production and operations management, services delivery, and product and process quality.

MyBizLab

Gain hands-on experience through an interactive, real-world scenario. This chapter's simulation entitled Improving a Business is located at www.mybizlab.com.

The Systems View of Business

One of the most important skills you can develop as a manager is the ability to view business from a systems perspective. A **system** is an interconnected and coordinated set of *elements* and *processes* that converts *inputs* into desired *outputs*. A company is made up of numerous individual systems in the various functional areas, not only in manufacturing or operations but also in engineering, marketing, accounting, and other areas that together constitute the overall system that is the company itself. Each of these individual systems can also be thought of as a *subsystem* of the overall business.

THINKING IN SYSTEMS

To grasp the power of systems thinking, consider a point, a line, and a circle (see Exhibit 1 on the next page). If you poked your head into a nearby office building, what would this snapshot tell you? You could see only one part of the entire operation—and only at this one point in time. You might see people in the advertising department working on plans for a new ad campaign or people in the accounting department juggling numbers in spreadsheets, but neither view would tell you much about what it takes to complete these tasks or how that department interacts with the rest of the company.

If you stood and observed for several days, though, you could start to get a sense of how people do their jobs in this department. In the advertising department, for instance, you could watch as the staff transforms ideas, information, and goals into a plan that leads to the creation of a new online advertising campaign. Your "point" view would thereby extend into a "line" view, with multiple points connected in sequence. However, you still wouldn't have a complete picture of the entire process in action. Was the campaign successful? What did the marketing department learn from the campaign that could help it do even better next time? To see the process operate over and over, you need to connect the end of the line (the completion of this ad campaign) back to the beginning of the line (the start of the next ad campaign) to create a circle. Now you're beginning to form a systems view of what this department does and how its performance can be improved.

This circular view helps you understand the advertising system better, but it still isn't complete, because it doesn't show you how the advertising system affects the rest of the company and vice versa. For instance, did the finance department provide enough money to run the ad campaign? Was the information technology group prepared to handle the surge in website traffic? Was the manufacturing department ready with enough materials

1 LEARNING OBJECTIVE

Explain the systems perspective, and identify seven principles of systems thinking that can improve your skills as a manager.

system An interconnected and coordinated set of *elements* and *processes* that converts *inputs* to desired *outputs*

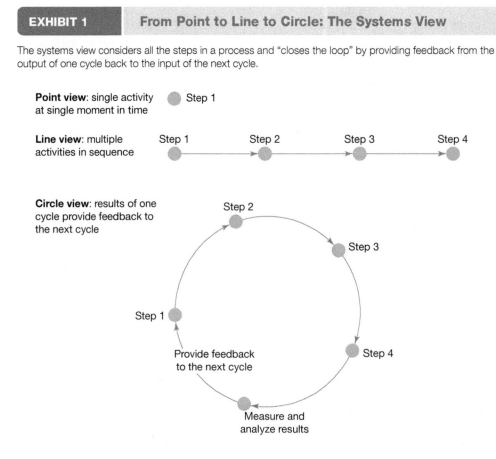

EXHIBIT 1 | **From Point to Line to Circle: The Systems View**

The systems view considers all the steps in a process and "closes the loop" by providing feedback from the output of one cycle back to the input of the next cycle.

Point view: single activity at single moment in time • Step 1

Line view: multiple activities in sequence   Step 1 → Step 2 → Step 3 → Step 4

Circle view: results of one cycle provide feedback to the next cycle

Step 1 · Step 2 · Step 3 · Step 4 · Provide feedback to the next cycle · Measure and analyze results

to build the product after customers started placing orders? Were the sales and customer service departments ready to handle the increase in their workloads? All of these subsystems connect to form the overall business system. Only by looking at the interconnected business system can you judge whether the ad campaign was a success for the company as a whole.

MANAGING SYSTEMS FOR PEAK PERFORMANCE

Much of the art and science of management involves understanding systems or creating new systems and figuring out ways to make them work more efficiently (using fewer resources) and more effectively (meeting goals more successfully). In some instances, systems analysis can run computer simulations to experiment with changes before making any resource decisions (see Exhibit 2). However, even without these formal techniques and tools, you can benefit from systems thinking by keeping these principles in mind:[2]

- **Help everyone see the big picture.** It's human nature for individual employees and departments to focus on their own goals and lose sight of what the company as a whole is trying to accomplish. Showing people how they contribute to the overall goal—and rewarding them for doing so—helps ensure that the entire system works efficiently.
- **Understand how individual systems really work and how they interact.** Managers need to avoid the temptation to jump in and try to fix systems without understanding how each one works and how they interact with other systems. For instance, as a wholesaling distribution manager, you might notice that delivery drivers are spending more time at retail sites than deliveries really take, so you instruct drivers to reduce the amount of time they spend. However, it might be that drivers are spending that time gathering market intelligence that they turn over to the sales staff. If you're not careful, you might improve the distribution system but damage the sales system.

EXHIBIT 2   Systems Diagram and Simulation

This example of a formal systems diagram models the flow of people at a ski resort, from arriving at the chairlift to taking the lift up the hill to skiing back down, then returning to the lift line. The resort is anticipating a boom in business and needs to figure out how to handle the additional skiers. By mathematically modeling the number of skiers at each point in the system, the resort can simulate several options: doing nothing, getting a faster chairlift, switching to triple chairs, or switching to quadruple chairs. Doing nothing would result in a long line waiting to get on the lift, while getting a faster lift (shown in the graph) would solve that problem but result in overcrowding on the slope. The optimum solution turns out to be switching to quad chairs.

Ski Resort Dynamics
Core Model Structure

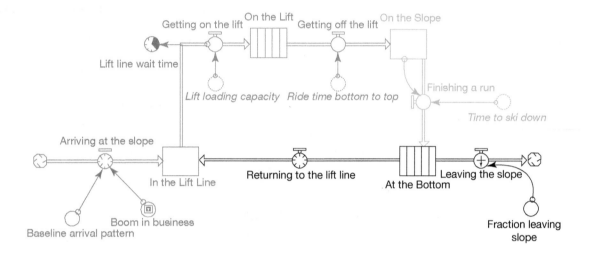

Ski Resort Dynamics
Simulate

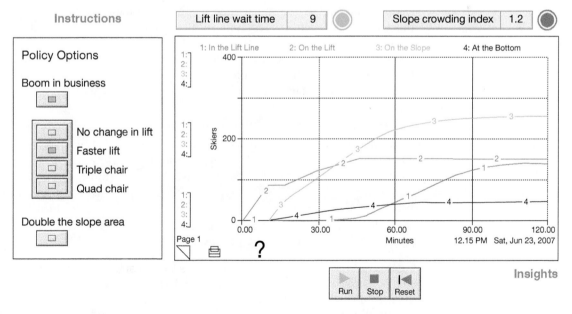

Source: Used with permission from Isee Systems, Inc., www.iseesystems.com.

- **Understand problems before you try to fix them.** The most obvious answer is not always the right answer, and poorly conceived solutions often end up causing more harm than good. When you analyze system behavior and malfunctions, make sure you focus on things that are *meaningful*, not merely things that are *measurable*. For instance, it's easy to measure how many reports employees write every month, but that might not be the most meaningful gauge of how well a process is working.

- **Understand the potential impact of solutions before you implement them.** Let's say you manage the customer support department, and to encourage high productivity, you run a weekly contest to see who can handle the most calls. Trouble is, you're essentially rewarding people based on how quickly they can get the customer off the phone, not on how quickly they actually solve customer problems. Customers who aren't happy keep calling back—which adds to the department's workload and *decreases* overall productivity.

- **Don't just move problems around—solve them.** When one subsystem in a company is malfunctioning, its problems are sometimes just moved around from one subsystem to the next, without ever getting solved. For example, if the market research department does a poor job of understanding customers, this problem will get shifted to the engineering department, which is likely to design a product that doesn't meet customer needs. The problem will then get shifted to the advertising and sales departments, which will struggle to promote and sell the product. The engineering, advertising, and sales departments will all underperform, but the real problem is back in the market research department. Market research in this case is a *leverage point*, where a relatively small correction could make the entire company perform better.

- **Understand how feedback works in the system.** Systems respond to *feedback*, which is information from the output applied back to the input. In the case of an ad campaign, the response from target customers is a form of feedback that helps the department understand whether the campaign is working. Feedback can work in unanticipated ways, too. A good example is managers sending mixed signals to their employees, such as telling them that customer satisfaction is the top priority but then criticizing anyone who spends too much time helping customers. Employees will respond to this feedback by spending less time with customers, leading to a decline in customer satisfaction.

- **Use mistakes as opportunities to learn and improve.** When mistakes occur, resist the temptation to just criticize or complain and then move on. Pull the team together and find out why the mistake occurred, and then identify ways to fix the system to eliminate mistakes in the future.

✓ Checkpoint

LEARNING OBJECTIVE 1: Explain the systems perspective, and identify seven principles of systems thinking that can improve your skills as a manager.

SUMMARY: The systems perspective involves looking at business as a series of interconnected and interdependent systems rather than as a lot of individual activities and events. Seven principles of systems thinking that can help every manager are (1) helping everyone see the big picture, (2) understanding how individual systems really work and how they interact, (3) understanding problems before you try to fix them, (4) understanding the potential impact of solutions before you implement, (5) avoiding the temptation to just move problems from one subsystem to the next without fixing them, (6) understanding how feedback works in a system so that you can improve each process by learning from experience, and (7) using mistakes as opportunities to learn and improve a system.

CRITICAL THINKING: (1) Why are leverage points in a system so critical to understand? (2) Why should a manager in marketing care about systems in the finance or manufacturing departments?

IT'S YOUR BUSINESS: (1) How could a systems approach to thinking help you get up to speed quickly in your first job after graduation? (2) Think back to your experience of registering for this class. How might you improve that system?

KEY TERM TO KNOW: system

Value Chains and Value Webs

2 **LEARNING OBJECTIVE**

Describe the *value chain* and *value web* concepts, and discuss the controversy over offshoring.

The essential purpose of a business is adding value—transforming lower-value inputs into higher-value outputs. The details vary widely from industry to industry, but all businesses focus on some kind of transformation like this (see Exhibit 3). The **value chain** is a helpful way to consider all the elements and processes that add value as input materials are transformed into the final products made available to the ultimate customer.[3] Each industry has a value chain, and each company has its own value chain as well.

value chain All the elements and processes that add value as raw materials are transformed into the final products made available to the ultimate customer

REDEFINING ORGANIZATIONS WITH VALUE WEBS

In the decades since Michael Porter introduced the value chain concept, many companies have come to realize that doing everything themselves is not always the most efficient or most successful way to run a business. Many now opt to focus on their core competencies and let other companies handle the remaining business functions—a strategy known as **outsourcing**. Hiring other firms to handle some tasks is not a new concept, to be sure;

outsourcing Contracting out certain business functions or operations to other companies

EXHIBIT 3	Business Transformation Systems

All businesses engage in a transformation process of some kind, converting one type of value (inputs) to another type (outputs).

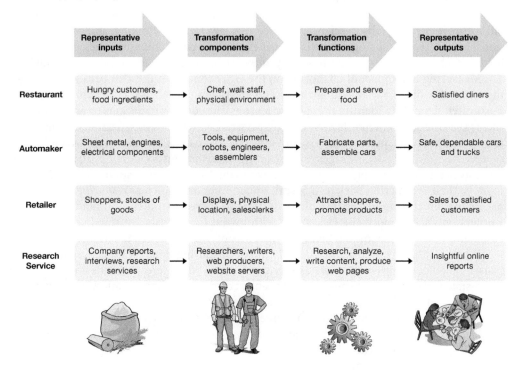

	Representative inputs	Transformation components	Transformation functions	Representative outputs
Restaurant	Hungry customers, food ingredients	Chef, wait staff, physical environment	Prepare and serve food	Satisfied diners
Automaker	Sheet metal, engines, electrical components	Tools, equipment, robots, engineers, assemblers	Fabricate parts, assemble cars	Safe, dependable cars and trucks
Retailer	Shoppers, stocks of goods	Displays, physical location, salesclerks	Attract shoppers, promote products	Sales to satisfied customers
Research Service	Company reports, interviews, research services	Researchers, writers, web producers, website servers	Research, analyze, write content, produce web pages	Insightful online reports

advertising, public relations, and transportation are among the services that have a long history of being handled by outside firms. The term *outsourcing* is usually applied when a firm decides to move a significant function that was previously done in house, such as information technology or manufacturing, to an outside vendor.

The combination of extensive globalization in many industries and the development of electronic networking has made it easy for companies to connect with partners around the world. Instead of the linear value chain, some businesses now think in terms of **value webs**, multidimensional networks of suppliers and outsourcing partners.[4] Value webs enable the virtual or network organization structures, and *unstructured organizations* can be viewed as dynamic value webs that grow, shrink, or change as the company's needs change.

value webs Multidimensional networks of suppliers and outsourcing partners

The outsourced, value web approach has several key advantages, including speed, flexibility, and the opportunity to access a wide range of talents and technologies that might be expensive or impossible to acquire otherwise. Established companies can narrow their focus to excel at their core competencies; entrepreneurs with product ideas can quickly assemble a team of designers, manufacturing plants, and distributors in far less time than it would take to build an entire company from scratch.

For all its potential advantages, outsourcing does carry some risks, particularly in terms of control. For example, to get its new 787 Dreamliner to market as quickly as possible, Boeing outsourced the manufacturing of many parts of the new plane to other manufacturers. Boeing managers initially decided not to impose the "Boeing way" on these suppliers, so it took a hands-off approach. However, the lack of control came to haunt the company. Many suppliers missed target dates and quality standards, throwing the Dreamliner off schedule by at least three years and costing Boeing billions of dollars in extra work, canceled sales, and delivery penalties.[5]

THE OFFSHORING CONTROVERSY

When companies outsource any function in the value chain, they usually eliminate many of the jobs associated with that function as well. In many cases, those jobs don't go across the street to another local company but rather around the world as companies pursue lower labor costs, a variation on outsourcing known as **offshoring**. (Offshoring can shift jobs to another company or to an overseas division of the same company.)

offshoring Transferring a part or all of a business function to a facility (a different part of the company or another company entirely) in another country

Offshoring has been going on for decades, but it began to be a major issue for U.S. manufacturing in the 1980s and then for information technology in the 1990s. Today, offshoring is affecting jobs in science, engineering, law, finance, banking, and other professional areas.[6] The offshoring debate is a great example of conflicting priorities in the stakeholder model; see Exhibit 4 for a summary of the key arguments for and against offshoring.

Measuring the impact of offshoring on the U.S. economy is difficult because isolating the effect of a single variable in such a complex system is not easy. For example, economists often struggle to identify the specific reasons one country gains jobs or another loses them. The emergence of new technology, phasing out of old technology, shifts in consumer tastes, changes in business strategies, and other factors can all create and destroy jobs.

As the offshoring debate rages on, the nature of offshoring is changing. The complexities and rising costs of long-distance manufacturing has prompted some U.S. companies to move their production back to U.S. soil, a phenomenon known as *reshoring*. For example, as manufacturing wages in China continue to increase and the demand for skilled workers outpaces supply, the U.S. states with lowest labor costs are starting to become cost-competitive with China when the total costs of offshoring are taken into account.[7]

While reshoring might reduce the amount of offshoring done by U.S. companies, globalized manufacturing is here to stay, so it's in everyone's best interest to make it work as well as possible for as many stakeholders as possible. For example, how should U.S. companies be taxed when they have operations all over the world? Also, should unions and regulatory agencies make it more difficult for companies to move jobs overseas, or would it be more beneficial in the long run to let companies compete as vigorously as possible and focus on retraining American workers for new jobs here? These issues are not simple, and you can expect this debate to continue.

EXHIBIT 4	The Offshoring Controversy

Offshoring, or shifting jobs performed by U.S. employees to countries with lower labor costs, is a complex controversy that pits some stakeholders against others. Here are the major arguments for and against the practice, along with some of the key stakeholder groups affected.

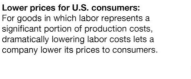 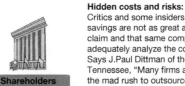

Arguments for Offshoring		Arguments Against or Concerns About Offshoring	
Stakeholders who benefit	**Argument**	**Stakeholders who suffer**	**Argument**
 Shareholders	**Responsibility to shareholder interests:** Companies that engage in offshoring say they have a duty to manage shareholder investments for maximum gain, so it would be irresponsible not to explore cost-saving opportunities such as offshoring.	 Workers	**Loss of well-paid U.S. jobs:** Opponents of offshoring say that companies are selling out the U.S. middle class in pursuit of profits and pushing a trend that can only harm the country.
 Consumers	**Lower prices for U.S. consumers:** For goods in which labor represents a significant portion of production costs, dramatically lowering labor costs lets a company lower its prices to consumers.	 Shareholders	**Hidden costs and risks:** Critics and some insiders say the real savings are not as great as proponents claim and that same companies fail to adequately analyze the costs and risks. Says J. Paul Dittman of the University of Tennessee, "Many firms are rethinking the mad rush to outsource . . . the long supply lines, incredibly volatile fuel costs, exchange rates, the geopolitical risks have all come home to roost."
 Shareholders	**Lack of choice in competitive industries:** Given the pricing advantage that offshoring can give U.S. companies, as soon as one company in an industry does it, the others are put under pressure to lower their prices—and offshoring might be the only way for some to lower costs enough to do so.	 Shareholders	**Business agility and responsiveness:** When companies rely on operations halfway around the world, marketplace trends and customer service matters.
 Shareholders	**Support for local customers around the world:** Some companies say that as they expand into other countries, they have no choice but to hire overseas employees in order to support local customers.	Shareholders	**Knowledge transfer and theft risk:** By hiring other companies to perform technical and professional services, U.S. companies transfer important knowledge to these other countries— making them more competitive and potentially depleting the pools of expertise in the United States. Offshoring can also increase the risks of product piracy and theft of intellectual property.
U.S. economy	**U.S. competitiveness:** Proponents say that offshoring is crucial to the survival of many U.S. companies and that it saves other U.S. jobs by making U.S. companies more competitive in the global marketplace.	U.S. economy	
		 Consumers	**Product safety issues:** Moving more production beyond U.S. borders increases concerns about the ability of regulators to oversee vital health and safety issues.
		United States	**National security and public health concerns:** The weapons and systems used for national defense require lots of steel, semiconductors, and other manufactured materials, and the health-care industry requires a vast supply of materials. What if the United States comes to rely too heavily on other countries for things it needs to protect its borders and its people?
		Consumers	

Sources: Adapted from J. Paul Dittmann, "WT100 and the University of Tennessee Supply Chain Survey," *World Trade 100*, July 2011, 42; Hayden Bush, "Reliance on Overseas Manufacturers Worries Supply Chain Experts," *Hospitals & Health Networks*, July 2011, 13; William T. Dickens and Stephen J. Rose, "Blinder Baloney," *The International Economy*, Fall 2007, 18+; "Supply Chain News: The Seven Timeless Challenges of Supply Chain Management," *SupplyChainDigest*, 2 June 2009, www.scdigest .com; Phil Fersht, Dana Stiffler, and Kevin O'Marah, "The Ins and Outs of Offshoring," *Supply Chain Management Review*, March 2009, 10–11; Ajay K. Goel, Nazgol Moussavi, and Vats N. Srivatsan, "Time to Rethink Offshoring?" *McKinsey Quarterly*, 2008 Issue 4, 108–111; Anita Hawser, "Offshoring Industry Faces New Opponent: Its Clients," *Global Finance*, November 2007, 6; Alan S. Brown, "A Shift in Engineering Offshore," *Mechanical Engineering*, March 2009, 24–29; John Ferreira and Len Prokopets, "Does Offshoring Still Make Sense?" *Supply Chain Management Review*, January/February 2009, 20–27; Dan Gilmore, "Can—and Should—Western Manufacturing Be Saved?" *SupplyChainDigest*, 28 May 2009, www.scdigest.com; Geri Smith and Justin Bachman, "The Offshoring of Airplane Care," *BusinessWeek*, 10 April 2008, www.businessweek .com; Susan Carey and Alex Frangos, "Airlines, Facing Cost Pressure, Outsource Crucial Safety Tasks," *Wall Street Journal*, 21 January 2005, A1, A5.

✓ Checkpoint

LEARNING OBJECTIVE 2: Describe the *value chain* and *value web* concepts, and discuss the controversy over offshoring.

SUMMARY: The *value chain* includes all the elements and processes that add value as input materials are transformed into the final products made available to the ultimate customer. The *value web* concept expands this linear model to a multidimensional network of suppliers and outsourcing partners. In the complex argument over *offshoring*, the transfer of business functions to entities in other countries in pursuit of lower costs, proponents claim that (a) companies have a responsibility to shareholder interests to pursue the lowest cost of production, (b) offshoring benefits U.S. consumers through lower prices, (c) many companies don't have a choice once their competitors move offshore, (d) some companies need to offshore in order to support customers around the world, and (e) offshoring helps U.S. companies be more competitive. Those who question the value or wisdom of offshoring raise points about (a) the future of good jobs in the United States, (b) hidden costs and risks, (c) diminished responsiveness, (d) knowledge transfer and theft issues, (e) product safety issues, and (f) national security and public health concerns.

CRITICAL THINKING: (1) Do U.S. companies have an obligation to keep jobs in the United States? Why or why not? (2) Will global labor markets eventually balance out, with workers in comparable positions all over the world making roughly the same wages? Explain your answer.

IT'S YOUR BUSINESS: (1) In your own long-term career planning, have you taken the "offshorability" of your target profession into account? (2) Should such concerns affect your career planning?

KEY TERMS TO KNOW: value chain, outsourcing, value webs, offshoring

---

3 **LEARNING OBJECTIVE**

Define *supply chain management* and explain its strategic importance.

supply chain A set of connected systems that coordinates the flow of goods and materials from suppliers all the way through to final customers

supply chain management (SCM) The business procedures, policies, and computer systems that integrate the various elements of the supply chain into a cohesive system

Supply Chain Management

Regardless of how and where it is structured, the lifeblood of every production operation is the **supply chain**, a set of connected systems that coordinates the flow of goods and materials from suppliers all the way through to final customers. Companies with multiple customer bases can also develop a distinct supply chain to serve each segment.[8]

Supply chain management (SCM) combines business procedures and policies with information systems that integrate the various elements of the supply chain into a cohesive system. As companies rely more on outsourcing partners, SCM has grown far beyond the simple procurement of supplies to become a strategic management function that means the difference between success and failure. Successful implementation of SCM can have a profound strategic impact on companies and the broader economy, in several important ways:[9]

- **Managing risks.** SCM can help companies manage the complex risks involved in a supply chain, risks that include everything from cost and availability to health and safety issues.
- **Managing relationships.** SCM can coordinate the numerous relationships in the supply chain and help managers focus their attention on the most important company-to-company relationships.
- **Managing trade-offs.** SCM helps managers address the many trade-offs in the supply chain. These trade-offs can be a source of conflict within the company, and SCM helps balance the competing interests of the various functional areas. This holistic view helps managers balance both capacity and capability along the entire chain.

- **Promoting sustainability.** As the part of business that moves raw materials and finished goods around the world, supply chains have an enormous effect on resource usage, waste, and environmental impact. A major effort is underway in the field of SCM to develop greener supply chains. A key player in this effort is the giant retailer Walmart, which buys products from more than 100,000 suppliers and has tremendous influence on global supply chains. The company now works with its suppliers to help them meet sustainability targets in the areas of energy and climate, material efficiency, natural resources, and people and community.[10]

SUPPLY CHAINS VERSUS VALUE CHAINS

The terms *supply chain* and *value chain* are sometimes used interchangeably, and the distinction between them isn't always clear in everyday usage. One helpful way to distinguish between the two is to view the supply chain as the part of the overall value chain that acquires and manages the goods and services needed to produce whatever it is the company produces and then deliver it to the final customer. Everyone in the company is part of the value chain, but not everyone is involved in the supply chain.[11]

Another way to distinguish the two is that the supply chain focuses on the "upstream" part of the process, collecting the necessary materials and supplies with an emphasis on reducing waste and inefficiency. The value chain focuses on the "downstream" part of the process and on adding value in the eyes of customers.[12]

Yet a third way that has recently emerged is talking about value chains as a strategic win-win business partnership rather than the more tactical, deal-driven arrangement of a supply chain. In this usage, "value" also encompasses *values*, including sustainability practices that make products more worthy and appealing in the eyes of customers.[13]

SUPPLY CHAIN SYSTEMS AND TECHNIQUES

The core focus of SCM is getting the right materials at the right price in the right place at the right time for successful production. Unfortunately, you can't just pile up huge quantities of everything you might eventually need, because **inventory**, the goods and materials kept in stock for production or sale, costs money to purchase and to store. On the other hand, not having an adequate supply of inventory can result in expensive delays. This balancing act is the job of **inventory control**, which tries to determine the right quantities of supplies and products to have on hand and then tracks where those items are. One of the most important technologies to emerge in inventory control in recent years is *radio frequency identification (RFID)*. RFID uses small antenna tags attached to products or shipping containers; special sensors detect the presence of the tags and can track the flow of goods through the supply chain.

Procurement, or *purchasing*, is the acquisition of the raw materials, parts, components, supplies, and finished products required to produce goods and services. The goal of purchasing is to make sure that the company has all the materials it needs, when it needs them, at the lowest possible cost. A company must always have enough supplies on hand to cover a product's *lead time*—the period that elapses between placing the supply order and receiving materials.

To accomplish these goals, operations specialists have developed a variety of systems and techniques over the years:

- **Material requirements planning (MRP).** MRP helps a manufacturer get the correct materials where they are needed, when they are needed, without unnecessary stockpiling. Managers use MRP software to calculate when certain materials will be required, when they should be ordered, and when they should be delivered so that storage costs

inventory Goods and materials kept in stock for production or sale

inventory control Determining the right quantities of supplies and products to have on hand and tracking where those items are

procurement The acquisition of the raw materials, parts, components, supplies, and finished products required to produce goods and services will be minimal. These systems are so effective at reducing inventory levels that they are used almost universally in both large and small manufacturing firms.

- **Manufacturing resource planning (MRP II).** MRP II expands MRP with links to a company's financial systems and other processes. For instance, in addition to managing inventory levels successfully, an MRP II system can help ensure that material costs adhere to target budgets.[14] Because it draws together all departments, an MRP II system produces a companywide game plan that allows everyone to work with the same numbers. Moreover, the system can track each step of production, allowing managers throughout the company to consult other managers' inventories, schedules, and plans.

- **Enterprise resource planning (ERP).** ERP extends the scope of resource planning and management even further to encompass the entire organization. ERP software programs are typically made up of modules that address the needs of the various functional areas, from manufacturing to sales to human resources. Some companies deploy ERP on a global scale, with a single centralized system connecting all their operations worldwide.[15]

✓ Checkpoint

LEARNING OBJECTIVE 3: Define *supply chain management* **and explain its strategic importance.**

SUMMARY: Supply chain management (SCM) combines business procedures and policies with information systems that integrate the various elements of the supply chain into a cohesive system. SCM helps companies manage risks, relationships, and trade-offs throughout their supply chains, building partnerships that help everyone in the supply chain succeed.

CRITICAL THINKING: (1) Why can't companies just stockpile huge inventories of all the parts and materials they need rather than carefully manage supply from one day to the next? (2) Why would a company invest time and money in helping its suppliers improve their business practices? Why not just dump underperformers and get better suppliers?

IT'S YOUR BUSINESS: (1) In any current or previous job, what steps have supervisors taken to help you understand your role in the supply chain? (2) Is it dehumanizing to your colleagues and business partners to be participants in a supply chain? Why or why not?

KEY TERMS TO KNOW: supply chain, supply chain management (SCM), inventory, inventory control, procurement

---

4 **LEARNING OBJECTIVE**

Identify the major planning decisions in production and operations management.

production and operations management Overseeing all the activities involved in producing goods and services

Production and Operations Management

The term *production* suggests factories, machines, and assembly lines making automobiles, computers, furniture, motorcycles, or other tangible goods. With the growth in the number of service-based businesses and their increasing importance to the economy, however, the term *production* is now used to describe the transformation of resources into both goods and services. The broader term **production and operations management**, or simply *operations management*, refers to overseeing all the activities involved in producing goods and services. Operations managers are responsible for a wide range of strategies and decisions, from locating production facilities to managing the supply chain.

FACILITIES LOCATION AND DESIGN

Choosing the location of production facilities is a complex decision that must consider such factors as land, construction, availability of talent, taxes, energy, living standards, transportation, and proximity to customers and business partners. Support from local communities and governments often plays a key role in location decisions as well. To provide jobs and expand their income and sales tax bases, local, state, and national governments often compete to attract companies by offering generous financial incentives such as tax reductions.

After a site has been selected, managers turn their attention to *facility layout*, the arrangement of production work centers and other elements (such as materials, equipment, and support departments) needed to process goods and services. Layout planning includes such decisions as how many steps are needed in the process, the amount and type of equipment and workers needed for each step, how each step should be configured, and where the steps should be located relative to one another.[16]

Well-designed facilities help companies operate more productively by reducing wasted time and wasted materials, but that is far from the only benefit. Smart layouts support close communication and collaboration among employees and help ensure their safety, both of which are important for employee satisfaction and motivation. In the delivery of services, facility layout can be a major influence on customer satisfaction because it affects the overall service experience.[17]

FORECASTING AND CAPACITY PLANNING

Using customer feedback, sales orders, market research, past sales figures, industry analyses, and educated guesses about the future behavior of customers and competitors, operations managers prepare *production forecasts*—estimates of future demand for the company's products. After product demand has been estimated, management must balance that with the company's capacity to produce the goods or services. The term *capacity* refers to the volume of manufacturing or service capability that an organization can handle. **Capacity planning** is the collection of long-term strategic decisions that establish the overall level of resources needed to meet customer demand. When managers at Boeing plan for the production of an airliner, they have to consider not only the staffing of thousands of people but also massive factory spaces, material flows from hundreds of suppliers around the world, internal deliveries, cash flow, tools and equipment, and dozens of other factors. Because of the potential impact on finances, customers, and employees—and the difficulty of reversing major decisions—capacity choices are among the most important decisions that top-level managers make.[18]

capacity planning Establishing the overall level of resources needed to meet customer demand

SCHEDULING

In any production process, managers must do *scheduling*—determining how long each operation takes and deciding which tasks are done in which order. Manufacturing facilities often use a *master production schedule (MPS)* to coordinate production of all the goods the company makes. Service businesses use a variety of scheduling techniques as well, from simple appointment calendars for a small business to the comprehensive online systems that airlines and other large service providers use.

To plan and track projects of all kinds, managers throughout a company can use a *Gantt chart*, a special type of bar chart that shows the progress of all the tasks needed to complete a project (see Exhibit 5 on the next page). For more complex projects, the *program evaluation and review technique (PERT)* is helpful. PERT helps managers identify the optimal sequencing of activities, the expected time for project completion, and the best use of resources. To use PERT, managers map out all the activities in a network diagram (see Exhibit 6 on the next page). The longest path through the network is known as the **critical path** because it represents the minimum amount of time needed to complete the project. Tasks in the critical path usually receive special attention because they determine when the project can be completed.[19] (If anyone ever says that *you* are in the critical path, make sure you stay on schedule!)

critical path In a PERT network diagram, the sequence of operations that requires the longest time to complete

LEAN SYSTEMS

Throughout all the activities in the production process, operations managers pay close attention to **productivity**, or the efficiency with which they can convert inputs to outputs. (Put another way, productivity is equal to the value of the outputs divided by the value of the inputs.) Productivity is one of the most vital responsibilities in operations management because it is a key factor in determining the company's competitiveness and profitability.

productivity The efficiency with which an organization can convert inputs to outputs

EXHIBIT 5 — Gantt Charts for Project Management

A Gantt chart is a handy tool in project and production management because it shows the order in which tasks must be completed and which tasks are dependent on other tasks. For the new product launch shown here, for example, the analysis task is dependent on all three tasks before it, which means those tasks must be completed before analysis can begin. With periodic updates, it's also easy to show a team exactly where the project stands at any particular moment.

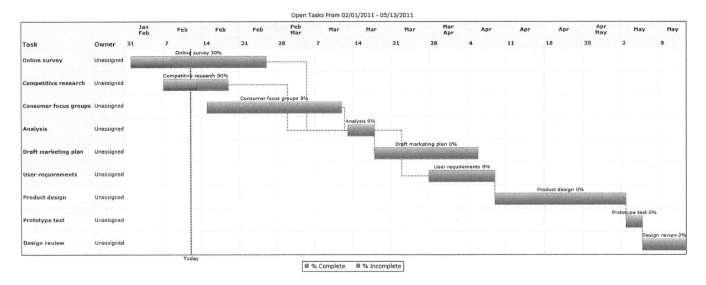

EXHIBIT 6 — Simplified PERT Diagram for a Store Opening

This PERT diagram shows a subset of the many tasks involved in opening a new retail store. The tasks involved in staffing are on the critical path because they take the longest time to complete (51 days), whereas the promotion tasks can be completed in 38 days, and the merchandise tasks can be completed in 39 days. In other words, some delay can be tolerated in the promotion or merchandise tasks, but any delay in any of the staffing tasks will delay the store's opening day.

lean systems Systems (in manufacturing and other functional areas) that maximize productivity by reducing waste and delays

just-in-time (JIT) Inventory management in which goods and materials are delivered throughout the production process right before they are needed

Companies that can produce similar goods or services with fewer resources have a distinct advantage over their competitors. Moreover, high productivity in the fullest sense also requires low waste, whether it's leftover materials, shoddy products that must be scrapped, or excess energy usage. Consequently, productivity improvements and sustainability improvements often complement each other.

Lean systems, which maximize productivity by reducing waste and delays, are at the heart of many productivity improvement efforts. Many lean systems borrow techniques from Toyota; the *Toyota Production System* is world renowned for its ability to continually improve both productivity and quality (see Exhibit 7).[20] Central to the notion of lean systems is **just-in-time (JIT)** inventory management, in which goods and materials are delivered

EXHIBIT 7	Conceptual Diagram of the Toyota Production System

The Toyota Production System, one of the most influential production strategies in modern business history, has been studied, duplicated, and adapted by companies in a variety of industries around the world. Toyota refined the system over decades, but it has always been based on the two fundamental principles of just-in-time inventory management, so that expensive inventory doesn't pile up when it isn't being used, and *jidoka*, or "automation with a human touch," whereby the highly automated process can be stopped by any worker any time a problem appears, to avoid making more defective parts or cars. However, for all its abilities to reduce manufacturing defects, the system has not been able to prevent all failures—particularly now that cars are vast software systems as well as mechanical systems.

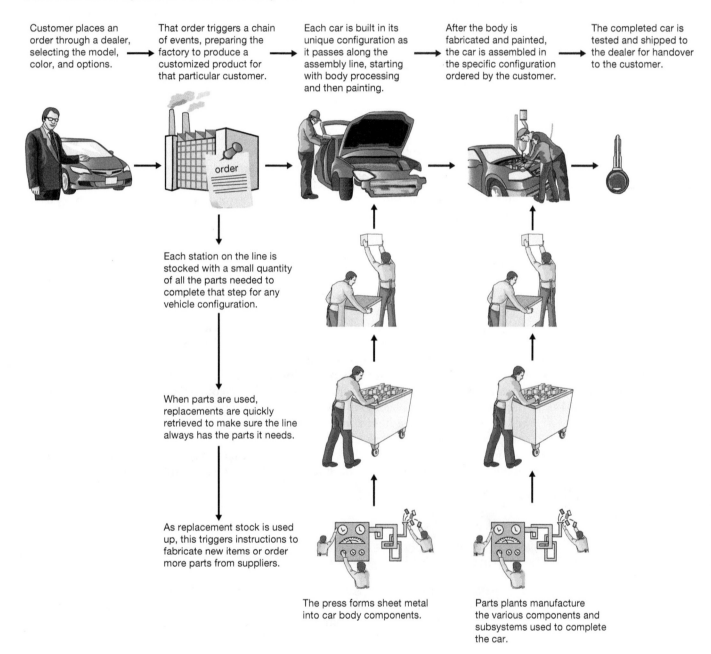

Customer places an order through a dealer, selecting the model, color, and options.

That order triggers a chain of events, preparing the factory to produce a customized product for that particular customer.

Each car is built in its unique configuration as it passes along the assembly line, starting with body processing and then painting.

After the body is fabricated and painted, the car is assembled in the specific configuration ordered by the customer.

The completed car is tested and shipped to the dealer for handover to the customer.

Each station on the line is stocked with a small quantity of all the parts needed to complete that step for any vehicle configuration.

When parts are used, replacements are quickly retrieved to make sure the line always has the parts it needs.

As replacement stock is used up, this triggers instructions to fabricate new items or order more parts from suppliers.

The press forms sheet metal into car body components.

Parts plants manufacture the various components and subsystems used to complete the car.

Source: Adapted from "Toyota Production System," Toyota Global website, accessed 25 August 2011, www.toyota-global.com.

throughout the production process right before they are needed rather than being stockpiled in inventories. Reducing stocks to immediate needs reduces waste and forces factories to keep production flowing smoothly. (For more on quality at Toyota, see "Quality and Complexity" later in this chapter.)

Achieving such benefits requires constant attention to quality and teamwork because with no spare inventory, there is no room for delays or errors.[21] Without stockpiles of extra parts and materials, each stage in the production process goes idle if the stages before it have not delivered on time.

MASS PRODUCTION, CUSTOMIZED PRODUCTION, AND MASS CUSTOMIZATION

mass production The creation of identical goods or services, usually in large quantities

customized production The creation of a unique good or service for each customer

mass customization A manufacturing approach in which part of the product is mass produced and the remaining features are customized for each buyer

Both goods and services can be created through *mass production*, *customized production*, or *mass customization*, depending on the nature of the product and the desires of target customers. In **mass production**, identical goods or services are created, usually in large quantities, such as when Apple churns out a million identical iPhones. Although not normally associated with services, mass production is also what American Airlines is doing when it offers hundreds of opportunities for passengers to fly from, say, Dallas to Chicago every day: Every customer on these flights gets the same service at the same time.

At the other extreme is **customized production**, sometimes called *batch-of-one production* in manufacturing, in which the producer creates a unique good or service for each customer. If you order a piece of furniture from a local craftsperson, for instance, you can specify everything from the size and shape to the types of wood and fabric used. Or you can hire a charter pilot to fly you wherever you want, whenever you want. Both products are customized to your unique requirements.

Mass production has the advantage of economies of scale, but it can't deliver many of the unique goods and services that today's customers demand. On the other hand, fully customized production can offer uniqueness but usually at a much higher price. An attractive compromise in many cases is **mass customization**, in which part of the product is mass produced and then the remaining features are customized for each buyer. With design and production technologies getting ever more flexible, the opportunities for customization continue to grow. For instance, the Italian motorcycle maker Ducati can now scan a customer's body shape and create the perfect seat to fit.[22] And as you'll read at the end of the chapter, this is the approach Carvin has taken: Customers get the same basic guitar bodies but with their own individual combinations of woods, fingerboard styles, finishes, and electronic components.

✓ Checkpoint

LEARNING OBJECTIVE 4: Identify the major planning decisions in production and operations management.

SUMMARY: The major decisions in operations management include (1) facilities location and design; (2) forecasting and capacity planning to match resources with demand; (3) scheduling; (4) lean system design to reduce waste and delays; and (5) the choice of mass production, customized production, or mass customization.

CRITICAL THINKING: (1) Why is it essential to identify tasks in the critical path of a project? (2) How does mass customization help a company balance productivity and customer satisfaction?

IT'S YOUR BUSINESS: (1) The phrase "lean and mean" is sometimes used to describe lean systems. What are the risks of using such language? (2) Is this course an example of mass production, customization, or mass customization? Explain.

The Unique Challenges of Service Delivery

5 LEARNING OBJECTIVE

Explain the unique challenges of service delivery.

With the majority of workers in the United States now involved in the service sector, managers in thousands of companies need to pay close attention to the unique challenges of delivering services: perishability, location constraints, scalability challenges, performance variability and perceptions of quality, and customer involvement and service provider interaction.

PERISHABILITY

Most services are *perishable*, meaning that they are consumed at the same time they are produced and cannot exist before or after that time. For example, if a 200-seat airliner takes off half empty, those 100 sales opportunities are lost forever. The airline can't create these products ahead of time and store them in inventory until somebody is ready to buy. Similarly, restaurants can seat only so many people every night, so empty tables represent revenue lost forever. This perishability can have a profound impact on the way service businesses are managed, from staffing (making sure enough people are on hand to help with peak demands) to pricing (using discounts to encourage people to buy services when they are available).

LOCATION CONSTRAINTS

Perishability also means that for many services, customers and providers need to be in the same place at the same time. The equipment and food ingredients used in a restaurant can be produced just about anywhere, but the restaurant itself needs to be located close to customers. One of the most significant commercial advantages of the Internet is the way it has enabled many service businesses to get around this constraint. Online retailers, information providers, and other e-businesses can locate virtually anywhere on the planet.

SCALABILITY CHALLENGES AND OPPORTUNITIES

Any business that wants to grow must consider the issue of **scalability**, the potential to increase production by expanding or replicating its initial production capacity. Scaling up always creates some challenges, but service businesses that depend on the skills of specific professionals can be particularly difficult to scale. Examples range from chefs and interior designers to business consultants and graphic designers, particularly when the business is built around the reputation of a single person.

scalability The potential to increase production by expanding or replicating its initial production capacity

Of course, many goods businesses also rely on highly skilled production workers, but the potential to mechanize goods production can make it easier to scale up manufacturing in some cases. For example, by using computer-controlled routers to carve the bodies of its guitars, Carvin frees itself from the constraint of hiring enough skilled carvers to do it all by hand.

PERFORMANCE VARIABILITY AND PERCEPTIONS OF QUALITY

For many types of services, the quality of the service performance can vary from one instance to the next—and that quality is in the eye of the beholder and often can't be judged until after the service has been performed. If you manufacture scissors, you can specify a certain

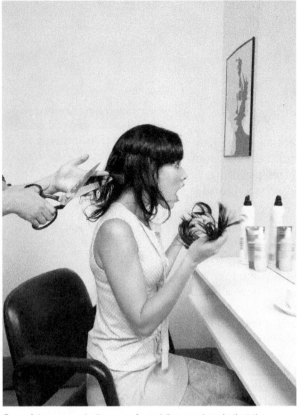

One of the many challenges of providing services is that the evaluation of quality is often subjective.

grade of steel from your suppliers and use automated machinery to produce thousands of identical pairs of scissors of identical quality. Many key attributes such as the size and strength of the scissors are *objective* and measurable, and customers can experience the *subjective* variables such as the feel and action before they buy. In other words, there is little mystery and little room for surprise in the purchase.

However, if you create a haircut using a pair of those scissors, perceptions of quality become almost entirely subjective *and* impossible to judge until after the service is complete. Plus, hair styling is a good example of a service in which *quality of experience* is an important part of customer perceptions as well, which is why, for instance, most salons pay a lot of attention to architecture, interior design, lighting, music, and other amenities that have nothing to do with the actual haircut itself.

CUSTOMER INVOLVEMENT AND PROVIDER INTERACTION

Finally, one of the biggest differences between goods and services production is the fact that customers are often involved in—and thereby can affect the quality of—the service delivery. For instance, personal trainers can instruct clients in the proper way to exercise, but if the clients don't follow directions, the result will be unsatisfactory. Similarly, a business consultant relies on accurate information from managers in a client organization; lacking that, he or she will be unable to craft the most effective advice.

When customers and service providers interact, the quality of the interpersonal experience also affects customer perceptions of quality. In this sense, service delivery is something of a performance that needs to instill confidence in the client. Weak communication skills or poor etiquette can create dissatisfaction with a service that is satisfactory or even exceptional in all other respects.

✓ Checkpoint

LEARNING OBJECTIVE 5: Explain the unique challenges of service delivery.

SUMMARY: The delivery of services presents a number of unique challenges, including (1) perishability, which means that services are consumed at the same time they are produced; (2) location constraints, which often require that customers and service providers be in the same place at the same time; (3) scalability challenges, which can make some types of service businesses more difficult to expand; (4) performance variability and perceptions of quality, which heighten the challenge of delivering consistent quality and increase the subjectivity of the customer experience; and (5) customer involvement and service provider interaction, which can put some of the responsibility for service quality on the customer's shoulders and increase the importance of good interpersonal skills.

CRITICAL THINKING: (1) How can technology help some service businesses address the challenge of scalability? (2) If customers are paying for a service, why should they ever have to share in the responsibility of ensuring quality results?

IT'S YOUR BUSINESS: (1) Do you think you have a natural personality for working in a service business? Why or why not? (2) If you're not a "natural," what steps could you take to succeed in a service job anyway?

KEY TERM TO KNOW: scalability

Product and Process Quality

6 **LEARNING OBJECTIVE**

Define *quality*, explain the challenge of quality and product complexity, and identify four major tools and strategies for ensuring product quality.

The term *quality* is often used in a vague sense of "goodness" or "excellence," but to be meaningful from a managerial standpoint, it needs to be defined in context. Hyundai and Aston Martin both make quality automobiles, but quality means dramatically different things to the makers and buyers of these two car brands. People who spend $15,000 or $20,000 on a Hyundai are likely to be satisfied with the quality they receive in return, but people who spend 10 times that much on an Aston Martin have very different expectations. Accordingly, **quality** is best defined as the degree to which a product or process meets reasonable or agreed-upon expectations. Within the framework of this general definition, a specific set of parameters can be identified that define quality in each situation.

quality The degree to which a product or process meets reasonable or agreed-upon expectations

Defining those expectations of quality and then organizing the resources and systems needed to achieve that level are vital responsibilities in today's competitive, resource-constrained environment. With numerous choices available in most product categories, consumers and business buyers alike tend to avoid or abandon products and companies that can't meet their expectations. Moreover, poor quality wastes time and money, squanders resources, frustrates customers and employees, erodes confidence in companies and their products, and can even put people in danger.

QUALITY AND COMPLEXITY

As many products become increasingly complex, defining and maintaining quality becomes an ever greater challenge. For example, even identical, mass-produced computers immediately become unique when their new owners start adding software, downloading files, and connecting to printers and other devices, each of which is a complex hardware/software system in its own right. All these changes and connections increase the chances that something will go wrong and thereby lower the functional quality of the product. In other words, even though the company verified the quality of the products before they left the factory, it could have thousands of quality issues on its hands over time.

Meeting expectations of quality in complicated, real-world operating conditions over time can present a sizable challenge but one that must be met to ensure buyer satisfaction. Dell, for example, has several dozen customer service specialists who monitor social media conversations for signs of discontent over its products. When they hear complaints, they jump in with advice and offers to help. This effort improves customer satisfaction and creates opportunities to sell additional goods and services—the company figures the program has generated more than $1 billion in additional sales—but it also gives Dell engineers valuable insights into how quality plays out in the messy real world outside the factory.[23]

The need to get feedback from the field and not just from the factory has been identified as one of the factors that contributed to quality issues that recently tarnished Toyota's reputation for safety and dependability—and prompted some observers to wonder whether the Toyota Production System was really all that effective at weeding out defects. The company made headlines in 2009 and 2010 by recalling millions of vehicles after complaints of unintended acceleration and other serious safety issues. A variety of causes were investigated, including floor mats being improperly installed by dealers or owners, software glitches, electromagnetic interference in the throttle control system (a problem that would affect virtually all new cars if it affected any), sticky pedals caused by humidity and material wear over time, driver error—the range of possibilities indicates how complex such problems can be. However, according to engineering professor Jeffrey Liker, who has researched and written extensively about Toyota, none of the recalls could be traced to production defects.[24]

One of the criticisms leveled at Toyota throughout these episodes is that the senior engineers in charge of design were isolated at company headquarters in Japan and too insulated from real-world feedback. In 2011, the company announced that North American engineering teams were being given more control over the development of vehicles designed for the North American market.[25]

STRATEGIES FOR ENSURING PRODUCT QUALITY

The traditional means of maintaining quality is called **quality control**—measuring quality against established standards after the good or service has been produced and weeding out

quality control Measuring quality against established standards after the good or service has been produced and weeding out any defective products

quality assurance A more comprehensive approach of companywide policies, practices, and procedures to ensure that every product meets quality standards

any defects. A more comprehensive and proactive approach is **quality assurance**, a holistic system of integrated policies, practices, and procedures designed to ensure that every product meets preset quality standards. Quality assurance includes quality control as well as doing the job right the first time by designing tools and machinery properly, demanding quality parts from suppliers, encouraging customer feedback, training and empowering employees, and encouraging employees to take pride in their work.

Companies can use a variety of tools and strategies to help ensure quality; four of the most significant are continuous improvement, statistical process control, Six Sigma, and ISO 9000.

Continuous Improvement

Delivering quality goods and services is as much a mindset as it is a technical challenge. Companies that excel tend to empower their employees to continuously improve the quality of goods production or service delivery, a strategy often expressed through the Japanese word *kaizen*. By making quality everyone's responsibility, the kaizen approach encourages all workers to look for quality problems, halt production when necessary, generate ideas for improvement, and adjust work routines as needed.[26]

Statistical Process Control

statistical process control (SPC) The use of random sampling and tools such as control charts to monitor the production process

Any quality control or improvement effort depends on reliable feedback that tells workers and managers how well products and processes are performing. Quality assurance often includes the use of **statistical process control (SPC)**, which involves taking samples from the process periodically and analyzing these data points to look for trends and anomalies. One of the most important SPC tools is the *control chart*, which plots measured data over time and helps identify performance that is outside the normal range of operating conditions and therefore in need of investigation.[27]

Six Sigma

Six Sigma A rigorous quality management program that strives to eliminate deviations between the actual and desired performance of a business system

Whereas *kaizen* is more of a general mindset and SPC is a set of analytical tools, **Six Sigma** is a comprehensive approach that encompasses a philosophy of striving toward perfection, a rigorous methodology for measuring and improving quality, and specific tools such as SPC to track progress.[28] (The term *six sigma* is used in statistics to indicate 3.4 defects per 1 million opportunities—near perfection, in other words.) Six Sigma is a highly disciplined, systematic approach to reducing the deviation from desired goals in virtually any business process, whether it's eliminating defects in the creation of a product or improving a company's cash flow.[29] Six Sigma efforts typically follow a five-step approach, known as DMAIC for short (see Exhibit 8).[30]

EXHIBIT 8	The DMAIC Process in Six Sigma Quality Management

The five-step process of *define, measure, analyze, improve,* and *control* (DMAIC) is at the heart of Six Sigma quality management efforts.

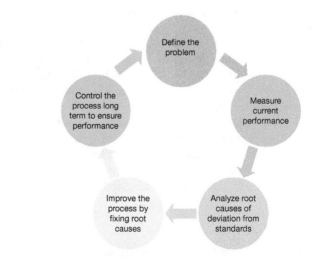

Source: Adapted from Kelly D. Sloan, "The Path to a Sustainable Playbook," *Industrial Engineer*, April 2011, 41–46.

Many companies now marry the concepts of lean production and Six Sigma, seeking to reduce waste and defects simultaneously. And moving beyond operations, this hybrid approach of *Lean Six Sigma* is also being applied at a strategic level to help identify opportunities in the marketplace and align the resources needed to pursue them.[31]

REAL-TIME UPDATES
Learn More by Watching This Video

Lean Six Sigma at Amazon.com

Learn how Amazon.com has applied Lean Six Sigma to build a customer-centric global operation. Go to http://real-timeupdates .com/bia6 and click on Learn More. If you are using MyBizLab, you can access Real-Time Updates within the chapter or under Student Study Tools.

ISO 9000

Buyers and business partners often want reassurance that the companies they do business with take quality seriously and have practices and policies in place to ensure quality outputs. **ISO 9000** is a globally recognized family of standards for quality management systems, administered by the International Organization for Standardization (ISO). ISO 9000 is based on eight quality management principles, including customer focus, a systematic approach to management, and fact-based decision making.[32]

Hundreds of thousands of organizations around the world have implemented ISO standards, making it a universally recognized indicator of compliance. Achieving ISO certification sends a reassuring signal to other companies that your internal processes meet these widely accepted standards, and many organizations now require that their supplies meet ISO standards. Even without the need to meet this requirement, ISO 9000 provides companies with a "tried and tested framework for taking a systematic approach to managing the organization's processes so that they consistently turn out products that satisfy customers' expectations."[33]

For the latest information on production systems, visit http://real-timeupdates.com/bia6.

ISO 9000 A globally recognized family of standards for quality management systems

✓ Checkpoint

LEARNING OBJECTIVE 6: Define *quality*, **explain the challenge of quality and product complexity, and identify four major tools and strategies for ensuring product quality.**

SUMMARY: Quality is the degree to which a product or process meets reasonable or agreed-upon expectations. As products become more complex, the challenges of defining what quality means, ensuring quality production or service performance, and ensuring quality once the product is out in the field all increase. Four major tools and strategies for ensuring product quality are (1) continuous process improvement, enabling employees to search for and correct quality problems; (2) statistical process control (SPC), the use of random sampling and tools such as control charts to monitor the production process; (3) Six Sigma, a rigorous quality management program that strives to eliminate deviations between the actual and desired performance of a business system; and (4) ISO 9000, a globally recognized family of standards for quality management systems.

CRITICAL THINKING: (1) How significant is the role of software in product quality today? (2) How can process simplicity contribute to quality?

IT'S YOUR BUSINESS: (1) Are the grades you get in your various classes an example of quality control or of quality assurance? Explain your answer. (2) Have you ever tried anything like the Six Sigma DMAIC process in your own life, even partially or informally?

KEY TERMS TO KNOW: quality, quality control, quality assurance, statistical process control (SPC), Six Sigma, ISO 9000

BEHIND THE SCENES

CARVIN'S PRODUCTION SYSTEM SATISFIES DEMANDING GUITARISTS

MyBizLab

Carvin has made a name for itself among serious guitarists by filling the gap between mass-produced and fully custom guitars. The company's secret has been perfecting the art and science of *mass customization*, the ability to adapt standardized products to the tastes of individual customers. In five to seven weeks, and for roughly $700 to $1,500, Carvin can customize one of several dozen models of guitars and basses. All are available in a wide variety of woods, paints, stains, finishes, electronics, and even the slight curvature in the fingerboard; there are so many choices that the discussion boards on Carvin's website buzz with debates about which combinations are "best" for specific styles of music.

Carvin's factory combines old-world craftsmanship with new-world technologies. Because the custom guitars are built on a standard set of body shapes and styles, Carvin can use computer-controlled cutting and milling machines that cut and shape the bodies and necks quickly and precisely. A diamond-surface finishing machine mills fingerboards to tolerances of a thousandth of an inch. A dehumidification chamber removes internal stresses from the wood used in the guitar necks to minimize the chance of warping years down the road. Experienced craftspeople with sensitive eyes and ears take over from there, performing such tasks as matching veneer pieces on guitar tops (veneers are thin sheets of wood, usually exotic or expensive species), adjusting the action (the feel of the strings against the frets), and listening to the tone quality of finished instruments.

With this blend of automation and human touch, Carvin produces more than 5,000 instruments a year that win rave reviews from appreciative customers. "Nothing can touch it in terms of sound quality and workmanship" and "I haven't seen anything close to this price that can outperform it" are typical of the comments that Carvin customers post online. Upon hearing a salesperson in another music store speak disparagingly of the brand, one indignant Carvin owner retrieved his guitar from his car and put on an impromptu concert for the store's sales staff to demonstrate just how good the Carvin product sounded. With a proven manufacturing approach and customer loyalty like that, Carvin will be fulfilling the musical dreams of guitarists for years to come.[34]

Critical Thinking Questions

1. If Carvin experienced an increase in orders from its website over a period of two weeks, should it expand its production capacity to make sure it can handle increased demand in the future? Why or why not?
2. Watch the video of Carvin's production in action at www.carvinchannel.com. How does this information help convince potential buyers to consider Carvin?
3. Wooden musical instruments have been carved by hand for hundreds of years. Why wouldn't Carvin want to continue this tradition?

LEARN MORE ONLINE

Visit the Carvin website, at www.carvinguitars.com. How does the company promote its customized products? Step through the process of customizing a guitar or bass. Would you feel comfortable purchasing a musical instrument in this manner? Review comments on www.carvinchannel.com and www.myspace.com/officialcarvin/comments. What are Carvin employees and customers talking about these days?

MyBizLab

Log on to www.mybizlab.com to access study and assessment aids associated with this chapter.

KEY TERMS

capacity planning
critical path
customized production
inventory
inventory control
ISO 9000
just-in-time (JIT)
lean systems
mass customization
mass production

offshoring
outsourcing
procurement
production and operations
    management
productivity
quality
quality assurance
quality control
scalability

Six Sigma
statistical process control
  (SPC)
supply chain

supply chain management (SCM)
system
value chain
value webs

TEST YOUR KNOWLEDGE

Questions for Review

1. What role does feedback play in a system?
2. Why is offshoring controversial?
3. What is mass customization?
4. What is a lean system?
5. What is scalability, in terms of managing a service business?

Questions for Analysis

6. Why is it important to monitor performance variables that are the most meaningful, not those that are the most easily measurable?
7. Why do some firms now think in terms of value webs instead of value chains?
8. How can supply chain management (SCM) help a company establish a competitive advantage?
9. How does perishability affect the delivery of services?
10. Ethical Considerations. How does society's concern for the environment affect a company's decisions about facility location and layout?

Questions for Application

11. Business is booming. Sales last month were 50 percent higher than the month before, and so far, this month is looking even better than last month. Should you hire more people to accommodate the increase? Explain your answer.
12. If 30 percent of the patrons eating at your restaurant say they won't eat there again, what steps would you take to define the problem(s) that needs to be solved, measure the relevant performance variables, and then analyze the root cause of the problems(s)?
13. You've developed a reputation as an outstanding math tutor, and you want to turn your talent into a full-time business after graduation. How will you address the challenge of scalability in your new venture?
14. Concept Integration. How might supply chain management issues influence your decision on how to expand your vitamin and nutritional supplements company internationally?

EXPAND YOUR KNOWLEDGE

Discovering Career Opportunities

Visit the *Occupational Outlook Handbook* at www.bls.gov/oco .com and locate "Industrial production managers" in the "Management" section.

1. What is the nature of the work for industrial production managers? Does the combination of people management and technical problem solving appeal to you?
2. What is the outlook for careers in this profession? If you were interested in this field, would you consider it, given the job outlook?
3. If you decide you want to work in a production-related job, what additional classes should you consider taking before you graduate?

Improving Your Tech Insights: Nanotechnology

Think small. Really small. Think about manufacturing products a molecule or even a single atom at a time. That's the scale of nanotechnology, a rather vague term that covers research and engineering done at nanoscale, or roughly 1/100,000 the width of a human hair.

The potential uses of nanotechnology range from the practical—smart materials that can change shape and heal themselves, more efficient energy generation and transmission, superstrong and superlight materials for airplanes, better cosmetics, smart medical implants, and ultrasmall computers—to the somewhat wilder—food-growing machines and microscopic robots that could travel through your body to cure diseases and fix injuries. (Like any new technology with lots of promise, nanotechnology also suffers from lots of hype.)

Well over 1,000 nanotechnology-enabled products have hit the market in a number of industries, from automotive materials to medicine to consumer products. Also, although they're slightly larger than the generally accepted scale of nanotechnology, *microelectromechanical systems (MEMS)* are having a major impact in some industries. These tiny machines (pumps, valves, and so on), some no bigger than a grain of pollen, are used in the nozzles of ink-jet printers, air bag sensors, and ultraprecise miniature laboratory devices.

Conduct research to identify a product currently on the market that uses nanotechnology in some fashion. In an email message to your instructor, describe the product, its target market, the role nanotechnology plays in the product's design, and any known safety concerns regarding the use of nanotechnology in this or similar products.[35]

257

PRACTICE YOUR SKILLS

Sharpening Your Communication Skills

As the newly hired manager of Campus Athletics, a shop featuring athletic wear bearing logos of colleges and universities, you are responsible for selecting the store's suppliers. Demand for merchandise with team logos and brands can be quite volatile. When a college team is hot, you've got to have merchandise. You know that selecting the right supplier is a task that requires careful consideration, so you have decided to host a series of selection interviews. Think about all the qualities you would want in a supplier, and develop a list of interview questions that will help you assess whether that supplier possesses those qualities.

Building Your Team Skills

Identify a company that has recently decided to offshore some part of its operations. (Search online news sources for "offshore outsourcing" or similar terms.) With the other members of your team, identify all the stakeholder groups that were or might be affected by this decision and speculate on the impact it had on each group. Weighing the effect on all the stakeholders, vote on whether this was a wise decision for the company. Be prepared to present your conclusions to the class.

Developing Your Research Skills

Seeking increased efficiency and productivity, a growing number of producers of goods and services are applying technology to improve the production process. Find an article in a business journal or newspaper that discusses how one company used computer-aided design (CAD), computer-aided engineering (CAE), computer-integrated manufacturing (CIM), robots, or other technological innovations to refit or reorganize its production operations.

1. What problems led the company to rethink its production process? What kind .of technology did it choose to address these problems? What goals did the company set for applying technology in this way?
2. Before adding the new technology, what did the company do to analyze its existing production process? What changes, if any, were made as a result of this analysis?
3. How did technology-enhanced production help the company achieve its goals for financial performance? For customer service? For growth or expansion?

REFERENCES

1. Carvin website, accessed 27 August 2011, www.carvinguitars .com; Carvin MySpace page, accessed 4 June 2009, www.myspace.com/officialcarvin; "Carvin AW175" (product reviews), Harmony Central website, accessed 18 March 2005, www.harmonycentral.com; "Carvin CT6M California Carved Top," *Guitar Player*, December 2004, www.guitarplayer.com; Rich Krechel, "Some Custom-Made Guitars Can Cost $4,000 to $8,000," *St. Louis Post Dispatch*, 27 September 2001, 16.
2. Adapted in part from Russell L. Ackoff, "Why Few Organizations Adopt Systems Thinking," Ackoff Center Weblog, 7 March 2007, http://ackoffcenter.blogs.com; Daniel Aronson, "Introduction to Systems Thinking," The Thinking Page website, accessed 21 June 2007, www.thinking.net; "What Is Systems Thinking?" The Systems Thinker website, accessed 21 June 2007, www .thesystemsthinker.com; Peter Senge, *The Fifth Discipline: The Art and Practice of the Learning Organization* (New York: Doubleday, 1994), 57–67.
3. Stephen P. Robbins and David A. DeCenzo, *Fundamentals of Management*, 4th ed. (Upper Saddle River, N.J.: Pearson Prentice Hall, 2004), 405.
4. Peter Fingar and Ronald Aronica, "Value Chain Optimization: The New Way of Competing," *Supply Chain Management Review*, September–October 2001, 82–85.
5. John Gillie, "Boeing Says Dreamliner Testing on Schedule for Third Quarter Delivery," *News Tribune* (Tacoma, Wash.), 25 February 2011, www.thenewstribune.com; Jeffrey Rothfeder, "Bumpy Ride," *Portfolio*, May 2009, www.portfolio.com.
6. Alan S. Brown, "A Shift in Engineering Offshore," *Mechanical Engineering*, March 2009, 24–29.
7. Lisa Harrington, "Is U.S. Manufacturing Coming Back?" *Inbound Logistics*, August 2011, www.inboundlogistics.com.
8. Bruce Constantine, Brian Ruwadi, and Josh Wine, "Management Practices That Drive Supply Chain Success," *McKinsey Quarterly*, no. 2 (2009): 24–26.
9. Tim Laseter and Keith Oliver, "When Will Supply Chain Management Grow Up?" *Strategy+Business*, Fall 2003, 32–36;

Robert J. Trent, "What Everyone Needs to Know About SCM," *Supply Chain Management Review*, 1 March 2004, www .manufacturing.net.
10. Ayse Bayat, Sekar Sundararajan, H. Robert Gustafson Jr., and Emory W. Zimmers Jr., "Sustainably Driven Supply Chains," *Industrial Engineer*, August 2011, 26–31; "Sustainability Index," Walmart, accessed 26 August 2011, http://walmartstores.com.
11. Trent, "What Everyone Needs to Know About SCM."
12. Andrew Feller, Dan Shunk, and Tom Callarman, "Value Chains Versus Supply Chains," *BPTrends*, March 2006, www .bptrends.com.
13. Patty Cantrell, "Sysco's Journey from Supply Chain to Value Chain," The Wallace Center, August 2009, www.ngfn.org.
14. Lee J. Krajewski and Larry P. Ritzman, *Operations Management: Processes and Value Chains*, 7th ed. (Upper Saddle River, N.J.: Pearson Prentice Hall, 2005), 744.
15. Malcolm Wheatley and Kevin Parker, "Rise in Global Enterprise Deployments Seen as Response to Far-Flung Supply Networks," *Manufacturing Business Technology*, May 2007, 26–27.
16. Krajewski and Ritzman, *Operations Management: Processes and Value Chains*, 299–300.
17. Russell and Taylor, *Operations Management: Focusing on Quality and Competitiveness*, 161.
18. Krajewski and Ritzman, *Operations Management: Processes and Value Chains*, 244–245.
19. Robert Kreitner, *Management*, 9th ed. (Boston: Houghton Mifflin, 2004), 202–203.
20. Krajewski and Ritzman, *Operations Management: Processes and Value Chains*, 482–483.
21. Russell and Taylor, *Operations Management: Focusing on Quality and Competitiveness*, 511.
22. Kenneth Korane, "Mass Production out, Mass Customization in," *Machine Design*, 21 August 2009, S2–S4.
23. Malcolm Wheatley, "Learning from Failure," *Engineering & Technology*, 11 September—24 September 2010, 56–58.

24. Jeffrey K. Liker, "The Way Back for Toyota," *Industrial Engineer*, May 2010, 28–33; Wheatley, "Learning from Failure."
25. Mark Rechtin, "Toyota Gives Development Clout to N.A.," *Automotive News*, 30 May 2011, 1, 23;
26. Russell and Taylor, *Operations Management*, 131.
27. Keith M. Bower, "Statistical Process Control," ASQ, accessed 27 August 2011, http://asq.org.
28. Donald W. Benbow and T. M. Kubiak, "Six Sigma," ASQ, accessed 27 August 2011, http://asq.org.
29. Steven Minter, "Six Sigma's Growing Pains," *IndustryWeek*, May 2009, 34–36; Tom McCarty, "Six Sigma at Motorola," *European CEO*, September–October 2004, www.motorola.com.
30. McCarty, "Six Sigma at Motorola"; General Electric, "What Is Six Sigma?" GE website, accessed 21 March 2005, www.ge.com.
31. George Byrne, Dave Lubowe, and Amy Blitz, "Driving Operational Innovation Using Lean Six Sigma," IBM, accessed 27 August 2011, www.ibm.com.
32. "Quality Management Principles," International Organization for Standardization website, accessed 27 August 2011, www.iso.org.
33. "ISO 9000 Essentials," International Organization for Standardization website, accessed 27 August 2011, www.iso.org.
34. See note 1.
35. Adapted from Project on Emerging Nanotechnologies website, accessed 27 August 2011, www.nanotechproject.org; National Nanotechnology Initiative website, accessed 28 June 2007, www.nano.gov; Barnaby J. Feder, "Technology: Bashful vs. Brash in the New Field of Nanotech," *New York Times*, 15 March 2004, www.nytimes.com; "Nanotechnology Basics," Nanotechnology Now website, accessed 16 April 2004, www.nanotech-now.com; Center for Responsible Nanotechnology website, accessed 16 April 2004, www.crnano.org; Gary Stix, "Little Big Science," *Scientific American*, 16 September 2001, www.sciam.com; Tim Harper, "Small Wonders," *Business 2.0*, July 2002, www.business2.com; Erick Schonfeld, "A Peek at IBM's Nanotech Research," *Business 2.0*, 5 December 2003, www.business2.com; David Pescovitz, "The Best New Technologies of 2003," *Business 2.0*, November 2003, 109–116.

GLOSSARY

capacity planning Establishing the overall level of resources needed to meet customer demand

critical path In a PERT network diagram, the sequence of operations that requires the longest time to complete

customized production The creation of a unique good or service for each customer

inventory Goods and materials kept in stock for production or sale

inventory control Determining the right quantities of supplies and products to have on hand and tracking where those items are

ISO 9000 A globally recognized family of standards for quality management systems

just-in-time (JIT) Inventory management in which goods and materials are delivered throughout the production process right before they are needed

lean systems Systems (in manufacturing and other functional areas) that maximize productivity by reducing waste and delays

mass production The creation of identical goods or services, usually in large quantities

mass customization A manufacturing approach in which part of the product is mass produced and the remaining features are customized for each buyer

offshoring Transferring a part or all of a business function to a facility (a different part of the company or another company entirely) in another country

outsourcing Contracting out certain business functions or operations to other companies

procurement The acquisition of the raw materials, parts, components, supplies, and finished products required to produce goods and services

productivity The efficiency with which an organization can convert inputs to outputs

production and operations management Overseeing all the activities involved in producing goods and services

quality The degree to which a product or process meets reasonable or agreed-upon expectations

quality assurance A more comprehensive approach of companywide policies, practices, and procedures to ensure that every product meets quality standards

quality control Measuring quality against established standards after the good or service has been produced and weeding out any defective products

scalability The potential to increase production by expanding or replicating its initial production capacity

Six Sigma A rigorous quality management program that strives to eliminate deviations between the actual and desired performance of a business system

statistical process control (SPC) The use of random sampling and tools such as control charts to monitor the production process

supply chain A set of connected systems that coordinates the flow of goods and materials from suppliers all the way through to final customers

supply chain management (SCM) The business procedures, policies, and computer systems that integrate the various elements of the supply chain into a cohesive system

system An interconnected and coordinated set of *elements* and *processes* that converts *inputs* to desired *outputs*

value chain All the elements and processes that add value as raw materials are transformed into the final products made available to the ultimate customer

value webs Multidimensional networks of suppliers and outsourcing partners

Distribution and Marketing Logistics

From Chapter 15 of *Business in Action*, Sixth Edition. Courtland L. Bovée, John V. Thill. Copyright © 2013 by Pearson Education, Inc. Published by Pearson Business. All rights reserved.

LEARNING OBJECTIVES   After studying this chapter, you will be able to

1 Explain the role of marketing intermediaries in contemporary business and list the eight primary functions that intermediaries can perform

2 Identify the major types of wholesalers and summarize four trends shaping the future of wholesaling

3 Identify the major retailing formats and summarize six trends shaping the future of retailing

4 Explain the strategic decisions that manufacturers must make when choosing distribution channels

5 Identify five key attributes of distribution channel design and management

6 Highlight the major components of physical distribution and logistics

MyBizLab

Where you see MyBizLab in this chapter, go to www.mybizlab.com for additional activities on the topic being discussed.

BEHIND THE SCENES COSTCO MAKES THE GOOD LIFE MORE AFFORDABLE

Costco shoppers have learned to look for great buys on both every-day items and an ever-changing mix of luxury and specialty goods.

Copyright © Mark Richards/Photoedit

www.costco.com

With an unusual mix of low prices and quality goods, Costco Wholesale has become the country's largest and most profitable warehouse club chain. The company knows that low prices on high-quality, high-end merchandise can transcend the common notion of "discount." And, in what amounts to a treasure hunt played out along Costco's cement-floor aisles, the high/low shopping experience is a powerful elixir for middle-class shoppers.

Once new members get the hang of the treasure hunt mentality, they get hooked on Costco, because even though they don't know what will be on display, they're sure it will be something at a price that will make the good life more affordable. Like other warehouse clubs, Costco Wholesale sells a mix of everything from giant boxes of cereal to patio furniture. In fact, Costco often asks vendors to change their factory runs to produce specially built packages that are bigger and less expensive. Unlike with other warehouse clubs, Costco shoppers can occasionally find $10,000 diamond rings and grand pianos along with mouthwash and laundry detergent. Costco also entices shoppers with in-store bakeries and ready-to-eat dishes, as well as optical departments, insurance, and other services that reflect the same high-quality, low-price model as the packaged merchandise.

If you were in charge of strategy at Costco, how would you keep Costco on the leading edge of retailing? How would you integrate your physical retail stores with your online e-commerce operation? What could you do to keep your bargain-conscious but demanding customers coming back for more?[1]

INTRODUCTION

Marketing intermediaries such as Costco (profiled in the chapter-opening Behind the Scenes) play an essential role in marketing products created by other companies. This chapter explores the many contributions these intermediaries make, both at the retailing stage that is visible to all consumers and at the less visible but no less important wholesaling stage. Manufacturers and other producers need to understand the distribution process in order to select the right intermediaries and work with them effectively. And, of course, wholesalers and retailers are business entities themselves, with their own strategic questions and operating challenges.

The Role of Marketing Intermediaries

A *distribution channel*, or *marketing channel*, is an organized network of firms that work together to get goods and services from producer to customer. Whether you're selling digital music files or scrap iron stripped out of old ships, your **distribution strategy**, or overall plan for moving products to buyers, will play a major role in your success.

Think of all the products you buy: food, cosmetics, clothing, sports equipment, train tickets, gasoline, stationery, appliances, music, books, and all the rest. How many of these products do you buy directly from the producer? For most people, the answer is not many. Most companies that create products do not sell these goods directly to the final users. Instead, producers in many industries work with **marketing intermediaries** to bring their products to market. Even some service companies rely on other firms to perform services on their behalf.

WHOLESALING VERSUS RETAILING

Intermediaries can be grouped into two general types: wholesalers and retailers. **Wholesalers** sell to organizational customers, including other wholesalers, companies, government agencies, and educational institutions. In turn, the customers of wholesalers either resell the products or use them to make products of their own.

Unlike wholesalers, **retailers** primarily sell products to consumers for personal use. Terminology in the distribution field can get a bit confusing, starting with the multiple uses of the term *wholesale*. For instance, even though Costco and other warehouse-type stores often use the "wholesale" label to describe themselves, they function as both wholesalers and retailers simultaneously. Small-business owners, for instance, are enthusiastic Costco shoppers because the store is a low-cost place to buy supplies and equipment. With these shoppers, Costco is functioning as a wholesaler. However, when selling to consumers, Costco is technically operating as a retailer, not a wholesaler. The distinction is important because business strategies for wholesaling and retailing are dramatically different in many ways. Even when they buy the same products, consumers and organizations usually make purchases for different reasons. Because their motivations and expectations are different, consumers (reached by retailers) and organizations (reached by wholesalers) don't respond to marketing programs the same way.

CONTRIBUTIONS OF MARKETING INTERMEDIARIES

Wholesalers and retailers are instrumental in creating three of the four forms of utility: They provide the items customers need in a convenient location (place utility), they save customers the time of having to contact each manufacturer to purchase a

---

1 LEARNING OBJECTIVE

Explain the role of marketing intermediaries in contemporary business, and list the eight primary functions that intermediaries can perform.

distribution strategy A firm's overall plan for moving products through intermediaries and on to final customers

marketing intermediaries Businesspeople and organizations that assist in moving and marketing goods and services between producers and consumers

wholesalers Intermediaries that sell products to other intermediaries for resale or to organizations for internal use

retailers Intermediaries that sell goods and services to individuals for their own personal use

good (time utility), and they provide an efficient process for transferring products from the producer to the customer (possession utility). In addition to creating utility, wholesalers and retailers perform the following distribution functions:

- **Matching buyers and sellers.** By making sellers' products available to multiple buyers, intermediaries such as Costco reduce the number of transactions between producers and customers. In the business-to-business market, the industrial distributor Grainger (www.grainger.com) is a good example of the enormous scale that can be achieved in bringing buyers and sellers together. Boasting a portfolio of more than 1 million products, Grainger connects some 3,000 suppliers with 2 million organizational customers.[2] These customers are saved the time and trouble of working with multiple suppliers, and the product suppliers get access to more customers than all but the very largest of them could ever hope to reach on their own. Although "cutting out the middleman" is sometimes used as a promotional slogan, intermediaries such as Grainger can actually make commerce more efficient by reducing the number of contact points between buyers and sellers (see Exhibit 1).
- **Providing market information.** Retail intermediaries, such as Amazon and Macy's, collect valuable data about customer purchases: who buys, how often, and how much.

EXHIBIT 1   **How Intermediaries Simplify Commerce**

Intermediaries actually reduce the price customers pay for many goods and services because they reduce the number of contacts between producers and consumers that would otherwise be necessary. They also create place, time, and possession utility.

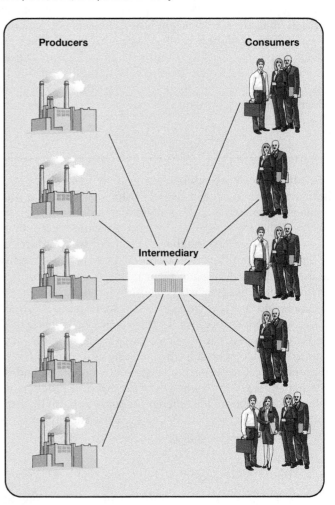

Number of transactions required when consumers buy directly from manufacturers

Number of transactions required when buying is conducted via intermediary

Source: Adapted from Philip Kotler, *Marketing Management*, 10th ed. (Upper Saddle River, N.J.: Pearson Prentice Hall, 2000), 491.

For example, e-commerce records and data from "frequent shopper" cards help retailers spot buying patterns, providing vital market information they can then share with producers to optimize product mixes and promotional efforts.

- **Providing promotional and sales support.** Many intermediaries assist with advertising, in-store displays, and other promotional efforts for some or all of the products they sell. Some also employ sales representatives who can perform a number of selling and customer relationship functions.

- **Gathering assortments of goods.** Many intermediaries receive bulk shipments from producers and break them into more convenient units (known as *breaking bulk*) by sorting, standardizing, and dividing bulk quantities into smaller packages.

- **Transporting and storing products.** Intermediaries often maintain inventories of merchandise that they acquire from producers so they can quickly fill customers' orders. In many cases, retailers purchase this merchandise from wholesalers who, in addition to breaking bulk, may also transport the goods from the producer to the retail outlets.

- **Assuming risks.** When intermediaries accept goods from manufacturers, they usually take on the risks associated with damage, theft, product perishability (in the sense of tangible goods that are vulnerable to rotting, for instance), and obsolescence.

- **Providing financing.** Large intermediaries sometimes provide loans to smaller producers.

- **Completing product solutions.** In some industries, producers rely on a class of intermediaries often called *value-added resellers (VARs)* or *system integrators* to complete or customize solutions for customers. For instance, Iris Professional Services (www.irisproservices.com) is a VAR for Apple, meaning it can combine Apple computers with other hardware and software elements to create information systems for its clients.[3] By partnering with companies such as Iris, Apple is able to reach a wider range of customers without the need to develop specialized expertise in multiple industries.

- **Facilitating transactions and supporting customers.** Intermediaries can perform a variety of functions that help with the selection, purchase, and use of products. Commercial real estate brokers, for example, can negotiate prices and contract terms on behalf of buyers and sellers. In a variety of industries, intermediaries help customers select the products that fit their needs and then provide customer support and technical assistance after the sale.

✔ Checkpoint

LEARNING OBJECTIVE 1: Explain the role of marketing intermediaries in contemporary business, and list the eight primary functions that intermediaries can perform.

SUMMARY: Intermediaries can be responsible for any and all aspects of distribution, one of the key elements in any firm's marketing mix. The two major categories are *wholesalers*, which buy from producers and sell to retailers, to other wholesalers, and to organizational customers such as businesses, government agencies, and institutions; and *retailers*, which buy from producers or wholesalers and sell the products to the final consumers. These marketing intermediaries bring products to market and help ensure that the goods and services are available in the right time, place, and amount. Depending on their position in the channel, intermediaries can perform the eight key functions of matching buyers and sellers; providing market information; providing promotional and sales support; sorting, standardizing, and dividing merchandise; transporting and storing products; assuming risks; providing financing; and completing production solutions.

CRITICAL THINKING: (1) Why wouldn't Apple develop the expertise to create professional video studios and other solutions that its channel partners now develop? (2) How can Costco be both a wholesaler and a retailer at the same time?

IT'S YOUR BUSINESS: (1) If you had the choice of buying a product directly from the manufacturer or from a local retailer, which would you choose? Why? (2) Have you ever had to work with more than one retailer to get a complete product solution (such as getting car parts or home improvement supplies from multiple stores)? Was the experience satisfactory?

KEY TERMS TO KNOW: distribution strategy, marketing intermediaries, wholesalers, retailers

Wholesaling and Industrial Distribution

2 LEARNING OBJECTIVE

Identify the major types of wholesalers, and summarize four trends shaping the future of wholesaling.

Although largely unseen by consumers, wholesaling is a huge presence in the economy. More than 5 million people work in wholesaling in the United States, and the sector sees several trillion dollars in sales volume every year.[4] By connecting producers with retailers and organizational customers, wholesalers play a vital role in nearly every industry in the world.

MAJOR TYPES OF WHOLESALERS

merchant wholesalers
Independent wholesalers that take legal title to goods they distribute

Most wholesalers are independent companies that can be classified as *merchant wholesalers*, *agents*, or *brokers*. The majority of wholesalers are **merchant wholesalers**, independently owned businesses that buy from producers, take legal title to the goods, and then resell them to retailers or to organizational buyers. Most merchant wholesalers are small businesses, but the field includes a handful of multibillion-dollar firms such as Grainger in industrial supplies, Avnet (www.avnet.com) in electronic components, McKesson (www.mckesson.com) in health care, and Supervalu (www.supervalu.com) in groceries.

Full-service merchant wholesalers provide a wide variety of services, such as storage, selling, order processing, delivery, and promotional support. *Rack jobbers*, for example, are full-service merchant wholesalers that set up displays in retail outlets, stock inventory, and perform other services such as marking prices on merchandise. *Limited-service merchant wholesalers*, on the other hand, provide fewer services. Natural resources such as lumber, grain, and coal are usually marketed through a class of limited-service wholesalers called *drop shippers*, which take ownership but not physical possession of the goods they handle.

distributors Merchant wholesalers that sell products to organizational customers for internal operations or the production of other goods, rather than to retailers for resale

Merchant wholesalers can also be distinguished by their customers. Supervalu and others that sell primarily to other intermediaries are usually known in the trade simply as *wholesalers*. In contrast, Avnet and others that sell goods to companies for use in their own products and operations are usually called **distributors**.

agents and brokers Independent wholesalers that do not take title to the goods they distribute but may or may not take possession of those goods

Unlike merchant wholesalers, **agents and brokers** never actually own the products they handle, and they perform fewer services. Their primary role is to bring buyers and sellers together; they are generally paid a commission (a percentage of the money received) for arranging sales. Producers of industrial parts often sell to business customers through brokers. *Manufacturers' representatives*, another type of agent, sell various noncompeting products to customers in a specific region. By representing several manufacturers' products, these reps achieve enough volume to justify the cost of a direct sales call.

THE OUTLOOK FOR WHOLESALING

The business of wholesaling is changing in ways that are helping some wholesalers and threatening others. Four trends in particular are likely to reshape the wholesaling business in the coming years:

- **Integrated logistics management.** The outsourcing trend is definitely having an impact in the wholesaling sector as *third-party logistics (3PL)* firms continue to take over a wide range of tasks in supply chain management, including not only traditional wholesaling activities but also order fulfillment, product repair, customer service, and other functions. These 3PL firms have been growing rapidly in recent years, as more companies look to offload supply chain functions to focus on core business activities.[5]

The emergence of 3PL is coming from two directions, as transportation companies such as UPS and FedEx and wholesalers such as Supervalu and McKesson expand the scope of their services. In fact, you'd be hard pressed from McKesson's description of itself to recognize that the company is in fact a major wholesaler, referring to itself as a "health-care services company."[6]

- **Threat of disintermediation.** For many years, and particularly since the advent of the Internet and the growth of e-commerce, various observers have predicted the widespread **disintermediation** of wholesalers, meaning their role would be taken over by manufacturers on the upstream end or by customers (retailers and other organizational buyers) on the downstream end. While this has certainly happened in specific instances in various industries, and the share of wholesaling activity performed by independent wholesalers appears to be shrinking somewhat, wholesalers as a group have not disappeared to the extent that some predicted.[7] Even as the sector evolves, intermediaries will continue to play an integral role in the distribution process as long as they can add value and perform essential services more effectively and more efficiently than either manufacturers or customers.[8]

disintermediation
The replacement of intermediaries by producers, customers, or other intermediaries when those other parties can perform channel functions more effectively or efficiently

- **Unbundling of services.** The conventional way that merchant wholesalers generate revenue and earn profits is by purchasing products from manufacturers at a discount and reselling them to retailers or organizational buyers at a markup. Whatever services a wholesaler provides are covered by that markup. However, a growing number of wholesaling customers would like to see these services "unbundled" so they can pay for specific distribution services individually.[9] If this trend catches on, it could change the business model for many wholesalers.

- **Industry consolidation.** With all the forces at play in the marketplace, consolidation seems likely as large firms with economies of scale buy up or drive out smaller, less-competitive firms. In addition, a growing number of customers are pursuing *strategic sourcing*, in which they forge closer relationships with a smaller number of strategic distribution partners.[10]

✓ **Checkpoint**

LEARNING OBJECTIVE 2: Identify the major types of wholesalers, and summarize four trends shaping the future of wholesaling.

SUMMARY: Most wholesalers can be classified as *merchant wholesalers*, *agents*, or *brokers*. Merchant wholesalers are independently owned businesses that buy from producers, take legal title to the goods, and then resell them to retailers or to organizational buyers. Merchant wholesalers can be distinguished by level of service (*full-service* versus *limited-service*) and target customers (*wholesalers* that sell goods to retailers for the purpose of then reselling them to consumers and *distributors* that sell goods to organizations for internal operation use or to make other products). In contrast to merchant wholesalers, agents and brokers do not assume ownership but focus on bringing buyers and sellers together. Four trends shaping wholesaling are integrated logistics management, the threat of disintermediation, the unbundling of services, and industry consolidation.

CRITICAL THINKING: (1) Why does McKesson promote itself as a health care services company, rather than as a logistics company? (2) Why might a manufacturer choose to hire a third-party logistics firm rather than a conventional wholesaler or distributor?

IT'S YOUR BUSINESS: (1) Considering the forces shaping wholesaling, would you consider a career in this sector? Why or why not? (2) If your family ran a small industrial products wholesaler that was facing the threat of disintermediation, how would you respond?

KEY TERMS TO KNOW: merchant wholesalers, distributors, agents and brokers, disintermediation

LEARNING OBJECTIVE

Identify the major retailing formats, and summarize six trends shaping the future of retailing.

Retailing

In addition to providing convenient access to products and supporting consumers with a variety of presale and postsale services, retailers play a major role in the buying process because many consumer buying decisions are made in the retail setting. Consequently, retailing involves a blend of the distribution and customer communication elements of the marketing mix. The term *shopper marketing*, or *in-store marketing*, refers to communication efforts directed at consumers while they are in the retail setting. These efforts can range from printed signs to in-store video screens to smartphone apps that help shoppers find products or stores in a mall, for example.[11] To be sure, the degree to which decision making occurs in the store varies across product categories, consumers, and purchasing situations. For example, consumers engaged in home remodeling projects typically have a clear idea of what they want to buy before they get to the store, so the in-store decisions relate more to specific colors and textures than to broad product categories.[12] In other instances, in-store signs, product labels, and other factors can influence the types of products and specific brands that consumers choose.

Given the importance of the shopping environment, retailers spend considerable time and money crafting physical spaces and shopping experiences that are intended to shape consumer behavior, addressing everything from lighting and color palettes to music, aromas, and employee attire. No detail seems to be too small. For instance, the attractiveness of employees and even other shoppers can influence consumer choices. Although consumers are generally put off by the realization that other shoppers have touched the products on display in a store, if they see an *attractive* person touch a product, people tend to think more highly of that product.[13]

RETAILING FORMATS

wheel of retailing An evolutionary process by which stores that feature low prices gradually upgrade until they no longer appeal to price-sensitive shoppers and are replaced by a new generation of leaner, low-price competitors

department stores Large stores that carry a variety of products in multiple categories, such as clothing, house wares, gifts, bedding, and furniture

specialty stores Stores that carry only a particular type of goods, often with deep selection in those specific categories

With so much effort directed toward influencing buying decisions across so many categories of products and diverse segments in the consumer market, the retail sector has evolved into a dizzying array of store types and formats. Much of this evolution can be explained by a concept called the **wheel of retailing**. In this model, an innovative retailer with low operating costs attracts a following by offering low prices and limited service. As this store adds more services to broaden its appeal, its prices creep upward, opening the door for a new generation of lower-priced competitors. Eventually, these competitors also upgrade their operations and are replaced by still other lower-priced stores that later follow the same upward pattern.[14]

For instance, Walmart reshaped retailing with low prices enabled by the company's extraordinary abilities at cost control and efficiency but now finds itself facing new low-price competition from the likes of Family Dollar Stores and Dollar General. For instance, after having added more than 4,000 stores over the past decade, Family Dollar gained market share during the recent recession, as more shoppers turned to it for food and household essentials.[15]

Regardless of product offerings or target markets, all retailing efforts can be divided into *store* formats—based in physical store locations—and *nonstore* formats—which take place anywhere and everywhere outside of physical stores. Exhibit 2 summarizes the most important store formats. **Department stores** are the classic major retailers in the United States, with the likes of Bloomingdale's, Macy's, Nordstrom, Dillard's, and Kohl's generally offering a range of clothing, accessories, bedding, and other products for the home. **Specialty stores** such as jewelers and bicycle shops offer a limited number of product lines but an extensive selection of brands, styles, sizes, models, colors, materials, and prices within each line. Huge specialty stores such as The Home Depot and Bed Bath & Beyond that tend to dominate those sectors of retail are known as *category killers*.

Retailers can also be distinguished by their pricing strategies. Family Dollar Stores and Walmart, for example, are

REAL-TIME UPDATES
Learn More by Reading This Article

Hope for a classic retailing format?

Can the former head of Apple's retailing operations work some of that magic on J.C. Penney and the aging department store format? Go to http://real-timeupdates.com/bia6 and click on "Learn More." If you are using MyBizLab, you can access Real-Time Updates within the chapter or under Student Study Tools.

EXHIBIT 2	Retail Store Formats	

The term *retailer* covers many types of outlets. This table shows some of the most common types.

Retail Format	Key Features	Examples
Department store	Store that offers a wide variety of merchandise under one roof in departmentalized sections and many customer services	Dillard's, J.C. Penney, Nordstrom
Specialty store	Store that offers a complete selection in a narrow range of merchandise, often with extensive customer services	Payless Shoes, R.E.I.
Category killer	Type of specialty store that focuses on specific products on a massive scale and dominating retail sales in respective product categories	Office Depot, Bed Bath & Beyond, Lowe's
Discount store	Store that offers a wide variety of merchandise at low prices with relatively fewer services	Dollar General, Target, Walmart
Off-price store	Store that offers designer and brand-name merchandise at low prices and with relatively fewer services	T.J. Maxx, Marshalls
Convenience store	Store that offers limited range of convenience goods, long service hours, and quick checkouts	7-Eleven, AM-PM
Factory/retail outlet	Large outlet store that sells discontinued items, overruns, and factory seconds	Nordstrom Rack, Nike outlet store
Supermarket	Large, self-service store that offers a wide selection of food and nonfood merchandise	Kroger, Safeway
Hypermarket	Giant store that offers both food and general merchandise at discount prices	Walmart Super Centers, Carrefour
Warehouse club	Large, warehouse-style store that sells food and general merchandise at discount prices; some require club membership	Sam's Club, Costco
Online retailer	Web-based store that offers anything from a single product line to comprehensive selections in multiple product areas; can be web-only (e.g., Amazon.com) or integrated with physical stores (e.g., REI.com)	Amazon.com, REI.com

discount stores, which feature a wide variety of aggressively priced everyday merchandise. **Off-price retailers** such as Filene's Basement and T.J. Maxx take a slightly different approach, offering more limited selections of higher-end products such as designer label clothing at steeply discounted prices.[16]

In the nonstore arena, **online retailers** can be either Internet-only operations such as fashion retailer Bluefly (www.bluefly.com) or online extensions of store-based operations, such as the sites run by J.C. Penney (www.jcpenney.com) and other department stores. Online stores still account for less than 10 percent of U.S. retail sales overall, but they have become a major force in some product categories—such as books, for example, where online sales now outpace store sales.[17] Electronic commerce, or **e-commerce**, is not limited to retailing, to be sure. Companies ranging from small specialty wholesalers to the world's largest distribution firms rely on the Internet as well.

Meanwhile, the mail-order firms that inspired e-commerce are still going strong in many industries. Attractive catalogs are a powerful marketing tool, but printing and mailing them is expensive, so many mail-order firms are working to integrate their catalog efforts with e-commerce to maximize sales. Vending machines and interactive kiosks are an important format for many food and convenience goods as well. Redbox, for example, now has nearly 30,000 movie rental machines positioned around the United States.[18]

discount stores Retailers that sell a variety of everyday goods below the market price by keeping their overhead low

off-price retailers Stores that sell designer labels and other fashionable products at steep discounts

online retailers Companies that use e-commerce technologies to sell over the Internet; includes Internet-only retailers and the online arm of store-based retailers

e-commerce The application of Internet technologies to wholesaling and retailing

THE OUTLOOK FOR RETAILING

Retailing has always been a challenging field, and it's not getting any easier for many companies in the sector. Of course, disruption for some can mean opportunities for others. Retailers that survive and succeed over the long term tend to do the same things well: (1) maintaining a clear sense of purpose in the minds of target customers, (2) crafting an overall shopping experience that complements the purchases customers are making, (3) protecting the credibility of the retail brand, and (4) adapting to consumer trends without overreacting to short-term fads.[19]

Here are six major forces shaping the future of retailing:

- **Overcapacity.** In too many categories, there are simply too many stores to support current levels of business activity. Shopping malls in particular, those icons of contemporary consumer life, have become a symbol for much of what ails retailing. A furious spate of mall building in the past couple decades left the country with hundreds more malls than the economy could really support, at the same time as the rise of online retailing and the growth of stand-alone discounters were drawing shoppers away from malls. In fact, 100 or so malls across the country are now considered "dead" because they have such low revenues and high vacancy rates.[20] However, mall operators are learning to adapt to the loss of department store anchors, web-enabled shopping, and other challenges. Top-performing malls remain profitable retailing centers.[21]

- **Continued growth in online retailing.** The growth rate of online retailing has outpaced store-based retailing in recent years, and that trend is likely to continue. Not only are more consumers buying online, but many store-based retailers are trying to reduce their fixed costs by shifting more activity to the Internet.[22] The companies most likely to succeed online are store-based retailers with strong reputations and loyal customers, Internet-only retailers such as Amazon (www.amazon.com) and the jewelry store Blue Nile (www.bluenile.com) that have achieved the economies of scale necessary to be profitable, and niche players that can combine unusual products and great customer service—sometimes while operating as affiliates of major players such as Amazon.[23]

- **Growth of multichannel retailing.** The growth in online retailing reflects the fact that today's consumers increasingly combine online and offline shopping, such as researching products online and then making the purchase in a physical store or the other way around.[24] To stay in contact with consumers as they move from one retail channel to the next, more companies now emphasize **multichannel retailing**, a term for any coordinated effort to reach customers through more than one retail channel.[25]

- **Format innovations.** As companies endlessly search for the magic formula to attract customers and generate profitable sales, they continue to experiment with retailing formats. Two interesting innovations are *hybrid stores* that combine different types of retailers or different retail companies in the same facility and *pop-up stores* that exist for only a short time and are designed more as attention-getting events than as ongoing retail operations.[26]

multichannel retailing
Coordinated efforts to reach consumers through more than one retail channel

retail theater The addition of entertainment or education aspects to the retail experience

- **Retail theater.** Increasingly, retail stores aren't just places to buy things; they're becoming places to research new technologies, learn about cooking, socialize, or simply be entertained for a few minutes while going through the drudgery of picking out the week's groceries—a tactic known as **retail theater.** Many of Apple's retail outlets look more like art galleries than stores, and they offer a multifaceted shopping and learning experience for both kids and adults.[27] CVS's Beauty 360 shops, which feel more like theater stages than traditional drug stores, give customers greater opportunities to learn about and experiment with various cosmetics.[28]

- **Threat of disintermediation.** Like wholesalers, retailers face the threat of disintermediation if suppliers or customers don't think they add sufficient value or if other types of retailers can do the job better.

Daniel Acker/Bloomberg Via Getty Images

Product demonstrations, in-store classes, and other "retail theater" events help attract shoppers and build store loyalty.

Checkpoint

LEARNING OBJECTIVE 3: Identify the major retailing formats, and summarize six trends shaping the future of retailing.

SUMMARY: Retailers come in many shapes and sizes, but the significant store formats include department stores, specialty stores, category killers, discount stores, and off-price retailers. The two most widely known nonstore retailers are online retailers and mail-order firms. The future of retailing is being shaped by such forces as overcapacity, continued growth in online retailing, the growth of multichannel retailing, format innovations such as hybrid stores, the use of retail theater, and the threat of intermediation.

CRITICAL THINKING: (1) Would it ever make sense for Amazon to open retail stores? Why or why not? (2) Moving into the future, what effect is online retailing likely to have on the oversupply of retail store space in the United States?

IT'S YOUR BUSINESS: (1) How have your shopping patterns changed in the past five years, in terms of how you research purchases and where you make those purchases? (2) Roughly what percentage of all your purchases do you make online? What could store-based retailers do to attract a greater portion of your business?

KEY TERMS TO KNOW: wheel of retailing, department stores, specialty stores, discount stores, off-price retailers, online retailers, e-commerce, multichannel retailing, retail theater

Distribution Strategies

4 LEARNING OBJECTIVE

Explain the strategic decisions that manufacturers must make when choosing distribution channels.

Manufacturers and other producers face some critical decisions when selecting marketing channels for their product. Should they sell directly to end users or rely on intermediaries? Which intermediaries should they choose? Should they try to sell their products in every available outlet or limit distribution to a few exclusive outlets? Should they use more than one channel?

Building an effective channel system can take years and, as with all other marketing relationships, it requires commitment. Successful *trading partners*, a general term for any group of companies involved in a distribution network, work to establish relationships that are mutually beneficial and built on trust.

The ideal **distribution mix**—number and type of intermediaries—varies widely from industry to industry and even from company to company within the same industry. For example, Black & Decker (www.blackanddecker.com) distributes its power tools through hundreds of hardware stores and home centers such as Lowe's and The Home Depot along with a wide range of online retailers, including Amazon.com.[29] Black & Decker sells to both consumers and professionals; it wants to reach a broad audience, and its products don't require extensive support from retailers, so these mass market intermediaries make perfect sense. In contrast, Felder (www.feldergroupusa.com), an Austrian company that manufacturers top-of-the line woodworking machines for professional use, makes its products available through only three company-owned stores in the entire United States.[30]

distribution mix A combination of intermediaries and channels a producer uses to reach target customers

CUSTOMER NEEDS AND EXPECTATIONS

The primary function of distribution channels is delivering value to customers, so channel strategy decisions should start with customer needs and expectations.[31] For instance, how do customers want and expect to purchase your product? If you have a food product, for example, are customers willing to drive to specialty stores to buy it, or does it need to be available in their regular grocery stores if you're to have any hope of selling it? Do customers expect to sample or try on products before they buy? Do they need help from trained product experts? What other goods and services do customers expect to be able to purchase at the same time or from the same supplier? By understanding these needs and expectations, producers can work backward, from their final customers back to their production facilities, to determine the right mix of channel features and functions.

PRODUCT SUPPORT REQUIREMENTS

Products vary widely in the amount of skilled support they may require before and after a sale. Laboratory instruments such as mass spectrometers require significant technical skills to sell and to support after the sale, which is why companies that make them, such as Agilent Technologies (www.agilent.com) generally sell them through their own salesforces.

SEGMENTATION, TARGETING, AND POSITIONING

Just as producers segment markets, choose target segments, and try to position their products within those segments, marketing intermediaries make strategic marketing decisions regarding their own businesses. For instance, Super Jock 'n Jill (www.superjocknjill.com) an athletic shoe retailer in Seattle, focuses on quality shoes and clothing for people who are serious about physical fitness. The store offers clinics on nutrition and injury prevention, sponsors races and running clubs, posts race results on its website, and takes other steps to support local walkers and runners.[32]

Super Jock 'n Jill doesn't sell shoes from its website because the company emphasizes individualized analysis and fitting by knowledgeable sales staff—and it offers the almost unheard-of option of letting shoppers lace on shoes and go for a run to test comfort and performance under real-life conditions. In other words, if you produce mass-market sneakers that are more about fashion than performance, this store won't help you reach your target audience.

COMPETITORS' DISTRIBUTION CHANNELS

Marketing managers must consider the distribution decisions that competitors have already made or are likely to make in the future. For instance, if you are a new producer trying to break into a particular market, you need to encourage buyers to consider your goods along with the products they already know about, so putting your products side-by-side with the competition in physical or online venues is probably the right choice. In other cases, you might want to distance yourself from competitors, either to make direct comparisons more difficult or to avoid being associated with competitive products.

Of course, marketing intermediaries have their own decisions to make about which products to carry and how to allocate their finite "bandwidth," whether it's the number of sales representatives or physical shelf space in a retail store. Because of these capacity limitations in the channel, producers often compete for the attention and resources of intermediaries. In some industries, channel capacity is at such a premium that retailers can demand payments from producers in exchange for carrying their products for an agreed-upon length of time. These *slotting allowances* are now common in the grocery business, for example, particularly for new products. Retailers are naturally reluctant to give up shelf space to unproven products, so slotting allowances help offset the financial risk of bringing in new products. Slotting allowances have grown common enough, in fact, that economic policymakers have begun to investigate their potential impact on competition and consumer prices.[33]

REAL-TIME UPDATES
Learn More by Visiting This Website

See how innovative retailers are embracing social media

Get an insider's view on how retailers use social media to find, connect with, and satisfy shoppers. Go to http://real-timeupdates .com/bia6 and click on "Learn More." If you are using MyBizLab, you can access Real-Time Updates within the chapter or under Student Study Tools.

ESTABLISHED INDUSTRY PATTERNS AND REQUIREMENTS

Over the years, all industries develop certain patterns of distribution. If you try to "buck the system," you might uncover a profitable new opportunity—or you might fail to reach your target customers entirely. Specific industries have other considerations as well, such as the need to get perishable food items to retail locations quickly or government regulations that dictate how and where certain products (hazardous chemicals and pharmaceuticals, for example) can be sold.

✔ Checkpoint

LEARNING OBJECTIVE 4: Explain the strategic decisions that manufacturers must make when choosing distribution channels.

SUMMARY: Defining a distribution strategy requires consideration of such issues as customer needs and expectations; product support requirements; segmentation, targeting, and positioning objectives; competitors' distribution channels; and established distribution patterns and requirements.

CRITICAL THINKING: (1) Would two manufacturers trying to reach the same customer segment with similar products use identical distribution mixes? Why or why not? (2) Is channel conflict necessarily always bad for everyone involved? Explain your answer.

IT'S YOUR BUSINESS: (1) You've probably seen television commercials advertising products that are "not available in stores." How does that lack of availability in stores affect your perception of those products? (2) Would knowing that a manufacturer had to pay a retailer to gain shelf space for a particular product change your perception of that product? Why or why not?

KEY TERM TO KNOW: distribution mix

Considerations in Channel Design and Management

5 LEARNING OBJECTIVE

Identify five key attributes of distribution channel design and management.

In addition to the strategic considerations discussed so far in this chapter, marketing managers need to consider five attributes that help define the function and effectiveness of any distribution channel: channel length, market coverage, distribution costs, channel conflict, and channel organization and control.

CHANNEL LENGTH

As you no doubt sense by now, distribution channels come in all shapes and sizes. Some channels are short and simple; others are long and complex. Many businesses purchase goods they use in their operations directly from producers, so those distribution channels are short. In contrast, the channels for consumer goods are usually longer and more complex (see Exhibit 3) on the next page.

The four primary channels for consumer goods are

- **Producer to consumer.** Producers that sell directly to consumers through catalogs, telemarketing, infomercials, and the Internet are using the shortest, simplest distribution channel. By selling directly to consumers, for example, Dell gains more control over pricing, promotion, service, and delivery. Although this approach eliminates payments to channel members, it also forces producers to handle distribution functions such as storing inventory and delivering products.

EXHIBIT 3	Common Distribution Channel Models

Producers can choose from a variety of distribution channel configurations. Channels in consumer markets tend to be longer (with more participants) than channels in organizational markets.

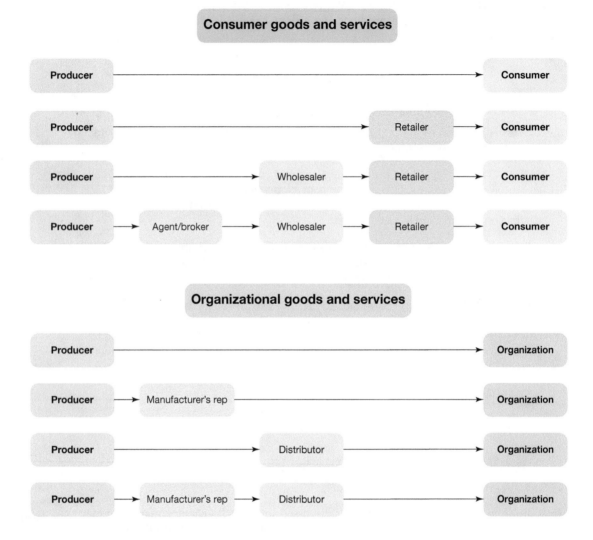

Consumer goods and services

Producer ────────────────────────────────→ Consumer

Producer ──────────────────→ Retailer → Consumer

Producer ──────→ Wholesaler → Retailer → Consumer

Producer → Agent/broker → Wholesaler → Retailer → Consumer

Organizational goods and services

Producer ────────────────────────────────→ Organization

Producer → Manufacturer's rep ──────────────→ Organization

Producer ──────→ Distributor ──────────────→ Organization

Producer → Manufacturer's rep → Distributor ──→ Organization

AP Photo/Rene Macura

Marketers of luxury products often use exclusive distribution through carefully selected stores to ensure an optimum shopping experience for their customers.

- **Producer to retailer to consumer.** Producers that don't want to be involved in sales to consumers can sell their products to retailers, who then resell them to consumers.
- **Producer to wholesaler to retailer to consumer.** Manufacturers or suppliers of supermarket and pharmaceutical items often rely on two intermediary levels to reach consumers. They sell their products to wholesalers such as Supervalu, which in turn sell to the retailers. This approach works particularly well for small producers that lack the resources to sell or deliver merchandise to individual retail sites. It is also beneficial to retailers that lack the space to store container-size shipments of each product they sell.
- **Producer to agent/broker to wholesaler to retailer to consumer.** Additional channel levels are common in certain industries, such as agriculture, where specialists are required to negotiate transactions or to perform interim functions such as sorting, grading, or subdividing the goods.

274

MARKET COVERAGE

The appropriate market coverage—the number of wholesalers or retailers that will carry a product—depends on a number of factors in the marketing strategy. Inexpensive convenience goods or organizational supplies such as computer paper and pens sell best if they are available in as many outlets as possible. Such **intensive distribution** requires wholesalers and retailers of many types. In contrast, shopping goods such as home appliances and autos require different market coverage, because customers shop for such products by comparing features and prices. For these items, the best strategy is usually **selective distribution**, selling through a limited number of outlets that can give the product adequate sales and service support. If producers of expensive specialty or technical products do not sell directly to customers, they may choose **exclusive distribution**, offering products in only one outlet in each market area. With any of these approaches, producers need to choose the optimum number of outlets carefully to balance cost and market coverage and then continue to monitor market conditions to maintain a healthy balance.

DISTRIBUTION COSTS

Performing all the functions that are handled by intermediaries requires time and resources, so cost plays a major role in determining channel selection. Small or new companies often cannot afford to hire a salesforce large enough to sell directly to end users or to call on a host of retail outlets. Neither can they afford to build large warehouses and distribution centers to store large shipments of goods. These firms need the help of intermediaries, who can spread the cost of such activities across a number of products. To cover their costs and turn a profit, intermediaries generally buy products at a discount and then resell them at higher prices, although as noted earlier, some wholesaling customers are starting to push for per-item cost structures.

CHANNEL CONFLICT

Individual channel members naturally focus on running their own businesses as profitably as possible, which can lead to **channel conflict**, or disagreement over rights and responsibilities of the organizations in a distribution channel. Channel conflict may arise for a number of reasons, such as producers providing inadequate support to their channel partners; markets being oversaturated with intermediaries; producers trying to expand sales by adding additional channels, either on their own or through new intermediaries; or some intermediaries bearing the cost of developing new markets or promoting products only to see the sales revenue go to other intermediaries.

For example, conflict between full-service and discount or online retailers continues to be an issue because shoppers can often take advantage of the opportunity to visit full-service retailers to examine products and get information from product experts—and they buy at lower prices from discounters or online stores. The full-service retailers not only lose the sale but end up helplessly helping their competitors make those sales—and websites and shopping apps on mobile phones are making this problem even worse for them.

CHANNEL ORGANIZATION AND CONTROL

To minimize costs and the potential for channel conflict, channel partners can take steps to work out issues of organization and control. Without some degree of coordination, the various companies involved will pursue their own economic interests, often to the detriment of the channel as a whole.

Producers and intermediaries can achieve this coordination through **marketing systems**, in which the channel participants agree to operate as a cohesive system under the leadership of one of the participants.[34] The agreement can be brought about through *ownership* (when the production and distribution firms are owned by a single company), *contracts* (when the participants have formal agreements that specify their rights and responsibilities, such as the franchising agreements, and *economic power* (when one player is so big that its

intensive distribution A market coverage strategy that tries to place a product in as many outlets as possible

selective distribution A market coverage strategy that uses a limited number of carefully chosen outlets to distribute products

exclusive distribution A market coverage strategy that gives intermediaries exclusive rights to sell a product in a specific geographic area

channel conflict Disagreement or tension between two or more members in a distribution channel, such as competition between channel partners trying to reach the same group of customers

marketing systems Arrangements by which channel partners coordinate their activities under the leadership of one of the partners

economic presence is enough to encourage or even force cooperation from the other participants in the channel).[35]

For example, one of the fundamentals of Costco's success is that it sells products in such high volume that many producers can't afford *not* to accommodate Costco's demands for specific price points and packaging configurations. If they don't play by Costco's rules, so to speak, they risk missing out on a major source of distribution for their products. Costco, Walmart, and other giant retailers offer enticing opportunities for manufacturers, but playing by their high-volume, low-cost rules can sometimes hurt a manufacturer more than help it.[36]

Exhibit 4 offers of a summary of the major factors to consider regarding distribution channels.

EXHIBIT 4	Factors That Influence Distribution Channel Choices

Designing a distribution mix is rarely a simple task; here are some of the most important factors to consider.

Factor	Issues to Consider
Customer needs and expectations	Where are customers likely to look for your products? How much customer service do they expect from the channel? Can you make your offering more attractive by choosing an unconventional channel?
Product support requirements	How much training do salespeople need to present your products successfully? How much after-sale support is required? Who will answer questions when things go wrong?
Segmentation, targeting, and positioning	Which intermediaries can present your products to target customers while maintaining your positioning strategy?
Competitors' distribution channels	Which channels do your competitors use? Do you need to use the same channels in order to reach your target customers, or can you use different channels to distinguish yourself?
Established industry patterns and requirements	Which intermediaries are already in place? Can you take advantage of them, or do you need to find or create alternatives? Will retailers demand that you use specific wholesalers or distributors?
Channel length	Do you want to deal directly with customers? *Can* you? Do you need to engage other intermediaries to perform vital functions?
Market coverage	Are you going for intensive, selective, or exclusive distribution? Are the right intermediaries available in your target markets? Can they handle the volumes at which you hope to sell?
Distribution costs	How much will intermediaries add to the price that final customers will eventually pay? Put another way, how much of a discount from the retail price will intermediaries expect from you?
Channel conflict	What are the potential sources of channel conflict, both now and in the future? If such conflict can't be avoided, how will you minimize its effect?
Channel organization and control	How much control do you need to maintain as products move through the channel—and how much can you expect to maintain with each potential intermediary? What happens if you lose control? Who leads the channel?

✔ Checkpoint

LEARNING OBJECTIVE 5: Identify five key attributes of distribution channel design and management.

SUMMARY: Five key attributes of channel design and management are channel length (the number of layers between producers and target customers), market coverage needs (intense, selective, or exclusive distribution), distribution costs (all the costs involved in using a particular channel), channel conflict (disagreement and tension between channel partners), and channel organization and control (attempts to coordinate the activities of a channel into a cohesive marketing system).

CRITICAL THINKING: (1) Does exclusive distribution limit the potential size of a manufacturer's market? Why or why not? (2) Is it ethical for one participant in a channel to have power over the marketing system through sheer economic power alone? Why or why not?

IT'S YOUR BUSINESS: (1) Does knowing that a product is available only in selected retail outlets affect your assessment of its quality? (2) Have you ever been skeptical of "shipping and handling" charges added to products you've ordered? Did these charges affect your buying decisions?

KEY TERMS TO KNOW: intensive distribution, selective distribution, exclusive distribution, channel conflict, marketing systems

Physical Distribution and Logistics

In addition to assembling and managing the organizations and systems that make up a distribution channel, any firm that deals in physical goods needs to figure out the best way to move those products so they are available to customers at the right place, at the right time, and in the right amount. **Physical distribution** encompasses all the activities required to move finished products from the producer to the consumer, including forecasting, order processing, inventory control, warehousing, and transportation (see Exhibit 5 on the next page).

Physical distribution may not be the most glamorous aspect of business, but it is one of the most critical. Behind every luxury storefront or cutting-edge e-commerce website is a vast network of facilities, vehicles, and information systems that make sure products arrive at their destinations. The secret to making it all happen on time is **logistics**, the planning and movement of goods and information throughout the supply chain. As managers try to squeeze cost efficiencies and competitive advantages everywhere they can, logistics has taken on key strategic importance for many companies.

Success in physical distribution requires achieving a competitive level of customer service at the lowest total cost. Doing so requires trade-offs because as the level of service improves, the cost of distribution usually increases. For instance, if you reduce the level of inventory to cut your storage costs, you run the risk of being unable to fill orders in a timely fashion. Or, if you use slower forms of transportation, you can reduce your shipping costs, but you might aggravate customers. The trick is to optimize the total cost of achieving the desired level of service. This optimization requires a careful analysis of each step in the distribution process in relation to every other step in the physical distribution process. Of course, when companies reduce mistakes and eliminate inefficiencies, they can lower costs *and* improve service, which is the goal of every logistics manager.

FORECASTING

To control the flow of products through the distribution system, a firm must have an accurate estimate of demand. To some degree, historical data can be used to project future sales, but despite heavy investments in information technology, forecasting remains a major logistical challenge that is part hard numbers and part managerial judgment.

6 | **LEARNING OBJECTIVE**

Highlight the major components of physical distribution and logistics.

physical distribution All the activities required to move finished products from the producer to the consumer

logistics The planning, movement, and flow of goods and related information throughout the supply chain

EXHIBIT 5	Steps in the Physical Distribution Process

Managing the physical distribution system is an attempt to balance a high level of customer service with the lowest overall cost.

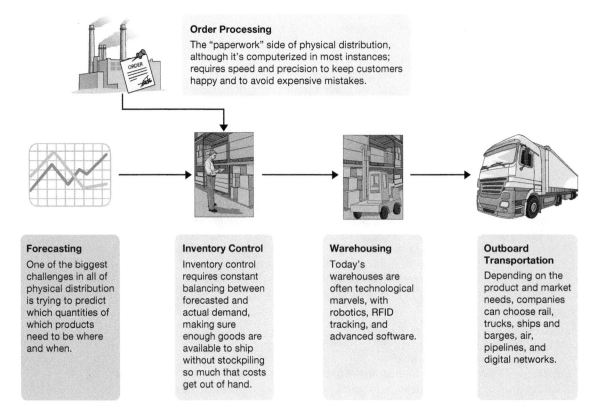

Order Processing
The "paperwork" side of physical distribution, although it's computerized in most instances; requires speed and precision to keep customers happy and to avoid expensive mistakes.

Forecasting
One of the biggest challenges in all of physical distribution is trying to predict which quantities of which products need to be where and when.

Inventory Control
Inventory control requires constant balancing between forecasted and actual demand, making sure enough goods are available to ship without stockpiling so much that costs get out of hand.

Warehousing
Today's warehouses are often technological marvels, with robotics, RFID tracking, and advanced software.

Outboard Transportation
Depending on the product and market needs, companies can choose rail, trucks, ships and barges, air, pipelines, and digital networks.

ORDER PROCESSING

order processing Functions involved in receiving and filling customer orders

Order processing involves preparing orders for shipment and receiving orders when shipments arrive. It includes a number of activities, such as checking the customer's credit, recording the sale, making the appropriate accounting entries, arranging for the item to be shipped, adjusting the inventory records, and billing the customer. Because order processing involves direct interaction with the customer, it affects a company's reputation for customer service. To keep buyers happy, companies should establish ambitious standards for accuracy and timeliness in order fulfillment.

INVENTORY CONTROL

As a just-in-time systems points out, in an ideal world, a company would always have just the right amount of goods on hand to fill the orders it receives. In reality, however, inventory and sales are seldom in perfect balance. For instance, many firms like to keep a ready supply of finished goods on hand so that they can fill orders as soon as they arrive. But how much inventory is enough? If your inventory is too large, you incur extra expenses for storage space, handling, insurance, and taxes; you also run the risk of product obsolescence. On the other hand, if your inventory is too low, you may lose sales when the product is not in stock. The objective of inventory control is to resolve these issues. Inventory managers decide how much product to keep on hand and when to replenish the supply of goods in inventory. They also decide how to allocate products to customers if orders exceed supply.

WAREHOUSING

warehouses Facilities for storing inventory

Products held in inventory are physically stored in **warehouses**, which may be owned by the manufacturer, by an intermediary, or by a private company that leases space to others. Some warehouses are almost purely holding facilities, in which goods are stored for relatively long periods. Other warehouses, known as **distribution centers**, serve as command posts for moving products to customers. In a typical distribution center, goods produced at a variety of locations are collected, sorted, coded, and redistributed to fill customer orders. Leading-edge distribution centers use some of the most advanced technologies in business today, including satellite navigation and communication, voice-activated computers, wireless data services, machine vision, robots, radio frequency identification (RFID) tags and scanners, and planning software that relies on artificial intelligence.

distribution centers Advanced warehouse facilities that specialize in collecting and shipping merchandise

TRANSPORTATION

For any business, the cost of transportation is normally the largest single item in the overall cost of physical distribution. When choosing a mode of transportation, managers must also evaluate other marketing issues, including storage, financing, sales, inventory size, speed, product perishability, dependability, flexibility, and convenience. Each of the six major modes of transportation has distinct advantages and disadvantages:

- **Rail.** Railroads can carry heavier and more diverse cargo and a larger volume of goods than any other mode of transportation. The obvious disadvantage of trains is that they are constrained to tracks, so they can rarely deliver goods directly to customers.
- **Trucks.** Trucks offer the convenience of door-to-door delivery and the ease and efficiency of travel on public highways. However, large, heavy loads are often better handled by water or rail, and some perishable loads may need to travel by air for the shortest possible delivery time over long distances.
- **Ships and barges.** The cheapest method of transportation is via water, and this is the preferred method for such low-cost bulk items as oil, coal, ore, cotton, and lumber. Water transport is slow, however, and like rail, must be combined with another mode of delivery for most shipments.
- **Air.** Air transport offers the primary advantage of speed over long distances, but it imposes limitations on the size, shape, and weight of shipments. It also tends to be the most expensive form of transportation; however, when speed is a priority, air is usually the only way to go.
- **Pipelines.** For products such as gasoline, natural gas, and coal or wood chips (suspended in liquid), pipelines are an effective mode of transportation. The major downsides are slow speeds and inflexible routes.
- **Digital networks.** Any product that exists in or can be converted to digital format, from books and movies to software to product design files, can be transported over the Internet and other digital networks. The range of digital products is fairly limited, of course, but the Internet has certainly revolutionized industries such as entertainment and publishing.

Shippers can also combine the benefits of multiple modes by using **intermodal transportation**. With *containerized shipping*, for instance, standard-size freight containers can be moved from trucks to railroads to ships for maximum flexibility.

For the latest information on wholesaling, retailing, and marketing logistics, visit http://real-timeupdates.com/bia6.

intermodal transportation The coordinated use of multiple modes of transportation, particularly with containers that can be shipped by truck, rail, and sea

✓ Checkpoint

LEARNING OBJECTIVE 6: Highlight the major components of physical distribution and logistics.

SUMMARY: The major components of a firm's distribution process are order processing, inventory control, warehousing, materials handling, and outbound transportation. When choosing the best method of outbound transportation, such as truck, rail, ship, airplane, or pipeline, you should consider cost, storage, sales, inventory size, speed, product perishability, dependability, flexibility, and convenience.

CRITICAL THINKING: (1) Given the huge volume of small packages that Amazon ships every year, should it consider starting its own transportation company instead of giving all that business to FedEx and other shippers? Why or why not? (2) If another high-tech company approached Dell with a partnership proposal to build and operate several distribution centers that would ship both companies' products to customers, what would you advise Dell to do? Why?

IT'S YOUR BUSINESS: (1) Online retailers sometimes use free shipping as a promotional appeal. Do you think most consumers really believe the shipping is "free" and not just factored into the product's price? (2) Have you ever paid extra for expedited shipping for an order placed on a website? Was it worth the extra expense?

KEY TERMS TO KNOW: physical distribution, logistics, order processing, warehouses, distribution centers, materials handling, intermodal transportation

BEHIND THE SCENES

MyBizLab

COSTCO PUSHES ITS SUPPLY CHAIN TO SATISFY CUSTOMERS

The merchandise sold at Costco may be similar to that of its two main competitors—Sam's Club and BJ's—but Costco aims to be a cut above by offering many unique and unusual items. Its stores also look slightly more upscale than other club stores, the brands it carries have more cachet, and the products are often a bit more expensive, but they still offer extremely good value. And unlike some other discounters, Costco does not have everything under the sun. The stores carry only about 4,000 products each, which is a small fraction of the more than 100,000 items stocked by other warehouse clubs and conventional discounters such as Target and Walmart. About 3,000 of Costco's products are a consistent array of carefully chosen basics, from canned tuna to laundry detergent to printer cartridges. The other 1,000 items are a fast-moving assortment of goods such as designer-label clothing, watches, and premium wines. These items change from week to week, reinforcing the idea of buying something when you see it because it'll probably be gone next week.

Costco prefers to offer name-brand products and has successfully introduced some branded luxury items such as Kate Spade and Coach purses. However, high-end suppliers such as Cartier and Cannondale flinch at the idea of their goods being sold in a warehouse setting, so carrying those brands isn't always possible. Some suppliers, hoping to protect their higher-end retail customers, have been known to spurn Costco's offers "officially," only to call back later to quietly cut a deal. In other cases, Costco goes on its own treasure hunts, using third-party distributors to track down hot products, even though these "gray market" channels can be unpredictable. And if that doesn't work, Costco can commission another manufacturer to create a lookalike product—leather handbags are one example—with its own Kirkland Signature label.

To give its millions of members the best prices on everything, Costco negotiates directly—and fiercely—with suppliers. Aiming to be known as the toughest negotiators in the business, Costco's buyers won't let up until they get their target price on

the merchandise. Often, the "right" price is determined by how much less expensively Costco can make a product itself. Using this approach, the company has managed to drive down price points in several categories, such as over-the-counter drugs. Costco then passes on the savings to customers, who never pay more than 15 percent above the company's cost. Cofounder and recently retired CEO Jim Sinegal was determined not to let the wheel of retailing take Costco for a spin, either. "When I started, Sears, Roebuck was the Costco of the country, but they allowed someone else to come in under them. We don't want to be one of the casualties. We don't want to turn around and say, 'We got so fancy we've raised our prices,' and all of a sudden a new competitor comes in and beats our prices."

Inventory turnover rate is also a key to Costco's financial success. By focusing on fast-selling items, the company moves its merchandise significantly faster than competitors—so quickly, in fact, that it often sells products to shoppers before it has to pay its suppliers.

Costco is rolling through its third decade with strong financial health, a dominant market position, and millions of consumers and business customers that rely on Costco bargains. Annual sales will break the $80 billion barrier soon, and $100 billion doesn't look too far out of reach. Online sales remain a fairly small fraction of total revenue, but the company expects those sales to pick up as the economy improves and consumers are more confident to spend on the more expensive items that are typically offered on the website. International expansion is another item on Costco's strategic menu, with sales recently growing at a faster clip outside the United States. Per-store sales are up in other countries, but the number of new store openings has tapered off over the past few years, thanks in part to the economy and in part to a cautious approach to finding the right locations. For instance, the company thinks Taiwan could support 20 Costco stores and Japan could support 50, but finding enough land for the giant footprint of a warehouse store—typically 15 acres—that is near population centers but not in areas with zoning regulations that prohibit big-box retailers is a particular challenge in some countries.[37]

Critical Thinking Questions

1. If customers repeatedly ask Costco to carry certain items that the company thinks are outside its price/quality "comfort zone" (because they're too expensive or not of high enough quality), should it give in and carry the items? Why or why not?

2. Most of the items on Costco's website are available only through Costco; should it expand its online product selection to include more commonly available products, since an online store doesn't have the physical constraints of a brick-and-mortar location? Why or why not?

3. If Costco can't find enough land in, say, Japan, to build its usual store format, should it leverage the Costco brand name anyway and build something such as conventional department stores or grocery stores in these areas? Why or why not?

LEARN MORE ONLINE

Explore the Costco website, at www.costco.com. What evidence do you see of "clicks-and-bricks" integration with the physical stores? Are sales promoted online? How much product information is available? Are nonmembers allowed to make purchases online? How does the online experience at Costco compare to that of another discounter, such as Walmart (www.walmart.com), or to a specialty retailer, such as Bluefly (www.bluefly.com)?

MyBizLab

Log on to www.mybizlab.com to access study and assessment aids associated with this chapter.

KEY TERMS

agents and brokers
channel conflict
department stores
discount stores
disintermediation
distribution centers
distribution mix
distribution strategy
distributors
e-commerce
exclusive distribution
intensive distribution
intermodal transportation
logistics
marketing intermediaries

marketing systems
merchant wholesalers
multichannel retailing
off-price retailers
online retailers
order processing
physical distribution
retail theater
retailers
selective distribution
specialty stores
warehouses
wheel of retailing
wholesalers

TEST YOUR KNOWLEDGE

Questions for Review

1. What is a distribution channel?
2. What are the two main types of intermediaries, and how do they differ from one another?
3. What forms of utility do intermediaries create?
4. What are some of the main causes of channel conflict?
5. How does a specialty store differ from a category killer and a discount store?

Questions for Analysis

6. How do marketing systems help avert channel conflict?
7. What are some of the challenges facing retailers and wholesalers today?
8. How might a once-valued intermediary find itself threatened with disintermediation?

9. How could strategic planning help a discount retailer avoid the pitfalls of the wheel of retailing?
10. Ethical Considerations. Manufacturers that have been selling to wholesalers and other intermediaries occasionally decide to start selling directly to end customers, which of course puts them in competition with the channel partners that have been selling for them. Even if this is legal, do you think such moves are ethical? Why or why not?

Questions for Application

11. Imagine that you own a small specialty store that sells hand-crafted clothing and jewelry. What are some of the nonstore retail options you might explore to increase sales? What are the advantages and disadvantages of each option?

12. Compare the prices of three products offered at a retail outlet with the prices charged if you purchase those products by mail order (catalog or phone) or over the Internet. Be sure to include extra costs such as handling and delivery charges. Which purchasing format offers the lowest price for each of your products?

13. This question was intentionally excluded from this edition.
14. This question was intentionally excluded from this edition.

EXPAND YOUR KNOWLEDGE

Discovering Career Opportunities

Retailing is a dynamic, fast-paced field with many career opportunities in both store and nonstore settings. In addition to hiring full-time employees when needed, retailers of all types often hire extra employees on a temporary basis for peak selling periods, such as the year-end holidays. You can find out about seasonal and year-round job openings by checking newspaper classified ads, looking for signs in store windows, browsing the websites of online retailers, and checking Craigslist (www.craigslist.org) and other sites.

1. Select a major retailer, such as a chain store in your area or a retailer on the Internet. Is this a specialty store, a discount store, a department store, or another type of retailer?
2. Visit the website of the retailer you selected. Does the site discuss the company's hiring procedures? If so, what are they? What qualifications are required for a position with the company?
3. Research your chosen retailer using library sources or online resources. Is this retailer expanding? Is it profitable? Has it recently acquired or been acquired by another firm? What are the implications of this acquisition for job opportunities?

Improving Your Tech Insights: Supply Chain Integration Standards

How do Amazon's computers know which book to reorder from its suppliers when you order one from Amazon's website?

Who makes sure RFID readers know how to detect RFID tags accurately and ensures that databases know what to do with the data? How does every one of the billions of barcodes now in use get the right combination of black and white stripes? All these decisions are guided by industry groups that define the standards and technologies that make sure supply chains work together, from producers to wholesalers to retailers.

Supply chain standardization might not be the most pulse-pounding technology from a consumer's point of view, but global business simply wouldn't work without it—and consumers benefit from the lower prices and better service that standards enable. Moving forward, advances in supply-chain integration promise to remove billions of dollars of errors and inefficiencies from supply chains in many industries.

Visit the website of GS1 (www.gs1.org) a global, not-for-profit organization that develops and oversees a number of supply chain standards. The brochure "What Is GS1?" available on the "About Us" page, explains the importance of global business standards and describes bar codes, RFID tagging, the Global Data Synchronization Network, and other efforts. In a brief email message to your instructor, describe one of the GS1 standards and explain how it helps businesses operate more efficiently and serve customers more effectively.

PRACTICE YOUR SKILLS

Sharpening Your Communication Skills

Sales of your DJ equipment (turntables, amplifiers, speakers, mixers, and related accessories) have been falling for months, even as more and more music fans around the world try their hand at being DJs. Magazine reviews and professional DJs give your equipment high marks, your prices are competitive, and your advertising presence is strong. Suspecting that the trouble is in the distribution channel, you and a half dozen fellow executives go on an undercover shopping mission at retail stores that carry your products—and you're appalled by what you see. The salespeople in these stores clearly don't understand your products, so they either give potential customers bad information about your products or steer them to products from your competitors. No wonder sales are falling off a cliff.

The executive team is split over the best way to solve this dilemma; you convince them that retraining your existing channel partners would be less expensive and less disruptive than replacing them. Now you have to convince store managers to let you pull their staffs off the sales floor for a half day so you can train them. Each store will lose a half day's revenue, and each sales rep will lose commissions for that time as well. Draft a short email message for the store managers, explaining why the training would be well worth their time. Make up any details you need to complete the message.

Building Your Team Skills

Complicated or confusing shopping experiences are one of the biggest challenges for online retailing. Customers who can't find what they're looking for or who get lost filling out order forms, for instance, often just click away and leave their virtual shopping carts. Unfortunately, consumers don't always perceive the shopping experience the same way, so it's not always easy for website developers to craft the ideal e-retail experience.

Your team's task is to analyze the shopping experience on three competitive e-retail sites and from that analysis decide how a new competitor in the market could create a better customer experience. First, choose a product that everyone in the group finds interesting but that none of you have purchased online before. Then identify three websites that are likely to offer the product. Next, individually (so you can't guide each other), each person in the group should shop the three sites for your chosen product. (If you can't find the exact model, choose something similar.) Answer the following questions about each site:

1. How difficult was it to find the product you wanted?
2. How much information was available? Complete product details or just a few highlights? A static photo or a three-dimensional (3D) virtual experience that lets you explore the product from all angles?
3. How easy was it to compare this product to similar products?
4. Could you find the store's privacy and return policies? Were they acceptable to you?
5. How long did it take to get from the site's homepage to the point at which you could place an order for the specific product?
6. What forms of help were available in case you had questions or concerns?

7. Go ahead and place your item in the shopping cart to simulate placing an order. (Don't actually buy the product, of course!)
8. What social commerce and social elements did you encounter on the website? Were they helpful in your search?

Summarize your impression of each of the three sites and then compare notes with your teammates. Based on the strengths and weaknesses of each site, identify four pieces of advice for a company that wants to compete against these sites.

Developing Your Research Skills

Find an article in a business journal or newspaper (online or print editions) that discusses changes a company is making to its distribution strategy or channels. For example, is a manufacturer selling products directly to consumers? Is a physical retailer offering goods via a company website? Is a company eliminating an intermediary? Has a nonstore retailer decided to open a physical store? Is a category killer opening smaller stores? Has a major retail tenant closed its store in a mall?

1. What changes in the company's distribution structure or strategy have taken place? What additional changes, if any, are planned?
2. What were the reasons for the changes? What role, if any, did e-commerce play in the changes?
3. If you were a stockholder in this company, would you view these changes as positive or negative? What, if anything, might you do differently?

REFERENCES

1. "Costco Wholesale Corp," *Bloomberg Businessweek*, accessed 8 September 2011, http://investing.businessweek.com; Mark Brohan, "Web Sales Rebound for Costco in Fiscal 2010," Internet Retailer, 8 October 2010, www.internetretailer.com; *Costco 2010 Annual Report*; Datamonitor, "Costco Wholesale Corporation: Company Profile," 12 April 2010, www.ebscohost.com; Costco website, accessed 8 September 2011, www.costco.com; "Analyst Picks and Pans: MCD, COST, YUM, TSN," *BusinessWeek*, 21 May 2009, www.businessweek.com; Michelle V. Rafter, "Welcome to the Club," *Workforce Management*, April 2005, 41–46; David Meier, "It's the Employees, Stupid," MotleyFool.com, 17 September 2004, www.fool.com; Steven Greenhouse, "How Costco Became the Anti-Wal-Mart," *New York Times*, 17 July 2005, www.nytimes.com; Jeff Malester, "Costco Sales Rise 10%, Hit $12.4 Billion in Fis. Q2," *Twice*, 7 March 2005, 53; Ilana Polyak, "Warehouse Sale," *Kiplinger's Personal Finance*, May 2005, 67; Suzanne Wooley, "Costco? More Like Costgrow," *Money*, August 2002, 44–46; "Costco: A Cut Above," *Retail Merchandiser*, July 2002, 44; Pete Hisey, "Costco.com Means Business," *Retail Merchandiser*, October 2001, 36; Shelly Branch, "Inside the Cult of Costco," *Fortune*, 6 September 1999, 184–188.
2. "Grainger at a Glance," Grainger website, accessed 7 September 2011, www.grainger.com.
3. Iris Professional Services website, accessed 7 September 2011, www.irisproservices.com.
4. "Manufacturing & Trade Inventories & Sales," U.S. Census Bureau website, accessed 7 September 2011, www.census.gov; "Wholesale Trade," U.S. Bureau of Labor Statistics website, accessed 7 September 2011, www.bls.gov.
5. Joseph O'Reilly, "3PL Perspectives 2011: The Power of Three," *Inbound Logistics*, July 2011, www.inboundlogistics.com; Philip Kotler and Gary Armstrong, *Principles of Marketing*, 13th ed. (Upper Saddle River, N.J.: Pearson Prentice Hall, 2010), 362–363; Bert Rosenbloom, "The Wholesaler's Role in the Marketing Channel: Disintermediation Vs. Reintermediation," *International Review of Retail, Distribution & Consumer Research*, September 2007, 327–339.
6. McKesson website, accessed 7 September 2011, www.mckesson.com.
7. Rosenbloom, "The Wholesaler's Role in the Marketing Channel: Disintermediation vs. Reintermediation."
8. Rosenbloom, "The Wholesaler's Role in the Marketing Channel: Disintermediation vs. Reintermediation."
9. Rosenbloom, "The Wholesaler's Role in the Marketing Channel: Disintermediation vs. Reintermediation."
10. "Wholesale Trade"; Rosenbloom, "The Wholesaler's Role in the Marketing Channel: Disintermediation vs. Reintermediation."
11. Richard Brunelli, "Shopper Marketing? There's an App for That . . . ," *Adweek*, 14 March 2011, S1–S3.
12. Jeneanne Rae, "New Thinking About Consumer Marketing," *BusinessWeek*, 30 June 2009, 16.
13. Jennifer J. Argo, Darren W. Dahl, and Andrea C. Morales, "Positive Consumer Contagion: Responses to Attractive Others in a Retail Context," *Journal of Marketing Research*, December 2008, 690–701.
14. Don E. Schultz, "Another Turn of the Wheel," *Marketing Management*, March/April 2002, 8–9.
15. "Investor Overview," Family Dollar website, accessed 7 September 2011, www.familydollar.com; Kerry Grace Benn,

"Family Dollar Earnings Jump 36%, Boosts Fiscal-Year View," *Wall Street Journal*, 8 July 2009, http://online.wsj.com.

16. Teri Agins, "What Is 'Off-Price'?" *Wall Street Journal*, 17 July 2009, http://online.wsj.com.

17. "Web to Become Top Sales Channel by 2012," *Bookseller*, 24 April 2009, 10; "Quarterly Retail E-Commerce Sales: 2nd Quarter 2011," U.S. Census Bureau, 16 August 2011, www.census.gov.

18. "Facts About Redbox," Redbox website, accessed 7 September 2011, www.redbox.com.

19. "What the Leaders Do Right," *Chain Store Age*, February 2008, 7A.

20. Kris Hudson and Vanessa O'Connell, "Recession Turns Malls into Ghost Towns," *Wall Street Journal*, 22 May 2009, http://online.wsj.com; Glen A. Bere, "Big Boxes Pop Up in Regional Malls, Altering Landscape for Chain Stores," *National Jeweler*, 16 May 2005, 1+; Bruce Horovitz and Lorrie Grant, "Changes in Store for Department Stores?" *USA Today*, 21 January 2005, B1–B2; Dean Starkman, "As Malls Multiply, Developers Fight Fiercely for Turf," *Wall Street Journal*, 19 April 2002, A1, A6; Robert Berner and Gerry Khermouch, "Retail Reckoning," *BusinessWeek*, 10 December 2001, 72–77.

21. David Bodamer, "The Mall Is Not Dead," *Retail Traffic*, May/ June 2011, 12.

22. Rick Braddock, "Lessons of Internet Marketing from FreshDirect," *Wall Street Journal*, 11 May 2009, http://online.wsj.com.

23. "Many-Stop Shopping? How Niche Retailers Are Thriving on Internet 2.0," Knowledge@Wharton, 11 May 2011, http://knowledge.wharton.upenn.edu; Cate T. Corcoran, "Delivering the Goods: E-Tailing Sales to Rise but Gains Seen Slowing," *Women's Wear Daily*, 5 May 2009, 1.

24. Jacques Bughin, Amy Guggenheim Shenkan, and Marc Singer, "How Poor Metrics Undermine Digital Marketing," *McKinsey Quarterly*, 2009 Issue 1, 106–107.

25. "Location-Free Shopping," *Chain Store Age*, February 2009, 13A.

26. Sharon Edelson, "Pop-ups Offer Retailers Multiple Benefits," *Women's Wear Daily*, 19 May 2009, 12.

27. Jim Dalrymple, "Inside the Apple Stores," *Macworld*, June 2007, 16–17; Andy Serwer, "The iPod People Have Invaded Apple's Stores," *Fortune*, 13 December 2004, 79.

28. Rob Eder, "CVS Unveils High-End Beauty 360 Store," *Drug Store News*, 17 November 2008, 1+.

29. Black & Decker website, accessed 7 September 2011, www.blackanddecker.com.

30. Felder website, accessed 7 September 2011, www.feldergroupusa.com.

31. Kotler and Armstrong, *Principles of Marketing*, 349.

32. Super Jock'n Jill website, accessed 26 October 2011, www.superjocknjill.com.

33. Øystein Foros and Hans Jarle Kind, "Do Slotting Allowances Harm Retail Competition?" *Scandinavian Journal of Economics* 110, no. 2 (2008), 367–384; U.S. Federal Trade Commission, "Slotting Allowances in the Retail Grocery Industry: Selected Case Studies in Five Product Categories," November 2003, www.ftc.gov.

34. Kotler and Armstrong, *Principles of Marketing*, 344.

35. Adapted from Kotler and Armstrong, *Principles of Marketing*, 344–345.

36. Andrew R. Thomas and Timothy J. Wilkinson, "The Devolution of Marketing," *Marketing Management*, Spring 2011, 19–25.

37. See note 1.

GLOSSARY

agents and brokers Independent wholesalers that do not take title to the goods they distribute but may or may not take possession of those goods

channel conflict Disagreement or tension between two or more members in a distribution channel, such as competition between channel partners trying to reach the same group of customers

department stores Large stores that carry a variety of products in multiple categories, such as clothing, house wares, gifts, bedding, and furniture

discount stores Retailers that sell a variety of everyday goods below the market price by keeping their overhead low

disintermediation The replacement of intermediaries by producers, customers, or other intermediaries when those other parties can perform channel functions more effectively or efficiently

distribution centers Advanced warehouse facilities that specialize in collecting and shipping merchandise

distribution mix A combination of intermediaries and channels a producer uses to reach target customers

distribution strategy A firm's overall plan for moving products through intermediaries and on to final customers

distributors Merchant wholesalers that sell products to organizational customers for internal operations or the production of other goods, rather than to retailers for resale

e-commerce The application of Internet technologies to wholesaling and retailing

exclusive distribution A market coverage strategy that gives intermediaries exclusive rights to sell a product in a specific geographic area

intensive distribution A market coverage strategy that tries to place a product in as many outlets as possible

intermodal transportation The coordinated use of multiple modes of transportation, particularly with containers that can be shipped by truck, rail, and sea

logistics The planning, movement, and flow of goods and related information throughout the supply chain

marketing intermediaries Businesspeople and organizations that assist in moving and marketing goods and services between producers and consumers

marketing systems Arrangements by which channel partners coordinate their activities under the leadership of one of the partners

merchant wholesalers Independent wholesalers that take legal title to goods they distribute

multichannel retailing Coordinated efforts to reach consumers through more than one retail channel

off-price retailers Stores that sell designer labels and other fashionable products at steep discounts

online retailers Companies that use e-commerce technologies to sell over the Internet; includes Internet-only retailers and the online arm of store-based retailers

order processing Functions involved in receiving and filling customer orders

physical distribution All the activities required to move finished products from the producer to the consumer

retail theater The addition of entertainment or education aspects to the retail experience

retailers Intermediaries that sell goods and services to individuals for their own personal use

selective distribution A market coverage strategy that uses a limited number of carefully chosen outlets to distribute products

specialty stores Stores that carry only a particular type of goods, often with deep selection in those specific categories

warehouses Facilities for storing inventory

wheel of retailing An evolutionary process by which stores that feature low prices gradually upgrade until they no longer appeal to price-sensitive shoppers and are replaced by a new generation of leaner, low-price competitors

wholesalers Intermediaries that sell products to other intermediaries for resale or to organizations for internal use

Financial Management

From Chapter 18 of *Business in Action*, Sixth Edition. Courtland L. Bovée, John V. Thill. Copyright © 2013 by Pearson Education, Inc. Published by Pearson Business. All rights reserved.

LEARNING OBJECTIVES After studying this chapter, you will be able to

1 Identify three fundamental concepts that affect financial decisions and identify the primary responsibilities of a financial manager

2 Describe the budgeting process, three major budgeting challenges, and the four major types of budgets

3 Compare the advantages and disadvantages of debt and equity financing and explain the two major considerations in choosing from financing alternatives

4 Identify the major categories of short-term debt financing

5 Identify the major categories of long-term debt financing

6 Describe the two options for equity financing and explain how companies prepare an initial public offering

MyBizLab

Where you see MyBizLab in this chapter, go to www.mybizlab.com for additional activities on the topic being discussed.

BEHIND THE SCENES CHARGING AHEAD: VISA SEARCHES FOR FUNDS

Visa faced the challenge of going public during the worst economic conditions in recent memory. The executive team is shown here at the New York Stock Exchange on the day the company went public.

www.visa.com

The story of Visa, Inc., is a story of big numbers. As the world's largest processor of credit and debit card transactions, Visa provides essential services to more than 16,000 financial institutions, which have issued 1.7 billion Visa-branded cards. The 28 million merchants that accept Visa ring up nearly 60 billion transactions a year.

Visa's history began in 1958, when Bank of America premiered the BankAmericard in Fresno, California, just as the concept of general-purpose credit cards was taking hold across the Unites States. (*Charge cards* issued and accepted by a single company, such as a gas station or department store, had been around for several decades by then.) These new *revolving* credit accounts, which let consumers charge purchases and pay them off over time, revolutionized consumer and business purchasing and changed the way consumers and companies manage their finances.

Over the next 50 years, the business venture that began as BankAmericard grew and transformed into the Visa International Service Association, a global payment-processing system jointly owned by thousands of member banks and other financial institutions. The BankAmericard became the Visa card, and Visa became one of the world's best-known and most valuable brands.

With growth and change came challenges, and by 2007 Visa had more than a few challenges on its hands. While Visa remained a privately held joint venture, archrival MasterCard had become a public company in 2006, raising $2.4 billion with its initial stock offering. MasterCard's stock price continued to climb, giving an already strong competitor more financial power and flexibility, including the ability to attract and motivate top employees with stock options. As competition—and opportunities—grew, Visa needed cash to keep investing in payment-processing technologies, including smart cards with embedded computer chips and phone-based mobile commerce payments. At the same time, Visa was also facing several billion dollars in liabilities from lawsuits filed by merchants and rival card companies American

Express and Discover. To top it off, the six major banks that were Visa's primary owners were facing a massive liquidity crisis after the subprime mortgage crisis and the global credit freeze that followed. They needed cash by the bucketful.

Selling stock for the first time through an initial public offering (IPO) of its own seemed like the obvious answer to Visa's funding challenges. However, did an IPO make sense when the global economy was in the process of falling off a cliff? Did Visa choose the right financing option and the right time to execute it? Would the IPO be another big number in a company history of big numbers, or would it be a big-time failure?[1]

INTRODUCTION

From the coffee shop down the street to the world's largest corporations, every business enterprise needs cash, although not always the billions of dollars that Visa needed. In this chapter, you'll learn about the major financial decisions companies make, starting with the process of developing a financial plan, then creating and maintaining budgets, and finally comparing ways to finance both ongoing operations and growth opportunities.

My BizLab

Gain hands-on experience through an interactive, real-world scenario. This chapter's simulation entitled Financial Management is located at **www.mybizlab.com**.

The Role of Financial Management

Planning for a firm's money needs and managing the allocation and spending of funds are the foundations of **financial management**, or *finance*. In most smaller companies, the owner is responsible for the firm's financial decisions, whereas in larger operations, financial management is the responsibility of the finance department. This department, which includes the accounting function, reports to a vice president of finance or a chief financial officer (CFO).

No matter what size the company, decisions regarding company finances must consider three fundamental concepts (see Exhibit 1 on the next page). First, if the firm spends too much money meeting short-term demands, it won't have enough money to make strategic investments for the future, such as building new facilities, developing the next generation of products, or being able to jump on a strategic acquisition. Conversely, if the firm spends too little in the short term, it can lose key employees to better-paying competitors, compromise product quality or customer service, or create other problems with long-term consequences.

Second, most financial decisions involve balancing potential risks against potential rewards, known as a **risk/return trade-off**. Generally speaking, the higher the perceived risk, the higher the potential reward, and vice versa. However, this situation doesn't always hold true. For example, a company with free cash could (a) invest it in the stock market, which offers potentially high returns but at moderate to high risk; (b) put the money in a bank account, which has little to no risk but very low return; or (c) invest in a new facility or a new product, which could yield high returns, moderate returns, or no returns at all. Moreover, the *safest* choice isn't always the *best* choice. For instance, if you're hording cash in a safe place while competitors are investing in new products or new stores, you could be setting yourself up for a big decline in revenue.

Third, financial choices can have a tremendous impact on a company's flexibility and resilience. For example, companies that are *highly leveraged* (that is, carrying a lot of debt) are forced to devote more of their cash flow to debt service and therefore can't spend that money on advertising, staffing, or product development. Heavy debt loads and low cash flow make a company especially vulnerable to economic downturns, too. In contrast, companies with lots of cash on hand can weather tough times and make strategic moves that their debt-constrained competitors can't make. In fact, well-funded companies often view recessions as opportunities to take market share from weaker competitors or simply to buy

1 LEARNING OBJECTIVE

Identify three fundamental concepts that affect financial decisions, and identify the primary responsibilities of a financial manager.

financial management Planning for a firm's money needs and managing the allocation and spending of funds

risk/return trade-off The balance of potential risks against potential rewards

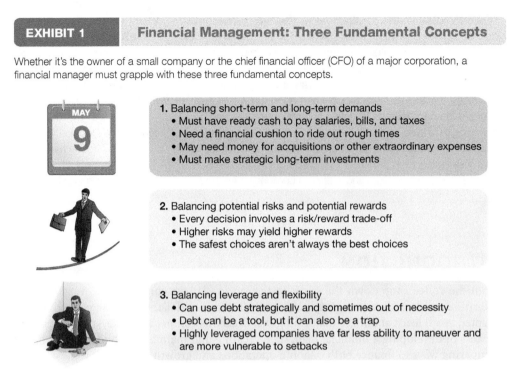

EXHIBIT 1   **Financial Management: Three Fundamental Concepts**

Whether it's the owner of a small company or the chief financial officer (CFO) of a major corporation, a financial manager must grapple with these three fundamental concepts.

MAY 9

1. Balancing short-term and long-term demands
- Must have ready cash to pay salaries, bills, and taxes
- Need a financial cushion to ride out rough times
- May need money for acquisitions or other extraordinary expenses
- Must make strategic long-term investments

2. Balancing potential risks and potential rewards
- Every decision involves a risk/reward trade-off
- Higher risks may yield higher rewards
- The safest choices aren't always the best choices

3. Balancing leverage and flexibility
- Can use debt strategically and sometimes out of necessity
- Debt can be a tool, but it can also be a trap
- Highly leveraged companies have far less ability to maneuver and are more vulnerable to setbacks

them outright.[2] The semiconductor giant Intel uses downturns to invest in major facility upgrades, enabling it to respond more aggressively when the economy turns around and demand picks up.[3]

DEVELOPING A FINANCIAL PLAN

Successful financial management starts with a **financial plan**, a document that outlines the funds a firm will need for a certain period of time, along with the sources and intended uses of those funds. The financial plan takes its input from three information sources:

- The strategic plan, which establishes the company's overall direction and identifies the need for major investments, expanded staffing, and other activities that will require funds
- The company's financial statements, including the income statement and the statement of cash flows, which tell the finance manager how much cash the company has now and how much it is likely to generate in the near future
- The external financial environment, including interest rates and the overall health of the economy

By considering information from these three sources, managers can identify how much money the company will need and how much it will have to rely on external resources to complement its internal resources over the span of time covered by the financial plan (see Exhibit 2).

MONITORING CASH FLOW

Overall income, as identified in the income statement, is important, but knowing precisely how much cash is flowing into and out of the company—and when—is critical because cash is necessary to purchase the assets and supplies a company needs to operate, to meet payroll, and to pay dividends to shareholders (for those corporations that pay dividends). Cash flow is generally related to net income; that is, companies with relatively high accounting profits generally have relatively high cash flow, but the relationship is not precise.

financial plan A document that outlines the funds needed for a certain period of time, along with the sources and intended uses of those funds

EXHIBIT 2 — Finding and Allocating Funds

Financial management involves finding suitable sources of funds and deciding on the most appropriate uses for those funds.

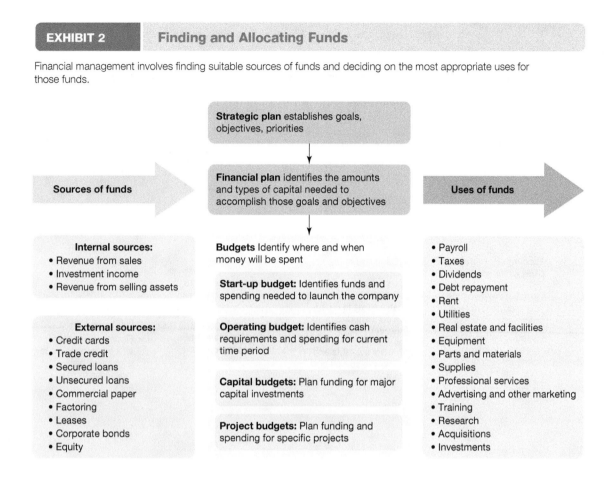

Strategic plan establishes goals, objectives, priorities

Sources of funds

Financial plan identifies the amounts and types of capital needed to accomplish those goals and objectives

Uses of funds

Internal sources:
- Revenue from sales
- Investment income
- Revenue from selling assets

External sources:
- Credit cards
- Trade credit
- Secured loans
- Unsecured loans
- Commercial paper
- Factoring
- Leases
- Corporate bonds
- Equity

Budgets Identify where and when money will be spent

Start-up budget: Identifies funds and spending needed to launch the company

Operating budget: Identifies cash requirements and spending for current time period

Capital budgets: Plan funding for major capital investments

Project budgets: Plan funding and spending for specific projects

- Payroll
- Taxes
- Dividends
- Debt repayment
- Rent
- Utilities
- Real estate and facilities
- Equipment
- Parts and materials
- Supplies
- Professional services
- Advertising and other marketing
- Training
- Research
- Acquisitions
- Investments

Companies that don't keep a close eye on cash flow can find themselves facing a *liquidity crisis*, having insufficient cash to meet their short-term needs. In the worst-case scenario, a firm in a liquidity crisis finds itself in a credit crisis, too, meaning it doesn't have the cash it needs and can't borrow any more. During the recent recession, many companies caught with no money and no way to borrow had no choice but to reduce their workforces. Whenever economic storm clouds are gathering, financial managers need to jump into action to strengthen balance sheets and do whatever they can to ensure positive cash flow as conditions deteriorate.[4]

A vital step in maintaining positive cash flow is monitoring *working capital accounts*: accounts receivable, accounts payable, inventory, and cash (see Exhibit 3 on the next page).

Managing Accounts Receivable and Accounts Payable

Keeping an eye on **accounts receivable**—the money owed to a firm by its customers—is one way to manage cash flow effectively. The volume of receivables depends on a financial manager's decisions regarding several issues: who qualifies for credit and who does not, how long customers are given to pay their bills, and how aggressive the firm is in collecting its debts. In addition to setting guidelines and policies for handling these issues, a financial manager analyzes the firm's outstanding receivables to identify patterns that might indicate problems and establishes procedures for collecting overdue accounts.

The flip side of managing receivables is managing **accounts payable**—the bills that the company owes to its suppliers, lenders, and other parties. Here the objective is generally to postpone paying bills until the last moment, because doing so allows the firm to hold on to its cash as long as possible. However, a financial manager also needs to weigh the advantages of paying promptly if doing so entitles the firm to cash discounts. In

accounts receivable Amounts that are currently owed to a firm

accounts payable Amounts that a firm currently owes to other parties

EXHIBIT 3	Monitoring the Working Capital Accounts

The working capital accounts represent a firm's cash on hand as well as economic value that can be converted to cash (inventory) or is expected from customers (accounts receivable), minus what it is scheduled to pay out (accounts payable).

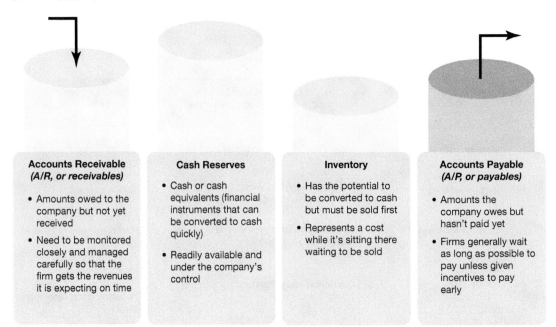

Accounts Receivable (A/R, or receivables)

- Amounts owed to the company but not yet received
- Need to be monitored closely and managed carefully so that the firm gets the revenues it is expecting on time

Cash Reserves

- Cash or cash equivalents (financial instruments that can be converted to cash quickly)
- Readily available and under the company's control

Inventory

- Has the potential to be converted to cash but must be sold first
- Represents a cost while it's sitting there waiting to be sold

Accounts Payable (A/P, or payables)

- Amounts the company owes but hasn't paid yet
- Firms generally wait as long as possible to pay unless given incentives to pay early

addition, paying on time is essential to maintaining a good credit rating, which lowers the cost of borrowing.

Managing Inventory

Inventory is another area in which financial managers can fine-tune the firm's cash flow. Inventory sitting on the shelf represents capital that is tied up without earning interest. Furthermore, the firm incurs expenses for storage and handling, insurance, and taxes. In addition, there is always a risk that inventory will become obsolete before it can be converted into finished goods and sold. Thus, the firm's goal is to maintain enough inventory to fill orders in a timely fashion at the lowest cost. To achieve this goal, financial managers work with operations managers and marketing managers to determine the *economic order quantity (EOQ)*, or quantity of materials that, when ordered regularly, results in the lowest ordering and storage costs.

MANAGING CASH RESERVES

Financial managers also serve as guardians of a company's cash reserves, whether that cash is from investors that have funded a start-up venture or from profitable product sales in an established company. The nature of this challenge varies widely, depending on the business, the firm's overall financial health, and management's predictions for the economy. For instance, start-ups usually have a finite pool of cash from their investors and need to manage that cash wisely so they don't run out of funds before the new business can start to generate cash on its own. At the other extreme, an established company with many successful and profitable products can generate more cash than it needs for both ongoing operations and "rainy day" emergency funds.

Checkpoint

SUMMARY: Decisions regarding company finances must take into account three fundamental concepts. First, every company has to balance short-term and long-term financial demands. Failure to do so can lead to serious cash flow problems and even bankruptcy. Second, most financial decisions involve a *risk/return trade-off* in which, generally speaking, the higher the perceived risk, the higher the potential reward, and vice versa. Third, financial choices can have a tremendous impact on a company's flexibility and resilience. Overburdening a company with debt limits its strategic options and makes it vulnerable to economic slowdowns. Financial managers are responsible for developing and implementing a firm's financial plan, monitoring cash flow and managing excess funds, and budgeting for expenditures and improvements. In addition, these managers raise capital as needed and oversee the firm's relationships with banks and other financial institutions.

CRITICAL THINKING: (1) What role does a company's strategic plan play in the process of financial management? (2) Does it ever make sense for a profitable company with positive cash flow to seek external financing? Why or why not?

IT'S YOUR BUSINESS: (1) What is your financial plan for getting through college? (2) How well do you budget your personal finances? If you don't budget, how do you monitor cash flow to make sure you don't run out of money each month?

KEY TERMS TO KNOW: financial management, risk/return trade-off, financial plan, accounts receivable, accounts payable

The Budgeting Process

In addition to developing a financial plan and monitoring cash flow, financial managers are responsible for developing a **budget**, a financial guide for a given period, usually the company's fiscal year, or for the duration of a particular project. Like a good personal or household budget, a company budget identifies where and when money will be spent throughout the year. Particularly in larger organizations, budgeting is often a combination of *top-down mandate*, in which top executives specify the amount of money each functional area can have based on the company's total available budget for the year, and *bottom-up requests*, in which individual supervisors and managers add up the amounts they need based on number of employees, project expenses, supplies, and other costs.

Finalizing a budget is usually a matter of negotiation and compromise in which financial managers try to reconcile the top-down and bottom-up numbers. After a budget has been developed, the finance manager compares actual results with projections to discover variances and recommends corrective action, a process known as **financial control**.

BUDGETING CHALLENGES

The budgeting process might sound fairly straightforward, but in practice, it can be an exhausting, time-consuming chore that everyone dreads and few managers find satisfactory. Budgeting is a challenge for several reasons (see Exhibit 4 on the next page). First, a company always has a finite amount of money available to spend each year, and every group in the company is fighting for a share of it. Consequently, individual department managers can spend a considerable amount of time making a case for their budgetary needs, and top executives frequently need to make tough choices that won't please everybody.

EXHIBIT 4	Budgeting Challenges

Budgeting can be a tough challenge that requires tough choices; here are three big issues managers usually face.

1. Every company has a limited amount of money to spend.
- Projects and departments are often in competition for resources.
- Managers need to make tough choices, occasionally taking money from one group and giving it to another.

2. Revenues and costs are often difficult to predict.
- Sales forecasts are never certain, particularly for new products or in sales into new markets.
- Fixed costs are easy to predict, but variable costs can be hard to predict, particularly more than a few months out.

3. It's not always clear how much should be spent.
- With some expenses, such as advertising, managers aren't always sure how much is enough.
- Uncertainty leads to budgeting based on past expenditures, which might be out of line with current strategic needs.

hedging Protecting against cost increases with contracts that allow a company to buy supplies in the future at designated prices

Second, managers often can't predict with complete accuracy how much revenue will come in or how much the various items covered by the budget will cost during the time frame covered by the budget. For instance, some expenses are routine and predictable, but others are variable and some can be almost impossible to predict. Fixed salaries are easy to predict month to month, but energy costs fluctuate—sometimes wildly so. In some cases, companies can protect themselves against future price increases by **hedging**, arranging contracts that allow them to buy supplies in the future at designated prices. The obvious risk of hedging against rising prices is that prices could instead drop over the duration of the contract, leaving a company paying more than it would have to otherwise.

Another alternative is *rolling forecasts*, in which the company starts the year with a budget based on revenue and cost assumptions made at that point but then reviews economic performance every month or every quarter to see whether the budget needs to be modified as the year progresses.[5] For example, Google CFO Patrick Pichette and his colleagues review projects every quarter, analyzing what has been accomplished in the past three months and what can be accomplished in the next three. Projects that appear to be losing momentum might get their funding reduced, whereas projects making strong headway might get a budget increase.[6]

Another effective tool in volatile situations is *scenario planning*, in which managers identify two or more possible ways that events could unfold—different scenarios, that is—and have a budgetary response ready for each one. Scenario planning is particularly valuable for long-range planning because the longer the time frame, the harder it is to pin down revenues and costs with any degree of accuracy.

Third, even if they can predict how much revenue will come in or how much various things will cost, managers can't always be sure how much they *should* spend in each part of the budget. A common practice is to take the amounts spent the previous year and raise or lower them by some amount to arrive at this year's budget. However, this practice is a bit like cost-plus pricing in that it is simple to do but can produce seriously flawed numbers by ignoring real-world inputs. This practice also encourages a "use it or lose it" mentality: At the end of the year managers hurriedly spend any remaining money in their budgets, even if doing so doesn't make financial sense, because they know if they don't spend it all, their budgets will be reduced for the next year.

A more responsive approach is **zero-based budgeting**, in which each department starts from zero every year and must justify every item in the budget.[7] This approach forces each department to show how the money it wants to spend will support the overall strategic plan. The downside to zero-based budgeting is the amount of time it takes. One practical alternative is a hybrid approach in which zero-basing is reserved for those areas of the budget with the greatest flexibility, such as advertising and various development projects.[8]

REAL-TIME UPDATES
Learn More by Reading This Article

Small business budgeting: how to make it work

Follow these six steps to create a better budget for your small business. Go to http://real-timeupdates.com/bia6 and click on Learn More. If you are using MyBizLab, you can access Real-Time Updates within the chapter or under Student Study Tools.

TYPES OF BUDGETS

A company can have up to four types of budgets, depending on the nature and age of its business:

- Before a new company starts business, the entrepreneurial team assembles a **start-up budget**, or *launch budget*, that identifies all the money it will need to spend to "get off the ground." A major concern at this stage is the *burn rate*, the rate at which the company is using up the funds from its initial investors. If the burn rate is too high, the firm risks running out of money before it can start generating sustainable sales revenues and become self-funding. Start-up budgets can be the most difficult of all because the company doesn't have any operating history to use as a baseline. Feedback from other entrepreneurs, experienced early-stage investors, and advisors such as SCORE executives or business incubators can be invaluable.

- After a company gets through the start-up phase, the financial manager's attention turns to the **operating budget**, sometimes known as the *master budget*, which identifies all sources of revenue and coordinates the spending of those funds throughout the coming year. Operating budgets help financial managers estimate the flow of money into and out of the business by structuring financial plans within a framework of estimated revenues, expenses, and cash flows. The operating budget incorporates any special budgets, such as *capital* and *project budgets*.

- A **capital budget** outlines expenditures for real estate, new facilities, major equipment, and other **capital investments**. For smaller capital purchases, a company might designate a certain percentage of its annual operating budget for capital items every year. Significant capital investments might require planning over the course of multiple years as the company assembles the necessary funds and makes payments on the purchases while maintaining its ongoing operating budget.

- Another special type of budget that has to be coordinated with the operating budget is the **project budget**, which identifies the costs needed to accomplish a particular project, such as conducting the research and development of a new product or moving a company to a new office building. Project managers typically request funding based on their estimates of the cost to complete the project and its value to the company. They then have the responsibility of making sure the project is completed on budget.

zero-based budgeting A budgeting approach in which each department starts from zero every year and must justify every item in the budget, rather than simply adjusting the previous year's budget amounts

start-up budget A budget that identifies the money a new company will need to spend to launch operations

operating budget Also known as the *master budget*, a budget that identifies all sources of revenue and coordinates the spending of those funds throughout the coming year

capital budget A budget that outlines expenditures for real estate, new facilities, major equipment, and other capital investments

capital investments Money paid to acquire something of permanent value in a business

project budget A budget that identifies the costs needed to accomplish a particular project

✓ **Checkpoint**

LEARNING OBJECTIVE 2: Describe the budgeting process, three major budgeting challenges, and the four major types of budgets.

SUMMARY: A budget is a financial guide for a given time period or project that indentifies how much money will be needed and where and when it will be spent. Budgeting often combines top-down mandates, whereby company executives identify how much money each functional area will have to spend, and bottom-up requests, whereby individual division or department managers add up the funding they'll need to meet their respective goals. Three major budgeting challenges are (1) reconciling the competing demands on the finite amount of money the company has to spend, (2) trying to predict future costs, (3) and deciding how much to spend in each area of the budget. Four major types of budgets are the *start-up budget*, which guides companies during the launch phase of a new company; the *operating* or *master budget*, which outlines all spending during a given time period (typically a year) and incorporates various special budgets; the *capital budget*, which plans expenditures on major capital purchases; and the *project budget*, which guides spending on projects such as new product launches.

CRITICAL THINKING: (1) What are some of the risks of failing to create and manage budgets? (2) How does zero-based budgeting help a company spend its cash in the most effective ways possible?

IT'S YOUR BUSINESS: (1) What steps would you take to identify the costs of a two-week trip to Scotland next summer? (2) Assume that you need to raise $3,000 between now and graduation for a down payment on a car. How would budgeting and financial control help you meet this objective?

KEY TERMS TO KNOW: budget, financial control, hedging, zero-based budgeting, start-up budget, operating budget, capital budget, capital investments, project budget

---

3 **LEARNING OBJECTIVE**

Compare the advantages and disadvantages of debt and equity financing, and explain the two major considerations in choosing from financing alternatives.

Financing Alternatives: Factors to Consider

Every firm's need for cash and its ability to get money from various external sources is unique, and it's up to financial executives to find the right source or combination of sources. This section explores the factors that finance managers consider when they are looking for outside funds, and the next three sections cover the three major categories of financing: short-term debt, long-term debt, and equity.

DEBT FINANCING VERSUS EQUITY FINANCING

debt financing Arranging funding by borrowing money

equity financing Arranging funding by selling ownership shares in the company, publicly or privately

The most fundamental decision a company faces regarding financing is whether it will obtain funds by **debt financing**, which is borrowing money, or by **equity financing**, which is selling ownership shares in the company. To meet their changing needs over time, many firms use a combination of debt and equity financing, and many use several kinds of debt financing at the same time for different purposes.

Note that business debt usually doesn't have the same negative connotations as consumer debt. Whereas consumers are advised to avoid most kinds of debt if at all possible, and being in debt is often a sign of financial trouble or financial mismanagement, robust and well-run businesses of all shapes and sizes use debt as a routine element of financial management. The key difference is that—unlike with nearly all consumer debt other than loans for education—businesses can make money by borrowing money. Of course, companies can get into debt trouble through bad choices and bad luck, just as consumers can, and it's up to financial managers to make smart borrowing choices.

When choosing between debt and equity financing, companies consider a variety of issues, including the prevailing interest rates, maturity, the claim on income, the claim on assets, and the desire for ownership control. Exhibit 5 summarizes these considerations.

EXHIBIT 5   Debt Financing Versus Equity Financing

When choosing between debt and equity financing, companies evaluate the characteristics of both types of funding.

Characteristic	Debt Financing	Equity Financing
Maturity	**Specific:** In most cases, specifies a date by which debt must be repaid.	**N/A:** Equity funding does not need to be repaid.
Claim on income	**Nondiscretionary, usually a recurring cost and usually fixed:** Debt obligations must be repaid, regardless of whether the company is profitable; payments can be regular (e.g., monthly), balloon (repaid all at once), or a combination.	**Discretionary cost:** At management's discretion and if company is profitable, shareholders may receive dividends after creditors have been paid; however, company is not required to pay dividends.
Claim on assets	**Priority:** Lenders have prior claims on assets.	**Residual:** Shareholders have claims only after the firm satisfies claims of lenders.
Influence over management	**Usually little:** Lenders usually have no influence over management unless debit vehicles come with conditions or management fails to make payments on time.	**Varies:** As owners of the company, shareholders can vote on some aspects of corporate operations, although in practice only large shareholders have much influence. Private equity holders (such as venture capitalists) can have considerable influence.
Tax consequences	**Deductible:** Debt payments reduce taxable income, lowering tax obligations.	**Not deductible:** Dividend payments are not tax deductible.
Employee benefit potential	**N/A:** Debt financing does not create any opportunities for compensation alternatives such as stock options.	**Stock options:** Issuing company shares creates the opportunity to use stock options as a motivation or retention tool.

Of course, not every firm has access to every financing option, and sometimes companies have to take whatever they can get. For instance, only companies that are already public or are prepared to go public (see "Public Stock Offerings" later in this chapter) can raise funds by selling shares on the open market. Similarly, as you'll read in the sections on debt financing, some debt options are not available to small companies.

LENGTH OF TERM

Financing can be either short term or long term. **Short-term financing** is financing that will be repaid within one year, whereas **long-term financing** is financing that will be repaid in a period longer than one year. The primary purpose of short-term financing is to ensure that a company maintains its liquidity, or its ability to meet financial obligations (such as inventory payments) as they become due. By contrast, long-term financing is used to acquire long-term assets such as buildings and equipment or to fund expansion via any number of growth options.

short-term financing Financing used to cover current expenses (generally repaid within a year)

long-term financing Financing used to cover long-term expenses such as assets (generally repaid over a period of more than one year)

COST OF CAPITAL

In general, a company wants to obtain money at the lowest cost and with the least amount of risk. However, lenders and investors want to receive the highest possible return on their investment, also at the lowest risk. A company's **cost of capital** is the average rate of interest it must pay on its debt and equity financing. For any form of financing to make economic sense, the expected returns must exceed the cost of capital. Consequently, financial managers study capital costs carefully in relation to the intended uses of those funds. At the same time, the potential sources of external funds, from banks to stock market investors to

cost of capital The average rate of interest a firm pays on its combination of debt and equity

suppliers who sell on credit, also analyze a company's plans and prospects to determine whether helping the company is a safe and sensible use of their capital.

During the recent credit crisis, when sources of available credit shrunk dramatically and the limited credit that was available became quite expensive, most companies were forced to rethink their approaches to financing.

Cost of capital depends on three main factors: the risk associated with the company, the prevailing level of interest rates, and management's selection of funding vehicles.

Risk

Lenders that provide money to businesses expect their returns to be in proportion to the two types of risk they face: the quality and length of time of the venture. Obviously, the more financially solid a company is, the less risk investors face and the less money they will demand in compensation. Just as with consumer credit, in which protecting your *credit score* is vital to securing credit at reasonable rates, companies must also guard their reputations as being good credit and investment risks.

In addition to perceived risk, time also plays a vital role. Because a dollar will be worth less tomorrow than it is today, lenders need to be compensated for waiting to be repaid. As a result, for a given type of debt, long-term financing generally costs a company more than short-term financing.

Interest Rates

prime interest rate The lowest rate of interest that banks charge for short-term loans to their most creditworthy customers

Regardless of how financially solid a company is, the cost of money will vary over time because interest rates fluctuate. The **prime interest rate** (often called simply the *prime*) is the lowest interest rate offered on short-term bank loans to preferred borrowers. The prime changes irregularly and, at times, quite frequently. Sometimes it changes because of supply and demand; at other times it changes because the prime rate is closely tied to the *discount rate*, the interest rate that the Federal Reserve charges on loans to commercial banks and other depository institutions (see page 464).

Companies must take such interest rate fluctuations into account when making financing decisions. For instance, a company planning to finance a short-term project when the prime rate is 3 percent would want to reevaluate the project if the prime rose to 6 percent a few months later. Even though companies try to time their borrowing to take advantage of drops in interest rates, this option is not always possible. A firm's need for money doesn't always coincide with a period of favorable rates. At times, a company may be forced to borrow when rates are high and then renegotiate the loan when rates drop. Sometimes projects must be put on hold until interest rates become more affordable.

Opportunity Cost

leverage The technique of increasing the rate of return on an investment by financing it with borrowed funds

Using a company's own cash to finance its growth has one chief attraction: No interest payments are required. Nevertheless, such internal financing is not free; using money for any particular purpose has an *opportunity cost*, defined in Chapter 2 as the value of the most appealing alternative from among those that weren't chosen. For instance, a company might be better off investing its excess cash in external opportunities, such as stocks of other companies, and borrowing money to finance its own growth. Doing so makes sense as long as the company can earn a greater *rate of return* (the percentage increase in the value of an investment) on those investments than the rate of interest paid on borrowed money. This concept is called **leverage** because the loan acts like a lever: It magnifies the power of the borrower to generate profits (see Exhibit 6).

capital structure A firm's mix of debt and equity financing

However, leverage works both ways: Borrowing may magnify your losses as well as your gains. Because most companies require some degree of external financing from time to time, the issue is not so much whether to use outside money; rather, it's a question of how much should be raised, by what means, and when. The answers to such questions determine the firm's **capital structure**, the total mix of debt and equity it uses to meet its short- and long-term needs.

EXHIBIT 6	Financial Leverage

Leverage can be your best friend if investments work out well—or it can be your worst enemy if they don't. Assume that you have $10,000 of your own funds to invest in the stock market or some business venture. You also have the opportunity to borrow an additional $50,000 at 6 percent interest. Should you invest just your own $10,000 or leverage your investment by borrowing the $50,000 so you can invest $60,000 instead? If the investment returns 12 percent after a year, you'll earn a healthy $1,200 if you invest just your own money. But with leverage, you would earn more than three and a half times that amount, even after you pay the cost of borrowing the $50,000. However, look at what happens if the investment turns sour. If it loses 12 percent that first year instead, the leveraging will wipe out your entire $10,000.

No leverage; 12% return			5x leverage; 12% return	
Funds	$10,000		Funds	$10,000
Debt	$0		Debt	$50,000
Total to invest	$10,000		Total to invest	$60,000
Annual return (12%)	$1,200		Annual return (12%)	$7,200
Cost of debt	$0		Cost of debt (6%)	($3,000)
Profit (loss)	$1,200		Profit (loss)	$4,200

No leverage; –12% return			5x leverage; –12% return	
Funds	$10,000		Funds	$10,000
Debt	$0		Debt	$50,000
Total to invest	$10,000		Total to invest	$60,000
Annual return (–12%)	($1,200)		Annual return (–12%)	($7,200)
Cost of debt	$0		Cost of debt (6%)	($3,000)
Profit (loss)	($1,200)		Profit (loss)	($10,200)

✓ Checkpoint

LEARNING OBJECTIVE 3: Compare the advantages and disadvantages of debt and equity financing, and explain the two major considerations in choosing from financing alternatives.

SUMMARY: Debt financing offers a variety of funding alternatives and is available to a wider range of companies than equity financing. It also doesn't subject management to outside influence the way equity financing does, and debt payments reduce a company's tax obligations. On the downside, except for trade credit, debt financing always puts a demand on cash flow, so finance managers need to consider whether a company can handle debt payments. The major advantages of equity financing are the fact that the money doesn't have to be paid back and the resulting discretionary drain on cash flow (publicly held companies don't have to pay regular dividends if they choose not to). The major disadvantages are the dilution of management control and the fact that equity financing—public equity financing in particular—is not available to many firms. The two major considerations in choosing financing alternatives are *length of term* (the duration of the financing) and *cost of capital* (the average cost to a company of all its debt and equity financing).

CRITICAL THINKING: (1) What factors might lead a company to gain additional funds through debt financing rather than through equity financing? (2) Why does consumer debt have a more negative connotation than business debt?

IT'S YOUR BUSINESS: (1) Do you know your credit score, or have you ever looked at your credit report? To learn more about free credit reports, visit www.ftc.gov/freereports. (2) How should the cost of capital figure into your decisions about attending college, buying cars, and buying housing?

KEY TERMS TO KNOW: debt financing, equity financing, short-term financing, long-term financing, cost of capital, prime interest rate, leverage, capital structure

Identify the major categories of short-term debt financing.

Financing Alternatives: Short-Term Debt

Financial managers have a number of options when it comes to short-term debt financing, including *credit cards, trade credit, secured loans, unsecured loans, commercial paper*, and an alternative to borrowing known as *factoring* (see Exhibit 7).

CREDIT CARDS

Half of all small companies and start-ups use credit cards to help fund their operations. Credit cards are one of the most expensive forms of financing, but they are sometimes the only form available to business owners. In the years leading up to the 2008 credit crunch, anyone with a pulse and mailbox could get multiple credit card offers, making cards a tempting way to get cash to start or expand a business, or simply to stay afloat during rough patches. However, card issuers recently began cutting credit limits for millions of card holders, even those with strong credit histories, and these cutbacks are affecting many small businesses whose owners use their personal credit cards to provide funds for their companies.[9]

EXHIBIT 7	Sources of Short-Term Debt Financing

Businesses have a variety of short-term debt financing options, each with advantages and disadvantages.

Source	Funding Mechanism	Length of Term	Advantages	Disadvantages and Limitations
Credit cards	Essentially creates a short-term loan every time cardholder makes purchases or gets a cash advance	Revolving (no fixed repayment date)	Widely available; convenient; no external scrutiny of individual purchases	High interest rates; availability decreasing since the credit crunch; ease of use and lack of external scrutiny can lead to overuse
Trade credit	Allows buyer to make purchases without immediately paying for them	Typically 30 to 90 days	Usually free (no interest) as long as payment is made by due date; enables purchaser to manage cash flow more easily; consolidates multiple purchases into a single payment	Buyer often needs to establish a payment history with seller before credit will be extended; availability and terms vary from seller to seller; some sellers may require promissory note and charge interest
Secured loans	Lender provides cash using borrower's assets (such as inventory or equipment) as collateral; also known as *asset-based loans*	Up to 1 year (for short-term loans)	Can provide financing for companies that don't qualify for unsecured loans or other alternatives	More expensive than some other options
Unsecured loans	Lender provides lump sum of cash via a promissory note or on-demand access to cash via a credit line	Up to 1 year (for short-term loans)	Provides cash or access to cash without requiring borrower to pledge assets as collateral	Cost varies according to borrower's credit rating; often not available to customers with unproven or poor credit history
Commercial paper	Participating in the global *money market*, large institutional investors provide unsecured, short-term loans to corporations	Up to 270 days (longer in special cases)	Less expensive and less trouble to get than conventional loans; can generate very large amounts of cash fairly quickly, from $100,000 to many millions	Available only to large corporations with strong credit ratings; proceeds can only be used to purchase current assets, not fixed assets
Factoring	Company sells its accounts receivable to an intermediary that collects from the customer	N/A	Frees up working capital; makes cash flow more predictable; can provide some protection from bad debts and customer bankruptcies; often can be arranged more quickly than a loan	Expensive (annualized costs can be 30–40 percent)

TRADE CREDIT

Trade credit, often called *open-account purchasing*, occurs when suppliers provide goods and services to their customers without requiring immediate payment. Such transactions create the accounts receivable. From the buyer's perspective, trade credit allows a company to get the goods and services it needs without immediately disrupting its cash flow. Trade credit can also lower transaction costs for buyers (as well as sellers) by consolidating multiple purchases into a single payment. In many cases, credit is extended at no interest for a short period (typically 30 days).

From the seller's perspective, offering credit terms is often a competitive necessity, and doing so can allow a supplier to sell more to each customer because purchase levels aren't constrained to buyers' immediate cash balances. However, like all other forms of credit, trade credit involves costs and risks. Allowing customers to delay payments affects the seller's cash flow and exposes it to the risk that some customers won't be able to pay when their bills come due. Extending trade credit can also reduce the company's own credit worthiness because lenders will look at how quickly it is closing its accounts receivable. Companies that offer trade credit should be sure to check the credit worthiness of all buyers, keep credit limits low for new customers until they establish a reliable payment history, and keep a close eye on every customer's payment status.[10]

trade credit Credit obtained by a purchaser directly from a supplier

SECURED LOANS

Secured loans are those backed by something of value, known as **collateral**, that may be seized by the lender in the event that the borrower fails to repay the loan. Common types of collateral include property, equipment, accounts receivable, inventories, and securities.

secured loans Loans backed up with assets that the lender can claim in case of default, such as a piece of property

collateral A tangible asset a lender can claim if a borrower defaults on a loan

UNSECURED LOANS

Unsecured loans are ones that require no collateral. Instead, the lender relies on the general credit record and the earning power of the borrower. To increase the returns on such loans and to obtain some protection in case of default, most lenders insist that the borrower maintain some minimum amount of money on deposit at the bank—a **compensating balance**—while the loan is outstanding.

A common example of an unsecured loan is a **line of credit**, which is an agreed-on maximum amount of money a bank is willing to lend a business. Once a line of credit has been established, the business may obtain unsecured loans for any amount up to that limit. The key advantage of a line of credit over a regular loan is that interest (or at least full interest) is usually not charged on the untapped amount.

unsecured loans Loans that require a good credit rating but no collateral

compensating balance The portion of an unsecured loan that is kept on deposit at a lending institution to protect the lender and increase the lender's return

line of credit An arrangement in which a financial institution makes money available for use at any time after the loan has been approved

COMMERCIAL PAPER

When businesses need a sizable amount of money for a short period of time, they can issue **commercial paper**—short-term *promissory notes*, or contractual agreements, to repay a borrowed amount by a specified time with a specified interest rate. Commercial paper is usually sold only by major corporations with strong credit ratings, in denominations of $100,000 or more and with maturities of up to 270 days (the maximum allowed by the Securities and Exchange Commission (SEC) without a formal registration process). Commercial paper is normally issued to secure funds for short-term needs such as buying supplies and paying rent rather than for financing major expansion projects. Because the amounts are generally large, these notes are usually purchased by various investment funds and not by individual investors.

commercial paper Short-term promissory notes, or contractual agreements, to repay a borrowed amount by a specified time with a specified interest rate

FACTORING AND RECEIVABLES AUCTIONS

Businesses with slow-paying trade credit customers—some organizational customers can take months to pay their bills—and tight cash flow have the option of selling their accounts receivable, a method known as **factoring**. Although it's not really a form of borrowing in the conventional sense, factoring is an alternative to short-term debt financing.

factoring Obtaining funding by selling accounts receivable

Factoring involves several steps. First, a *factor* or *factoring agent* purchases a company's receivables, paying the company a percentage of the total outstanding amount, typically 70 to 90 percent. Second, the factoring agent collects the amounts owed, freeing the company from the administrative tasks of collection. Third, after a customer pays the factor, the factor makes a second payment to the company, keeping a percentage as a fee for its services. Some factors assume the risk that customers won't ever pay (and their fees are naturally higher), while others don't, in which case the company has to refund the initial payment it received from the factor.[11]

The use of factoring has increased in recent years, particularly as banks and other lenders have reduced the level of credit that many businesses rely on to manage cash flow. Because it is a comparatively expensive method, factoring is generally best suited for profitable, growing companies with pressing cash flow needs and large, creditworthy customers (businesses or government agencies, not consumers) that are likely to pay their bills but are just slow in doing so.[12] Particularly for companies that sell to retailers, factoring is sometimes a necessity because they have contracts that require them to keep retailers supplied with inventory on a regular schedule and need the cash flow to do so.[13]

An innovative twist on factoring is the *receivables auction*, pioneered by The Receivables Exchange (www.receivablesxchange.com). Using an online format somewhat like eBay and other auction sites, companies post their receivables for investors to bid on. Those who offer the best combination of funding amount and fees win the business, and the sellers get their money the next day. The average auction duration is one day; the fastest deal was done in just three seconds.[14]

✓ Checkpoint

LEARNING OBJECTIVE 4: Identify the major categories of short-term debt financing.

SUMMARY: The major categories of short-term debt financing are *credit cards*, *trade credit* (the option to delay paying for purchases for 30 to 60 days or more), *secured loans* (loans backed by sellable assets such as land, equipment, or inventory), *unsecured loans* (loans and lines of credit extended solely on the borrower's creditworthiness), *commercial paper* (short-term promissory notes issued by major corporations), and *factoring* (selling a firm's accounts payable to a third-party financer; strictly speaking, not a form of debt financing).

CRITICAL THINKING: (1) How does getting a secured loan using accounts receivable as collateral differ from factoring? (2) Why would any seller offer trade financing, since it ties up working capital without generating any income through interest payments?

IT'S YOUR BUSINESS: (1) Would you launch a new company if the only way to finance it was through the use of your personal credit cards? Why or why not? (2) Which of the short-term debt alternatives identified in this section are available to you as a consumer?

KEY TERMS TO KNOW: trade credit, secured loans, collateral, unsecured loans, compensating balance, line of credit, commercial paper, factoring

---

5 LEARNING OBJECTIVE

Identify the major categories of long-term debt financing.

Financing Alternatives: Long-Term Debt

In addition to the various short-term debt alternatives, a number of long-term debt financing options are available as well. Although some of them are similar in concept to short-term debt, the longer time spans create a different set of decisions for both borrowers and lenders. The most common long-term debt alternatives are *long-term loans*, *leases*, and *corporate bonds* (see Exhibit 8).

EXHIBIT 8	Sources of Long-Term Debt Financing

Long-term debt financing can provide funds for major asset purchases and other investments needed to help companies grow.

Source	Funding Mechanism	Length of Term	Advantages	Disadvantages and Limitations
Long-term loans	Bank or other lender provides cash; borrower agrees to repay according to specific terms	From 1 to 25 years	Can provide substantial sums of money without diluting ownership through sale of equity; allows company to make major purchases of inventory, equipment, and other vital assets	Not all companies can qualify for loans and acceptable terms; payments tie up part of cash flow for the duration of the loan; purchases made via loans require substantial down payments
Leases	Company earns the right to use an asset in exchange for regular payments; arrangement can be directly between lessor and lessee or can involve a third party such as a bank	Typically several years for equipment and vehicles; longer for real estate	Usually require lower down payments than loans; can provide access to essential assets for companies that don't qualify for loans; let company avoid buying assets that are likely to decline in value or become obsolete; often free company from maintenance and other recurring costs	Can restrict how assets can be used; company doesn't gain any equity in return for lease payments, except in the case of lease-to-own arrangements; can be more expensive than borrowing to buy
Corporate bond	Company sells bonds to investors, with the promise to pay interest and repay the principle according to a set schedule	Typically from 10 to 30 years	Can generate more cash with longer repayment terms than are possible with loans	Available only to large companies with strong credit ratings

LONG-TERM LOANS

Long-term loans, sometimes called *term loans*, can have maturities between 1 and 25 years or so, depending on the lender and the purpose of the loan. (Some lenders designate loans with maturities between one and three years as *intermediate-term loans*.[15]) Common reasons for taking out long-term loans are to buy real estate, to build or expand facilities, to acquire other companies, to purchase equipment or inventory, to refinance existing debt at lower interest rates, or to provide working capital.[16] Long-term loans on real estate are called *mortgages*.

Long-term loans can be an attractive option for borrowers because such loans can provide substantial capital without the need to sell equity in the company. However, because they tie up a lender's capital for a long period of time and usually involve large sums of money, lending standards tend to be fairly stringent and not all companies can qualify. Lenders usually look at "the five Cs" when considering applications for these loans:[17]

- **Character.** This aspect includes not only the personal and professional character of the company owners but also their experience and qualifications to run the type of business for which they plan to use the loan proceeds.
- **Capacity.** To judge the company's capacity or ability to repay the loan, lenders scrutinize debt ratios, liquidity ratios, and other measures of financial health. For small businesses, the owners' personal finances are also evaluated.
- **Capital.** Lenders want to know how well *capitalized* the company is—that is, whether it has enough capital to succeed. For small-business loans in particular, lenders want to know how much money the owners themselves have already invested in the business.
- **Conditions.** Lenders look at the overall condition of the economy as well as conditions within the applicant's specific industry to determine whether they are comfortable with the business's plans and capabilities.

- **Collateral.** Long-term loans are usually secured with collateral of some kind. Lenders expect to be repaid from the borrower's cash flow, but in case that is inadequate, they look for assets that could be used to repay the loan, such as real estate or equipment.

An old joke about applying for bank loans suggests that the only way to qualify for a loan is to prove you don't need the money. This is an exaggeration, of course, but it is grounded in fact. Before they will part with their capital, particularly in tough economic conditions, responsible lenders want a high degree of assurance that they'll get their money back.

LEASES

lease An agreement to use an asset in exchange for regular payment; similar to renting

Rather than borrow money to purchase an asset, a firm may enter into a **lease**, under which the owner of an asset (the *lessor*) allows another party (the *lessee*) to use it in exchange for regular payments. (Leasing is similar to renting; a key difference is that leases fix the terms of the agreement for a specific amount of time.) Leases are commonly used for real estate, major equipment, and vehicles. In some cases, the lease arrangement is made directly between the asset owner and the lessee. In other cases, a bank or other financial firm provides leasing services to its clients and takes care of payments to the lessor.

Leasing may be a good alternative for a company that has difficulty obtaining a loan because of a poor credit rating or that is unwilling or unable to use its working capital for a down payment on a loan. A creditor is more willing to provide a lease than a loan because, should the company fail, the lessor need not worry about a default on loan payments; it can simply repossess the asset it legally owns. Some firms use leases to finance significant portions of their assets, particularly in industries such as airlines, where assets are mostly large, expensive pieces of equipment. Leasing can also provide more flexibility than purchasing through a loan. For instance, a growing company with expanding office space requirements can lease additional space when needed without the cost and delay of buying and selling real estate.

CORPORATE BONDS

bonds A method of funding in which the issuer borrows from an investor and provides a written promise to make regular interest payments and repay the borrowed amount in the future

secured bonds Bonds backed by specific assets that will be given to bondholders if the borrowed amount is not repaid

debentures Corporate bonds backed only by the reputation of the issuer

convertible bonds Corporate bonds that can be exchanged at the owner's discretion into common stock of the issuing company

When a company needs to borrow a large sum of money, it may not be able to get the entire amount from a single source. Under such circumstances, it may try to borrow from many individual investors by issuing **bonds**—certificates that obligate the company to repay a certain sum, plus interest, to the bondholder on a specific date. (Note that although bondholders buy bonds, they are acting as lenders.)

Companies issue a variety of corporate bonds. **Secured bonds**, like secured loans, are backed by company-owned property (such as airplanes or plant equipment) that passes to the bondholders if the issuer does not repay the amount borrowed. *Mortgage bonds*, one type of secured bond, are backed by real property owned by the issuing corporation. **Debentures** are unsecured bonds, backed only by the corporation's promise to pay. Because debentures are riskier than other types of bonds, the companies that issue them must pay higher interest rates to attract buyers. **Convertible bonds** can be exchanged at the investor's option for a certain number of shares of the corporation's common stock. Because of this feature, convertible bonds generally pay lower interest rates.

Of course, organizations that issue bonds must eventually repay the borrowed amount to the bondholders. Normally, this repayment is done when the bonds mature, but the cost of retiring the debt can be staggering because bonds are generally issued in quantity—perhaps thousands of individual bonds in a single issue. To ease the cash flow burden of redeeming its bonds all at once, a company can issue *serial bonds*, which mature at various times, as opposed to *term bonds*, which mature all at the same time.

Another way of relieving the financial strain of retiring many bonds all at once is to set up a *sinking fund*. When a corporation issues a bond payable by a sinking fund, it must set aside a certain sum of money each year to pay the debt. This money may be used to retire a few bonds each year, or it may be set aside to accumulate until the issue matures.

With most bond issues, a corporation retains the right to pay off the bonds before maturity. Bonds containing this provision are known as *callable bonds*, or *redeemable bonds*. If a company issues bonds when interest rates are high and then rates fall later on, it may want to pay off its high-interest bonds and sell a new issue at a lower rate. However, this feature carries a price tag: Investors must be offered a higher interest rate to encourage them to buy callable bonds.

✔ Checkpoint

LEARNING OBJECTIVE 5: Identify the major categories of long-term debt financing.

SUMMARY: The three major categories of long-term debt financing are *long-term loans* (substantial amounts of capital for major purchases or other needs, on terms up to 25 years, usually secured by assets), *leases* (similar to renting, conferring the rights to use an asset in exchange for regular payments), and *bonds* (certificates that obligate the company to repay a specified sum, plus interest, to the bondholder on a specific date).

CRITICAL THINKING: (1) How could rates of technological change affect a company's decision about whether to buy or lease equipment, vehicles, and other assets? (2) Why would lenders want to see that a business already has some level of capitalization before giving it access to more capital by means of a loan?

IT'S YOUR BUSINESS: (1) If you have just moved to a new city to start a new job, would you prefer to lease or rent an apartment? Why? (2) Assume you are in the market for a new car. Will you lease or buy? Why?

KEY TERMS TO KNOW: lease, bonds, secured bonds, debentures, convertible bonds

Financing Alternatives: Equity

6 LEARNING OBJECTIVE
Describe the two options for equity financing, and explain how companies prepare an initial public offering.

The most far-reaching alternative for securing funds is to sell shares of ownership in a company. Even the most thorough loan application reviews and strict repayment terms can't match the degree to which selling equity changes the way a company is managed. In the most extreme cases, selling equity can lead to the founders of a firm being ousted from the company. Even when owners retain control, equity financing can complicate operations by adding new layers of public scrutiny and accountability. Finally, the process of obtaining equity financing is expensive and time-consuming, so even companies that could obtain it don't always choose to do so—and some that sell equity to the public choose to reverse the decision by buying it back.

With all these caveats, why would any company bother with equity financing? The answer is the tremendous upside potential for the company as a whole and for any individual or organization that owns shares. Equity financing has fueled the growth of most of the major corporations in the world, and it has contributed to the financial security of millions of employees (and made millionaires out of thousands of employees, too). Plus, unlike debt financing, selling stock can continue to generate money for years if share prices continue to increase.

Although this option is available to only a small fraction of companies, it is one of the most powerful forms of financing. Moreover, it directly and indirectly plays a huge role in the economy by giving both individual and institutional investors the opportunity to increase their own capital by investing in company shares. This section takes a quick look at the private and public varieties of equity financing.

VENTURE CAPITAL AND OTHER PRIVATE EQUITY

Venture capitalists (VCs), as well as angel investors for companies that aren't yet ready for VC funding, are a key source of equity financing for a certain class of start-up companies. In exchange for a share of ownership, VCs can invest millions of dollars in companies long before those firms can qualify for most other forms of financing, so they represent an essential form of funding for high-growth ventures. VCs also provide managerial expertise and industry connections that can be crucial to new companies.

However, VCs are one of the most specialized and least widely available forms of funding, and most firms have no chance of getting venture capital. VCs typically look for privately held firms that are already well established enough to be able to use a significant amount of money and are positioned to grow aggressively enough to give the VCs a good shot at eventually selling their interests at an acceptable profit. Not all VC-backed firms grow enough to pay back their investors, so VCs count on getting very high returns from a handful of winners.

private equity Ownership assets that aren't publicly traded; includes venture capital

Venture capital is a specialized form of funding known as **private equity** (ownership assets that aren't publicly traded), and other forms of private equity can provide funding for companies that are beyond the start-up stage. Leveraged buyouts are usually done with private equity funds. Other uses of private equity are taking companies private by buying up all publicly held shares and rescuing companies that are on the verge of bankruptcy.

PUBLIC STOCK OFFERINGS

Going public, offering shares of stock to the public through a stock market such as the New York Stock Exchange, can generate millions or even billions of dollars in funding. As you can read in the Behind the Scenes wrap-up, this is the financing path Visa chose, and its initial public offering (IPO) raised a record $19.6 billion.[18]

However, going public is not for the faint of heart. The process takes months of management time and attention, it can cost several million dollars, and it exposes the company to rigorous scrutiny (which isn't necessarily a bad thing, of course). Complaining that the process had become too difficult in the wake of some high-profile accounting scandals that tightened oversight of public companies, former PayPal CEO Peter Thiel once remarked, "Going public today is a process I wouldn't wish upon my worst enemy."[19] Moreover, companies have no assurance that efforts to go public will pay off. Some offerings fail to sell at the hoped-for share price, and some offerings are withdrawn before going public because their backers don't think the market conditions are strong enough. Like the economy as a whole, the market for IPOs runs in cycles, and timing an IPO is one of the key factors for success (see Exhibit 9).

Despite the costs and risks, the potential rewards are so high that every year thousands of companies around the world attempt to go public. The legal, financial, and promotional steps in the process can be grouped into three phases:[20]

underwriter A specialized type of bank that buys the shares from the company preparing an IPO and sells them to investors

- **Preparing the IPO.** Preparing an offering involves assembling a team of advisors that includes legal experts, a public accounting firm to serve as auditor, and an **underwriter**, a specialized type of bank known as an *investment bank* that buys the shares from the company and sells them to investors. (To spread the risk, a lead underwriter usually assembles a syndicate of other underwriters.) Working with company management, this team prepares required financial statements, organizes a board of directors, hires a public relations firm to begin promoting the upcoming offering, and engages in *due diligence* to make sure the company's financial policies and systems meet the expectations and legal requirements of public ownership.

prospectus An SEC-required document that discloses required information about the company, its finances, and its plans for using the money it hopes to raise

- **Registering the IPO.** Before a company can sell shares to the public in the United States, it must first register with the SEC. This process includes submitting a **prospectus**, which discloses required information about the company, its finances, and its plans for using the money it hopes to raise. The SEC reviews the information and typically requests modifications and additional information to make the filing conform with all applicable regulations.

- **Selling the IPO.** Before the stock is officially offered for sale, the company and its team promote the offering privately to institutional investors through a series of meetings called the *road show*. Although the IPO is the first "public" offering, shares are usually offered only to institutional investors or selected individual investors before the IPO date. Based on the demand they perceive during the road show, the company and the underwriter decide how to price the IPO shares. After the SEC approves the registration, the stock begins trading on a designated stock exchange, and the company is now officially public.

As with corporate bonds, this chapter's coverage of stocks is from the stock issuer's perspective.

For the latest information on financial management and funding alternatives, visit http://real-timeupdates.com/bia6.

REAL-TIME UPDATES
Learn More by Visiting This Website

Get the inside scoop on IPO activity

Renaissance Capital is the go-to source for information on IPOs. Go to http://real-timeupdates.com/bia6 and click on Learn More. If you are using MyBizLab, you can access Real-Time Updates within the chapter or under Student Study Tools.

EXHIBIT 9	Global IPO Activity

The number of initial public offerings (IPOs) tends to track the stock market's ups and downs. This graph compares global IPO activity with the year-end level of the S&P 500 Index, a common composite measure of stock market values.

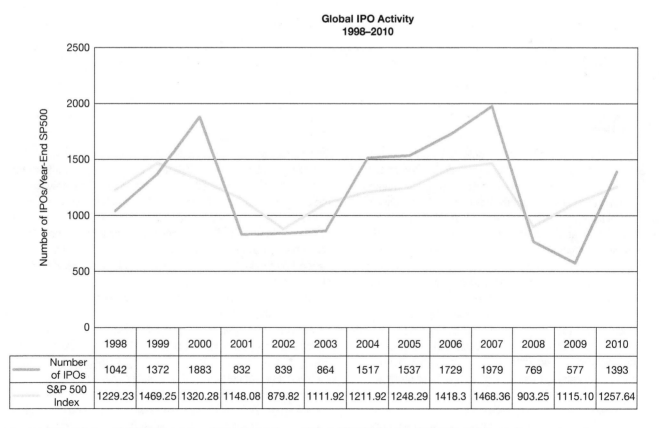

Global IPO Activity
1998–2010

	1998	1999	2000	2001	2002	2003	2004	2005	2006	2007	2008	2009	2010
Number of IPOs	1042	1372	1883	832	839	864	1517	1537	1729	1979	769	577	1393
S&P 500 Index	1229.23	1469.25	1320.28	1148.08	879.82	1111.92	1211.92	1248.29	1418.3	1468.36	903.25	1115.10	1257.64

Sources: IPO activity from *Global IPO Trends Report 2011*, Ernst & Young, 2011, 6; S&P 500 data from "S&P 500 Index," Google Finance, accessed 11 September 2011, www.google.com/finance.

✔ **Checkpoint**

LEARNING OBJECTIVE 6: Describe the two options for equity financing, and explain how companies prepare an initial public offering.

SUMMARY: Equity financing can be accomplished through *private equity* (ownership assets that aren't publicly traded the way shares of company stock are) or the issuance of public stock. Private equity investments such as venture capital are often used at specific points in a company's growth history, such as to get the company off the ground or to perform a leveraged buyout. Preparing for an initial public offering (IPO) involves a number of financial, legal, and promotional activities that fall into three stages: (1) preparing the IPO by assembling a team that includes a public auditor and an underwriter, preparing required financial statements, and making sure the company's financial statements and systems are up to public company standards; (2) registering the IPO with the SEC and responding to any demands for additional information from the SEC; and (3) selling the IPO, primarily through a *road show*, a series of presentations to institutional investors aimed at getting them interested in buying blocks of the soon-to-be-released stock.

CRITICAL THINKING: (1) High-technology firms tend to dominate IPO filings year after year; why do you suppose this is so? (2) Why does the volume of IPOs tend to track the ups and downs of the stock market?

IT'S YOUR BUSINESS: (1) If you had the choice between working at a company still in the pre-IPO stage, which is offering a lower salary but a share of ownership that will become shares of company stock after the IPO, or a higher paying job with no stock, what additional information would you need before you would be comfortable making a choice? (2) Choose any business that you might like to start as an entrepreneur. How would you make a compelling pitch to private equity investors to encourage them to invest in your company?

KEY TERMS TO KNOW: private equity, underwriter, prospectus

BEHIND THE SCENES

MyBizLab

VISA FUNDS ITS FUTURE WITH RECORD-SETTING IPO

If ever a company needed a few billion dollars, it was Visa in late 2007. Still operating as a privately held joint venture owned by its member banks, Visa didn't have access to the stock market as a fundraising mechanism. Archrival MasterCard was reaping the benefits of its recent IPO, generating several billion dollars in fresh capital and creating the opportunity to use stock options to recruit and reward employees. Moreover, after settling lawsuits brought against it by merchants and two other credit card companies, Visa had rung up more than $4 billion in legal liabilities. Plus, the six large banks that made up the primary ownership group within the Visa association were desperately in need of cash to help ride out the recession and the credit crunch. On top of these challenges, Visa had to keep investing in new payment-processing systems and technologies as consumers around the world continued to increase their use of conventional credit and debit cards and as promising new opportunities such as mobile commerce were coming up to speed.

An IPO could help solve all these funding dilemmas, but it would prove to be much more complicated than a normal IPO.

One of the essential steps was creating a company that could actually go public. In late 2007, Visa Inc., was spun off from the Visa association as a wholly owned subsidiary. This new firm is the company that actually filed the IPO—with the U.S. economy in the depths of the worst downturn since the Great Depression of the 1930s and the financial services industry in turmoil. One could hardly have picked a worse time to go public, as evidenced by the fact that the normal annual flow of IPOs had slowed to a trickle.

However, Visa had several factors working in its favor. First, with one of the world's best-known brand names and a half century of growth behind it, Visa didn't need to introduce itself to investors the way most companies do when pitching an IPO. Second, in investor-speak, Visa had a wide "economic moat," meaning its revenue-generating capacity was safeguarded by barriers to entry—including a powerful brand, established relationships with millions of companies worldwide, and a global transaction-processing network—that new market entrants would find hard to overcome. Third, and most important from the timing perspective, Visa isn't really a financial services company in the sense of lending money or issuing credit cards, so it wasn't exposed to the credit meltdown the way banks and credit card companies were. Although it is intertwined with the financial sector, Visa is actually more of a data processing company than a finance company.

In its prospectus, Visa indicated that it expected to net $16 or $17 billion from the IPO and intended to distribute $10 billion of that to its member institutions, use another $3 billion toward its legal liabilities, and reserve the remaining few billion for general corporate purposes. This was a staggering amount of money to generate in an IPO during the best of times and an almost unimaginable amount to generate during the worst of times.

But that is exactly what Visa did. It went public on March 19, 2008, and broke the record for the largest IPO ever by a U.S. company—over $19 billion after some optional shares were redeemed by the two lead underwriters on the giant deal, Goldman Sachs and JPMorgan Chase. As both an underwriter earning fees on the IPO and one of the cash-hungry member banks of the Visa association benefiting from the stock sale, JPMorgan Chase made over $1 billion on the deal.

In a turbulent stock market and an even rougher economy over the past several years, Visa's new stock has fared well, all things considered. By late 2011, it was up around 30 percent from its IPO price. Archrival MasterCard's stock did slightly better, and both companies were outpacing the overall stock market by a healthy margin.

Visa's growth in the coming years could be hampered by any protracted slowdown in consumer spending, because fewer purchases means fewer transactions for Visa to process. However, more transactions are shifting from cash to cards, mobile commerce is on the rise, and credit card use is only just beginning to ramp up in many areas around the world—and between its core processing business and recent acquisitions, Visa is positioned to benefit from all three trends.[21]

Critical Thinking Questions

1. How might Visa executives use scenario planning in the budgeting process?
2. Could Visa have accomplished its funding goals through short-term or long-term debt financing instead? Why or why not?
3. As Visa continues to explore growth opportunities, should it consider becoming a lender by issuing cards itself or lending money to banks that issue cards? Why or why not?

LEARN MORE ONLINE

Visit Visa's website, at www.visa.com, and locate the investors section. Has the company reported any significant financial news in the past year? Has it resolved its outstanding legal issues? What were its net income and earnings per share for the more recent fiscal year? Has company management expressed any concerns about ongoing cash flow issues?

MyBizLab

Log on to www.mybizlab.com to access study and assessment aids associated with this chapter.

KEY TERMS

accounts payable	hedging
accounts receivable	lease
bonds	leverage
budget	line of credit
capital budget	long-term financing
capital investments	operating budget
capital structure	prime interest rate
collateral	private equity
commercial paper	project budget
compensating balance	prospectus
convertible bonds	risk/return trade-off
cost of capital	secured bonds
debentures	secured loans
debt financing	short-term financing
equity financing	start-up budget
factoring	trade credit
financial control	underwriter
financial management	unsecured loans
financial plan	zero-based budgeting

TEST YOUR KNOWLEDGE

Questions for Review

1. What is the primary goal of financial management?
2. What types of investments and expenditures are typically considered in the capital budgeting process?
3. What is the difference between a secured loan and an unsecured loan?
4. What does it mean when someone refers to a company's *capital structure*?
5. How can factoring help a company manage its cash flow?

Questions for Analysis

6. Would it be wise for a young company that is growing quickly but still hasn't achieved profitability to attempt to issue bonds as a way to expand its working capital? Why or why not?
7. Why is careful management of accounts receivable and accounts payable so essential to ensuring positive cash flow?
8. How does factoring differ from short-term debt?
9. Why do lenders often refuse to finance 100 percent of the cost of a purchase, requiring borrowers to make a down payment that covers a portion (typically from 10 to 25 percent) of the purchase price? After all, a lender could potentially earn more by financing the entire purchase amount.
10. **Ethical Considerations.** Budget projections always involve a degree of judgment because managers can never predict the future with total accuracy. For instance, one manager with an optimistic view and another manager with a pessimistic view could look at the same set of facts and arrive at distinctly different conclusions about the company's financial prospects. When budgets will influence decisions made by investors or lenders, how should the people who prepare the budgets deal with the variance between optimistic and pessimistic viewpoints? On the one hand, being too pessimistic could result in lower levels of funding, which could be detrimental to employees, existing investors, existing creditors, and other financial stakeholders. On the other hand, being too optimistic could be detrimental to prospective investors or creditors. How do you find the right balance?

Questions for Application

11. The company you cofounded last year is growing rapidly and has strong prospects for an IPO in the next year or two. The additional capital that an IPO could raise would let you hire the brightest people in the industry and continue to innovate with new product research. There is one potential glitch: You and the rest of the executive team have been so focused on launching the business that you haven't paid much attention to financial control. You've had plenty of funds from venture capitalists and early sales, so working capital hasn't been a problem, but an experienced CEO in your industry recently told you that you'll never have a successful IPO unless you clean up the financial side of the house. Your cofounders say they are too busy chasing great opportunities right now, and they want to wait until right before the IPO to hire a seasoned financial executive to put things in order. What should you do and why?
12. Why might a company's board of directors decide to lease office space even though it would be more economical to purchase the property and finance it with a long-term loan?
13. You're getting ready to expand your woodworking hobby into a full-time business of building custom kitchen cabinets. To create top-quality cabinets, you know you'll need to upgrade from the consumer-grade machinery you have now to industrial-grade equipment. The new equipment will be much more expensive, but, if properly cared for, should last for decades, and you hope to be in business for at least 20 years. If the overall costs of leasing this equipment or borrowing money to buy it are roughly the same, which financing method would you choose? Why?
14. This question was intentionally excluded from this edition.

EXPAND YOUR KNOWLEDGE

Discovering Career Opportunities

People interested in entering the field of financial management can choose among a wide variety of careers with diverse responsibilities and challenges. Visit the "Financial Managers" page at www.bls.gov/oco/ocos010.htm to read more about career opportunities in financial management.

1. What are the day-to-day duties of this occupation? How would these duties contribute to the financial success of a company?
2. What skills and educational qualifications would you need to enter this occupation? How do these qualifications fit with your current plans, skills, and interests?
3. What kinds of employers hire people for this position? According to your research, does the number of employers seem to be increasing or decreasing? How do you think this trend will affect your employment possibilities if you choose this career?

Developing Your Tech Insights: Credit Scoring Software

Credit scoring software is a type of business intelligence software that measures the credit worthiness of applications for credit cards, mortgages, business loans, and other forms of credit. It has the dual objective of filtering out applications that don't meet a lender's criteria and speeding up the process for applications that do meet the criteria.

Using sophisticated mathematical models based on historical records, credit scoring software helps lenders decide which applicants to accept and how much credit to extend to each one. In addition, software with *predictive modeling* or *predictive analytics* helps predict which applicants will make the best customers (lowest risk and highest profit potential) for a given lender. Explore the credit scoring and risk assessment products offered by Fair Isaac (www.fico.com), Equifax (www.equifax.com), or another company in this industry. Choose one product. In a brief email message to your instructor, explain how this tool can help lenders make better decisions.

PRACTICE YOUR SKILLS

Sharpening Your Communication Skills

You've just been hired as the CFO of a start-up company that is a few months away from launching its first products. Unfortunately, the company is running short of cash and doesn't have enough to pay for initial manufacturing costs. Your boss, Connie Washington, is getting frantic. She has worked for several years to get to this point, and she doesn't want the company to collapse before it even starts selling products. She comes to you, asking for ideas to generate some funds—immediately. Several investors have expressed interest in helping with financing, but Washington doesn't want to surrender any control by using equity financing. She wants to start applying for loans, or even stacks of credit cards, if that's what it takes.

However, you don't think piling on debt is a wise idea at this point. The company doesn't have any revenue yet, and there's no guarantee that the new products will be successful. You'd rather share the risk with some equity investors, even if doing so means that Washington will have to give up some of her managerial authority. Draft a short memo to her, explaining why you think equity financing is a better option at this stage (make up any details you need).

Building Your Team Skills

You and your team are going to build an operating expense budget worksheet for a neighborhood Domino's Pizza franchise. Begin by brainstorming a list of expenses that are typical of a franchise delivery restaurant. One way to do so is to think about the company's process—from making the pizza to delivering it. List the types of expenses and then group your list into categories such as delivery, marketing, manufacturing, financing, and so on. Leave the budget dollar amounts blank. Finally, develop a list of capital investments your company will make over the next three to five years. Compare your budget worksheets to those of the other teams in your class. Which operating and capital expenses did other teams have that your team didn't? Which expenses did your team have that other teams didn't? Did all the teams categorize the expenses in a similar manner?

Developing Your Research Skills

Choose a recent article from a business journal or newspaper (print or online editions) that discusses the financing arrangements or strategies of a particular company.

1. What form of financing did the company choose? Does the article indicate why the company selected this form of financing?
2. Who provided the financing for the company? Was this arrangement considered unusual, or was it routine?
3. What does the company intend to do with the arranged financing—purchase equipment or other assets, finance a construction project, finance growth and expansion, or do something else?

REFERENCES

1. Michael Kon, "Visa Is Set to Benefit from the Growth in Electronic Payments," Morningstar, 17 August 2011, www.morningstar.com; "Visa Inc.," Google Finance, accessed 11 September 2011, www.google.com/finance; "Visa Inc. Posts Strong Fiscal Third Quarter 2011 Earnings Results and Authorizes New $1 Billion Share Repurchase Program," press release, 27 July 2011, http://investor.visa.com; *Visa Inc. Annual Report 2010*, Visa website, accessed 11 September 2011, http://investor.visa.com; *Visa Inc. Annual Report 2008*, Visa website, accessed 2 September 2009, www.visa.com; "Visa Inc, Corporate Overview," Visa website, accessed 2 September 2009, www.visa.com; Katie Benner, "Visa's Record IPO Rings up 28% Gain," *Fortune*, 19 March 2008, http://money.cnn.com; Tami Luhby, "JPMorgan Chase makes $1B-plus on Visa IPO," CNNMoney.com, 21 March 2008, http://money.cnn.com; M.J. Stephey, "A Brief History of: Credit Cards," *Time*, 23 April 2009, www.time.com. "Form S-1 Registration Statement, Visa Inc." U.S. Securities and Exchange Commission website, accessed 2 September 2009, www.sec.gov; *Visa Inc.*, Datamonitor, 9 March 2009.
2. Emily Thornton and Frederick Jespersen, "Corporate Cash: Big Stockpiles for Tough Times," *BusinessWeek*, 5 March 2009, 11.
3. David McCann, "For Intel, the Future Is Now," *CFO*, 25 August 2009, www.cfo.com.
4. Janice DiPietro, "Protecting Liquidity in Tough Times," *Financial Executive*, June 2009, 61.
5. Mahmut Akten, Massimo Giordano, and Mari A. Scheiffele, "Just-in-Time Budgeting for a Volatile Economy," *McKinsey Quarterly*, 2009, Issue 3, 115–121.
6. James Manyika, "Google's CFO on Growth, Capital Structure, and Leadership," *McKinsey Quarterly*, August 2011, www.mckinseyquarterly.com;
7. Martin Labbe, "Budgeting the Proper Way," *Fleet Owner*, December 2008, 39.
8. Akten, et al., "Just-in-Time Budgeting for a Volatile Economy."

9. "Banks Cut Credit for 58M Card Holders in 1 Year," *New York Times*, 20 August 2009, www.nytimes.com.
10. "How to Create a Smart Credit Policy," *Inc.*, March 2009, 37–40.
11. "Turn Your Receivables into Quick Cash," CNNMoney.com, 21 November 2008, http://money.cnn.com/smallbusiness; David Worrell, "Taking the Sting out of Receivables," Investopedia.com, accessed 28 August 2009, www.investopedia.com.
12. Maureen Farrell, "The Check Is in the Mail," *Forbes*, 11 May 2009, 56–57; "Invoice Factoring Basics," Invoice Factoring Group, accessed 28 August 2009, http://factoring.qlfs.com; "Turn Your Receivables into Quick Cash"; Worrell, "Taking the Sting out of Receivables."
13. "Demand for Factoring High," *The Secured Lender*, April 2009, 26–29.
14. "How It Works," The Receivables Exchange, accessed 11 September 2011, www.receivablesxchange.com.
15. "Bank-Term Loans," *Entrepreneur*, accessed 29 August 2009, www.entrepreneur.com.
16. "Small Business Administration (SBA) Loans," U.S. Bank website, accessed 29 August 2009, www.usbank.com.
17. "Bank-Term Loans"; "Financing for Your Future—The Five C's of Credit," PNC website, accessed 29 August 2009, www.pnc.com.
18. Ben Steverman, "IPOs: Back from the Dead?" *BusinessWeek*, 9 March 2008, 12.
19. Marguerite Rigoglioso, "The Risky Business of Going Public," *Stanford GSB News*, March 2003, www.gsb.stanford.edu.
20. "The Corporate Handbook Series: Going Public," U.S. Securities and Exchange Commission website, accessed 29 August 2009, www.sec.gov; Matt H. Evans, "Excellence in Financial Management: Course 13: Going Public," Excellence in Financial Management website, accessed 29 August 2009, www.exinfm.com.
21. See note 1.

GLOSSARY

accounts payable Amounts that a firm currently owes to other parties

accounts receivable Amounts that are currently owed to a firm

bonds A method of funding in which the issuer borrows from an investor and provides a written promise to make regular interest payments and repay the borrowed amount in the future

budget A planning and control tool that reflects expected revenues, operating expenses, and cash receipts and outlays

capital budget A budget that outlines expenditures for real estate, new facilities, major equipment, and other capital investments

capital investments Money paid to acquire something of permanent value in a business

capital structure A firm's mix of debt and equity financing

collateral A tangible asset a lender can claim if a borrower defaults on a loan

commercial paper Short-term *promissory notes*, or contractual agreements, to repay a borrowed amount by a specified time with a specified interest rate

compensating balance The portion of an unsecured loan that is kept on deposit at a lending institution to protect the lender and increase the lender's return

convertible bonds Corporate bonds that can be exchanged at the owner's discretion into common stock of the issuing company

cost of capital The average rate of interest a firm pays on its combination of debt and equity

debentures Corporate bonds backed only by the reputation of the issuer

debt financing Arranging funding by borrowing money

equity financing Arranging funding by selling ownership shares in the company, publicly or privately

factoring Obtaining funding by selling accounts receivable

financial control The process of analyzing and adjusting the basic financial plan to correct for deviations from forecasted events

financial management Planning for a firm's money needs and managing the allocation and spending of funds

financial plan A document that outlines the funds needed for a certain period of time, along with the sources and intended uses of those funds

hedging Protecting against cost increases with contracts that allow a company to buy supplies in the future at designated prices

lease An agreement to use an asset in exchange for regular payment; similar to renting

leverage The technique of increasing the rate of return on an investment by financing it with borrowed funds

line of credit An arrangement in which a financial institution makes money available for use at any time after the loan has been approved

long-term financing Financing used to cover long-term expenses such as assets (generally repaid over a period of more than one year)

operating budget Also known as the *master budget*, a budget that identifies all sources of revenue and coordinates the spending of those funds throughout the coming year

prime interest rate The lowest rate of interest that banks charge for short-term loans to their most creditworthy customers

private equity Ownership assets that aren't publicly traded; includes venture capital

project budget A budget that identifies the costs needed to accomplish a particular project

prospectus An SEC-required document that discloses required information about the company, its finances, and its plans for using the money it hopes to raise

risk/return trade-off The balance of potential risks against potential rewards

secured bonds Bonds backed by specific assets that will be given to bondholders if the borrowed amount is not repaid

secured loans Loans backed up with assets that the lender can claim in case of default, such as a piece of property

short-term financing Financing used to cover current expenses (generally repaid within a year)

start-up budget A budget that identifies the money a new company will need to spend to launch operations

trade credit Credit obtained by a purchaser directly from a supplier

underwriter A specialized type of bank that buys the shares from the company preparing an IPO and sells them to investors

unsecured loans Loans that require a good credit rating but no collateral

zero-based budgeting A budgeting approach in which each department starts from zero every year and must justify every item in the budget, rather than simply adjusting the previous year's budget amounts

LEARNING OBJECTIVES   After studying this chapter, you will be able to

1 Discuss what it means to practice good business ethics and highlight three factors that influence ethical decision making

2 Define *corporate social responsibility (CSR)* and explain the difference between philanthropy and strategic CSR

3 Distinguish among the four perspectives on corporate social responsibility

4 Discuss the role of business in protecting the natural environment and define *sustainable development*

5 Identify four fundamental consumer rights and the responsibility of business to respect them

6 Explain the responsibilities businesses have toward their employees

MyBizLab

Where you see MyBizLab in this chapter, go to www.mybizlab.com for additional activities on the topic being discussed.

BEHIND THE SCENES   NIKE'S GLOBAL PRESENCE PUTS IT ON THE FRONT LINES OF CORPORATE SOCIAL RESPONSIBILITY

KRISTOPHER SKINNER/KRTC/Newscom

Nike has taken a leadership role in improving workplace conditions and environmental stewardship in factories around the globe.

www.nike.com

Imagine yourself in this dilemma. Much of the appeal of your products is based on their association with famous athletes, whose fame allows them to charge considerable sums for their endorsement of your products. Add this to your costs of doing business. You're in a ferociously competitive, trend-driven business, where you can drop off the public radar practically overnight if you don't invest heavily in constant promotion. Add this to your costs of doing business. Many of your products are technically innovative, which requires ongoing research and development. Add this to your costs of doing business. Finally, consumers want to be able to buy your products from thousands of retail outlets, at a moment's notice, wherever they like to shop, so you must keep a vast distribution network supplied with inventory. Add this to your costs of doing business.

Add up all these costs, and you still haven't paid for somebody to actually *make* your products. You could make them in the United States, with its comparatively high labor costs, which would force you to raise prices in order to sustain the profit margin your investors expect in return for the money they have entrusted to you. Of course, raise them too high, and consumers will decide that, as cool as your products are, they can get a better deal from your competitors.

Or you could move production to a country with significantly lower labor costs, taking the pressure off your prices and profit margins and allowing you to maintain high levels of investments in other areas. Looks great on paper, but you know that every decision in business involves trade-offs. Moving production overseas and into the hands of other companies entails a significant loss of control over the manufacturing process, materials sourcing, and working conditions.

You can measure financial costs and product quality, providing clear feedback on some important performance parameters. But what about the way your production partners conduct business? Do they conduct themselves in a manner that is consistent with your values and your public image? Do they treat workers humanely? Do they steward shared natural resources in a responsible manner? Do they minimize negative impacts on their communities?

You don't have direct control over how these companies perform, and you don't always know what they're up to, but you know one thing for certain: People are going to hold you accountable for the performance and behavior of these subcontractors, even if they are independent companies operating in other countries. Big companies make big targets, and you've been the focus of a number of campaigns by advocacy groups and other nongovernmental organizations.

Welcome to a day in the life of Mark Parker, president and CEO of Nike, the athletic footwear and apparel giant based in Beaverton, Oregon. If you were in Parker's Nikes, how would you balance the competing demands of investors, employees, retailers, advocacy groups, and business partners? How would you keep Nike on its path of strong growth while also being a responsible corporate citizen in the 160 countries where it does business?[1]

INTRODUCTION

Like Nike's Mark Parker (profiled in the chapter-opening Behind the Scenes), managers in every industry today must balance the demands of running a profitable business with the expectations of running a socially responsible company. As a future business leader, you will face some of the challenges discussed in this chapter, and your choices won't always be easy. You may struggle to find ethical clarity in some situations, to even understand what your choices are and how each option might affect your company's various stakeholders. You may need to muster the courage to stand up to colleagues, bosses, or customers if you think ethical principles are being violated. Fortunately, by having a good understanding of what constitutes ethical behavior and what society expects from business today, you'll be better prepared to make these tough choices. This chapter explores the basic ideas of business ethics and corporate social responsibility and then takes a closer look at business's responsibility toward the natural environment, consumers, and employees.

1 LEARNING OBJECTIVE

Discuss what it means to practice good business ethics, and highlight three factors that influence ethical decision making.

Ethics in Contemporary Business

Assessing the ethics of contemporary business is no simple matter, partly because of disagreement over what constitutes ethical behavior and partly because the behavior of individual companies runs the gamut from positive to neutral to negative. However, it is safe to say that there is significant concern about the ethics of current (and future) business leaders. Harvard Business School professor Rakesh Khurana probably speaks for many when he says, "One way of looking at the problem with American business today is that it has succeeded in assuming many of the appearances and privileges of professionalism, while evading the attendant constraints and responsibilities."[2] By and large, the general public seems to agree (see Exhibit 1).

The news is not all bad, of course. The vast majority of businesses are run by ethical managers and staffed by ethical employees whose positive contributions to their communities are unfortunately overshadowed at times by headline-grabbing scandals. Companies around the world help their communities in countless ways, from sponsoring youth sports teams to raising millions of dollars to build hospitals.

Moreover, even when companies are simply engaged in the normal course of business—and do so ethically—they contribute to society by making useful products, providing employment, and paying taxes. Business catches a lot of flak these days, some of it deserved, but overall, its contributions to the health, happiness, and well-being of society are beyond measure.

EXHIBIT 1	Public Perceptions of Business Ethics

One can argue whether public perceptions of business ethics accurately reflect the behavior of the entire community of business professionals or simply the behavior of businesses and individuals that make headlines. However, there is no argument on this point: The general public doesn't think too highly of business. This graph shows the percentage of Americans who rate the honesty and ethics of a particular profession as either "high" or "very high." Several business professions are shown, with several nonbusiness professions for comparison.

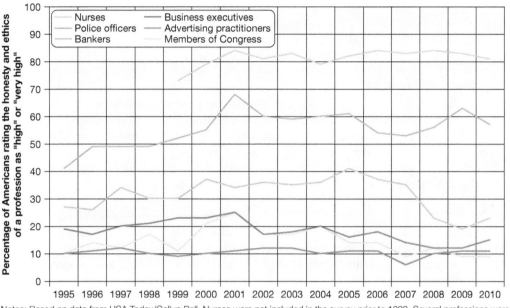

Notes: Based on data from USA Today/Gallup Poll. Nurses were not included in the survey prior to 1999. Several professions were asked about in two separate polls in 2002; for those professions, the 2002 figure shown in the graph is the average of the two scores for that year.
Source: Data from "USA Today/Gallup Poll, November Wave 1, Final Topline, 19–21 November 2010," www.gallup.com.

WHAT IS ETHICAL BEHAVIOR?

Ethics are the principles and standards of moral behavior that are accepted by society as right versus wrong. Practicing good business ethics involves, at a minimum, competing fairly and honestly, communicating truthfully, being transparent, and not causing harm to others:

ethics The rules or standards governing the conduct of a person or group

- **Competing fairly and honestly.** Businesses are expected to compete fairly and honestly and to not knowingly deceive, intimidate, or misrepresent themselves to customers, competitors, clients, employees, or the media.
- **Communicating truthfully.** Communicating truthfully is a simple enough concept: Tell the truth, the whole truth, and nothing but the truth. However, matters sometimes aren't so clear. For instance, if you plan to introduce an improved version of a product next year, do you have an obligation to tell customers who are buying the existing product this year? Suppose you do tell them, and so many decide to delay their purchases that you end up with a cash flow problem that forces you to lay off several employees. Would that be fair for customers but unfair for your employees?
- **Being transparent.** Business communication ethics often involve the question of **transparency**, which can be defined as "the degree to which information flows freely within an organization, among managers and employees, and outward to stakeholders."[3] For example, Facebook found itself the subject of criticism for a behind-the-scenes attempt to generate public outrage regarding alleged privacy violations by Google. After the company's use of a public relations agency to encourage bloggers and the news media to write critical stories about Google was exposed, Facebook admitted, "The issues are serious and we should have presented them in a serious and transparent way."[4]
- **Not causing harm to others.** All businesses have the capacity to cause harm to employees, customers, other companies, their communities, and investors. Problems can start when managers make decisions that put their personal interests above those of other stakeholders, underestimate the risks of failure, or neglect to consider potential

transparency The degree to which affected parties can observe relevant aspects of transactions or decisions

insider trading The use of unpublicized information that an individual gains from the course of his or her job to benefit from fluctuations in the stock market

effects on other people and organizations. For example, **insider trading**, in which company insiders use confidential information to gain an advantage in stock market trading, harms other investors. (Insider trading is illegal, in addition to being unethical.) Of course, harm can also result even when managers have acted ethically—but they are still responsible for these negative outcomes.

FACTORS INFLUENCING ETHICAL BEHAVIOR

Of the many factors that influence ethical behavior, three warrant particular attention: cultural differences, knowledge, and organizational behavior.

Cultural Differences

Globalization exposes businesspeople to a variety of cultures and business practices. What does it mean for a business to do the right thing in Thailand? In Nigeria? In Norway? What may be considered unethical in one culture could be an accepted practice in another. Managers may need to consider a wide range of issues, including acceptable working conditions, minimum wage levels, product safety issues, and environmental protection. (See the Nike Behind the Scenes wrap-up for more on this important topic.)

Knowledge

As a general rule, the more you know and the better you understand a situation, the better your chances of making an ethical decision. In the churn of daily business, though, it's easy to shut your eyes and ears to potential problems. However, as a business leader, you have the responsibility not only to pay attention but to actively seek out information regarding potential ethical issues. Ignorance is never an acceptable defense in the eyes of the law, and it shouldn't be in questions of ethics, either.

Organizational Behavior

Companies with strong ethical practices create cultures that reward good behavior—and don't intentionally or unintentionally reward bad behavior.[5] At United Technologies (www .utc.com), a diversified manufacturer based in Hartford, Connecticut, ethical behavior starts at the top; executives are responsible for meeting clearly defined ethical standards, and their annual compensation is tied to how well they perform.[6] To help avoid ethical breaches, many companies develop programs to improve ethical conduct, typically combine training, communication, and a **code of ethics** that defines the values and principles that should be used to guide decisions (see Exhibit 2 for an example).

code of ethics A written statement that sets forth the principles that guide an organization's decisions

Employees who observe unethical or illegal behavior within their companies and are unable to resolve the problems through normal channels may have no choice but to resort to **whistle-blowing**—expressing their concerns internally through formal reporting mechanisms or externally to the news media or government regulators. However, the decision to "blow the whistle" on one's own employer is rarely easy or without consequences. More than 80 percent of whistle-blowers in one survey said they were punished in some way for coming forward with their concerns.[7] In addition, the laws governing whistle-blowing are a complicated web of federal and state legislation that can be difficult for employees and employers to navigate through.[8]

whistle-blowing The disclosure of information by a company insider that exposes illegal or unethical behavior by others within the organization

Although whistle-blowing is sometimes characterized as "ratting on" colleagues or managers, it has an essential function. According to international business expert Alex MacBeath, "Often whistle-blowing can be the only way that information about issues such as rule breaking, criminal activity, cover-ups, and fraud can be brought to management's attention before serious damage is suffered."[9]

ETHICAL DECISION MAKING

When the question of what is right and what is wrong is clear, ethical decisions are easy to make: You simply choose to do the right thing. (At least making the decision is simple; *implementing* the decision may be another story.) If you choose the wrong course, such as cheating on your taxes or stealing from your employer, you commit what is known as an **ethical lapse**. The choices were clear, and you made the wrong one.

ethical lapse A situation in which an individual or a group makes a decision that is morally wrong, illegal, or unethical

AT&T's Code of Ethics (excerpts)

AT&T's Code of Ethics addresses nine areas of conduct and decision making. Selected guidelines for each of the nine principles are shown here; you can see the complete code at www.att.com (look in the "Investor Relations" section).

Principle	Selected Guidelines
I. Honest and Ethical Conduct	Each director, officer and employee owes a duty to the Company to act with integrity. Integrity requires, among other things, being honest and ethical.
II. Conflicts of Interest	A "conflict of interest" arises when an individual's personal interest interferes or appears to interfere with the interests of the Company. A conflict of interest can arise when a director, officer or employee takes actions or has personal interests that may make it difficult to perform his or her Company work objectively and effectively.
III. Disclosure	Each director, officer or employee . . . must not knowingly misrepresent, or cause others to misrepresent, facts about the Company to others, whether within or outside the Company, including to the Company's independent auditors, governmental regulators and self-regulatory organizations.
IV. Compliance	It is the Company's policy to comply with all applicable laws, rules and regulations. It is the personal responsibility of each employee, officer and director to adhere to the standards and restrictions imposed by those laws, rules and regulations in the performance of their duties for the Company, including those relating to accounting and auditing matters and insider trading.
V. Reporting and Accountability	Each director, officer or employee must: • Notify the appropriate Code of Ethics contact promptly of any existing or potential violation of this Code. • Not retaliate against any other director, officer or employee for reports of potential violations that are made in good faith.
VI. Corporate Opportunities	Employees, officers and directors are prohibited from taking (or directing to a third party) a business opportunity that is discovered through the use of corporate property, information or position, unless the Company has already been offered the opportunity and turned it down.
VII. Confidentiality	Employees, officers and directors must maintain the confidentiality of all information so entrusted to them, except when disclosure is authorized or legally mandated.
VIII. Fair Dealing	Each employee, officer and director should endeavor to deal fairly with the Company's customers, service providers, suppliers, competitors and employees.
IX. Protection and Proper Use of Company Assets	All employees, officers and directors should protect the Company's assets and ensure their efficient use. All Company assets should be used only for legitimate business purposes.

Source: Adapted from "AT&T Inc. Code of Ethics," AT&T website, accessed 2 August 2011, www.att.com.

However, you will encounter situations in which choices are not so clear. An **ethical dilemma** is a situation in which you must choose between conflicting but arguably valid options, or even situations in which all your options are unpleasant. As Exhibit 3 on the next page suggests, stakeholders' needs often conflict, requiring managers to make tough decisions about resource allocation.

ethical dilemma A situation in which more than one side of an issue can be supported with valid arguments

Consider the following points to help find the right answer whenever you face with an ethical dilemma:

• Make sure you frame the situation accurately, taking into account all relevant issues and questions.
• Identify all parties who might be affected by your decision, and consider the rights of everyone involved.
• Be as objective as possible. Make sure you're not making a decision just to protect your own emotions, and don't automatically assume you're viewing a situation fairly and objectively.
• Don't assume that other people think the way you do. The time-honored "Golden Rule" of treating others the way you want to be treated can cause problems when others don't *want* to be treated the same way you do.
• Watch out for **conflicts of interest**, situations in which competing loyalties can lead to ethical lapses. For instance, if you are in charge of selecting an advertising agency to handle your company's next campaign, you would have an obvious conflict of interest if your husband or wife worked for one of the agencies under consideration.

conflict of interest A situation in which competing loyalties can lead to ethical lapses, such as when a business decision may be influenced by the potential for personal gain

Exhibit 4 identifies six well-known approaches to resolving ethical dilemmas.

EXHIBIT 3	Stakeholders' Rights: A Difficult Balancing Act

Balancing the individual needs and interests of a company's stakeholders is one of management's most difficult tasks. Consider how these three examples could affect each of these five stakeholder groups in a different way. (Note that some people may fall into multiple groups. Employees, for example, are taxpayers and members of the local community, and they may also be shareholders. Also, these scenarios and outcomes offer a simplified view of what is likely to happen in each case, but they illustrate the mixed effects that can result from management decisions.)

Decision	Shareholders (entrust money to the company in anticipation of a positive return on their investment)	Employees (devote time, energy, and creativity to the company's success)	Customers (expect to receive quality products and maximum value for prices paid)	Local Community (can be affected both positively and negatively by the company's presence and actions)	Taxpayers (affected indirectly by the amount of tax revenue that local, state, and federal governments get from the company)
Company decides to *offshore* some of its production to another country with lower labor costs; lays off significant number of employees	⬆ Stand to benefit from lower production costs, which could increase sales, profits, or both, probably leading to increases in share price	⬇ Some employees lose their jobs; morale likely to suffer among those who keep theirs	⬆ Benefit from lower prices	⬇ Suffers from loss of spendable income in the local economy and taxes paid to local government; exodus of employees can drive down home values	⬇⬆ Might be hurt or helped by the move, depending on whether loss of income tax paid by U.S. employees is offset by increased income tax paid by the company, for example
Company institutes a generous pay and benefits increase to improve employee morale	⬇⬆ Might be hurt in the short term as the stock market punishes the company for increasing its cost structure and diverting funds away from development; could help over the long term if the moves boost employee productivity	⬆ Benefit from higher pay and more valuable benefits	⬇⬆ Could be hurt by higher prices if prices are raised to cover the added costs; could benefit from higher levels of employee satisfaction, leading to improved customer service	⬆ Benefits from more spendable income in the local economy and taxes paid to local government; better employee benefits could also mean less drain on community resources such as health clinics	⬆ Benefit from more money paid into government treasuries through higher income taxes
Company installs a multimillion-dollar waste water recirculation system that surpasses regulatory requirements; system will pay for itself in lower water bills, but not for 10 years	⬇⬆ Probably hurt as stock market punishes an investment with no immediate payback; increased goodwill and long-term cost savings help in years ahead	⬇⬆ Probably hurt in the short term as less money is available for raises and benefits; likely to benefit in the long term as the costs are recovered	⬇ Hurt as higher costs are passed along as higher prices	⬆ Helped by the company's efforts to conserve a shared natural resource	⬇ Hurt as the company writes off the cost of the system, thereby lowering the taxes it pays to the government

EXHIBIT 4	Approaches to Resolving Ethical Dilemmas

These approaches can help you resolve ethical dilemmas you may face on the job. Be aware that in some situations, different approaches can lead to different ethical conclusions.

Approach	Summary
Justice	Treat people equally or at least fairly in a way that makes rational and moral sense
Utilitarianism	Choose the option that delivers the most good for the most people (or protects the most people from a negative outcome)
Individual rights	To the greatest possible extent, respect the rights of all individuals, particularly their right to control their own destinies
Individual responsibilities	Focus on the ethical duties of the individuals involved in the situation
The common good	Emphasize qualities and conditions that benefit the community as a whole, such as peace and public safety
Virtue	Emphasize desirable character traits such as integrity and compassion

Sources: Adapted from Manuel Velasquez, Claire Andre, Thomas Shanks, and Michael J. Meyer, "Thinking Ethically: A Framework for Moral Decision Making," Markkula Center for Applied Ethics, Santa Clara University, accessed 3 June 2009, www.scu.edu; Ben Rogers, "John Rawls," *The Guardian*, 27 November 2002, www.guardian.co.uk; Irene Van Staveren, "Beyond Utilitarianism and Deontology: Ethics in Economics," *Review of Political Economy*, January 2007, 21–35.

✔ Checkpoint

LEARNING OBJECTIVE 1: Discuss what it means to practice good business ethics, and highlight three factors that influence ethical decision making.

SUMMARY: Three essential components of good business ethics are competing fairly and honestly, communicating truthfully, and not causing harm to others. Three major influences on ethical decision making are culture, knowledge, and organizational culture. When facing an ethical dilemma, you can often find clarity by starting with universal standards of justice, considering the rights of everyone involved, being as objective as possible, not assuming that other people think the way you do, and avoiding conflicts of interest.

CRITICAL THINKING: (1) If you go to work tomorrow morning and your boss asks you to do something you consider unethical, what factors will you take into consideration before responding? (2) How can you balance the business need to inspire employees to compete aggressively with the moral need to avoid competing unethically?

IT'S YOUR BUSINESS: (1) In your current job (or any previous job you've held), in what ways does your employer contribute to society? (2) Have you ever encountered an ethical dilemma in your work? If so, how did you resolve it?

KEY TERMS TO KNOW: ethics, transparency, insider trading, code of ethics, whistle-blowing, ethical lapse, ethical dilemma, conflicts of interest

Corporate Social Responsibility

2 LEARNING OBJECTIVE

Corporate social responsibility (CSR) is the notion that business has obligations to society beyond the pursuit of profits. There is a widespread assumption these days that CSR is both a moral imperative for business and a good thing for society, but the issues aren't quite as clear as they might seem at first glance.

Define *corporate social responsibility (CSR),* and explain the difference between philanthropy and strategic CSR.

corporate social responsibility (CSR) The idea that business has obligations to society beyond the pursuit of profits

THE RELATIONSHIP BETWEEN BUSINESS AND SOCIETY

What does business owe society, and what does society owe business? Any attempt to understand and shape this relationship needs to consider four essential truths:

- Consumers in contemporary societies enjoy and expect a wide range of benefits, from education and health care to credit and products that are safe to use. Most of these benefits share an important characteristic: They require money.

321

- Profit-seeking companies are the economic engine that powers modern society; they generate the vast majority of the money in a nation's economy, either directly (through their own taxes and purchases) or indirectly (through the taxes and purchases made by the employees they support).
- Much of what we consider when assessing a society's standard of living involves goods and services created by profit-seeking companies.
- Conversely, companies cannot hope to operate profitably without the many benefits provided by a stable, functioning society: talented and healthy employees, a legal framework in which to pursue commerce, a dependable transportation infrastructure, opportunities to raise money, and customers with the ability to pay for goods and services, to name just some of them.

Business and society clearly need each other—and each needs the other to be healthy and successful.

PHILANTHROPY VERSUS STRATEGIC CSR

philanthropy The donation of money, time, goods, or services to charitable, humanitarian, or educational institutions

Companies that engage in CSR activities can choose between two courses of action: general philanthropy or strategic CSR. **Philanthropy** involves donating money, employee time, or other resources to various causes without regard for any direct business benefits for the company. For instance, a company might support the arts in its hometown in the interest of enhancing the city's cultural richness. In addition to free products, employee time, use of company facilities, and other non-cash contributions, U.S. companies donate billions of dollars to charity every year.[10]

strategic CSR Social contributions that are directly aligned with a company's overall business strategy

In contrast to generic philanthropy, **strategic CSR** involves social contributions that are directly aligned with a company's overall business strategy. In other words, the company helps itself and society at the same time. This approach can be followed in a variety of ways. A company can help develop the workforce by supporting job training efforts, for example. A company can also help develop markets for its goods and services, as the British firm Thames Water did by assisting groups trying to improve water supplies in Africa.[11] And a company can make choices that address social concerns while giving it a competitive advantage. As you can read in the "Improving Your Tech Insights" activity at the end of the chapter, IBM and Microsoft are among the many companies that invest in *assistive technologies* that help people with disabilities while expanding market opportunities and access to employee talent.

Strategic CSR makes more sense than general philanthropy or an antagonistic business-versus-society mindset, for several reasons. First, because business and society are mutually dependent, choices that weaken one or the other will ultimately weaken both. Second, investments that benefit the company are more likely to be sustained over time. Third, making sizable investments in a few strategically focused areas will yield greater benefits to society than will spreading smaller amounts of money around through generic philanthropy.[12] Thames Water CEO Bill Alexander emphasizes, "Philanthropy won't be enough. To achieve real scale we need a new business model."[13]

Exactly how much can or should businesses contribute to social concerns? This is a difficult decision because all companies have limited resources that must be allocated to a number of goals, such as upgrading facilities and equipment, developing new products, marketing existing products, and rewarding employee efforts, in addition to contributing to social causes.

✓ **Checkpoint**

LEARNING OBJECTIVE 2: Define *corporate social responsibility (CSR),* **and explain the difference between philanthropy and strategic CSR.**

SUMMARY: Corporate social responsibility (CSR) is the notion that business has obligations to society beyond the pursuit of profits. However, there is no general agreement over what those responsibilities are or which elements of society should determine those obligations or benefit from them. Philanthropy involves donating time, money, or other resources, without regard for any direct business benefits. In contrast, strategic CSR involves contributions that are aligned with the company's business needs and strategies.

CRITICAL THINKING: (1) Given that "society" is not an organized entity, how can society decide what the responsibilities of business are in a CSR context? (2) Is philanthropy morally superior to strategic CSR? Why or why not?

IT'S YOUR BUSINESS: (1) Have a company's philanthropic or CSR efforts ever influenced your purchasing behavior? (2) Have you ever benefited personally from a company's philanthropic or CSR efforts?

KEY TERMS TO KNOW: corporate social responsibility (CSR), philanthropy, strategic CSR

Perspectives on Corporate Social Responsibility

3 **LEARNING OBJECTIVE**

Distinguish among the four perspectives on corporate social responsibility.

To encourage ethical behavior and promote a mutually beneficial relationship between business and society, it is clearly necessary to establish expectations about how businesses should conduct themselves. However, both business and society are still grappling with exactly what those expectations should be. "Social responsibility" certainly sounds admirable, but it's not always clear which segments of society this involves or what those responsibilities are.[14] Approaches to CSR can be roughly categorized into four perspectives (see Exhibit 5), from minimalist through proactive.

EXHIBIT 5	Perspectives on Corporate Social Responsibility

The perspectives on CSR can be roughly divided into four categories, from minimalist to proactive. Companies that engage in CSR can pursue either *generic philanthropy* or *strategic CSR*.

Response: Philanthropy	Perspective (Motivation to Act)	Response: Strategic CSR
	Minimalist Companies do not have social responsibilities beyond earning money and obeying the law.	
Giving money to causes unrelated to the company's lines of business	**Cynical** Companies use CSR as a marketing ploy to distract attention from their self-centered behavior.	
Giving money to causes unrelated to the company's lines of business	**Defensive** Companies engage in CSR only after being shamed or forced into it.	
Giving money to causes unrelated to the company's lines of business	**Proactive** Companies have a responsibility to help society beyond simply paying taxes and obeying the law.	Investing in areas that are aligned with the company's business mission

MINIMALIST CSR

According to what might be termed the *minimalist* view, the only social responsibility of business is to pay taxes and obey the law. In a 1970 article that is still widely discussed today, Nobel Prize–winning economist Milton Friedman articulated this view by saying, "There is only one social responsibility of business: to use its resources and engage in activities designed to increase its profits so long as it stays within the rules of the game, which is to say, engages in open and free competition without deception or fraud."[15]

This view might seem selfish and even antisocial, but it raises a couple of important questions. First, any business that operates ethically and legally provides society with beneficial goods and services at fair prices. One can argue that doing so fulfills a company's primary obligation to society.

Second—and this is a vital point to consider even if you reject the minimalist view—should businesses be in the business of making social policy and spending the public's money? Proponents of the minimalist view claim that this is actually what happens when companies make tax-deductible contributions to social causes. For example, assume that in response to pressure from activists, a company makes a sizable contribution that nets it a $1 million tax break. That's $1 million taken out of the public treasury, where voters and their elected representatives can control how money is spent, and put it into whatever social cause the company chooses to support. In effect, the corporation and the activists are spending the public's money, and the public has no say in how it is spent. Would it be better for society if companies paid full taxes and let the people (through their elected representatives) decide how their tax dollars are put to work?

DEFENSIVE CSR

nongovernmental organizations (NGOs) Nonprofit groups that provide charitable services or promote social and environmental causes

Many companies today face pressure from a variety of activists and **nongovernmental organizations (NGOs)**, nonprofit groups that provide charitable services or promote causes, from workers' rights to environmental protection. One possible response to this pressure is to engage in CSR activities as a way to avoid further criticism. In other words, the company may take positive steps to address a particular issue only because it has been embarrassed into action by negative publicity.

Note that companies can engage in proactive CSR (see below) and still receive criticism from advocacy groups. A company and an NGO might disagree about responsibilities or outcomes, or in some cases an NGO might target a company for a problem that the company has already been working on. In other words, don't immediately conclude that a company is simply being defensive when it engages in CSR while in the glare of public criticism. (For an example, see the Nike Behind the Scenes wrap-up at the end of the chapter.)

CYNICAL CSR

One possible approach to CSR is purely cynical, in which a company accused of irresponsible behavior promotes itself as being socially responsible without making substantial improvements in its business practices. For example, environmental activists use the term *greenwash* (a combination of *green* and *whitewash*, a term that suggests covering something up) as a label for publicity efforts that present companies as being environmentally friendly when their actions speak otherwise. Ironically, some of the most ardent antibusiness activists and the staunchly probusiness advocates of the minimalist view tend to agree on one point: Many CSR efforts are disingenuous. Thirty-five years after his provocative article, Friedman said he believed that "most of the claims of social responsibility are pure public relations."[16]

REAL-TIME UPDATES
Learn More by Reading This Article

Taking the junk out of junk food

Learn how PepsiCo's nutritional scientists are working to create healthy—but still tasty—versions of soft drinks, potato chips, and other products that consumers can't seem to stop eating. Go to http://real-timeupdates.com/bia6 and click on Learn More. If you are using MyBizLab, you can access Real-Time Updates within the chapter or under Student Study Tools.

PROACTIVE CSR

In the fourth approach, proactive CSR, company leaders believe they have responsibilities beyond making a profit, and they back up their beliefs and proclamations with actions taken on their own initiative. Laurie Erickson is the founder and CEO of The Finest Accessories, a North Bend, Washington, company that markets handmade barrettes and other hair accessories to high-end department stores. After a customer asked Erickson if she sold any products for women who had lost their hair to chemotherapy, Erickson not only created a fashionable scarf that fit the bill but also launched a program of offering a free scarf to any cancer patient who asks for one. The company has now given away thousands of scarves, each accompanied with a get-well card signed by every employee in the company.[17]

RESOLVING THE CSR DILEMMA

So what's the right answer? Of the four perspectives on CSR, we can instantly eliminate the cynical approach simply because it is dishonest and therefore unethical. Beyond that, the debate is less clear, but the opinions are certainly strong. Some proponents of the minimalist view equate CSR with *collectivism*, a term that suggests socialism and even communism. Some consider CSR demands from activist groups and other outsiders to be little more than extortion.[18] Professor Alexei Marcoux of Loyola University in Chicago says that CSR is "fundamentally antagonistic to capitalist enterprise."[19] At the other extreme, some critics of contemporary business seem convinced that corporations can never be trusted and that every CSR initiative is a cynical publicity stunt.

A two-tiered approach to CSR can yield a practical, ethical answer to this complex dilemma. At the first tier, companies must take responsibility for the consequences of their actions and limit the negative impact of their operations. This approach can be summarized as "do no harm," and it is not a matter of choice. Just as a society has a right to expect certain behavior from all citizens, it has a right to expect a basic level of responsible behavior from all businesses, including minimizing pollution and waste, minimizing the depletion of shared natural resources, being honest with all stakeholders, offering real value in exchange for prices asked, and avoiding exploitation of employees, customers, suppliers, communities, and investors. Some of these issues are covered by laws, but others aren't, thereby creating the responsibility of ethical decision making by all employees and managers in a firm.

At the second tier, moving beyond "do no harm" becomes a matter of choice. Companies can choose to help in whatever way that investors, managers, and employees see fit, but the choices are up to the company and should not be the result of pressure from outside forces.

For the latest information on CSR, visit http://real-timeupdates.com/bia6.

✓ Checkpoint

LEARNING OBJECTIVE 3: Distinguish among the four perspectives on corporate social responsibility.

SUMMARY: The spectrum of viewpoints on CSR can be roughly divided into minimalist (business's only obligation is to compete to the best of its abilities without deception or fraud), defensive (in which businesses engage in CSR efforts only in response to social pressure), cynical (in which businesses engage in CSR as a public relations ploy), and proactive (in which businesses contribute to society out of a belief that they have an obligation to do so).

CRITICAL THINKING: (1) Do you agree that giving companies tax breaks for charitable contributions distorts public spending by indirectly giving companies and activists control over how tax revenues are spent? Why or why not? (2) If Company A takes a cynical approach to CSR while Company B takes a proactive approach but they make identical contributions to society, is one company "better" than the other? Why or why not?

IT'S YOUR BUSINESS: (1) Have you ever suspected a company of engaging in greenwashing or other disingenuous CSR activities? How would you prove or disprove such a suspicion? (2) If you were the head of a small company and wanted to give back to society in some way, how would you select which organizations or causes to support?

KEY TERM TO KNOW: nongovernmental organizations (NGOs)

---

4 **LEARNING OBJECTIVE**

Discuss the role of business in protecting the natural environment, and define *sustainable development*.

CSR: The Natural Environment

In the past few decades, few issues in the public dialog have become as politicized and polarized as pollution and resource depletion. Environmentalists and their political allies sometimes portray business leaders as heartless profiteers who would strip the Earth bare for a few bucks. Corporate leaders and their political allies, on the other hand, sometimes cast environmentalists as "tree huggers" who care more about bunnies and butterflies than about people. As is often the case, the shouting match between these extreme positions obscures real problems—and opportunities for real solutions.

To reach a clearer understanding of this situation, keep three important points in mind. First, the creation, delivery, use, and disposal of products that society values virtually always generate pollution and consume natural resources. For example, it's tempting to assume that web-based businesses are "clean" because there is no visible pollution. However, the Internet and all the computers attached to it have a voracious appetite for electricity; Google is one of the largest users of electricity in the world, for example.[20] (See more about Google's energy conservation efforts under "Efforts to Conserve Resources and Reduce Pollution.") Moreover, generation of electricity seriously affects the environment, as over 70 percent of the electricity used in the United States is generated by burning coal, oil, or natural gas (see Exhibit 6).[21]

Second, "environmental" causes are often as much about human health and safety as they are about forests, rivers, and wildlife. The availability of clean air, water, and soil affects everyone, not just people concerned with wild spaces.

Third, many of these issues are neither easy nor simple. They often require tough trade-offs, occasional sacrifice, disruptive change, and decision making in the face of uncertainty. Meeting these challenges will require people to be clear-headed, open-minded, adaptable, and courageous.

EFFORTS TO CONSERVE RESOURCES AND REDUCE POLLUTION

Concerns over pollution and resource depletion have been growing since the dawn of the Industrial Age in the 19th century. However, widespread concern for the environment really dates to the 1960s, when *ecology*, the study of the relationship between organisms and the natural environment, entered mainstream discussion. In 1963, federal, state, and

REAL-TIME UPDATES

Learn More by Exploring This Interactive Website

Create a more sustainable product with Nike's interactive tool

Nike's Environmental Design Tool measures the environmental impact of a manufactured product and helps design teams improve the sustainability of their products. You can plug in data from your own apparel to see how your clothing scores. Go to http://real-timeupdates.com/bia6 and click on Learn More. If you are using MyBizLab, you can access Real-Time Updates within chapter or under Student Study Tools.

EXHIBIT 6	Green and Clean? Where Our Electricity Comes From

Most of the electricity generated in the United States is produced by burning fossil fuels. Nuclear and hydroelectric power provide most of the rest. Renewable sources such as solar and wind have grown over the past decade, but they remain minor sources of electricity at this point.

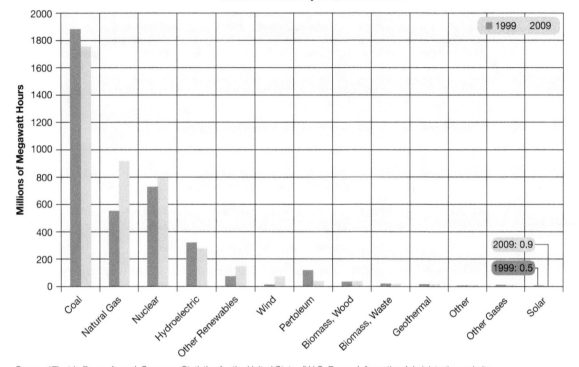

Sources of Electricity in the United States

Source: "Electric Power Annual, Summary Statistics for the United States," U.S. Energy Information Administration website, accessed 3 August 2011, www.eia.gov.

local governments began enacting laws and regulations to reduce pollution (see Exhibit 7 on the next page). Many states and cities have also passed their own tough clean-air laws.

You've no doubt heard the phrase "reduce, reuse, recycle" as advice for conserving resources and minimizing pollution. Google offers a great example of what businesses can do in this regard. As a major consumer of energy, the company is taking responsibility for that consumption in a number of significant ways, including reducing energy usage in its data centers (massive complexes that house the thousands of computers that make Google searches possible) by more than half, investing in renewable energy in ways that help this fledgling industry grow, using its position as a major corporation to help shape energy policy and public awareness, and sharing the results of its considerable research efforts with other companies to help them reduce resource usages as well.[22]

In addition to technological solutions to reduce pollution and resource consumption, businesses, governments, and NGOs are pursuing a variety of political and economic solutions. For example, **cap and trade** programs try to balance free-market economics with government intervention. Lawmakers first establish a maximum allowable amount of a particular pollutant that a designated group of companies or industries is allowed to emit (the "cap") and then distribute individual emission allowances to all the companies in that group. If a company lowers its emissions enough to stay under its prescribed limit, it can

cap and trade A type of environmental policy that gives companies some freedom in addressing the environmental impact of specified pollutants, by either reducing emissions to meet a designated cap or buying allowances to offset excess emissions

EXHIBIT 7	Major Federal Environmental Legislation

Since the early 1960s, major federal legislation aimed at the environment has focused on providing cleaner air and water and reducing toxic waste. (Many of these laws have been amended since their original passage dates.)

LEGISLATION	KEY PROVISIONS
Clean Air Act (1963)	Assists states and localities in formulating control programs; sets federal standards for auto-exhaust emissions; sets maximum permissible pollution levels; authorizes nationwide air-pollution standards and limitations to pollutant discharge; requires scrubbers in new coal-fired power plants; directs EPA to prevent deterioration of air quality in clean areas; sets schedule and standards for cutting smog, acid rain, hazardous factory fumes, and ozone-depleting chemicals
Solid Waste Disposal Act (1965)	Authorizes research and assistance to state and local control programs; regulates treatment, storage, transportation, and disposal of hazardous waste
National Environmental Policy Act (1969)	Establishes a structure for coordinating all federal environmental programs
Resource Recovery Act (1970)	Subsidizes pilot recycling plants; authorizes nationwide control programs
Clean Water Act (1972)	Authorizes grants to states for water-pollution control; gives federal government limited authority to correct pollution problems; authorizes EPA to set and enforce water-quality standards
Noise Control Act (1972)	Requires EPA to set standards for major sources of noise and to advise Federal Aviation Administration on standards for airplane noise
Endangered Species Act (1973)	Establishes protections for endangered and threatened plants and animals
Safe Drinking Water Act (1974)	Sets standards of drinking-water quality; requires municipal water systems to report on contaminant levels; establishes funding to upgrade water systems
Toxic Substances Control Act (1976)	Requires chemicals testing; authorizes EPA to restrict the use of harmful substances
Resource Conservation and Recovery Act (1976)	Gives the EPA authority to control hazardous waste
Comprehensive Environmental Response, Compensation, and Liability Act (1980)	Establishes the "Superfund" program to oversee the identification and cleanup of uncontrolled or abandoned hazardous waste sites
Nuclear Waste Policy Act (1982)	Establishes procedures for creating geologic repositories of radioactive waste
Marine Protection, Research, and Sanctuaries Act (1988)	Prohibits ocean dumping that could threaten human health or the marine environment
Oil Pollution Act (1990)	Sets up liability trust fund; extends operations for preventing and containing oil pollution

Source: U.S. Environmental Protection Agency website, accessed 3 August 2011, www.epa.gov.

sell, trade, or save leftover allowances (the "trade"). If a company exceeds its emission allowances, it must buy or trade for enough allowances to cover the excess emissions. In this way, companies can choose the lowest-cost means of taking responsibility for their emissions.[23] During the 1990s, a cap and trade program to reduce sulfur dioxide emissions from coal-burning power plants, a leading cause of acid raid, reduced emissions by 50 percent.[24]

THE TREND TOWARD SUSTAINABILITY

sustainable development

Operating business in a manner that minimizes pollution and resource depletion, ensuring that future generations will have vital resources

Efforts to minimize resource depletion and pollution are part of a broader effort known as *sustainability*, or **sustainable development**, which the United Nations has defined as development that "meets the needs of the present without compromising the ability of future generations to meet their own needs."[25]

Sustainable development can certainly require changes to the way companies conduct business, but paying attention to a broader scope of stakeholders and managing for the longer term doesn't automatically mean that companies have to take a financial hit to go "green." Many businesses are discovering that taking steps now to reduce consumption and pollution can end up saving money down the road by reducing everything from cleanup and litigation expenses to ongoing production costs. As Xerox CEO Ursula Burns puts it, "The greener we get, the more we can reduce costs and boost efficiency."[26]

In other words, in addition to better stewardship of shared natural resources, sustainable development is also a smart business strategy. By taking a broad and long-term view of their companies' impact on the environment and stakeholders throughout the world, managers can ensure the continued availability of the resources their organizations need and be better prepared for changes in government regulations and shifting social expectations. In fact, some experts believe sustainability is a good measure of the quality of management in a corporation. According to investment researcher Matthew J. Kiernan, companies that take a sustainable approach "tend to be more strategic, nimble, and better equipped to compete in the complex, high-velocity global environment."[27]

When you upgraded your smartphone or laptop, where did the old one go?

✔ Checkpoint

LEARNING OBJECTIVE 4: Discuss the role of business in protecting the natural environment, and define *sustainable development*.

SUMMARY: As major users of natural resources and generators of waste products, businesses play a huge role in conservation and pollution-reduction efforts. Many businesses are making an effort to reduce, reuse, and recycle, and governments are trying market-based approaches such as *cap and trade* to encourage businesses to reduce emissions. All these efforts are part of a trend toward *sustainable development*, which can be defined as meeting the needs of the present without compromising the ability of future generations to meet their own needs.

CRITICAL THINKING: (1) Should all industries be required to meet the same levels of pollution control? Why or why not? (2) How would you respond to critics who say that cap and trade programs allow polluters to buy their way out of the responsibility of cleaning up their operations?

IT'S YOUR BUSINESS: (1) In what ways could your employer (or your college, if you're not currently working) take steps to reduce resource depletion? (2) How did you dispose of the last electronic product you stopped using?

KEY TERMS TO KNOW: cap and trade, sustainable development

CSR: Consumers

The 1960s activism that awakened business to its environmental responsibilities also gave rise to **consumerism**, a movement that put pressure on businesses to consider consumer needs and interests. (Note that some people use *consumerism* in a negative sense, as a synonym for *materialism*.) Consumerism prompted many businesses to create consumer affairs departments to handle customer complaints. It also prompted state and local agencies to set up bureaus to offer consumer information and assistance. At the federal level, President John F. Kennedy announced a "bill of rights" for consumers, laying the foundation for a wave of consumer-oriented legislation (see Exhibit 8 on the next page).

5 **LEARNING OBJECTIVE**

Identify four fundamental consumer rights and the responsibility of business to respect them.

consumerism A movement that pressures businesses to consider consumer needs and interests

329

EXHIBIT 8	Major Federal Consumer Legislation

Major federal legislation aimed at consumer protection has focused on food and drugs, false advertising, product safety, and credit protection.

LEGISLATION	MAJOR PROVISIONS
Food, Drug, and Cosmetic Act (1938)	Puts cosmetics, foods, drugs, and therapeutic products under Food and Drug Administration's jurisdiction; outlaws misleading labeling
Cigarette Labeling and Advertising Act (1965)	Mandates warnings on cigarette packages and in ads
Fair Packaging and Labeling Act (1966, 1972)	Requires honest, informative package labeling; labels must show origin of product, quantity of contents, uses or applications
Truth in Lending Act (Consumer Protection Credit Act) (1968)	Requires creditors to disclose finance charge and annual percentage rate; limits cardholder liability for unauthorized use
Fair Credit Reporting Act (1970)	Requires credit-reporting agencies to set process for assuring accuracy; requires creditors to explain credit denials
Consumer Product Safety Act (1972)	Creates Consumer Product Safety Commission
Magnuson-Moss Warranty Act (1975)	Requires complete written warranties in ordinary language; requires warranties to be available before purchase
Alcohol Beverage Labeling Act (1988)	Requires warning labels on alcohol products, saying that alcohol impairs abilities and that women shouldn't drink when pregnant
Children's Online Privacy Protection Act (1988)	Gives parents control over the collection or use of information that websites can collect about children
Nutrition Education and Labeling Act (1990)	Requires specific, uniform product labels detailing nutritional information on every food regulated by the FDA
American Automobile Labeling Act (1992)	Requires carmakers to identify where cars are assembled and where their individual components are manufactured
Deceptive Mail Prevention and Enforcement Act (1999)	Establishes standards for sweepstakes mailings, skill contests, and facsimile checks to prevent fraud and exploitation
Controlling the Assault of Non-Solicited Pornography and Marketing Act (2003)	Known as CAN-SPAM, attempts to protect online consumers from unwanted and fraudulent email
Consumer Product Safety Improvement Act (2008)	Strengthens standards for lead in children's products; mandates safety testing for imported children's products; creates a searchable database for reporting accidents, injuries, and illnesses related to consumer products
Dodd-Frank Wall Street Reform and Consumer Protection Act (2010)	Amends a number earlier acts and regulations in an attempt to improve stability of the banking and investment industries; establishes the Consumer Financial Projection Bureau

Sources: U.S. Food and Drug Administration website, accessed 3 August 2011, www.fda.gov; U.S. House of Representatives, Office of the Law Revision Counsel website, accessed 3 August 2011, http://uscode.house.gov; U.S. Federal Trade Commission website, accessed 3 August 2011, www.ftc.gov; U.S. Consumer Product Safety Commission website, accessed 3 August 2011, www.cpsc.com; Alcohol and Tobacco Tax and Trade Bureau website, accessed 3 August 2011, www.ttb.gov; U.S. Consumer Financial Projection Bureau website, accessed 3 August 2011, www.consumerfinance.gov.

THE RIGHT TO BUY SAFE PRODUCTS—AND TO BUY THEM SAFELY

As mentioned previously, doing no harm is one of the foundations of corporate social responsibility. The United States and many other countries go to considerable lengths to ensure the safety of the products sold within their borders. The U.S. government imposes many safety standards that are enforced by the Consumer Product Safety Commission (CPSC), as well as by other federal and state agencies. Companies that don't comply with these rules are forced to take corrective action, and the threat of product-liability suits and declining sales motivates companies to meet safety standards.

Product safety concerns range from safe toys, food, and automobiles to less-tangible worries such as online privacy and **identity theft**, in which criminals steal personal information and use it to take out loans, request government documents, get expensive medical procedures, and commit other types of fraud. According to Federal Trade Commission estimates, some 9 million Americans are victims of identity theft every year.[28] Companies—e-commerce websites in particular—play a vital role in fighting this crime because they frequently collect the information that identity thieves use to commit their fraud, including credit card and Social Security numbers. Any company that collects such information has a clear ethical obligation to keep it safe and secure.

REAL-TIME UPDATES

Learn More by Exploring This Interactive Website

Can you outsmart online crooks?

Play these games to find out how much you know about protecting your identity and your privacy online. Go to http://real-timeupdates.com/bia6 and click on Learn More. If you are using MyBizLab, you can access Real-Time Updates within the chapter or under Student Study Tools.

identity theft A crime in which thieves steal personal information and use it to take out loans and commit other types of fraud

THE RIGHT TO BE INFORMED

Consumers have a right to know what they're buying, how to use it, and whether it presents any risks to them. They also have a right to know the true price of goods or services and the details of purchase contracts. Accordingly, numerous government regulations have been put in place to make sure buyers get the information they need to make informed choices. Of course, buyers share the responsibility here, at least morally if not always legally. Not bothering to read labels or contracts or not asking for help if you don't understand them is no excuse for not being informed.

Fortunately, both consumers and businesses can turn to a wide range of information sources to learn more about the goods and services they purchase. The spread of social media and their use in *social commerce*, in which buyers help educate one another, has helped shift power from sellers to buyers. For just about every purchase you can envision these days, you can find more information about it before you choose.

THE RIGHT TO CHOOSE WHICH PRODUCTS TO BUY

Especially in the United States, the number of products available to consumers is staggering, even sometimes overwhelming. But how far should the right to choose extend? Are we entitled to choose products that are potentially harmful, such as cigarettes, alcoholic beverages, guns, sugary soft drinks, or fatty fried foods? Should the government take measures to make such products illegal, or should consumers always be allowed to decide for themselves what to buy?

Consider cigarettes. Scientists determined long ago that the tar and nicotine in tobacco are harmful and addictive. In 1965, the Federal Cigarette Labeling and Advertising Act was passed, requiring all cigarette packs to carry the Surgeon General's warnings. Over the years, tobacco companies have spent billions of dollars to defend themselves in lawsuits brought by smokers suffering from cancer and respiratory diseases. Lawsuits and legislative activity surrounding tobacco products continue to this day—and are likely to continue for years. Meanwhile, consumers can still purchase cigarettes in the marketplace. As one tobacco company executive put it, "Behind all the allegations . . . is the simple truth that we sell a legal product."[29]

THE RIGHT TO BE HEARD

The final component of consumer rights is the right to be heard. As with the challenge of gathering information, social media give consumers numerous ways to ask questions, voice concerns, provide feedback, and—if necessary—demand attention. Savvy companies monitor Twitter, blogs, and other online venues to catch messages from dissatisfied customers. Companies that fail to respond or that respond in defensive, inward-looking ways are likely to lose business to competitors that embrace this new media environment and the power it gives today's consumers.

✓ Checkpoint

LEARNING OBJECTIVE 5: Identify four fundamental consumer rights and the responsibility of business to respect them.

SUMMARY: Four fundamental consumer rights that form the basis of much of the consumer-related legislation in the United States are the right to safe products, the right to be informed, the right to choose, and the right to be heard. Many specific aspects of these rights are now embodied in government regulations, but others rely on business professionals to practice ethical and responsive decision making.

CRITICAL THINKING: (1) Is there a point at which responsibility for product safety shifts from the seller to the buyer? Explain your answer. (2) If providing full information about products raises prices, should businesses still be required to do so? Why or why not?

IT'S YOUR BUSINESS: (1) Do you rely on social media when making purchases? (2) Have you ever lodged a complaint with a business? What was the outcome?

KEY TERMS TO KNOW: consumerism, identity theft

---

6 | **LEARNING OBJECTIVE**

Explain the responsibilities businesses have toward their employees.

CSR: Employees

The past few decades have brought dramatic changes in the attitudes and composition of the global workforce. These changes have forced businesses to modify their recruiting, training, and promotion practices, as well as their overall corporate values and behaviors. This section discusses some key responsibilities that employers have regarding employees.

THE PUSH FOR EQUALITY IN EMPLOYMENT

discrimination In a social and economic sense, denial of opportunities to individuals on the basis of some characteristic that has no bearing on their ability to perform in a job

The United States has always stood for economic freedom and the individual's right to pursue opportunity. Unfortunately, in the past many people were targets of economic **discrimination**, being relegated to low-paying, menial jobs and prevented from taking advantage of many opportunities solely on the basis of their race, gender, disability, or religion.

The Civil Rights Act of 1964 established the Equal Employment Opportunity Commission (EEOC), the regulatory agency that addresses job discrimination. The EEOC is responsible for monitoring hiring practices and for investigating complaints of job-related discrimination. It has the power to file legal charges against companies that discriminate and to force them to compensate individuals or groups who have been victimized by unfair practices. The Civil Rights Act of 1991 amended the original act in response to a number of Supreme Court decisions that had taken place in the intervening quarter-century. Among its key provisions are limiting the amount of damage awards, making it easier to sue for discrimination, giving employees the right to have a trial by jury in discrimination cases, and extending protections to overseas employees of U.S. companies.[30]

Affirmative Action

affirmative action Activities undertaken by businesses to recruit and promote members of groups whose economic progress has been hindered through either legal barriers or established practices

In the 1960s, **affirmative action** programs were developed to encourage organizations to recruit and promote members of groups whose past economic progress has been hindered through legal barriers or established practices. Affirmative action programs address a variety of situations, from college admissions to hiring to conducting business with government agencies. Note that while affirmative action programs address a variety of population segments, from military veterans with disabilities to specific ethnic groups, in popular usage, "affirmative action" usually refers to programs based on race.

Affirmative action remains a controversial and politicized issue, with opponents claiming that it creates a double standard and can encourage reverse discrimination against white males; proponents say that it remains a crucial part of the effort to ensure equal opportunities for all. One of the key points of contention is whether affirmative action programs are still needed, given the various antidiscrimination laws now in place. Opponents assert that everyone has an equal shot at success now, so the programs are unnecessary and, if anything, should be based on income, not race; proponents argue that laws can't remove every institutionalized barrier and that discrimination going back decades has left many families and communities at a long-term disadvantage.[31]

Policy debates aside, well-managed companies across the country are finding that embracing diversity in the richest sense is simply good business.

People with Disabilities

In 1990, people with a wide range of physical and mental difficulties got a boost from the passage of the federal Americans with Disabilities Act (ADA), which guarantees equal opportunities in housing, transportation, education, employment, and other areas for the estimated 50 to 75 million people in the United States who have disabilities. As defined by the 1990 law, *disability* is a broad term that protects not only those with physical handicaps but also those with cancer, heart disease, diabetes, epilepsy, HIV/AIDS, drug addiction, alcoholism, emotional illness, and other conditions. In most situations, employers cannot legally require job applicants to pass a physical examination as a condition of employment. Employers are also required to make reasonable accommodations to meet the needs of employees with disabilities, such as modifying workstations or schedules.[32]

OCCUPATIONAL SAFETY AND HEALTH

Every year several thousand U.S. workers lose their lives on the job and many thousands more are injured (see Exhibit 9).[33] During the 1960s, mounting concern about workplace hazards resulted in the passage of the Occupational Safety and Health Act of 1970, which set mandatory standards for safety and health and also established the Occupational Safety and Health Administration (OSHA) to enforce them. These standards govern everything

| EXHIBIT 9 | Fatal Occupational Injuries |

Transportation accidents are the leading cause of death on the job in the United States. Overall, U.S. workers suffer fatal on-the-job injuries at a rate of 3.5 deaths per 100,000 full-time employees per year.

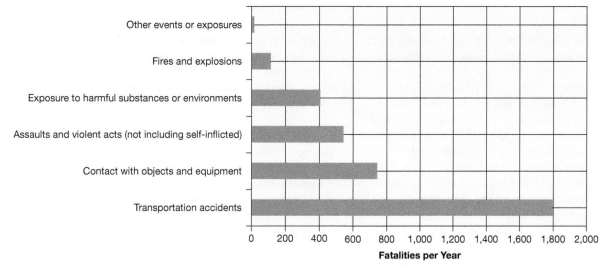

Source: "Census of Fatal Occupational Injuries," U.S. Bureau of Labor Statistics website, accessed 3 August 2011, www.bls.gov.

from hazardous materials to *ergonomics*, the study of how people interact with computers and other machines.

Concerns for employee safety can extend beyond a company's own workforce, and this concern is particularly acute for the many U.S. companies that contract out production to factories in Asia, Latin America, and parts of the United States to make products under their brand names. A number of these companies have been criticized for doing business with so-called *sweatshops*, a disparaging term applied to production facilities that treat workers poorly. As discussed in the Behind the Scenes wrap-up below, Nike is one of many companies taking positive steps to improve conditions in the factories that make their products. American colleges have been influential in this effort, too. More than 200 schools have joined the Fair Labor Association (www.fairlabor.org) to ensure that school-logo products are manufactured in an ethical manner.[34]

✔ Checkpoint

LEARNING OBJECTIVE 6: Explain the responsibilities businesses have toward their employees.

SUMMARY: In addition to the impact a company has on its external stakeholders, corporate social responsibility applies within the company as well, to the way employees are treated. Major issues include the push for equal opportunity, which includes affirmative action programs and regulations to protect the rights of people with disabilities, and occupational safety and health.

CRITICAL THINKING: (1) Does affirmative action seem like a fair approach? Why or why not? (2) Should employees automatically get paid more to work in hazardous jobs? Why or why not?

IT'S YOUR BUSINESS: (1) Have you ever experienced or observed discrimination on the job? If so, how did you handle the situation? (2) Has this chapter changed your perspective about the relationship between business and society? Why or why not?

KEY TERMS TO KNOW: discrimination, affirmative action

BEHIND THE SCENES

MyBizLab

NIKE BUILDS A SUSTAINABLE BUSINESS THROUGH SUSTAINABLE DESIGN AND MANUFACTURING

Nike CEO Mark Parker would surely agree that any examination of Nike's business–society relationship needs to include a look at the massive scale of the company's operations. With annual revenues in the neighborhood of $20 billion, a strong presence in every continent except Antarctica, and billions of products sold since its founding in the 1960s, Nike is one of the world's largest and most visible corporations. (Starting right now, see how long you can go without seeing a Nike logo.) In addition to the 36,000 employees who work directly for the company, another 800,000 work in the 900 contract factories across nearly 50 countries that manufacture the company's products. With millions of shoes, garments, sporting goods, and other "Swoosh"-branded products rolling off those production lines every month, the company oversees a vast supply chain that sources a wide variety of natural and synthetic materials and uses almost every mode of transportation imaginable.

It's safe to say that Nike and the global community are stuck with each other—and Nike needs a vibrant, stable world economy as much as the global community needs Nike to be a well-managed and well-behaved corporate citizen.

Workplace conditions and sustainable manufacturing are two issues in particular that highlight the impact Nike has on stakeholders and the considerable investments the company continues to make toward improving its entire "business ecosystem." In the matter of workplace conditions, the first wave of improvement efforts focused on building monitoring systems so that companies such as Nike could get a better sense of how workers were being treated in contract factories. Across a number of industries, some of these "sweatshop" factories had been accused of forcing employees to work 24 hours or more at a time, employing young children in unsafe conditions, or virtually imprisoning workers in conditions that have at times been compared to slavery. Mattel, Reebok, Patagonia, Liz Claiborne, and Gap are among the other industry leaders that have been working at improving monitoring of contract factories.

However, Nike began to realize that setting standards and monitoring operations weren't improving conditions in its contract factories sufficiently, and the company is now working closely with vendors to improve their operations and practices. As the company explains, "What we've learned, after nearly a decade, is that monitoring alone hasn't solved the problems. And many of the problems are recurring in the industry. Our focus now is getting to the root of the problems."

A key part of that effort is an in-depth auditing process conducted by Nike inspectors, who look for evidence of compliance with Nike's own environmental safety, and health codes. Nike inspectors examine factory operations and interview supervisors as well as employees to make sure contract manufacturers are living up to the expectations outlined in Nike's *Code of Conduct*. Nike doesn't leave compliance to chance, either. The company's *Code Leadership Standards* is a comprehensive manual that describes exactly what a factory needs to do to meet Nike's standards. If a factory is out of compliance, Nike teams work with local management to help them figure where their processes are breaking down and how to improve.

In the area of sustainable manufacturing, Nike calls its efforts "considered design," which it describes as "reducing or eliminating toxics and waste, increasing the use of environmentally preferred materials and using Nike's innovation to create a future with more sustainable products." For example, the company's materials experts have worked for years to analyze and document the environmental impact of a wide variety of garment and shoe materials, and its designers now have a handy software tool to help them choose fabrics and other components that maximize product performance and resource sustainability. After spending several million dollars developing it, Nike released this tool for free public use to help other companies improve their design practices. (You can try this software yourself, actually—it's the Environmental Design Tool featured in the Real-Time Updates Learn More item.)

Recycling is another area of concentration for the company. Nike collects and grinds up millions of pairs of worn-out sneakers every year to produce shock-absorbing materials that are used in running tracks, tennis courts, playgrounds, and other playing surfaces. Nike designers are also ramping up their use of recycled polyester from discarded plastic bottles, keeping hundreds of millions of them out of landfills.

Fabric manufacturing uses enormous volumes of water, and Nike has had a water stewardship program in place since 2001 to help factories minimize water usage and to do a more responsible job of "borrowing" water, as the company phrases it. Given the number of factories it works with worldwide, Nike figures its efforts to improve water stewardship influence the usage of more than 500 billion gallons of water a year.

Even with the considerable investments it has made and the measurable progress that has come from those efforts, the scale of its operations and the visibility of its brand ensure that Nike will continue to attract the attention of stakeholders and advocacy groups. For example, Greenpeace recently launched a "detox challenge" publicity campaign in which the environmental advocacy group challenged Nike and arch-rival Adidas to reduce the discharge of toxic fabric-treatment chemicals from contract factories in China.

Nike's response included a comprehensive report on its progress toward eliminating toxic chemicals from the manufacturing process—efforts that had been underway for more than a decade. These included the process research and chemistry patents it has freely shared with other manufacturers through the GreenXchange intellectual property collaborative and an offer to work with Greenpeace and other NGOs on water usage issues.

Parker talks frankly of the lessons Nike has learned along the way. Reflecting on pressure the company received in the 1990s from worker rights groups, he says, "Our critics were smart (and right) to focus on the industry leader." After first defending conditions in the factories as just the way business was done in those countries, the company realized that change was needed, and it had to be fundamental change affecting every part of the company. Parker now welcomes collaboration with stakeholders and promotes the value of transparency, so that affected groups can see what the company is doing, and the company can learn from anybody who has great ideas to share. "For all the athletic and cultural and financial successes of the company," he says, "I believe our work in sustainable business and innovation has equal potential to shape our legacy."[35]

Critical Thinking Questions

1. This chapter covers three factors that influence ethical decisions: cultural differences, knowledge, and organizational behavior. How have these factors shaped Nike's CSR actions over the past two decades?
2. How does Mark Parker's phrase "sustainable business" relate to sustainable manufacturing?
3. Is it ethical for NGOs to put pressure on just one company in an industry when they are trying to effect change across the entire industry, given that responding to that pressure is likely to cost that one company more than its competitors?

LEARN MORE ONLINE

Visit Nike's consumer-oriented website, www.nike.com, and its corporate website, www.nikebiz.com. Study the messages presented on the two sites. How does Nike reach out to different stakeholder groups using these two separate sites? Read the "Letter to Shareholders" from Nike's latest annual report (available in the "Investors" section of its corporate website). How does Nike present itself to this vital stakeholder group? How does the company present its CSR efforts in a way that appeals to a reader whose primary interest is financial investment?

MyBizLab

Log on to www.mybizlab.com to access study and assessment aids associated with this chapter.

KEY TERMS

affirmative action
cap and trade
code of ethics
conflict of interest
consumerism
corporate social responsibility (CSR)
discrimination
ethical dilemma
ethical lapse

ethics
identity theft
insider trading
nongovernmental organizations (NGOs)
philanthropy
strategic CSR
sustainable development
transparency
whistle-blowing

TEST YOUR KNOWLEDGE

Questions for Review

1. How does ethics differ from corporate social responsibility?
2. What is a conflict of interest?
3. How do companies support ethical behavior?
4. How are businesses responding to the environmental issues facing society?
5. What is identity theft, and what responsibilities do businesses have to prevent it?

Questions for Analysis

6. Why can't legal considerations resolve every ethical question?
7. How do individuals employ philosophical principles in making ethical business decisions?
8. Why does a company need more than a code of ethics to be ethical?
9. Why is it important for a company to balance its social responsibility efforts with its need to generate profits?
10. Ethical Considerations. Is it ethical for companies to benefit from their efforts to practice corporate social responsibility?

Why or why not? How can anyone be sure that CSR efforts aren't just public relations ploys?

Questions for Application

11. What steps could a bookstore take to engage in strategic CSR?
12. Based on what you've learned about corporate social responsibility, what effect will CSR considerations have on your job search?
13. Concept Integration. If an employee leaves a company to work for a competitor, what types of knowledge would be ethical for the employee to share with the new employer, and what types would be unethical to share?
14. Concept Integration. Is it ethical for state and city governments to entice specific businesses to relocate their operations to that state or city by offering them special tax breaks that are not extended to other businesses operating in that area?

EXPAND YOUR KNOWLEDGE

Discovering Career Opportunities

Businesses, government agencies, and not-for-profit organizations offer numerous career opportunities related to ethics and social responsibility. How can you learn more about these careers?

1. Search the *Occupational Outlook Handbook* at www.bls.gov/oco for "occupational health and safety specialists and technicians," jobs concerned with a company's responsibility toward its employees. What are the duties and qualifications of the jobs you have identified? Are the salaries and future outlooks attractive for all of these jobs?
2. Select one job from the *Handbook* and search blogs, websites, and other sources to learn more about it. Try to find real-life information about the daily activities of people in this job. Can you find any information about ethical dilemmas or other conflicts in the duties of this position? What role do you think people in this position play within their respective organizations?
3. What skills, educational background, and work experience do you think employers are seeking in applicants for the specific job you are researching? What keywords do you think employers would search for when reviewing résumés submitted for this position?

Improve Your Tech Insights: Assistive Technologies

The term *assistive technologies* covers a broad range of devices and systems that help people with disabilities perform activities that might otherwise be difficult or impossible. These include technologies that help people communicate orally and visually, interact with computers and other equipment, and enjoy greater mobility, along with myriad other specific functions.

Assistive technologies create a vital link for thousands of employees with disabilities, giving them opportunities to pursue a greater range of career paths and giving employers access to a broader base of talent. Plus, the economy and society benefit when everyone who can make a contribution is able to, and assistive technologies will be an important part of the solution.

Research some of the technologies now on the market. AssistiveTech.net, www.assistivetech.net, is a great place to explore the thousands of assistive products now available; it also provides links to a variety of other sites. The Business Leadership Network (USBLN), www.usbln.org, helps companies develop policies and practices to encourage the full participation and advancement of employees with disabilities and to market goods and services to consumers with disabilities. Also visit the Rehabilitation Engineering and Assistive Technology Society of North America (RESNA), www.resna.org. (USBLN and RESNA sponsor annual conferences that bring together some of the best minds in the field of assistive technologies, too.) For a look at the federal government's efforts to promote these technologies, visit the National Institute on Disability and Rehabilitation Research, www.ed.gov/about/offices/list/osers/nidrr. Technology companies such as IBM, www.ibm.com/able, and Microsoft, www.microsoft.com/enable, also devote significant resources to developing assistive technologies and making information technology more accessible. Choose one assistive technology, and in a brief email to your instructor, explain how this technology can help companies support employees or customers with disabilities.[36]

PRACTICE YOUR SKILLS

Sharpening Your Communication Skills

Your employer makes a grand show of promoting strong ethics, with regular classes, posters in the hallways, a toll-free hotline, and more. However, as the economy has slowed down over the past few months, you've noticed that company managers aren't always practicing what they preach. They're cutting corners on product quality and squeezing suppliers by not paying bills on time. They even launched a frivolous lawsuit against an upstart competitor that will do little more than drain the new firm of funds and delay its entry into the market. This isn't the same company you were once so proud to work for. Write a brief email message to your immediate supervisor, requesting a meeting to discuss your concerns.

Building Your Team Skills

Every organization can benefit from having a code of ethics to guide decision making. But whom should a code of ethics protect, and what should it cover? In this exercise, you and the rest of your team are going to draft a code of ethics for your college or university.

Start by thinking about who will be protected by this code of ethics. What stakeholders should the school consider when making decisions? What negative effects might decisions have on these stakeholders? Then think about the kinds of situations you want your school's code of ethics to cover. One example might be employment decisions; another might be disclosure of confidential student information.

Next, using Exhibit 2 as a model, draft your school's code of ethics; identify general principles and then provide specific guidelines. Write a general introduction explaining the purpose of the code and who is being protected. Next, write a positive statement to guide ethical decisions in each situation you identified earlier in this exercise. Your statement about promotion decisions, for example, might read: "School officials will encourage equal access to job promotions for all qualified candidates, with every applicant receiving fair consideration."

Compare your code of ethics with the codes drafted by your classmates. Did all the codes seek to protect the same stakeholders? What differences and similarities do you see in the statements guiding ethical decisions?

Developing Your Research Skills

Articles on corporate ethics and social responsibility regularly appear in business journals and newspapers. Find one or more articles discussing one of the following ethics or social responsibility challenges faced by a business:

- Environmental issues, such as pollution, acid rain, and hazardous-waste disposal
- Employee or consumer safety measures
- Consumer information or education
- Employment discrimination or diversity initiatives
- Investment ethics
- Industrial spying and theft of trade secrets
- Fraud, bribery, and overcharging
- Company codes of ethics

1. What is the nature of the ethical challenge or social responsibility issue presented in the article? Does the article report any wrongdoing by a company or agency official? Was the action illegal, unethical, or questionable? What course of action would you recommend the company or agency take to correct or improve matters now?
2. What stakeholder group(s) is affected? What lasting effects will be felt by (a) the company and (b) this stakeholder group(s)?
3. Writing a letter to the editor is one way consumers can speak their mind. Review some of the letters to the editor in newspapers or journals. Why are letters to the editor an important feature for that publication?

REFERENCES

1. "Nike, Inc.'s Response to Greenpeace Report," 18 July 2011, Nike website, www.nikebiz.com; *Nike 2011 Annual Report*, accessed 4 August 2011, www.nikebiz.com; "Detox Campaign," Greenpeace, accessed 4 August 2011, www.greenpeace.org; *Nike Code Leadership Standard*, Nike website, accessed 7 August 2011, www.nikebiz.com; Nike corporate website, accessed 4 August 2011, www.nikebiz.com; GreenXchange, accessed 4 August 2011, www.greenxchange.cc; "Workers & Factories: Improving Conditions in Our Contract Factories," Nike website, accessed 4 August 2011, www.nike.com; Abigail Goldman, "Sweat, Fear, and Resignation Amid All the Toys," *Los Angeles Times*, 26 November 2004, A1, A30–A32; Edward Iwata, "How Barbie Is Making Business a Little Better," *USA Today*, 27 March 2006, B1–B2; "Nike Corporate Responsibility/Compliance ESH CLS Audit" worksheet, accessed 4 August 2011, www.nikebiz.com.

2. Rakesh Khurana, "The Future of Business School," *BusinessWeek*, 26 May 2009, www.businessweek.com.

3. James O'Toole and Warren Bennis, "What's Needed Next: A Culture of Candor," *Harvard Business Review*, June 2009, 54–61.

4. Barbara Ortutay, "Facebook Tries Dirty Tricks on Google But Is Found Out," *Seattle Times*, 12 May 2011, www.seattletimes.com.

5. O'Toole and Bennis, "What's Needed Next: A Culture of Candor," 59.

6. "Ethics and Business Practices," United Technologies website, accessed 3 August 2011, www.utc.com.

7. Ben Levisohn, "Getting More Workers to Whistle," *BusinessWeek*, 28 January 2008, 18.

8. Alan D. Berkowitz, Claude M. Tusk, J. Ian Downes, and David S. Caroline, "Whistleblowing," *Employee Relations Law Journal*, Vol. 36, No. 4, Spring 2011, 15–32.

9. "Less Than Half of Privately Held Businesses Support Whistleblowing," Grant Thornton website, accessed 13 October 2008, www.internationalbusinessreport.com.

10. Ian Wilhelm, "A Surge in Corporate Giving," *Chronicle of Philanthropy*, 17 August 2006, http://find.galegroup.com.

11. David Grayson and Adrian Hodges, "Forget Responsibility, Think Opportunities," *The Observer*, 4 June 2004, http://observer.guardian.co.uk.

12. Michael Porter and Mark Kramer, "Strategy & Society: The Link Between Competitive Advantage and Corporate Social Responsibility," *Harvard Business Review*, December 2006, 78–92.

13. "New Initiative Creates Partnerships on Water Projects Across Africa," Greenbiz.com, 7 June 2004, www.greenbiz.com.

14. Timothy M. Devinney, "Is the Socially Responsible Corporation a Myth? The Good, the Bad, and the Ugly of Corporate Social Responsibility," *Academy of Management Perspectives*, May 2009, 44–56.

15. Milton Friedman, "The Social Responsibility of Business Is to Increase Its Profits," *New York Times Magazine*, 13 September 1970, www.umich.edu/~thecore.

16. "Social Responsibility: 'Fundamentally Subversive'?" Interview with Milton Friedman, *BusinessWeek*, 15 August 2005, www.businessweek.com.

17. Krisi Heim, "In Person: Laurie Erickson Is a 'Wrap' Star to Cancer Patients," *Seattle Times*, 24 April 2011, www.seattletimes.com.

18. Henry G. Manne, "Milton Friedman Was Right," *WSJ Opinion Journal*, 24 November 2006, www.opinionjournal.com.

19. Alexei M. Marcoux, "Business Ethics Gone Wrong," *Cato Policy Report*, May/June 2000, www.cato.org.

20. Kas Thomas, "Google Uses More Electricity Than Most Countries on Earth," assertTrue() blog, 9 March 2009, http://asserttrue.blogspot.com; Rich Miller, "Google Data Center FAQ," Data Center Knowledge website, 26 August 2008, www.datacenterknowledge.com.

21. "Electric Power Annual," U.S. Department of Energy website, accessed 20 June 2007, www.energy.gov.

22. Urs Hölzle, "Energy and the Internet," The Official Google Blog, 11 May 2009, http://googleblog.blogspot.com; eSolar website, accessed 1 June 2009, www.esolar.com; "Google's Green PPAs: What, How, and Why," 29 April 2011, Google website, www.google.com; "Step 5: An Efficient and Clean Energy Future," Google website, accessed 1 June 2009, www.google.com; "Google Data Centers, Best Practices," Google website, accessed 3 August 2011, www.google.com.

23. Cap and Trade 101, U.S. Environmental Protection Agency website, accessed 1 June 2009, www.epa.gov.

24. John M. Broder, "From a Theory to a Consensus on Emissions," *New York Times*, 16 May 2009, www.nytimes.com.

25. "Report of the World Commission on Environment and Development," United Nations General Assembly, 96th Plenary Meeting, 11 December 1987, www.un.org.

26. Ursula M. Burns, "Is the Green Movement a Passing Fancy?" *BusinessWeek*, 27 January 2009, www.businessweek.com.

27. Pete Engardio, "Beyond the Green Corporation," *BusinessWeek*, 29 January 2007, www.businessweek.com.

28. "About Identity Theft," Federal Trade Commission website, accessed 30 May 2009, www.ftc.gov.

29. Action on Smoking and Health website, accessed 15 March 2005, www.ash.org; Chris Burritt, "Fallout from the Tobacco Settlement," *Atlanta Journal and Constitution*, 22 June 1997, A14; Jolie Solomon, "Smoke Signals," *Newsweek*, 28 April 1997, 50–51; Marilyn Elias, "Mortality Rate Rose Through '80s," *USA Today*, 17 April 1997, B3; Mike France, Monica Larner, and Dave Lindorff, "The World War on Tobacco," *BusinessWeek*, 11 November 1996; Richard Lacayo, "Put Out the Butt, Junior," *Time*, 2 September 1996, 51; Elizabeth Gleick, "Smoking Guns," *Time*, 1 April 1996, 50.

30. "The Civil Rights Act of 1991," U.S. Equal Employment Opportunity Commission website, accessed 7 August 2011, www.eeoc.gov.

31. Lorraine Woellert, "Anger on the Right, Opportunity for Bush," *BusinessWeek*, 7 July 2003, www.businessweek.com; Roger O. Crockett, "The Great Race Divide," *BusinessWeek*, 14 July 2003, www.businessweek.com; Earl Graves, "Celebrating the Best and the Brightest," *Black Enterprise*, February 2005, 16.

32. "Disability Discrimination," Equal Employment Opportunity Commission website, accessed 12 June 2007, www.eeoc.gov.

33. "Injuries, Illnesses, and Fatalities," Bureau of Labor Statistics, accessed 31 May 2009, www.bls.gov/iif.

34. Fair Labor Association website, accessed 4 August 2011, www.fairlabor.org.

35. See note 1.

36. Adapted from IBM Human Ability and Accessibility Center, accessed 4 August 2011, www.ibm.com/able; AssistiveTech.net, accessed 4 August 2011, www.assistivetech.net, Business Leadership Network website, accessed 4 August 2011, www.usblin.org; National Institute on Disability and Rehabilitation Research website, accessed 4 August 2011, www.ed.gov; Rehabilitation Engineering and Assistive Technology Society of North America website, accessed 4 August 2011, www.resna.org; Microsoft Accessibility, accessed 4 August 2011, www.microsoft.com/enable.

GLOSSARY

affirmative action Activities undertaken by businesses to recruit and promote members of groups whose economic progress has been hindered through either legal barriers or established practices

cap and trade A type of environmental policy that gives companies some freedom in addressing the environmental impact of specified pollutants, by either reducing emissions to meet a designated cap or buying allowances to offset excess emissions

code of ethics A written statement that sets forth the principles that guide an organization's decisions

conflict of interest A situation in which competing loyalties can lead to ethical lapses, such as when a business decision may be influenced by the potential for personal gain

consumerism A movement that pressures businesses to consider consumer needs and interests

corporate social responsibility (CSR) The idea that business has obligations to society beyond the pursuit of profits

discrimination In a social and economic sense, denial of opportunities to individuals on the basis of some characteristic that has no bearing on their ability to perform in a job

ethical dilemma A situation in which more than one side of an issue can be supported with valid arguments

ethical lapse A situation in which an individual or a group makes a decision that is morally wrong, illegal, or unethical

ethics The rules or standards governing the conduct of a person or group

identity theft A crime in which thieves steal personal information and use it to take out loans and commit other types of fraud

insider trading The use of unpublicized information that an individual gains from the course of his or her job to benefit from fluctuations in the stock market

nongovernmental organizations (NGOs) Nonprofit groups that provide charitable services or promote social and environmental causes

philanthropy The donation of money, time, goods, or services to charitable, humanitarian, or educational institutions

strategic CSR Social contributions that are directly aligned with a company's overall business strategy

sustainable development Operating business in a manner that minimizes pollution and resource depletion, ensuring that future generations will have vital resources

transparency The degree to which affected parties can observe relevant aspects of transactions or decisions

whistle-blowing The disclosure of information by a company insider that exposes illegal or unethical behavior by others within the organization

Risk Management

The Business of Risk

All businesses face the risk of loss. Fire, lawsuits, accidents, natural disasters, theft, illness, disability, interest rate changes, credit freezes, contract defaults, and deaths of key employees can devastate any business if it is not prepared. Misjudging or mismanaging risks can damage careers, companies, and entire economies. For example, referring to the subprime mortgage mess, the editors of the *Harvard Business Review* were blunt: "Of all the management tasks that were bungled in the period leading up to the global recession, none was bungled more egregiously than the management of risk."[1]

In fact, financial risk was so misunderstood and mismanaged that the very tools some banks used to protect themselves from risk often made them more vulnerable instead.[2] Attempts to reduce human error by relying on advanced statistical models and algorithms to predict outcomes sometimes had the unfortunate effect of removing human judgment from the decision making as well. Without experienced minds actively engaged in the process to grapple with uncertainties and the nuances of individual situations, in some cases these algorithms produced disastrous decisions.[3]

UNDERSTANDING RISK

Although the formal definition of **risk** is the variation, based on chance, in possible outcomes of an event, it's not unusual to sometimes hear the term used to mean *exposure to loss*. This second definition is helpful because it explains why people purchase **insurance**, a contractual arrangement whereby one party agrees to compensate another party for losses. In the broadest sense, insurance can range from the home and auto policies that consumers buy to hedging strategies and credit default swaps.

Speculative risk refers to exposures that offer the prospect of making a profit or loss—such as investments in stock. **Pure risk**, on the other hand, is the threat of loss without the possibility of gain. Disasters such as an earthquake or a fire at a manufacturing plant are examples of pure risk. Nothing good can come from an exposure to pure risk.

An **insurable risk** is a risk that meets certain requirements in order for the insurer to provide protection, whereas an **uninsurable risk** is one that an insurance company will not cover (see Exhibit 1). Generally speaking, most speculative risks are not insurable, but many pure risks are. For example, most insurance companies are unwilling to cover potential losses that can occur from general economic conditions such as a recession (although strategies such as financial hedging might help in such scenarios). In order for a type of loss exposure to present a desirable business opportunity for an insurance company, it needs to meet the following criteria:[4]

- **The potential loss must be accidental.** Replacing an automobile that is totaled in a crash is an insurable event; replacing an automobile that fell apart through neglect is not.
- **The loss must be significant and measurable.** The loss of a building is quantifiable because the property has a measurable market value. In contrast, the pain and suffering associated with a loss may well be significant, but they are not quantifiable and therefore are not insurable.
- **The same threat must be faced by a large number of similar persons or organizations.** In order for the likelihood of a loss to be predictable, insurance companies must be able to compile data on the frequency and severity of losses posed by a particular threat. For example, by tracking the shipping industry year to year, a provider of marine insurance can collect enough data to be able to predict losses due to storms, accidents, piracy, and other threats.
- **The likely frequency of catastrophic losses must be low.** Insurance companies are able to stay in business only if the amounts they pay out in **claims** (customer demands to pay for insured losses) are less than the **premiums** (fees paid by customers to get insurance) they collect. As a simple example, a property insurance company can't survive if it takes in $10 million in premiums every year but 20 or 30 customers lose $1 million buildings every year.

Because not all calamities in life are insurable, businesses can't insure themselves against every potential loss. Even when they can buy coverage, insurance represents a recurring financial burden that must be considered carefully. Consequently, smart companies do everything they can to reduce the financial exposure created by risk through **risk management**, which includes assessing, controlling, and financing risk by shifting it to an insurance company or another outside party or by *self-insuring* to cover possible losses.

EXHIBIT 1 **EXHIBIT 1** | **Insurable and Uninsurable Risk**

Some of the risks that businesses and individuals face are insurable, but many others aren't.

Generally Insurable	Generally Uninsurable
Property risks: Uncertainty surrounding the occurrence of loss from perils that cause 1. Direct loss of property 2. Loss of use of or benefits of property **Personal risks:** Uncertainty surrounding the occurrence of loss due to 1. Premature death 2. Physical disability 3. Old age **Legal liability risks:** Uncertainty surrounding the occurrence of loss arising out of 1. Use of automobiles 2. Occupancy of buildings 3. Employment 4. Manufacture of products 5. Professional misconduct	**Market risks:** Factors that may result in loss of property or income, such as 1. Price changes, both seasonal and cyclical 2. Consumer indifference 3. Style changes 4. Increased competition **Political risks:** Uncertainty surrounding the occurrence of 1. Overthrow of a government 2. Restrictions imposed on free trade 3. Unreasonable or punitive taxation 4. Restrictions of free exchange of currencies **Production risks:** Uncertainties surrounding the occurrence of 1. Failure of machinery to function economically 2. Failure to solve technical problems 3. Exhaustion of raw-material resources 4. Strikes, absenteeism, and labor unrest **Personal risks:** Uncertainty surrounding the occurrence of 1. Unemployment 2. Poverty from factors such as divorce, lack of education or opportunity, and loss of health from military service

ASSESSING RISK

One of the first steps in managing risk is to identify the source of the threat. Areas of risk in which a potential for loss exists are called **loss exposures**. Some types of exposures are common to all businesses, such as fires, floods, and the death of key personnel. Other risks vary from industry to industry. For example, financial firms have to assess *credit risk* (the risk that borrowers will not repay loans), *market risk* (the risk that investments will lose value), and *operational risk* (the risk that anything from computer hackers to hurricanes will disrupt trading operations). Manufacturers have many of these loss exposures as well, plus such added risks as product liability and inventory losses during storage or transportation. Retailers worry about *shrinkage*, the loss of inventory due to shoplifting or internal theft. Medical firms face the possibility of lawsuits from *malpractice* claims.

Risk managers also need to understand the breadth or extent of a risk, because this determines how much control they have—if any. **Systemic risk** exists throughout an entire market or economy, such as the possibility that interest rates might rise and thereby increase capital costs for everyone. In contrast, **nonsystemic risk** threatens only a single company or a single industry. However, nonsystemic risk can become systemic if the scope of the threat grows beyond the single company or industry. This is what happened in the subprime mortgage market, when so many investment banks transferred their credit default risks to the insurance company AIG. Eventually, so many companies became dependent on AIG that its instability became a risk for the entire financial sector and eventually for the entire economy.

Finally, managers need to estimate the *probability* that a potential threat could become real and the magnitude of its *impact* if it does become real. For example, chemical spills are much more likely in facilities that use chemicals in processing or manufacturing than in facilities that use chemicals only for cleaning. And the impact of spilling a gallon of cleaning fluid is obviously less severe than the impact of a train derailment that spills the contents of a tanker car.

After managers have characterized a potential for risk, they have three possible responses: accept the risk and go on with business as usual (which can be a reasonable response for low-probability, low-impact risks, for example), take steps to control the risk, or shift some or all of the responsibility for the risk to a third party. Combining the last two steps, controlling and shifting risk, is common.

CONTROLLING RISK

If a risk is controllable and significant enough to warrant attention, managers can use a number of *risk-control techniques* to minimize the organization's losses:

- **Risk avoidance.** A risk manager might try to eliminate the chance of a particular type of loss, such as when a bank chooses not to lend money to new companies that haven't yet proven their ability to sustain profitable sales. The implication of risk avoidance is that it can mean not pursuing particular business opportunities—but that isn't always a bad thing.
- **Loss prevention.** A risk manager may try to reduce (but not totally eliminate) the *chance* of a given loss by removing hazards or taking preventive measures. Security guards at banks, warnings on medicines and dangerous chemicals, and safety locks are examples of physical loss prevention measures. Banks can use tighter lending standards to prevent instances of loan defaults.
- **Loss reduction.** A risk manager may try to reduce the *severity* of losses that do occur. Examples include installing overhead sprinklers to reduce damage during a fire and paying the medical expenses of an injured consumer to reduce the likelihood of litigation and punitive damages.

SHIFTING RISK TO A THIRD PARTY

If a company can't prevent or reduce potential losses to an acceptable level, the next option is to finance the risk by paying another company to assume part or all of it. You do the same thing when you buy an insurance policy for your car: You're paying an insurance company to hold the risk of losses caused by thefts or accidents. (Companies can shift risk in a variety of ways; this appendix focuses on the use of insurance.)

In many cases, though, transferring one type of risk creates another type of risk.[5] For instance, buying an insurance policy against some possible calamity shifts some or all of that risk to the insurer—but then creates a new risk that the insurer won't be able to pay up when disaster strikes. AIG offers a good example of these interdependent risks. Investment banks transferred the risk of mortgage defaults to AIG, which then couldn't pay up when the subprime market collapsed. For your personal insurance needs, it's vital to investigate the financial health of an insurer to make sure the company will be around when you need it. Websites such as Insure.com (www.insure.com) let you check on the financial strength ratings of insurance companies.

Insurance companies don't count on making a profit on any particular policy, nor do they count on paying for a single policyholder's losses out of the premium paid by that particular policyholder. Rather, the insurance company pays for a loss by drawing the money out of the pool of funds it has received from all its policyholders in the form of premiums. In this way, the insurance company redistributes the cost of predicted losses from a single individual or company to a large number of policies. To determine premium amounts, insurers rely on **actuaries**—loss-assessment specialists who determine how much income insurance companies need to generate from premiums by compiling statistics of losses—to forecast the funds needed to pay claims over a given period.

The types of insurance that a company needs depend on the nature of the business and its ability to withstand specific types of losses. Most companies protect themselves against the loss of property, loss of income, liability, and loss of services of key personnel (see Exhibit 2).

Property Insurance

Property insurance covers physical damage, destruction, or theft of company property. These policies vary in how much funding is providing. *Replacement-cost coverage* provides enough money to replace or restore property, without any reductions for depreciation in the property's value since it was put into service.[6] In contrast, *actual cash value coverage* pays only what the property is currently worth—which could be far less than the money needed to replace it. Because actual cash value coverage pays less, such policies understandably cost less than replacement-cost policies.

EXHIBIT 2	**Business Risks and Protection**

Here are some of the most common types of business insurance purchased.

Risk	Protection
Loss of property	
Due to destruction or theft	Fire insurance Disaster insurance Marine insurance Automobile insurance
Due to dishonesty or nonperformance	Fidelity bonding Surety bonding Credit life insurance Crime insurance
Loss of income	Business interruption insurance Extra-expense insurance
Liability	Comprehensive general liability insurance Automobile liability insurance Workers' compensation insurance Umbrella liability insurance Professional liability insurance
Loss of services of key personnel	Key-person insurance

Business Interruption Insurance

In addition to the direct losses they inflict, fires, floods, criminal acts, and other events can cause significant indirect losses if they disrupt business operations. Short-term disruptions cause the loss of immediate sales revenue, and longer-term disruptions can cost a company permanent market share as customers seek out new suppliers.[7] To get some level of reimbursement for lost revenue, companies can purchase **business interruption insurance**. For example, when a fire at its Universal City, California, studios destroyed a sound stage and a streetscape used in the production of television shows and movies, NBC Universal was able to file business interruption claims with its insurance company to mitigate its revenue losses.[8]

Liability Insurance

A variety of insurance policies are available to protect against **liability losses**, financial losses that occur when companies or their employees are found to be responsible for damage or injury to another party (which can include a company's own employees):

- **Commercial general liability** policies provide financial protection in the event a company is sued for damaging property or causing injury. For some companies, a general liability policy provides adequate coverage for their entire scope of operations, but other companies add specific types of liability coverage as well.[9]
- **Product-liability coverage** provides financial protection in the event that a company's products cause injury, disease, or death. Claims can result from defects in design, packaging, materials, labeling, safety warnings, and user instructions.[10]
- Also known as *malpractice insurance* or *errors and omissions insurance*, **professional liability insurance** covers people who might be found liable for professional negligence. This insurance applies to specialties such as accounting and medicine, as well as top management in public corporations. To protect corporate officers and members of corporate boards from lawsuits stemming from claims of mismanagement, companies can purchase *directors' and officers' liability insurance*, often called *D&O insurance*.[11]
- **Employment practices liability insurance** reimburses employers for a variety of claims related to employment practices, including negligent hiring, wrongful termination, and negligent employee evaluations.[12]
- Finally, just to be safe, businesses sometimes purchase **umbrella policies** to provide coverage for loss exposures not covered by all their other liability policies.[13]

Key-Person Insurance

If an employee or executive is essential to a company's ability to generate revenue, the firm can purchase **key-person insurance** to cushion the financial blow of losing that person's services in the event of death, disablement, or unexpected departure. Of course, if a person is that essential to the company, the management team should also take steps to have potential replacements ready to step in if needed.[14]

SELF-INSURING AGAINST RISK

Rather than finance risk through a third party, companies sometimes choose to address risk through **self-insurance**, which attempts to replicate the coverage provided by an independent insurer. The primary advantage of self-insurance is cost, because the company doesn't have to pay for risky behaviors of an insurance company's other clients or the insurer's own profit margins.[15] When insurance rates climb, more companies typically look to self-insure. For example, when the cost of *windstorm insurance* jumped after a tough hurricane season, many oil drilling companies with platforms in the Gulf of Mexico opted to self-insure rather than renew policies with higher rates.[16]

Companies with strong balance sheets are obviously in the best position to self-insure. Microsoft, for instance, uses self-insurance programs or no insurance at all in many instances because it has so much cash on hand to cover emergencies. In general, the company uses commercial insurers only for potentially catastrophic losses or when it can find great deals on policies.[17]

Insuring the Health and Well-Being of Employees

In addition to protecting company property and assets, many businesses look out for the well-being of employees by providing them with health, disability, workers' compensation, and life insurance coverage. Disease and disability may cost employees huge sums of money unless they are insured. In addition, death carries the threat of financial hardship for an employee's family.

HEALTH INSURANCE

Health care costs are one of the most pressing issues facing managers today, and health insurance represents one of the biggest concerns in health care—for people who are covered by health insurance and for the millions of Americans who aren't covered. Exhibit 3 identifies the most common forms of health insurance.

Health insurance and health care services are available from a variety of sources, including government programs, private not-for-profit organizations, and for-profit commercial providers. The largest health insurer in the United States is the Blue Cross and Blue Shield Association, www.bcbs.com, an organization of independent local insurance providers.[18]

Another major source of health coverage are **health maintenance organizations (HMOs)**, which are prepaid, group-practice medical plans in which consumers pay a set fee and, in return, receive many services as needed for either no additional

EXHIBIT 3	Common Types of Health Insurance

Here are five of the most common types of health insurance policies sold by insurers.

Types	Purpose
Basic medical	Designed to pay for most inpatient hospital costs (when the patients stays in the hospital) and some outpatient costs (when care is given in a doctor's office or another setting)
Major medical	Protects the insured against catastrophic financial losses by covering medical expenses that exceed the coverage limits of the basic policies
Disability income	Designed to protect against the loss of short-term or long-term income while the insured is disabled as a result of an illness or accident
Medicare supplemental	Designed specifically to supplement benefits provided under the Medicare program
Long-term care	Designed to cover stays in long-term care facilities

Source: Adapted from Mark S. Dorfman, *Introduction to Risk Management and Insurance*, 8th ed. (Upper Saddle River, N.J.: Pearson Prentice Hall, 2005), 296–301.

cost or for a modest co-payment. For patients, a key attraction of HMOs is paying the same monthly fees, regardless of usage level. To maintain profitability, therefore, HMOs usually place a high priority on wellness and disease prevention.[19]

As an alternative to HMOs, some employers opt for **preferred-provider organizations (PPOs)**, health care providers that contract with employers, insurance companies, or other third-party payers to deliver health care services to employees.[20] The "preferred providers" are medical specialists and medical facilities who have opted to join that particular PPO network. Employees generally aren't required to use in-network providers, but they pay more for using out-of-network services.[21]

Several million people are now covered by **health savings accounts (HSAs)**, a recent innovation that allows employees to save a portion of their earnings in a special account that can be used for medical expenses when needed.[22] Contributions to HSA accounts are usually tax deductible, so they also give employees a financial incentive.[23]

Finally, major efforts are currently under way at the national level to reform health care insurance coverage, including finding ways to reduce costs and to provide some level of coverage for the uninsured. Reforming the health care system is an urgent national priority because health costs are consuming an ever-growing portion of the gross domestic product (GDP). However, with many different parties pushing to protect their interests, reform is not going to be easy, nor will changes be welcomed by everyone to the same degree.

DISABILITY INCOME AND WORKERS' COMPENSATION INSURANCE

Two forms of insurance exist to help employees who are temporarily or permanently unable to work. **Disability income insurance** replaces a portion of an employee's income, typically up to 60 percent or so, with possible supplemental coverage up to 70 or 80 percent.[24] The length of coverage varies widely; some policies are designed only for short-term disabilities, whereas others provide benefits for a number of years.

In contrast to disability insurance, which is provided as part of an employer's overall health insurance package or purchased by individuals, **workers' compensation insurance** programs are administered by state governments. The intent of "workers' comp" is to replace some portion of an employee's income and to pay for some or all necessary medical costs if he or she is unable to work as the result of a job-related accident or illness. Every employer that is required to participate (different states exempt various categories of businesses) pays into an insurance fund based on the number of employees, the types of work those employees perform, and the company's *experience rating*—essentially a running tally of its safety record. Companies with higher accident rates pay higher insurance rates and vice versa.[25]

LIFE INSURANCE

Life insurance provides financial support to family members and others in the event of a person's death. Some employers include life insurance in their benefits packages, and many people buy policies on their own as well. The range of life insurance products is quite varied, from simple term life insurance to more complicated policies that combine investment with insurance:

- The simplest form of life insurance, **term life insurance**, offers coverage for a specific period of time—the *term* of the policy. Unlike other types of life insurance, term life is insurance only, with no savings or investment components. Term life is usually the least expensive, but it must be renewed after the term expires, and renewal rates increase as buyers get older. A great use of term life is investing the money you save (compared to other insurance policies) so that by the time the term is up, you have accumulated enough assets to protect your loved ones without relying on life insurance.[26]

- **Whole life insurance** differs from term in two important ways: It provides coverage until the insured person dies (meaning that, unlike term policies, whole life policies always pay out benefits), and part of the premiums paid accumulate in a savings plan. The policyholder can borrow against this amount or cash in the policy, if needed.[27]

- **Universal life insurance** is a combination life insurance and investment product, in which customers purchase an insurance policy and invest additional funds (typically in government bonds). The combination of insurance and investments gives customers some flexibility—depending on the performance of the investments—in the size and frequency of premiums and the size of the death benefits.[28] A similar concept, *variable life insurance*, gives policyholders more control over the investments made with their paid-in premiums.

TEST YOUR KNOWLEDGE

Questions For Review

1. What is the difference between pure risk and speculative risk?
2. What is risk management?
3. What are the four general requirements of insurability?
4. What are the three steps to controlling risk?
5. What is the difference between workers' compensation insurance and disability income insurance?

Questions for Analysis

6. How do insurance companies calculate their premiums?
7. Is self-insurance the same as going without insurance? Why or why not?

8. Why is it a good idea to purchase business interruption insurance?
9. Does every worker or consumer need life insurance? Why or why not?
10. Ethical Considerations. Life insurance can be one of the most complex purchases a consumer ever makes. It is also an expensive purchase and often sold by salespeople working on commission, which means they are motivated to make the sale. Whose responsibility is it to make sure purchasers understand the options available to them and understand all the details and ramifications of the specific policies they choose? Why?

APPENDIX GLOSSARY

risk Uncertainty of an event or exposure to loss

insurance A written contract that transfers to an insurer the financial responsibility for losses for specific events, up to specified limits and within specified conditions

speculative risk Risk that involves the chance of both loss and profits

pure risk Risk that involves the chance of loss only

insurable risk Risk that an insurance company might be willing to cover

uninsurable risk Risk that few, if any, insurance companies will assume because it likely cannot be covered profitably

claims Demands for payments from an insurance company based on the terms in an insurance policy

premiums Fees that insured parties pay insurers for coverage against losses

risk management A process business firms and individuals use to address their exposures to loss

loss exposures Areas of risk in which a potential for loss exists

systemic risk Risk that exists throughout an entire market

nonsystemic risk Risk that threatens only a single company or a single industry

actuaries Risk analysts employed by insurance companies to forecast expected losses and to calculate the cost of premiums

property insurance Insurance that provides coverage for physical damage to or destruction of property and for its loss by theft

business interruption insurance Insurance that covers losses resulting from temporary business closings

liability losses Financial losses suffered by a business firm or an individual held responsible for property damage or injuries suffered by others

commercial general liability Policies that provides protection against all forms of liability not specifically excluded under the terms of the policy

product-liability coverage Insurance that protects companies from claims that result from use of a product the company manufactures or distributes

professional liability insurance Insurance that covers claims for damages or injuries caused by professionals in the course of their work

employment practices liability insurance Insurance that reimburses employers for a variety of claims related to employment practices

umbrella policies Insurance that provides businesses with coverage beyond what is provided by a basic liability policy

key-person insurance Insurance that provides a business with funds to compensate for the loss of a key employee by unplanned retirement, resignation, death, or disability

self-insurance A financial protection strategy in which a company maintains enough funds to pay for potential losses on its own, rather than purchasing insurance coverage

health maintenance organizations (HMOs) Prepaid medical plans in which consumers pay a set fee in order to receive a full range of medical care from a group of medical practitioners

preferred-provider organizations (PPOs) Health care providers offering reduced-rate contracts to groups that agree to obtain medical care through the providers' organization

health savings accounts (HSAs) Special savings accounts that allow employees to save a portion of their earnings to use for medical expenses when needed

disability income insurance Short-term or long-term insurance that replaces some of the income lost when an individual is unable to perform his or her work due to illness or injury

workers' compensation insurance Insurance that partially replaces lost income and that pays for employees' medical costs and rehabilitation expenses for work-related injuries

life insurance Insurance that provides financial support to family members and others in the event of a person's death

term life insurance Life insurance that provides death benefits for a specified period

whole life insurance Insurance that provides both death benefits and savings for the insured's lifetime

universal life insurance A combination life insurance and investment product in which customers purchase an insurance policy and invest additional funds

REFERENCES

1. "Spotlight on Risk," *Harvard Business Review*, October 2009, 67.
2. Nassim N. Taleb, Daniel G. Goldstein, and Mark W. Spitznagel, "The Six Mistakes Executives Make in Risk Management," *Harvard Business Review*, October 2009, 78–81.
3. Amar Bhidé, "The Judgment Deficit," *Harvard Business Review*, September 2010, 44–53.
4. Mark S. Dorfman, *Introduction to Risk Management and Insurance*, 8th ed. (Upper Saddle River, N.J.: Pearson Prentice Hall, 2005), 19–24.
5. Robert S. Kaplan, Anette Mikes, Robert Simons, Peter Tufano, and Michael Hofmann, "Managing Risk in the New World," *Harvard Business Review*, October 2009, 69–75.
6. Dorfman, *Introduction to Risk Management and Insurance*, 153.
7. Nick Whitfield, "Business Interruption May Cost More Than Damage," *Business Insurance*, 4 August 2008, 17–19.
8. Roberto Ceniceros, "Studio Fire Sparks Business Interruption Losses," *Business Insurance*, 9 June 2008, 4.
9. "Business Liability Insurance: Different Kinds for Different Businesses," Nationwide, accessed 20 December 2011, www.nationwide.com.
10. Karen E. Klein, "Is Liability Insurance a Must to Go Global?" *BusinessWeek*, 18 June 2008, www.businessweek.com.
11. Dorfman, *Introduction to Risk Management and Insurance*, 391.
12. Dorfman, *Introduction to Risk Management and Insurance*, 394.
13. "Understanding General Liability Insurance."
14. "Key Person Insurance Can Help Companies Mourning an Owner or Executive," Insure.com, 28 May 2009, www.insure.com; Dorfman, *Introduction to Risk Management and Insurance*, 51.
15. Nancy L. Bolton, "Self-Insurance Survival: Creating a Health Plan in Unsuccessful Times," *Employee Benefit News*, July 2009, 14–16.
16. Zack Phillips, "In Tight Market Energy Firms Drop Cover, Cross Fingers," *Business Insurance*, 31 August 2009, 1+.
17. Joanne Wojcik, "Microsoft Relies on Self-Insurance for Most Exposures," *Business Insurance*, 20 April 2009, 34–37.
18. Blue Cross and Blue Shield Association website, accessed 13 October 2009, www.bcbs.com.
19. Dorfman, *Introduction to Risk Management and Insurance*, 73.
20. Dorfman, *Introduction to Risk Management and Insurance*, 74.
21. "CIGNA Preferred Provider Organization (PPO)," Cigna website, accessed 13 October 2009, www.cigna.com.
22. "Fact Sheet: Dramatic Growth of Health Savings Accounts (HSAs)," U.S. Department of the Treasury website, accessed 13 October 2009, www.ustreas.gov.
23. "Individual: The HSA for Life Health Savings Account," Bank of America website, accessed 13 October 2009, www.bankofameric.com.
24. Stacey L. Bradford, "Do You Need Disability Insurance?" *SmartMoney*, 10 September 2008, www.smartmoney.com.
25. Dorfman, *Introduction to Risk Management and Insurance*, 461–468.
26. Jack Hough, "Should You Hurry to Buy Life Insurance?" *SmartMoney*, 18 September 2009, www.smartmoney.com; Miriam Gottfried, "Should You Buy Term Life Insurance?" *SmartMoney*, 10 September 2009, www.smartmoney.com; Dorfman, *Introduction to Risk Management and Insurance*, 256–260.
27. Ginger Applegarth, "Term or Permanent Life Insurance?" MSN Money, 21 July 2009, http://articles.moneycentral.msn.com.
28. Dorfman, *Introduction to Risk Management and Insurance*, 263–265.

Information Systems

Information represents one of the most intriguing challenges you'll face as both an employee and a manager. Many companies now find themselves drowning in an ocean of data—but struggling to find real insights that can mean the difference between success and failure.

The first step in turning information into a competitive advantage is understanding the difference between **data** (recorded facts and statistics), **information** (useful knowledge, often extracted from data), and **insight** (a deep level of understanding about a particular situation). The transformation of data into insight requires a combination of technology, information-management strategies, creative thinking, and business experience—and companies that excel at this transformation have a huge advantage over their competitors. In fact, entire industries can be created when a single person looks at the same data and information everyone else is looking at but sees things in a new way, yielding insights that no one has ever had before (see Exhibit 1).

Businesses collect data from a wide array of sources, from checkout scanners and website clicks to research projects and electronic sensors. A single customer order can generate hundreds of data points, from a credit card number to production statistics to accounting totals that end up on a tax form. Even a small business can quickly amass thousands or millions of individual data points; large companies generate billions and even trillions of data points.[1]

To keep all these data points under control and to extract useful information from them, companies rely on **databases**, computerized files that collect, sort, and cross-reference data. In addition to helping with the daily chores of sending out bills, ordering new parts, and doing everything else that keeps the company running, databases can also be used for *data mining*, a powerful computerized analysis technique that identifies previously unknown relations among individual data points.[2]

Most large organizations employ a top-level manager, often called a **chief information officer (CIO)**, whose job is to understand the company's information needs and to create systems and procedures to deliver that information to the right people at the right time. This manager is expected to deliver quality information, which can be defined as *relevant* (directly pertinent to the recipient's needs), *accurate* (both current and free from errors), *timely* (delivered in time to make a difference), and *cost-effective* (costs a reasonable amount of money compared to the value it offers).

How Businesses Use Information

Companies invest heavily in information for the simple reason that they can't live without it. Here's a small sample of the ways managers rely on information:

- **Research and development.** In a sense, the cycle of information use starts with understanding customer needs

EXHIBIT 1	From Data to Information to Insight

Businesses generate massive amounts of data, but a key challenge is transforming all those individual data points into useful information and then applying creative thinking (sometimes with the additional help of computers) to extract deeper insights from the information.

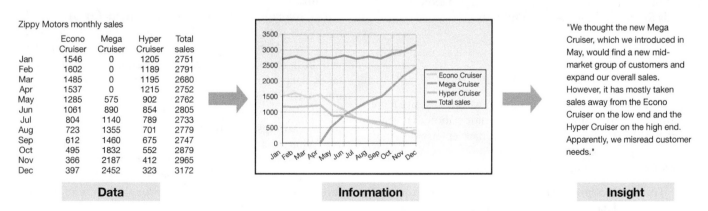

Zippy Motors monthly sales

	Econo Cruiser	Mega Cruiser	Hyper Cruiser	Total sales
Jan	1546	0	1205	2751
Feb	1602	0	1189	2791
Mar	1485	0	1195	2680
Apr	1537	0	1215	2752
May	1285	575	902	2762
Jun	1061	890	854	2805
Jul	804	1140	789	2733
Aug	723	1355	701	2779
Sep	612	1460	675	2747
Oct	495	1832	552	2879
Nov	366	2187	412	2965
Dec	397	2452	323	3172

Data

Information

"We thought the new Mega Cruiser, which we introduced in May, would find a new mid-market group of customers and expand our overall sales. However, it has mostly taken sales away from the Econo Cruiser on the low end and the Hyper Cruiser on the high end. Apparently, we misread customer needs."

Insight

and then moves to developing new goods and services to meet those needs. Information is vital at every step, from researching markets to analyzing competitors to testing new products.

- **Planning and control.** Two of the most important functions of management are planning and control—deciding what to do and making sure it gets done. Accounting managers need accurate financial information, sales managers need to know if their teams are meeting their sales goals, human resource managers need to make sure the company has enough of the right kind of employees, and so on.

- **Marketing and sales.** Thanks to technology, marketing and sales have evolved from "gut feel" activities to more scientific, information-driven functions.

- **Communication and collaboration.** Throughout an organization, employees, managers, and teams of every size and shape rely on information to communicate and collaborate. In fact, information technology is changing the very definition of what an organization means, thanks to the Internet's ability to connect people from every corner of the globe.

Types of Business Information Systems

Over the years, the collective label for the technologies used to manage information has changed; what used to be called *data processing* is now called either **information systems (IS)** or **information technology (IT)**, depending on the context. The types of information systems used by a company generally fall into two major categories: (1) operational systems and (2) professional and managerial systems. (The specific systems you'll encounter in your career are likely to have their own names, often arcane acronyms that make no sense to outsiders.) Most systems meet the information needs of people at specific levels in the organization. In contrast, *enterprise systems* are designed to connect everyone in the organization, giving each person the information he or she needs to meet specific job responsibilities.

OPERATIONAL SYSTEMS

Operational systems are the "frontline" workhorses of IT, collecting and processing the data and information that represent the day-to-day work of the business enterprise. These systems typically support daily operations and decision making for lower-level managers and supervisors:

- **Transaction processing systems.** Much of the daily flow of data into and out of the typical business organization, particularly regarding sales, is handled by a *transaction processing system (TPS)*, which captures and organizes raw data and converts these data into information. Common transaction processing systems take care of customer orders, billing, employee payroll, inventory changes, and other essential transactions. Such systems are a vital part of supply chain management.

- **Process and production control systems.** Operational systems are also used to make routine decisions that control operational processes. *Process control systems* monitor conditions such as temperature or pressure change in physical processes. *Production control systems* are used to manage the production of goods and services by controlling production lines, robots, and other machinery and equipment.

- **Office automation systems.** *Office automation systems* address a wide variety of typical office tasks. Office automation systems range from a single personal computer with word-processing software to *content management systems* that help companies organize the content on their websites.

- **Customer relationship management systems.** *Customer relationship management (CRM) systems* capture, organize, and capitalize on all the interactions that a company has with its customers, from marketing surveys and advertising through sales orders and customer support. Companies continue to find ways to integrate social media into customer communication, too, from using Twitter to answer customer support questions to offering coupons and other special deals on Facebook pages.

PROFESSIONAL AND MANAGERIAL SYSTEMS

In contrast to operational systems, *professional and managerial systems* help with such higher-level tasks as designing new products, analyzing financial data, identifying industry trends, and planning long-term business needs. These systems are used by professionals such as engineers and marketing specialists and by managers up to the top executive and board of directors. An important advance for many professionals is the idea of a *knowledge management (KM) system*, which collects the expertise of employees across an organization.

A **management information system (MIS)** provides managers with information and support for making routine decisions. (Note that *MIS* is sometimes used synonymously with both *IS* and *IT* to describe an overall IT effort.) An MIS takes data from a database and summarizes or restates it into useful information such as monthly sales summaries, daily inventory levels, product manufacturing schedules, employee earnings, and so on.

Whereas an MIS typically provides structured, routine information for managerial decision making, a *decision support system (DSS)* assists managers in solving highly unstructured and nonroutine problems through the use of decision models and specialized databases. Compared with an MIS, a DSS is more interactive (allowing the user to interact with the system instead of simply receiving information), and it usually relies on both internal and external information. Similar in concept to a DSS is an *executive support system (ESS)*, which helps top executives make strategic decisions.

Employee performance management systems help managers set employee performance goals, develop improvement plans, and reward employees based on measurable performance. By making performance evaluation more transparent and objective, such systems can help companies improve employee retention and job satisfaction.[3]

One of the most intriguing applications for computers in decision making and problem solving is the development of **artificial intelligence**—the ability of computers to solve problems through reasoning and learning and to simulate human sensory perceptions. For instance, an *expert system* mimics the thought processes of a human expert to help less-experienced individuals make decisions.

Information Systems Management Issues

As you already know from your experiences as a student and a consumer, technology can deliver some amazing benefits and every year seems to bring new technological miracles. As a business manager or entrepreneur, you can capitalize on all these benefits as well, but you'll also be responsible for a variety of legal, ethical, and administrative issues, starting with the challenge of ensuring privacy and security.

ENSURING SECURITY AND PRIVACY

Linking computers via networking technology creates enormous benefits for businesses and consumers, but there's a dark side to connecting everyone everywhere. Managers need to be constantly vigilant these days to make sure their computer systems remain secure and that data on them remain private. In recent years, millions of employee and customer records have been stolen or exposed, and billions of dollars have been lost to damage from computer viruses. The financial damage from computer-based crime is estimated to be as much as $100 billion annually and is getting worse every year.[4] Moreover, the collection, storage, and use of private information raises a host of legal and ethical issues that managers must consider.

The sources of potential trouble seem to multiply with every passing year and each new technological breakthrough:

- **Malicious software.** **Malware**, short for *malicious software*, is the term often applied to the diverse and growing collection of computer programs designed to disrupt websites, destroy information, or enable criminal activity. **Viruses** are invasive programs that reproduce by infecting legitimate programs; *worms* are a type of virus that can reproduce by themselves. *Trojan horses* allow outsiders to hijack infected computers and use them for purposes such as retransmitting spam email. *Spyware* sneaks onto computers with the intent of capturing passwords, credit card numbers, and other valuable

information. Chances are you've also met spyware's less-malicious cousin, *adware*, which creates pop-up ads on your computer screen.

- **Security breaches.** Any time a computer is connected to any network, it becomes vulnerable to security breaches. Given the enormous value of information stored on business information systems, particularly credit card numbers and other personal data that can be used for identity theft, there is financial motivation for outsiders to break in and insiders to sell out. For example, a security breach at United Health Services gave identity thieves access to the personal data of students enrolled in a health insurance program at the University of California, Irvine. The thieves used the information to collect bogus tax refunds by filing false tax returns.[5]

- **Unauthorized software and services.** IT departments in many companies face a constant battle with employee use of unauthorized software and online services. Employees not only expose their companies to security risks but also legal risks if they download or transmit inappropriate content on company networks.

- **Social media.** Social media technologies such as wikis, social networking sites, and video-sharing sites help companies create a more open communication environment for employees, customers, and other communities. Unfortunately, these technologies also create new system vulnerabilities, such as virus-infected Facebook pages and employee blogs that divulge company secrets.[6]

- **Misuse of information systems.** Companies must monitor for intentional or unintentional misuse of information systems, such as sending inappropriate files through email or using company resources for personal communication. Many employers now monitor both internal and external email. This monitoring can involve both automated scans using software programmed to look for sensitive content and manual scans in which selected email messages are actually read by security staff.[7]

- **Poor security planning and management.** Many viruses and worms are able to wreak their havoc and gain intruders access because computer owners haven't bothered to install available security patches in their software or haven't installed *firewalls*, hardware or software devices that block access to intruders. As larger companies with more resources and expertise work to improve their security, many criminals are now going after small businesses.[8] As the networking options multiply, so do the areas of risk; new areas of concern include viruses sent through VoIP Internet phone service, viruses on smartphones (including viruses downloaded from ringtone websites, viruses transmitted from phone to phone over Bluetooth wireless, and viruses hiding inside software apps), nasty things lurking on public wireless networks, and hacked accounts on Twitter, Facebook, and other social networking sites.[9]

- **Lack of physical control.** Software and network security isn't enough. Some of the most egregious security lapses involve the loss or theft of laptops that contain sensitive data such as employee or customer records.

Whether it's human issues such as background checks on new hires and ongoing security training or technical issues such as firewalls, encryption, or disaster recovery plans, all managers need to devote time and energy to potentially harmful side effects of IT. Sadly, as long as criminals can profit from digital theft and malware writers can amuse themselves by destroying the hard work of others, the problems are likely to get worse.

PROTECTING PROPERTY RIGHTS

Digital technology has increased concerns over the protection of digital products (including software and entertainment products available in digital format) and intellectual property (which includes a wide range of creative outputs with commercial value, such as design ideas, manufacturing processes, brands, and chemical formulas). One of the most controversial issues in this area is *digital rights management (DRM)*, the protection of owners' rights in products that are in digital format. DRM limits the ways consumers can use music files, movies, and other digital purchases, and critics worry that major corporations are using DRM to stifle creativity and control popular culture. Intellectual property protection remains a contentious and complex issue, as copyright owners, privacy advocates, and consumer groups battle over how digital products can or can't be used.

GUARDING AGAINST INFORMATION OVERLOAD

From simple RSS newreaders to enterprise-wide sales reporting systems, it's not uncommon for businesspeople to be stunned by how quickly their computerized systems start piling up data and information. The overuse or misuse of communication technology can lead to *information overload*, in which people receive more information than they can effectively process. Information overload makes it difficult to discriminate between useful and useless information, lowers productivity, and amplifies employee stress both on the job and at home—even to the point of causing health and relationship problems.[10]

Anyone who has sampled today's electronic media offerings has probably experienced this situation: You find a few fascinating blogs, a few interesting people to follow on Twitter, a couple of podcast channels with helpful business tips, and then *wham*—within a few hours of signing up, your computer is overflowing with updates. Even if every new item is useful (which is unlikely), you receive so many that you can't stay ahead of the incoming flood. Between Twitter updates, newsfeeds, email, instant messaging, and social networks—not to mention a desk phone and a mobile phone—today's business professionals could easily spend their entire days just trying to keep up with incoming messages and never get any work done.

To keep social media from turning into a source of stress and information anxiety, consider these tips:

- **Understand what information you really need in order to excel in your current projects and along your intended career path.** Unfortunately, taking this advice is even trickier than it sounds because you can't always

know what you need to know, so you can't always predict which sources will be helpful. However, don't gather information simply because it is interesting or entertaining; collect information that is useful or at least potentially useful.
- **Face the fact that you cannot possibly handle every update from every potentially interesting and helpful source.** You have to set priorities and make tough choices to protect yourself from information overload.
- **Add new information sources slowly.** Give yourself a chance to adjust to the flow and judge the usefulness of each new source.
- **Prune your sources vigorously and frequently.** Bloggers run out of things to say; your needs and interests change; higher-priority sources appear.
- **Remember that information is an enabler, a means to an end.** Collecting vast amounts of information won't get you a sweet promotion with a big raise. *Using* information creatively and intelligently will.

MONITORING PRODUCTIVITY

Facebook, Twitter, and other technologies are key parts of what has been called the "information technology paradox," in which tools designed to save time can waste as much time as they save. For instance, many employers are so concerned about productivity losses from personal use of the Internet at work that they place restrictions on how employees can use it, such as installing software that limits Internet access to business-related sites during working hours.[11]

Managers also need to guide their employees in productive use of information tools. The speed and simplicity of these tools is also one of their greatest weaknesses: It's simply too easy to send too many messages and to subscribe to too many blog feeds, Twitter follows, and other information sources. The flood of messages from an expanding array of electronic sources can significantly affect employees' ability to focus on their work. In one study, in fact, workers exposed to a constant barrage of emails, IMs, and phone calls experienced an average 10-point drop in their functioning intelligence quotient (IQ).[12]

MANAGING TOTAL COST OF OWNERSHIP

The true costs of IT are a concern for every company. The *total cost of ownership (TCO)* of IT systems, which includes the purchase costs of hardware, software, and networking plus expenses for installation, customization, training, upgrades, and maintenance, can be three to five times higher than the purchase price.[13] And that's for IT that companies really need and actively use. Managers also need to guard against the all-too-common problems of buying technology they don't need and building poorly planned systems that are redesigned or even scrapped before being completed.

DEVELOPING EMPLOYEE SKILLS

With the pervasiveness of IT, virtually everyone from the mailroom to the executive suite is expected to have some level of technology skills. Not only will you need to keep your own skills up to date so that you can manage yourself and others efficiently, but you'll also need to make sure your employees have the skills they need. With so much business communication taking place through electronic channels these days, managers and employees need more skills than ever to stay connected.

MAINTAINING THE HUMAN TOUCH

Technology can do wonderful things for business, but it can also get in the way of communication and collaboration. Even in the best circumstances, technology can't match the rich experience of person-to-person contact. Let's say you IM a colleague, asking how she did with her sales presentation to an important client, and her answer comes back simply as "Fine." What does *fine* mean? Is an order expected soon? Did she lose the sale and doesn't want to talk about it? Was the client rude, and she doesn't want to talk about it? If you communicate in person, she might provide additional information, or you might be able to offer advice or support during a difficult time. As technological options increase, people seem to need the human touch even more. In fact, some firms have taken such steps as banning email one day a week to force people to communicate in person or at least over the phone.

Moreover, in-person communication is important to your career. You can create amazing documents and presentations without ever leaving your desk or meeting anyone in person. But if you stay hidden behind technology, people won't get to know the real you. Jill Smart, an executive with the consulting firm Accenture, often takes advantage of the company's advanced telepresence facilities but still travels frequently to meet with clients—particularly clients in other countries and cultures. "You get things from being there, over breakfast and dinner, building relationships face to face."[14]

TEST YOUR KNOWLEDGE

Questions for Review

1. What is the difference between data and information?
2. What is the key difference between a management information system and a decision support system?
3. What is information overload?
4. What is the purpose of data mining?
5. How do operational information systems differ from managerial systems?

Questions for Analysis

6. Why do social media technologies present a potential information security threat?

7. What steps can you take to balance the need for relevant, timely information with the need to protect your productivity?
8. Why would a firm invest in an expert system if it already employs the experts whose knowledge and experience would be used to develop the system's decision support capabilities?
9. Why is new information technology sometimes considered both a benefit and a curse?
10. Ethical Considerations. Should employees be allowed to use company-owned information technologies for personal use during work hours? Why or why not?

APPENDIX GLOSSARY

data Facts, numbers, statistics, and other individual bits and pieces of data that by themselves don't necessarily constitute useful information

information Useful knowledge, often extracted from data

insight A deep level of understanding about a particular subject or situation

databases Computerized files that collect, sort, and cross-reference data

chief information officer (CIO) A high-level executive responsible for understanding a company's information needs and creating systems and procedures to deliver that information to the right people at the right time

information systems (IS) A collective label for all technologies and processes used to manage business information

information technology (IT) A generally accepted synonym for information systems; many companies use *IT* to refer to the department that manages information systems

management information system (MIS) A computer system that provides managers with information and support for making routine decisions

artificial intelligence The ability of computers to solve problems through reasoning and learning and to simulate human sensory perceptions

malware Short for *malicious software*; computer programs that are designed to disrupt websites, destroy information, or enable criminal activity

viruses Invasive programs that reproduce by infecting legitimate programs

MyBizLab

For an interactive, real-world example of this topic, access this chapter's simulation entitled Technolgy Direction, located at **www.mybizlab.com**.

REFERENCES

1. Daniel Lyons, "Too Much Information," *Forbes*, 13 December 2004, 110–115.
2. Irma Becerra-Fernandez, Avelino Gonzalez, and Rajiv Sabherwal, *Knowledge Management* (Upper Saddle River, N.J.: Pearson Prentice Hall, 2004), 200.
3. Victoria Murphy Barret, "Fight the Jerks," *Forbes*, 2 July 2007, 52–54.
4. "Cyber-Gloom on the Horizon," *Accountancy*, January 2009, 59; Spencer E. Ante and Brian Grow, "Meet the Hackers," *BusinessWeek*, 29 May 2006, www.businessweek.com.
5. Robert McMillan, "Data Scam Hits Grad Students," *Computerworld*, 9 June 2008, 6.
6. Jenny Williams, "Top Three Internet Scams to Avoid in 2011," ComputerWeekly.com, 12 January 2011, www.computerweekly .com; "Boom Time for Cybercrime," *Consumer Reports*, June 2009, 18–21; Sharon Gaudin, "The Move to Web 2.0 Increases Security Challenges," *InformationWeek*, 24 May 2007, www.informationweek.com.
7. Greg Burns, "For Some, Benefits of Email Not Worth Risk," *San Diego Union-Tribune*, 16 August 2005, A1, A8; Pui-Wing Tam, Erin White, Nick Wingfield, and Kris Maher, "Snooping Email by Software Is Now a Workplace Norm," *Wall Street Journal*, 9 March 2005, B1+.
8. Jeffrey Gangemi, "Cybercriminals Target Small Biz," *BusinessWeek*, 11 December 2006, www.businessweek.com.
9. Williams, "Top Three Internet Scams to Avoid in 2011"; Todd Wasserman, "Facebook Says 600,000 Accounts Compromised per Day," Mashable, 28 October 2011, http://mashable.com; Al Senia, "High-Tech Handsets Are Hacker Bait," *BusinessWeek*, 10 January 2007, www.businessweek.com; Ken Belson, "Hackers Are Discovering a New Frontier: Internet Telephone Service," *New York Times*, 2 August 2004, C4; Yuki Noguchi, "Hold the Phone: Hackers Starting to Infect Our Cells," *Seattle Times*, 26 November 2004, www.seattletimes.com; Steven Ranger, "Mobile Virus Epidemic Heading This Way," *Test Bed Blog*, 10 February 2005, www.vnunet.com; Stephanie N. Mehta, "Wireless Scrambles to Batten Down the Hatches," *Fortune*, 18 October 2004, 275–280.
10. Tara Craig, "How to Avoid Information Overload," *Personnel Today*, 10 June 2008, 31; Jeff Davidson, "Fighting Information Overload," *Canadian Manager*, Spring 2005, 16+.
11. Sushil K. Sharma and Jatinder N. D. Gupta, "Improving Workers' Productivity and Reducing Internet Abuse," *Journal of Computer Information Systems*, Winter 2003–2004, 74–78.
12. Jack Trout, "Beware of 'Infomania,'" *Forbes*, 11 August 2006, www.forbes.com.
13. Laudon and Laudon, *Management Information Systems*, 208.
14. Steve Lohr, "As Travel Costs Rise, More Meetings Go Virtual," *New York Times*, 22 July 2008, www.nytimes.com.

Taking Control of Your Financial Life

In your years as a consumer and a wage earner, even if you've had only part-time jobs so far, you've already established a relationship with money. How would you characterize that relationship? Is it positive or negative? Are you in control of your money, or does money—and a frequent lack of it—control you? Unfortunately, too many people find themselves in the second situation, with heavy debt loads, a constant cycle of struggle from one paycheck to the next, and worries about the future.

The good news is that with some basic information in hand, you can start to improve your financial well-being and take control of your money. The timing might seem ironic, but the best time to establish a positive relationship with money is right now, when you're still a student. If you build good habits now, when money is often scarce, you'll be taking a major step toward getting set for life. Conversely, if you fall into bad habits, you could find yourself struggling and worrying for years to come.

This appendix will help you understand the basic principles of personal finances and give you a solid foundation for managing your money. Before exploring some helpful strategies for each stage of your life, you'll learn three lessons that every consumer and wage earner needs to know and get a brief look at the financial planning process.

Three Simple—but Vital— Financial Lessons

If you've ever read a copy of the *Wall Street Journal* or another financial publication, you might have gotten the sense that money management is complex and jargon infested. However, unless you become a financial professional, you don't need to worry about the intricacies of "high finance." A few simple lessons will serve you well, starting with three ideas that will have enormous impact on your financial future: (1) The value of your money is constantly changing, so you need to understand how time affects your financial health, (2) small sacrifices early in life can have a huge payback later in life, and (3) every financial decision you make involves trade-offs. Taking these three ideas to heart will improve every aspect of your money management efforts, no matter how basic or sophisticated your finances.

THE VALUE OF YOUR MONEY IS CONSTANTLY CHANGING

If you remember only one thing from this discussion of personal finance, make sure this thought stays with you: A dollar today does not equal a dollar tomorrow. If you've successfully invested a dollar, it will be worth a little more tomorrow. However, if you charged a dollar's worth of purchases on a credit card, you're going to owe a little more than a dollar tomorrow. And even if you hold it tightly in your hand, that dollar will be worth a little less tomorrow, thanks to *inflation*—the tendency of prices to increase over time. When prices go up, your *buying power* goes down, so that dollar will buy less and less with each passing day.

These effects are so gradual that they are virtually impossible to notice from one day to the next, but they can have a staggering impact on your finances over time. Put time to work for you, and you'll join that happy segment of the population whose finances are stable and under control. Let time work against you, and you could get trapped in an endless cycle of stress and debt.

A simple example will demonstrate the power of time. Let's say you inherit $10,000 today and have two choices: hide it under your mattress or invest it in the stock market. Now fast-forward 10 years. If you hid the $10,000 under your mattress, it might now be worth only $7,000 or so (assuming that today's inflation rates stay about the same). It will still *look* like $10,000, but because of inflation, it'll *spend* like $7,000. On the other hand, if you invested it in the stock market, you could have $15,000 or more, assuming that the stock market tracks long-term historical patterns. That's a difference of $8,000 between the two choices—almost as much as your inheritance to begin with.

Now let's say you didn't get that inheritance, but you did get the urge to treat your best friends to a relaxing vacation. You don't have the cash, but lucky you—a shiny new credit card with a $10,000 limit just arrived in the mail, so away you go, spending right up to your limit. The bill arrives a few days after you return home, and you start paying a modest amount, say $150 a month. At 13 percent interest, which is not unusual for a credit card, it'll take you just about 10 years to pay off the $10,000 you borrowed—and you'll end up paying $18,000, nearly twice what you thought that vacation was costing you. Doesn't seem so relaxing now, does it?

Depending on the financial decisions you make, then, time can be your best friend or your worst enemy. The **time value of money** refers to increases in money as a result of accumulating interest.[1] Time is even more powerful when your investment or debt is subject to **compounding**, which occurs when new interest is applied to interest that has already accumulated. Financial planners often talk about the "magic of compounding," and it really can feel like magic—good magic if it's compounded interest on savings or bad magic if it's compounded interest on debt. Saving is about the only legitimate way to earn money by doing nothing.

SMALL SACRIFICES EARLY IN LIFE CAN PRODUCE BIG PAYOFFS

If you're currently living the life of a typical college student, you probably can't wait to move on and move up in life. You'll land that first "real" job, and then you'll get a nicer apartment, buy a new car, replace those ratty clothes you've been wearing for years, and stop eating ramen seven nights a week. This might be the last thing you want to hear, but if you can convince yourself to continue your frugal ways for a few more years, you'll benefit tremendously in the long run. Keep your expenses down and start saving as aggressively as you can.

Of course, saving during the early years of your career is no easy task, and it may be impossible, depending on your starting salary. In addition to the endless temptations to spend, you may also face the costs of starting a family, for instance. However, you'd be amazed at how much you can save every month by skipping that new car, renting a cheaper apartment, buying fewer clothes, and watching your entertainment expenses closely. A few simple choices may be able to free up hundreds of dollars every month. Even if you can save only a few hundred dollars a month early in your career, the sooner you start, the better off you'll be. Just keep increasing your monthly investment every time your salary increases, and do everything you can to take advantage of the time value of money.

EVERY DECISION INVOLVES TRADE-OFFS

By now, you've probably noticed that the time value of money and frugal living involve lots of choices. In fact, virtually every financial decision you make, from buying a cup of coffee to buying a house, involves a trade-off, in which you have to give up one thing to gain something else. If your family and friends give you $2,000 for graduation, should you run right out and buy alloy wheels and a custom exhaust system for your car? Or should you invest that $2,000 in the stock market and invest another $200 every month, so that in five or six years you could have enough to buy a new car—in cash, with no monthly payments? If you choose the second option, while your friends are shelling out $400 or $500 in payments for their new cars, you can be investing that amount every month and build up enough money to start your own business or perhaps retire a few years early.

Even the smallest habits and choices have consequences. Addicted to potato chips? Let's say you spend $3.19 for a big bag two or three times a week. Kick that habit now and invest that $400 or so a year instead. Over the course of 40 years, you could earn enough to treat yourself to a new car when you retire. Sounds crazy, but over many years, even tiny amounts of money can add up to large sums.

Not all your choices will be so simple, of course. Most of the examples presented so far have involved trading current pleasures and luxuries for future financial gain—a dilemma you'll be facing most of your life, by the way. Other choices involve risks versus rewards. Should you buy life insurance to provide for your family or invest the money and hope it'll grow fast enough to provide your loved ones with enough to get by on in the event of your death? Should you invest your money in a safe but slow-growing investment or an investment that offers the potential for high growth but also high risk of losing everything? As you gain experience with financial choices, you'll recognize your own level of *risk tolerance*. For instance, if you're lying awake at night, worrying about a high-risk stock you just purchased, you may have a lower level of risk tolerance, and you'll probably want to stick with safer, saner investments.

Figuring out the best choice is difficult in many cases but simply recognizing that every decision involves a trade-off will improve your decision making. Too often, people get into trouble by looking at *only* the risk (which can stop them from making choices that might in fact be better for them in the long run) or *only* the potential rewards (which can lure them into making choices that are too risky). Consider all the consequences of every choice you make, and you'll start making better financial decisions.

You'll pick up many other financial tips as you start investing, buying houses, selecting insurance, and making other financial choices, but these three concepts will always apply. With those thoughts in mind, it's time to take a look at the financial planning process.

Creating Your Personal Financial Plan

Creating and following a sensible financial plan is the only sure way to stay in control of your finances. A good plan can help you get the most from whatever amount of money you have, identify the funds you'll need in order to get through life's major expenses, increase your financial independence and confidence, minimize the time and energy needed to manage your finances, and answer a question that vexes millions of people every year: Where did all my money go?

Many people discover they'd rather turn the task over to a professional financial planner. Even if you do most of your planning yourself, you may encounter special situations or major transactions in which you'd like the advice of an expert. The right advice at the right time can make a huge difference. However, before you sign on with anyone, make sure you understand what advice you need and who can provide it. Ask about references, professional credentials, investing strategies, and how the adviser is paid.[2]

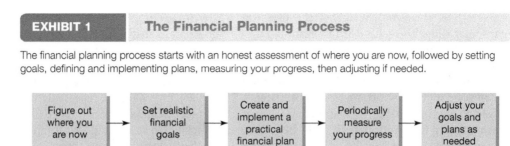

EXHIBIT 1   **The Financial Planning Process**

The financial planning process starts with an honest assessment of where you are now, followed by setting goals, defining and implementing plans, measuring your progress, then adjusting if needed.

Fee-only planners charge you for their services, either an hourly rate or a percentage of the assets they're managing for you. In theory, the major advantage of fee-only planners is complete objectivity, as they don't make money on the specific decisions they recommend for you. In contrast, **commission-based planners** are paid commissions on the financial products they sell you, such as insurance policies and mutual funds. While you can certainly receive good advice from a commission-based planner, make sure he or she has a wide range of offerings for you. Otherwise, you're likely to be hampered by limited choices.[3] Of course, since these types of planners are selling you something, it's important to make sure their recommendations are really the best choices for your financial needs. If you can't get a good recommendation from family members or colleagues, consider a matchmaker such as www.wiseradvisor.com, an impartial service that helps investors find advisers.

Even if you decide to rely on a full-service financial adviser to guide your decisions, you need to stay informed and actively involved. Lawsuits against financial advisers have risen dramatically in recent years, as clients seek compensation for losses in the stock market, for recommendation of *tax shelters* (investments designed primarily to reduce tax obligations) that the Internal Revenue Service (IRS) later ruled "abusive," and for other financial missteps. Keep in mind that even if you get advice, you are ultimately responsible for—and in control of—the choices involving your money. Don't count on anyone else to secure your financial future for you.

Planning can be as simple or as complex as you're inclined to make it, as long as you follow the basic steps shown in Exhibit 1.[4] The following sections discuss each step in more detail.

FIGURE OUT WHERE YOU ARE NOW

Successful financial planning starts with a careful examination of where you stand right now, financially speaking. Before you can move ahead, you need to add up what you own and what you owe, where your money is going, and how you're using credit. You might not like what you see, but if your finances are heading downhill, the sooner you learn that, the sooner you can fix it.

Start by listing your *assets*—the things you own—and your *liabilities*—the amounts of money you owe. Assets include both *financial assets*, such as bank accounts, mutual funds, retirement accounts, and money that people owe you, and *physical assets*, such as cars, houses, and artwork. Liabilities include credit card debts, car loans, home mortgages, and student loans. After you've itemized everything you own and everything you owe, calculate your **net worth** by subtracting your liabilities from your assets. The balance sheet in Exhibit 2 shows Devon Anderson's net worth. It is currently negative, but that's certainly not uncommon for college students. The important thing for Devon at this point is that she knows how much she's worth, so she has a baseline to build on.

EXHIBIT 2   Devon Anderson's Net Worth

Devon Anderson's net worth is currently negative, driven in large part by her school loans. However, she now knows exactly where she stands and can start working to improve her balance.

Assets

Cash accounts	Checking account	$ 450.67
	Savings account	927.89
Investments	50 shares Microsoft	1,302.50
Retirement accounts	(none)	
Automobiles	2001 Escort	5,500.00
Personal property	Jewelry	1,800.00
	Furniture	2,000.00
	Computer	450.00
Total assets		**$ 12,431.06**

Liabilities

Current bills (due within 30 days)	Rent	$ 650.00
	Visa	120.00
	MasterCard	195.00
	Car payment	327.25
Credit card debt	Visa	1,185.34
	MasterCard	2,431.60
Housing debt	(none)	
Automobile loans	2001 Escort	3,880.10
Other debt	Student loans	22,560.00
Total liabilities		**$ 31,349.29**
Net worth (total assets − total liabilities)		**($ 18,918.23)**

Your balance sheet gives you a snapshot of where you stand at a particular time. The second major planning tool is your **income and expense statement**, or simply *income statement*. This statement answers the all-important question of where your money is going month by month. Start by adding up all your sources of income from jobs, parents, investments, and so on. If you have irregular income, such as a one-time cash infusion from your parents at the beginning of each semester, you can divide it by the number of months it needs to cover to give you an average monthly value. Next, list all your expenses. If you're in the habit of using debit cards, credit cards, or a checkbook for most of your expenses, this task is fairly easy, since your statements will show where the money is going. However, if you tend to use cash for a lot of purchases, you'll need to get in the habit of keeping receipts and recording those purchases. (Using cash has the major advantage of limiting your spending to money that you actually have, but it doesn't leave a "paper trail" the way credit and debit cards do, so you have to keep track of the spending yourself.) Exhibit 3 shows Devon's income and expense statement.

Assembling your balance sheet and your income and expense statement can be a chore the first time around, but updating it as you make progress is much easier. A variety of software programs and websites can simplify these tasks, but they're not absolutely necessary. You can do all your recordkeeping in a spreadsheet (the software is probably already on your computer) or simply keep records in a notebook. How you record your data is less important than making sure you do it.

SET REALISTIC FINANCIAL GOALS

Now that you've finished assessing your current financial situation, the next step is setting goals. Take some time with this step. Your goals will drive all your financial decisions from here on out, so make sure they're the right ones for you. For instance, saving up for an early retirement requires a different financial strategy than saving up to take a year off in the middle of your career. Think carefully about what you really value in life. Discuss your dreams and plans with family and friends. Is making a million dollars by the time you're 40 your most important goal, and are you willing to work around the clock to get there? Or would you rather accumulate wealth more slowly and live at a more relaxed pace? Do you want to start a family when you're 25? 35? Perhaps being able to take care of an aging relative is important to you. You can't have it all, but you can make trade-offs that are compatible with your personal goals and values.

No matter what they might be, effective financial goals have two aspects in common: They are *specific* and they are *realistic*. "I want to be rich" and "I just don't want to have to worry about money" are not good goal statements because both are too general to give you any guidance. For one person, "not worrying about money" could require $100,000 a year, but another person might get by on $50,000 a year. You can certainly start with a general desire, such as wealth or freedom from worry, but you need to translate that into real numbers so you can craft a meaningful plan.

In addition to making them specific, make sure your goals are realistic. Lots of young people start out life saying they'd like to make a million dollars by age 30 or retire by age 40. These are wonderful desires, but for most people, they simply aren't realistic. The problem with having unrealistic goals is that you'll be repeatedly frustrated by your inability to meet them, and you're more likely to give up on your financial plan as a result.[5] While amassing a million dollars in the first 10 years of your career is highly unlikely, amassing a million dollars in 40, 30, or sometimes even 20 years is quite attainable for many professional wage earners. A few minutes with a financial calculator will help you assess the various possibilities and determine what is reasonable for you. (You can also visit www.choosetosave.org, which offers a wide variety of online calculators. In fact, just playing around with the many calculators on this site will teach you a fair amount about financial planning.)

EXHIBIT 3	Devon Anderson's Income and Expense Statement

Devon was surprised to learn that she has been spending over $800 more every month than she takes in. Since she can't work any more hours without compromising her studies and she is reluctant to ask her parents for more money, the only solution is to cut expenses. After some careful thought, she realizes that by cutting her cell-phone usage in half (or finding a better deal), dropping the sailing club, economizing on groceries, and cutting way back on entertainment, fast food, and new clothes she can almost break even every month.

Income

Wages (take home, average per month)	$ 1,230.00
Help from the parents	450.00
Total income	$ 1,680.00

Expenses (Average Monthly)

Rent	$ 650.00
Gas bill	34.00
Electric bill	76.00
Mobile phone	98.00
Food	315.00
Misc. household supplies	45.00
School materials & supplies	22.00
Car payment	327.25
Gasoline	38.00
Sailing club	78.25
Clothes	188.00
Entertainment & fast food	325.00
Visa payment	120.00
MasterCard payment	195.00
Total expenses	**$ 2,511.50**
Monthly difference	**($ 831.50)**

Many people find it helpful to divide financial objectives into short-, medium-, and long-term goals. Your personal time frame for each might vary, but in general, short-term goals will get you through your current financial situation, medium-term goals will get you into the next stage in your life, and long-term goals will get you completely set for life. The important thing is to consider the phases in your life and establish goals for each phase. Also, think carefully about the type of goals you wish to achieve. For instance, acquiring a ranch might be a significant goal for you, whereas someone who loves to travel may have little interest in real estate. Similarly, if you find that you have a low tolerance for risk or if a number of loved ones depend on you, comprehensive insurance coverage might be a significant goal. So go ahead and earn that million if you want to, but make sure you know *why* you're earning it.

CREATE AND IMPLEMENT A PRACTICAL PLAN TO MEET YOUR GOALS

You've thought about your goals and defined some that are specific and realistic. You're inspired and ready to start. What's next? For all the thousands of books, television shows, magazines, software products, and websites devoted to money, financial success really boils down to one beautifully—and brutally—simple formula: Earn more, spend less, and make better choices with what you have left over. On the plus side, this is an easy concept to understand. On the minus side, it's completely unforgiving. If you're spending more than you're earning or making bad choices with your savings and investments, you're never going to reach your goals until you can turn things around. The sections on life stages later in this appendix explore some of the details of these three components, but here's a brief overview to put it all in context:

- **Earn more.** Particularly in the early stages of your career, pay from your job will probably provide most or all of your income, so be sure to maximize your earning potential. As you get more established and have the opportunity to invest, you can start earning income from real estate, stocks and other investments, and perhaps businesses that you either own yourself or with others. As you move into retirement, your sources of income will shift to returns from your own investments, perhaps along with employer- and government-funded retirement plans.
- **Spend less.** Regardless of how much control you have over your income (and there are times and circumstances in life when you probably can't expect to change your earning power), you always have some control over how you spend your money. The first and most important step to spending less is maintaining a personal budget. For most people, budgeting sounds like about as much fun as having root canal surgery, but it shouldn't be that way. Don't think of budgeting as a straightjacket that crimps your style; think of it as a way to free up more cash so that you can accomplish those wonderful goals

you've set for yourself. When you skip a night out at the clubs or squeeze another year out of your car, think of that ranch in Montana you want to buy or that business you want to start. As with dieting, exercise, and other personal improvement regimes, sticking to a budget is difficult at first, but as you start to see some positive results, you'll be motivated to continue. Another important aspect of budgeting is understanding *why* you spend money, particularly on things you don't need and can't afford.[6] Don't try to spend your way out of depression, for instance. "Retail therapy" never solves anything and only makes financial matters worse. If you're prone to budget meltdowns, try to make everything as automatic as possible. For example, have your employer invest part of your salary in a company-sponsored investment program or have a mutual fund company pull money from your checking account every month.
- **Make better choices with what you have left over.** Once you've maximized your income and minimized your expenses, success largely comes down to making better choices with the money you have to save and invest. Investing can be a complex subject, with literally thousands of places to put your money. As with everything else in personal finance, the more you know, the better you're likely to perform. Don't make investments that you don't understand, whether it's some exotic financial scheme or simply the stock of a company that doesn't make sense to you. Proceed at your own pace, such as starting with an *index mutual fund* (which tracks the overall performance of the stock market) instead of trying to pick individual stocks.

In addition to your other healthy financial habits, get in the habit of keeping good records of income, expenses, investments, and other financial matters. Doing so will not only help you track your progress, but the IRS requires you to keep a variety of tax-related records. For a good overview of both suggested and required records, refer to Publication 552 (for personal records) and Publication 583 (for business records), both of which are available online at www.irs.gov.

Finally, make sure that anyone who plays a role in your financial plan, whether roommates sharing grocery costs or family members sharing all aspects of finances, buys into the plan. One of the most critical aspects of successful financial planning is discipline, and a plan will fall apart if some people follow it and some don't. Money is one of the most common issues in relationship problems and divorces, so talk things over calmly and honestly with your partner or spouse. Getting everyone to agree to—and commit to—the plan will reduce stress and increase the chances of success.[7]

PERIODICALLY MEASURE YOUR PROGRESS

To make sure you're on track to meet your goals, get in the habit of periodically checking your progress. Is your net worth increasing? (It might still be moving up toward zero, but that's progress!) Are your expenses under control?

However, don't obsess over your finances. Life's too short, and there are too many other pleasurable and productive ways to spend your time. You don't need to check your stock portfolio a dozen times a day or lie in bed every night dreaming up new ways to snip nickels and dimes out of your budget. After a while, you'll get a sense of how often you need to measure your progress to make sure you stay on track toward your goals. In general, check your income and expenses at least once a month to make sure you're staying within budget. For larger assets such as your house, you might want to verify approximate values once or twice a year.

However, don't put off checking your financial health so long that you don't notice problems such as poorly performing investments or small expenses that have somehow ballooned into big expenses. If you're using a financial planner, don't wait for an annual statement. Find out where you stand at least once a quarter.

ADJUST YOUR GOALS AND PLANS AS NEEDED

At various points in your life, you'll find that your goals or your financial status have changed enough to require adjustments to your plan. Whenever you pass through one of life's major transitions, such as getting married, having children, changing jobs, or buying a house, chances are you'll need to make some revisions. For instance, many first-time home buyers are surprised by the amount of money it takes to maintain a house, particularly a "fixer-upper" that needs a lot of work. To keep your income and expenses in balance, you may find you need to make sacrifices elsewhere in your budget.

If you're like most college students, you'll go through at least four major stages in your financial life: getting through college, establishing a financial foundation, building your net worth and preparing for life's major expenses, and planning for retirement. (If you're back in college after having been in the workforce for a while, your situation might vary.) The following sections give you an overview of the decisions to consider at each major stage in your life.

Life Stage 1: Getting Through College

With tuition and expenses rising rapidly these days, completing your education can be a mammoth struggle, to be sure. Costs are getting so high that some people are even beginning to wonder if the effort is worth it, particularly if you need to borrow heavily. Consider the eye-opening statistics discussed in the following sections and then think about your specific situation.

FINANCING YOUR EDUCATION

On the plus side, on average, college graduates earn more than 80 percent more per year than people with only high school educations.[8] Over the course of a 40- or 45-year career, this difference can be huge.

However, this doesn't tell the whole story. First, the 80 percent differential is only an average; a college education increases your chances of making more money, but it is by no means a guarantee. Quite a few people with only high school educations make more than people with college educations, and the income variations among people with different majors can be dramatic.[9]

Second, while you're in college, people who went to work right out of high school are already earning wages. By the time you graduate, those full-time workers who didn't go to college might be $100,000 or more ahead of you in cumulative earnings to that point.

Third, chances are you're going to be saddled with some debt when you graduate, setting you even further behind. With costs continuing to climb, more students are forced to borrow in ever-larger amounts to complete their education. Is it a good idea to borrow money to get through college? The only honest answer these days is that it depends. For starters, you need to compare education costs with potential income. Yes, a college education is likely to boost your income, and your education should ideally be about more than simply career training, but the reality of the situation is that your education needs to be paid for somehow. If you take on a lot of debt and need many years to pay off your student loans, you need to think about how this will affect your life plans.

Moreover, while education costs have gone up, forcing more students to borrow more, so have the costs of borrowing. Make sure you understand the true cost of any loan before you sign on the dotted line. In general, *private loans*, those that aren't guaranteed by a government agency, are more expensive than those that are. In recent years, some students have been stunned to discover they were paying as much as 18 percent interest or more on student loans.[10] If you're not sure what the true cost of a loan is, ask a financial aid counselor or another trusted adviser before you sign. And remember that a loan is not a gift; it's a serious financial commitment that will affect your life for years.

The worst of all possible outcomes is borrowing a lot of money and then not getting your degree. This situation will saddle you with big loan payments *and* the likelihood of lower income. Once you commit to getting your degree, make sure you get it. Ask for advice—and help—if you need it. Many people find doing so uncomfortable or embarrassing, but you're almost guaranteed to regret it later if you don't ask for help now. Talk to a counselor in your school's financial aid office, and make sure you explore every available option for financial assistance. Ask friends and family members for advice. If you have a job, see whether your employer is willing to help with school expenses.

Our intent here isn't to scare you out of school, by any means, but rather to make sure you understand the reality of the situation so that you can make choices that are best for you, your family, and your future.

STAYING OUT OF THE CREDIT CARD BLACK HOLE

Speaking of borrowing, every college student needs to be aware of the dangers of credit card debt. Far too many students dig themselves into giant holes with such debt. If you find yourself in this situation, don't panic—but stop digging any deeper. Your first step to recovery is to recognize that you're at a make-or-break point in both your college career and your life as a whole. No amount of extracurricular fun is worth the damage that a credit card mess can inflict on your life. Excessive credit card debt from college can follow you for decades, severely limiting your financial options.

Don't assume that you can easily pay off those balances when you start working, either. Many graduates entering the workforce are disappointed to find themselves bringing home less and paying out more than they expected. You'll be facing a host of new expenses, from housing to transportation to a business-quality wardrobe. You can't afford to devote a big chunk of your new salary to paying off your beer and pizza bills—with interest—from the previous four or five years.

Your second step is to compile your income and expense statement, as described earlier, so you know where all that borrowed money is going. Do a thorough and honest evaluation of your expenses: How much of your spending is going to junk food, clubbing, concert tickets, video games, and other nonessentials? At first, it won't seem possible that these small-ticket items can add up to big trouble, but it happens to thousands of college students every year. Most colleges and college towns offer a wide spectrum of free and low-cost entertainment options. With a little effort and creativity, anyone can find ways to reduce nonessential expenses, often by hundreds of dollars a month. As noted earlier, a few sacrifices now can make a big difference.

Life Stage 2: Building Your Financial Foundation

Whew, you made it: You scraped by to graduation, with any luck found a decent job, and now are ready to get really serious about financial planning. First, give yourself a pat on the back; it's a major accomplishment in life. Second, dust off that financial plan you put together in college. It's time to update it to reflect your new status in life. Third, don't lose those frugal habits you learned in college. Keep your *fixed expenses*, the bills you have to pay every month no matter what, as low as possible. Some of these expenses are mandatory, such as transportation and housing, but others may not be. Such things as gym memberships and added services on your mobile phone have a tendency to creep into your budget and gradually raise your expenses. Before you know it, you could be shelling out hundreds of dollars a month on these recurring but often nonessential expenses. In addition, if your income temporarily drops, the lower your fixed expenses are, the more easily you can handle the setback.

Among the important decisions you may need to make at this stage involve paying for transportation and housing, taking steps to maximize your earning power, and managing your cash and credit wisely.

PAYING FOR TRANSPORTATION

Transportation is likely to be one of your biggest ongoing expenses, if for you that means owning or leasing a vehicle. The *true cost* of owning a vehicle is significantly higher than the price tag. You'll probably have to finance it, you'll definitely need to insure it, and you'll face recurring costs for fuel and maintenance. And, unfortunately, unlike houses, which often *appreciate* in value, cars always *depreciate* in value (except in extremely rare cases, such as with classic cars). In fact, that lovely new ride can lose as much as 20 percent of its value the instant you drive away from the dealership. If you pay $25,000 for a car, for example, your net worth could drop $5,000 before you've driven your first mile. And if you took out a five-, six-, or seven-year loan, you'll probably owe more than the car is worth for the first several years.

There is good news, however: Most cars tend not to depreciate much during their second, third, and fourth years, but their value plummets again after five years. You can take advantage of this effect by looking for a used car that is about a year old, driving it for three years, and then selling it.[11] Automotive websites such as www.edmunds.com offer a wealth of information about depreciation and other costs, including the true cost of owning any given model. Also check with your insurance company before buying any car, as some models cost considerably more to insure.

Negotiating the purchase of a car ranks high on most consumers' list of dreaded experiences. You can level the playing field, at least somewhat, by remembering two important issues. First, most buyers worry only about the monthly payment, which can be a costly mistake. Salespeople usually negotiate with four or even five variables at once, including the monthly payment, purchase price, down payment, value of your trade-in, and terms of your loan. If you don't pay attention to these other variables, you can get a low monthly payment and still get a bad deal. Experts suggest that you arrange your financing ahead of time and then negotiate only the purchase price when you're at the dealership.[12] If you're not comfortable negotiating, consider using a car-buying service such as CarsDirect.com (www.carsdirect.com).

Leasing, rather than buying, is a popular option with many consumers, but it's not always a money-smart option. In general, the biggest advantage of leasing is lower monthly payments than with a purchase (or a nicer car for the same monthly payment, depending on how you look at it). However, leases are even more complicated than purchases and often more expensive, so it's even more important to know what you're getting into. Also, leases usually aren't the best choice for consumers who want to minimize their long-term costs.

PAYING FOR HOUSING

Housing also presents you with a lease-versus-buy decision, although purchasing a house has two huge advantages that purchasing a car doesn't have: Houses *can* appreciate in value over the long term, while cars *always* drop in value (unless you have a rare collector's car). The interest on a home mortgage is also tax deductible. And compared to renting, buying your own place also lets you build *equity*, the portion of the house's value that you own. However, there are times when renting makes better financial sense. The **closing costs** for real estate—the fees and commissions associated with buying or selling a house—can be considerable. Closing costs can represent from 3 to 6 percent of the price of a home. Depending on how fast your house's value rises, you may need to stay in it several years just to recoup your closing costs before selling.

If you think that a job change, an upcoming marriage, or any other event in your life might require you to move in the near future, plug your numbers into a "rent versus own" calculator to see which option makes more sense. You can find several of these calculators at www.choosetosave.org.

When you are ready to buy, take your time. Buying a house is the most complicated financial decision many people will ever make, involving everything from property values in the neighborhood to the condition of the home to the details of the financial transaction. Fortunately, you can learn more about home ownership from a number of sources. Check local lenders and real estate agencies for free seminars. Online sources include the U.S. Department of Housing and Urban Development (www.hud.gov) and MSN Real Estate (http://realestate.msn.com). Buying your own house can and should be a wonderful experience, but don't let emotional factors lead you to a decision that doesn't make financial sense. Keep in mind that a house is both a home and an investment.

MAXIMIZING YOUR EARNING POWER

Why do some people peak at earning $40,000 or $50,000 a year, while others go on to earn 2 or 3 or 10 times that much? Because your salary is likely to be the primary "engine" of your financial success, this question warrants careful consideration. The profession you choose is one of the biggest factors, of course, but even within a given profession, you'll often find a wide range of income levels. A number of factors influence these variations, including education, individual talents, ambition, location, contacts, and good old-fashioned luck. You can change some of these factors throughout your career, but some you can't. However, compensation experts stress that virtually everyone can improve his or her earning power by following these tips:[13]

- **Know what you're worth.** The more informed you are about your competitive value in the marketplace, the better chance you have of negotiating a salary that reflects your worth. Several websites offer salary-level information that will help you decide your personal value, including www.bls.gov, www.salary.com, www.vault.com, and www.salaryexpert.com. (Some of these sites charge a modest fee for customized reports, but the information might be worth many times what you pay for it.)

- **Be ready to explain your value.** In addition to knowing what other people in your profession make, you need to be able to explain to your current employer or a potential new employer why you're worth the money you think you deserve. Collect concrete examples of how you've helped your company or previous employers earn more or spend less in the past—and be ready to explain how you can do so in the future. Moreover, seek out opportunities that let you increase and demonstrate your worth.

- **Don't overlook the value of employee benefits, performance incentives, and perks.** For instance, even if you can't negotiate the salary you'd really like, maybe you can negotiate extra time off or a flexible schedule that would allow you to run a home-based business on the side. Or perhaps you can negotiate a bonus arrangement that rewards you for higher-than-average performance.

- **Understand the salary structure in your company.** If you hope to rise through the ranks and make $200,000 as a vice president, for instance, but the chief executive officer (CEO) is making only $150,000, your goal is obviously unrealistic. Some companies pay top performers well above market average, whereas others stick closely to industry norms.

- **Study top performers.** Some employees have the misperception that top executives must have "clawed their way" to the top or stepped on others on their way up. In most cases, the opposite is true. Employees and managers who continue to rise through an organization do so because they make people around them successful. Being successful on your own is one thing; helping an entire department or an entire company be successful is the kind of behavior that catches the attention of the people who write the really big paychecks.

MANAGING CASH

When paychecks start rolling in, you'll need to set up a system of **cash management**, a personal system for handling cash and other liquid assets, which are those that can be quickly and easily converted to cash. You have many alternatives today for storing cash, from a basic savings account to a variety of investment funds, but most offer interest rates that are below the average level of inflation. In other words, if you were to keep all your money in such places, your buying power would slowly but surely erode over time. Consequently, the basic challenge of cash management is keeping enough cash or other liquid assets available to cover your near-term needs without keeping so much cash that you lose out on investment growth opportunities or fall prey to inflation. Once again, your budget planning will come to the rescue by showing you how much money you need month to month. Financial experts also recommend keeping anywhere from three to six months' worth of basic living expenses in

EXHIBIT 4	Places to Stash Your Cash

You can find quite a few places to park your cash, but they're not all created equal.

Type of Account	Advantages	Disadvantages
Checking account (demand deposit)	Convenient, usually no minimum balance needed to open, often provides online banking and access via ATMs, insured against losses due to bank failure	Does not earn any interest
Checking account (NOW account)	Convenience of a regular checking account, plus you earn interest on your balance; insured	Some institutions require a minimum balance to open an account; modest interest rates
Savings account	Slightly higher interest rate than on typical checking account, often linked to a checking account for simple transfers; insured	Low interest rates; not as liquid as checking accounts (except for linked accounts, in which you can easily transfer funds to checking)
Money market deposit account	Higher interest rates than checking or savings accounts; insured	High minimum balances; limited check writing; fees can limit real returns
Money market mutual fund	Higher interest rates than many other cash management options	Not insured (but limited exposure to risk); minimum balance requirements; limited check writing
Asset management account	Convenience of having cash readily available for investment purposes; higher interest rates than regular checking or savings accounts; consolidated statements show most of your cash management and investing activity	Expensive (high monthly fees); large minimum balances; restrictions on check writing privileges (such as high minimum amounts) can limit usefulness as regular checking account; not insured against losses
Certificate of deposit	Higher interest rates that are fixed and therefore predictable; insured	Minimum balance requirements; limited liquidity (your money is tied up for weeks, months, or years)

Sources: Adapted from Lawrence J. Gitman and Michael D. Joehnk, *Personal Financial Planning*, 10th ed. (Mason, Ohio: Thomson South-Western, 2005), 139–143; Jack R. Kapoor, Les R. Dlabay, and Robert J. Hughes, *Personal Finance*, 7th ed. (New York: McGraw-Hill/Irwin, 2004), 141; Arthur J. Keown, *Personal Finance: Turning Money into Wealth*, 3rd ed. (Upper Saddle River, N.J.: Prentice Hall, 2003), 150.

an *emergency fund* that you can access if you find yourself between jobs or have other unexpected needs.

You can choose from several different options for holding cash (see Exhibit 4 for a summary of their advantages and disadvantages):[14]

- **Checking accounts.** Whether it's a traditional checking account from your neighborhood bank, an online account at an Internet bank, or a brokerage account with check-writing privileges, your checking account will serve as your primary cash management tool. A checking account can be either a demand deposit, which doesn't pay interest, or an interest-bearing or negotiable order of withdrawal (NOW) account.
- **Savings accounts.** Savings accounts are convenient places to store small amounts of money. Many savings accounts can be linked to a checking account for quick access to your cash. Although they're convenient and safe, savings accounts nearly always offer interest rates below average inflation rates, so the buying power of your account steadily diminishes.
- **Money market accounts.** Money market accounts, sometimes called money market deposit accounts, are an alternative to savings accounts; the primary difference is that they have variable interest rates that are usually higher than savings account rates.

- **Money market mutual funds.** Money market mutual funds, sometimes called money funds, are similar to stock mutual funds, although they invest in *debt instruments* such as bonds, rather than stocks.
- **Asset management accounts.** Brokerage firms and mutual fund companies frequently offer **asset management accounts** as a way to manage cash that isn't currently invested in stocks or stock mutual funds.
- **Certificate of deposits.** With a certificate of deposit (CD), you are essentially lending a specific amount of money to a bank or another institution for a specific length of time and at a specific interest rate. The length of time can range from a week to several years; the longer the time span and the larger the amount, the higher the interest rate.

No matter which types of accounts you choose, make sure you understand all the associated fees—which might not be clearly labeled as fees. Some accounts charge a fee every month, some charge fees when your balance drops below a certain amount or when you write too many checks, and so on. For accounts with checking capability, **overdraft fees** can chew up hundreds of dollars if you bounce checks frequently. Also, be sure to verify your account statement every month and **reconcile** your checking account to make sure you and the bank agree on the balance.

363

MANAGING CREDIT

Even if you never want to use a credit card or borrow money, it's increasingly difficult to get by without credit in today's consumer environment. For instance, car rental companies usually require a credit card before you can rent a car, most hotels require a credit card upon check-in, and landlords want to verify your **credit history**, a record of your mortgages, consumer loans (such as financing provided by a home appliance store), credit card accounts, and bill-paying performance. Banks and other companies voluntarily provide this information to credit rating agencies, businesses that compile **credit reports**. An increasing number of employers are looking into the credit histories of job applicants as well. Moreover, you may find yourself in need of a loan you didn't anticipate, and getting a loan without a credit history is not easy. Consequently, a solid credit history needs to be a part of your lifetime financial plan.

To build a good credit history, apply for a modest amount of sensible credit (a credit card, an auto loan, or a line of credit at a bank, for instance) and use that credit periodically. Also, if you are married or in a domestic partnership where expenses are shared, make sure that at least some credit is being established in your name so that you establish an independent credit record. Most important of all is to pay all your bills on time. If you find that you can't pay a particular bill by the due date, call the company and explain your situation. You may get some leniency by showing that you're making a good-faith effort to pay your bill.

Experts also recommend that you verify the accuracy of your credit report once a year. Mistakes do creep into credit reports from time to time, and you also need to make sure you haven't been a victim of *identity theft*, in which someone illegally applies for credit using your name. Actually, you don't have just one credit report. The three major credit reporting agencies in the United States each keep a file on you and provide their own credit reports to lenders, landlords, and others with a valid need to see them. You are entitled to one free credit report every 12 months from each of the three companies; visit www.annualcreditreport .com for more information. You can also directly visit the three bureaus: Experian (www.experian.com), TransUnion (www.transunion.com), and Equifax (www.equifax.com).

Managing your credit wisely will help you avoid one of the most traumatic events that can befall a consumer: **personal bankruptcy**. You have several options for declaring bankruptcy, but none of them is desirable, and all should be avoided by every means possible. Declaring bankruptcy, even if for an unavoidable reason such as medical costs or loss of a spouse, is sometimes called "the 10-year mistake" because it stays on your credit record for 10 years.[15] Bankruptcy is not a simple cure-all, as it is sometimes presented. If you are considering bankruptcy, talk to a counselor first. Start with the National Foundation for Credit Counseling (www.nfcc.org). Wherever you turn for advice, make sure you understand it thoroughly and understand why the organization would be motivated to give you that particular advice. You've probably seen ads (and a torrent of spam email) offering ways to get out from under your debt. Many of these schemes involve declaring bankruptcy, which may not be the right choice for you.[16]

After years of growing concern about the number of U.S. consumers filing for personal bankruptcy, Congress modified the bankruptcy filing process in 2005, with the intent of making it considerably more difficult for many people to file. Consumers seeking bankruptcy protection must first submit to *credit counseling*, which is designed to explore alternatives to bankruptcy. The outcome of credit counseling is likely to depend largely on household income: Those with high incomes will be encouraged to get their spending under control, those with moderate incomes will be encouraged to apply for a *debt-management plan* (an agreement to stop using credit cards and pay off existing balances, possibly in exchange for reduced interest rates), and those with lower incomes and therefore less hope of paying off their debts over time will be directed toward bankruptcy filing.[17]

Stage 3: Increasing Your Net Worth and Preparing for Life's Major Expenses

With your basic needs taken care of and a solid foundation under your feet, the next stage of your financial life is to increase your net worth and prepare for both expected and unexpected expenses. Some of the major decisions at this stage include investments, taxes, insurance, your children's education, and emergency planning.

INVESTING: BUILDING YOUR NEST EGG

The various cash management options described earlier can help you store and protect money you already have, but they aren't terribly good at generating more money. That's the goal of *investing*, in which you buy something of value with the idea that it will increase in value before you sell it to someone else. The most common financial investment vehicles are: stocks, mutual funds, and bonds. Real estate is the other major category of investment for most people—not only their own homes but also rental properties and commercial real estate. The final category of investments includes precious metals (primarily gold), gems, and collectibles such as sports or movie memorabilia.

The details of successful investing in these various areas differ widely, but six general rules apply to all of them:

- **Don't invest cash that you may need in the short term.** You may not be able to *liquidate* the investment (selling it to retrieve your cash) in time, or the value may be temporarily down, in which case you'll permanently lose money.
- **Don't invest in anything you don't understand or haven't thoroughly evaluated.** If you can't point to

specific reasons that the investment should increase in value, you're simply guessing or gambling.

- **Don't invest on emotion.** You might love eating at a certain restaurant chain, shopping at a particular on-line retailer, or collecting baseball cards, but that doesn't mean any of these is automatically a good investment.

- **Understand the risks.** Aside from Treasury bills and U.S. savings bonds, virtually no investment can guarantee that you'll make money or even protect the money you originally invested. You could lose most or all of your money, thanks to the risk/reward trade-off discussed earlier. To give yourself the opportunity to realize higher gains, you nearly always need to accept higher levels of risk.

- **Beware of anybody who promises guaranteed results or instant wealth.** Chances are that person will profit more by snaring you into the investment than you'll earn from the investment yourself.

- **Given the risks involved, don't put all your eggs in one basket.** Diversify your investments to make sure you don't leave yourself vulnerable to downturns in a single stock or piece of real estate, for instance.

If you plan to invest in a specific area, you would be wise to take a course about it or commit to learning on your own. Most of the websites mentioned throughout this appendix offer information, and some offer formal courses you can take online. Working with an investment club is an increasingly popular way to learn and pool your resources with other individual investors. In the beginning, don't worry about the details of particular stocks or the intricacies of real estate investment trusts and other more advanced concepts. Focus on the fundamentals: Why do stock prices increase or decrease? What effect do interest rates have on bonds? How can a particular house increase in value dramatically while another in the same neighborhood stays flat?

You can also practice investing without risking any money. This is a smart move early in your career, when you're still getting on your feet and may not have much money to invest yet. After you've learned the basics of stock investing, for instance, set up a "mock portfolio" on one of the many online sites that provide free portfolio tracking. Month by month, monitor the performance of your choices. Whenever you see a big increase or decrease, dig deeper to understand why. By practicing first, you can learn from your mistakes before those mistakes cost you any money.

TAXES: MINIMIZING THE BITE

Taxes will be a constant factor in your personal financial planning. You pay *sales tax* on many of the products you buy (in all but five states); you pay federal *excise taxes* on certain purchases, such as gasoline and phone service; you pay *property tax* on real estate; and you pay *income tax* on both earned income (wages, salaries, tips, bonuses, commissions, and business profits) and investment income. The total taxes paid by individuals vary widely, but you can safely assume that taxes will consume 30 to 40 percent of your income.

Your personal tax strategy should focus on minimizing the taxes you are required to pay, without running afoul of the law or harming your financial progress. (For instance, you usually don't want to skip an investment opportunity just because you'll have to pay tax on your gains.) Put another way, you are expected to pay your fair share of taxes, but no one expects you to pay more than your share.

You can reduce taxes in three basic ways: (1) by reducing your consumption of goods and services that are subject to either sales tax or excise taxes, (2) by reducing your *taxable income*, or (3) by reducing your tax through the use of *tax credits*. Reducing consumption is a straightforward concept, although there are obviously limits to how far you can reduce consumption and therefore this portion of your tax obligation.

Reducing your taxable income (the part of your income that is subject to local, state, or federal income tax, not reducing your overall income level) is more complicated but can have a great impact on your finances. Authorities such as the IRS allow a variety of **deductions**, such as interest paid on home mortgages and the costs associated with using part of your home for office space. Qualifying deductions can be subtracted from your *gross income* to lower your taxable income. A portion of your income is also *exempt* from federal income tax, based on the number of dependents in your household. The more **exemptions** you can legally claim, the lower your taxable income. You can also lower your taxable income by investing a portion of your income in *tax-exempt* or *tax-deferred* investments. With **tax-exempt investments** (which are primarily bonds issued by local governments), you don't have to pay federal income tax on any income you earn from the investment. With **tax-deferred investments**, such as 401(k) plans and individual retirement accounts (IRAs), you can deduct the amount of money you invest every year from your gross income, and you don't have to pay tax on income from the investment until you withdraw money during retirement.

Unlike deductions, which only reduce your taxable income and therefore reduce your tax burden by your tax rate, **tax credits** reduce your tax obligation directly. In other words, a $100 *deduction* reduces your tax bill by $28 (if you're in the 28 percent tax bracket, for instance), whereas a $100 *credit* reduces your tax bill by $100.

Personal tax software can guide you through the process of finding deductions and credits. For more complex scenarios, though, it's always a good idea to get the advice of a professional tax adviser.

INSURANCE: PROTECTING YOURSELF, YOUR FAMILY, AND YOUR ASSETS

Unfortunately, things go wrong in life, from accidents to health problems to the death of an income provider. Insurance is designed to protect you, your family, and your assets if and when these unpleasant events occur. In a sense, insurance is the ultimate risk/reward trade-off decision. If you had an ironclad guarantee that you would never get sick or injured, you would have no need for health insurance.

EXHIBIT 5	Understanding Your Insurance Options

You can buy insurance for every eventuality from earthquake damage to vacation interruptions, but the most common and most important types include medical, disability, auto, home owners', and life insurance.

Category	Highlights
Medical insurance	Usually purchased as part of group coverage, such as through an employer or a union; individual or single family is available but often more expensive; most plans offer a variety of cost and coverage options—for instance, to lower your monthly costs you can select a higher deductible, which is the amount you have to pay before insurance coverage kicks in; selecting the right plan requires a careful analysis of your needs and financial circumstances
Disability insurance	Temporarily replaces a portion of your salary if you are unable to work; various policies have different definitions of "disability" and restrictions on coverage and payments
Auto insurance	Most states now have *compulsory liability insurance laws*, meaning that you have to prove that you are covered for any damage you might cause as a driver; coverage for your vehicle can be both *collision* (damages resulting from collisions) and *comprehensive* (other damages or theft); you can also buy coverage to protect yourself from illegally uninsured motorists
Homeowner's insurance	Most policies include both *property loss coverage* (to replace or repair the home and its contents) and *liability coverage* (to protect you in case someone sues you); often required by the lender when you have a mortgage
Life insurance	Primary purpose is to provide for others in the event that your death would create a financial hardship for them; common forms are *term life* (limited duration, less expensive, no investment value), *whole-life* (permanent coverage, builds cash value over time, more expensive than term life), and *universal life* (similar to whole-life but more flexible)

However, there's a reasonable chance that you will need medical attention at some point, and major injuries and illness can generate many thousands of dollars of unplanned expenses. Consequently, most people consider it a reasonable trade-off to pay for health insurance to protect themselves from catastrophic financial blows. Exhibit 5 provides a brief overview of your most significant insurance options.

Another vital step to protecting your family—and one that is often overlooked by younger people—is preparing a **will**, a legal document that specifies what will happen to your assets, who will execute your estate (carry out the terms of your will), and who will be the legal guardian of your children, if you have any, in the event of your death.

Stage 4: Plan for a Secure, Independent Retirement

Retirement? You're only 25 years old (or 35 or 45). Yes, but as you saw earlier, in the discussion of compound interest, it's never too early to start planning for retirement. It's tempting to picture retirement as a carefree time when you can finally ditch your job and focus on hobbies, travel, volunteer work, and the hundreds of other activities you haven't had time for previously in your life. Sadly, the reality for millions of retired people today is much different. Between skyrocketing medical costs, a sluggish economy, and lower-than-expected company pensions in some cases, retirement for many people is a never-ending financial struggle, with little hope for improvement.

Perhaps the most important step you can take toward a more positive retirement is to shed the misconceptions that people often have about retirement planning, including the following:[18]

- **My living expenses will drop, so I'll need less money.** Some of your expenses may well drop, but rising health-care costs will probably swamp any reductions you have in housing, clothing, and other personal costs.
- **I'll live for roughly 15 years after I retire.** The big advantage of the health care that costs so much today is that people are living longer and longer. You could live for 20 or 30 years after you retire.
- **Social Security will cover my basic living expenses.** Social Security probably won't cover even your basic requirements, and the entire system is in serious financial trouble. While it's unlikely that political leaders would ever let Social Security collapse, the safest bet is to not count on it at all.
- **My employer will keep funding my pension and health insurance.** Thousands of retirees in recent years have been devastated by former employers either curtailing or eliminating pension and health coverage.
- **I can't save much right now, so there's no point in saving anything at all.** If you find yourself thinking this, remind yourself of the magic of compounding. Over time, small

amounts grow into large amounts of money. Do whatever it takes to get started now.

- **I have plenty of time to worry about retirement later.** Unfortunately, you don't. The longer you wait, the harder it will become to ensure a comfortable retirement. If you're not prepared, your only option will be to continue working well into your 70s or 80s.

In other words, the situation is serious. However, that doesn't mean it's hopeless—not by any means. You control your destiny, and you don't need to abandon all pleasures and comforts now to make it happen. But you do need to put together a plan and start saving now. Make retirement planning a positive part of your personal financial planning—part of your dream of living the life you want to live.

TEST YOUR KNOWLEDGE

Questions for Review

1. What does the *time value of money* mean?
2. What is compounding?
3. What is the major advantage of using a fee-only financial planner?
4. What is credit counseling?
5. What is the difference between a tax deduction and a tax credit?

Questions for Analysis

6. Should you borrow at any cost to get through college? Explain your answer.

7. What are the risks of relying on credit cards for living expenses while in college?
8. Why is it essential to keep a close eye on fixed expenses?
9. Why do you need to be able to explain your value to potential employers?
10. **Ethical Considerations.** Is it unethical for lenders to get students to sign up for loans that the students may not fully understand? Why or why not?

APPENDIX GLOSSARY

time value of money The increasing value of money as a result of accumulating interest

compounding The acceleration of balances caused by applying new interest to interest that has already accumulated

fee-only planners Financial advisers who charge a fee for their services rather than earning a commission on financial services they sell you

commission-based planners Financial advisers who are paid commissions on the financial products they sell you, such as insurance policies and mutual funds

net worth The difference between your assets and your liabilities

income and expense statement A listing of your monthly inflows (income) and outflows (expenses); also called an *income statement*

closing costs Fees associated with buying and selling a house

cash management All the planning and activities associated with managing your cash and other liquid assets

asset management accounts Cash management accounts offered by brokerage firms and mutual fund companies, frequently as tools to manage cash that isn't currently invested elsewhere

overdraft fees Penalties charged against your checking account when you write checks that total more than your available balance

reconcile To compare the balance you believe is in your account with the balance the bank believes is in your account

credit history A record of your mortgages, consumer loans, credit card accounts (including credit limits and current balances), and bill-paying performance

credit reports Reports generated by credit bureaus, showing an individual's credit usage and payment history

personal bankruptcy A condition in which a consumer is unable to repay his or her debts; depending on the type of bankruptcy, a court will either forgive many of the person's debts or establish a compatible repayment plan

deductions Opportunities to reduce taxable income by subtracting the cost of a specific item, such as business expenses or interest paid on home mortgages

exemptions Reductions to taxable income based on the number of dependents in the household

tax-exempt investments Investments (usually municipal bonds) whose income is not subject to federal income tax

tax-deferred investments Investments such as 401(k) plans and IRAs that let you deduct the amount of your investments from your gross income (thereby lowering your taxable income); you don't have to pay tax on any of the income from these investments until you start to withdraw money during retirement

tax credits Direct reductions in your tax obligation

will A legal document that specifies what will happen to your assets, who will execute your estate (carry out the terms of your will), and who will be the legal guardian of your children, if you have any, in the event of your death

My BizLab

For an interactive, real-world example of this topic, access this chapter's simulation entitled Personal Finance, located at **www.mybizlab.com**.

REFERENCES

1. Jack R. Kapoor, Les R. Dlabay, and Robert J. Hughes, *Personal Finance*, 7th ed. (New York: McGraw-Hill/Irwin, 2004), 18.
2. "Interview Tips," WiserAdvisor.com, accessed 14 October 2009, www.wiseradvisor.com.
3. Arthur J. Keown, *Personal Finance: Turning Money into Wealth*, 3rd ed. (Upper Saddle River, N.J.: Prentice Hall, 2003), 52–53.
4. Kapoor et al., *Personal Finance*, 11; Lawrence J. Gitman and Michael D. Joehnk, *Personal Financial Planning*, 10th ed. (Mason, Ohio: Thomson South-Western, 2005), 5.
5. Gitman and Joehnk, *Personal Financial Planning*, 15.
6. Deborah Fowles, "The Psychology of Spending Money," About .com, accessed 22 May 2004, www.about.com.
7. Gitman and Joehnk, *Personal Financial Planning*, 15.
8. "Study Puts Dollar Amounts on Earning Power of College Majors," OregonLive.com, 24 May 2011, www.oregonlive.com; Kathy Kristof, "Crushed by College," *Forbes*, 2 February 2009, 60–65.
9. "Study Puts Dollar Amounts on Earning Power of College Majors"; Kristof, "Crushed by College."
10. Ben Elgin, "Study Now—And Pay and Pay and Pay Later," 21 May 2007, *BusinessWeek*, 66–67; Kristof, "Crushed by College."
11. Philip Reed, "Drive a (Nearly) New Car for (Almost) Nothing," Edmunds.com, accessed 22 May 2004, www.edmunds.com.
12. Chandler Phillips, "Confessions of a Car Salesman," Edmunds .com, accessed 22 May 2004, www.edmunds.com.
13. Eryn Brown, "Hot to Get Paid What You're Worth," *Business 2.0*, May 2004, 102–110, 134.
14. Keown, *Personal Finance: Turning Money into Wealth*, 143–148; Gitman and Joehnk, *Personal Financial Planning*, 140–147.
15. Kapoor et al., *Personal Finance*, 222.
16. "Ads Promising Debt Relief May Be Offering Bankruptcy," FTC Consumer Alert, accessed 23 May 2004, www.ftc.gov.
17. Christopher Conkey, "Bankruptcy Overall Means Tougher Choices," *Wall Street Journal*, 22 May 2005, www.wsj.com.
18. Kapoor et al., *Personal Finance*, 582.

Index